Innovation and

Entrepreneurship

WILEY PLUS

... a powerful online tool providing instructors and students with an integrated suite of teaching and learning resources, including an online version of the text, in one easy-to-use website.

WileyPLUS is organised around the essential activities you perform in class:

- **Prepare & Present:** Create class presentations using a wealth of Wiley-provided resources - such as an online version of the textbook, PowerPoint slides and interactive simulations - making your preparation time more efficient. You may easily adapt, customise, and add to this content to meet the needs of your course.

- **Create Assignments:** Automate the assigning and grading of homework or quizzes by using Wiley-provided question banks, or by writing your own. Student results will be automatically graded and recorded in your grade book. WileyPLUS can link homework problems to the relevant section of the online text, providing students with context-sensitive help.

- **Track Student Progress:** Keep track of your students' progress via an instructor's gradebook, which allows you to analyse individual and overall class results to determine their progress and level of understanding.

Innovation and Entrepreneurship

John Bessant

Joe Tidd

BICENTENNIAL
1807
WILEY
2007
BICENTENNIAL

John Wiley & Sons, Ltd

Other Wiley Editorial Offices

John Wiley & Sons Inc., 111 River Street, Hoboken, NJ 07030, USA

Jossey-Bass, 989 Market Street, San Francisco, CA 94103-1741, USA

Wiley-VCH Verlag GmbH, Boschstr. 12, D-69469 Weinheim, Germany

John Wiley & Sons Australia Ltd, 42 McDougall Street, Milton, Queensland 4064, Australia

John Wiley & Sons (Asia) Pte Ltd, 2 Clementi Loop #02-01, Jin Xing Distripark, Singapore 129809

John Wiley & Sons Canada Ltd, 6045 Freemont Blvd, Mississauga, Ontario, L5R 4J3, Canada

Wiley also publishes its books in a variety of electronic formats. Some content that appears in print may not be available in electronic books.

Library of Congress Cataloging-in-Publication Data

Bessant, J. R.
Innovation and entrepreneurship/John Bessant, Joe Tidd.
    p. cm.
 Includes bibliographical references and index.
 ISBN-13: 978-0-470-03269-5 (pbk. : alk. paper)
 ISBN-10: 0-470-03269-3 (pbk. : alk. paper)
 1. Creative ability in business. 2. Entrepreneurship. I. Tidd, Joseph,
 1960- II. Title.
 HD53.B476 2007
 658.4'21 – dc22
                                        2006036087

British Library Cataloguing in Publication Data

A catalogue record for this book is available from the British Library

ISBN: 978-0-470-03269-5

Typeset in 9/13 Galliard by Laserwords Private Limited, Chennai, India
Printed and bound in Great Britain by Scotprint, Haddington, East Lothian
This book is printed on acid-free paper responsibly manufactured from sustainable forestry
in which at least two trees are planted for each one used for paper production.

CONTENTS

PREFACE

This book has been developed to be an accessible and more highly structured introduction to innovation and entrepreneurship, suitable for students of business and management, or engineering students studying courses on these subjects. It is designed to complement our best-selling text *Managing Innovation: Integrating Technological, Market and Organizational Change* (3rd end., John Wiley & Sons Ltd, Chichester, 2005), which is focused more on the needs of postgraduate and post-experience audiences.

There are a few good existing texts on innovation management, and many more on entrepreneurship in various guises. However, most texts tend to be too theoretical, whereas innovation and entrepreneurship are inherently about management practice and creating change. Much of this theory of innovation has been derived from studies of large manufacturing firms in developed economies, and is very much concerned with the successful development of products, whereas theories of entrepreneurship focus too much on small business creation, rather than the broader issue of creating new ventures and managing change in the corporate, public and third sectors. Moreover, too much emphasis is typically placed on the (important) roles of national systems and institutions, which are difficult for managers to influence in any significant way.

We believe that this text is unique in two significant respects. First, how it treats and applies the key theories and research on innovation and entrepreneurship. Second, the pedagogy and approach to learning. In this text we review and synthesize the theory and research, where relevant, but put far greater emphasis on the practice of innovation and entrepreneurship applied in a much broader context, including the corporate and public services, emerging technologies and economies, and for sustainability and development. The book is structured in four parts:

I. Principles

II. Context

III. Practice

IV. Action

In Principles we review the key theories and recent research relevant to understanding the dynamics and practice of innovation and entrepreneurship. In the first chapter we begin by mapping out different definitions and types of innovation, and identify the relationships between innovation, entrepreneurship and the performance of organizations in the private and public sectors. We develop a process for innovation and entrepreneurship that consists of three phases – generating new ideas, selecting the best ones, and implementing these. In Chapter 2 we focus on the relative roles of individuals, groups and organizations in innovation and entrepreneurship, and identify the key characteristics of creative people, and the factors which contribute to an innovative organization, including trust, challenge, support, conflict and debate, risk-taking and freedom. Chapter 3 examines innovation and entrepreneurship in the wider context of networks of individuals and organizations, and identifies the role and influence of different regional, national and global institutions and actors in both the rate and direction of innovation and enterprise.

In Context, we show how the generic model from Part I needs to be adapted to different environments, focusing on the similarities and differences between the manufacturing sector, where most research and experience is, to the service sector, which is highly differentiated, and includes private firms, public organizations and other third-sector bodies such as non-governmental organizations (NGOs), which includes charities and the voluntary sectors. In many advanced economies the service sector, broadly defined, accounts for 60–75% of employment, and more than half of this is in public and third-sector services.

In the Practice section we apply the material from the first two parts to explore some central themes: creating and sharing knowledge and intellectual property; exploiting systems and networks (e.g. for sustainability); anticipating disruptive, pervasive innovations (e.g. the potential of information and telecommunications technologies); and the globalization of innovation (e.g. role in development and emerging economies). Finally, in Part IV we identify the steps necessary to make innovation and entrepreneurship happen, and suggest an action plan for translating ideas into practice.

Throughout the book, the pedagogy and approach to learning we adopt is a combination of the tried and tested and the more novel. Like any good text, each chapter includes clear learning objectives, key terms, a guide to further resources and individual reflective questions and suggested group assignments. However, in addition to these, each chapter has four key elements:

■ *Exploring Innovation in Action* – contemporary anchor case study;

■ *Developing Personal Capabilities* – to help students reflect and develop skills;

■ *Advice for Future Managers* – practical implications and advice;

■ *Strategic and Social Impact* – broader strategic and social relevance.

The text is also fully integrated with an interactive web resource, which includes for each chapter:

■ Interactive multiple choice-type questions, assessed online;

■ Additional case studies with questions, as a basis of seminars and tutorials;

■ Links to relevant tools and techniques to support innovation and entrepreneurship;

■ Exercises to apply the lessons learned.

www.wileyeurope.com/college/bessant

This book is written as an accessible yet comprehensive introduction to innovation and entrepreneurship, specifically aimed at students of business and management, or the business courses on engineering programmes. We provide examples of good and not-so-good practice, drawn from a range of sectors and countries. Our analysis and prescriptions are based on the systematic analysis of the latest management research and practice, and our own research, consulting and teaching experiences at SPRU – Science and Technology Policy Research, at the University of Sussex, UK – and the Tanaka Business School at Imperial College, London, as well as our experience in the USA, Europe, Asia, Latin America and South Africa. In 2002 SPRU joined CENTRIM (Centre for Research in Innovation Management) in the £12 million purpose-built Freeman Centre at Sussex University, to create one of the greatest concentrations of researchers in the field of technology and innovation and management and policy. For details of our current teaching and research please visit us at www.sussex.ac.uk/spru and www.imperial.ac.uk. However, remember, this is a dynamic and evolving field, and this text is designed to encourage and support experimentation and learning, and not to substitute for it. We would appreciate your feedback.

John Bessant and Joe Tidd
Brighton, Sussex, UK, February 2007

ACKNOWLEDGEMENTS

We would like to thank all those colleagues and students at SPRU, CENTRIM, Tanaka, Imperial College and elsewhere who have provided feedback on our work. We are also grateful for the more formal reviews by Professors Jan van den Ende of ERASMUS, Rotterdam, Ken Green of Manchester University, Peter Jennings of the School of Management at Southampton University, Charlie Nagelschmit of Champlain College, USA, Han van der Meer of the University of Twente, Dr J. Faber of the University of Utrecht, plus the other anonymous reviewers. Our special thanks also to the extended team at Wiley, who have practised what we preach with their seamless cross-functional working, especially Steve Hardman, Deb Egleton, Mark Styles, Nicola Thompson, Peter Hudson, Debbie Scott and Emma Cooper.

Part 1
Principles

Chapter 1
The Innovation Imperative

This chapter

- Introduces the concept of innovation and its importance as a survival and growth imperative.
- Looks at the challenge of managing the innovation process.
- Explores four key themes in successful innovation management:
  - Understanding what it is we are trying to manage (what is innovation?);
  - Creating the conditions for making innovation happen (how do we organize innovation?);
  - Strategy for innovation (where, why and when do we innovate?);
  - Innovation as a dynamic capability (learning to manage innovation).
- Provides a map of the rest of the book.

Learning Objectives

By the end of this chapter you will develop an understanding of:

- What innovation is and how it enables survival and growth.
- Innovation as a process rather than a single flash of inspiration.
- The difficulties in managing what is an uncertain and risky process.
- The key themes in thinking about how to manage this process effectively.

Innovation – Everybody's Talking About It...

> *We're continuing to drive P&G's business with breakthrough innovations and excellent in-market execution. This...positions P&G to deliver its growth objectives in fiscal year 2007 and beyond. (A.G. Lafley, Chairman, President and CEO, Procter & Gamble, reporting on five years of sustained growth)*

> *We're measuring GE's top leaders on how imaginative they are. Imaginative leaders are the ones who have the courage to fund new ideas, lead teams to discover better ideas, and lead people to take more educated risks. (J. Immelt, Chairman and CEO, General Electric)*

> *We are always saying to ourself...we have to innovate. We've got to come up with that breakthrough. (Bill Gates, Microsoft)*

> *Innovation distinguishes between a leader and a follower. (Steve Jobs, Apple)*

> *John Deere's ability to keep inventing new products that are useful to customers is still the key to the company's growth. (Robert Lane, CEO, John Deere)*

Innovation Matters...

You don't have to look far before you bump into the innovation imperative. It leaps out at you from a thousand mission statements and strategy documents, each stressing how important innovation is to 'our customers/our shareholders/our business/our future' and most often, 'our survival and growth'. Innovation shouts at you from advertisements for products ranging from hairspray to hospital care. It nestles deep in the heart of our history books, pointing out how far and for how long it has shaped our lives. And it is on the lips of every politician, recognizing that our lifestyles are constantly shaped and reshaped by the process of innovation.

INNOVATION IN ACTION

...and It's a Big Issue

- OECD countries spend US$700 billion/year on R&D
- More than 16 000 firms in the USA currently operate their own industrial research labs, and there are at least 20 firms that have annual R&D budgets in excess of US$1 billion.

This isn't just hype or advertising babble. Innovation does make a huge difference to organizations of all shapes and sizes. The logic is simple – if we don't change what we offer the world (products and services) and how we create and deliver them, we risk being overtaken by others who do. At the limit it's about survival – and history is very clear on this point; survival is not compulsory! Those enterprises which survive do so because they are capable of regular and focused change. It's worth noting that Microsoft – currently one of the biggest and most successful companies in the world – takes the view that it is always only two years away from extinction! Or, as Andy Groves, one of the founders of Intel points out, 'Only the paranoid survive!'

INNOVATION IN ACTION

It's a Top National Priority . . .

Companies that do not invest in innovation put their future at risk. Their business is unlikely to prosper, and they are unlikely to be able to compete if they do not seek innovative solutions to emerging problems. (Australian Government website, 2006)

Innovation is the motor of the modern economy, turning ideas and knowledge into products and services. (UK Office of Science and Technology, 2000)

In Canada, the success of many high-growth, small and medium-sized enterprises (SMEs) is significantly connected to innovation. According to Statistics Canada, the following factors characterize successful small and medium-sized enterprises:

- Innovation is consistently found to be the most important characteristic associated with success.
- Innovative enterprises typically achieve stronger growth or are more successful than those that do not innovate.
- Enterprises that gain market share and increasing profitability are those that are innovative. (Government of Manitoba, Canada, 2006)

On the plus side innovation is also strongly associated with *growth*. New business is created by new ideas, by the process of creating competitive advantage in what a firm can offer. Economists have argued for decades over the exact nature of the relationship but they are generally agreed that innovation accounts for a sizeable proportion of economic growth. In a recent book William Baumol pointed out that 'virtually all of the economic growth that has occurred since the eighteenth century is ultimately attributable to innovation'.

The survival/growth question poses a problem for established players but a huge opportunity for newcomers to rewrite the rules of the game. One person's problem is another's opportunity and the nature of innovation is that it is fundamentally about *entrepreneurship*. The skill to spot opportunities and create new ways to exploit them is at the heart of the innovation process. Entrepreneurs are risk-takers – but they calculate the costs of taking a bright idea forward against the potential gains if they succeed in doing something different – especially if that involves upstaging the players already in the game.

INNOVATION IN ACTION

'We always eat elephants' is a surprising claim made by Carlos Broens, founder and head of a successful tool-making and precision engineering firm in Australia with an enviable growth record. Broens Industries is a small/medium-sized company of 130 employees which survives in a highly competitive world by exporting over 70% of its products and services to technologically demanding firms in aerospace, medical and other advanced markets. The quote doesn't refer to strange dietary habits but to their confidence in 'taking on the challenges normally seen as impossible for firms of our size' – a capability which is grounded in a culture of innovation in products and the processes which go to produce them.

Of course not all games are about win/lose outcomes. Public services like healthcare, education and social security may not generate profits but they do affect the quality of life for millions of people. Bright ideas well-implemented can lead to valued new services and the efficient delivery of existing ones – at a time when pressure on national purse strings is becoming ever tighter. New ideas – whether wind-up radios in Tanzania or micro-credit financing schemes in Bangladesh – have the potential to change the quality of life and the availability of opportunity for people in some of the poorest regions of the world. There's plenty of scope for innovation and entrepreneurship – and at the limit we are talking here about real matters of life and death.

INNOVATION IN ACTION

When the Tasman Bridge collapsed in Hobart, Tasmania, in 1975 Robert Clifford was running a small ferry company and saw an opportunity to capitalize on the increased demand for ferries – and to differentiate his by selling drinks to thirsty cross-city commuters. The same entrepreneurial flair later helped him build a company – Incat – which pioneered the wave-piercing design which helped them capture over half the world market for fast catamaran ferries. Continuing investment in innovation has helped this company from a relatively isolated island build a key niche in highly competitive international military and civilian markets.

Innovation is driven by the ability to see connections, to spot opportunities and to take advantage of them. Sometimes this is about completely new possibilities – for example, by exploiting radical breakthroughs in technology. New drugs based on genetic manipulation have opened a major new front in the war against disease. Mobile phones, PDAs and other devices have revolutionized where and when we communicate. Even the humble window pane is the result of radical technological innovation – almost all the window glass in the world is made these days by the Pilkington float glass process which moved the industry away from the time-consuming process of grinding and polishing to get a flat surface

Equally important is the ability to spot where and how new markets can be created and grown. Alexander Bell's invention of the telephone didn't lead to an overnight revolution in communications – that depended on developing the market for person-to-person communications. Henry Ford may not have invented the motor car but in making the Model T – 'a car for Everyman' at a price most people could afford – he grew the mass market for personal transportation. And eBay justifies its multi-billion-dollar price tag not because of the technology behind its online auction idea but because it created and grew the market.

Innovation isn't just about opening up new markets – it can also offer new ways of serving established and mature ones. Low-cost airlines are still about transportation – but the innovations which firms like Southwest Airlines, Easyjet and Ryanair have introduced have revolutionized air travel and grown the market in the process.

INNOVATION IN ACTION

Despite a global shift in textile and clothing manufacture towards developing countries the Spanish company, Inditex (through its retail outlets under various names including Zara) have pioneered a highly flexible, fast turnaround clothing operation with over 2000 outlets in 52 countries. It was founded by Amancio Ortega Gaona who set up a small operation in the west of Spain in La Coruna – a region not previously noted for textile production – and the first store opened there in 1975. Central to the Inditex philosophy is close linkage between design, manufacture and retailing and their network of stores constantly feeds back information about trends which are used to generate new designs. They also experiment with new ideas directly on the public, trying samples of cloth or design and quickly getting back indications of what is going to catch on. Despite their global orientation, most manufacturing is still done in Spain, and they have managed to reduce the turnaround time between a trigger signal for an innovation and responding to it to around 15 days.

And it isn't just about manufactured products; plenty of examples of turnaround through innovation can be found in services. In most economies the service sector accounts for the vast majority of activity so there is likely to be plenty of scope. And the lower capital costs often mean that the opportunities for new entrants and radical change are greatest in the service sector. Online banking and insurance have become commonplace but they have radically transformed the efficiencies with which those sectors work and the range of services they can provide. New entrants riding the Internet wave have rewritten the rule book for a wide range of industrial games – for example, Amazon in retailing, eBay in market trading and auctions, Google in advertising, Skype in telephony. Others have used the Web to help them transform business models around things like low-cost airlines, online shopping and the music business.

The challenge which the Internet poses is not only one for the major banks and retail companies, although those are the stories which hit the headlines. It is also an issue – and quite possibly a survival one – for thousands of small businesses. Think about your local travel agent and the cosy way in which it used to operate. Racks full of glossy brochures through which people can browse, desks at which helpful sales assistants sort out the details of selecting and booking a holiday, procuring the tickets, arranging insurance and so on. And then think about how all of this can be accomplished at the click of a mouse from the comfort of home – and that it can be done with more choice and at lower cost.

Innovation offers huge challenges – and opportunities – for the public sector. Pressure to deliver more and better services without increasing the tax burden is a puzzle likely to keep many civil servants awake at night. But it's not an impossible dream – right across the spectrum there are examples of innovation changing the way the sector works. For example, in healthcare there have been major improvements in efficiencies around key targets such as waiting times. Hospitals like the Leicester Royal Infirmary in the UK or the Karolinska Hospital in Stockholm, Sweden, have managed to make radical improvements in the speed, quality and effectiveness of their care services – such as cutting waiting lists for elective surgery by 75% and cancellations by 80% – through innovation.

. . . but it isn't Easy!

It's a disturbing thought – but the majority of companies have a lifespan significantly shorter than that of a human being. Even the largest firms can show worrying signs of vulnerability and, for the smaller firm, the mortality statistics are bleak. Sometimes it is individual firms which face the problem – sometimes it is whole sectors. We only have to consider the sad fate of European and US industries like motorcycles, machine tools, coal mining and toys, to realize how shaky the foundations of most of our industrial base really are. What goes up can come down just as fast.

Many small and medium-sized enterprises (SMEs) fail because they don't see or recognize the need for change. They are inward-looking, too busy fighting fires and dealing with today's crises to worry about emerging storm clouds on the horizon. Even if they do talk to others about the wider issues it is very often to people in the same network and with the same perspectives – for example, the people who supply them with goods and services or their immediate customers. The trouble is that by the time they realize there is a need to change it may be too late.

And it isn't just a small-firm problem – there is no guaranteed security in size or in previous technological success. Take the case of IBM – a giant firm which can justly claim to have laid the foundations of the IT industry and one which came to dominate the architecture of hardware and software and the ways in which computers were marketed. But such core strength can sometimes become an obstacle to seeing the need for change – as proved to be the case when, in the early 1990s, the company moved slowly to counter the threat of networking technologies – and nearly lost the business in the process. Thousands of jobs and billions of dollars were lost and it has taken another 10 years to bring the share price back to the high levels which investors had come to expect.

A common problem for successful companies occurs when the very things which helped them achieve success – their 'core competence' – become the things which make it hard to see or accept the need for change. Sometimes the response is what is sometimes called 'not invented here' – the new idea is recognized as good but in some way not suited to the business. (A famous example of this was the case of Western Union who, in the nineteenth century, were probably the biggest communications company in the world. They were approached by one Alexander Graham Bell who wanted them to consider helping him commercialize his new invention. After mounting a demonstration to senior executives he received a written reply which said that 'after careful consideration of your invention, which is a very interesting novelty, we have come to the conclusion that it has no commercial possibilities ... We see no future for an electrical toy'. Within four years of the invention there were 50 000 telephones in the USA and, within 20 years, 5 million. Over the next 20 years the company which Bell formed grew to become the largest corporation in the USA).

Sometimes the pace of change appears slow and the old responses seem to work well. It appears, to those within the industry, that they understand the rules of the game and that they have a good grasp of the relevant technological developments likely to change things. But what can sometimes happen here is that change comes along from *outside* the industry – and by the time the main players inside have reacted it is often too late. For example, in the late nineteenth century there was a thriving industry in New England based upon the harvesting and distribution of ice. In its heyday it was possible for ice harvesters to ship hundreds of tons of ice around the world on voyages that lasted as long as six months – and still have over half the cargo available for sale. By the late 1870s the 14 major firms in the Boston area of the USA were cutting around 700 000 tons per year and employing several thousand people. But the industry was completely overthrown by the new developments which followed from the invention of refrigeration and the growth of the modern cold storage industry. The problem is that the existing players often fail to respond fast enough to the new signals coming from outside their industry – as was the case for many of the old ice industry players.

Of course for others these conditions provide an opportunity for moving ahead of the game and writing a new set of rules. Think about what has happened in online banking, call-centre linked insurance or low-cost airlines – in each case the existing stable pattern has been overthrown, disrupted by new entrants coming in with new and challenging business models. For many managers, business model innovation is seen as the biggest threat to their competitive position, precisely because they need to learn to let go of their old models as well as learn new ones.

By the time they do so they may well have been overtaken by newcomers for whom this is the only business model and one they are well-placed to exploit.

It's not all doom and gloom though – there are also plenty of stories of new firms and new industries emerging to replace those which die. And in many cases the individual enterprise can renew itself, adapting to its environment and moving into new things. Consider a firm like Nokia – once a humble timber company and now a major player in the global business of mobile telephones. Or the example of the Stora company in Sweden which was founded in the twelfth century as a timber-cutting and processing operation but which is still thriving today – albeit in the very different areas of food-processing and electronics.

The challenge is one of dealing with an uncertain world by constantly trying new things. At first sight this seems obvious – firms which don't recognize the need for change simply disappear – while those which recognize that 'we must change' can use this to build new and growing businesses. But sometimes that 'change' is pretty dramatic, challenging the roots of where the company began and overturning a lot in the process. TUI is the largest European travel and tourism services company owning, among others Thomson Holidays, Britannia Airways and Lunn Poly travel agents. Its origins however go back to 1917 where it began as the Prussian state-owned lead-mining and smelting company! Nokia's key role as a leader in mobile telephony hides its origins as a diverse timber products conglomerate with interests as wide as rubber boots and toilet paper!

ADVICE FOR FUTURE MANAGERS

'Only the paranoid survive!' These words – the title of Andy Grove's autobiography (one of the founders of Intel) – stress the need for managers to be constantly searching not just for innovation opportunities but for the early warning signals that someone else's innovation may pose a threat. But rather than just running around in a blind panic, smart managers use tools and techniques to research their environment – carrying out R&D to keep ahead on the shifting technological frontier, using market research and competitor analysis to keep track of the context in which they are playing, and futures tools – forecasting, scenarios, and so on – to avoid being caught out or blindsided by unpleasant surprises when the world doesn't turn out quite as they had expected.

Can we do it? One indicator of the possibility of doing this comes from the experiences of organizations which have survived for an extended period of time. While most organizations have comparatively modest lifespans there are some which have survived at least one and sometimes multiple centuries. Looking at the experience of these '100 club' members – firms like 3M, Corning, Procter & Gamble, Reuters, Siemens, Philips and Rolls-Royce – we can see that much of their longevity is down to having developed a capacity to innovate on a continuing basis. They have learned – often the hard way – how to manage the process and, importantly, how to repeat the trick. Any organization gets lucky once but sustaining it for a century or more suggests there's a bit more to it than just luck.

Managing Innovation

If you asked most people about innovation they would readily sign up to its importance and the need for them to do it in order to survive and grow. What these and many other examples show is that simply wishing it to happen may not be enough – they need to actively *manage* the process. So how do we do this?

At its heart innovation is about three core themes:

- Generating new ideas
- Selecting the good ones
- Implementing them.

Looked at in this way we can see a parallel with biology and Darwin's theory of evolution. Organisms survive and grow through generating variation, selecting those new elements which help with adapting to a particular environment and propagating these across the species. Those that do it right survive, those that don't, disappear. Survival of the fittest, pure and simple.

But there's an important difference. In the case of the organizations we build and work in – unlike natural evolution – we have the chance to intervene in the process. Instead of random mutations and lucky accidents we can be a bit more strategic and purposive, searching and generating our own variety, making choices about which innovations to pursue and managing the process of implementation and diffusion to make sure they succeed.

Of course we shouldn't underestimate the task – for example:

- Generating new ideas – these could come from inspiration, from transferring from another context, from listening to user needs, from frontier research or by combining existing ideas into something new. And they could come through building alternative models for the future and exploring options opened up within these alternative worlds. But if we're going to succeed we need to build rich and varied ways of picking up on all the potential trigger signals which offer us interesting variation opportunities.

- Selecting the best of these sounds simple enough – except that we don't know which of them is best until we try. Innovation is fraught with uncertainty and guesswork and the only way to find out whether or not something is a good bet is to start developing it. So the process of strategic choice – Which of the many possibilities should we back, given that we only have limited resources? – is a big challenge. And if we get it wrong we could end up out of the game.

- And implementing the new idea – taking it from a gleam in the eye into a fully fledged product or service or a process people use. That's a long haul and a journey where Murphy's law dominates – if something is going to go wrong there's a good chance that it will! It's not just a matter of project management – balancing resources against time and budget – but doing so against this background of uncertainty. Even if we can steer a project through the rocks of making it real in terms of a new product, service or process proposition there's no guarantee that people will adopt it and it will diffuse widely.

This book is about what we've learned – and what we still need to understand – around the theme of managing innovation.

What Do We Know about Managing Innovation?

Success in innovation appears to depend upon two key ingredients – resources (people, equipment, knowledge, money, etc.) *and* the capabilities in the organization to manage them. It's the second which is the hardest to get a handle on – but it is the one which makes or breaks the process. So what is involved – and how do we know?

Innovation is the specific tool of entrepreneurs, the means by which they exploit change as an opportunity for a different business or service. It is capable of being presented as a discipline, capable of being learned, capable of being practised. (Peter Drucker, 1985, Innovation and Entrepreneurship[1])

An innovative business is one which lives and breathes 'outside the box'. It is not just good ideas, it is a combination of good ideas, motivated staff and an instinctive understanding of what your customer wants. (Richard Branson – DTI Innovation lecture, 1998)

Over the past hundred years there have been many attempts to answer the question – drawing on a wide range of studies. People have looked at case examples, at sectors, at big firms and small firms, at success and failure – but above all, they have looked at the world of *experience*. What we've learned comes from the laboratory of practice rather than some deeply-rooted theory.

Although these studies give us a wealth of other insights, four core themes emerge which are critical. If we want to succeed in managing innovation we need to:

- Understand *what* we are trying to manage – the better our mental models the more likely what we do with them in the way of building and running organizations and processes will work.

- Understand the *how* – creating the conditions (and adapting/configuring them) to make it happen.

- Understand the *what, why* and *when* of innovation activity – strategy shaping the innovation work that we do.

- Understand that it is a moving target – managing innovation is about building a *dynamic capability*.

What happens if we ignore these? Put simply, we run the risk of our good ideas running into the ground. For example, if we believe that innovation is simply about having the initial idea – some version of the cartoon characters, with a light bulb flashing on above their heads – then we shouldn't be too surprised when we find we can't turn that idea into a technical reality. Or when we do, that people won't necessarily see it as the best thing since sliced bread. We need richer mental models than that if we are to design and run an innovation process.

Or if we simply innovate in any direction that takes our fancy – in other words, we have no idea of where or why we want to innovate – then we shouldn't be surprised to find a large hole in our bank balance where the money used to be. Innovation consumes resources – time, energy, ideas and money – and no organization has infinite resources. So we need to think about being *strategic* in innovation activities.

Or if we believe that innovation is simply about letting it all hang out, creating a wacky space where people play basketball, lie around on sofas and have random conversations over endless cups of coffee, then we shouldn't be surprised if we have a bunch of people with some interesting ideas which never actually go anywhere. Innovation is about organizing different pieces of a knowledge jigsaw puzzle and particularly about balancing creativity with the discipline of making something happen.

ADVICE FOR FUTURE MANAGERS

'You can't make an omelette without breaking eggs' – and you can't innovate without taking risks. But what separates good innovation managers from the gamblers is the recognition that there is a core process involved which can be organized and managed. Anyone can get lucky once with innovation – just by being in the right place at the right time. But repeating the trick requires skills and understanding – and in particular smart innovation managers:

- Understand what we are trying to manage – the better our mental models the more likely what we do with them in the way of building and running organizations and processes will work.
- Understand the how – creating the conditions (and adapting/configuring them) to make it happen.
- Understand the what, why and when of innovation activity – strategy shaping the innovation work that we do.
- Understand that it is a moving target – managing innovation is about building a dynamic capability.

And if we don't reflect on and learn from the process – even if we get it wrong – then we risk being condemned to keep on making the same mistakes into the future. We operate in a world of massive complexity – where the sheer number of important elements is increasing and where their interactions make life extremely hard to predict. So we need to innovate – but we also need to innovate in our thinking about how to organize and manage the process. Not for nothing do we talk about the ability to organize and manage the process as a *dynamic capability*!

Whether we are thinking about starting our own business based on a bright idea or we are working in a giant public or private sector organization concerned with renewing itself the challenges remain the same. These four themes matter – so let's take a closer look at each of them in turn.

Understanding the What

So what is this innovation thing – and how can we use a better understanding of it to help us manage it better? The dictionary defines it as change – it comes from Latin *in* and *novare* – to make something new, to change. Helpful but a bit vague if we're trying to manage it. The definitions below get a bit closer to its meaning for us – in particular the simple DTI one about it being the successful exploitation of ideas.

> *Innovation is the successful exploitation of new ideas. (Innovation Unit, UK Department of Trade and Industry, 2004)*

> *Industrial innovation includes the technical, design, manufacturing, management and commercial activities involved in the marketing of a new (or improved) product or the first commercial use of a new (or improved) process or equipment. (Chris Freeman, 1982, The Economics of Industrial Innovation, 2nd edn. Frances Pinter, London)*

> *Innovation does not necessarily imply the commercialization of only a major advance in the technological state of the art (a radical innovation) but it includes also the utilization of even small-scale changes in technological know-how (an improvement or incremental innovation). Roy Rothwell and Paul Gardiner, 1985, Invention, innovation, re-innovation and the role of the user, Technovation, 3, 168.[2]*

One important point about innovation is that we often tend to think about it both as the *output* – a new product, for example – and also the *process* of making it happen. It's worth thinking about both of these – what we're going to change and the process of change itself.

What Can Be Changed in Innovation?

Innovation can take many forms but it can be reduced to four dimensions of change (the 4Ps of innovation):

- *Product innovation* – changes in the things (products/services) which an organization offers;
- *Process innovation* – changes in the ways in which things (products/services) are created and delivered;
- *Position innovation* – changes in the context in which the products/services are introduced;
- *Paradigm innovation* – changes in the underlying mental models which frame what the organization does.

For example, a new design of car, a new insurance package for accident-prone babies and a new home entertainment system would all be examples of product innovation. And change in the manufacturing methods and equipment used to produce the car or the home entertainment system, or in the office procedures and sequencing in the insurance case, would be examples of process innovation.

Sometimes the dividing line is somewhat blurred – for example, a new jet-powered sea ferry is both a product and a process innovation. Services represent a particular case of this where the product and process aspects often merge – for example, is a new holiday package a product or process change?

Innovation can also take place by repositioning the perception of an established product or process in a particular user context. For example, an old-established product in the UK is Lucozade – originally developed as a glucose-based drink to help children and invalids in convalescence. These associations with sickness were abandoned by the brand owners, Beechams (now part of Glaxo Smith Kline), when they relaunched the product as a health drink aimed at the growing fitness market where it is now presented as a performance-enhancing aid to healthy exercise. This shift is a good example of position innovation.

Sometimes opportunities for innovation emerge when we reframe the way we look at something. Henry Ford fundamentally changed the face of transportation not because he invented the motor car (he was a comparative latecomer to the new industry) nor because he developed the manufacturing process to put one together (as a craft-based specialist industry, car-making had been established for around 20 years). His contribution was to change the underlying model from one which offered a hand-made specialist product to a few wealthy customers to one which offered a car for Everyman at a price he/she could afford. The ensuing shift from craft to mass production was nothing short of a revolution in the way cars (and later countless other products and services) were created and delivered. Of course making the new approach work in practice also required extensive product and process innovation – for example, in component design, in machinery building, in factory layout and particularly in the social system around which work was organized.

Recent examples of paradigm innovation – changes in mental models – include the shift to low-cost airlines, the provision of online insurance and other financial services, and the repositioning of drinks like coffee and fruit juice as premium 'designer' products. Although in its later days Enron became infamous for financial malpractice it originally came to prominence as a small gas pipeline contractor which realized the potential in paradigm innovation in the utilities business. In a climate of deregulation and with global interconnection through grid distribution systems energy and other utilities like telecommunications bandwidth increasingly became commodities which could be traded much as sugar or cocoa futures.

Paradigm innovation can be triggered by many different things – for example, new technologies, the emergence of new markets with different value expectations, new legal rules of the game, new environmental conditions (climate change, energy crises), and so on. For example, the emergence of Internet technologies made possible a complete reframing of how we carry out many businesses. In the past similar revolutions in thinking were triggered by technologies like steam power, electricity, mass transportation (via railways and, with motor cars, roads) and microelectronics. And it seems very likely that similar reframing will happen as we get to grips with new technologies like nanotechnology or genetic engineering.

From Incremental to Radical Innovation

One other thing to think about is the degree of novelty involved. Clearly, updating the styling on our car is not the same as coming up with a completely new concept car which has an electric engine and is made of new composite materials as opposed to steel and glass (radical innovation). Similarly, increasing the speed and accuracy of a lathe is not the same thing as replacing it with a computer-controlled laser forming process. There are degrees of novelty in these, running from minor, incremental improvements (incremental innovation) right through to radical changes which transform the way we think about and use them. Sometimes these changes are common to a particular sector or activity, but sometimes they are so radical and far-reaching that they change the basis of society – for example the role played by steam power in the Industrial Revolution or the ubiquitous changes resulting from today's communications and computing technologies.

and Components and Systems

Finally we need to think about innovation often being like those Russian dolls – we can change things at the level of components or we can change the architecture of the whole system. For example, we can put a faster transistor on a microchip on a circuit board for the graphics display in a computer (component innovation). Or we can change the way several boards are put together into the computer to give it particular capabilities – a games box, an e-book, a media PC. Or we can link the computers into a network to drive a small business or office. Or we can link the networks to others into the Internet (architecture innovation). There's scope for innovation at each level – but changes in the higher-level systems often have implications for lower down. For example, if cars – as a complex assembly – were suddenly designed to be made out of plastic instead of metal it would still leave scope for car assemblers – but would pose some sleepless nights for producers of metal components!

Figure 1.1 illustrates the range of choices, highlighting the point that such change can happen at component or sub-system level or across the whole system.

ADVICE FOR FUTURE MANAGERS

Innovation is often thought of as radical or breakthrough stuff – because that's what makes good headlines and soundbites. But the reality is that most innovation is about incremental changes, doing what we do but better. And most of it involves working within established rules of the game, improving on our particular pieces of the overall jigsaw puzzle. But sometimes radical change is needed – or happens because someone else has introduced it. And sometimes the underlying architecture of a system changes and the old rules no longer apply. (See the case study on the music industry later in this chapter for an example of this.) Smart managers don't wait for innovation to be forced upon them to happen but explore a portfolio of innovation possibilities, from incremental through to radical and from component through to architecture.

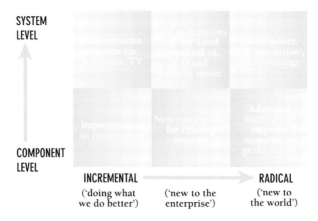

Figure 1.1   Types of innovation.

What Has to Be Managed?

Let's switch our attention to understanding innovation as a verb – a 'doing word'. What are the actions involved in innovation and how can we use this understanding to help us manage the process better? What comes into our minds when we think of innovation taking place in an organization?

If someone asked you 'When did you last use your Spengler?' they might well be greeted by a quizzical look. But if they asked you when you last used your 'Hoover' – the answer would be fairly easy. Yet it was not Mr Hoover who invented the vacuum cleaner in the late nineteenth century but one J. Murray Spengler. Hoover's genius lay in taking that idea and making it into a commercial reality. In similar vein the father of the modern sewing machine was not Mr Singer, whose name jumps to mind and is emblazoned on millions of machines all round the world. It was Elias Howe who invented the machine in 1846 and Singer who brought it to technical and commercial fruition. Perhaps the godfather of them all in terms of turning ideas into reality was Thomas Edison who during his life registered over 1000 patents. Products for which his organization was responsible include the light bulb, 35 mm cinema film and even the electric chair. Many of the inventions for which he is famous weren't in fact invented by him – the electric light bulb for example – but were developed and polished technically and their markets opened up by Edison and his team. More than anyone else Edison understood that invention is not enough – simply having a good idea is not going to lead to its widespread adoption and use.

ADVICE FOR FUTURE MANAGERS

Unlike Messrs Spengler, Howe and the many others who tried and failed to get their inventions across, smart managers realize that innovation is an extended process with a number of key stages. More important, they avoid thinking in partial or simplistic terms about the process and instead develop rich and integrated models of how it works – which they can then use to organize and manage the process. Take a look at Table 1.1 and think about how you would design a system for innovation which avoided some of the traps on the right-hand side.

One of the problems we have in managing anything is that how we think about it shapes what we do about it. So if we have a simplistic model of how innovation works – for example, that it's just about invention – then that's what we will organize and manage. We might end up with the best invention department in the world – but there is no guarantee that people would ever actually want any of our wonderful inventions! If we are serious about managing innovation, then we need to check on our mental models and make sure we're working with as complete a picture as possible. Otherwise we run risks like those in Table 1.1.

Rather than the cartoon image of a light bulb flashing on above someone's head, we need to think about innovation as an extended sequence of activities – a *process*. At heart innovation is a sequence of such activities involved in turning ideas and possibilities into reality.

To make this happen organizations need to generate, select and implement. And this involves things like:

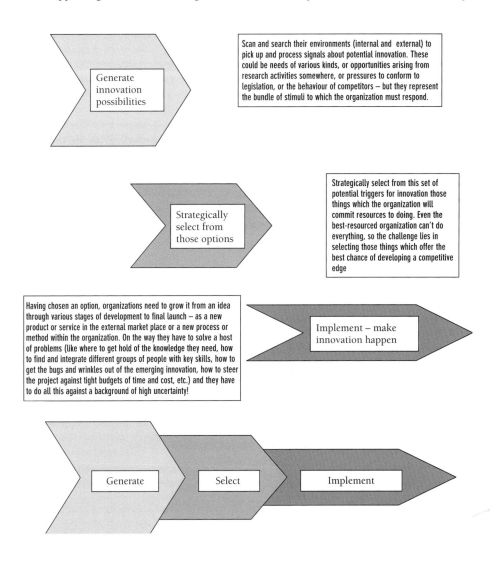

Generate innovation possibilities

Scan and search their environments (internal and external) to pick up and process signals about potential innovation. These could be needs of various kinds, or opportunities arising from research activities somewhere, or pressures to conform to legislation, or the behaviour of competitors – but they represent the bundle of stimuli to which the organization must respond.

Strategically select from those options

Strategically select from this set of potential triggers for innovation those things which the organization will commit resources to doing. Even the best-resourced organization can't do everything, so the challenge lies in selecting those things which offer the best chance of developing a competitive edge

Having chosen an option, organizations need to grow it from an idea through various stages of development to final launch – as a new product or service in the external market place or a new process or method within the organization. On the way they have to solve a host of problems (like where to get hold of the knowledge they need, how to find and integrate different groups of people with key skills, how to get the bugs and wrinkles out of the emerging innovation, how to steer the project against tight budgets of time and cost, etc.) and they have to do all this against a background of high uncertainty!

Implement – make innovation happen

Generate   Select   Implement

Table 1.1   The problem with partial models

If innovation is only seen as . . .	. . . the result can be
Strong R&D capability	Technology which fails to meet user needs and may not be accepted – 'the better mousetrap which nobody wants'
The province of specialists in white coats in the R&D laboratory	Lack of involvement of others, and a lack of key knowledge and experience input from other perspectives
Meeting customer needs	Lack of technical progression, leading to inability to gain competitive edge
Technology advances	Producing products which the market does not want or designing processes which do not meet the needs of the user and so users resist adopting them
The province only of large firms	Weak small firms with too high a dependence on large customers
Only about 'breakthrough' changes	Neglect of the potential of incremental innovation. Also an inability to secure and reinforce the gains from radical change because the incremental performance ratchet is not working well
Only associated with key individuals	Failure to utilize the creativity of the remainder of employees, and to secure their inputs and perspectives to improve innovation
Only internally generated	The 'not invented here' effect, where good ideas from outside are resisted or rejected
Only externally generated	Innovation becomes simply a matter of filling a shopping list of needs from outside and there is little internal learning or development of technological competence

The core process shown in the diagram on page 16 is the minimum we need to make innovation happen – but how do we do so in different kinds of organizations? And what factors can help – or hinder – its effective operation? That's the subject of our next section.

Creating the Conditions for Effective Innovation

As we mentioned earlier, there has been plenty of research around this question and at the end of the chapter there are some links to good examples of these studies. But one of the most important points to make at the outset is that firms aren't born with the capability to organize and manage this process – they learn and develop it over time, and mainly through a process of trial and error. They hang on to what works and develop their capabilities in that – and they try and drop those things which don't work. For example, successful innovation correlates strongly with how a firm selects and manages projects, how it coordinates the inputs of different functions, how it links up with its customers, and so on. Successful innovators acquire and accumulate technical resources and managerial capabilities over time; there are plenty of opportunities for learning – through doing, using, working with other firms, asking the customers, and so on – but they all depend upon the readiness of the firm to see innovation less as a lottery than as a process which can be continuously improved.

Another critical point to emerge from research is that innovation needs managing in an *integrated* way; it is not enough just to be good at one thing. It's less like running a 100 metres sprint than developing the range of skills to compete effectively in a range of events in the pentathlon.

So what things should organizations think about as they build and develop their innovation process? Let's take it stage by stage:

Searching for Signals to Generate Innovation Possibilities

Innovation triggers come in all shapes and sizes ands from all sorts of directions. They could take the form of new technological opportunities, or changing requirements on the part of markets; they could be the result of legislative pressure or competitor action. They could be a bright idea occurring to someone as they sit, Archimedes-like, in their bathtub. Or they could come as a result of buying in a good idea from someone outside the organization.

The message here is clear – if we are going to pick up these trigger signals – then we need to develop some pretty extensive antennae for searching and scanning around us and that includes some capability for looking into the future.

Strategically Selecting Which Possibilities to Take Forward

The trouble with innovation is that it is by its nature a risky business. You don't know at the outset whether what you decide to do is going to work out or even that it will run at all. Yet you have to commit some resources to begin the process – so how do you build a portfolio of projects which balance the risks and the potential rewards? (Of course this decision is even more tough for the first-time entrepreneur trying to launch a business based on his or her great new idea – the choice there is whether or not to go forward and commit what may be a huge investment of personal time, the mortgage, family life, and so on. Even if they succeed there is then the problem when they try and grow the business and need to develop more good ideas to follow the first.)

So this stage is very much about *strategic* choices – does the idea fit a business strategy, does it build on something we know about (or where we can get access to that knowledge easily) and do we have the skills and resources to take it forward?

Implementation – Turning the Idea into Reality

Having picked up relevant trigger signals and made a strategic decision to pursue some of them the next key phase is actually turning those potential ideas into some kind of reality – a new product or service, a change in process, a shift in business model, and so on. In some ways this implementation phase is a bit like weaving a kind of 'knowledge tapestry' – gradually pulling together different threads of knowledge – about technologies, markets, competitor behaviour – and weaving them into a picture which gradually emerges as a successful innovation.

Early on it is full of uncertainty but gradually the picture becomes clearer – but at a cost. We have to invest time, money and people to find out via research and development, market studies, competitor analysis, prototyping, testing and so on in order to gradually improve our understanding of the innovation and whether or not it will work. Eventually it is in a form which can be launched into its intended context – internal or external market – and then further knowledge about its adoption (or otherwise) can be used to refine the innovation.

Throughout this implementation phase we have to balance creativity – finding bright ideas and new ways to get around the thousand and one problems which emerge and get the bugs out of the system – with control – making sure we keep to some kind of budget on time, money, resources. This balancing act means that skills in project management around innovation – with all its inherent uncertainties – are always in high demand! This phase is also where we need to bring together different knowledge sets from many different people – so combining them in ways which help rather than hinder the process, raising big questions around team-building and management.

It would be foolish to throw good money after bad so most organizations make use of some kind of risk management as they implement innovation projects. By installing a series of 'gates' as the project moves from a gleam in the eye to an expensive commitment of time and money it becomes possible to review – and if necessary redirect or even stop something which is going off the rails.

Eventually the project is launched into some kind of marketplace – externally people who might use the product or service, and internally people who make the choice about whether or not to 'buy in' to the new process being presented to them. Either way we don't have a guarantee that just because the innovation works and we think it is the best thing since sliced bread others will feel the same way. Innovations diffuse across user populations over time – usually the process follows some kind of S-curve shape. A few brave souls take on the new idea and then gradually, assuming it works for them, others get on the bandwagon until finally there are just a few diehards – laggards – who resist the temptation to change. Managing this stage well means that we need to think ahead about how people are likely to react and build these insights into our project before we reach the launch stage – or else work hard at persuading them after we have launched it!

The Context of Success

It's all very well putting a basic process for turning ideas into reality in place. But it doesn't take place in a vacuum – it is subject to a range of internal and external influences which shape what is possible and what actually emerges. This process doesn't take place in a vacuum – it is shaped and influenced by a variety of factors. In particular innovation needs:

- Clear strategic leadership and direction, plus the commitment of resources to make this happen. Innovation is about taking risks, about going into new and sometimes completely unexplored spaces. We don't want to gamble – simply changing things for their own sake or because the fancy takes us. No organization has resources to waste in that scattergun fashion – innovation needs a strategy. But equally we need to have a degree of courage and leadership, steering the organization away from what everyone else is doing or what we've always done and into new spaces.

- An innovative organization in which the structure and climate enables people to deploy their creativity and share their knowledge to bring about change. It's easy to find prescriptions for innovative organizations which highlight the need to eliminate stifling bureaucracy, unhelpful structures, brick walls blocking communication and other factors stopping good ideas getting through. But we must be careful not to fall into the chaos trap – not all innovation works in organic, loose, informal environments or 'skunk works' – and these types

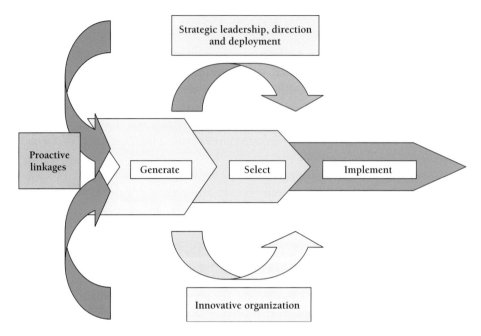

Figure 1.2   Simplified model for managing innovation.

of organization can sometimes act against the interests of successful innovation. We need to determine appropriate organization – that is, the most suitable organization given the operating contingencies. Too little order and structure may be as bad as too much.

■ Proactive links across boundaries inside the organization and to the many external agencies who can play a part in the innovation process – suppliers, customers, sources of finance, skilled resources and of knowledge, and so on. Twenty-first-century innovation is most certainly not a solo act but a multi-player game across boundaries inside the organization and to the many external agencies who can play a part in the innovation process. These days it's about a global game and one where connections and the ability to find, form and deploy creative relationships is of the essence.

Figure 1.2 shows the resulting model – what we need to pay attention to if we are going to manage innovation well.

Learning to Manage Innovation

Whatever their size or sector, all firms are trying to find ways of managing this process of renewal. There is no right answer, but each firm needs to aim for the most appropriate solution for its particular circumstances. Firms develop their own particular ways of doing things and some work better than others do. Any organization can get lucky once but the real skill in innovation management is being able to repeat the trick. And while there are no guarantees there is plenty of evidence to suggest that firms can and do learn to manage the process for success – by consciously building and developing their 'innovation capability'.

ADVICE FOR FUTURE MANAGERS

If we want to manage innovation we ought to ask ourselves the following check questions:

- Do we have effective enabling mechanisms for the core process?
- Do we have strategic direction and commitment for innovation?
- Do we have an innovative organization?
- Do we build rich proactive links?
- Do we learn and develop our innovation capability?

These questions apply across the board – though the answers may take us in different directions depending on where we start from. A new start-up business may not need much in the way of a formal and structured process for organizing and managing innovation. But a firm the size of Nokia will need to pay careful attention to structures and procedures for building a strategic portfolio of projects to explore and for managing the risks as they move from ideas into technical and commercial reality. Equally a large firm may have extensive resources to build a global set of networks to support its activities, whereas a new start-up may be vulnerable to threats from elements in its environment it simply didn't know about, never mind connected to.

Throughout the book we'll look at how these play out in different types of innovative organizations and how an understanding of them can help improve the chances of long-term innovation success. But for now let's turn our attention to the question of innovation *strategy*.

What, Why and When – the Challenge of Innovation Strategy

Building a capability to organize and manage innovation is a great achievement – but unless that capability is pointed in a suitable direction the organization risks being all dressed up with nowhere to go! The last theme we need to consider is where and how innovation can be used to strategic advantage. Table 1.2 gives some examples of the different ways in which this can be achieved – you might like to add your own ideas to the list.

Table 1.2　Strategic advantages through innovation

Mechanism	Strategic advantage	Examples
Novelty in product or service offering	Offering something no one else can	Introducing the first ... Walkman, fountain pen, camera, dishwasher, telephone bank, on-line retailer, etc. ... to the world

(continued overleaf)

Table 1.2 (*continued*)

Mechanism	Strategic advantage	Examples
Novelty in process	Offering it in ways others cannot match – faster, lower cost, more customized, etc.	Pilkington's float glass process, Bessemer's steel process, Internet banking, online bookselling, etc.
Complexity	Offering something which others find difficult to master	Rolls-Royce and aircraft engines – only a handful of competitors can master the complex machining and metallurgy involved
Legal protection of intellectual property	Offering something which others cannot do unless they pay a licence or other fee	Blockbuster drugs like Zantac, Prozac, Viagra, etc.
Add to/extend range of competitive factors	Move basis of competition – e.g. from price of product to price and quality, or price, quality, choice.	Japanese car manufacturing, which systematically moved the competitive agenda from price to quality, to flexibility and choice, to shorter times between launch of new models, and so on – each time not trading these off against each other but offering them all
Timing	First-mover advantage – being first can be worth significant market share in new product fields	Amazon.com, Yahoo – others can follow, but the advantage 'sticks' to the early movers
	Fast follower advantage – sometimes being first means you encounter many unexpected teething problems, and it makes better sense to watch someone else make the early mistakes and move fast into a follow-up product	Palm Pilot and other personal digital assistants (PDAs) which have captured a huge and growing share of the market. In fact the concept and design was articulated in Apple's ill-fated Newton product some five years earlier – but problems with software and especially handwriting recognition meant it flopped
Robust/platform design	Offering something which provides the platform on which other variations and generations can be built	Walkman architecture – through minidisk, CD, DVD, MP3, iPod
		Boeing 737 – over 30 years old, the design is still being adapted and configured to suit different users – one of the most successful aircraft in the world in terms of sales
		Intel and AMD with different variants of their microprocessor families

Table 1.2   (*continued*)

Mechanism	Strategic advantage	Examples
Rewriting the rules	Offering something which represents a completely new product or process concept – a different way of doing things – and makes the old ones redundant	Typewriters vs. computer word processing, ice vs. refrigerators, electric vs. gas or oil lamps
Reconfiguring the parts of the process	Rethinking the way in which bits of the system work together – e.g. building more effective networks, outsourcing and coordination of a virtual company	Zara, Benetton in clothing, Dell in computers, Toyota in its supply-chain management
Transferring across different application contexts	Recombining established elements for different markets	Polycarbonate wheels transferred from application market like rolling luggage into children's toys – lightweight micro-scooters
Others?	Innovation is all about finding new ways to do things and to obtain strategic advantage – so there will be room for new ways of gaining and retaining advantage	Napster. This firm began by writing software which would enable music fans to swap their favourite pieces via the Internet – the Napster program essentially connected person to person (P2P) by providing a fast link. Its potential to change the architecture and mode of operation of the Internet was much greater, and although Napster suffered from legal issues followers developed a huge industry based on downloading and file-sharing.

The problem isn't the shortage of ways of gaining competitive advantage through innovation but rather which ones will we choose and why? It's a decision which any organization has to take – whether a start-up deciding the (relatively) simple question of go/no-go in terms of trying to enter a hostile marketplace with their new idea, or a giant firm trying to open up new market space through innovation. Police forces need to think strategically about how they will deploy their scarce resources to contain crime and stabilize law and order, while hospital managements are concerned to balance limited resources against the increasing demands of healthcare expectations.

We can think about strategy as a process of exploring the space defined by our four innovation types – the 4 Ps mentioned earlier. Each of our 4Ps of innovation can take place along an axis running from incremental through to radical change; the area indicated by the circle in Figure 1.3 is the potential innovation space within which an organization can operate. Where it actually explores and why – and which areas it leaves alone – are all questions for innovation strategy.

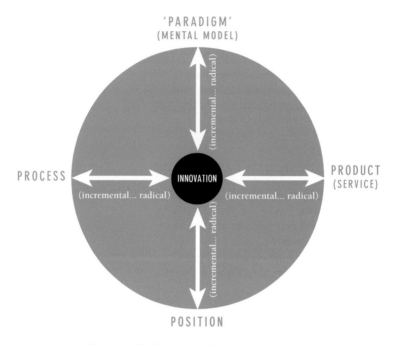

Figure 1.3   Exploring innovation space.

How can we choose which options might make sense for us? We need to ask the question against a backdrop of two key themes: Where are we trying to go as an organization – what's our overall 'business strategy' – and how will innovation help us get there? And do we know anything about the direction we want to go in – does it build on something we have some competence in (or have access to)? These form the basis for the strategic discussion which needs to go on.

Beyond the Steady State – the Challenge of Discontinuous Change

	Do it better	Do it differently
Product (service)	*Product improvement*	*... and now for something completely different*
Process	*Getting lean, the quest for 'excellence'*	*Radical process change*
Position	*Extend, deepen, segment markets*	*Find new playing fields*
Paradigm (business concept)	*Change the business model*	*Rewrite the rules*

The risk is that even if firms recognize and accept the need for continuous innovation they may find difficulties in framing an appropriate strategic innovation agenda. With limited resources they may find themselves putting scarce eggs into too few or the wrong baskets. Innovation can take many forms – from simple, incremental development of what is already there to radical development of totally new options.

The challenge is for firms to be aware of the extensive space within which innovation possibilities exist and to try and develop a strategic portfolio which covers this territory effectively, balancing risks and resources.

Most of the time innovation takes place within a set of rules of the game which are clearly understood, and involves players trying to innovate by doing what they already do (product, process, position, etc.) but better. Some manage this more effectively than others but the 'rules of the game' are accepted and do not change.

But occasionally something happens which dislocates this framework and changes the rules of the game. By definition these are not everyday events but they have the capacity to redefine the space and the boundary conditions – they open up new opportunities but also challenge existing players to reframe what they are doing in the light of new conditions.

ADVICE FOR FUTURE MANAGERS

Most of the time managing innovation is about the 'steady state' – doing what we do but better under a set of rules which everybody plays by. But we know that the carpet does get pulled out from under us on occasions, triggered by violent shifts in the technological, political or market context. So smart managers work to build not only the capability to manage innovation under stable conditions but also to create at least some capacity to pick up on, and do something about discontinuous conditions. They create resources for 'blue sky' project research, they send out scouts to pick up on early warning about radical developments, they fund internal entrepreneurs and venture capital. And at the limit they find ways to ask uncomfortable questions like 'how would we destroy this business?' – and use that to seek out potential areas of vulnerability.

What seems to happen is that for a given set of technological and market conditions there is a long period of relative stability during which a continuous stream of variations around a basic innovation theme take place. Essentially this is product/process improvement along the lines of 'doing what we do, but better'. For example, the Bic ballpoint pen was originally developed in 1957 but remains a strong product with daily sales of 14 million units worldwide. Although superficially the same shape closer inspection reveals a host of incremental changes that have taken place in materials, inks, ball technology, safety features, and so on.

But these 'steady-state' innovation conditions are punctuated by occasional discontinuities – and when these occur one or more of the basic conditions (technology, markets, social, regulatory, etc.) shifts dramatically. In the process the underlying 'rules of the game' change and a new opportunity space for innovation opens up. 'Do different' conditions of this kind occur, for example, when radical change takes place along the technological frontier or when completely new markets emerge.

Chapter 7 looks in more detail at this question of discontinuous innovation and how we might manage it. The important message is that under such conditions (which thankfully don't emerge every day) we need different approaches to organizing and managing innovation. If we try and use established models which work under steady state conditions we find we are increasingly out of our depth and risk being upstaged by new and more agile players.

STRATEGIC AND SOCIAL IMPACT

Much of the innovation that we hear about is around commercial products and services – more gadgets added to our mobile phones, faster or more fuel-efficient cars, increasing customization of our retail experience or lower-cost flying, banking, insurance or bookselling. But apart from its role as an engine for economic growth, innovation has wider social implications which make understanding and managing the process a key challenge for all of our futures. For example:

■ Innovation in micro-credit in poor countries like Bangladesh or Tanzania has revolutionized parts of the financial sector and opened up access to start-up capital for thousands of people who go on to grow their businesses, create employment opportunities and develop the wider local economy.

■ Innovation in sustainable energy systems offers a way out of the trap being sprung by spiralling fossil fuel prices and declining availability.

■ Growing desire for 'green' products and services is fuelling demand for innovation across a range of sectors – to the point where a major consulting firm, Arthur D. Little, describe sustainability as 'the new high ground' for innovation.

■ Massively increased life expectancies coupled with static or declining birth rates and inadequate pension provision means a time bomb is ticking away under many 'developed' economies. Meeting expectations in fields like healthcare and social welfare on the back of limited resources is going to require radical innovation across the board, not only in products and services but also in the underlying models of how such care is organized and delivered – and paid for.

■ Law and order top the list of concerns in many inner cities and are sometimes painted as a losing battle. But the experience of the New York Police Department in the 1990s suggests that innovation can play a decisive role here too. When William Bratton was appointed as police commissioner in 1994 murders were at an all-time high and muggings, thefts and armed robberies had reached the point where many felt the city was in irreversible decline. The 36 000 staff felt demoralized and unable to cope and the organization was prone to in-fighting and blame swapping. Yet in less than two years he introduced innovations which turned the tide – murder rates fell by 50%, felonies by 39% and thefts by 35%, while public confidence grew from 37% to 73%. And after his departure in 1996 the figures have continued in this positive direction.

These – and many other examples – point to the importance of innovation as a social shaper and driver. But getting the benefits and minimizing the negative consequences depends critically on how we approach the challenge of understanding and *managing* the innovation process itself.

Developing Personal Capabilities

Innovation doesn't happen by accident, as we've seen in this chapter. It results from a systematic and organized process of managed change, taking new ideas forward to successful reality. Entrepreneurial skills lie at the heart of this process – whether in terms of starting a new business, renewing or reinventing an established firm or opening up new possibilities for community development through social entrepreneurship. But entrepreneurship isn't just another name for gambling – instead it involves motivated and focused energy and commitment – and a core skill set which includes:

- A well-developed understanding of the process and its different elements.

- Project planning and management – against a background of uncertainty.

- Project team working – the ability to work with others under uncertain conditions.

- Strategic leadership – having a vision and being able to share it.

- Learning skills – the ability to analyse what works and why and to feed this back into the system to improve capability for next time.

Finally it's worth remembering some useful advice from an old but wise source. In his famous book *The Prince* Niccolo Machiavelli gave a warning to would-be innovators:

> *It must be remembered that there is nothing more difficult to plan, more doubtful of success, nor more dangerous to management than the creation of a new system. For the initiator has the enmity of all who would profit by the preservation of the old institution and merely lukewarm defenders in those who gain by the new ones.*

Chapter Summary

- Innovation is a survival imperative. If an organization doesn't change what it offers the world and the ways in which it creates and delivers its offerings it could well be in trouble. And innovation contributes to competitive success in many different ways – it's a *strategic* resource to getting the organization where it is trying to go, whether it is delivering shareholder value for private sector firms, or providing better public services, or enabling the start-up and growth of new enterprises.

- But innovation doesn't happen simply because we hope it will – it's a complex process which carries risks and needs careful and systematic *management*. The core process involves three steps – getting hold of new ideas, selecting the good ones and implementing them. The challenge comes in doing this in organized fashion and in being able to repeat the trick.

- Research repeatedly suggests that if we want to succeed in managing innovation we need to:
    - Understand *what* we are trying to manage – the better our mental models the more likely what we do with them in the way of building and running organizations and processes will work.
    - Understand the *how* – creating the conditions (and adapting/configuring them) to make it happen.
    - Understand the *what*, *why* and *when* of innovation activity – strategy shaping the innovation work that we do.
    - Understand that it is a moving target – managing innovation is about building a *dynamic capability*.

- Innovation can take many forms but it can be reduced to four dimensions of change (the 4Ps):
    - *Product innovation* – changes in the things (products/services) which an organization offers.
    - *Process innovation* – changes in the ways in which things (products/services) are created and delivered.

- *Position innovation* – changes in the context in which the products/services are introduced.
- *Paradigm innovation* – changes in the underlying mental models which frame what the organization does.

■ Within any of these dimensions innovations can be positioned on a spectrum from 'incremental' – doing what we do but better – through to 'radical' – doing something completely different. And they can be stand-alone component innovations or they can form part of a linked 'architecture' or system which brings many different components together in a particular way.

■ Innovation isn't a single event, like the light bulb going off above a cartoon character's head. It's an extended process of picking up on ideas for change and turning them into effective reality – a new product or service people use and value, a new process they buy into working with. We can think of this in terms of a simplified three stage model:
  - Searching for signals to generate innovation possibilities.
  - Strategically selecting which possibilities to take forward.
  - Implementation – turning the idea into reality.

■ But this core process doesn't take place in a vacuum – we know it is strongly influenced by many factors. In particular innovation needs:
  - Clear strategic leadership and direction, plus the commitment of resources to make this happen.
  - An innovative organization in which the structure and climate enable people to deploy their creativity and share their knowledge to bring about change.
  - Proactive links across boundaries inside the organization and to the many external agencies who can play a part in the innovation process – suppliers, customers, sources of finance, skilled resources and of knowledge, and so on.

■ Any organization can get lucky once but the real skill in innovation management is being able to repeat the trick. So if we want to manage innovation we ought to ask ourselves the following check questions:
  - Do we have effective enabling mechanisms for the core process?
  - Do we have strategic direction and commitment for innovation?
  - Do we have an innovative organization?
  - Do we build rich proactive links?
  - Do we learn and develop our innovation capability?

■ Building a capability to organize and manage innovation is a great achievement – but we also need to consider where and how innovation can be used to strategic advantage. Two key themes are important here – first, what is our overall 'business strategy' and how will innovation help us get there? And second, do we know anything about the direction we want to go in – does it build on something we have some competence in (or have access to)?

■ Most of the time innovation takes place within a set of rules of the game which are clearly understood, and involves players trying to innovate by doing what they already do (product, process, position, etc.) but better. But occasionally something happens which changes the rules of the game – for example, when radical change takes place along the technological frontier or when completely new markets emerge. When this happens we need different approaches to organizing and managing innovation. If we try and use established models which work under steady-state conditions we find we are increasingly out of our depth and risk being upstaged by new and more agile players.

Key Terms Defined

Architecture innovation Changes in the whole system – for example, moving from that computer design to a completely different way of processing information.

Component innovation Changes at the level of components in a bigger system – for example a faster transistor in a microchip in a computer.

Discontinuous innovation Radical innovations which change the 'rules of the game' and open up a new game in which new players are often at an advantage.

Incremental innovation Small improvements to existing products, services or processes – 'doing what we do but better'.

Innovation The process of translating ideas into useful – and used – new products, processes or services.

Invention Coming up with a new idea.

Paradigm innovation Changes in the underlying mental models which frame what the organization does.

Position innovation Changes in the context in which the products/services are introduced.

Process innovation Changes in the ways in which they are created and delivered.

Product innovation Changes in the things (products/services) which an organization offers.

Radical innovation – significantly different changes to products, services or processes – 'do what we do differently'

Further Reading and Resources

The importance of innovation as a strategic imperative comes through in many case examples – some good ones can be found in the following:

Christensen, C. (1997) *The Innovator's Dilemma*. Harvard Business School Press, Boston, Mass.

Dell, M. (1999) *Direct from Dell*. HarperCollins, New York.

Dyson, J. (1997) *Against the Odds*. Orion, London.

Garr, D. (2000) *IBM Redux: Lou Gerstner and the Business Turnaround of the Decade*. HarperCollins, New York.

Hamel, G. (2000) *Leading the Revolution*. Harvard Business School Press, Boston, Mass.

Kim, W. and Mauborgne, R. (2005) *Blue Ocean Strategy: How to Create Uncontested Market Space and Make the Competition Irrelevant*. Harvard Business School Press, Boston, Mass.

Tidd, J. and Hull, F. (eds) (2003) *Service innovation: Organizational Responses to Technological Opportunities and Market Imperatives*. Imperial College Press, London.

Utterback, J. (1994) *Mastering the Dynamics of Innovation*. Harvard Business School Press, Boston, Mass.

Von Stamm, B. (2003) *The Innovation Wave*. John Wiley & Sons, Ltd, Chichester.

Womack, J., Jones, D. et al. (1991) *The Machine that Changed the World*. Rawson Associates, New York.

More detailed discussion of the 4Ps approach is in: Francis, D. and Bessant, J. (2005) Targeting innovation and implications for capability development. *Technovation*, **25** (3), 171–183.

Incremental and radical innovation themes are covered well in sources like: Benner, M.J. and Tushman, M.L. (2003) Exploitation, exploration, and process management: the productivity dilemma revisited. *Academy of Management Review*, **28** (2), 238.

Imai, K. (1987) *Kaizen*. Random House, New York.

Leifer, R., McDermott, C. et al. (2000). *Radical Innovation*, Harvard Business School Press, Boston, Mass.

The idea of component and architectural innovation was originally discussed in: Henderson, R. and Clark, K. (1990) Architectural innovation: the reconfiguration of existing product technologies and the failure of established firms. *Administrative Science Quarterly*, **35**, 9–30.

Seeing innovation as a process and the ways in which we think about how that process works are discussed in: Rothwell, R. (1992) Successful industrial innovation: critical success factors for the 1990s. *R&D Management*, **22** (3), 221–239; and Van de Ven, A. (1999) *The Innovation Journey*. Oxford University Press, Oxford. A good view of some of the twenty-first-century challenges can be found in Chesborough, H. (2003) *Open Innovation: The New Imperative for Creating and Profiting from Technology*. Harvard Business School Press, Boston, Mass.

Innovation strategy is discussed later in this book but for more background, see: Burgelman, R., Christensen, C. et al. (eds.) (2004) *Strategic Management of Technology and Innovation*. McGraw Hill Irwin, Boston.

The theme of 'discontinuous' innovation is explored, for example, in: Foster, R. and Kaplan, S. (2002) *Creative Destruction*. Harvard University Press, Cambridge; Bessant, J., Lamming, R. et al. (2005) Managing innovation beyond the steady state. *Technovation*, **25** (12), 1366–1376; and Day, G. and Schoemaker, P. (2000). *Wharton on Managing Emerging Technologies*. John Wiley & Sons, Ltd, New York.

References

1 Drucker, P. (1985) *Innovation and Entrepreneurship*. Harper & Row, New York.

2 Rothwell, R. and Gardiner, P. (1985) Invention, innovation, re-innovation and the role of the user. *Technovation*, **3**, 167–186.

Discussion Questions

1 Is innovation manageable or just a random gambling activity where you sometimes get lucky? If it is manageable, how can firms organize and manage it – what general principles might they use?

2 'Build a better mousetrap and the world will beat a path to your door!' Will it? What are the limitations of seeing innovation simply as coming up with bright ideas? Illustrate your answer with examples drawn from manufacturing and services.

3 What are the key stages involved in an innovation process? And what are the characteristic sets of activities which take place at each stage? How might such an innovation process look for:
   ■ A fast-food restaurant chain
   ■ An electronic test equipment maker
   ■ A hospital
   ■ An insurance company
   ■ A new entrant biotechnology firm.

4 Fred Bloggs was a bright young PhD scientist with a patent on a new algorithm for monitoring brainwave activity and predicting the early onset of a stroke. He was convinced of the value of his idea and took it to market having sold his car, borrowed money from family and friends and taken out a large loan. He went

bankrupt despite having a demonstration version which doctors he showed it to were impressed by. Why might his failure be linked to having a partial model of how innovation works – and how could he avoid making the same mistake in the future?

5 How does innovation operate as a knowledge creation and transfer process? Illustrate your answer with relevant case examples.

6 If innovation is increasingly a matter of knowledge management, what sorts of challenges does this approach pose for managing the process?

7 How can knowledge be used to provide competitive advantage in a competitive marketplace – and how might this advantage be protected and preserved?

8 How does innovation contribute to competitive advantage? Support your answer with illustrations from both manufacturing and services.

9 Does innovation matter for public services? Using examples indicate how and where it can be an important strategic issue.

10 You are a newly appointed director for a small charity which supports homeless people. How could innovation improve the ways in which your charity operates?

11 Innovation can take many forms. Give examples of product/service, process, position and paradigm (mental model) innovations.

12 The low-cost airline approach has massively changed the way people choose and use air travel – and has been both a source of growth for new players and a life-threatening challenge for some existing players. What types of innovation have been involved in this?

13 You have been called in as a consultant to a medium-sized toy manufacturer whose range of construction toys (building bricks, etc.) has been losing market share to other types of toys. What innovation directions would you recommend to this company to restore their competitive position? (Use the 4Ps framework to think about possibilities.)

14 Innovation is about big leaps forward, 'eureka' moments and radical breakthroughs – or is it? Using examples from manufacturing and services make a case for the importance of incremental innovation.

15 Describe, with example, the concept of platforms in product and process innovation and suggest how such an approach might help spread the high costs of innovation across a longer time period.

16 What are the challenges which managers might face in trying to organize for a long-term steady stream of incremental innovation?

Team Exercises

1 Strategic Advantage through Innovation

Think about an organization with which you are familiar and about the other firms or players in its sector. How do they choose to try and position themselves for strategic advantage – and how do they use technology to help them do so? They may try and offer the lowest prices – and have heavy investments in clever machines which help them achieve this. Or they may try and offer the best designs – and back this up with a commitment to design and R&D.

Try and research the strategies not only of one firm but of several within the sector and build up a picture of how the sector is shaped by firms using technology to try and gain competitive advantage. You might like to use Table 1.2 to help you think about how they are doing so – and to record your thoughts.

2 Forces for Strategic Innovation

Thinking about an organization with which you are familiar, try and list the 'driving forces' for strategic technological innovation. What are the main sources of demand and how are they pulling particular responses from competing firms? What are the main trends in technology and how are these shaping new opportunities which firms can exploit to advantage? Jot your ideas down in the spaces provided. Then add a future dimension – thinking 5, 10, 20 years ahead what can you see on the horizon? Is it more of the same or might there be possible points where new demand issues or new technology opportunities change the rules of the game?

Timescale	Demand forces pulling innovation	Technology push creating opportunities
Now		
5 years ahead		
10 years ahead		
20 years ahead		

3 On the chart below try and list as many ways as possible which a firm might be able to exploit knowledge for strategic advantage. What would be needed to create and sustain such advantage?

Source of competitive advantage	Examples	What has to be managed to build and sustain such advantage?
e.g. Having a design no-one else has thought of	Dyson's vacuum cleaner	How to protect it legally – patents, copyright, etc.

Assignment and Case Study Questions

1 Sector Innovation Patterns

Imagine you work for a firm involved in children's toy manufacturing. Now try and list the major changes in that sector over the past 25 years in terms of what contributes to competitiveness. Who (which firms) have been the winners and losers and why? You are trying to get a feel in this for how technological change can shape the competitive dynamics of an industry so think about questions like these:

■ How has the industry changed – and how has technology helped (or could it help) deal with these changes?
■ What new technologies have emerged – and how have they been used?
■ What are the main market demands (e.g. price, quality, design, customization, speed of response, etc.) and how has technology affected the ability of firms to offer these?
■ If a new entrant came into the industry what would he or she have to offer to become a market leader – and how might technology help him or her do so?

You may need to spend some time researching the wider sector to build up this picture. Try and summarize your research in the form of short 'bullet points' which highlight the strategic role which technology plays. You might like to use the framework below which is partially filled in.

Major changes in the industry	Major new technologies	Main market demands and how technology affects them	How to become a market leader
Big influence of TV and films – increasing tie-ins Price pressures push actual manufacturing to the Far East Fashion industry with high risks – and benefits for the right products. Costs of new technologies mean fewer players can stay in the game of new product development – so consolidation of the industry	Electronics and programmability TV/video and computer games – as competitors to traditional toys but also as complements which can extend their range – e.g. Lego bricks plus computer = programmable toys.	Strong price pressure – pushes manufacturing to low-cost locations – technology relevant in keeping costs low while enabling consistent quality Major emphasis on design technologies	Close market understanding and the ability to communicate this deep into the organization and configure products to meet these demands Broad knowledge base – especially in newer technologies like computers and software but also in design of parts Access to distribution networks Strong design and marketing capability

2 Innovation Success and Failure

Innovations don't happen by accident – and they don't always succeed. They are influenced by a variety of factors – organizational structures, project team dynamics, strategic decision-making, technological and market events, and so on. Using any case examples and/or your own experience, list the key management/organizational factors which appear to affect the outcome of innovation in products or processes.

CASE STUDY 1

Exploring Innovation in Action: The Changing Nature of the Music Industry

1 April 2006. Apart from being a traditional day for playing practical jokes, this was the day on which another landmark in the rapidly changing world of music was reached. 'Crazy' – a track by Gnarls Barkley – made pop history as the UK's first song to top the charts based on download sales alone. Commenting on the fact that the song had been downloaded more than 31 000 times but was only released for sale in the shops on 3 April. Gennaro Castaldo, spokesman for retailer HMV, said: 'This not only represents a watershed in how the charts are compiled, but shows that legal downloads have come of age . . . if physical copies fly off the shelves at the same rate it could vie for a place as the year's biggest seller.'

One of the less visible but highly challenging aspects of the Internet is the impact it has had – and is having – on the entertainment business. This is particularly the case with music. At one level its impacts could be assumed to be confined to providing new 'e-tailing' channels through which you can obtain the latest CD of your preference – for example from Amazon.com or CD-Now or 100 other websites. These innovations increase the choice and tailoring of the music purchasing service and demonstrate some of the 'richness/reach' economic shifts of the new Internet game.

But beneath this updating of essentially the same transaction lies a more fundamental shift – in the ways in which music is created and distributed and in the business model on which the whole music industry is currently predicated. In essence the old model involved a complex network in which songwriters and artists depended on A&R (artists and repertoire) to select a few acts, production staff who would record in complex and expensive studios, other production staff who would oversee the manufacture of physical discs, tapes and CDs, and marketing and distribution staff who would ensure the product was publicized and disseminated to an increasingly global market.

Several key changes have undermined this structure and brought with it significant disruption to the industry. Old competencies may no longer be relevant while acquiring new ones becomes a matter of urgency. Even well-established names like Sony find it difficult to stay ahead while new entrants are able to exploit the economics of the Internet. At the heart of the change is the potential for creating, storing and distributing music in digital format – a problem which many researchers have worked on for some time. One solution, developed by one of the Fraunhofer Institutes in Germany, is a standard based on the Motion Picture Experts Group (MPEG) level 3 protocol – MP3. MP3 offers a powerful algorithm for managing one of the big problems in transmitting music files – that of compression. Normal audio files cover a wide range of frequencies and are thus very large and not suitable for fast transfer across the Internet – especially with a population who may be using only relatively slow modems. With MP3 effective compression is achieved by cutting out those frequencies which the human ear cannot detect – with the result that the files to be transferred are much smaller.

As a result MP3 files can be moved across the Internet quickly and shared widely. Various programmes exist for transferring normal audio files and inputs – such as CDs – into MP3 and back again.

What does this mean for the music business? In the first instance aspiring musicians no longer need to depend on being picked up by A&R staff from major companies who can bear the costs of recording and production of a physical CD. Instead they can use home recording software and either produce a CD themselves or else go straight to MP3 – and then distribute the product globally via newsgroups, chatrooms, and so on. In the process they effectively create a parallel and much more direct music industry which leaves existing players and artists on the sidelines.

Such changes are not necessarily threatening. For many people the lowering of entry barriers has opened up the possibility of participating in the music business – for example, by making and sharing music without the complexities and costs of a formal recording contract and the resources of a major record company. There is also scope for innovation around the periphery – for example, in the music publishing sector where sheet music and lyrics are also susceptible to lowering of barriers through the application of digital technology. Journalism and related activities become increasingly open – now music reviews and other forms of commentary become possible via specialist user groups and channels on the Web whereas before they were the province of a few magazine titles. Compiling popularity charts – and the related advertising – is also opened up as the medium switches from physical CDs and tapes distributed and sold via established channels to new media such as MP3 distributed via the Internet.

As if this were not enough the industry is also challenged from another source – the sharing of music between different people connected via the Internet. Although technically illegal this practice of sharing between people's record collections has always taken place – but not on the scale which the Internet threatens to facilitate. Much of the established music industry is concerned with legal issues – how to protect copyright and how to ensure that royalties are paid in the right proportions to those who participate in production and distribution. But when people can share music in MP3 format and distribute it globally the potential for policing the system and collecting royalties becomes extremely difficult to sustain.

It has been made much more so by another technological development – that of person-to-person or P2P networking. Sean Fanning, an 18-year-old student with the nickname 'the Napster', was intrigued by the challenge of being able to enable his friends to 'see' and share between their own personal record collections. He argued that if they held these in MP3 format then it should be possible to set up some kind of central exchange programme which facilitated their sharing.

The result – the Napster.com site – offered sophisticated software which enabled P2P transactions. The Napster server did not actually hold any music on its files – but every day millions of swaps were made by people around the world exchanging their music collections. Needless to say this posed a huge threat to the established music business since it involved no payment of royalties. A number of high-profile lawsuits followed but while Napster's activities have been curbed the problem did not go away. There are now many other sites emulating and extending what Napster started – sites such as Gnutella, Kazaa, Limewire took the P2P idea further and enabled exchange of many different file formats – text, video, and so on. In Napster's own case the phenomenally successful site concluded a deal with entertainment giant Bertelsman which paved the way for subscription-based services which provide some revenue stream to deal with the royalty issue.

Expectations that legal protection would limit the impact of this revolution have been dampened by a US Court of Appeal ruling which rejected claims that P2P violated copyright law. Their judgement said, 'History has shown that time and market forces often provide equilibrium in balancing interests, whether the new technology be a player piano, a copier, a tape recorder, a video recorder, a PC, a karaoke machine or an MP3 player' (*Personal Computer World*, November 2004, p. 32).

Significantly the new opportunities opened up by this were seized not by music industry firms but by computer companies, especially Apple. In parallel with the launch of their successful iPod personal MP3 player they opened a site called iTunes which offered users a choice of thousands of tracks for download at 99 cents each. In its first weeks of operation it recorded 1 million hits in February 2006. The billionth song, 'Speed of Sound', was purchased as part of Coldplay's *X&Y* album by Alex Ostrovsky from West Bloomfield, Michigan. 'I hope that every customer, artist and music company executive takes a moment today to reflect on what we've achieved together during the past three years,' said Steve Jobs, Apple's CEO. 'Over 1 billion songs have now been legally purchased and downloaded around the globe, representing a major force against music piracy and the future of music distribution as we move from CDs to the Internet.'

This has been a dramatic shift, reaching the point where more singles were bought as downloads in 2005 than as CDs, and where the overall shift to a majority of purchases being by download is expected to take place during 2006. New players are coming to dominate the game – for example, Tesco and Microsoft. And the changes don't stop there. In February 2006 the Arctic Monkeys topped the UK album charts and walked off with a fistful of awards from the music business – yet their rise to prominence had been entirely via 'viral marketing' across the Internet rather than by conventional advertising and promotion. Playing gigs around the northern English town of Sheffield, the band simply gave away CDs of their early songs to their fans, who then obligingly spread them around on the Internet. 'They came to the attention of the public via the Internet, and you had chatrooms, everyone talking about them,' says a slightly worried Gennaro Castaldo of HMV Records. David Sinclair, a rock journalist suggests that 'It's a big wakeup call to all the record companies, the establishment, if you like.... This lot caught them all napping...We are living in a completely different era, which the Arctic Monkeys have done an awful lot to bring about.'

The writing may be on the wall for the music industry in the same way as the low-cost airline business has transformed the travel business. And behind the music business the next target may be the movie and entertainment industry where there are already worrying similarities. Or the growing computer games sector with shifts towards more small-scale developers emulating the Arctic Monkeys and using viral marketing to build a sales base.

Case Study Questions

1 In the chapter we looked at the idea that innovations can be 'architectural' – changes in the ways different things are put together into a whole system. Examples might be a motor car, a mobile phone business, a hospital. And innovations can also be at the 'component' level – the parts which go into those systems – for example, the engine, brakes, fuel tank, electrics, which go into a car. Changes at the component level may take place independently but when the whole architecture changes there are often major winners and losers.

Looking at the case study, try and identify which of the changes are architectural and which are component. What are the implications for different players in terms of the likely threat to them and the ways in which they could respond?

Use the framework at the top of the next page to capture your answers.

	Architectural innovation	Component innovation
Likely threat/opportunity for player 1 – and why		
Likely threat/opportunity for player 2 – and why		
Etc.		

2 Competence-destroying and Competence-enhancing Innovation

Try and review the case in terms of the following questions.

■ To what extent are the changes involved competence-enhancing (i.e. building on what a player in the industry already knows so they can strengthen their position) or competence-destroying (i.e. something completely new which requires learning some new tricks) innovations?

■ And for whom? (Think about the different players in the music industry – who are the likely winners and losers?)

■ What strategies might a firm use to exploit the opportunities? (Again think about the different players in the industry and how they might defend their positions or open up new opportunities.)

Use the following framework to capture your answers.

	An established record company	A newcomer wanting to offer entertainment on the Web	A music publishing company (responsible for copyrights on sheet music, etc.)	Other examples ...
Is the change competence-enhancing? Why?				
Is the change competence-destroying? Why?				
What might you do about this to secure and improve your position?				

3 Can you map the different kinds of innovation in the case study? Which were incremental and which radical/discontinuous? Why? Give examples to support your answer.

4 Strategic advantage in innovation can come through combinations of four basic types of innovation – product/offering, process, position and paradigm (mental model). (Look at page **11** to remind yourself about this). Giving examples to illustrate your answer, how has the pattern of strategic advantage changed in the music industry?

5 Is the 'revolution' in the music industry a result of the development of new technologies? Or is it happening because of changes on the demand side – shifts in what people want and are prepared to pay for? Or is it a mixture of both? What lessons might that offer to someone wanting to enter the industry as a new player? And what might an established player do to preserve their position? Illustrate your answer with examples.

Chapter 2

Organizing Innovation and Entrepreneurship

Innovation is the specific tool of entrepreneurs, the means by which they exploit change as an opportunity for a different business or service. It is capable of being presented as a discipline, capable of being learned, capable of being practiced – Peter Drucker

This chapter

■ Looks at key themes in organizing and managing entrepreneurship and innovation.

■ Explores individual creativity and how it can be promoted.

■ Reviews the key processes, strategies and stages in creativity.

■ Examines how to create a climate for innovation.

Learning Objectives

When you have completed this chapter you will be able to:

■ Understand the relationships between individual creativity, entrepreneurship and innovation.

■ Appreciate what factors make an individual more or less creative.

■ Identify the key characteristics of an entrepreneur.

■ Follow a process to help translate ideas into innovations.

■ Develop an organizational environment that supports creativity, entrepreneurship and innovation.

Linking Creativity, Entrepreneurship and Innovation

Innovation and entrepreneurship are not just about having a bright idea. Conventional approaches to entrepreneurship too often assume that the business idea and concept have already been identified, and that the main job to do is to develop a business plan and to raise resources to implement this. However, in our experience, identifying, assessing and refining an idea and developing this into a business concept is a big part of the problem. Many of the problems entrepreneurs and innovations experience can be traced to weaknesses in the early part of the process.

This has major implications for how we manage creativity and translate ideas into innovations. While the initial idea may require a significant creative leap, much of the rest of the process will involve hundreds of small problem-finding and -solving exercises – each of which needs creative input. And though the former may need the skills or inspiration of a particular individual the latter requires the input of many different people over a sustained period of time. Developing the light bulb or the Post-it note or any successful innovation is actually the story of the combined creative endeavour of many individuals.

Broadly speaking, the practice and study of innovation and entrepreneurship can be approached from three different perspectives:

- Personal or individual, which emphasizes the role of creativity and entrepreneurship;

- Collective or social, which stresses the contribution of teams and groups;

- Contextual, which focuses on the structures, climate, processes and tools.

One critical issue arising from these different perspectives is the relative effort needed between the individual, social and organizational contributions to innovation and entrepreneurship, and the interaction between these three levels.

We will use the following definition of creativity:

> *Creativity is the making and communicating of meaningful new connections to help us think of many possibilities; to help us think and experience in varied ways and using different points of view; to help us think of new and unusual possibilities; and to guide us in generating and selecting alternatives. These new connections and possibilities must result in something of value for the individual, group, organization, or society.*

Note that being creative at work is not the same as having a creative job. Jobs typically thought to be creative include design, development and advertising, but creativity in most organizations is essentially down to an individual choice between the routine and novel. It is based on the belief that one has the ability to produce productive creative outcomes. It includes the confidence to adopt non-conformist perspectives, to take risks and act without dependence on social approval, and can encourage broader information search and sustain effort. Also, the creativity of all workers responds positively to support for creativity from managers and co-workers.

Research has provided many insights into many aspects of creativity, the most relevant being an understanding and nurturing of the creative process. This focus includes consideration of mental operations, heuristics and problem-solving strategies (among other items). Those who study creativity often refer to three overlapping themes:

- *Personality*, which has led to the identification of many personality characteristics, cognitive abilities and behavioural or biographical events associated with individual creativity.

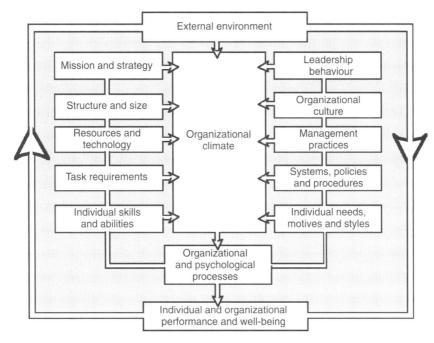

Figure 2.1   Factors which contribute to a creative organization.

Source: Isaksen, S. and Tidd, J (2006) *Meeting the innovation Challenge. John Wiley & Sons, Ltd, Chichester*.

■ *Process* of creative thinking, with various stages and strategies.

■ *Environmental* factors that facilitate or inhibit creative performance, such as climate and culture.

Together, these factors interact to either encourage, or to constrain, innovation and entrepreneurship (Figure 2.1).

Personality: Promoting Individual Creativity

Studies of innovation and entrepreneurship have tended to focus on the role of key individuals; in particular, inherent or given traits of inventors or entrepreneurs. Archetypical inventors include Thomas Edison and Alexander Graham Bell, or more recently James Dyson or Steve Jobs. Each of these examples of inventors was also an innovator, translating the original technical inventions into new products, but each was also an entrepreneur, in the sense that they created and developed successful businesses based on the inventions and innovations.

Typically, an entrepreneur:[1]

■ Passionately seeks to identify new opportunities and ways to profit from change and disruption.

■ Pursues opportunities with discipline and focuses on a limited number of projects, rather than opportunistically chasing every option.

■ Focuses on action and execution, rather than endless analysis.

■ Involves and energizes networks of relationships, exploiting the expertise and resources of others, while helping others to achieve their own goals.

These characteristics are consistent with what research tells us about the cognitive abilities necessary for creativity and innovation:

■ Information acquisition and dissemination, including the capture of information from a wide range of sources, requiring attention and perception.

■ Intelligence, the ability and capability to interpret, process and manipulate information.

■ Sense-making, giving meaning to information.

■ Unlearning, the process of reducing or eliminating pre-existing routines or behaviours, including discarding information.

■ Implementation and improvization, autonomous behaviour, experimentation, reflection and action. Using information to solve problems, for example, during new product development or process improvement.

Personal orientation includes what is traditionally thought of as characteristics of the creative person as well as the creative abilities associated with creativity. These include personality traits traditionally associated with creativity such as openness to experience, tolerance of ambiguity, resistance to premature closure, curiosity and risk-taking, among others. They also include such creative-thinking abilities as fluency, flexibility, originality and elaboration. Expertise, competence and knowledge base also contribute to creative efforts. Traditionally, people have been assessed and selected for different tasks on the basis of such characteristics, for example, using psychometric questionnaires or tests. For example, the Kirton Adapter-Innovator (KAI) scale assesses different dimensions of creativity, including originality, attention to detail and reliance on rules.

The Kirton Adapter-Innovator (KAI) scale is a psychometric approach for assessing the creativity of individuals. By a series of questions it seeks to identify an individual's attitudes towards originality, attention to detail and following rules. It seeks to differentiate 'adaptive' from 'innovative' styles:

■ *Adaptors* characteristically produce a sufficiency of ideas based closely on existing agreed definitions of a problem and its likely solutions, but stretching the solutions. These ideas help to improve and 'do better'.

■ *Innovators* are more likely to reconstruct the problem, challenge the assumptions and to emerge with a much less expected solution which very probably is also at first less acceptable. Innovators are less concerned with doing things better than with doing things differently.

It is important to recognize that creativity is an attribute that we all possess, but the preferred *style* of expressing it varies widely. Recognizing the need for different kinds of individual creative styles is an important aspect of developing successful innovations and new ventures. It is clear from a wealth of psychological research that every human being comes with the capability to find and solve complex problems, and where such creative behaviour can be harnessed among a group of people with differing skills and perspectives extraordinary things can be achieved. Some people are comfortable with ideas which challenge the whole way in which the universe works, while others prefer smaller increments of change – ideas about how to improve the jobs they do or their working environment in small incremental steps.

A focus on creative style reveals more on preferred mode or manner of applying creativity. This distinction between the style of problem-solving and level or capacity is important, and studies confirm that creative cognitive style and capacity are different. Once we understand our own style preferences, we can approach the task of challenging the way we think and respond more constructively, rather than viewing the task merely as attaining proficiency with an externally imposed, fixed set of tools or techniques. If we can assess our own strengths and needs more effectively it becomes easier to understand and accept the principle that there is more than one 'right way'.

There is no doubt that certain individuals are more creative than others but, as with physical development and training, it is possible for almost anyone to improve their creativity. It can be encouraged by paying attention to the climate for creativity, the environment in which people work, the projects and challenges they face and the systems and techniques used to support them at work.

Creative productivity does not come about (or fail to come about) only as a result of what is present (or absent) within the individual; it is influenced by time, other people, places, settings, domain-specific knowledge and strategies that people can use individually or in groups. Therefore, no one is, in an absolute sense, always more or less creative. We must ask, creative at what, when, how, where, why and with whom. We shouldn't 'look for' creativity as something fixed and static; it waxes and wanes dependent on a combination of multiple factors. Thus, the goal of profiling is *not* to ask, 'How creative is this person?', but 'How is this person creative?'. It is to help identify, for a particular task or goal, in a certain setting and under particular circumstances, the person's creative strengths or talents, the best ways to put them to use, and plans to enable us to incorporate those talents into a meaningful and effective instructional or training experience.

Changing mindset and refocusing organizational energies requires the articulation of a new vision, and there are many cases where this kind of leadership is credited with starting or turning round organizations. Examples include Jack Welch of GE, Steve Jobs (Pixar/Apple), Andy Groves (Intel) and Richard Branson (Virgin). While we must be careful of vacuous expressions of 'mission' and 'vision', it is also clear that in cases like these there has been a clear sense of, and commitment to, shared organizational purpose arising from such leadership. Creativity is not just something that happens to people; it is actively and deliberately employed, monitored and managed. Creativity can be enhanced and nurtured. Research has demonstrated that specific process tools and strategies can be used to increase creative-thinking skills.

For example, research on successful entrepreneurs has identified some of the factors that affect the likelihood of establishing a venture, and these include a combination of those which are largely inherent or given, and those which can be more easily learnt or influenced:

- ■ Family and ethnic background;
- ■ Psychological profile;
- ■ Formal education and early work experience.

ENTREPRENEURSHIP IN ACTION

Personal Creativity and Entrepreneurship

A study of 800 senior managers revealed that there were significant differences between those in the top quartile (25%) and the rest of the sample. The more successful managers had achieved their goals within 8 years, and most were in senior management positions by their early thirties. The key differences associated with the more successful managers were personality and cognitive, in particular the breadth and creativity of their thinking, and their social skills. However, the study does not conclude that creative thinking and social skills are inherent personality traits, but rather dispositions, which can be developed and improved significantly.

Such abilities are critical in many contexts, including large organizations and small start-up companies. For example, Eon, the world's largest energy services company, has created a graduate training programme to help to assess and develop their new recruits. Following psychometric assessment, graduate recruits follow specific programmes aimed at improving their personal and social skills, including placements in different parts of the business. Alex Oakley, head of human resources at Eon, believes: 'In this way we get a balance between skills and personal attributes that helps people do the job. We don't just concentrate on skills.' Similarly, Jamie Malcolm, an entrepreneur who co-founded the garden centre Shoots in Sussex, argues that:

anything new and innovative, like a start-up business, needs to take risks – you just can't succeed without it. I'll always be prepared to take risk in order to innovate. The innovation required to grow the business is what drives me. Risk can be dangerous if you're taking it because of your personal desire to do so. You don't have to lower your appetite for risk as the business grows – you just have to analyse it more as there's more at stake.

Source: Kaisen Consultants, 2006, www.kaisen.co.uk

Background

A number of other studies confirm that both family background and religion affect an individual's propensity to establish a new venture. A significant majority of technical entrepreneurs have a self-employed or professional parent. Studies indicate that 50–80% have at least one self-employed parent. For example, one seminal study found that four times as many technical entrepreneurs have a parent who is a professional, compared with other groups of scientists and engineers.[2] The most common explanation for this observed bias is that the parent acts as a role model and may provide support for self-employment.

The effect of religious and ethnic background is more controversial, but it is clear that certain groups are over-represented in the population of entrepreneurs. For example, in the USA and Europe, Jews are more likely to establish new ventures, and Chinese are more likely to in Asia. Whether this observed bias is the result of specific cultural or religious norms, or the result of minority status, is the subject of much controversy but little research. Research suggests that dominant cultural values are more important than minority status, but even this work indicates that the effect of family background is more significant than religion. In any case, and perhaps more importantly, there appears to be no significant relationship between family and religious background and the subsequent probability of success of a new venture.

Psychological Profile

Much of the research on the psychology of entrepreneurs is based on the experience of small firms in the USA, so the generalizability of the findings must be questioned. However, in the specific case of technical entrepreneurs there appears to be some consensus regarding the necessary personal characteristics. The two critical requirements appear to be an internal locus of control and a high need for achievement. The former characteristic is common in scientists and engineers, but the need for high levels of achievement is less common. Entrepreneurs are typically motivated by a high need for achievement (so-called 'nAch'), rather than a general desire to succeed. This behaviour is associated with moderate risk-taking, but not gambling or irrational risk-taking. A person with a high nAch:

- Likes situations where it is possible to take personal responsibility for finding solutions to problems.

- Has a tendency to set challenging but realistic personal goals and to take calculated risks.

- Needs concrete feedback on personal performance.

However, a US study of almost 130 technical entrepreneurs and almost 300 scientists and engineers found that not all entrepreneurs have high nAch, only some do.[3] Technical entrepreneurs had only moderate nAch, but low need for affiliation (nAff). This suggests that the need for independence, rather than success, is the most significant motivator for technical entrepreneurs. Technical entrepreneurs also tend to have an internal locus of control. In other words, technical entrepreneurs believe that they have personal control over outcomes, whereas someone with an external locus of control believes that outcomes are the result of chance, powerful institutions or others. More sophisticated psychometric techniques such as the Myers–Briggs type indicators (MBTI) confirm the differences between technical entrepreneurs and other scientists and engineers.

Education and Experience

The levels of education of technical entrepreneurs do not differentiate them from other scientists and engineers, but education and training are major factors that distinguish the founders of technical ventures from other types of entrepreneur. The median level of education of technical entrepreneurs is a master's degree, and with the important exception of biotechnology-based new ventures, a doctorate was superfluous. Significantly, potential technical entrepreneurs tend to have higher levels of productivity than their technical work colleagues, measured in terms of papers published or patents granted. This suggests that potential entrepreneurs may be more driven than their corporate counterparts.

In addition to a master's-level education, on average, a technical entrepreneur will have around 13 years of work experience before establishing a new venture. In the case of Route 128, the entrepreneurs' work experience is typically with a single incubator organization, whereas technical entrepreneurs in Silicon Valley tend to have gained their experience from a larger number of firms before establishing their own venture. This suggests that there is no ideal pattern of previous work experience. However, experience of development work appears to be more important than work in basic research. As a result of the formal education and experience required, a typical technical entrepreneur will be aged between 30 and 40 years when establishing his or her first venture. This is relatively late in life compared to other types of venture, and is due to a combination of ability and opportunity. On the one hand, it typically takes between 10 and 15 years for a potential entrepreneur to attain the necessary technical and business experience. On the other hand, many people begin to have greater financial and family responsibilities at this time, which reduces the appetite for risk. Thus there appears to be a window of opportunity to start a new venture some time in the mid-thirties. Moreover, different fields of technology have different entry and growth potential. Therefore the choice of a potential entrepreneur will be constrained by the dynamics of the technology and markets. The capital requirements, product lead times and potential for growth are likely to vary significantly between sectors.

Numerous surveys indicate that around three-quarters of technical entrepreneurs claim to have been frustrated in their previous job. This frustration appears to result from the interaction of the psychological predisposition of the potential entrepreneur and poor selection, training and development by the parent organization. Specific events may also trigger the desire or need to establish a new venture, such as a major reorganization or downsizing of the parent organization (Figure 2.2).

Figure 2.2   Factors which influence the creation of new ventures.
Source: Tidd, J., Bessant, J. and Pavitt, K. (2005) *Managing Innovation*. John Wiley & Sons, Ltd, Chichester**.**

Processes: Strategies and Stages of Creativity

Stimulating creativity and innovation consists of much more than a set of tools and techniques to help generate ideas. The process focuses on the methodology and strategies needed, a pathway towards some solution or outcome. Effective practitioners have long since passed the view of the process as a fixed sequence of prescribed steps and activities but, to be effective, it is necessary to make deliberate decisions about the components, stages and techniques that will be appropriate and valuable, given the purpose and intended outcomes of the process.

A number of models of the creative process can be helpful to those who need to engage in innovation and entrepreneurship. One proven and practical process for challenging the way we perceive things includes three main stages:[4]

- ■ Understanding the opportunity;
- ■ Generating ideas;
- ■ Planning for action.

Understanding the Opportunity

Understanding the opportunity or problem includes a systematic effort to define, construct or formulate a problem. This is not necessarily the first step, nor is it necessarily undertaken by all people. Rather than prescribing an essential problem-finding process, this involves active construction by the individual or group through analysing the task at hand (including outcomes, people, context and methodological options) to determine whether and when deliberate problem-structuring efforts are needed. This stage includes the three components:

- ■ *Opportunity construction* is a broad statement of a goal or direction that can be constructed as broad, brief and beneficial. The opportunity generally describes the basic area of need or challenge on which the problem-solver's efforts will be focused, remaining broad enough to allow many perspectives to emerge as one (or a group) looks more closely at the situation.

■ *Exploring data* includes the generating and answering of questions to bring out key data (information, impressions, observations, feelings, etc.) to help the problem-solver(s) focus more clearly on the most challenging aspects and concerns of the situation.

■ *Framing problems* includes the seeking of a specified or targeted question (problem statement) on which to focus subsequent effort. Effectively worded problem statements invite an open or wide-ranging search for many, varied and novel options. They are stated concisely and are free from specific limiting criteria. This component has been widely applied to assist in strategic decision-making and problem-solving. Management teams have considered many, varied and unique opportunities and focused on those that offer the best future organizational results. These teams have explored a variety of data to better understand their market, competition and internal strengths and weaknesses.

For example, in quality management a number of proven tools and techniques exist to support a better understanding of problems or opportunities. These include tools such as Pareto analysis and cause and effect analysis.

Pareto analysis is used to prioritize areas for improvement by identifying the factors that will have the greatest impact on quality. A Pareto diagram simply ranks problems or causes of problems according to their frequency or significance. In some but not all cases, the frequency of a problem is a good guide to its significance, but in some cases frequency and significance are not the same. Pareto analysis is useful as it helps to identify and focus attention on the critical few rather than the trivial but commonplace. A common interpretation of the Pareto principle is the 80/20 rule: in many cases 80% of errors or failures can be traced to 20% of the causes. For example, in Figure 2.3 the most common problem is delays to repairs which accounts for 75% of complaints to a car dealership. This analysis would suggest that quality improvement should begin with an identification of the root causes of such delays.

Having identified the most pressing quality problems using the Pareto analysis, we can now begin to search for their causes. Cause and effect diagrams are a useful way of searching for the root cause of a particular problem (Figure 2.4). They are also known as fish bone (because of the way the diagram looks) or Ishikawa diagrams (after the Japanese person who promoted the technique).

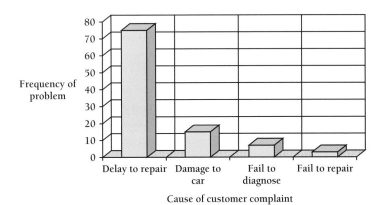

Figure 2.3   Example of a Pareto analysis for quality problems at a car dealership.

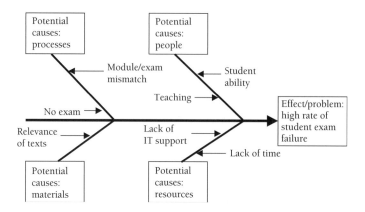

Figure 2.4   Example of cause and effect analysis for exam failure.

There are a number of simple steps in cause and effect analysis:

■ Clearly state a specific problem, that is, the 'effect'.

■ Next identify the main classes of potential causes. Commonly used classification schemes are 'methods, machinery, materials, manpower and money', or alternatively 'processes, people, materials and resources'.

■ Under each of these headings, identify potential causes by means of data collection and group discussion.

■ Change and refine the potential causes as necessary.

■ Finally, produce a shortlist of the most likely candidates for further analysis.

Another popular and proven method to assist problem definition is the mind map or spider diagram. This is simply a graphical way of identifying and exploring relationships between different factors. Mind or cognitive maps are a specific application of spider diagrams used to make explicit the relationships and assumptions within a given context. In both cases you begin with a central theme or key word which is written in the centre of a large sheet of paper, a whiteboard or screen. Next, generate related concepts or themes and write these around the central theme. Finally, draw lines to represent potential relationships between the different concepts. Used by an individual, this is a very effective way of clarifying thoughts. Used by a group, it helps to identify shared assumptions and to highlight differences in perceptions.

Cognitive-mapping techniques aim to provide a tool for revealing people's subjective beliefs in a meaningful way so that they can be examined not only by the individual for whom the map is constructed, but also by other individuals and groups. Individual decision-makers might be encouraged to reflect on their own, perhaps rather narrow, under-standing of a particular problem. The resultant cognitive map will not represent an entire belief system (this would be impossible), but hopes to portray those beliefs that are held to be most significant by the stakeholders concerned. In this way, valuable knowledge can be entered into the decision-making process that might otherwise remain hidden.

Another potential use of cognitive-mapping techniques is to allow decision-makers to look at maps that have been constructed for other stakeholders so that they can begin to understand and appreciate alternative perspectives on the problem. This insight, however crude, into the way that others are thinking about the problem can encourage negotiation and help to reduce conflict. An advantage of cognitive-mapping techniques (over, say, simply asking someone what they think) is that they allow knowledge to be externalized in some sort of graphical form that is then open for critical reflection. In this way subjective knowledge can be to some extent 'objectified' and therefore discussed in a less threatening way than direct questioning. In this way, if used as the decision-making process unfolds, cognitive-mapping techniques may help the process to be managed.

Generating Ideas

Generating ideas includes the generating of options in answer to an open-ended or invitational statement of the problem. This stage contains both a generating and a focusing phase. During the generating phase, the person or group produces many options (fluent thinking), a variety of possible options (flexible thinking), novel or unusual options (original thinking), or a number of detailed or refined options (elaborative thinking). The focusing phase of generating ideas provides an opportunity for examining, reviewing, clustering and selecting promising options. Although this stage includes a focusing phase, its primary emphasis is generative.

Generating Ideas has also been widely applied to assist those who engage in strategic decision-making and problem-solving. Brainstorming is the widely known tool to assist groups in generating ideas, but it can be applied whenever a group needs to consider many, varied and unusual alternatives.

A very wide range of specific tools and techniques has been developed to assist idea generation. Most are now available as software or as proprietary consultancy training packages. However, our experience suggests that simple, low-technology exercises are just as effective in practice. There is no mystery to applying these tools or techniques, and individuals and groups will improve with experience and practice.

There is no shortage of management consultants, gurus and training packages which claim to promote creativity. However, many of these consist of little more than team-building or brainstorming. In addition, many advocate superficial and unproven methods, for example, drama workshops, humour workshops or just being zany.

While there may be some value in these, they should not be considered training in creativity and problem-solving. De Bono introduced the term lateral thinking to describe alternatives to logical thought, and has a long and distinguished career promoting applied creative thinking. In his 1996 book *Serious Creativity* he argues that creativity training in a business environment is not about artistic creativity/right-brain or simply being crazy/a rebel. Unlike most gurus of creativity, De Bono argues that most of us are not inherently creative, but rather that our brains are proficient at identifying, developing and subsequently following patterns or regularities. In most cases such mental models and patterned behaviour are efficient, but for problem-solving and creativity they can be dysfunctional. There is a great deal of research to support this view, and our experience confirms this. It follows that it is not sufficient to free the mind from constraints. Instead, we must force or provoke alternative ways of thinking. Specific methods of encouraging alternative ideas or solutions include the following:

- *Remove or suspend an assumption or goal* – what could we do differently if we temporarily ignore a key objective or assumption?

- *Reverse objectives or methods* – what would we do to achieve the exact opposite, and then reverse this?

- *Exaggerate the problem or goal* – what might we do if the goal or problem was much larger or smaller?

- *Distort the relationships or cause and effect* – what would the implications be?

- *Generate random inputs* – what new ideas does the introduction of a random word help create?

- *Use a metaphor or character* – what would a chosen famous character do in these circumstances?

In general, the more approaches used to generate ideas, the better. Planning and promotion of such schemes are critical to their success, and management support, feedback and rewards are associated with successful idea generation (Table 2.1).

Table 2.1 Assessing the effectiveness of schemes to promote idea generation

Scheme features	Perceived success of scheme	Rate of generation of new ideas
Planning of scheme	17.6	8.5
Promotion of scheme	31.2	21.5
Management support	28.6	3.2
Feedback to staff	34.3	5.2
Rewards – recognition	23.8	3.8
Rewards – monetary	4.1	2.3(+)
Rewards – non-monetary	31.3	9.3

Notes: N = 182

Numbers are F values of the mean success scores, all are statistically significant at 5% level, except +

Source: Derived from Leach, D.J., Stride, C.B. and Wood, S.J. (2006) The effectiveness of idea capture schemes, *International Journal of Innovation Management*, **10** (3), 325–350.

Planning for Action

Planning for action is appropriate when a person or group recognizes a number of interesting or promising options that may not necessarily be useful, valuable or valid without extended effort and productive thinking. The need may be to make or develop effective choices, or prepare for successful implementation and acceptance by different stakeholders. This stage includes two components: *developing solutions* and *building acceptance.*

In developing solutions, promising options are analysed, refined or developed. If there are many options the emphasis may be on compressing or condensing them so that they are more manageable. If there are only a few promising options, the challenge may be to strengthen each as much as possible. There may be a need to rank or prioritize a number of possible options. Specific criteria may be generated and selected upon which to evaluate and develop promising options or select from a larger pool of available alternatives. Although there may be some generating in this stage, the emphasis is primarily on focusing. Once the new concepts and ideas have been developed, the next logical focus of attention is to prepare them for the marketplace and acceptance from key stakeholders.

Building acceptance involves searching several potential sources of assistance and resistance for possible solutions. The aim is to help prepare an option or alternative for improved acceptance and value. This stage helps the problem-solver identify ways to make the best possible use of assisters and avoid or overcome possible sources of resistance. From considering these factors, a plan of action is developed and evaluated for implementation.

Although techniques to support more creative strategic decision-making and problem-solving can be taught and learned, they are best suited for the solution of real-life problems. This requires interest, influence and imagination. To be interesting, a problem must be 'real', and be owned by someone. A problem becomes 'real' only when it involves an emotional or affective commitment as well as an intellectual or cognitive one; it must have a personal frame of reference. The owners of the problem must also have some degree of influence, authority and decision-making responsibility for implementing the solutions. It also means that the problem owner is motivated and willing to submit the challenge to systematic problem-solving efforts and is interested in following through on the results. Finally, the search and solutions must engage the imagination, and there must be a deliberate and explicit search for something new. The purpose of a 'real' problem is to contribute something new or bring about some sort of innovation. A good example of this process is the development of a business plan for a new venture.

Developing a Business Plan

The primary reason for developing a formal business plan for a new venture is to attract external funding. However, it serves an important secondary function. A business plan can provide a formal agreement between founders regarding the basis and future development of the venture. A business plan can help reduce self-delusion on the part of the founders, and avoid subsequent arguments concerning responsibilities and rewards. It can help to translate abstract or ambiguous goals into more explicit operational needs, and support subsequent decision-making and identify trade-offs. Of the factors *controllable* by entrepreneurs, business planning has the most significant positive effect on new venture performance. However, there are of course many *uncontrollable* factors, such as market opportunity, which have an even more significant influence on performance. Pasteur's advice still applies: 'Chance favours only the prepared mind.' In such cases contingencies need to be identified and their potential impact on the venture assessed.

No standard business plan exists, but in many cases venture capitalists will provide a pro forma for the business plan. Typically a business plan should be relatively concise, say no more than 10 sides, begin with an executive summary, and include sections on the product, markets, technology, development, production, marketing, human resources, financial estimates with contingency plans, and the timetable and funding requirements. Most business plans submitted to venture capitalists are strong on the technical considerations, often placing too much emphasis on the technology relative to other issues. As Roberts notes, 'Entrepreneurs propose that they can do *it* better than anyone else, but may forget to demonstrate that anyone wants *it*.'[5] He identifies a number of common problems with business plans submitted to venture capitalists: marketing plan, management team, technology plan and financial plan.

There were found to be serious inadequacies in all four of these areas, but the worst were in marketing and finance. Less than half of the plans examined provided a detailed marketing strategy, and just half included any sales plan. Three-quarters of the plans failed to identify or analyse any potential competitors. As a result most business plans contain only basic financial forecasts, and just 10% conducted any sensitivity analysis on the forecasts. The lack of attention to marketing and competitor analysis is particularly problematic as research indicates that both factors are associated with subsequent success.

While there is general agreement about the main components of a good business plan, there are some significant differences in the relative weights attributed to each component. General venture capital firms typically only accept 5% of the technology ventures they are offered, and the specialist technology venture funds are even more selective, accepting around 3%. The main reasons for rejecting technology proposals compared to more general funding proposals are the lack of intellectual property, the skills of the management team and size of the potential market. A survey of venture capitalists in North America, Europe and Asia found major similarities in the criteria used, but also identified several interesting differences in the weights attached to some criteria (Table 2.2). The criteria are similar to those discussed earlier, grouped into five categories:

- The entrepreneur's personality.
- The entrepreneur's experience.
- Characteristics of the product.
- Characteristics of the market.
- Financial factors.

Table 2.2   Criteria used by venture capitalists to assess proposals

Criteria	European (n = 195)	American (n = 100)	Asian (n = 53)
Entrepreneur able to evaluate and react to risk	3.6	3.3	3.5
Entrepreneur capable of sustained effort	3.6	3.6	3.7
Entrepreneur familiar with the market	3.5	3.6	3.6
Entrepreneur demonstrated leadership ability*	3.2	3.4	3.0
Entrepreneur has relevant track record*	3.0	3.2	2.9
Product prototype exists and functions*	3.0	2.4	2.9
Product demonstrated market acceptance*	2.9	2.5	2.8
Product proprietary or can be protected*	2.7	3.1	2.6
Product is 'high technology'*	1.5	2.3	1.4
Target market has high growth rate*	3.0	3.3	3.2
Venture will stimulate an existing market	2.4	2.4	2.5
Little threat of competition within three years	2.2	2.4	2.4
Venture will create a new market*	1.8	1.8	2.2
Financial return >10 times within 10 years*	2.9	3.4	2.9
Investment is easily made liquid* (e.g. made public or acquired)	2.7	3.2	2.7
Financial return >10 times within 5 years*	2.1	2.3	2.1

1 = irrelevant, 2 = desirable, 3 = important, 4 = essential. * Denotes significant at the 0.05 level.

Source: Adapted from Knight, R. (1992) Criteria used by venture capitalists, in Khalil, T. and Bayraktar, B. (eds), *Management of Technology III: The key to global competitiveness*. Industrial Engineering & Management Press, Georgia, 574–583.

Overall, the survey confirmed the importance of a bundle of personal, market and financial factors, which were consistently ranked as being most significant: a proven ability to lead others and sustain effort; familiarity with the market; and the potential for a high return within 10 years. The personality and experience of the entrepreneurs were consistently ranked as being more important than either product or market characteristics, or even financial considerations. However, there were a number of significant differences between the preferences of venture capitalists from different regions. Those from the USA placed greater emphasis on a high financial return and liquidity than their counterparts in Europe or Asia, but less emphasis on the existence of a prototype or proven market acceptance. Perhaps surprisingly, all venture capitalists are averse to technological and market risks. Being described as a 'high-technology' venture was rated very low in importance by the US venture capitalists, and the European and Asian venture capitalists rated this characteristic as having a negative influence on funding. Similarly, having the potential to create an entirely new market was considered a drawback.

At each of the different stages of developing a new venture there are different significant challenges to overcome in order to make a successful transition to the next stage, what the researchers call 'critical junctures':

Opportunity recognition – at the interface of the research and opportunity framing phases. This requires the ability to connect a specific technology or know-how to a commercial application, and is based on a rather rare combination of skill, experience, aptitude, insight and circumstances. A key issue here is the ability to synthesize scientific knowledge and market insights, which increases with the entrepreneur's social capital – linkages, partnerships and other network interactions.

Entrepreneurial commitment – acts and sustained persistence that bind the venture champion to the emerging business venture. This often demands difficult personal decisions to be made, for example, whether or not to remain an academic, as well as evidence of direct financial investments to the venture.

Venture credibility – is critical for the entrepreneur to gain the resources necessary to acquire the finance and other resources for the business to function. Credibility is a function of the venture team, key customers and other social capital and relationships. This requires close relationships with sponsors, financial and other, to build and maintain awareness and credibility. Lack of business experience, and failure to recognize their own limitations are a key problem here. One solution is to hire the services of a 'surrogate entrepreneur'. As one experienced entrepreneur notes: 'The not so smart or really insecure academics want their hands over everything. These prima donnas make a complete mess of things, get nowhere with their companies and end up disappointed professionally and financially.'

ENTREPRENEURSHIP IN ACTION

Opportunity and Planning at Innocent

Innocent develops and sells fruit smoothies, healthy, premium pulped-fruit drinks, with no additives. The company was created in 1999 by three friends from university, Adam Balon, Richard Reed and Jon Wright. The company was founded with the help of £200 000 of venture capital, but Balon, Reed and Wright still own 70% of the company. In 2006 Innocent had sales of around £70 million, representing a market share of 60%, and the company was valued at £175 million. It has since recruited more experienced managers from larger firms, and now employs 100 staff in West London. It also has bases in France and Denmark, and plans to open offices in Germany and Austria in 2007. All production and packaging is outsourced, and the company focuses on development and marketing.

The company has cultivated a funky liberal image, in contrast to the large multinational firms that dominate the drinks market. They give 10% of company profits to charities, such as the Rainforest Alliance, and have developed a healthy dialogue with their customers through a weekly e-mail newsletter. In 2005 Reed won the title 'Most Admired Businessman' from the UK National Union of Students. However, beneath the hippy image there is a well-educated and experienced management team. After university

> Reed, now aged 33, gained experience in the advertising industry, and Balon and Wright both worked for large management consultants, respectively McKinsey and Bain. The likely exit or harvest for the business will be a trade sale, similar to other so-called 'ethical brands' such as Ben and Jerry's which was bought by Unilever, and Green and Blacks acquired by Cadburys. However, so far they have resisted offers to acquire the business, and they plan to float the business in 2010.

Environment: Creating a Climate for Innovation

A climate for creativity and innovation is that which promotes the generation, consideration and use of new products, services and ways of working. This kind of climate supports the development, assimilation and utilization of new and different approaches, practices and concepts. It is associated with a wide range of innovative outputs: new ideas, improved processes, new products or new ventures.

Many researchers have looked at the conditions under which creativity thrives or is suppressed. Kanter provides a list of environmental factors that contribute to stifling innovation; these include:[6]

- Dominance of restrictive vertical relationships;

- Poor lateral communications;

- Limited tools and resources;

- Top-down dictates;

- Formal, restricted vehicles for change;

- Reinforcing a culture of inferiority (i.e. innovation always has to come from outside to be any good);

- Unfocused innovative activity;

- Unsupportive accounting practices.

The effect of these environmental factors is to create and reinforce the behavioural norms which inhibit creativity and lead to a culture lacking in innovation. It follows from this that developing an innovative climate is not a simple matter since it consists of a complex web of behaviours and artefacts. And changing this culture is not likely to happen quickly or as a result of single initiatives (such as restructuring or mass training in a new technique).

Culture is a complex concept, but it basically equates to the pattern of shared values, beliefs and agreed norms which shape behaviour – in other words, it is 'the way we do things round here' in any organization. Many writers have offered a variety of definitions of culture. Thankfully, there are consistent themes among this diversity. Culture consists of deep and enduring patterns of how individuals and groups make decisions and demonstrate priorities about value differences. In general, culture is something that is shared by all or most of the members of some social group, and shapes behaviour and structures perceptions of the world.

As such culture can be described as collective programming of the mind or, as Geert Hofstede has called it, 'software of the mind'.[7] This collective software of the mind distinguishes the members of one social group from another. Many writers see culture as something that is stable, deep, and reinforced by a history of decisions, use of power and learned strategies for answering fundamental questions. Schein suggests that culture can be understood as an hierarchy of interlinked levels:[8]

Values, Beliefs and Deeply Held Assumptions

Values are general beliefs that function to define what is right or wrong, or specify general preferences. They influence behaviour because they are broad tendencies to prefer certain states of affairs over others. They are similar to deeply held assumptions.

In an organizational context, values can sometimes be specific and explicit. When we first started consulting with DuPont's Innovation Initiative in the early 1990s we were impressed with the many successes with new product development. There were, however, some challenges in implementing some of the strategies included within the innovation initiative. We also ran into a number of rules when we visited numerous factories and locations. We could not run on DuPont property, for example. When we looked deeper into the culture, it became very clear to us that DuPont held a strong value for safety. Later, we were able to visit the site of the founding of the E. I. Du Pont de Nemours gunpowder manufactury in Wilmington, Delaware. It was a pretty location on the Brandywine River, which served as the power source in the early 1800s. We noticed that in the buildings in which the gunpowder was produced, three walls were made of very thick stone, but the side facing the river was made of thin wood. Not a single nail was used in the construction of these buildings for fear that a small piece of metal could fall and make a spark.

The family home was not very far from the buildings that made the gunpowder. So, from the very founding of the company, there was always a great concern for safe operations and limiting the risk of harm to people. This is an example of how many deeply held values are embedded in organizations.

Rituals and Heroes

Rituals and customs are activities that seem non-essential to the actual functioning of the group, but they are considered socially necessary. These behaviours are reinforced over time – forming traditions that are filled with implicit meaning. In an organizational context this could include the way greetings and initial social exchanges occur during meetings. Heroes are people who can be either dead or living, real or imaginary, who possess highly valued characteristics. As such, they serve as role models for preferred or desired ways of behaving.

Symbols and Artefacts

Symbols are words, gestures, pictures or other objects that carry and convey meaning to a particular group that share a common culture. In an organizational context they can include flags, status symbols, manner of dress and so on. Rituals, heroes and symbols are visible to the observer, although their meaning is invisible and may require interpretation.

However, organizational culture is a different concept from national or social culture. Most people have exercised a choice to join a place of work whereas people are born into particular societies. People who work in organizations usually have limits on how much time they spend there (or at work) and have other discretionary time available. People are generally free to leave an organization and may do so more easily than leaving a society. Organizational cultures should describe the shared mental programming of those within the same organization, particularly if they share the same nationality. Research has shown that organizational cultures can and do differ in six important areas:

- *Process versus results orientation* – focus on the means or the way things are done, such as quality management or process improvement, versus a bias for action and results, such as 'management by objectives'.

- *Employee versus job* – the classic tension between concern for people, versus concern for the task, for example, the so-called 'European Social Model' versus the 'Anglo-Saxon' liberal market approach.

■ *Parochial versus professional* – identity derived from the internal organization, versus identity with a specific type of job.

■ *Open versus closed systems* – broad definition of organizational boundaries with a high degree of interaction with the environment, versus a narrow organizational focus, for example, the 'not invented here' syndrome.

■ *Loose versus tight control* – a high degree of autonomy regarding ends and means, versus a more prescriptive and directive approach.

■ *Normative versus pragmatic* – a focus on following the bureaucratic rules and procedures, versus meeting the needs of the task or customer.

Can Culture Be Changed?

Culture is maintained over time through the attraction, selection and attrition of staff, and this provides clues to how culture may be changed over the longer term. This means that applicants are attracted to a certain type of organization; and the organization is more likely to select those that fit the organization; and those that do not fit are more likely to leave, therefore reinforcing the existing culture. Since culture is such a deep, stable, complex set of shared assumptions that are built over relatively long periods of time, it is not an easy task to change it. Further, many definitions of culture specifically exclude behaviour.

When we see what leaders have done to influence culture change, they have actually focused their efforts more on the working climate. For example, Schein identified the primary mechanisms that leaders use to embed a culture. These include things like what leaders pay attention to, measure and control, as well as a number of other observed behaviours like the criteria leaders use to allocate scarce resources and rewards.

Given this model it is clear that management cannot directly change culture; but it can intervene at the level of artefacts – by changing structures or processes – and by providing models and reinforcing preferred styles of behaviour. Such 'culture change' actions are now widely tried in the context of change programmes towards total quality management and other models of organization which require more participative culture.

Climate Versus Culture

Climate is defined as the recurring patterns of behaviour, attitudes and feelings that characterize life in the organization. At the individual level of analysis the concept is called psychological climate. At this level, the concept of climate refers to the intrapersonal perception of the patterns of behaviour, attitudes and feelings as experienced by the individual. When aggregated, the concept is called work unit or organizational climate. These are the objectively shared perceptions that characterize life within a defined work unit or in the larger organization. Climate is distinct from culture in that it is more observable at a surface level within the organization and more amenable to change and improvement efforts. Culture refers to the deeper and more enduring values, norms and beliefs within the organization.

The two terms, culture and climate, have been used interchangeably by many writers, researchers and practitioners. We have found that the following distinctions may help those who are concerned with effecting change and transformation in organizations:

■ *Different levels of analysis* Culture is a rather broad and inclusive concept. Climate can be seen as falling under the more general concept of culture. If your aim is to understand culture, then you need to look at the entire organization as a unit of analysis. If your focus is on climate, then you can use individuals and their shared perceptions of groups, divisions or other levels of analysis. Climate is recursive or scalable.

■ *Different disciplines involved* Culture is within the domain of anthropology and climate falls within the domain of social psychology. The fact that the concepts come from different disciplines means that different methods and tools are used to study them.

■ *Normative versus descriptive* Cultural dimensions have remained relatively descriptive, meaning that one set of values or hidden assumptions were neither better nor worse than another. This is because there is no universally held notion or definition of the best society. Climate is often more normative in that we are more often looking for environments that are not just different, but better for certain things. For example, we can examine different kinds of climates and compare the results against other measures or outcomes such as innovation, motivation and growth.

■ *More easily observable and influenced* Climate is distinct from culture in that it is more observable at a surface level within the organization and more amenable to change and improvement efforts.

What is needed is a commonsense set of levers for change that leaders can exert direct and deliberate influence over.

Climate and culture are different: Traditionally studies of organizational culture are more qualitative, whereas research on organizational climate is more quantitative, but a multidimensional approach helps to integrate the benefits of each perspective.

Research indicates that organizations exhibit larger differences in practices than values, for example, the levels of uncertainty avoidance.

Table 2.3 summarizes some research on how climate influences innovation. Many dimensions of climate have been shown to influence innovation and entrepreneurship, but here we discuss six of the most critical factors.

Trust and Openness

The trust and openness dimension refers to emotional safety in relationships. These relationships are considered safe when people are seen as both competent and sharing a common set of values. When there is a strong level of trust, everyone in the organization dares to put forward ideas and opinions. Initiatives can be taken without fear of reprisals and ridicule in case of failure. The communication is open and straightforward. Where trust is missing, count on high expenses for mistakes that may result. People also are afraid of being exploited and robbed of their good ideas.

Table 2.3   Climate factors influencing innovation

Climate factor	Most innovative (score)	Least innovative (score)	Difference
Trust and openness	253	88	165
Challenge and involvement	260	100	160
Support and space for ideas	218	70	148
Conflict and debate	231	83	148
Risk-taking	210	65	145
Freedom	202	110	92

Source: Derived from Isaksen, S. and Tidd, J (2006). *Meeting the Innovation Challenge*. John Wiley & Sons, Ltd, Chichester.

Trust can make decision-making more efficient as it allows positive assumptions and expectations to be made about competence, motives and intentions, and thereby economizes on cognitive resources and information-processing. Trust can also influence the effectiveness of an organization through structuring and mobilizing.

Trust helps to structure and shape the patterns of interaction and coordination within and between organizations. Trust can also motivate employees to contribute, commit and cooperate, by facilitating knowledge- and resource-sharing and joint problem-solving. When trust and openness are too low you may see people hoarding resources (i.e. information, software, materials, etc.). There may also be a lack of feedback on new ideas for fear of having concepts stolen. Management may not distribute the resources fairly among individuals or departments. One cause for this condition can be that management does not trust the capabilities and/or integrity of employees. It may be helpful to establish norms and values that management can follow regarding the disbursement of resources, and a means to assure that resources are wisely used.

However, trust can bind and blind. If trust and openness are too high, relationships may be so strong that time and resources at work are often spent on personal issues. It may also lead to a lack of questioning each other that, in turn, may lead to mistakes or less productive outcomes. Cliques may form where there are isolated 'pockets' of high trust. One cause of this condition may be that people have gone through a traumatic organizational experience together and survived (e.g. down-sizing, a significant product launch, etc.). In this case it may help to develop forums for interdepartmental and inter-group exchange of information and ideas.

Trust is partly the result of an individual's own personality and experience, but can also be influenced by the organizational climate. For example, we know that the nature of rewards can affect some components of trust. Individual competitive rewards tend to reduce information-sharing and raise suspicions of others' motives, whereas group or cooperative rewards are more likely to promote information-sharing and reduce suspicions of motives. Similarly, the frequency of communication within an organization influences trust, and in general the higher the frequency of communication, the higher the levels of trust. In a climate of low communication, the level of trust is much more dependent on the general attitudes of individuals towards their peers.

Trust is also associated with employees having some degree of role autonomy. Role autonomy is the amount of discretion that employees have in interpreting and executing their jobs. Defining roles too narrowly constrains the decision-making latitude. Role autonomy can also be influenced by the degree to which organizational socialization encourages employees to internalize collective goals and values, for example, a so-called 'clan' culture focuses on developing shared values, beliefs and goals among members of an organization so that appropriate behaviours are reinforced and rewarded, rather than specifying task-related behaviours or outcomes. This approach is most appropriate when tasks are difficult to anticipate or codify, and it is difficult to assess performance. Individual characteristics will also influence role autonomy, including the level of experience, competence and power accumulated over time working for the organization.

Trust may exist at the personal and organizational levels, and researchers have attempted to distinguish different levels, qualities and sources of trust. For example, the following bases of organizational trust have been identified:

- *Contractual* – honouring the accepted or legal rules of exchange, but can also indicate the absence of other forms of trust.
- *Goodwill* – mutual expectations of commitment beyond contractual requirements.
- *Institutional* – trust based on formal structures.
- *Network* – because of personal, family or ethnic/religious ties.
- *Competence* – trust based on reputation for skills and know-how.
- *Commitment* – mutual self-interest, committed to the same goals.

These types of trust are not necessarily mutually exclusive, although over-reliance on contractual and institutional forms may indicate the absence of the other bases of trust. In the case of innovation, problems may occur where trust is based primarily on the network, rather than competence or commitment.

Challenge and Involvement

Challenge and involvement relates to the degree to which people are involved in daily operations, long-term goals and visions. High levels of challenge and involvement mean that people are intrinsically motivated and committed to making contributions to the success of the organization. The climate has a dynamic, electric and inspiring quality. People find joy and meaningfulness in their work and, therefore, they invest much energy. In the opposite situation, people are not engaged and feelings of alienation and indifference are present. The common sentiment and attitude is apathy and lack of interest in work and interaction is both dull and listless.

If challenge and involvement are too low, you may see that people are apathetic about their work, are not generally interested in professional development, or are frustrated about the future of the organization. One of the probable causes for this might be that people are not emotionally charged about the vision, mission, purpose and goals of the organization. One of the ways to improve the situation might be to get people involved in interpreting the vision, mission, purpose and goals of the organization for themselves and their work teams.

On the other hand, if the challenge and involvement are too high you may observe that people are showing signs of burnout, they are unable to meet project goals and objectives, or they spend 'too many' long hours at work. One of the reasons for this is that the work goals are too much of a stretch. A way to improve the situation is to examine and clarify strategic priorities.

Building and maintaining a challenging climate involves systematic development of organizational structures, communication policies and procedures, reward and recognition systems, training policy, accounting and measurement systems and deployment of strategy. Leaders who focus on work challenge and expertise rather than formal authority result in climates that are more likely to be assessed by members as being innovative and high-performance. Studies suggest that output controls such as specific goals, recognition and rewards have a positive association with innovation. A balance must be maintained between creating a climate in which subordinates feel supported and empowered, with the need to provide goals and influence the direction and agenda. Leaders who provide feedback that is high on developmental potential, for example, provide useful information for subordinates to improve, learn and develop, resulting in higher levels of creativity.

Intellectual stimulation is one of the most underdeveloped components of leadership, and includes behaviours that increase others' awareness of and interest in problems, and develops their propensity and ability to tackle problems in new ways. Intellectual stimulation by leaders can have a profound effect on organizational performance under conditions of perceived uncertainty, and is also associated with commitment to an organization.

However, innovation is too often seen as the province of specialists in R&D, marketing, design or IT, but the underlying creative skills and problem-solving abilities are possessed by everyone. If mechanisms can be found to focus such abilities on a regular basis across the entire organization, the resulting innovative potential is enormous. Although each individual may only be able to develop limited, incremental innovations, the sum of these efforts can have far-reaching impacts.

Since much of such employee involvement in innovation focuses on incremental change it is tempting to see its effects as marginal. Studies show, however, that when taken over an extended period it is a significant factor in the strategic development of the organization. For example, a study of firms in the UK that have acquired the 'Investors in People' award (an externally assessed review of employee involvement practices) showed a correlation between this and higher business performance. On average, these businesses increased their sales and profits per employee by three-quarters. Another study involved over 1000 organizations in a total of 7 countries, and found that those that had formal employee involvement programmes, for example, featuring support and training in idea generation and problem-finding and solving, reported performance gains of 15-20%. But there is also an important secondary effect of high-involvement: the more people are involved in change, the more receptive they become to it. Since the turbulent nature of most organizational environments is such that increasing levels of change are becoming the norm, greater formal involvement of employees may provide a powerful aid to effective management of change.

INNOVATION IN ACTION

Increasing Challenge and Involvement in an Electrical Engineering Division

The organization was a division of a large, global electrical power and product supply company head-quartered in France. The division was located in the south-east of the USA and had 92 employees. Its focus was to help clients automate their processes particularly within the automotive, pharmaceutical, microelectronics and food and beverage industries. For example, this division would make the robots that put cars together in the automotive industry or provide public filtration systems.

When this division was merged with the parent company, it was losing about US$8 million a year. A new general manager was bought in to turn the division around and make it profitable quickly.

An assessment of the organization's climate identified that they were strongest on the debate dimension but were very close to the stagnated norms when it came to challenge and involvement, playfulness and humour, and conflict. The quantitative and qualitative assessment results were consistent with their own impressions that the division could be characterized as conflict-driven, uncommitted to producing results, and people were generally despondent. The leadership decided, after some debate, that they should target challenge and involvement, which was consistent with their strategic emphasis on a global initiative on employee commitment. It was clear to them that they also needed to soften the climate and drive a warmer, more embracing, communicative and exuberant climate.

The management team re-established training and development and encouraged employees to engage in both personal and business-related skills development. They also provided mandatory safety training for all employees. They committed to increase communication by holding monthly all-employee meetings, sharing quarterly reviews on performance, and using cross-functional strategy review sessions. They implemented mandatory 'skip level' meetings to allow more direct interaction between senior managers and all levels of employees. The general manager held 15-minute meetings with all employees at least once a year. All employee suggestions and recommendations were invited and feedback and recognition was required to be immediate. A new monthly recognition and rewards programme was launched across the division for both managers and employees that was based on peer nomination. The management team formed employee review teams to challenge and craft the statements in the hopes of encouraging more ownership and involvement in the overall strategic direction of the business.

In 18 months the division showed a US$7 million turnaround, and in 2003 won a worldwide innovation award. The general manager was promoted to a national position.

Source: Isaksen, S. and Tidd, J. (2006) *Meeting the Innovation Challenge: Leadership for Transformation and Growth*. John Wiley & Sons Ltd, Chichester.

Support and Space for Ideas

Idea time is the amount of time people can (and do) use for elaborating new ideas. In the high idea-time situation, the possibilities exist to discuss and test impulses and fresh suggestions that are not planned or included in the task assignment and people tend to use these possibilities. When idea time is low, every minute is booked and specified. The time pressure makes thinking outside the instructions and planned routines impossible. Research confirms that individuals under time pressure are significantly less likely to be creative.

If there is insufficient time and space for generating new ideas you may observe that people are only concerned with their current projects and tasks. They may exhibit an unhealthy level of stress. People see professional development and training as hindrances to their ability to complete daily tasks and projects. You may also see that management avoids new ideas because they will take time away from the completion of day-to-day projects and schedules. One of the possible reasons for this could be that project schedules are so intense that they do not allow time to refine the process to take advantage of new ideas. Individuals are generally not physically or mentally capable of performing at 100%. A corrective action could be to develop project schedules that allow time for modification and development.

Conversely, if there is too much time and space for new ideas you may observe that people are showing signs of boredom, that decisions are made through a slow, almost bureaucratic, process because there are too many ideas to evaluate, or the management of new ideas becomes such a task that short-term tasks and projects are not adequately completed. Individuals, teams and managers may lack the skills to handle large numbers of ideas and then converge on the most practical idea(s) for implementation. You may be able to provide training in creativity and facilitation, especially those tools and skills of convergence or focusing.

This suggests that there is an optimum amount of time and space to promote creativity and innovation. The concept of *organizational slack* was developed to identify the difference between resources currently needed and the total resources available to an organization. When there is little environmental uncertainty or need for change, and the focus is simply on productivity; too much organizational slack represents a static inefficiency. However, when innovation and change is needed, slack can act as a dynamic shock absorber, and allows scope for experimentation. This process tends to be self-reinforcing due to positive feedback between the environment and organization.

When successful, an organization generates more slack, which provides greater resource (people, time, money) for longer-term, significant innovation; however, when an organization is less successful, or suffers a fall in performance, it tends to search for immediate and specific problems and their solution, which tends to reduce the slack necessary for longer-term innovation and growth.

The research confirms that an appropriate level of organizational slack is associated with superior performance over the longer term. For high-performance organizations the relationship between organizational slack and performance is an inverted 'U' shape, or curvilinear: too little slack, for example being too lean or too focused, does not allow sufficient time or resource for innovation, but too much provides little incentive or direction to innovation. However, for low-performance organizations any slack is simply absorbed and therefore simply represents an inefficiency rather than an opportunity for innovation and growth. Managers too often view time as a constraint or measure of outcomes, rather than as a variable to influence which can both trigger and facilitate innovation and change. By providing some, but limited, time and resources, individuals and groups can minimize the rigidity that comes from work overload, and the laxness that stems from too much slack.

Idea time helps to generate new ideas, but support is needed to assess and develop these ideas. In a supportive climate, ideas and suggestions are received in an attentive and kind way by bosses and workmates. People listen to each other and encourage initiatives. Possibilities for trying out new ideas are created. The atmosphere is constructive and positive.

When idea support is low, the reflexive 'no' prevails. Every suggestion is immediately refuted by a counter-argument. Fault-finding and obstacle-raising are the usual styles of responding to ideas. Where there is little idea support, people shoot each other's ideas down, keep ideas to themselves, and idea-suggestion systems are not well utilized. It could be that, based on past experience, people don't think anything will be done. You may need to carefully plan a relaunch of your suggestion system with a series of case studies of what has been acted upon and why.

A supportive climate is vital for gaining information, material resources, organizational slack and political support. This can reduce the energy wasted by individuals through non-legitimate acquisition and support strategies, such as bootlegging (within the organization), or moonlighting (outside the organization). Without appropriate support for new ideas, potential innovators grow frustrated: 'If they speak out too loudly, resentment builds towards them; if they play by the rules and remain silent, resentment builds inside them.' It is not sufficient simply to have a policy or process of support, it is necessary for managers to provide the time and resources to generate and test new ideas.

However, some situations may have too much idea support. In these cases you may observe that people are only deferring judgement. Nothing is getting done and there are too many options because appropriate judgement is not being applied. Too many people may be working in different directions. One of the reasons for this condition may be that people are avoiding conflict and staying 'too open'. You may need to help people apply affirmative judgement so that a more balanced approach to evaluation prevails.

In many cases innovation happens in spite of the senior management within an organization, and success emerges as a result of guerrilla tactics rather than a frontal assault on the problem. Much has been made of the dramatic turnaround in IBM's fortunes under the leadership of Lou Gerstner who took the ailing giant firm from a crisis position to one of leadership in the IT services field and an acknowledged pioneer of e-business. But closer analysis reveals that the entry into e-business was the result of a bottom-up team initiative led by a programmer called Dave Grossman. It was his frustration with the lack of response from his line managers that eventually led to the establishment of a broad coalition of people within the company who were able to bring the idea into practice and establish IBM as a major e-business leader. The message for senior management is as much about leading through creating space and support within the organization as it is about direct involvement.

Conflict and Debate

Conflict in an organization refers to the presence of personal, interpersonal or emotional tensions. Although conflict is a negative dimension, all organizations have some level of personal tension.

Conflicts can occur over tasks, process or relationships. Task conflicts focus on disagreements about the goals and content of work, the 'what?' needs to be done and 'why?'. Process conflicts are around 'how?' to achieve a task, means and methods. Relationship or affective conflicts are more emotional, and characterized by hostility and anger. In general, some task and process conflict is constructive, helping to avoid groupthink, and to consider more diverse opinions and alternative strategies. However, task and process conflict have a positive effect on performance only in a climate of openness and collaborative communication, otherwise it can degenerate into relationship conflict or avoidance. Relationship conflict is generally energy-sapping and destructive, as emotional disagreements create anxiety and hostility.

If the level of conflict is too high, groups and individuals dislike or hate each other and the climate can be characterized by 'warfare'. Plots and traps are common in the life of the organization. There is gossip and back-biting going on. You may observe gossiping at water coolers (including character assassination), information-hoarding, open aggression, or people lying or exaggerating about their real needs. In these cases, you may need to take the initiative to engender cooperation among key individuals or departments.

If conflict is too low you may see that individuals lack any outward signs of motivation or are not interested in their tasks. Meetings are more about 'tell' and not consensus. Deadlines may not be met. It could be that too many ineffective people are entrenched in an overly hierarchical structure. It may be necessary to restructure and identify leaders who possess the kinds of skills that are desired by the organization.

So the goal is not necessarily to minimize conflict and maximize consensus, but to maintain a level of constructive conflict consistent with the need for diversity and a range of different preferences and styles of creative problem-solving. Group members with similar creative preferences and problem-solving styles are likely to be more harmonious but much less effective than those with mixed preferences and styles. So if the level of conflict is constructive, people behave in a more mature manner. They have psychological insight and exercise more control over their impulses and emotions.

Debate focuses on issues and ideas (as opposed to conflict which focuses on people and their relationships). Debate involves the productive use and respect for diversity of perspectives and points of view. Debate involves encounters, exchanges or clashes among viewpoints, ideas and differing experiences and knowledge. Many voices are heard and people are keen on putting forward their ideas. Where debates are missing, people follow authoritarian patterns without questioning. When the score on the debate dimension is too low you may see constant moaning and complaining about the way things are, rather than how the individual can improve the situation. Rather than open debate, you may see more infrequent and quiet one-on-one conversation in hallways. In these conditions, there will be a lack of willingness by individuals to engage others in conversation regarding new ideas, thoughts or concepts. One of the reasons for this situation is that people may have had bad experiences when they have interacted in the past. It may help to clarify the rationale of debate in the organization and begin to model the behaviour.

However, if there is too much debate you are likely to see more talk than implementation. Individuals will speak with little or no regard for the impact of their statements. The focus on conversation and debate becomes more on individualistic goals than on cooperative and consensus-based action. One reason for this may be too much diversity or people holding very different value systems. In these situations it may be helpful to hold structured or facilitated discussions and affirm commonly held values.

The mandate for legitimating challenge to the dominant vision may come from the top – such as Jack Welch's challenge to 'destroy your business'. Perhaps building on their earlier experiences Intel now has a process called 'constructive confrontation', which essentially encourages a degree of dissent. The company has learned to value the critical insights which come from those closest to the action rather than assume senior managers have the 'right' answers every time.

This has important implications for managers trying to cope more effectively with complexity and change:

■ Given uncertainty, explore the implications of a *range* of possible future trends;

■ Ensure broad participation and informal channels of communication;

■ Encourage the use of multiple sources of information, debate and scepticism;

■ Expect to change strategies in the light of new (and often unexpected) evidence.

INNOVATION IN ACTION

Developing a Creative Climate in a Medical Technology Company

A Finnish-based global healthcare organization had 55 000 employees and US$50 billion in revenue. Its mission was to develop, manufacture and market products for anaesthesia and critical care.

The senior management team of one division conducted an assessment, and found that they had been doing well on quality and operational excellence initiatives in manufacturing and had improved their sales and marketing results, but were still concerned that there were many other areas on which they could improve, in particular creativity and innovation.

We held a workshop with the senior team to present the results and engage them to determine what they needed to do to improve their business. We met with the CEO prior to the workshop to highlight the overall results and share the department comparisons. She was not surprised by the results but was very interested to see that some of the departments had different results.

During the workshop, the team targeted challenge and involvement, freedom, idea time and idea support as critical dimensions to improve to enable them to meet their strategic objectives. The organization was facing increasing competition in their markets and significant advances in technology. Although major progress had been made in the manufacturing area, they needed to improve their product development and marketing efforts by broadening involvement internally and cross-functionally and externally by obtaining deep consumer insight. The main strategy they settled upon was to jump-start their innovation in new product development for life support.

Key personnel in new product development and marketing were provided training in creative problem-solving, and follow up projects were launched to apply the learning to existing and new projects. One project was a major investment in re-engineering their main product line. Clinicians were challenged with the current design of the equipment. The initial decision was to redesign the placement of critical control valves used during surgery. The project leader decided to use a number of the tools to go out and clarify the problem with the end-users, involving project team members from research and development as well as marketing. The result was a redefinition of the challenge and the decision to save the millions of dollars involved in the re-engineering effort and instead develop a new tactile tool to help the clinicians' problem of having their hands full. Since the professionals in the research and development lab were also directly involved in obtaining and interpreting the consumer insight data, they understood the needs of the end-users and displayed an unusually high degree of energy and commitment to the project.

We also observed a much greater amount of cross-functional and informal working across departments. Some human resource personnel were replaced and new forms of reward and recognition were developed. Not only was there more consumer insight research going on, but there were more and closer partnerships created with clinicians and end-users of the products. During this period of time the CEO tracked revenue growth and profitability of the division and reported double-digit growth.

Source: Isaksen, S. and Tidd, J. (2006) *Meeting the Innovation Challenge: Leadership for Transformation and Growth*. John Wiley & Sons Ltd, Chichester.

Risk-taking

Tolerance of uncertainty and ambiguity constitutes risk-taking. In a high risk-taking climate, bold new initiatives can be taken even when the outcomes are unknown. People feel that they can 'take a gamble' on some of their ideas. People will often 'go out on a limb' and be first to put an idea forward.

In a risk-avoiding climate there is a cautious, hesitant mentality. People try to be on the 'safe side'. They decide 'to sleep on the matter'. They set up committees and they cover themselves in many ways before making a decision. If risk-taking is too low, employees offer few new ideas or few ideas that are well outside of what is considered safe or ordinary. In risk-avoiding organizations people complain about boring, low-energy jobs and are frustrated by a long, tedious process used to get ideas to action.

These conditions can be caused by the organization not valuing new ideas, or having an evaluation system that is bureaucratic, or people being punished for 'colouring outside the lines'. It can be remedied by developing a company plan that would speed 'ideas to action'.

Conversely, if there is too much risk-taking, you will see that people are confused. There are too many ideas floating around, but few are sanctioned. People are frustrated because nothing is getting done. There are many loners doing their own thing in the organization and no evidence of teamwork. These conditions can be caused by individuals not feeling they need a consensus or buy-in from others on their team in their department or organization. A remedy might include some team-building and improving the reward system to encourage cooperation rather than individualism or competition.

A recent study of organizational innovation and performance confirms the need for this delicate balance between risk and stability. Risk-taking is associated with a higher relative novelty of innovation (how different it was from what the organization had done before), and absolute novelty (how different it was from what *any* organization had done before), and that both types of novelty are correlated with financial and customer benefits. However, the same study concludes that 'incremental, safe, widespread innovations may be better for internal considerations, but novel, disruptive innovations may be better for market considerations ... absolute novelty benefits customers and quality of life, relative innovation benefits employee relations (but) risk is detrimental to employee relations'.

This is consistent with the real options approach to investing in risky projects, because investments are sequential and managers have some influence on the timing, resourcing and continuation or abandonment of projects at different stages. By investing relatively small amounts in a wide range of projects, a greater range of opportunities can be explored. Once uncertainty has been reduced, only the most promising projects should be allowed to continue. The goal is not to calculate or optimize, but rather to help to identify risks and pay-offs, key uncertainties, decision points and future opportunities that might be created. Combined with other methods, such as decision trees, a real-options approach can be particularly effective where high volatility demands flexibility, placing a premium on the certainty of information and timing of decisions.

Research on new product and service development has identified a broad range of strategies for dealing with risk. Both individual characteristics and organizational climate influence perceptions of risk and propensities to avoid, accept or seek risks. Formal techniques such as failure mode and effects analysis (FMEA), potential problem analysis (PPA) and fault tree analysis (FTA) have a role, but the broader signals and support from the organizational climate are more important than the specific tools or methods used.

Freedom

Freedom is described as the independence in behaviour exerted by the people in the organization. In a climate with much freedom, people are given autonomy to define much of their own work. They are able to exercise discretion in their day-to-day activities. They take the initiative to acquire and share information, make plans and decisions about their work. In a climate with little freedom, people work within strict guidelines and roles. They carry out their work in prescribed ways with little room to redefine their tasks.

If there is not enough freedom people demonstrate very little initiative for suggesting new and better ways of doing things. They may spend a great deal of time and energy obtaining permission and gaining support (internally and externally) or perform all their work 'by the book' and focus too much on the exact requirements of what they are told to do. One of the many reasons could be that the leadership practices are very authoritarian or overly bureaucratic. It might be helpful to initiate a leadership improvement initiative including training, 360-degree feedback with coaching, skills of managing and so on.

If there is too much freedom you may observe people going off in their own independent directions. They have an unbalanced concern weighted toward themselves rather than the work group or organization. People may do things that demonstrate little or no concern for important policies/procedures, performing tasks differently and independently redefining how they are done each time. In this case people may not know the procedures, they could be too difficult to follow or the need to conform may be too low. You may start to reward improvement of manuals, process improvements, and ways to communicate and share best practices to help correct the situation.

Developing Personal Capabilities

Complete the questionnaire below, being as honest as possible. Then calculate your score using the guide in the answer. How innovative are you?

How Creative Are You?

(Please tick yes or no)

	Yes	No
1 Are you constantly on the look-out for new ideas?	☐	☐
2 Do you get bored with doing things in the same old ways?	☐	☐
3 Do you get satisfaction from making improvements?	☐	☐
4 Are you afraid of making mistakes?	☐	☐
5 Do you worry about appearing foolish?	☐	☐
6 Do you enjoy playing around with ideas?	☐	☐
7 Do you resent criticism of your ideas?	☐	☐
8 Do you welcome ideas from other people?	☐	☐

9 Do you like solving problems in unorthodox ways? ☐ ☐

10 Do you give up early when you run into difficulties? ☐ ☐

11 Are you discouraged from acting because of lack of resources? ☐ ☐

12 Should we have more respect for traditional methods? ☐ ☐

13 Do you prefer a quiet life to a challenge? ☐ ☐

14 Do you feel that it's not your job to be critical of established practice? ☐ ☐

15 Do you fear new situations with unpredictable consequences? ☐ ☐

16 Do you mistrust your own or other people's intuition? ☐ ☐

17 Do you find it hard to accept disorder and confusion? ☐ ☐

18 Do you dislike complexity? ☐ ☐

19 Are you afraid of being looked upon as being pushy? ☐ ☐

20 Are you reluctant to express your opinions? ☐ ☐

21 Are you afraid of having your ideas ridiculed? ☐ ☐

22 Are you easily discouraged by hostile criticism? ☐ ☐

23 Do you have a difficulty in thinking broadly? ☐ ☐

24 Are you quick to point out why an idea won't work? ☐ ☐

25 Do you set yourself specific innovation objectives? ☐ ☐

26 Do you keep abreast of new ideas in your field? ☐ ☐

Answer

This is not a very sophisticated test, but if completed honestly does help to identify weaknesses.

Score one point for answering 'yes' to questions 1, 2, 3, 6, 8, 9, 25, 26.
Score one point for answering 'no' to questions 4, 5, 7, and 10 to 24.

Overall score	above 20	high levels of creativity
	15-19	above average
	11-14	average
	7-10	below average
	less than 7	low creativity

The overall score is less important than the answers to specific questions. Using some of the approaches and tools in the next section can help you to overcome these weaknesses.

ADVICE FOR FUTURE MANAGERS

Developing a business plan will not always be enough to ensure effective and successful implementation. Research has identified several factors to help increase the power of your implementation plan. For example, Everett Rogers identified five factors to increase the effectiveness of your planning and implementation. He suggested that if your plan shows the relative advantage of your solutions over previous approaches and their compatibility or consistency with existing values, experiences or needs, the likelihood of them being implemented increase. Also, as you make the plan easy to understand and use (less complex), observable, and give people a chance to try parts of it, the greater the change of successful implementation.[9]

We have used these five categories to develop a checklist to help you examine the effectiveness of your plan and to identify places where it might be strong or need improvement or modification.

Relative advantage Being better than the previous solution: How well does my plan show how much better off people will be when they adopt the plan?

- Why is this plan better than what has been done before?
- What advantages or benefits might there be to accepting the plan?
- Who will gain from the implementation of the plan?
- How will I (or others) be rewarded by adopting the plan?
- How might I emphasize the plan's benefits to all?

Compatibility Consistent with values, experiences, and needs: How well does my plan demonstrate that it is compatible with current values, past experiences, and needs?

- Is the plan consistent with current practice?
- Does the plan meet the needs of a particular group?
- Does it offer better ways to reach our common goals?
- Who will naturally support and agree with the plan?
- Can it be favourably named, packaged or presented?

Complexity Being difficult to understand and use: How well does my plan provide for easy communication, comprehension and use?

- Is the plan easy for others to understand?
- Can it be explained clearly to many different people?
- Will the plan be easily communicated?
- How might the plan be made more simple or easy to understand?
- Is the plan easy to use or follow?

Trialability May be experimented with on a limited basis: How well does my plan allow for trialability?

- Can the plan be tried out or tested?
- Can uncertainty be reduced?
- Can we begin with a few parts of the plan?
- How might others be encouraged to try out the plan?
- Can the plan be modified by you or others?

Observability Results are visible to others: How well does my plan provide results that are easily observed and visible to others?

- Is the plan easy for others to find or obtain?
- Can the plan be made more visible to others?
- How might I make the plan easier for others to see?
- Will others be able to see the effects of the plan?
- Are there good reasons for not making the entire plan visible?

Other questions The following are some general questions that will help your planning and implementation efforts:

- What other resources will I need; how might I get them?
- What obstacles exist; how might we prevent or overcome them?
- What new challenges might be created; and dealt with?
- How might I encourage commitment to the plan?
- What feedback about the plan is needed?

Source: Isaksen, S. and Tidd, J. (2006) *Meeting the Innovation Challenge: Leadership for Transformation and Growth*. John Wiley & Sons Ltd, Chichester.

STRATEGIC AND SOCIAL IMPACT

Managers are facing broadening demands on their time and attention to a dynamic and uncertain environment. No organization is insulated from the requirements of being able to broaden their responsiveness to change. Organizations in both the private and public sectors face an increasingly ambiguous environment. Under these conditions, managers must learn how to become more flexible and agile in order to respond successfully.

Organizations have typically viewed creativity and entrepreneurial ability as belonging to a gifted few (usually placed within the design, research and development or marketing functions). As a result, the development and implementation of innovation has been limited. There is increasing recognition of the need to move beyond this narrow view of who has creative talent to how a broader range of talents might be applied. Organizations need to find ways to recognize and apply the full spectrum of creative talent represented in the entire employee population.

Innovation and change are at the forefront of the agenda for many who work within organizations, whether in the private or public sectors, or manufacturing or services, small or large. In his work on disruptive innovation, Clayton Christensen identifies the many challenges organizations now face, and why so many fail to respond to these.[10] Today everyone seems to be involved in planning or implementing some sort of change programme or innovation initiative. At the same time organizations must competently manage existing operations and businesses, what Michael Tushman calls the 'ambidextrous organization'.[11]

However, organizing innovation and change is not easy, and many fail. Research confirms what many of us already suspected. For example, a study of change efforts of Fortune 100 companies between 1980 and 1995 found that virtually all had implemented at least one change programme with an average investment of US$1 billion per organization, but only 30% produced an improvement in bottom-line results that exceeded the company's cost of capital, and 50% failed to market performance.[12] Similarly, most major programmes of business process re-engineering (BPR) have failed to deliver the promised improvements in productivity or quality, for example two-thirds of 600 BPR cases studied experienced marginal or zero benefit, and many have simply been used as an excuse for rationalization and down-sizing; typically 20% reduction in staff is experienced.[13] Most recently, many large private and public organizations have invested in some form of enterprise resource planning (ERP) as a catalyst for change, but 'such systems force change on an organization structure, working practices, policies and procedures that can hinder innovation'.[14]

In this chapter we have discussed the need for a more systemic approach, rather than simply trying to pull a single lever. Our research and experience confirm that those who initiate change need to have a good understanding of the nature of organizations, as well as the dynamics of innovation and change. This means that we must have a workable model for how organizations function that includes the key levers or factors for innovation and change.

Chapter Summary

- The organization of innovation and entrepreneurship is much more than a set of tools and techniques. Too often it is reduced to a simple methodology, such as developing a plan for a new business or development of a new product or service.

- The successful practice of innovation and entrepreneurship demands the interaction and integration of three different perspectives: personal, social and contextual.
  - Personal or individual attributes include creative style, and the ability to identify, assess and develop new ideas and concepts.
  - Collective or social issues involve the contribution of teams, groups and processes necessary to translate ideas and concepts into new products, services or businesses.
  - Contextual factors consist of the climate and resources needed to support the creation and growth of innovation and entrepreneurship.

Key Terms Defined

Cause and effect diagram A useful structured way of searching for the root cause of a particular problem, also known as fish bone (because of the way the diagram looks) or Ishikawa diagrams (after the Japanese person who promoted the technique).

Climate Recurring patterns of behaviour, attitudes and feelings that characterize life in the organization. These are the objectively shared perceptions that characterize life within a defined work unit or in the larger organization. Climate is distinct from culture in that it is more observable at a surface level within the organization and more amenable to change and improvement efforts.

Cognitive-mapping techniques which aim to provide a tool for revealing people's subjective beliefs in a meaningful way so that they can be examined not only by the individual for whom the map is constructed, but also by other individuals and groups. Another potential use of cognitive-mapping techniques is to allow decision-makers to look at maps that have been constructed for other stakeholders.

Culture The deeper and more enduring values, norms and beliefs within the organization.

Creativity The making and communicating of meaningful new connections to help us think of many possibilities; to help us think and experience in varied ways and using different points of view; to help us think of new and unusual possibilities; and to guide us in generating and selecting alternatives.

Lateral thinking Methods and tools to support alternatives to logical thought, to promote applied creative thinking.

Kirton Adapter-Innovator (KAI) scale A psychometric approach for assessing the creativity of individuals. By a series of questions it seeks to identify an individual's attitudes towards originality, attention to detail and following rules. It seeks to differentiate 'adaptive' from 'innovative' styles.

Pareto analysis Used to prioritize areas for improvement by identifying the factors that will have the greatest impact on quality. A Pareto diagram simply ranks problems or causes of problems according to their frequency or significance.

Further Reading and Resources

The research and practice of organizing innovation and entrepreneurship is rather fragmented, and tends to reflect the different disciplines relevant to the subject, ranging from psychology, which focuses on the individual issues such as cognition; sociology, which is more concerned with group processes and power; and economics, which only adequately deals with structures and exchanges or transaction between individuals and organizations. If you do not have a background in psychology, sociology or a dedicated course on organizational behaviour, we recommend you consult a good text on organizational behaviour. There are many suitable texts, but here is a selection we would recommend:

■ Buchanan, D. and Huczynski, A. (2004) *Organizational Behaviour*, 5th edn. FT Prentice Hall, Harlow, Essex. An excellent synthesis of the main issues, with a good balance of managerial and more critical social science approaches. Chapters 15, 16 and 18 are especially relevant.

■ Pugh, D.S. (1997) *Organization Theory: Selected Readings*, Penguin, London. A cheap text that covers a wide range of classical papers on organization, albeit a little dated.

■ Sorge, A. (2002) *Organization*, Thomson Learning London. A text of edited contributions from both classic and contemporary writers. Less managerial and more critical than the previous two texts.

A more detailed treatment of the issues covered in this chapter can be found in our recent text (2006) *Meeting the Innovation Challenge: Leadership for Transformation and Growth* (John Wiley & Sons, Ltd, Chichester), written with Scott Isaksen. Katz, R. (2003) *The Human Side of Managing Technological Innovation* (Oxford University Press, Oxford) is an excellent collection of readings; and Van de Ven, A.H., Polley, Angle H.L. and Poole, M.S. (2000) *Research on the Management of Innovation* (Oxford University Press, Oxford) provides a comprehensive review of a seminal study in the field, and includes a discussion of individual, group and organizational issues.

References

1 Kaplan, J.M. (2007) *Patterns of Entrepreneurship*, 2nd edn. John Wiley & Sons, Inc., New Jersey.

2 Roberts, E.B. (1991) *Entrepreneurs in High Technology: Lessons from MIT and beyond*. Oxford University Press, Oxford.

3 Roberts, *Entrepreneurs in High Technology*.

4 Isaksen, S. and Tidd. J. (2006) *Meeting the Innovation Challenge: Leadership for Transformation and Growth*. John Wiley & Sons, Ltd, Chichester.

5 Roberts, E.B. (1991) *Entrepreneurs in High Technology*. Lessons from MIT and beyond. Oxford University Press, Oxford.

6 Kanter, R.M. (2003) *Rosabeth Moss Kanter on the Frontiers of Management*. Harvard Business School Press, Boston, Mass. (1992) *The Change Masters: Corporate Entrepreneurs at Work*. International Thomson Business Press, London.

7 Hofstede, G. (2003) *Culture's Consequences: Comparing Values, Behaviors, Institutions, and Organizations across Nations*. SAGE Thousand Oaks, CA, Hofstede, G. (1994) *Cultures and Organizations – Software of the Mind: Intercultural Cooperation and its Importance for Survival*. McGraw-Hill, New York.

8 Schein, E.H. (2004) *Organizational Culture and Leadership*. John Wiley & Sons, Ltd, Chichester.

9 Rogers, E.M. (2003). *Diffusion of Innovations*, 4th edn. Simon & Schuster International, New York.

10 Christensen, C. and Raynor, M. (2003) *The Innovator's Solution: Creating and Sustaining Successful Growth*. Harvard Business School Press, Boston, Mass.

11 Tushman, M.L. (2002) *Winning through Innovation*. Harvard Business School Press, Boston, Mass.

12 Nohria, N. (1996) From the M-form to the N-form: taking stock of changes in the large industrial corporation. *Harvard Business School Working Paper 96–054*.

13 CSC Index (1994) *The State of Re-Engineering*. CSC Index, London.

14 Trott, P. and Hoecht, A. (2004) Enterprise Resource Planning (ERP) and its impact on the innovative capability of the firm. *International Journal of Innovation Management*, **8** (4), 380–398.

Discussion Questions

1 What are the key similarities, differences and relationships between entrepreneurship and innovation?

2 Why is the creative style of an individual more important than any assessment of absolute creativity?

3 What are the relevant influences of an individual's characteristics and their environment on entrepreneurship?

4 List the key components of a process for identifying, developing and assessing new ideas, and suggest a tool or technique to support each stage.

5 What is the difference between culture and climate, and why is this distinction critical for innovation and entrepreneurship?

6 What factors contribute to the development of a creative climate – and what factors might block it?

Team Exercise: Brainstorming and Spider Diagrams

Construct a spider diagram to help to identify the key issues related to the implementation of a new IT system.

You will probably be familiar with brainstorming. However, it is often not conducted very well. Brainstorming is the rapid generation and pooling of all and any ideas that a group of people can come up. It can be used to solve problems or to generate new ideas. Every idea is recorded no matter how obvious, irrational or bizarre. The critical thing to do when brainstorming, which is often not done well, is to *temporarily suspend any discussion or judgement*. This happens later. The keys to successful brainstorming are:

■ Keep a relaxed atmosphere. Meetings should be disciplined but informal. If possible, choose an informal venue.

■ Get the right size of team. The technique seems to work best with groups of five to seven people.

■ Choose a neutral (ideally external) chairperson. The chair checks that everyone understands what is going on and why. Avoid senior managers, as this might restrict the flow of ideas.

■ Define the problem or objectives clearly.

■ Generate as many ideas as possible.

■ Do not allow any evaluation and discussion.

■ Give everyone equal opportunity to contribute.

■ Write down *every* idea – clearly and where everyone can see them.

■ When all the ideas are listed, review them for clarification, making sure everyone understands each item. At this point you can eliminate duplications and remove ideas the group feels are no longer appropriate.

■ Allow ideas to incubate. Brainstorm in sessions with perhaps a few days in between. This gives time for the team to let the ideas turn over in their mind, which often results in new ideas at a later session.

The evaluation of the ideas happens later, usually with a smaller group and using clear criteria for selection, review or rejection.

Here is a list of potential issues to get you started:

■ Role of consultants

■ Maintenance and support

■ Financing and timing

■ Training and new skills

■ Software and data compatibility.

Assignment and Case Study Questions

1 Propose some new services for mobile telephony. Use each of the following six methods to help to provoke alternatives:

   ■ *Remove or suspend an assumption or goal* – what could we do differently if we temporarily ignore a key objective or assumption?

   ■ *Reverse objectives or methods* – what would we do to achieve the exact opposite, and then reverse this?

   ■ *Exaggerate the problem or goal* – what might we do if the goal or problem was much larger or smaller?

   ■ *Distort the relationships or cause and effect* – what would the implications be?

   ■ *Generate random inputs* – what new ideas does the introduction of a random word help create?

   ■ *Use a metaphor or character* – what would a chosen famous character do in these circumstances?

CASE STUDY 2

Exploring Innovation in Action: Creative Problem-solving in Technical Consultancies

Technical consultancies (TCs) provide services to support design, development, and maintenance. Examples include employee-owned firms such as Mott MacDonald or publicly listed firms companies such as Atkins, although there are numerous much smaller firms focusing on fewer or even single markets. Collectively these firms provide services for the total life cycle of client assets. TCs are an excellent example of the interaction of individual expertise and creativity, and organizational innovation.

Technical services are an important contributor to most advanced and emerging economies, and TCs are large employers of a wide range of engineering talent and disciplines. For example Atkins alone was recently reported as requiring a further 3000 engineers – more than the entire UK output of civil engineers annually. TCs operate in many distinct sectors of the economy, including energy, transport, utilities and infrastructure projects, although many of the roles they play in these sectors are broadly similar, and include opportunity and risk assessment, and project specification, design, management and execution.

However, innovation by TCs is not the same as more conventional manufacturing firms as they do not produce products as such, but rather projects and services. Therefore the usual measures of innovation such as R&D expenditure, new products or patents are less appropriate.

As project-based consultancies, these firms do not have dedicated R&D departments or formal product development processes. Instead innovation is distributed both within client-focused projects and as part of internally sponsored activities. On the basis of submissions to the Inland Revenue, estimates for R&D activity appear to be in the range of 2–5% of turnover. Although successful innovation is grounded in technical expertise, in such professional environments it is also dependent on advocacy, mentoring and learning from experience, and conveying that understanding to the customers through precedent and reputation. As these companies become more global, a challenge is to transfer skills to local staff to remain competitive, and to gain access to local knowledge and networks. Indeed some have learned to compete effectively for government research funding as part of client-led consortia, or university–business research schemes or even on their own. With few formal R&D staff or facilities, most TCs have developed informal or formal venture schemes to fund internal exploratory projects by buying out staff from project work for short periods of time. The fruits of such schemes often leverage the intellectual capital of the firm and are used during projects, across projects and indeed beyond project work all together.

Table 2.4 identifies some of the types of innovation by TCs. Innovation is often project-based, but with such a diversity of market sectors and clients there is much variation, and innovation is not frequently part of the brief of the TC when engaged by the client. Therefore where innovation is generated it is generally through mediation with the client. Some of the most innovative work undertaken by TCs is in partnership with well-informed and experienced clients. Moreover some TCs claim to be able to influence clients and other stakeholders to use more innovative approaches that will save the client time (including delays), money, and perhaps enhance fees for other stakeholders. This emphasis on being able to be convincing and be trusted is important because, by definition, innovation is about applying new ideas or old ideas to new situations. As such, innovation is often perceived as 'risky' especially in large capital-intensive projects where profit margins may be rapidly eroded by mistakes.

While innovation within the project mix may be often difficult ('it has to be shoe-horned in' according to one TC director), failure to use innovation means losing the ability to cut client costs and thereby enhance reputation and chances of repeat business. Furthermore innovation brings cumulative benefits – through the accumulation of competencies and their combined application, as when a series of marginal savings through the application of techniques adds up to significant savings in large projects. In a globalizing marketplace, where TCs compete in bids far away from their country of origin, the ability to be innovative is often seen as key to competitive advantage, to enhance margins and to attract and retain staff.

Choosing innovative projects, partners and clients can also enhance reputation and credibility, critical for TECs. Particular value is placed on gaining credibility or goodwill from governments, customers, market analysts, and even from the company's own top management, academic institutions and potential recruits. This can create a virtuous circle of reputation, capability and performance. However, the converse cycle is also observed; poor performance leading to greater caution, less innovative and challenging projects, and a loss of capability and reputation.

Individual Talent and Creativity

Individual technical experience and expertise are necessary, but not sufficient for successful innovation in TCs. In addition, staff need to develop more generic problem-solving skills and strategies, and 'soft skills' such as client relationship-building, personal and institutional trust, as well as reliance on reputation and an ability to listen to others and adapt, rather than impose an off-the-shelf solution. The development of such a skill set in engineers is of key competitive advantage, but too often depends on the initiative and drive of individual consultants, rather than the firm. However, some TCs have invested in the development of such skills. For example, Atkins, one of the largest multidisciplinary TCs in Europe, has been voted one of the top 20 best companies to work for: 'When so much is invested in your training and development, it's easy to see why everyone is so motivated and enthusiastic ... I've always had the latitude to shape my own role ... ensuring as you progress you are given more responsibility without being out of your depth.'

Processes to Support Innovation

A central problem facing all project-based firms is how to capture knowledge from projects in order to develop corporate capabilities for future projects, often referred to as project-to-business (P2B) learning. Few TCs have any formal R&D or technical support functions, and instead rely upon a combination of individual expertise, technical communities of practice and expert groups to help coordinate knowledge capture and reuse. These tend to suffer unless sufficient resources – time and funding – are provided to support existing groups and help to create new groups. TCs find there is strong sharing of knowledge and experience within communities of practice, even across national boundaries. Gatekeepers for these communities act as expert technical 'gurus'.

Intranets were widely used by TCs to encourage sharing across communities of practice, but proved to be a very poor substitute for personal and social mechanisms. For example, one of the larger inter-national TCs had for the past six years established a wide range of knowledge management initiatives to encourage sharing of know-how and experience across projects. These initiatives range from orga-nizational processes and mechanisms, such as cross-functional communications meetings and skills networks, to technology-based approaches, such as an expert database and intranet. The former has been significantly more successful than the latter. For example, a survey of engineers in one TC indi-cated that in design and problem-solving, discussions with colleagues were rated as being twice as valuable as use of the knowledge databases, and consequently engineers were four times more likely to rely on colleagues than on the technology. Nonetheless, intranets are successfully used to communi-cate information across international business units, and as a means to socialize and develop younger engineers.

Organization Context to Promote Innovation and Entrepreneurship

Relationships with clients and other stakeholders are critical aspects of organization for TCs. Lead users are critical to the development and adoption of complex products. As the title suggests, lead users demand new requirements ahead of the general market of other users, but are also positioned in the market to significantly benefit from the meeting of those requirements. Where potential users have high levels of sophistication, for example in business to business markets such as scientific instruments, capital equipment and IT systems, lead users can help to co-develop innovations, and are therefore often early adopters of such innovations. This suggests that those TCs seeking to develop innovative complex products and services should identify potential lead users with such characteristics to contribute to the co-development and early adoption of the innovation.

Case Study Questions

1 What are some of the key characteristics required to become a successful technical consultant?

2 How do processes and technology help to encourage multidisciplinary working in projects?

3 What influences, positive and negative, might exposure to key clients have on creativity and innovation?

Sources: Tidd, J. and Hopkins, M. (2006). Managing Innovation in Technology and Engineering Consultancies, 15th International Association of Management of Technology (IAMOT 15) Conference, Beijing, May 2006; Managing Knowledge to Capture Value in Technology and Engineering Consultancies, IEEE International Conference on Management of Innovation and Technology (ICMIT 2006), Singapore, June 2006.

Table 2.4   Modes of innovation by TCs and key benefits

Mode	Example of innovation	Benefit
(a) Business models	1 Focus on long-term client relationship and repeat business as opposed to competitive bidding	Reduced cost of acquiring new business to TC. Greater trust and understanding of business needs for the client
	2 Dual strategy of consultancy and internal R&D	Uses consultancy to inform R&D, and R&D to develop licensing revenues and better platforms to underlie consultancy offerings
	3 The multidisciplinary consultancy – becoming a one-stop shop for clients, and operating in multiple market sectors	Increased capability of TC to deal with complex innovation Opportunity for client to benefit from greater integration of skill sets required for a given project. Reduction of impact on TC's financial performance if a slow-down in a single market occurs
(b) Internal processes	1 Establishment of knowledge management systems such as online forums for communities of practice (e.g. for all electrical engineers across a company's divisions)	In large firms these leverage the global knowledge base and deliver technical expertise rapidly to the locality required

(continued overleaf)

Table 2.4 (*continued*)

Mode	Example of innovation	Benefit
	2 End of project reviews and learning, for example via team-based appraisals and reporting	Brings the lessons learned by project teams into the open and facilitates identification of diffusion of best practice
(c) Techniques/ platforms	Wide range of tools including: bespoke or modified software for modelling; prefabricated components for speeding site work; electronically enhanced data-collection on site; rapid decision-making/risk-assessment methodologies during projects	Provides opportunities to leverage/reuse existing knowledge and reduce staff time or project duration during client projects – saves client money and enhances margins for TCs
(d) Products/ widgets	Development of a tangible product (e.g. software package, vehicle part) that can be licensed out or sold directly	Creation of intellectual property assets, licensing income for TC and possible opportunities for spin-off ventures
(e) Project partnering	1 Expanding the role of the client's engineer in a tender adjudication role to allow them to do some of the detailed design rather than merely producing specifications for the tender competition	This approach reduces the chances of overspend and overruns later in projects, reducing risk for client and contractors. This attracts more competitors to bid. The TC benefits from more fees and greater engineer satisfaction than is typical in the client-engineer role – but sacrifices opportunity of entering the higher-risk/ higher-reward competition to be awarded the design engineer role
	2 New combinations of partners in project environments – such as forming a joint venture between design engineer and a maintenance engineer to approach a client together	Could provide more optimal management of asset repairs for a client than might be the case if the client hired them both individually. TCs get first-mover advantage to exploit novel offering in marketplace
(f) Design features	Application of new technical feature – such as aesthetic and insulating	Can be reused by the TC, and some features win prizes which enhance reputation.

Table 2.4 (*continued*)

Mode	Example of innovation	Benefit
	properties of the inflatable roof at the UK's Eden Project	Can enhance client value too, through life-cycle or build-phase cost savings, through status or visitor appeal.
(g) Solution extension	Using past experience to adjudicate a Public–Private Investment (PFI) tender competition in a country with no PFI experience Building a larger version of an existing solution such as a coffer dam to retain earth	Extensions such as larger-scale applications of known solutions leverage existing knowledge and can also win prizes and enhance reputation (e.g. tunnel-jacking under live rail lines during the Boston central artery project won Mott MacDonald many awards)

Chapter 3
Networks and Systems

This chapter

- ◼ Introduces the concept of networking as an increasingly powerful mechanism for enabling innovation and entrepreneurship.

- ◼ Looks at why networking matters – in terms of increasing and enabling knowledge flows within and between organizations.

- ◼ Reviews different types of innovation network, both inside and between organizations.

- ◼ Explores key mechanisms for designing and operating innovation networks.

Learning Objectives

By the end of this chapter you will develop an understanding of:

- ◼ How networking helps the process of innovation through improving the range and scale of knowledge interaction.

- ◼ How different types of network can contribute to the process.

- ◼ How effective networks can be designed and operated.

- ◼ How drivers such as globalization and the emergence of Internet-infrastructures are shaping an increasingly networked model of innovation.

No man is an Island . . .

Eating out in the days of living in caves was not quite the simple matter it has become today. For a start there was the minor difficulty of finding and gathering the roots and berries – or, being more adventurous, hunting and (hopefully) catching your mammoth for the stew pot. And raw meat isn't necessarily an appetizing or digestible dish so cooking it helps – but for that you need fire and for that you need wood, not to mention cooking pots and utensils. If any single individual tried to accomplish all of these tasks alone they would quickly die of exhaustion, never mind starvation! We could elaborate but the point is clear – like almost all human activity, putting food on the table is dependent on others. But it's not simply about spreading the workload – for most of our contemporary activities the key is shared creativity – solving problems together, and exploiting the fact that different people have different skills and experiences which they can bring to the party.

INNOVATION IN ACTION

Take any group of people and ask them to think of different uses for an everyday item – a cup, a brick, a ball. Working alone they will usually develop an extensive list – but then ask them to share the ideas they have generated. The resulting list will not only be much longer but will also contain much greater diversity of possible classes of solution to the problem. For example, uses for a cup might include using it as a container (vase, pencil holder, drinking vessel, etc.), a mould (for sandcastles, cakes, etc.), a musical instrument, a measure, a template around which one can draw, a device for eavesdropping (when pressed against a wall) and even, when thrown, a weapon!

The psychologist J.P.Guilford classed these two traits as 'fluency' – the ability to produce ideas – and 'flexibility' – the ability to come up with different types of idea (Guilford, 1967). The above experiment will quickly show that working as a group people are usually much more fluent and flexible than any single individual. When working together people spark off each other, jump on and develop each other's ideas, encourage and support each other through positive emotional mechanisms like laughter and agreement – and in a variety of ways stimulate a high level of shared creativity.

(This is the basis of 'brainstorming' and a wide range of creativity enhancement techniques which have been developed over many years.)

It's easy to think of innovation as a solo act – the lone genius, slaving away in a garret or lying, Archimedes-like, in the bath before that moment of inspiration when they run through the streets proclaiming their 'Eureka!' moment. But although that's a common image it lies a long way from the reality. In reality taking any good idea forward relies on all sorts of inputs from different people and perspectives.

For example, the technological breakthrough which makes a better mousetrap is only going to mean something if people can be made aware of it and persuaded that this is something they cannot live without – and this requires all kinds of inputs from the marketing skill set. Making it happen is going to need skills in manufacturing, in procurement of the bits and pieces to make it, in controlling the quality of the final product. None of this will happen without some funding so other skills round getting access to finance – and the understanding of how to spend the money wisely – become important. And coordinating the diverse inputs needed to turn the mousetrap into a successful reality rather than a gleam in the eye will require project management skills, balancing resources against the clock and facilitating a team of people to find and solve the thousand and one little problems which crop up as you make the journey.

Innovation is not a solo act but a multiplayer game. Whether it is the entrepreneur who spots an opportunity or an established organization trying to renew its offerings or sharpen up its processes, making innovation happen depends on working with many different players. This raises questions about team-working, bringing the different people together in productive and creative ways inside an organization – a theme we discussed in Chapter 2. But increasingly it's also about links *between* organizations, developing and making use of increasingly wide networks. Smart firms have always recognized the importance of linkages and connections – getting close to customers to understand their needs, working with suppliers to deliver innovative solutions, linking up with collaborators, research centres, even competitors to build and operate innovation systems. But in an era of global operations and high-speed technological infrastructures populated by people with highly mobile skills, building and managing networks and connections becomes *the* key requirement for innovation. It's not about knowledge creation so much as knowledge *flows*. Even major research and development players like Siemens or GlaxoSmithKline are realizing that they can't cover all the knowledge bases they need and instead are looking to build extensive links and relationships with players around the globe.

This chapter explores some of the emerging themes around the question of innovation as a network-based multiplayer game. And of course, in the twenty-first century this game is being played out on a vast global stage but with an underlying networking technology – the Internet – which collapses distances, places geographically far-flung locations right alongside each other in time and enables increasingly exciting collaboration possibilities. However, just because we have the technology to make and live in a global village doesn't necessarily mean we'll be able to do so – much of the challenge, as we'll see, lies in organizing and managing networks so that they perform. Rather than simply being the coming together of different people and organizations, successful networks have what are called emergent properties – the whole is greater than the sum of the parts.

The Spaghetti Model of Innovation

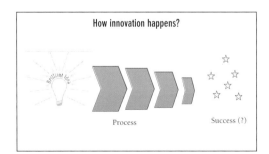

How innovation happens?

Brilliant idea

Process

Success (?)

As we showed in Chapter 1, innovation is a core process with a defined structure and a number of influences. That's helpful in terms of simplifying the picture into some clear stages and recognizing the key levers we might have to work with if we are going to manage the process successfully. But like any simplification, the model isn't quite as complex as the reality. While our model works as an aerial view of what goes on and has to be managed, the close-up picture can look a lot more like the picture on the right. The ways knowledge actually flows around an innovation project are complex and interactive, woven together in a kind of social spaghetti where different people talk to each other in different ways, more or less frequently, and about different things.

This complex interaction is all about *knowledge* and the ways it flows and is combined and deployed to make innovation happen. Whether it's our entrepreneur building a network to help him get his mousetrap to market or a company like Apple bringing out the latest generation iPod, the process will involve building and running knowledge networks. And as the innovation becomes more complex so the networks have to

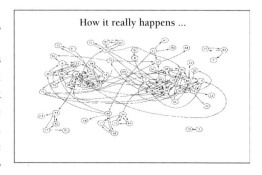

How it really happens ...

Table 3.1 **Rothwell's five generations of innovation models**[1]

Generation	Key features
First/second	Simple linear models – need pull, technology push
Third	Coupling model, recognizing interaction between different elements and feedback loops between them
Fourth	Parallel model, integration within the company, upstream with key suppliers and downstream with demanding and active customers, emphasis on linkages and alliances
Fifth	Systems integration and extensive networking, flexible and customized response, continuous innovation

involve more different players, many of whom may lie outside the firm. By the time we get to big complex projects – like building a new aeroplane or hospital facility – the number of players and the management challenges the networks pose get pretty large. There is also the complication that increasingly the networks we have to learn to deal with are becoming more virtual, a rich and global set of human resources distributed and connected by the enabling technologies of the Internet, broadband and mobile communications and shared computer networks.

Networking of this kind is something which Roy Rothwell, for many years a key researcher at Sussex University's Science Policy Research Unit, foresaw in his pioneering work on models of innovation which predicted a gradual move away from thinking about (and organizing) a linear science/technology push or demand pull process to one which saw increasing interactivity. At first, this exists across the company with cross-functional teams and other boundary-spanning activities. Increasingly, it then moves outside it with links to external actors. Rothwell's vision of the 'fifth-generation' innovation is essentially the one in which we now need to operate, with rich and diverse network linkages accelerated and enabled by an intensive set of information and communication technologies.

Types of Innovation Networks

A network can be defined as *a complex, interconnected group or system*, and networking involves using that arrangement to accomplish particular tasks. As we've suggested, innovation has always been a multiplayer game and we can see a growing number of ways in which such networking takes place. At its simplest networking happens in an informal way when people get together and share ideas as a by-product of their social and work interactions. But we'll concentrate our attention on more formal networks which are deliberately set up to help make innovation happen, whether it is creating a new product or service or learning to apply some new process thinking more effectively within organizations.

Innovation networks are more than just ways of assembling and deploying knowledge in a complex world. They can also have what are termed 'emergent properties' – that is, the potential for the whole to be greater than the sum of its parts. Being in an effective innovation network can deliver a wide range of benefits beyond the collective knowledge efficiency mentioned above. These include getting access to different and complementary knowledge sets, reducing risks by sharing them, accessing new markets and technologies and otherwise pooling complementary skills and assets. Without such networks it would be nearly impossible for the lone inventor to bring his or her idea successfully to market. And it's one of the main reasons why established businesses are increasingly turning to cooperation and alliances – to extend their access to these key innovation resources.

INNOVATION IN ACTION

Cosworth are a well-known producer of high-performance engines for motor-racing and performance-car applications. They were seeking a source of aluminium castings which were cheap enough for volume use but of high enough precision and quality for their product; having searched throughout the world they were unable to find a suitable stockist. Either they took the low-price route and used some form of die-casting which often lacked precision and accuracy, or they went along the investment-casting route which added significantly to the cost. Eventually Cosworth decided to go right back to basics and design their own manufacturing process; they set up a small pilot facility and employed a team of metallurgists and engineers with the brief to come up with an alternative approach that could meet their needs. After three years' work and a very wide and systematic exploration of the problem the team came up with a process which combined conventional casting approaches with new materials (especially a high grade of sand) and other improvements. The breakthrough was, however, the use of an electromagnetic pump which forced molten metal into a shell in such a way as to eliminate the air which normally led to problems of porosity in the final product. This innovation came from well outside the foundry industry, from the nuclear power field where it had been used to circulate the liquid sodium coolant used in the fast-breeder reactor programme! The results were impressive; not only did Cosworth meet their own needs, they were also able to offer the service to other users of castings and to license the process to major manufacturers such as Ford and Daimler-Benz.[2]

Consider another example from the motor-sport industry: leading race-car makers are continually seeking innovation in support of enhanced performance and may take ideas, materials, technology or products from very different sectors. Indeed some have people (called 'technological antennae') whose sole responsibility is to search for new technologies that might be used. For instance, recent developments in the use of titanium components in Formula 1 engines have been significantly advanced by lessons learned about the moulding process from a company producing golf clubs.

For example, participating in innovation networks can help companies bump into new ideas and creative combinations – even for mature businesses. It is well known, in studies of creativity, that the process involves making associations. And sometimes, the unexpected conjunction of different perspectives can lead to surprising results. The same seems to be true at the organizational level; studies of networks indicate that getting together in such a fashion can help open up new and productive territory.

INNOVATION IN ACTION

Learning together has its advantages. For example, in the UK, the Society of Motor Manufacturers and Traders has run the successful Industry Forum for many years, helping a wide range of businesses adopt and implement process innovations around world-class manufacturing. This model has been rolled out (with support from the Department of Trade and Industry) to sectors as diverse as ceramics, aerospace, textiles and tourism. Many regional development agencies (such as Advantage West Midlands with its 'Innovation Networks' programme) now try and use networks and clusters as a key aid to stimulating economic growth through innovation. The same principles can help to diffuse innovative practices along supply chains; companies such as IBM and BAE Systems have made extensive efforts to make 'supply chain learning' the next key thrust in their supplier development programmes.

Another way in which networking can help innovation is in providing support for shared learning. A lot of process innovation is about configuring and adapting what has been developed elsewhere and applying it to your processes – for example, in the many efforts which organizations have been making to adopt world-class manufacturing (and increasingly, service) practice. While it is possible to go it alone in this process, an increasing number of companies are seeing the value in using networks to give them some extra traction on the learning process.

INNOVATION IN ACTION

The case of the Italian furniture industry is one in which a consistently strong export performance has been achieved by companies with an average size of less than 20 employees. Keeping their position at the frontier in terms of performance is the result of sustained innovation in design and quality enabled by a network-based approach. This isn't an isolated case – one of the most respected research institutes in the world for textiles is CITER, based in Emilia Romagna. Unlike so many world-class institutions, this was not created in top-down fashion but evolved from the shared innovation concerns of a small group of textile producers who built on the network model to share risks and resources. Their initial problems with dyeing and with computer-aided design helped them to gain a foothold in terms of innovation in their processes. In the years since its founding in 1980, it has helped its 500 (mostly small business) members develop a strong innovation capability.

Innovation is about taking risks and deploying what are often scarce resources on projects which may not succeed. So, another way in which networking can help is by helping to spread the risk and, in the process, extending the range of things which might be tried. This is particularly useful in the context of smaller businesses where resources are scarce and it is one of the key features behind the success of many industrial clusters.

Long-lasting innovation networks can create the capability to ride out major waves of change in the technological and economic environment. We think of places like Silicon Valley, Cambridge in the UK or the island of Singapore as powerhouses of innovation but they are just the latest in a long-running list of geographical regions which have grown and sustained themselves through a continuous stream of innovation.

INNOVATION IN ACTION

Michael Best's fascinating account of the ways in which the Massachusetts economy managed to reinvent itself several times is one which places innovation networking at its heart. In the 1950s the state suffered heavily from the loss of its traditional industries of textiles and shoes but by the early 1980s the 'Massachusetts miracle' led to the establishment of a new high-tech industrial district. It was a resurgence enabled in no small measure by an underpinning network of specialist skills, high-tech research and training centres (the Boston area has the highest concentration of colleges, universities, research labs and hospitals in the world) and by the rapid establishment of entrepreneurial firms keen to exploit the emerging 'knowledge economy'. But in turn this miracle turned to dust in the years between 1986 and 1992 when around one third of the manufacturing jobs in the region disappeared as the minicomputer and defence-related industries collapsed. Despite gloomy predictions about its future the region built again on its rich network of skills, technology sources and a diverse local supply base which allowed rapid new product development to emerge again as a powerhouse in high technology such as special-purpose machinery, optoelectronics, medical laser technology, digital printing equipment and biotech.[3]

Table 3.2 gives an idea of the different ways in which networks can be configured to help with the innovation process. In the following section we'll look a little more closely at some of these, how they operate and the benefits they can offer.

Table 3.2   Types of innovation networks

Network type	Examples
Entrepreneur-based	Bringing different complementary resources together to help take an opportunity forward. Often a combination of formal and informal, depends a lot on the entrepreneur's energy and enthusiasm in getting people interested to join – and stay in – the network.
Internal project teams	Formal – and informal – networks of knowledge and key skills which can be brought together to help enable some opportunity to be taken forward – essentially like entrepreneur networks but on the inside of established organizations. May run into difficulties because of having to cross internal organizational boundaries.
Communities of practice	These are networks which can involve players inside and across different organizations – what binds them together is a shared concern with a particular aspect or area of knowledge.
Spatial clusters	Networks which form because of the players being close to each other – for example, in the same geographical region. Silicon Valley is a good example of a cluster which thrives on proximity – knowledge flows among and across the members of the network – but is hugely helped by geographical closeness and the ability of key players to meet and talk.

(continued overleaf)

Table 3.2 *(continued)*

Network type	Examples
Sectoral networks	Networks which bring different players together because they share a common sector – and often have the purpose of shared innovation to preserve competitiveness. Often organized by sector or business associations on behalf of their members. Shared concern to adopt and develop innovative good practice across a sector or product market grouping – for example, the SMMT Industry Forum or Logic (Leading Oil and Gas Industry Competitiveness), a gas and oil industry forum.
New product or process development consortium	Sharing knowledge and perspectives to create and market a new product or process concept – for example, the Symbian consortium (Sony, Ericsson, Motorola and others) working towards developing a new operating system for mobile phones and PDAs.
Sectoral forum	Working together across a sector to improve competitiveness through product, process and service innovation.
New technology development consortium	Sharing and learning around newly emerging technologies – for example, the pioneering semiconductor research programmes in the USA and Japan.
Emerging standards	Exploring and establishing standards around innovative technologies – for example, the Motion Picture Experts Group (MPEG) working on audio and video compression standards.
Supply-chain learning	Developing and sharing innovative good practice and possibly shared product development across a value chain – for example, the SCRIA initiative in aerospace.

Networks at the Start-up

The idea of the lone inventor pioneering his or her way through to market success is something of a myth – not least because of the huge efforts and different resources needed to make innovation happen. While individual ideas, energy and passion are key requirements, most successful entrepreneurs recognize the need to network extensively and to collect the resources they need via complex webs of relationships. They are essentially highly skilled at networking, both in building and in maintaining those networks to help build a sustainable business model.

INNOVATION IN ACTION

Many Minds Make Light Work...

Say the name Thomas Edison – and people instinctively imagine a great inventor, the lone genius who gave us so many twentieth-century products and services – the gramophone, the light bulb, electric power. But he was actually a very smart networker. His 'invention factory' in Menlo Park, New Jersey, employed a team of engineers in a single room filled with workbenches, shelves of chemicals, books and other resources. The key to his undoubted success was bringing together a group of young, entrepreneurial and enthusiastic men from very diverse backgrounds – and allowing the emerging community to tackle a wide range of problems. Ideas flowed across the group and were combined and recombined into an astonishing array of inventions.

Networks on the Inside

'If only x knew what x knows...' You can fill the x in with the name of almost any large contemporary organization – Siemens, Philips, GSK, Citibank – they all wrestle with the paradox that they have hundreds or thousands of people spread across their organizations with all sorts of knowledge. The trouble is that – apart from some formal project activities which bring them together – many of these knowledge elements remain unconnected, like a giant jigsaw puzzle in which only a small number of the pieces have so far been fitted together. This kind of thinking was behind the fashion for 'knowledge management' in the late 1990s and one response, popular then, was to make extensive use of information technology to try and improve the connectivity. Trouble is that while the computer and database systems were excellent at storage and transmission, they didn't necessarily help make the connections that turned data and information into useful – and used – knowledge. Increasingly firms are recognizing that – while advanced information and communications technology can support and enhance – the real need is for improved knowledge networks inside the organization.

It's back to the spaghetti model of innovation – how to ensure that people get to talk to others and share and build on each other's ideas. This might not be too hard in a three- or four-person business but it gets much harder across a typical sprawling multinational corporation. Although this is a long-standing problem there has been quite a lot of movement in recent years towards understanding how to build more effective innovation networks within such businesses.

Networks on the Outside

Creating and combining different knowledge sets has always been the name of the game both inside and outside the firm. But there has been a dramatic acceleration in recent years led by major firms like Procter & Gamble, GSK, 3M, Siemens and GE towards what has been termed open innovation. The idea – first put forward by US professor Henry Chesbrough – is that even large-scale R&D in a closed system like an individual firm isn't going to be enough in the twenty-first-century environment.[4] Knowledge production is taking place at an exponential rate and the OECD countries spend getting on for US$1 trillion on R&D in the public and private sector – a figure which is probably an underestimate since it ignores the considerable amount of 'research' which is not captured in official statistics. How can any single organization keep up with – or even keep tabs on – such a sea of knowledge? And this is happening in widely distributed fashion – R&D is no longer the province of the advanced industrial nations like USA, Germany or Japan but is increasing most rapidly in the newly growing economies like India and China. In this kind of context it's going to be impossible to pick up on every development and even smart firms are going to miss a trick or two.

INNOVATION IN ACTION

Procter & Gamble is a firm which has not exactly been a slouch where innovation is concerned – continually renewing its product offerings across a wide palette and spending around $3 billion a year on some 7000 researchers worldwide to help them do this. Yet during the past 5 years they have radically changed their game from 'research and develop' to 'connect and develop', and they have set themselves the ambitious target of sourcing 50% of their innovations from outside the company. So far the move has paid off – they now get around 35% of their innovations through a rich network of external links and seem to be leveraging significant market success as a result. The Crest Spinbrush – a battery-operated toothbrush which sells for around $5 and has grown a huge presence (worth around $200m per year) – originated as a derivative of a rotating lollipop and was introduced by a small team of entrepreneurs who approached P&G. Their ideas plus P&G's marketing and distribution strengths seem to have paid off handsomely.[5]

And of course innovation isn't just about the R&D side – it's also about market knowledge around customer needs and wishes. Globalization has meant that markets are increasingly fragmented so understanding the demand side for innovation becomes massively more complex. Not to mention the fact that the rapid rise of the Internet as a virtual marketplace changes the rules radically – new markets emerge with high speed out of nowhere as information flows in and across complex networks. A band like the Arctic Monkeys can rise to prominence and top the album charts with a product originally available only in digital download form and a reputation built not via conventional PR and publicity but by the sheer pace and scale of viral marketing via the Web. What will this mean for players in the media, information and entertainment industries in the near future? How does even an established player like the BBC try and deal with the challenge of new digital media – who creates it, with what content, for which audience reached by what route? Rather than attempt to second-guess this massively complex game they too are deploying an open innovation strategy, with projects like BBC Backstage aimed at working with a wide range of software developers to try and surface and at least get early warning of emerging Internet-led trends.

INNOVATION IN ACTION

BBC Backstage is an example of one of the projects trying to do with new media development what the open source community did with LINUX and other software development. The model is deceptively simple – developers are invited to make free use of various elements of the BBC's site (such as live news feeds, weather, TV listings, etc.) to integrate and shape innovative applications. The strap line is 'use our stuff to build your stuff' – and since the site was launched in May 2005 it has already attracted interest from hundreds of software developers and led to some high-potential product ideas. Ben Metcalf, one of the programme's founders, summed up the approach.

> *Top line, we are looking to be seen promoting innovation and creativity on the Internet, and if we can be seen to be doing that, we will be very pleased. In terms of projects coming out of it, if we could see a few examples that offered real value to our end users to build something new, we would be happy with that as well.*

And if someone is doing something really innovative, we would like to invite them into the BBC and see if some of that value can be incorporated into the BBC's core propositions.

The logic of open innovation is that organizations need to open up their innovation processes, searching widely outside their boundaries and working towards managing a rich set of network connections and relationships right across the board. Their challenge becomes one of improving the knowledge *flows* in and out of the organization, trading in knowledge as much as goods and services. Great in theory – but what it implies is that firms need to raise their game around finding and forming relevant connections and networks – and in building high-performance relationships with which to enable innovation.

INNOVATION IN ACTION

Perhaps the key to effective innovation management in the twenty-first century is going to be developing 'spaghetti skills' – building and running complex and rich networks along which knowledge flows. This is certainly the view of many senior managers. In a recent IBM survey of 750 CEOs around the world, 76% ranked business partner and customer collaboration as top sources for new ideas while internal R&D ranked only eighth. The study also indicated that 'outperformers' – in terms of revenue growth – used external sources 30% more than underperformers. It's not hard to see why – the managers interviewed listed the clear benefits from collaboration with partners as things like reduced costs, higher quality and customer satisfaction, access to skills and products, increased revenue, and access to new markets and customers. As one CEO put it,

'We have at our disposal today a lot more capability and innovation in the marketplace of competitive dynamic suppliers than if we were to try to create on our own' while another stated simply, 'If you think you have all of the answers internally, you are wrong'.

P&G's successes with 'connect and develop' owe much to their mobilizing rich linkages between people who know things within their giant global operations and increasingly outside it. They use communities of practice – Internet-enabled 'clubs' where people with different knowledge sets can converge around core themes, and they deploy a small army of innovation 'scouts' who are licensed to act as prospectors, brokers and gatekeepers for knowledge to flow across the organization's boundaries. Intranet technology links around 10 000 people in an internal 'ideas market' while sites like Innocentive.com extend the principle outside the firm and enable a world of new collaborative possibilities. 3M – another firm with a strong innovation pedigree dating back over a century – similarly put much of their success down to making and managing connections. Larry Wendling, Vice President for Corporate Research, talks of 3M's 'secret weapon' – the rich formal and informal networking which links the thousands of R&D and market-facing people across the organization. Their long-history of breakthrough innovations – from masking tape, through Scotchgard, Scotch tape, magnetic recording tape to Post-Its and their myriad derivatives – arise primarily out of people making connections.

Networks into the Unknown

Much of the time the challenge in innovation is one of 'doing what we do, but better' – continuously improving products and services and enhancing our processes. The scope here is enormous – both in terms of incremental modifications and additions of features and enhancements and in delivering on cost savings and quality improvements. Taken on their own these may not be as eye-catching as the launch of a radically new product but the historical evidence is that continuous incremental innovation of this kind has enormous economic impact. It's the glacier model rather than the violently fast-running stream – but in the long run the impact on the economic geography is significant.

We've learned a lot about how to manage this kind of 'steady-state' innovation and the kinds of thing which make for 'good practice'. The trouble is that from time to time there are *discontinuous* shifts in the environment – events which pull the carpet out from under our feet and rewrite the rules of the game. For example, some bright spark invents a radical new technology which changes the underlying knowledge base on which the firm operates. Or a completely new market emerges at the fringes and becomes mainstream – in the process disrupting the cosy arrangements among established players who are suddenly wrong-footed. Or business models change – as we have seen with low-cost airlines, the music industry or across the Internet. Or government changes the rules of the game through the regulatory environment. Discontinuities arise from many sources and we know they will happen – we just don't know when or where!

But we also know we can't simply ignore the possibility – the evidence is clear that when discontinuous events occur existing players do badly and it is the new kids on the block who succeed. Under these conditions the natural reaction is often to redouble our efforts along tried and tested pathways – to work twice as hard to get close to customers and build their requirements into our products and services. We do even better at our existing technologies, wringing extra performance out of them, and we persevere with established business models refining them with even more bells and whistles. Unfortunately the evidence is that enhancing our ways of managing 'steady-state' innovation may not help but even actively hinder our abilities to deal with new challenges. As Clayton Christensen showed in his work on disruptive innovation,[6] when new markets emerge they do so at the fringe of existing ones and are often easy to ignore and dismiss as not being relevant. So working on getting even closer to existing customers actually takes you further away from what becomes the site of the real action.

Under these conditions organizations need a different approach to managing innovation – much more exploratory, agile, flexible in thinking and deciding, being able to turn on an organizational sixpence. In short they need to be like a new entrant firm, an entrepreneurial opportunity-seeker but backed with more extensive resources and experience.

How do firms deal with this kind of innovation – how do they work at the edge of chaos where new threats and opportunities are only dimly visible? And how do they search for innovation triggers or pick up on weak signals about emerging – but possibly radically different – futures? One way is to mobilize precisely the kind of 'open innovation' approaches described earlier – to cast the net wide and concentrate on finding and forming new networks. Another is to find active users and work alongside them to co-evolve new possibilities for products, services or better delivery processes. (We'll explore these questions in more detail in Chapter 7.)

Learning Networks

In principle firms have a number of opportunities available to them to enable learning – through experiment (e.g. R&D), through transfer of ideas from outside, through working with different players (suppliers, partners, customers), through reflecting and reviewing previous projects and even from failure. Studies of organizational learning suggest that it can be supported by structures, procedures and so on to facilitate the operation of the learning cycle – for example, through challenging reflection, facilitated sharing of experiences or planned experimentation.

INNOVATION IN ACTION

'The trouble with small firms isn't that they're small, it's that they're isolated!' A powerful point – we know that small firms have lots of advantages in terms of focus, energy and fast decision-making. But they often lack resources to achieve their full potential. This is where a concept which the economists call 'collective efficiency' comes in – the idea that you don't have to have all the resources under your own roof, only to know where and how to get hold of them. Working with others can get you a lot further. For example, the Italian furniture industry is a world-beater and has been for decades. Competing at the high end of the market, with great designs and customized products, they have topped the export league tables and are the envy of many other countries. Yet the average firm size in this sector is 12 people. They achieve their success not through individual excellence but through collective efficiency, sharing design facilities, materials purchasing, advertising and marketing costs, and so on. The same is true all round the world – for example, in one town in Pakistan 12% of the world's surgical instruments are made. This isn't low-cost manufacturing but high-precision, design-intensive work – but these small firms work together in a cooperative cluster.

Experience and research suggests that shared learning can help deal with some of the barriers to learning which individual firms might face. For example,

- In shared learning there is the potential for challenge and structured critical reflection from different perspectives.

- Different perspectives can bring in new concepts (or old concepts which are new to the learner).

- Shared experimentation can reduce perceived and actual costs risks in trying new things.

- Shared experiences can provide support and open new lines of inquiry or exploration.

- Shared learning helps explicate the systems principles, seeing the patterns, separating 'the wood from the trees'.

- Shared learning provides an environment for surfacing assumptions and exploring mental models outside of the normal experience of individual organizations – helps prevent 'not invented here' and other effects.

■ Shared learning can reduce costs (e.g. in drawing on consultancy services and learning about external markets) which can be particularly useful for SMEs and for developing country firms.

A key element in shared learning is the active participation of others in the process of challenge and support. Its potential as an aid to firms trying to cope with a challenging and continuing learning agenda has led to a number of attempts to establish formal arrangements for inter-organizational learning. For example, the experience of regional clusters of small firms, which have managed to share knowledge about product and process technology and to extend the capabilities of the sector as a whole, is recognized as central to their abilities to achieve export competitiveness. In work on supply-chain development there is a growing recognition that the next step after moving from confrontational to cooperative relationships within supply chains is to engage in a process of shared development and learning.

Learning is often involved as a 'by-product' of network activities – for example, emerging through exchange of views or through shared attempts at problem-solving. But it is also possible to see learning as the primary purpose around which a network is built; this concept of a learning network can be expressed as *a network formally set up for the primary purpose of increasing knowledge*. Such networks share a number of characteristics:

■ They are formally established and defined.

■ They have a primary learning target – some specific learning/knowledge which the network is going to enable.

■ They have a structure for operation, with boundaries defining participation processes which can be mapped onto the learning cycle.

■ They have measurement of learning outcomes which feeds back to operation of the network and which eventually decides whether or not to continue with the formal arrangement.

Examples include 'best practice' clubs (whose members have formed together to try and understand and share experiences about new production concepts), 'co-laboratories' (shared pre-competitive R&D projects), supplier associations and sectoral research organizations (where the aim is to upgrade knowledge across a system of firms). Learning may also involve 'horizontal' collaboration (between like firms) or 'vertical' cooperation (as in supply-chain learning programmes), or a combination of the two.

Making Networks Happen – Networks by Design

Whatever the purpose in setting it up, actually operating within an innovation network is not easy – it needs a new set of management skills and it depends on the starting point. For example, there is a big difference between the demands for an innovation network working at the frontier where issues of intellectual property management and risk are critical, and one where there is an established innovation agenda. But the challenges are about building trust and sharing key information – as might be the case in using supply chains to enhance product and process innovation. We can map some of these different types of innovation network on to a simple diagram (Figure 3.1) which positions them in terms of:

■ How radical the innovation target is with respect to current innovative activity.

■ The similarity of the participating companies.

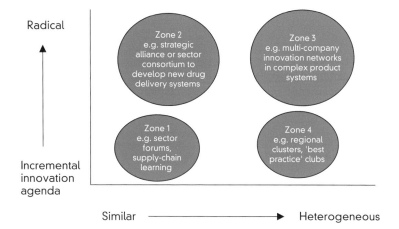

Figure 3.1   Types of innovation network.

By making this distinction, we can see that different types of networks have different issues to resolve. For example, in zone 1 we have firms with a broadly similar orientation working on tactical innovation issues. Typically, this might be a cluster or sector forum concerned with adopting and configuring 'good practice' manufacturing. Issues here would involve enabling them to share experiences, disclose information, develop trust and transparency and build a system-level sense of shared purpose around innovation.

Zone 2 activities might involve players from a sector working to explore and create new product or process concepts – for example, the emerging biotechnology/pharmaceutical networking around frontier developments and the need to look for interesting connections and synthesis between these adjacent sectors. Here, the concern is exploratory and challenges existing boundaries but will rely on a degree of information-sharing and shared risk-taking, often in the form of formal joint ventures and strategic alliances.

In Zone 3, the players are highly differentiated and bring different key pieces of knowledge to the party. Their risks in disclosing can be high so ensuring careful intellectual property (IP) management and establishing ground rules will be crucial. At the same time, this kind of innovation is likely to involve considerable risk and so putting in place risk- and benefit-sharing arrangements will also be critical. For example, in a recent review of 'high-value innovation networks' (Zone 4 in our figure) in the UK, researchers from the Advanced Institute of Management Research (AIM)[7] found the following characteristics were important success factors:

- Highly diverse: network partners from a wide range of disciplines and backgrounds who encourage exchanges about ideas across systems.

- Third-party gatekeepers: science partners, such as universities but also consultants and trade associations, who provide access to expertise and act as neutral knowledge-brokers across the network.

- Financial leverage: access to investors via business angels, venture capitalist firms and corporate venturing which spreads the risk of innovation and provides market intelligence.

- Proactively managed: participants regard the network as a valuable asset and actively manage it to reap the innovation benefits.

STRATEGIC AND SOCIAL IMPACT

Innovation isn't a solo act but a multiplayer game. And the theory of systems and networks talks about 'emergent properties' – essentially where the whole is greater than the sum of the parts. In innovation networks there are plenty of ways such emergent properties might help – for example:

- Bringing together different knowledge sets to solve a particular complex problem.

- Maximizing problem-solving capabilities by getting more (and different) minds on the job.

- Sharing the risks around exploring and exploiting new ideas.

- Transmitting learning across a group of players – for example, improving quality or delivery performance across a whole supply chain.

Given the scale of many of today's innovation challenges it is unlikely that any single enterprise – and certainly no single individual – will be able to deal with them all. But networking offers the chance to leverage other kinds of resources – knowledge, skills, finance, distribution – to help make things happen. It's particularly an opportunity for small firms – competing in a turbulent global marketplace can be very tough, not to mention lonely. But – as one commentator put it – 'The problem for small firms isn't so much that they're small as that they're isolated.' Networking offers the chance to build 'collective efficiency' – a model which has been used with great success in small-firm clusters around the world.

And in the field of social entrepreneurship, where the challenge isn't so much about making money as creating social value – changing the world – the potential of networking is equally powerful. As we'll see in Chapter 9, mobilizing the kinds of resources to make a difference, often against the odds, depends critically on the skills and abilities to engage others in the network.

ADVICE FOR FUTURE MANAGERS

Learning to Manage Innovation Networks

We have enough difficulties trying to manage within the boundaries of a typical business. So, the challenge of innovation networks takes us well beyond this. The challenges include:

- How to manage something we don't own or control.

- How to see system-level effects, not narrow self-interests.

- How to build trust and shared risk-taking without tying the process up in contractual red tape.

- How to avoid 'free riders' and information 'spillovers'.

It's a new game and one in which a new set of management skills becomes important.

Innovation networks can be broken down into three stages of a life cycle. Table 3.3 looks at some of the key management questions associated with each stage.

Table 3.3   Challenges in managing innovation networks

Set-up stage	Operating stage	Sustaining (or closure) stage
Issues here are around providing the momentum for bringing the network together and clearly defining its purpose. It may be crisis-triggered – for example, perception of the urgent need to catch up via adoption of innovation. Equally, it may be driven by a shared perception of opportunity – the potential to enter new markets or exploit new technologies. Key roles here will often be played by third parties – network brokers, gatekeepers, policy agents and facilitators.	The key issues here are about trying to establish some core operating processes about which there is support and agreement. These need to deal with: Network boundary management – how the membership of the network is defined and maintained. Decision-making – how (where, when, who) decisions get taken at the network level. Conflict resolution – how conflicts are resolved effectively. Information-processing – how information flows among members and is managed. Knowledge management – how knowledge is created, captured, shared and used across the network. Motivation – how members are motivated to join/remain within the network. Risk/benefit-sharing – how the risks and rewards are allocated across members of the network. Coordination – how the operations of the network are integrated and coordinated	Networks need not last forever – sometimes they are set up to achieve a highly specific purpose (e.g. development of a new product concept) and once this has been done the network can be disbanded. In other cases there is a case for sustaining the networking activities for as long as members see benefits. This may require periodic review and 're-targeting' to keep the motivation high. For example, CRINE, a successful development programme for the offshore oil and gas industry, was launched in 1992 by key players in the industry such as BP, Shell and major contractors with support from the DTI with the target of cost reduction. Using a network model, it delivered extensive innovation in product/ services and processes. Having met its original cost-reduction targets, the programme moved to a second phase with a focus aimed more at capturing a bigger export share of the global industry through innovation.

Developing Personal Capabilities

Innovation isn't a solo act – it's a multiplayer game. But that means we need to develop skills around networking – and in particular to think about three key tasks:

- Finding – who should we recruit and why – for example, sources of complementary expertise, finance, access to key markets, opinion leaders.

- Forming – how will we establish a working relationship with them? What's in it for them? Do we need to tie this up with some form of contract or is the network more open-ended, as in a learning network, where people share on a voluntary basis? How do we build trust and manage the core processes of decision-making, conflict resolution, risk- and benefit-sharing, and so on?

■ Performing – how can we retain and develop the relationship over the long term? How do we sustain things after the initial project? Is there a point where we need to end the relationship and move on?

Use of this simple checklist – finding, forming, performing – allows us to build a map of the networks we need to build, or to ensure we have a rich-enough and robust network already in place.

Chapter Summary

■ Innovation is not a solo act but a multiplayer game. Whether it is the entrepreneur who spots an opportunity or an established organization trying to renew its offerings or sharpen up its processes, making innovation happen depends on working with many different players. This raises questions *between* organizations, developing and making use of increasingly wide *networks*.

■ The ways knowledge actually flows around an innovation project are complex and interactive, woven together in a kind of social spaghetti where different people talk to each other in different ways, more or less frequently, and about different things. As the innovation becomes more complex so the networks have to involve more different players, many of whom may lie outside the firm.

■ Increasingly the networks we have to learn to deal with are becoming more virtual, a rich and global set of human resources distributed and connected by the enabling technologies of the Internet, broadband and mobile communications and shared computer networks.

■ Innovation networks are more than just ways of assembling and deploying knowledge in a complex world. They can also have what are termed 'emergent properties' – that is, the potential for the whole to be greater than the sum of its parts. These include getting access to different and complementary knowledge sets, reducing risks by sharing them, accessing new markets and technologies and otherwise pooling complementary skills and assets.

■ Operating within an innovation network is not easy – it needs a new set of management skills and it depends on the starting point. The challenges include:
   ■ How to manage something we don't own or control.
   ■ How to see system-level effects, not narrow self-interests.
   ■ How to build trust and shared risk-taking without tying the process up in contractual red tape.
   ■ How to avoid 'free riders' and information 'spillovers'.

Key Terms Defined

Clusters Networks which form because of the players being close to each other – for example, in the same geographical region. Silicon Valley is a good example of a cluster which thrives on proximity – knowledge flows among and across the members of the network but is hugely helped by the geographical closeness and the ability of key players to meet and talk.

Communities of practice Networks which can involve players inside and across different organizations – what binds them together is a shared concern with a particular aspect or area of knowledge.

Emergent properties Principle in systems that the whole is greater than the sum of the parts.

Learning network A network formally set up for the primary purpose of increasing knowledge.

Network A complex, interconnected group or system; and networking involves using that arrangement to accomplish particular tasks.

Open innovation Approach which seeks to mobilize innovation sources inside and outside the enterprise.

Supply-chain learning Developing and sharing innovative good practice and possibly shared product development across a value chain.

Further Reading and Resources

The work of Andrew Hargadon has highlighted the importance of networks and brokers going back to the days of Edison and Ford.
Hargadon, A. (2003) *How Breakthroughs Happen*. Harvard Business School Press, Boston, Mass.

One of the strong examples of this approach today is IDEO, the design consultancy which Kelley has described in detail.
Kelley, T., Littman, J. et al. (2001) *The Art of Innovation: Lessons in Creativity from Ideo, America's Leading Design Firm*. Currency, New York.

Conway, S. and Steward, F. (1998) Mapping innovation networks. *International Journal of Innovation Management*, **2** (2), 165–196 look at the concept of innovation networks and this theme is also picked up by:

Swan, J. and Newell, S. et al. (1999) Knowledge management and innovation: networks and networking. *Journal of Knowledge Management*, **3** (4), 262.

Learning networks are discussed in: Bessant and Tsekouras (2001) Developing learning networks, *A.I. and Society*, **15** (2), 82–98; and their use in sectors, supply chains and regional clusters in:

Morris, M. and Bessant, J. et al. (2006). Using learning networks to enable industrial development: case studies from South Africa. *International Journal of Operations and Production Management*, **26** (5), 557–568.

High-value innovation networks in several reports from AIM – the Advanced Institute for Management Research (www.aimresearch.org).

References

1 Rothwell, R. (1992) Successful industrial innovation: critical success factors for the 1990s. *R&D Management*, **22** (3), 221–239.

2 Delbridge, R. (2004) *How Motorsport Companies Collaborate and Share Knowledge*. AIM and Government Motorsport Unit, London.

3 Best, M. (2001) *The New Competitive Advantage*. Oxford University Press, Oxford.

4 Chesborough, H. (2003) *Open Innovation: The New Imperative for Creating and Profiting From Technology*. Harvard Business School Press, Boston, Mass.

5 Huston, L. and Sakkab, N. (2006) Connect and develop: inside Procter & Gamble's new model for innovation. *Harvard Business Review*, March.

6 Christensen, C. (1997) *The Innovator's Dilemma*. Harvard Business School Press, Boston, Mass.

7 AIM (2004) i- works: How high value innovation networks can boost UK productivity. ESRC/EPSRC Advanced Institute of Management Research, London.

Discussion Questions

1 Michael Dell didn't invent the computer – but he built one of the most successful businesses selling them. Discuss how he makes use of a networking approach to build and sustain a competitive edge in his business.

2 Why might Joe Bloggs, famous inventor, need help in getting his great idea into widespread use? And how might a networking approach help him?

3 Innovation is a solo act – the product of the lone genius? Show how successful entrepreneurs make use of networks to help take their ideas forward.

4 List three advantages of cooperating across networks in innovation as opposed to a 'go-it-alone' approach.

5 Jane Wilson has come up with a great new idea for a medical sensor to help in monitoring babies while they sleep. How could she improve her chances of success with her new product idea by using a networking approach to taking it forward?

Team Exercises

1 'Many hands make light work' – or 'Too many cooks spoil the broth'? Using examples show why networking may be a positive or negative element in enabling successful innovation. Split the group to present both sides of this argument and run the discussion as a debate.

2 Try and construct a map of the innovation network which leads to creating and delivering a new product like a new mobile phone or MP3 player.

Assignment and Case Study Questions

1 'The problem for small firms isn't that they're small – it's that they're isolated.' How might networking help deal with the challenges of being an innovative small firm and what advantages might this approach offer?

2 XYZ Electronics want to launch a supplier development programme to get their 180 suppliers to participate more fully in the innovation process – contributing new ideas for products and services and helping improve processes around quality, delivery and cost reduction. What issues should they think about in designing and implementing such a programme?

3 'Open innovation' is becoming a fashionable approach to innovation, building on the advantages of networking. But what problems might the implementation of such an approach throw up?

CASE STUDY 3

Exploring Innovation in Action: Connect and Develop at Procter & Gamble

Next time you go into a supermarket, think about innovation. Not only are you likely to encounter a massive range of products – food, drink, homecare, personal care, luxury goods and so on – but you're likely to find them constantly changing. Watch any category and see how much the offer changes – the range, the packaging, the branding and advertising/promotional storyline and, of course, the products themselves. Most of this change is incremental – you'll have to look closely to pick up on the minor shifts in the shape of the coffee jar or the improved seal on a toothpaste cap. But from time to time there are radical shifts – a new generation of an established product but embodying new technology or sometimes the emergence of a whole new product category.

Now think about the challenge this poses for the manufacturers of those products – a game played out every week in thousands of supermarkets where they compete with other manufacturers for the attention (and hopefully the purchases) of an army of shoppers. Innovation is very much the name of the game and it's a relentless quest for novelty. It's a powerful force driving a company like Procter & Gamble (P&G) forward – as their Chief Technology Officer, G. Gilbert Cloyd, comments,

> We're facing an ever-faster pace of innovation in consumer-product markets. We think the pace of innovation has roughly doubled in the past 10 years. So when we make an innovation and bring it into the marketplace, it has a much shorter market life than what it had previously. We need to be moving to upgrade our brands even more frequently . . . the competition is very fierce. Fifteen years ago, when we had a lot of generic brands or private labels, they were often not true brands; they were products. Now the brands that we face from retailers, from regional competitors, are very well-developed brands.

P&G have been players in the household and consumer goods market for nearly 200 years. They started life making candles at a time when these were still a common source of domestic lighting. But they moved on from those to other, related products – soaps and cleaning products. Today their range is a little wider – P&G have around 300 brands include Crest oral care, Pampers nappies and baby products, Tide and Ariel washing powders, Tampax sanitary products, Flash and Vanish cleaners – the list goes on a long way!

To keep a range as wide as this refreshed and to develop new and improved products to feature on the supermarket stages around the world needs a powerful innovation engine. P&G have built a worldwide R&D operation which involves some 7500 scientists and a spend of around US$3 billion per year. Maybe not as much as the high-technology pharmaceutical industry but still very impressive for its sector. Nor is it simply throwing money at the problem – P&G has some very effective systems and structures to ensure efficient project selection and progression.

The engine has worked well for them. They have an impressive record on new product launches and many of their new categories have gone on to reach the magic number of becoming billion-dollar brands – products whose annual sales can be as high as US$150–200 million.

The Birth of 'Connect and Develop'

But in the late 1990s there were concerns about this approach to innovation. While it worked, there were worries – not least the rapidly rising costs of carrying out R&D. In a world where technology is changing so fast and across so many frontiers it becomes increasingly hard to keep up. It's important in a diverse product company to try and cover all the bases – but which bases? – and how do you afford to cover all of them when getting on them carries a significant price tag? And what about the ones that get away – the new product ideas which are offered to the firm, or even developed in its own labs, but which don't appear to have enough market promise and so are not backed? For P&G there were many instances of innovations which they might have made but which they passed on – only to find someone else doing so and succeeding. As CEO Alan Lafley explained in a recent article:

> *Our R&D productivity had levelled off, and our innovation success rate – the percentage of new products that met financial objectives – had stagnated at about 35 percent. Squeezed by nimble competitors, flattening sales, lacklustre new launches, and a quarterly earnings miss, we lost more than half our market cap when our stock slid from US$118 to US$52 a share. Talk about a wake-up call. (Harvard Business Review, March 2006)*

Chesbrough's principles of open innovation can be summarized as:

■ Not all the smart people work for you.

■ External ideas can help create value, but it takes internal R&D to claim a portion of that value for you.

■ It is better to build a better business model than to get to market first.

■ If you make the best use of internal and external ideas, you will win.

■ Not only should you profit from others' use of your intellectual property, you should also buy others' IP whenever it advances your own business model.

■ You should expand R&D's role to include not only knowledge generation, but knowledge brokering as well.

Source: Chesbrough, H. (2003) *Open Innovation*. Harvard Business School Press, Boston, Mass.

Thinking along these lines led them to take a radically different approach to innovation. Instead of their traditional 'research and develop' model they moved to what they have called 'connect and develop' – an innovation process based on the principles of 'open innovation'. This idea originated in the work of Henry Chesbrough and basically challenges the dominant mode in which firms operate a 'closed' system, carrying out R&D but keeping it in-house so that they can exploit the benefits and control the use of ideas. This works but creates the kind of rising costs and insulation from new ideas which P&G were experiencing.

They recognized that much important innovation was being carried out in small entrepreneurial firms, or by individuals, or in university labs – essentially there was a great deal going on outside the company. They also saw other major players like IBM, Cisco, Eli Lilly and Microsoft beginning to go down the route of opening up their innovation systems.

That rang bells with their own experience as well. They recognized that in the past some of their best innovations had come from connecting ideas across internal businesses. So the idea of 'connect and develop' was born – not with the intention of outsourcing R&D but rather to increase their leverage in innovation by working better across internal and external networks.

Did it work? Lafley's original stretch goal was to get 50% of innovations coming from outside the company; by 2006 more than 35% of new products had elements which originated from outside, compared with 15% in 2000. Over 100 new products in the past 2 years came from outside the firm and 45% of innovations in the new product pipeline have key elements which were discovered or developed externally. They estimate that R&D productivity has increased by nearly 60% and their innovation success rate has more than doubled. One consequence is that they have increased innovation while reducing their R&D spend, from 4.8% of turnover in 2000 to 3.4%. And 5 years after the stock suffered a serious setback the share price has doubled and they now have a portfolio of 22 billion-dollar brands.

How Does It Work?

Pretty successful on anyone's scale – but how have they made it happen? How does the new innovation engine operate? The key lies in harnessing the power of innovation networks. As Cloyd explained,

> It has changed how we define the organization . . . We have 9000 people on our R&D staff and up to 1.5 million researchers working through our external networks. The line between the two is hard to draw . . . We're . . . putting a lot more attention on what we call 360-degree innovation.

Among their successes in internal networking was the Crest Whitestrips product – essentially linking oral care experts with researchers working on film technology and others in the bleach and household cleaning groups. Another is Olay Daily Facials which linked the surface-active agents expertise in skin care with people from the tissue and towel areas and from the fabric property-enhancing skills developed in Bounce, a fabric-softening product.

Making it happen as part of daily life rather than as a special initiative is a big challenge. They use multiple methods including extensive networking via an intranet site called 'Ask me' which links 10 000 technical people across the globe. It acts as a signposting and Web market for ideas and problems across the company. They also operate 21 'communities of practice' built around key areas of expertise such as polymer chemists, biological scientists, people involved with fragrances. And they operate a global-technology council, which is made up of representatives of all of their business units.

External links are built through an increasingly diverse set of mechanisms. One powerful approach is a group of 80 'technology entrepreneurs' whose task is to roam the globe and find and make interesting connections. They visit conferences and exhibitions, talk with suppliers, visit universities, scour the Internet – essentially a no-holds-barred approach to searching for new possible connections.

They also make extensive use of the Internet. One is their involvement as founder members of a site called InnoCentive (www.innocentive.com) originally set up by the pharmaceutical giant Eli Lilly in 2001. This is essentially a Web-based marketplace where problem-owners can link up with problem-solvers – and it currently has around 90 000 solvers available around the world. The business model is simple:–companies – like P&G, Boeing, DuPont – post their problems on the site and if any of the solvers can help they pay for the idea. Payments can range from US$10 000 to US$1 00 000 – and the model appears to work. From the outset, InnoCentive threw open the doors to other firms eager to access the network's trove of ad hoc experts. Companies like Boeing, DuPont and Procter & Gamble now post their most ornery scientific problems on InnoCentive's Website; anyone on InnoCentive's network can take a shot at cracking them. Importantly the solvers are a very wide mix, from corporate and university lab staff through to lone inventors, retired scientists and engineers and professional design houses. Jill Panetta,

InnoCentive's chief scientific officer, says more than 30% of the problems posted on the site have been cracked, 'which is 30% more than would have been solved using a traditional, in-house approach'.

Other mechanisms include a website called Yourencore which allows companies to find and hire retired scientists for one-off assignments. NineSigma is an online marketplace for innovations, matching seeker companies with solvers in a marketplace similar to InnoCentive. As P&G Chief Technology Officer, Gil Cloyd, comments, 'NineSigma can link us to solutions that are more cost efficient, give us early access to potentially disruptive technologies, and facilitate valuable collaborations much faster than we imagined.' And yet2com looks for new technologies and markets across a broad frontier, involving around 40% of the world's major R&D players in their network.

What is significant about the P&G use of these mechanisms is that it is part of a deliberate networking strategy to open up their innovation system. As Larry Huston comments,

> *People mistake this for outsourcing, which it most definitely is not ... Outsourcing is when I hire someone to perform a service and they do it and that's the end of the relationship. That's not much different from the way employment has worked throughout the ages. We're talking about bringing people in from outside and involving them in this broadly creative, collaborative process. That's a whole new paradigm.*

Case Study Questions

1 'Open innovation' is becoming a fashionable approach to innovation, building on the advantages of networking. But what problems might the implementation of such an approach throw up?

2 ABC Electronics has heard about 'open innovation' and sees this as a possible solution to its flagging innovation efforts. How might they think about implementing such a programme – and what issues would they watch out for?

3 What might the downside be for taking an open innovation approach like that of P&G?

Part 2
Context

Chapter 4
Innovative Manufacturing

This chapter

- Looks at the changing face of manufacturing and the persistence of the innovation imperative within it.

- Highlights key trends shaping the way we create and deliver manufactured goods in the twenty-first century.

- Underlines the core challenges for innovative manufacturing.
    - Moving to more agility.
    - Moving to more involvement in the innovation process.
    - Moving to more knowledge-intensity.
    - Moving to a 'design-make-serve' pattern.
    - Moving to a globalized, networked model.
    - Moving to a computer-integrated model.

Learning Objectives

By the end of this chapter you will develop an understanding of:

- The continuing role and importance of innovation within manufacturing.

- The changing nature of the innovation challenges to be managed.

- The relevance of core principles of entrepreneurship and innovation – the game may be changing dramatically but the underlying management challenges remain the same.

Images of Manufacturing

For most people the word 'manufacturing' conjures up images of belching smokestacks, urban sprawl, lines of unfriendly looking machinery – and all with a uniform colour scheme based on very drab grey! And as for how people fit into this puzzle that image is probably best captured by the immortal shot in *Modern Times* where Charlie Chaplin literally becomes a cog in the giant industrial machine.

INNOVATION IN ACTION

It's a Hot Topic for Politicians...

Trade liberalization and a rapid fall in communication and transport costs mean that the UK must increasingly compete against countries not only with much lower labour costs but also with well-educated labour forces. Wages in China are less than 5% of those in the UK and educational participation rates are high. Labour costs in Korea are just over half UK levels and the proportion of graduates in the working age population is almost identical and is particularly high in engineering and technology.

(From a UK Government report stressing the urgent need for UK manufacturers to become more knowledge-based and compete in the new 'knowledge economy'.)

The reality is that manufacturing is changing – of course. It has always been changing, since the earliest days when we began to try and reproduce simple operations like iron-making around our cave fires. There are periods of slow, incremental change punctuated by radical jumps in the ways we can produce things – for example, the massive acceleration around the time of the Industrial Revolution as a result of steam power.

It's also been a restless business – ever since we began to trade in manufactured goods the relative advantages of different places have played out. Those with better access to raw materials, to cheap energy or – most recently – cheap labour are in a better competitive position and so there is a shift in their direction. China is the current star but the massive upsurge in manufacturing activity there and the decline in so many other places is just the latest instalment of a long-running saga. Previous instalments of the story include the location across various parts of South East Asia for electronics assembly, and Africa and Latin America as preferred locations for car and car-component factories.

In fact manufacturing has come a long way from the Industrial Revolution days when elements of the picture painted above could be seen. If you were to visit the BMW factory in Leipzig, for example, you'd find a building designed by an award-winning architect; it has spacious halls, glass almost everywhere and the car-assembly track weaving its aerial way in and out of the office space. Customers are invited to enjoy the experience of seeing their cars being made as well as owning and driving them. And the product itself has come a long way from Henry Ford's famous limited choice – one Model T design with two or four doors and 'Any colour you like – as long as it's black!' Prospective BMW owners begin by sitting with sales staff in a 'design suite' in which they together configure their particular and personalized choice from the thousands of permutations of model, engine, interior trim, exterior features and add-on extras – and only when they are happy with the virtual design is it committed to physical production.

Whether it is making cars, carpets, cookers or cardboard boxes, the process of manufacturing is the same – a sequence of operations which bridge design with physical production and configuration before final distribution to end-users. What has changed is the ways in which this is carried out – Table 4.1 gives some examples of the major shifts which have taken place in recent years.

Table 4.1 The changing face of manufacturing

Dimensions of manufacturing	Nature of recent changes
Location	Since the Industrial Revolution where European manufacturers dominated, the location of 'the workshop of the world' has been shifting around the planet with accelerating speed. For example, the electronics assembly industry moved rapidly around South East Asia, repeatedly jumping across to locations with lower labour costs. At present many of the roads lead to China where the labour-cost advantages coupled with a huge domestic market opportunity make it a preferred location – but there are other trends around location, such as the need to be close to centres of knowledge which make places like Ireland another destination. The key point is that the game is now seriously global and mobile in nature.
Operations – what's involved in manufacturing	Moves from direct physical manufacturing and assembly of components to an extended network of activities ranging from design activities at the early stages, through various physical processes and assembly and out into distribution and after-sales service and support. The emerging picture is less one of 'making' than 'design/make/serve'.
Number and arrangement of players	For all but the simplest product, manufacturing requires a number of specialist suppliers of ideas, goods and services which need to be configured and coordinated rather as tributaries to a large river. In the case of something like a motor car we are talking of tens of thousands of components, for example. This means that we are talking about a multiplayer game but we are also seeing moves from vertical integration to organizing and managing extended and often globally distributed networks.
Drivers	In the early days of manufacturing the challenge was simply one of satisfying demand and price was the dominant factor shaping competitiveness in the marketplace for manufactured goods. These days the role of non-price factors like design, choice, delivery speed and after-sales service means that manufacturers have to differentiate themselves by playing in several games simultaneously – while not losing sight of the price challenge.
Technology	The earliest manufacturers made use of simple physical tools like hammers and axes. But these days the world of physical equipment has become immensely sophisticated and recent

(continued overleaf)

Table 4.1 *(continued)*

Dimensions of manufacturing	Nature of recent changes
	developments in information and communications technology mean that the game is increasingly played out in virtual space. Most design activity is done via computer and simulation so that, by the time metal is cut or plastic is moulded, problems have been explored and dealt with. Making the items is almost all done under computer control and the complex support activities – coordinating the arrival and payment for parts and materials, sales-order processing and customer-invoicing and so on – are all done with the aid of technologies like the Internet.

There's nothing new or surprising in the fact that manufacturing is changing – it has always been a powerful focus for innovation and entrepreneurship. It goes right back to basics – if you can make something no one else can but that people want, there are enormous entrepreneurial opportunities. And pretty soon others will want to imitate and enter the market, accelerating the growth of both the market and the pace of incremental innovation. Similarly, being able to make it better in some way – faster, cheaper, more variety – will stimulate innovation.

Misunderstood Manufacturing?

One common misperception is that manufacturing is declining, particularly in the more advanced industrial economies. This isn't strictly true. The share of *employment* in manufacturing has certainly fallen consistently so that it accounts for a relatively minor – 10 to 15% – share of the total. But that doesn't mean that people don't still want manufactured goods. Just as with agriculture the diffusion of increasingly sophisticated innovations has meant that very few people work directly in that sector – 2% typically. People still have to eat and they have more choice than ever. What has happened, of course, is that the change has been in the ways the sector works, and especially in the employment patterns. The same is true in manufacturing – people need clothes, washing machines, iPods – and with increasing world trade has come a massive expansion in demand for these goods. But producing them has become more efficient and more dependent on sophisticated equipment, less on direct manual labour. And, as we'll see later, even that needs a closer look – manufacturing is more than just putting things together (assembly) and some of the other components like design and service remain in their old locations.

The question we are concerned with in this chapter isn't whether or not manufacturing is changing – of course it is, driven by a strong spirit of innovation and entrepreneurship. Creativity in thinking about how and what to make is alive and well. Our interest is in *how* those changes are happening and where they are now playing out across a global and richly networked stage. What do successful manufacturers have in common in the ways they are approaching the question of organizing and managing the process? And how, in particular, are they dealing with the following key trends?

- Shifting from craft production to agile manufacturing.

- Increasing employee involvement in manufacturing innovation.

- Managing the move from physical to virtual manufacturing.

■ Changing from concentration on 'make' to 'design/make/serve' as the new manufacturing task.

■ Building and running effective manufacturing networks.

From Craft to Agile

At the start of the twentieth century, manufacturing saw a period of dramatic expansion. New industries were blossoming as entrepreneurs sought to provide people with a range of new products and services never before available on a large scale – cars, home entertainment, new food products, and so on. As the world moved through the increasing militarization which culminated in the First World War, the expansion in military products was even more dramatic, including new machines, armour-plating, aircraft, chemical weapons, explosives, food preservation, large-scale clothing manufacture and various synthetic substitutes for scarce items. When the war was finally over the mass production capacity for these industries had to look for other outlets, providing another stimulus for market expansion and development.

For a manufacturer supplying such rapidly growing markets, the key concern was output – produce as much as possible at as keen and competitive a price as possible. Emphasis was placed on economies of scale, the theory being that the bigger the plant, the cheaper it became to produce a single unit of product. Typical of the products available at this time – and in many ways a symbol of the whole era – was Henry Ford's Model T. A car for Everyman, it represented the triumph of the manufacturing system over small-scale craftsman production. And its manufacture required a new pattern of production technology and organization.

This shift was influenced by the ideas of industrial theorists like Adam Smith, Charles Babbage and Andrew Ure, all of whom saw the factory as a complex machine in which people were to be seen as parts, interchangeable with and replaceable by machines.

The industrial engineer, Frederick Taylor, with his 'principles of Scientific Management' extended this principle, stressing the need to remove discretion wherever possible – 'All possible brain work should be removed from the shop and centred in the planning and laying out department.' His principle of layers of functional management introduced the separation of indirect as opposed to direct workers and the pyramidal structure of management.

'The Machine that Changed the World'

That the convergent blueprint for manufacturing has come to be known as 'Fordism' reflects the enormous influence of Henry Ford in the way in which he (and his gifted team of engineers) developed and systematized such approaches. His model for the manufacture of cars was based on a number of innovations which reduced the need for skilled labour, mechanized much of the assembly process, integrated preparation and manufacturing operations for both components and finished product and systemized the entire process. Actually the basic elements of the Ford system were largely already in existence; the key was in *synthesizing* them into a new system.

For example, the idea of flow production lines for motor cars was first used in the Olds Motor Works in 1902, while Leland's Cadillac design of 1906 won an award for the innovation of using interchangeable, standardized parts. The challenge of the high-volume, low-cost production of the Model T led Ford engineers to extend the application of these ideas to new extremes – involving heavy investment in highly specialized machine tools and handling systems, and extending the division and separation of labour to provide workers whose main tasks were feeding the machines. The dramatic impact of this pattern on productivity can be seen in the case of the first assembly line, installed in 1913 for flywheel assembly, where the assembly time fell from 20 man-minutes to 5.

By 1914, 3 lines were being used in the chassis department to reduce assembly time from around 12 hours to less than 2.

This approach extended beyond the actual assembly operations to embrace raw material supply (such as steelmaking) and transport and distribution. At its height a factory operating on this principle was able to turn out high volumes (8000 cars/day) with short lead times. For example, as a consequence of the smooth flow which could be achieved it took only 81 hours to produce a finished car from raw iron ore – and this included 48 hours for the raw materials to be transported from the mine to the factory! In the heyday of the integrated plants such as at River Rouge, productivity, quality, inventory and other measures of manufacturing performance were at levels which would still be the envy even of the best organized car plants today.

INNOVATION IN ACTION

The Challenge of Change

Changing over to the new Model A was a massive undertaking and involved crippling investments of time and money – since the blueprint for the highly integrated and productive Ford factories was designed to make only one model well. During the year it took to change over, Ford lost U$200 million and was forced to lay off thousands of workers – 60 000 in Detroit alone – 15 000 machine tools were scrapped and a further 25 000 had to be rebuilt, and even though the Model A eventually became competitive, Ford lost its market leadership to General Motors.

Arguably, Ford's plants represented the most efficient response to the market environment of its time. But that environment changed rapidly during the 1920s, so that what had begun as a winning formula for manufacturing began gradually to represent a major obstacle to change. Production of the Model T began in 1909 and for 15 years or so it was the market leader. Despite falling margins the company managed to exploit its blueprint for factory technology and organization to ensure continuing profits. But growing competition (particularly from General Motors with its strategy of product differentiation) was shifting away from trying to offer the customer low-cost personal transportation and towards other design features – such as the closed body – and Ford was increasingly forced to add features to the Model T. Eventually it was clear that a new model was needed and production of the Model T stopped in 1927.

The Only Certainty Is Change!

This highlights one of the key lessons about the manufacturing environment – nothing stays the same for ever! Just as the environment of the 1900s differed radically from that of the nineteenth century, so the emerging picture in the twenty-first century poses new and unexpected challenges. We have seen the massive increase in competition with many more providers of goods and services, both in the domestic market and overseas. And 'overseas' no longer means simply a handful of firms in the advanced industrialized nations serving largely dependent and captive colonial/imperial markets. Now we have many newly industrializing countries competing aggressively for a share not only of their local markets but also those in the heartland of the old established manufacturing nations. The model of Japan for export-led economic growth provided an example successfully followed by nations on the Pacific Rim (such as South Korea) – and is now at the heart of Chinese expansion.

This international position is further complicated by the presence of the massive transnational corporations (TNCs), some of whom have a sales turnover exceeding the GNP of many substantially sized countries. Their elaborate network of manufacturing, sales and distribution operations is spread throughout the world and their facility to move between these geographical locations to secure optimum trading conditions adds another key element to the complex environment of the twenty-first century.

Keeping the Customer Satisfied

For the customer the range of choice of products and services is bewildering but it is becoming clear that such competition for custom puts a degree of power in their hands. They can now begin to demand better levels of service, better-quality products, better delivery and support and greater specificity in what they buy. Such power is often increasingly concentrated in the hands of key groups, such as food retailers, which can exert enormous influence on manufacturers in terms of what they are asked to produce.

And *when* they produce it. Increasing interest has been shown in supply and distribution chain management with the emphasis on cutting out buffer stocks and inventory-holding 'just in case' of problems; instead the move is now to producing and delivering 'just in time' for something to be used or sold.

Even the products themselves are no longer something to be taken for granted. Whereas the life of a typical product might once have been measured in years or even decades, the life cycle of many products today is down to months. Some consumer products – like television sets or hi fi systems – go through several changes every year. It has been estimated that up to 80% of the new products which we will be buying in 10 years' time have yet to be invented! The effect of this is to challenge the idea that industries go through phases, moving from being new young and innovative sectors associated with new products to mature industries in which the product and the way in which it is made are well established. Pressure for shorter product life cycles means that industries now need to find ways of constant renewal.

All of this poses enormous challenges for manufacturers – and takes them a long way from the kind of world in which Henry Ford was operating 80 years ago. Perhaps the key feature of this is the shift away from emphasis on price factors and output and towards *non-price* factors. If the world is a market square, then what determines whether a shopper buys from stall A or stall B – assuming they offer the same price – will be other features like the quality of the product; the design and packaging; the selling ability of the stallholder; the degree of service which the customer is offered, during purchase and after sales; and the degree to which the stallholder is able to offer the customer something specifically tailored to their needs rather than simply taken off-the shelf as a standard item.

INNOVATION IN ACTION

Costs – and Price – Still Matter

It is important to see this trend as complementary to that of 'lean manufacturing'. Manufacturing firms have been implementing process innovations aimed at 'doing what we do but better' for 30 years, using a bundle of approaches loosely grouped under the headings of 'Japanese manufacturing techniques', 'world-class manufacturing' and most recently 'lean'. These represent a consistent attack on waste and a quest for continuous process improvement. It's through the use of these process innovations that year-on-year cost reductions of 10% or more have been achieved – and why the relative price of many manufactured goods has remained constant.

Although some of the words are new, involving phrases like 'knowledge economy', the underlying challenge is a long-term one. For example, a major report for the UK Government back in the 1960s identified design and other non-price factors as increasingly relevant to UK competitiveness. What has changed is the growing emphasis on multiple bundles of non-price factors becoming the default requirement; the expectation now is not for trade-offs (e.g. quality vs. price, or delivery reliability vs. variety) but rather for 'bundles' of 'order-winning' factors. The situation has evolved to the point where strong demand and widespread and globally available supply mean that markets can demand not only this bundling of advantage but also a degree of 'agility' on the part of manufacturers – that is, the ability to change and reconfigure the bundle of offerings.

The trend is now to do much more in the way of extending the repertoire of capability – not only doing things better but adding new things. Competitive edge comes from offering more variety, delivery flexibility, more frequent model updates and eventually radical product innovation. Being able to move to new positions on this framework is increasingly a source of competitive advantage and without such mobility firms risk being trapped in positions where – even if they can perform well in terms of cost or quality performance – it will not be sufficient. Innovation is the ability to offer something which others cannot – and it confers a short term advantage but one which is increasingly competed away by imitators. So we have seen the frontier for manufacturing competitiveness move from price to non-price and now to *bundling*; each of these 'revolutions 'is hard to implement but essential for survival.

At the centre of this lies the ability to frame and reconfigure – dynamic capability – around what are seen by the demand side as a set of 'value propositions'. These represent bundles of non-price factors which particular market segments find valuable. Figure 4.1 illustrates this.

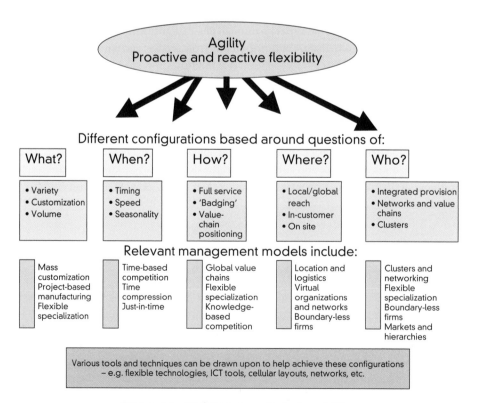

Figure 4.1   Building manufacturing ability.

Personalized Products for Everyone?

Mass customization (MC) is a widely used term which captures some elements of this. MC is the ability to offer highly configured bundles of non-price factors configured to suit different market segments (with the ideal target of total customization – i.e. a market size of one) – but to do this without incurring cost penalties and the setting up of a trade-off of agility versus prices.

ADVICE FOR FUTURE MANAGERS

One of the common mistakes we make in thinking about innovation is that we assume users are passive. But while not everyone may be able to design and build their own motor car, people do have wishes and aspirations which they'd like to see built into products. And they often have good ideas about particular features which they'd find useful or valuable – and which they would be prepared to pay for if they could see them implemented somewhere. So increasingly smart firms are realizing the potential of working with users, capturing their ideas and co-creating products and services. This isn't going to happen just by advertising slogans – firms need to develop ways of finding who are the 'lead users' whose ideas and wishes would be worth capturing because they reflect the wider needs of a particular market. And they need new ways of working alongside them – for example, via design studios, using the Web to get ideas and discuss new concepts. In the future an increasingly important skill set will be around:

- Lead user identification;
- Lead user design methods;
- Co-design and co-creation tools;
- Deployment of technologies like rapid prototyping, computer-aided design and manufacture.

Of course there are different levels of customizing – from simply putting a label 'specially made for...(insert your name here)' on a standard product right through to sitting down with a designer and co-creating something truly unique. Table 4.2 gives some examples.

Table 4.2   Options in customization (after Mintzberg and Lampel)[1]

Type of customization	Characteristics	Examples
Distribution customization	Customers may customize product packaging, delivery schedule and delivery location. The actual product is standardized.	Sending a book to a friend from Amazon.com. They will receive an individually wrapped gift with a personalized message from you – but it's actually all been done online and in their distribution warehouses.

(continued overleaf)

Table 4.2 (*continued*)

Type of customization	Characteristics	Examples
Assembly customization	Customers are offered a number of pre-defined options. Products are made to order using standardized components.	Buying a computer from Dell or another online retailer. You choose and configure to suit your exact requirements from a rich menu of options – but Dell only start to assemble this (from standard modules and components) when your order is finalized.
Fabrication customization	Customers are offered a number of pre-defined designs. Products are manufactured to order.	Buying a luxury car like a BMW, where you are involved in choosing ('designing') the configuration which best meets your needs and wishes – for example engine size, trim levels, colour, fixtures and extras, and so on. Only when you are satisfied with the virtual model you have chosen does the manufacturing process begin – and you can even visit the factory to watch your car being built.
Design customization	Customer input stretches to the start of the production process. Products do not exist until initiated by a customer order.	Co-creation, where you may not even be sure what it is you want but where – sitting down with a designer – you co-create the concept and elaborate it. It's a little like having some clothes made but rather than choosing from a pattern book you actually have a designer with you and you create the concept together. Only when it exists as a firm design idea does it then get made.

From Hands to High-Involvement

The word 'manufacture' comes from the Latin – meaning to make by hand. And that's pretty much how the game started, with craftsmen producing the things people wanted – shoes, knives, crockery. But as the population grew and demand increased, so too did the opportunities to innovate in production methods. Sometimes these were changes in the tools used, sometimes in the methods. And sometimes the power source was a target, moving through clever gears and pulleys to amplify manpower and then go to horses or water. By the time of the Industrial Revolution there was a massive acceleration, fuelled by steam power and by increasingly smart uses of materials like cast iron.

It wasn't just changes in the physical production – there were also changes in the way we thought about organizing and managing the process. The gradual drift towards the cities and the increasing use of machinery led to a rethink of how operations were managed. The rise of the modern factory organization origins can be traced back to Adam Smith and his famous observations of the pin-making process which marked the emergence of the concept of the division of labour. By breaking up the task into smaller, specialized tasks performed by a skilled worker or special machine, productivity could be maximized. During the next 100 years or so considerable emphasis was placed on trying to extend this further, by splitting tasks up and then mechanizing the resulting smaller tasks wherever possible to eliminate variation and enhance overall managerial control.

The resulting model saw people increasingly involved as only one of several 'factors of production' – and in a rapidly mechanizing world, often in a marginal 'machine-minding' role. At the same time the need to coordinate different operations in the emerging factories led to a rise in indirect activity and a separation between doing and thinking/deciding. This process accelerated with the increasing demand for manufactured goods throughout the nineteenth century, and much work was done to devise ways of producing high volumes in reproducible quality and at low prices.

A consequence of this was that by the turn of the twentieth century it was possible for people to speak of 'thinkers' and 'doers'. Developments in manufacturing organization and technology moved rapidly and the emergence of a 'scientific management' approach meant that skilled specialists were able to analyse and devise 'the one best way' to accomplish a wide range of tasks. It is hard to argue with the results they were able to achieve – for example, in a series of famous experiments Frederick Taylor was able to increase dramatically the productivity of businesses as diverse as steelmaking, dock handling and engineering.

INNOVATION IN ACTION

Characteristics of the Ford/Taylor system for manufacturing, *circa* 1920.

- Standardization of products and components, of manufacturing process equipment, of tasks in the manufacturing process, and of control over the process.

- Time and work study, to identify the optimum conditions for carrying out a particular operation and job analysis, to break up the task into small, highly controllable and reproducible steps.

- Specialization of functions and tasks within all areas of operation. Once job analysis and work-study information was available, it became possible to decide which activities were central to a particular task, and to train an operator to perform these smoothly and efficiently. Those activities which detracted from this smooth performance were separated out and became, in turn, the task of another worker. So, for example, in a machine shop the activities of obtaining materials and tools, or maintenance of machines, or of progressing the part to the next stage in manufacture, or quality control and inspection were all outside the core task of actually operating the machine to cut metal. Thus there was considerable narrowing and routinization of individual tasks and an extension of the division of labour. One other consequence was that training for such narrow tasks became simple and reproducible and thus new workers could quickly be brought on stream and slotted into new areas as and when needed.

- Uniform output rates and systemization of the entire manufacturing process. The best example of this is probably the assembly line for motor cars, where the speed of the line determined all activity.

- Payment and incentive schemes based on results – on output, on productivity and so on.

- Elimination of worker discretion and passing of control to specialists.

- Concentration of control of work into the hands of management within a bureaucratic hierarchy with extensive reliance on rules and procedures – doing things by the book.

Faced with the challenge of a widely differing workforce, many of whom lacked manufacturing skills and in a lot of cases spoke poor English as a second language, Ford and his engineers used scientific management principles to develop an alternative approach to making cars. From a highly variable activity with low productivity and variable quality, the 'mass-production' system changed car manufacturing dramatically.

There is little doubt that this was a 'better' way of making cars – at least in terms of the overall production figures (although the conditions under which manufacturing took place are perhaps more open to question). But the trap it set was to help embed the powerful belief that this was something which only specialists could be involved in designing and refining. Henry Ford is reputed to have once complained, 'How come when I want a pair of hands I get a human being as well?' The justification for this separation of hand and brain was that a well-designed system should not be interfered with through the introduction of unnecessary variation. A consequence – easy to see with hindsight but less so in the context of what were significant improvements in productivity and quality – was that many early mass-production factories came to resemble giant machines staffed by an army of human robots.

The paradox which this raises is simple to express but hard to understand. Organizations need creativity and active learning in order to survive in a hostile environment. In today's turbulent times with challenges coming from all directions – uncertainty in competing in a global market, uncertainty in political and social stability, technological frontiers being pushed back at a dizzying pace – the one certainty is that we need all the creativity and learning capacity that we can get.

> *Our findings were eye-opening. The Japanese plants require one-half the effort of the American luxury-car plants, half the effort of the best European plant, a quarter of the effort of the average European plant, and one-sixth the effort of the worst European luxury car producer. At the same time, the Japanese plant greatly exceeds the quality level of all plants except one in Europe – and this European plant required four times the effort of the Japanese plant to assemble a comparable product. (Womack et al., 1991[2])*

This seems an obvious point – but one which manufacturers continued to miss. For example, research on the global automobile industry in the 1980s showed that there were very significant performance differences between the best plants in the world (almost entirely Japanese-operated at that time) and the rest. The gaps were not trivial; on average the best plants were twice as productive (based on labour hours/car), used half the materials and space and the cars produced contained half the number of defects. Not surprisingly this triggered a search for explanations of this huge difference, and people began looking to see if scale of operations or specialized automation equipment or government subsidy might be behind it. What they found was that there were few differences in areas like automation – indeed; in many cases non-Japanese plants had higher levels of automation and use of robots. But there were major differences in three areas – design of the product for manufacturability, the way work was organized and in the approach taken to human resources.

ADVICE FOR FUTURE MANAGERS

Building a culture which supports high-involvement doesn't happen overnight – and it needs a strong lead from the top. 3M is a widely recognized innovator with an enviable record on high-involvement. But it owes much to one of the early CEOs, William McKnight, whose views are well summarized in the following quote:

As our business grows, it becomes increasingly necessary to delegate responsibility and to encourage men and women to exercise their initiative. This requires considerable tolerance. Those men and women, to whom we delegate authority and responsibility, if they are good people, are going to want to do their jobs in their own way.

Mistakes will be made. But if a person is essentially right, the mistakes he or she makes are not as serious in the long run as the mistakes management will make if it undertakes to tell those in authority exactly how they must do their jobs.

Management that is destructively critical when mistakes are made kills initiative. It's essential that we have many people with initiative if we are to continue to grow.

The idea that people can contribute to innovation through suggesting and implementing their ideas isn't new. Attempts to utilize this approach in a formal way can be traced back to the eighteenth century, when the eighth shogun, Yoshimune Tokugawa, introduced the suggestion box in Japan. In 1871 Denny's shipyard in Dumbarton, Scotland, employed a programme of incentives to encourage suggestions about productivity-improving techniques; they sought to draw out 'any change by which work is rendered either superior in quality or more economical in cost'. In 1894 the National Cash Register Company made considerable efforts to mobilize the 'hundred-headed brain' which their staff represented, while the Lincoln Electric Company started implementing an 'incentive management system' in 1915. NCR's ideas, especially around suggestion schemes, found their way back to Japan where the textile firm of Kanebuchi Boseki introduced them in 1905.

Harnessing the 'Hundred-headed Brain'

While there are a number of detailed company-level studies of high-involvement innovation there is relatively little information about the 'bigger picture'. How far has this approach diffused? Why do organizations choose to develop it? What benefits do they receive? And what barriers prevent them moving further along the road towards high-involvement?

Questions like these provided the motivation for a large survey carried out in a number of European countries and replicated in Australia during the late 1990s. It was 1 of the fruits of a co-operative research network which was established to share experiences and diffuse good practice in the area of high-involvement innovation. The survey involved over 1000 organisations in a total of 7 countries and provides a useful map of the take-up and experience with high-involvement innovation. Some of the key findings were:[3]

- Overall around 80% of organisations were aware of the concept and its relevance, but its actual implementation, particularly in more developed forms, involved around half of the firms.

- The average number of years which firms had been working with high-involvement innovation on a systematic basis was 3.8, supporting the view that this is not a 'quick fix' but something to be undertaken as a major strategic commitment. Indeed, those firms which were classified as continuous improvement innovators – 'CI innovators' – operating well-developed high-involvement systems – had been working on this development for an average of nearly 7 years.

- High-involvement is still something of a misnomer for many firms, with the bulk of efforts concentrated on shop-floor activities as opposed to other parts of the organisation. There is a clear link between the level of maturity and development of high-involvement here – the 'CI innovators' group was much more likely to have spread the practices across the organization as a whole.

Motives for making the journey down this road vary widely but cluster particularly around the themes of quality improvement, cost reduction and productivity improvement. This supports the view that high-involvement innovation is an 'engine for innovation' which can be hooked up to different strategic targets but it also underlines its main role as a source of 'doing what we do better' innovation rather than the more radical 'do different' type.

In terms of the outcome of high-involvement innovation there is clear evidence of significant activity, with an average per capita rate of suggestions of 43/year of which around half were actually implemented. This is a difficult figure since it reflects differences in measurement and definition but it does support the view that there is significant potential in workforces across a wide geographical range – it is not simply a Japanese phenomenon. Firms in the sample also reported indirect benefits arising from this including improved morale and motivation, and a more positive attitude towards change.

What these suggestions can do to improve performance is, of course, the critical question and the evidence from the survey suggests that key strategic targets were being impacted upon. On average improvements of around 15% were reported in process areas like quality, delivery, manufacturing lead time, and overall productivity, and there was also an average of 8% improvement in the area of product cost. Of significance is the correlation between performance improvements reported and the maturity of the firm in terms of high-involvement behaviour. The 'CI innovators' – those which had made most progress towards establishing high-involvement as 'the way we do things around here' – were also the group with the largest reported gains – averaging between 19 and 21% in the above process areas.

Almost all high-involvement innovation activities take place on an 'in-line' basis – that is, as part of the normal working pattern rather than as a voluntary 'off-line' activity. Most of this activity takes place in some form of group work although around a third of the activity is on an individual basis. (Boer, Berger et al., 1999)

But although a simple principle, it was neglected in much Western manufacturing until the last part of the twentieth century. In Japan, on the other hand, it thrived and became a powerful engine for innovation for firms like Kawasaki Heavy Engineering (reporting an average of nearly 7 million suggestions per year, equivalent to nearly 10 per worker per week), Nissan (6 million/3 per worker per week), Toshiba (4 million) and Matsushita (also with 4 million). Joseph Juran, one of the pioneers of the quality movement in the USA and Japan, pointed out the significance of 'the gold in the mine', suggesting that each worker in a factory could potentially contribute a valuable and continuing stream of improvements – provided they were enabled to do so. But it took a long time before the lessons which the Japanese had worked so hard at learning migrated to the rest of the world.

INNOVATION IN ACTION

A comprehensive study of UK experience carried out for the Chartered Institute of Personnel and Development collected evidence to support the contention that in the twenty-first century 'Tayloristic task management gives way to knowledge management; the latter seeking to be cost-efficient by developing an organisation's people assets, unlike the former which views labour as a cost to be minimised' (CIPD,

2001). They observe that although the task of convincing sceptical managers and shareholders remains difficult:

> more than 30 studies carried out in the UK and US since the early 1990s leave no room to doubt that there is a correlation between people management and business performance, that the relationship is positive, and that it is cumulative: the more and the more effective the practices, the better the result. (Caulkin, 2001[4])

These days, of course, most organizations have attempted to implement some form of employee involvement and the gains from doing so are becoming increasingly apparent. For example, the national UK Workplace Employee Relations Survey found a link between the use of more human resource management (HR) practices and a range of positive outcomes, including greater employee involvement, satisfaction and commitment, productivity and better financial performance. Another UK study concludes that 'practices that encourage workers to think and interact to improve the production process are strongly linked to increased productivity'. The use of tools such as lean manufacturing, and Six Sigma approaches to total quality management has become widespread.

INNOVATION IN ACTION

'Pretty in Pink'

Walking through the plant belonging to Ace Trucks (a major producer of forklift trucks) in Japan the first thing which strikes you is the colour scheme. In fact you would need to be blind not to notice it – among the usual rather dull greys and greens of machine tools and other equipment there are flashes of pink. Not just a quiet pastel tone but a full-blooded, shocking pink which would do credit to even the most image-conscious flamingo. Closer inspection shows these flashes and splashes of pink are not random but associated with particular sections and parts of machines – and the eye-catching effect comes in part from the sheer number of pink-painted bits, distributed right across the factory floor and all over the different machines.

What is going on here is not a bizarre attempt to redecorate the factory or a failed piece of interior design. The effect of catching the eye is quite deliberate – the colour is there to draw attention to the machines and other equipment which have been modified. Every pink splash is the result of a *kaizen* project to improve some aspect of the equipment, much of it in support of the drive towards 'total productive maintenance' (TPM) in which every item of plant is available and ready for use 100% of the time. This is a goal like 'zero defects' in total quality – certainly ambitious, possibly an impossibility in the statistical sense, but one which focuses the minds of everyone involved and leads to extensive and impressive problem-finding and -solving. TPM programmes have accounted for year-on-year cost savings of 10–15% in many Japanese firms and these savings are being ground out of a system which is already renowned for its lean characteristics.

Painting the improvements pink plays an important role in drawing attention to the underlying activity in this factory, in which systematic problem-finding and -solving is part of 'the way we do things around here'. The visual cues remind everyone of the continuing search for new ideas and improvements, and often provide stimulus for other ideas or for places to which the displayed pink idea can be transferred. Closer inspection around the plant shows other forms of display – less visually striking but powerful nonetheless – charts and graphs of all shapes and sizes which focus attention on trends and problems as well as celebrating successful improvements. Photographs and graphics which pose problems or offer suggested improvements in methods or working practices. And flipcharts and whiteboards covered with symbols and shapes of fishbones and other tools being used to drive the improvement process forward.

So how can organizations develop and sustain a higher level of involvement of their workforce in innovation? Research suggests that there are a number of stages in this journey, progressing in terms of the development of systems and capability to involve people but also progressing in terms of the bottom-line benefits which can be expected. Each of these takes time to move through, and there is no guarantee that organizations will progress to the next level. Moving on means having to find ways of overcoming the particular obstacles associated with different stages.[5]

Figure 4.2 shows the model in outline. The first stage – level 1 – is characterized by little, if any, innovative involvement going on, and when it does happen it is essentially random in nature and occasional in frequency. People do help to solve problems from time to time – for example, they will pull together to iron out problems with a new system or working procedure, or getting the bugs out of a new product. But there is no formal attempt to mobilize or build on this activity, and many organizations may actively restrict the opportunities for it to take place. The normal state is one in which innovation is not looked for, not recognized, not supported – and often, not even noticed. Not surprisingly, there is little impact associated with this kind of change.

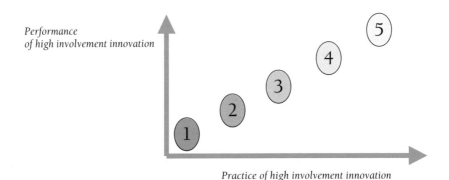

Figure 4.2   The five stage model.

Level 2, on the other hand, represents an organization's first serious attempts to mobilize high-involvement innovation. It involves setting up a formal process for finding and solving problems in a structured and systematic way – and training and encouraging people to use it. Supporting this will be some form of reward/recognition arrangement to motivate and encourage continued participation. Ideas will be managed through some form of system for processing and progressing as many as possible and handling those which cannot be implemented. Underpinning the whole set-up will be an infrastructure of appropriate mechanisms (teams, task forces or whatever), facilitators and some form of steering group to enable it to take place and to monitor and adjust its operation over time. None of this can happen without top management support and commitment of resources to back that up.

Dutton Engineering

This does not, at first sight, seem a likely candidate for world class. A small firm with 28 employees, specializing in steel cases for electronic equipment, it ought to be among the ranks of hand-to-mouth metal-bashers of the kind which you can find all round the world. Yet Dutton has been doubling its turnover; sales per employee have doubled in an 8-year period, rejects are down from 10% to 0.7%, and over 99% of deliveries are made within 24 hours – compared to only 60% being achieved within 1 week a few years ago. This transformation has not come overnight – the process started in 1989 – but it has clearly been successful and Dutton are now held up as an example to others of how typical small engineering firms can change.

At the heart of the transformation which Ken Lewis, the original founder and architect of the change has set in train is a commitment to improvements through people. The workforce are organized into 4 teams who manage themselves, setting work schedules, dealing with their own customers, costing their own orders and even setting their pay! The company has moved from traditional weekly pay to a system of 'annualised hours' where they contract to work for 1770 hours in year – and tailor this flexibly to the needs of the business with its peaks and troughs of activity. There is a high level of contribution to problem-solving, encouraged by a simple reward system which pays £5–£15 for bright ideas, and by a bonus scheme whereby 20% of profits are shared. (Lewis and Lytton, 1994[6])

Level 2 is all about establishing the habit of innovation within at least part of the organization. It certainly contributes improvements but these may lack focus and are often concentrated at a local level, having minimal impact on more strategic concerns of the organization. The danger is that, once having established the habit, the high-involvement innovation process may lack any clear target and begin to fall away.

Level 3 involves coupling high-involvement innovation to the strategic goals of the organization such that all the various local-level improvement activities of teams and individuals can be aligned. In order to do this, two key behaviours need to be added to the basic suite – those of strategy deployment and of monitoring and measuring. Strategy (or policy) deployment involves communicating the overall strategy of the organization and breaking it down into manageable objectives towards which activities in different areas can be targeted. Linked to this is the need to learn to monitor and measure the performance of a process and use this to drive the continuous improvement cycle.

INNOVATION IN ACTION

At first sight XYZ systems does not appear to be anyone's idea of a 'world-class' manufacturing outfit. Set in a small town in the Midlands with a predominately agricultural industry, XYZ employs around 30 people producing gauges and other measuring devices for the forecourts of filling stations. Their products are used to monitor and measure levels and other parameters in the big fuel tanks underneath the stations, and on the tankers which deliver to them. Despite their small size (although they are part of a larger but decentralized group) XYZ have managed to command around 80% of the European market. Their processes are competitive against even large manufacturers; their delivery and service level the envy of the industry. They have a fistful of awards for their quality and yet manage to do this across a wide range of products, some dating back 30 years, which still need service and repair. They use technologies from complex electronics and remote sensing right down to basics – they still make a wooden measuring stick, for example.

Their success can be gauged from profitability figures but also from the many awards which they receive and continue to receive as one of the best factories in the UK.

Yet if you go through the doors of XYZ you would have to look hard for the physical evidence of how they achieved this enviable position. This is not a highly automated business – it would not be appropriate. Nor is it laid out in modern facilities; instead they have clearly made much of their existing environment and organized it and themselves to best effect.

Where does the difference lie? Fundamentally in the approach taken with the workforce. This is an organization where training matters – investment is well above the average and everyone receives 50 hours per year, not only in their own particular skills area but across a wide range of tasks and skills. One consequence of this is that the workforce are very flexible, having been trained to carry out most of the operations they can quickly move to where they are most needed. The payment system encourages such cooperation and team-working, with its simple structure and emphasis on payment for skill, quality and team-working. The strategic targets are clear and simple, and are discussed with everyone before being broken down into a series of small manageable improvement projects in a process of policy deployment. All around the works there are copies of the 'bowling chart' which sets out simply – like a tenpin-bowling score sheet – the tasks to be worked on as improvement projects and how they could contribute to the overall strategic aims of the business. And if they achieve or exceed those strategic targets – then everyone gains thorough a profit-sharing and employee-ownership scheme.

Being a small firm there is little in the way of hierarchy but the sense of team-working is heightened by active leadership and encouragement to discuss and explore issues together – and it doesn't hurt that the Operations Director practises a form of MBWA – management by walking about!

Perhaps the real secret lies in the way in which people feel enabled to find and solve problems, often experimenting with different solutions and frequently failing – but at least learning and sharing that information for others to build on. Walking round the factory it is clear that this place isn't standing still – while major investment in new machines is not an everyday thing, little improvement projects – kaizens as they call them – are everywhere. More significant is the fact that the Operations Director is often surprised by what he finds people doing – it is clear that he has not got a detailed idea of which projects people are working on and what they are doing. But if you ask him if this worries him the answer is clear – and challenging. 'No, it doesn't bother me that I don't know in detail what's going on. They all know the strategy; they all have a clear idea of what we have to do (via the "bowling charts"). They've all been trained, they know how to run improvement projects and they work as a team. And I trust them.'

Level 3 activity represents the point at which high-involvement innovation makes a significant impact on the bottom line – for example, in reducing throughput times, scrap rates, excess inventory and so on. It is particularly effective in conjunction with efforts to achieve external measurable standards (such as ISO 9000) where the disciplines of monitoring and measurement provide drivers for eliminating variation and tracking down root-cause problems. The majority of 'success stories' (such as those of Japanese firms) can be found at this level – but it is not necessarily the end of the journey.

One of the limits of level 3 is that the direction of activity is still largely set by management and within prescribed limits. Activities may take place at different levels, from individuals through small groups to cross-functional teams, but they are still largely responsive and steered externally. The move to level 4 introduces a new element – that of 'empowerment' of individuals and groups to experiment and innovate on their own initiative.

Clearly this is not a step to be taken lightly, and there are many situations where it would be inappropriate – for example, where established procedures are safety-critical. But the principle of 'internally directed' innovation as opposed to externally steered activity is important, since it allows for the open-ended learning behaviour which we normally associate with professional research scientists and engineers. It requires a high degree of understanding of, and commitment to, the overall strategic objectives, together with training to a high level to enable effective experimentation. It is at this point that the kinds of 'fast learning' organizations described in some 'state-of-the-art' innovative company case studies can be found – places where everyone is a researcher and where knowledge is widely shared and used.

An organization at level 5 is one where HII is the dominant culture – constantly searching for ways to improve things and not leaving things as they are unless there is a good reason. The motto could almost be 'It it ain't being fixed, it's broke!' HII is part of individual behaviour in recognition of the fact that the world outside is constantly moving on and the survival and growth of the organization depends on constant learning and change.

Table 4.3 illustrates the key elements in each stage:

Table 4.3   Stages in the evolution of high-involvement innovation (HII) capability

Stage of development	Typical characteristics
1 'Natural'/background HII	Problem-solving random No formal efforts or structure Occasional bursts punctuated by inactivity and non-participation Dominant mode of problem-solving is by specialists Short-term benefits No strategic impact
2 Structured HII	Formal attempts to create and sustain HII Use of a formal problem-solving process Use of participation Training in basic HII tools Structured idea management system Recognition system Often parallel system to operations
3 Goal-oriented HII	All of the above, plus formal deployment of strategic goals Monitoring and measurement of HII against these goals In-line system

(continued overleaf)

Table 4.4 (*continued*)

Stage of development	Typical characteristics
4 Proactive/empowered HII	All of the above, plus responsibility for mechanisms, timing and so on, devolved to problem-solving unit Internally directed rather than externally directed HII High levels of experimentation
5 'Best practice' HII	HII is the dominant culture – 'the way we do things around here' Highly systematic problem-finding and solving HII linked to strategy and occurs at all levels of the organization

ADVICE FOR FUTURE MANAGERS

Implementing high-involvement innovation will need skills in dealing with questions like these:

Question	Response required
What's in it for people?	Putting in place some form of recognition/reward system which acknowledges their contribution
How to do it?	Training and skills development around problem-finding and -solving and related innovation capabilities Setting up suitable vehicles – problem-solving teams, quality circles or whatever – to carry through HI activities
Who is going to help support them?	Identification and training of suitable facilitators Commitment of senior management to support and champion the cause
How will this fit in?	Ensuring that organizational structures and systems support rather than block HI behaviour Making space and time available to carry out HI activities
How will the flow of ideas be managed?	Putting in place some form of idea management system
How to maintain momentum?	Ensuring this is more than another 'fashion statement' by the organization Planning for long-term strategic development of HI capability Linking HI to the organizational development strategy
Where and how to get started?	Identifying suitable pilot areas/teams/projects

From Things to Knowledge

Manufacturing is about physically working with things to produce other things people need. Or is it? If we think more closely about even a simple product we realize that it is a flow of activities which involves both tangible and intangible elements.

INNOVATION IN ACTION

Think about a camera. While some of the activity is certainly about assembling the item there's also:

- Design and product development;
- Procurement of different components and sub-assemblies;
- Logistics to get all these different bits to the right place just in time to be put together;
- Sales and distribution;
- After-sales service and support;
- Branding – telling a 'story' to particular customer groups.

Increasingly we have come to realize that the skill in manufacturing is in bringing these different knowledge sets together in the most efficient and effective way. And the scope for innovation lies in each of the knowledge areas as well as in their overall combination. With this background there is plenty of room for coming up with new ideas, both in the products we design and offer and in the ways we produce them.

Take a firm like Rolls-Royce. An offshoot of the famous motor-car partnership, the company specialized in aero engines and later moved into large-scale power generation systems for electricity generation and similar applications. Famous for high-quality, high-performance engines which power around half the aircraft in the skies today, the company has a tradition of innovation going right back to its foundation. Radical product innovations included many families of engines which enabled breakthroughs in aviation technology – the commercial jetliner engines in the Comet, the variable thrust engines which powered the vertical take-off Harrier and perhaps the biggest stretch (which bankrupted the company and required state aid to refloat the business) – the RB211 family which enabled the jumbo jet era.

Their innovation portfolio wasn't just about products though – in parallel they pioneered many of the core process technologies around designing and machining exotic and expensive alloys, introducing carbon fibre and other composites, and installing ever more complex and integrated manufacturing systems. Their Advanced Integrated Manufacturing System in the 1990s led the field in terms of linking robotics, automated guided vehicles, computer-controlled machine tools and links with computer-aided design and engineering. Their current activities place huge emphasis on supplier development and integration, taking out waste in the extensive supply chain but also leveraging the skills, experience and core knowledge of their suppliers.

INNOVATION IN ACTION

Southern Antique Supplies (SAS) is a small manufacturer of paints and varnishes for furniture restoration. It also buys in brushes, cloths and other items so that it can offer a complete range of products which are likely to be used by both amateur and professional restorers. Over recent years the business has declined considerably, and the margins being made have shrunk to the point where the overall viability of the concern is in doubt.

One consequence was that they called in the Innovation Counsellor from their local Business Link (a government-backed network of advice and assistance for smaller UK firms). He spent time going through the business strategy, balance sheet, and so on and was coming round to the same opinion about the future of the firm. But he noticed that during the entire time of his visit one of the sales staff appeared to be on the same telephone call. Intrigued, he asked about the subject and found that the customer had already bought some varnish and brushes but had rung up to enquire about how he could best use them to get optimum results. The half-hour phone call was essentially concerned with the sales person giving extensive advice and encouragement to the amateur restorer.

At this an idea took shape in the Innovation Counsellor's mind and he asked about how often this sort of thing happened. On finding out that it was a frequent occurrence he suggested that they might think about charging for this service. From this seed a new business has grown which is proving far more successful than the old supplies operation – although that is still in existence. While there are many professional restorers who simply require the retailing of equipment and supplies, there are many more people with leisure time and a hobby interest in antique restoration. SAS has developed a completely new – and very successful – service operation with consultants, videos, books and other ways of accessing its deep knowledge base about how to restore furniture well. In essence they have moved from being a supplier of products to a knowledge-based business where people are prepared to pay handsomely for their accumulated knowledge and experience. The fact that in doing so it also creates a new market for its supplies is almost incidental!

But perhaps the biggest recent shift in Rolls-Royce's approach to innovation has been to reframe the whole business. If we map their development onto the 4Ps framework from Chapter 1 – where innovation can be in product, process, position or 'paradigm' – we can see they have been moving around this space, constantly seeking new ways to develop competitive advantage. They have worked on product and process innovation and opened up new market space by position innovation. But they have recently – along with General Electric, their major competitor – moved to an approach which is about providing key customers with 'power by the hour'.

They realized that, while their interests and strengths lay in product and process technologies, from their customers' standpoint the critical thing was having serviceable and reliable jet engines keeping their aircraft flying – and earning them money. The customers' major concern was in buying in the service of keeping their planes aloft rather than in the particular features of the engines themselves. From this came the development of a range of services around maintenance and support, even extending to leasing and other financial dealings. These days Rolls-Royce earns the majority of its revenues – around 60% – from the bundle of services they wrap around their beautifully engineered products.

This pattern – the 'servicization' of manufacturing – has been going on for some time and an increasing number of firms in engineering, telecommunications and other complex systems fields have moved towards service-oriented models. The model these days is one of 'design/make/serve' – and it moves manufacturing from being increasingly sidelined as a low-employment fringe activity to the centre of the stage. And with it comes major new opportunities for innovation and entrepreneurship.

INNOVATION IN ACTION

You Are What You Know

Plasco Automotive are a medium-sized company with factories in several UK locations and in Spain and Belgium. Their origins are as 'trade moulders' – essentially providing a service to manufacturers in producing plastic mouldings; from this they have grown to become one of the automotive industry's preferred or 'first-line' suppliers. They are now responsible for the bumpers, wing mirrors and other external parts and for the dashboard, door panels and other items of interior trim. Turnover is around the £40m mark and their volumes of work extend to production of hundreds of thousands of mouldings for all the major European, US and Japanese manufacturers.

Their survival and growth has been the result of careful attention to strategy and in particular to climbing a knowledge ladder. Moulding an object in plastic is not easy but it is something which an increasing number of firms can do and at competitive prices. Basically the process involves someone producing a design and from this making a mould and related tooling to ensure that the object can be made. This is highly specialized work and requires a high degree of understanding and of combining different key knowledge sets:

- What the customer wants in terms of looks and appeal – the aesthetics of the design.
- Functionality – what the product has to do and the strength and other properties which it has to have.
- What the polymer is capable of and its particular strengths and weaknesses for this kind of application.
- What the manufacturing process will permit and its limitations.
- Quality required in terms of tolerances.
- Cost minimization – via value analysis of waste sources and so on.

Once the tool and product are specified the tool needs to be made – again involving specialized knowledge and skills in design and manufacturing to high tolerances and with specialist metals.

The tools and so on are then fitted to a moulding machine – and again specialized knowledge is needed to choose the correct process for the part being made. Most production involves some variation on injection-moulding where granules of the chosen polymer (which have been premixed with chemicals to provide colour and other properties) are fed from a hopper into a chamber in the machine where they are heated until they become plastic. A ram then forces the molten plastic into the mould and the item is allowed to cool enough to set before being ejected. Finally there are various trimming and other post-processing operations.

Understanding each of these stages and how to control them is the heart of the mouldings business. Historically trade moulders would receive tools and specifications from a customer and simply mould to order – a process not without its knowledge demands but one where entry barriers are low. Moulding machines are increasingly sophisticated so that if someone has enough money to buy a state-of-the-art machine then fitting a mould and doing a production run is possible. There will still be scope for learning and improving control over variables like temperature, mix and other parameters – and these manufacturing skills are increasingly relevant for high-specification, high-quality parts like those demanded by the auto industry. For many products, however, the quality requirements are relatively low and firms can enter the market and secure a position by exploiting a low-cost base – often using older machinery and low-cost labour, materials and so on.

The result is that trade moulding is a highly competitive sector with low entry barriers and little chance for differentiation except on price. For firms that wish to grow and develop the challenge is to find customers who value higher quality and precision and to offer a better manufacturing service based on tighter control and quality assurance. This was Plasco's approach during the early stages of development and they built up good relationships with many auto producers; unfortunately the pressures on such producers meant that they increasingly began demanding high quality and product performance but accompanied by continuing price reductions. Relationships between auto component producers and auto assemblers became difficult as assemblers began to source products more widely and on the basis of low cost and high quality; with the entry of many new countries into auto component production this put pressure on established players like Plasco. It was particularly challenging for sectors like plastics moulding where entry barriers were low since there was little scope for differentiation and relatively little room for further cost reduction compared to other developing and industrializing countries.

Under these conditions the threat to Plasco forced them to look at managing their knowledge base and developing skills and capabilities which would help them differentiate. Their strategy was to move further up the design chain and to concentrate on developing close relationships with customers and playing a key role in the early thinking about new products. They already knew a great deal abut manufacturing and could bring this specialized knowledge about how to get the best out of plastics mouldings while also making them cheap to manufacture without compromising quality. As the industry began looking to more sophisticated use of plastics in cars so Plasco worked alongside the assemblers – and in the process learned a great deal. They pushed the frontiers of technical possibilities – getting involved in experiments to see what was possible. Some of these succeeded and they found themselves able to offer sophisticated moulding techniques (such as binding cloth and polymer to make a 'soft' finish to interior trim components such as door panels) – but others turned out to be costly failures. Nonetheless this process of moving upstream in terms of their knowledge base began to pay off. In the late 1990s they achieved preferred supplier status which meant that they were increasingly part of the inner circle with auto producers, invited to participate in early design discussions and to explore together with the assemblers the new concepts which would eventually find their way into new models.

This process required a significant investment by Plasco in R&D – not in the formal sense as might be funding in a research-based sector like pharmaceuticals – but in staff time, specialist equipment, interruptions to production while testing is carried out. The overheads this represents – together with the costs of experiments which failed but which the end customer would not pay for, and the costs of quoting for business not gained – can be built up into a figure which represents the investment in developing new products and production capability. In the case of Plasco this moved from a very low level – perhaps 1-2% of turnover and not even identified as a separate cost – to close to 10%.

We can draw out a number of key points from this story:

■ The strategic need to move from commodity production where there are many and increasing numbers of competitors.

■ The challenge in making the move in terms of investment in knowledge and in the skills and equipment to take them up the knowledge ladder.

- Letting go of the simpler – and easier – parts of the business – taking the risk to go for higher technology.

- Building new kinds of relationships with customers to ensure they receive information and understand the problems they will have to solve.

- Invest in design centre and get close to producers at early stages – concept development.

- Develop close links with toolmakers and other specialists to ensure they have access to and learn from them.

- Develop links with polymer firms and work with them to colonize the knowledge.

- Capitalize on areas of acquired knowledge which may become relevant in future – for example, in recycling technology.

From Hand Tools to Intelligent Manufacturing

Innovation in manufacturing has been taking place ever since the Stone Age as new and better ways of doing things are discovered and developed. But there is a qualitative difference between innovations which are primarily associated with 'doing what we've always done but a little better' and those which fundamentally change the nature of the process to which they are applied. In the former case we are really talking about a *substitution* process – a typical example here would be replacing a machine with one designed to work faster or more accurately. In the latter case the machine could be radically extended in its capability; for example, by making it able to perform several functions instead of one, or by adding an 'intelligent' controller.

The distinction is one of *integration*. Through a synthesis of different elements the whole becomes greater than the sum of its parts. Figure 4.3 illustrates this trend. As we move from substitution towards more integrated forms, so we bring together more of the previously separate functions in the manufacturing process. At the same time, the benefits which the technology offers increase with higher levels of integration. We move from 'more of the same but a little better' – faster, more accurate and so on – to radically new opportunities which offer significant improvements across a broad front in quality, flexibility, productivity and so on. In systems theory terms, more integrated systems have 'emergent properties', only appearing at the higher levels of integration of sub-systems.

We can see this in a number of examples. In the field of manufacturing, for example, the earliest machines built upon the integration of craftsman's tools with new sources of motive power. Subsequent development enabled a single machine to perform multiple functions, so that although its cost and complexity rose, it replaced several older-generation machines. Nor was this process confined to the physical technology alone. As we have seen the process of organizing production and the use of labour within a pattern of work organization was also gradually integrated in such a fashion that by the 1920s the Ford lines represented the triumph of integration, linking men and machines into a complex but, even by today's standards, an extremely efficient integrated system. This also involved the integration of supply chains and distribution.

Other developments in machinery in more recent years have included the integration of 'intelligence', gradually substituting the judgement of individual craftsmen by the incorporation of some form of machine controller – originally 'numerical control' (NC), then computer numerical control, direct numerical control (CNC/DNC), then 'flexible manufacturing systems' (FMS), and now artificial intelligence. Over a period of

From discrete and loosely linked activities and players . . .

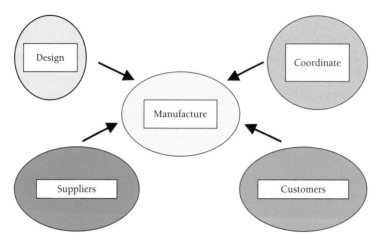

. . . to integration within the business and beyond . . .

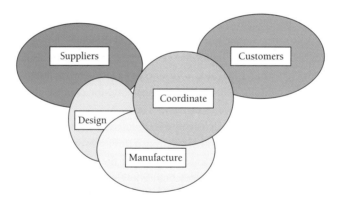

Figure 4.3   The trend to integrated automation.

150 years or so we have moved via this integrating process from a single machine tool to a complete manufacturing system. In the process the range of benefits emerging from the innovation have moved from better and faster machining to much more powerful and strategic advantages such as lead-time reduction, quality improvement, flexibility improvement and inventory saving.

The same trend can be observed in other areas of manufacturing. For example, in the field of design the various tasks associated with this complex process have gradually become integrated into computer-aided design systems. In this process the traditional drawing office with its rows of draughtsmen crouched over drawing boards has been replaced in many cases by computer-aided design in which the designers work with computer terminals. This changes a great deal of their work, although superficially they are still doing the same task except with an electronic pencil.

The first change is that the activities of design and drafting have converged. Whereas before much of the design department's work was laborious drawing out of ideas and redrawing to accommodate changes and improvements, this can all now be done using the computer system. More important, the drawing on which a team of designers are working at any moment is automatically updated with the results of changes made by any other designer. This means that for the first time all designers are working on the same project and, in the design of complex assemblies like motor cars, such a feature can mean significant savings.

But even allowing for the very powerful contribution of computer-aided design (CAD) to the drafting and design process, its real significance emerges as IT facilitates its integration with the manufacturing process itself. Since CAD systems make use of information coded in electronic form, it follows that other systems such as those for computer-aided manufacturing which also use such information can be linked in via some form of network. This is the basis of CAD/CAM (computer-aided design and manufacture) in which not only can the product be designed on a computer screen but, when the design is finally refined, the necessary instructions can be generated and sent to the machine tools and other devices which will actually manufacture it.

The advantages of this kind of integration are enormous and extend beyond the generation of designs and the relevant information necessary for controlling the manufacturing process to those for other activities – for example, for managing the various coordination and control activities such as material requirements planning, capacity planning and quality control. Benefits arising from this include significantly reduced lead times, improved quality, better machine utilization and much improved customer service.

One other feature worthy of comment here is that whereas Ford was able to achieve very high levels of productivity and efficiency in his plant through integrating different physical elements into the assembly line, this led to rigidity and centralization which ultimately acted against the company's competitiveness. By contrast, today's systems can offer – as a consequence of network technology – the possibilities for *flexible integration*, in which systems can be at once tightly coupled and highly centralized and also highly decentralized and autonomous.

Computer-integrated manufacturing

Until recently such integration took place *within* particular functional areas of manufacturing. So the major changes in design have largely remained in the design and drawing area. Improvements in machining systems have mostly been confined to the factory floor and to specific areas within that. However, recent developments have blurred the lines between functions – as in CAD/CAM systems, for example. They make use of the feature that IT-based systems use a common electronic language and can thus be configured to communicate with each other via some form of network.

INNOVATION IN ACTION

Computer-integrated manufacturing (CIM) can be defined as:

> the integration of computer-based monitoring and control of all aspects of the manufacturing process, drawing on a common database and communicating via some form of computer network.

Of course, such integration does not stop at the boundaries of the firm. Integration via electronic means can also extend backwards along the supply chain (with, for example, shared design processes or electronic components ordering linked to inventory management computers) or forwards into the distribution chain, using what is termed 'electronic data interchange' (EDI) to speed the flow of products to outlets while also minimizing the inventory held within the chain.

Such developments towards CIM do not just offer considerable improvements in traditional ways of making things. They also open up completely new and often highly integrated options. And the contribution which such changes can make to dealing with the problems of the twenty-first-century market environment are equally significant. Pressures on firms to be more flexible, to offer high quality, better customer service and improved delivery performance, to emphasize design and other non-price factors all pose major challenges to manufacturers to add to the 'traditional' burden of ensuring effective use of inputs of energy, materials, labour and capital. CIM in this context is seen a major and valuable competitive weapon.

But it's not simply a machine-based solution – in order to make CIM work there needs to be parallel development of the organization. Early experience with implementing CIM highlighted the importance of these changes. Expectations of radical improvement were often unmet by simply installing the equipment, and a growing number of studies pointed to dissatisfaction among users. Closer examination of the problem suggested that investment was unlikely to succeed unless it was accompanied by relevant parallel organizational change.

This should not have come as a surprise; after all the principle that radical technological change requires some form of parallel organizational change was at the heart of the 1960s work by the Tavistock Centre researchers which led to the development of the concept of 'socio-technical systems design'. When the UK National Coal Board tried to introduce a radical new automated method for mining coal the tests suggested it would offer a massive improvement in productivity. But in practice it didn't – and it was only when the researchers pointed out that the old and tight-knit teamwork structures were effectively taken away in the new model that things began to change. By paying attention to the social and team-working aspects they were able to redesign the new system to work effectively and achieve its productivity targets.

The nature of the organizational changes required depends on the scale of technological shift (small changes can often be absorbed with only slight variations on the existing pattern whereas larger shifts require a fundamental rethink of the way the organization operates). Equally, technologies which span more than one functional boundary are likely to pose problems of organizational integration; for example, one of the major requirements in effective computer-aided design and manufacture (CAD/CAM) utilization is the organization of a multidisciplinary, multifunctional design process to enable close cooperation and integration.

ADVICE FOR FUTURE MANAGERS

In order to deal with this changing pattern of integration, managers need to develop a new skill set along the following lines:

From...	To...
(a) In work organization...	
Single skill	Multi-skill
High division of labour – break tasks up	Highly integrated tasks
Long skill life cycle	Short skill life cycle – people need 'retooling' several times in their working lifetime
Skill life = employee working life	Skill life = less than employee working life
Payment by results	Alternative payment systems – e.g. pay for quality, innovation

From . . .	To . . .
Individual work and accountability	Teamwork and accountability
Supervisor controller	Supervisor-supported
Low work discretion	High work discretion
(b) In management organization	
Sharp line/staff boundary	Blurred boundaries, broad scope jobs
Steep pyramid	Flat structures
Vertical communication	360-degree communication, networks
Formal control	Mutual adjustment, decentralized focus and autonomy
Functional structures	Product/project/customer-based structures
Status differentiated	Single status
Rigid and non-participative	Flexible and participative cultures
(c) Inter-organizational relationships	
Tight boundaries between firms	Blurred boundaries
'Arm's-length' relationships	Cooperative and close links
Short-term relationships	Long-term relationships
Confrontation and adversarial	Cooperative and partnership
Lack of customer involvement	High customer involvement, co-creation

From Solo Act to Network

No man is an island – and these days few businesses are either, as we saw in Chapter 3. Companies operate in a complex web involving a host of different players – suppliers, customers, competitors, regulators, collaborators and many others. The challenge is no longer how to manage the business but how to manage it in the wider context of networking.

And there is evidence that learning to play the networking game can pay dividends. Dell's business model for creating a world-class computer business owes less to high-tech manufacturing techniques than to sophisticated use of a network model (enabled by IT) to allow fast and customized procurement, configuration and support for its growing market. At the other end of the scale, small Italian firms continue to dominate the export league table for furniture – their success coming not by being individually strong but by working together, sharing key resources and collaborating in order to compete externally.

Studies of such collective efficiency highlight the power of this model. For example, one town (Salkot) in Pakistan plays a dominant role in the world market for specialist surgical instruments made of stainless steel. From a core group of 300 small firms, supported by 1500 even smaller suppliers, 90% of production (1996) was exported and took a 12% share of the world market, second only to Germany. In another case the Sinos valley in Brazil contains around 500 small firm manufacturers of specialist high-quality leather shoes. Between 1970 and 1990 their share of the world market rose from 0.3% to 12.5% and they now export some 70% of total production. In each case the gains are seen as resulting from close interdependence in a cooperative network.

INNOVATION IN ACTION

Conceived as a response to the 1992 oil crisis, CRINE (Cost Reduction Initiative for the New Era) was a joint effort involving government and key industry players in the UK oil and gas sector representing contractors, suppliers, consultants, trade associations and others. The project was successful on a number of dimensions – for example, by 1997 the cost of field developments had fallen by 40% on a barrel/barrel basis. 'Since its inception CRINE has had a dramatic effect on the safety, efficiency and economics of North Sea oil and gas field development and operation,' was the response of one senior manager.

It's not simply a matter of regional cooperation – networking can also operate at the level of sectors or supply chains. Much of Toyota's success derives from an active supplier association which has been responsible for sustained learning and development of supplier firms over an extended period of time. Sector studies – in fields as far apart as wine, food, aerospace, electronics and chemicals – provide further examples of the power of network cooperation.

But how do we set up and run effective manufacturing networks? We have enough difficulties trying to manage within the boundaries of a typical business. The challenges include:

■ How to manage something we don't own or control.

■ How to see system level effects not narrow self-interests.

■ How to build trust and shared risk-taking without tying the process up in contractual red tape.

■ How to avoid 'free riders' and information 'spillovers'.

INNOVATION IN ACTION

A learning network has been established to help the emerging South African automotive components supply industry improve its competitiveness. Using a process of benchmarking to identify key areas for development, linked to regular inputs of training and plant-level change projects, the industry has managed to close the gap against suppliers from outside the country to the extent that in a number of key areas the country is a net exporter. Significantly, while the sector as a whole has been going through a process of rapid learning and development the rate of improvement among firms which are members of this actively managed learning network appear to be considerably higher than the industry average.

It's a new game and one in which, once again, a new set of management skills becomes important – as we saw in Chapter 3.

The Future of Manufacturing Innovation...?

Manufacturing today is no more like the images of belching smokestacks or Chaplinesque cogs in the machine than those pictures were like the mediaeval craft workshops. But although the pattern may look different, underneath the challenge remains one of how to find and develop an effective way of organizing and managing the process of manufacturing.

STRATEGIC AND SOCIAL IMPACT

Manufacturing is a central part of civilization, and its development over the centuries has brought with it great shifts – in where we live, in how we work, in the living standards we have come to expect. Changes like those in the eighteenth and nineteenth century were so big they came to be called the Industrial Revolution – not an exaggeration given the huge social and economic transitions involved. But the pattern persists today with major challenges in terms of globalization, customization, virtualization and so on. And there are likely to be winners – and losers – in the game. Part of managing manufacturing innovation requires an awareness of these trends and some innovative responses to dealing with them.

For example, clothing manufacturing has always been a major source of employment because the soft textures of fabrics make automation more difficult than in sectors like, for example, metalworking. But inevitably labour-intensive operations like this move to where labour costs are lowest – so recent years have seen this industry moving around Latin America, Africa and parts of Asia, with a growing concentration now in China. This has implications not only for their economic development but also for the clothing industries left behind in higher-wage-cost economies. One solution has been to increase the skills and value-adding components – such as design and brand-led distribution – carried out in these countries and source the low-cost assembly elsewhere.

But firms like Zara and Benetton have pioneered alternative models which suggest that there are more options. Using the old concept of regional clusters and local economic systems they have created and sustained an industry which is still based largely in Europe, particularly Spain, Italy and Portugal. These models not only carry out high-skill knowledge-based activities like design but also extend their network into various manufacturing and assembly operations. In the case of Zara around 2500 people are employed directly in the La Coruna region of Spain but a further 6000 are employed as part of a network of small village and household enterprises. Critics argue that these often operate on very low wage levels but other factors, like preserving small communities, also need to be taken into the equation.

Within firms there is also the challenge – do we continue to see people simply as pairs of hands and migrate manufacturing activities to wherever those are cheapest? Or do we recognize the increasingly important knowledge component and try and build on the fact that 'with every pair of hands you get a free brain'? If we do, how will we create the structures and systems to enable people to contribute their creativity and entrepreneurship in the factories of the future?

Developing Personal Capabilities

Manufacturing isn't dead – but it is changing. The game is still the same – creating physical goods and the services around them to meet general and increasingly specific needs. But how this game gets played out is constantly changing – and so a key skill in managing innovative manufacturing is flexibility in thinking about both the problem and how to configure solutions. This twenty-first-century skill set includes:

- Understanding the core operations involved in manufacturing but also how they can be spread out across the globe.

- Integrating these different elements of an extended enterprise into effective manufacturing systems and managing the relationships between different elements.

■ Creating the enabling conditions in which a high proportion of the workforce can contribute not only with their hands but with their heads. Enabling and sustaining high-involvement innovation requires extensive work on human resource development via structures, reward systems, career and training policies and so on.

■ Understanding how strategic advantage can be built up through emphasizing not just the making part of manufacturing but the design and service elements.

■ Developing innovation strategies which are not just about process innovation but which extend into products and services, into marketing and into renewing and changing the underlying business models.

Although automation may take increasing numbers of people off the direct factory floor, the day of the people-less factory remains a long way off. Instead we've seen major shifts in the composition and distribution of the workforce with a growing emphasis on high skills and high flexibility, and an increase in networking. We are also seeing a shift in mindset in more advanced economies where the recognition is that remaining in the manufacturing game requires climbing up the knowledge ladder and emphasizing innovation. While people might once have been seen as an unavoidable expense which might be eliminated through more use of technology, the trend in manufacturing today sees a central role for them as sources of flexibility and creativity.

Chapter Summary

■ Whether it is making cars, carpets, cookers or cardboard boxes the process of manufacturing is the same – a sequence of operations which bridge design with physical production and configuration before final distribution to end-users. What change are the ways in which this is carried out – the consequence of continuing innovation.

■ This chapter has covered *how* those changes are happening and in particular the following key trends
  ■ Shifting from craft production to agile manufacturing.
  ■ Increasing employee involvement in manufacturing innovation.
  ■ Managing the move from physical to virtual manufacturing.
  ■ Changing from concentration on 'make' to 'design/make/serve' as the new manufacturing task.
  ■ Building and running effective manufacturing networks.

■ Strong demand and widespread and globally available supply means that markets can demand emphasis on both price and *non-price* factors like design, speed, customization and variety. Competitive edge comes from offering more variety, delivery flexibility, more frequent model updates and eventually radical product innovation.

■ The idea that people can contribute to innovation through suggesting and implementing their ideas isn't new. Many organizations have attempted to implement some form of employee involvement and the gains from doing so are becoming increasingly apparent. But making the journey towards high-involvement innovation involves a long-term shift in organizational structure and processes, supported by clear and committed leadership.

■ Increasingly we have come to realize that the skill in manufacturing is in bringing these different knowledge sets together in the most efficient and effective way. And the scope for innovation lies in each of the knowledge areas as well as in their overall combination. With this background there is plenty of room for coming up with new ideas, both in the products we design and offer and in the ways we produce them. This pattern – the 'servicization' of manufacturing – has been going on for some time and an increasing number of firms in engineering, telecommunications and other complex systems fields have moved towards service-oriented models. The model these days is one of 'design/make/serve' – and it moves manufacturing from being increasingly sidelined as a low-employment fringe activity to the centre of the stage. And with it comes major new opportunities for innovation and entrepreneurship.

■ Much manufacturing innovation involves a *substitution* process – a typical example here would be replacing a machine with one designed to work faster or more accurately. But sometimes we move from this to something completely different – for example, the machine could be radically extended in its capability; for example, by making it able to perform several functions instead of one, or by adding an 'intelligent' controller. The distinction is one of *integration*. As we move from substitution towards more integrated forms, so we bring together more of the previously separate functions in the manufacturing process. Until recently such integration took place *within* particular functional areas of manufacturing. Such integration does not stop at the boundaries of the firm. Integration via electronic means can also extend backwards along the supply chain (with, for example, shared design processes or electronic components ordering, linked to inventory management computers) or forwards into the distribution chain, or working directly with customers. But it's not simply a machine-based solution – in order to make computer-integrated manufacturing work there needs to be parallel development of the organization.

■ Companies operate in a complex web involving a host of different players – suppliers, customers, competitors, regulators, collaborators and many others. The challenge is no longer how to manage the business but how to manage it in the wider context of networking. It's not simply a matter of regional cooperation – networking can also operate at the level of sectors or supply chains. Questions we need to deal with include:
  ■ How to manage something we don't own or control.
  ■ How to see system level effects not narrow self-interests.
  ■ How to build trust and shared risk-taking without tying the process up in contractual red tape.
  ■ How to avoid 'free riders' and information 'spillovers'.

■ Manufacturing today is no more like the images of belching smokestacks or Chaplinesque cogs in the machine than those pictures were like the mediaeval craft workshops. But although the pattern may look different, underneath the challenge remains one of how to find and develop an effective way of organizing and managing the process of manufacturing. And that will require high levels of entrepreneurship and innovation.

Key Terms Defined

Agile manufacturing Approach to manufacturing which offers high flexibility along several dimensions (variety, delivery speed, customization, etc.) *and* the ability to switch between combinations of these.

Collective efficiency Where a group of (often small) players work together to share resources, risks and so on.

Computer-integrated manufacturing (CIM) The integration of computer-based monitoring and control of all aspects of the manufacturing process, drawing on a common database and communicating via some form of computer network.

Craft production Approach to manufacturing in which goods were made, often by hand, in low volume.

Design/make/serve Philosophy which sees manufacturing as involving an end-to-end process rather than simply assembling physical goods. Blurs the line between manufacturing and service sectors.

Division of labour Principle (originally identified by Adam Smith) that by breaking up the task into smaller, specialized tasks performed by a skilled worker or special machine, productivity could be maximized.

High-involvement innovation Approaches which try and mobilize the creativity of the entire workforce in an organization.

Lean manufacturing Minimal waste approaches – focus on eliminating non-value-adding activities in physical and business processes.

Mass customization The ability to offer highly configured bundles of non-price factors (variety, speed, features, etc.) configured to suit different market segments–but to do this without incurring cost penalties.

Mass production Approach developed by Henry Ford and others to supply high volume of standardized goods to meet high market demand

Non-price factors Factors other than price which influence the purchase of manufactured goods; for example, design, choice, speed of delivery, quality.

Six Sigma Advanced statistical approach to total quality management developed in companies like Motorola and General Electric.

Further Reading and Resources

A number of books and reports look at the challenges in today's manufacturing environment. The challenges around agility are explored in:

Best, M. (2001) *The New Competitive Advantage*. Oxford University Press, Oxford.
Brown, S., Bessant, J. et al. (2004) *Strategic Operations Management*, 2nd edn. Butterworth Heinemann, Oxford.
Mascitelli, R. (1999) *The Growth Warriors. Creating Sustainable Global Advantage for America's Technology Industries*. Technology Perspectives, Northridge, California.

The challenges of lean thinking and its emergence from the automobile industry are well tracked in:

Womack, J., Jones, D. et al. (1991) *The Machine that Changed the World*. Rawson Associates, New York.
High-involvement innovation is explored in detail in books by:
Bessant, J. (2003) *High-Involvement Innovation*. John Wiley & Sons, Ltd, Chichester.
Boer, H., Berger, A. et al. (1999). *CI Changes: From Suggestion Box to the Learning Organisation*. Ashgate, Aldershot.
Gallagher, M. and Austin, S. (1997) *Continuous Improvement Casebook*. Kogan Page, London.
Imai, K. (1987) *Kaizen*. Random House, New York.
Schroeder, A. and Robinson, D. (2004) *Ideas Are Free: How the Idea Revolution Is Liberating People and Transforming Organizations*. Berrett Koehler, New York.

Websites include the CINet, a network of researchers co-operating on the question of implementing high-involvement innovation within and between organizations. (www.continuous-innovation.net)

The moves towards design/make/serve and the growing knowledge component in manufacturing are explored in:

Davies, A. and Hobday, M. (2005) *The Business of Projects: Managing Innovation in Complex Products and Systems.* Cambridge University Press, Cambridge.

References

1 Lampel, J. and Mintzberg, H. (1996) Customizing, customization. *Sloan Management Review,* **38** (1), 21–30.

2 Womack, J., Jones, D. et al. (1991). *The Machine that Changed the World.* Rawson Associates, New York.

3 Boer, H., Berger, A. et al. (1999). *CI Changes: From Suggestion Box to the Learning Organisation.* Ashgate, Aldershot.

4 Caulkin, S. (2001) *Performance through People.* Chartered Institute of Personnel and Development, London.

5 Bessant, J. (2003) *High-Involvement Innovation.* John Wiley & Sons, Ltd, Chichester.

6 Lewis, K. and Lytton, S. (1994). *How to Transform Your Company.* Management Books 2000, London.

Discussion Questions

1 Manufacturing is a dying art? Using examples with which you are familiar, show how you would argue that there's still plenty of scope for innovation and entrepreneurship.

2 How would you convince a young school-leaver that there's a worthwhile career in manufacturing – one that demands high levels of creativity and entrepreneurial skills?

3 The government is worried that not enough school-leavers want to go into manufacturing careers. You've been hired as an advertising agency to create an ad campaign which highlights the potential for innovation and entrepreneurship. What are your key ideas?

4 'Manufacturing is a creative industry' – how would you convince someone that this is still the case?

5 You have just been appointed MD of the XYZ Widget Company. In developing your strategy your team recognizes that it is losing market share to a Chinese competitor offering much lower cost for your standard product. So how could you change what you offer/how you offer it (product and process innovation) to regain a competitive edge?

6 What are Lampel and Mintzberg's four types of customization? Give an example of each.

7 'The beauty of it is that with every pair of hands you get a free brain!' This quote from a manager highlights the potential of employee involvement, but the fact remains that most organizations still do not manage to engage their workforce on a systematic and sustained basis. What are the main barriers to doing so – and what would you do, as a manager, to try and increase active employee involvement in continuous improvement of the business?

8 What would you do if you wanted to ensure that no one ever offered or implemented a new idea in the workplace?

Team Exercises

1 Dark Satanic mills? *Modern Times?* Powerful images of yesterday's manufacturing world. You're a small film-making firm given the job of coming up with powerful and exciting images for promoting twenty-first-century manufacturing. What's your storyboard/images?

2 Your last programme was so successful you've been asked back to do another. What's your storyboard/ideas for presenting along the following theme?

'You can have any colour you like as long as it's black!' Henry Ford's famous saying doesn't necessarily apply in today's world of manufacturing. How has manufacturing changed/is changing to give more choice? Give examples of the different kinds of choice now available.

Assignment and Case Study Questions

1 Many pictures of the future stress themes like 'the learning organization' or 'the knowledge-based business'. Such visions are likely to depend on human resources and achieving them poses challenges for how such resources are recruited, developed and managed. How can managers contribute to the design and operation of such organizations?

2 In the 1980s there was great enthusiasm for the 'lights out' factory – a totally automated operation in which almost no people would be required. Why do you think this idea has fallen from favour, and why are advanced organizations in many sectors now seeing people as a key resource in their businesses?

3 You're a senior civil servant in Denmark. The country is a typical high-wage cost and high living standards economy but it still depends on manufacturing for a lot of its wealth creation. What policy advice would you provide to the Minister for Industry in his forthcoming speech on 'Competing in the global knowledge economy'?

CASE STUDY 4

Exploring Innovation in Action: Sewing up the Competition – Innovation in the Textile and Clothing Industry

Manufacturing doesn't get much older than the textile and clothing industry. Since the earliest days when we lived in caves there's been a steady demand for something to wrap around us to keep warm and to protect the more sensitive bits of our anatomy from the worst of the elements. What began with animal hides and furs gradually moved into a more sophisticated activity with fabrics woven from flax or wool – and with people increasingly specializing in the business.

In its early days this was very much a cottage industry – quite literally people would spin wool gathered from sheep and weave simple cloths on home-made looms. But the skill base – and the technology – began to develop and many of the family names we still have today – Weaver, Dyer, Tailor, for example – remind us of the importance of this sector. And where there were sufficient cottages and groups of people with such skill we began to see concentrations of manufacturing – for example the Flemish weavers or the lace-makers in the English Midlands. As their reputation – and the quality of their goods – grew so the basis of trading internationally in textiles and clothing was established.

The small-scale nature of the industry changed dramatically during the Industrial Revolution. Massive growth in population meant that markets were becoming much bigger while at the same time significant developments in technology (and the science underpinning the technology) meant that making textiles and clothing became an increasingly industrialized process. Much of the early Industrial Revolution was around the cotton and wool industries in England and many of the great innovations and machinery – such as the spinning jenny – were essentially innovations to support a growing international industry. And the growth of the industry fuelled scientific research and led to developments like the invention of synthetic dyes (which allowed a much broader range of colour) and the development of bleaching agents.

There's a pattern in this in which certain manufacturing innovation trajectories play a key role. For example, the growing mechanization of operations, their linking together into *systems* of production and the increasing attempts to take human intervention out through automation. Of course this was easier to do in some cases than others – for example one of the earliest forms of programmable control, long before the invention of the computer, was the Jacquard punched-card system which could control the weaving of different threads across a loom. But actually making material into various items of clothing is more difficult simply because material doesn't have a fixed and controllable shape – so this remained increasingly a labour-intensive process.

By the twentieth century, the industries had become huge and well established, with growing international trade in raw materials such as cotton and in finished goods. The role of design became increasingly important as basic demand was satisfied and certain regions – for example, France and Italy – began to assume strong reputations for design. Branding became increasingly important in a world where mass communications began to make the telling of stories and the linking of images and other elements into advertising, which fuelled demand for clothing as much more than a basic necessity purchase.

Mass production methods and the scientific management approaches underpinning them diffused rapidly and, in the case of clothing assembly which remained a labour-intensive process, led to the quest for lower-wage-cost locations. So began the migration of clothing manufacture around the world, visiting and settling in ever cheaper locations across the Far East, through much of Africa and Latin America to its present home in China.

Today this is a global industry embracing design activities, cutting and processing operations, assembly, distribution and sales – all fuelled by a huge demand for differentiation and personalization. This is an industry in which price is only one element – non-price factors such as variety, speed, brand and quality matter. And it's an industry dominated by the need for high-frequency product innovation – fashion collections no longer run along the old seasonal track with winter and summer collections. In some cases the range is changed every month and innovation in information and communications technology means that this cycle is getting shorter still.

All of this has shaped an industry which is highly networked across global 'value chains' and coordinated by a few major players. Much of the 'front' end of the industry is about major brands and retail chains while the 'backroom' operations are often small-scale subcontractors often in low-wage-cost areas of the world. Like so many industries it has become somewhat footloose and wandered from its origins – leaving behind only a small reminder of its original dominance. Compared with countries like India and China today's European clothing industry is a small player on the global stage.

There are some exceptions to this – and they underline the power of innovation and entrepreneurship. Just because the dominant trends lead in one direction doesn't mean that there isn't scope for someone to spot and deploy ways of bucking this trend. One such player was a young clerk working in a small clothing retailing business in northern Spain. Frustrated with his career prospects Amancio Ortega Gaona decided to strike out on his own and in 1963 invested his savings – the princely sum of US$25 – into a small manufacturing operation making pyjamas and lingerie. In classic fashion he peddled (and pedalled – his earliest transport was a bicycle!) his wares around the region and built the business over the next 10 years and then decided to move into retailing as well, opening his first shop in the north-western town of La Coruna in 1975.

Things have moved on somewhat since then. Industria de Diseno Textil – Inditex – the holding company which he established – is now worth around US$8 billion and has just opened its two-thousandth store in Hong Kong. Active in nearly 70 countries this textile and clothing business has 8 key brand groups, each targeted at particular segments or product types – for example, 'Pull and Bear' for children, 'Massimo Dutti' for older men and women or 'Oysho' in lingerie. Best known of these is 'Zara' – a global brand with strong design and fashion identity running through both the clothes and the stores in which they are sold.

Its clothes combine stylish designs with a strong link to current high fashion themes with moderate prices. As Lotte Freddie, fashion editor of the Danish daily newspaper *Berlingske Tidende*, commented, 'If you want a classic, Italianate look in tune with current styles and at a reasonable price go to Zara.'

Zara's successful growth is not simply a matter of low cost or of standardization but rather of *innovation*. The company have become leaders by exploiting some of the key non-price trends in the industry – for example, variety and product innovation. For example, over 10 000 different clothing models are created and sold every year – this is most certainly not a case of 'one size fits all' or of long-lasting product types! Ortega has taken the entire system for creating clothes and built a business – and originally did so in an area which did not previously have any textile tradition.

At an early stage in the development of the manufacturing business he moved back into textile-finishing operations to make sure that the colours and quality of the material he used to make the clothes were up to scratch. Not only did this give better quality control but it also opened up the road to offering exciting and different fabric designs and textures. There are now 18 textile-designing and -finishing operations in the group as well as the clothing manufacturing.

A major part of the company's success comes from a strong commitment to design – they employ over 200 designers and make extensive play of this commitment. It's a theme which doesn't stop with the clothes themselves but also extends to the presentation of the stores, their window displays, their catalogues, Internet advertising and so on. Part of the headquarters building in Arteixo La Coruna, Spain contains 25 full-size shop windows with display platforms and lighting which allow the team to see what real store windows would look like – not only under normal conditions but also on rainy days, at night and so on.

Another key aspect of Zara's success is the flexibility which comes from having a very different model for manufacturing. Around 2500 employees work directly in manufacturing operations – but behind them is a much larger workforce spread across villages and small communities in Spain and northern Portugal. Once the new design has been approved the fabric is cut and then distributed to this network of small workshops – and these represent an outsource capability delivering a high degree of flexibility. Pre-cut pieces and easy-to-follow instructions are given to workers in what is still largely an informal economy – and their output then flows back into the massive Zara distribution centre like tributaries to a fast-flowing river. (This is not a small operation – the centre has around 200 kilometres of moving rails on which the products flow. Highly automated and with extensive in-line quality checking, the process transfers the incoming pieces into production lots which are then allocated to a fleet of trucks for fast shipment, mostly by air from the nearby airport at Santiago de Compostella.)

Needless to say this places significant demands on a highly flexible and innovative coordination system which Zara have developed in-house. In this way they make use of a model which dates back hundreds of years (the idea of industrial districts and clusters) but use twenty-first-century technologies to make it work to give them huge flexibility in both the volume and variety of the things they make. Where competitors such as H&M and Gap have to start planning and producing their new lines three to five months before goods finally make it to the stores, Zara manages the whole process in less than three weeks!

Their flexibility is also based on rapid response and extensive use of information and communication technologies. At the end of the day as the customers leave their 950 stores around the world the sales staff use wireless handsets to communicate inventory levels to the store manager who then transmits this intelligence back to Spain as a feed into the design order and distribution system. This gives an up-to-the-minute idea of what is selling – and what isn't, so the stores can be highly responsive to customer preferences – which colours 'work', which themes are popular, which designs aren't hitting the spot. But it's not just following the market – Zara also push the game by making sure that no model is kept on sale for more than four weeks – no matter how well it is selling. This has a strong impact on their brand – they are seen as very original and design-led – but it puts even more pressure on their ability to be agile in design and manufacture.

Case Study Questions

1 Is the Zara model sustainable? What would you do to preserve their edge over the next 5–10 years, given that many other players are now looking to follow their example? If you don't think it can survive, give your reasons for why you think the model is unsustainable and will fail.

2 You have been hired as a consultant to a small clothing manufacturer who wants to emulate the success of Zara and Benetton. She wants advice on an innovation strategy which takes the key lessons from these successful firms. What would you offer?

3 Zara Home has just opened using the same basic business model and deploying the same innovative approach as the rest of the business but in the home goods field. Do you think it might succeed and why?

Chapter 5

New Product and Service Development

This chapter

- Explores the nature of service versus product development.

- Reviews service development strategies.

- Looks at success factors and organization for development and delivery of services.

- Describes processes for new service development.

- Provides a review of tools and technology to support service innovation.

Learning Objectives

When you have completed this chapter you will be able to:

- Describe the main differences between services and products, and how these differences influence development.

- Identify the main strategies and factors influencing the success of new services.

- Understand the organization and processes required to develop and deliver new services successfully.

- Select and apply the tools and technologies most appropriate in different service contexts and cases.

In this chapter we examine the process of new product and service development. We review a very large body of management research on the subject, and identify a number of generic factors that influence success (and failure). Based on this evidence we identify a 'good practice' process for developing new products and services which includes a number of distinct stages separated by decision points of gates at which selection criteria are applied. However, the generic factors and process need to be adapted for different contexts, and the specific context will influence the most appropriate factors, process and organization for new product and service development. Therefore we begin with a discussion of the main differences between products and services. Finally, we review a range of tools and methods to support the development process, and identify how the novelty of the product or service affects the utility of these tools.

Service Versus Product Development

Employment trends in all the so-called advanced countries indicate a move away from manufacturing, construction, mining and agriculture, towards a range of services, including retail, finance, transportation, communication, entertainment, professional and public services. This trend is in part because manufacturing has become so efficient and highly automated, and therefore generates proportionately less employment; and partly because many services are characterized by high levels of customer contact and are reproduced locally, and are therefore often labour-intensive.

In the most advanced service economies such as the USA and UK, services create up to three-quarters of the wealth and 85% of employment, and yet we know relatively little about managing innovation in this sector. The critical role of services, in the broadest sense, has long been recognized, but service innovation is still not well understood.

Innovation in services is much more than the application of information technology (IT). In fact, the disappointing returns to IT investments in services have resulted in a widespread debate about causes and potential solutions – the so-called 'productivity paradox' in services. Frequently service innovations, which make significant differences to the ways customers use and perceive the service delivered, will demand major investments in process innovation and technology by service providers, but also demand investment in skills and methods of working to change the business model, as well as major marketing changes. Estimates vary, but returns on investment on IT alone are around 15%, with a typical lag of 2 to 3 years, when productivity often falls, but when combined with changes in organization and management these returns increase to around 25%.[1]

In the service sector the impact of innovation on growth is generally positive and consistent, with the possible exception of financial services. The pattern across retail and wholesale distribution, transport and communication services, and the broad range of business services is particularly strong (Figure 5.1).

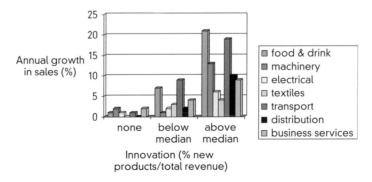

Figure 5.1   Innovation and growth in the service sector.
Source: EU Community Innovation Survey, 2000. Based on a survey of 2000 UK service businesses.

Most research and management prescriptions have been based on the experience of manufacturing and high-technology sectors. Most simply assume that such practices are equally applicable to managing innovation in services, but some researchers argue that services are fundamentally different. There is a clear need to distinguish what, if any, of what we know about managing innovation in manufacturing is applicable to services, what must be adapted, and what is distinct and different.

We will argue that generic good practices do exist, which apply to both the development of manufactured and service offerings, but that these must be adapted to different contexts, specifically the scale, complexity and degree of customization of the offerings, and the uncertainty of the technological and market environments. It is critical to match the configuration of management and organization of development to the specific technology and market environment.

The service sector includes a very wide range and a great diversity of different activities and businesses, ranging from individual consultants and shopkeepers, to huge multinational finance firms and critical non-profit public and third-sector organizations such as government, health and education. Therefore great care needs to be taken when making any generalization about the service sectors. We will introduce some ways of understanding and analyzing the sector later, but it is possible to identify some fundamental differences between manufacturing and service operations:

- *Tangibility* Goods tend to be tangible, whereas services are mostly intangible, even though you can usually see or feel the results. Therefore *perceptions* of performance are often more important than more objective measures.

- *Perceptions* of performance and quality are more important in services, in particular the difference between expectations and perceived performance. A customer is likely to regard a service as being good if it exceeds their expectations. Perceptions of service quality are affected by:
  - Tangible aspects – appearance of facilities, equipment and staff;
  - Responsiveness – prompt service and willingness to help;
  - Competence – the ability to perform the service dependably;
  - Assurance – knowledge and courtesy of staff and ability to convey trust and confidence;
  - Empathy – provision of caring, individual attention.

- *Simultaneity* The lag between production and consumption of goods and services is different. Most goods are produced well in advance of consumption, to allow for distribution, storage and sales. In contrast, many services are produced and almost immediately consumed. This creates problems of quality management and capacity planning. It is harder to identify or correct errors in services, and more difficult to match supply and demand.

- *Storage* Services cannot usually be stored; for example, a seat on an airline, although some, such as utilities, have some potential for storage. The inability to hold stocks of services can create problems matching supply and demand – capacity management. These can be dealt with in a number of ways. Pricing can be used to help smooth fluctuations in demand; for example, by providing discounts at off-peak times. Where possible, additional capacity can be provided at peak times by employing part-time workers or outsourcing. In the worst cases, customers can simply be forced to wait for the services, by queuing.

- *Customer contact* Most customers have low or no contact with the operations which produce goods. Many services demand high levels of contact between the operations and ultimate customer, although the level and timing of such contact varies. For example, medical treatment may require constant or frequent contact, but financial services only sporadic contact.

- *Location* Because of the contact with customers and near simultaneous production and consumption of services, the location of service operations is often more important than for operations which produce goods.

For example, restaurants, retail operations and entertainment services all favour proximity to customers. Conversely, manufactured goods are often produced and consumed in very different locations. For these reasons the markets for manufactured goods also tend to be more competitive and global, whereas many personal and business services are local and less competitive. For example, only around 10% of services in the advanced economies are traded internationally.

These service characteristics should be taken into account when designing and managing the organization and processes for new service development, as some of the findings from research on new product development will have to be adapted or may not apply at all. Also, because of the diversity of service operations, we need also to tailor the organization and management to different types of service context.

Services differ from manufactured goods in many ways, but the two characteristics that most influence innovation management are their intangibility and the interaction between production and consumption. The intangibility of most services makes differentiation more difficult as it is harder to identify and control attributes. The near simultaneous production and consumption of many service offerings blurs the distinction between process (how) and product (what) innovation, and demands the integration of back-end (support services) and front-end (customer-facing) operations.

For example, in our study of 108 service firms in the UK and USA, we found that a strategy of rapid, reiterative redevelopment (RRR) was associated with higher levels of new service development success and higher service quality. This approach to new service development combines many of the benefits of the polar extremes of radical and incremental innovation, but with lower costs and risks. This strategy is less disruptive to internal functional relationships than infrequent but more radical service innovations, and encourages knowledge reuse through the accumulation of numerous incremental innovations. For example, the American Express Travel Service Group implemented a strategy of RRR. A vice-president of product development was created, cross-functional teams were established, a formal development process adopted, and computer tools, including prototyping and simulation, were deployed. In the previous decade, the group had introduced only two new service products. Since the strategy was implemented the group has developed and launched more than eighty new service offerings, and has become the market leader.[2]

In practice, most operations produce some combination of goods and services, as we discussed in the previous chapter. It is possible to position any operation on a spectrum from 'pure' products or goods, through to 'pure' services. For example, a restaurant or retail operation both have real goods on offer, but in most cases the service provided is at least equally important. Conversely, most manufacturers now offer some after-sales service and support to customers.

However, the distinction between goods and services remains important because the differences in their characteristics demand a different approach to management and organization. It is perhaps better to think of any business or operation as offering a bundle of benefits, some of which will be tangible, some not, and from this decide the appropriate mix of products and services to be produced.

The service sector includes a wide range of very different operations, including low-skilled personal services such as cleaners, higher-skilled personal services such as tradesmen, business services such as lawyers and bankers, and mass consumer services such as transportation, telecommunications and public administration. The service–process matrix provides a useful way of identifying the key management challenges of an operation. The matrix classifies operations in terms of two dimensions (Figure 5.2). The first dimension is the labour intensity of the operations, that is the ratio of labour costs to equipment costs. The second dimension is the degree of customization or interaction with customers. Combining these dimensions produces four distinct types of service operation, which demand different approaches to operations management.

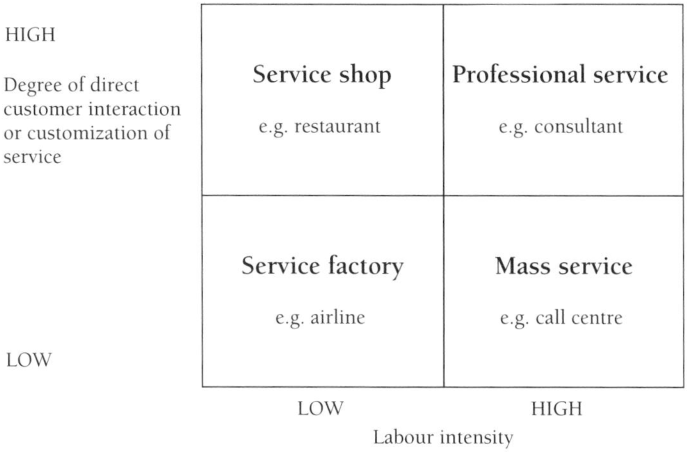

Figure 5.2 Characterizing service operations based on labour intensity and degree of customer interaction or customization.

Source: Derived from Schmenner R. W. (1986) How can service businesses survive and prosper? MIT. *Sloan Management Review*, **27**, (3), 21–32.

This framework is useful for two purposes. First, to help characterize different types of service operation, even within the same business. Second and more importantly, to help to identify the scope for improvement or change. For example, if the levels of customization and labour intensity are both high, what is the scope to reduce the level of customization or labour intensity to help reduce costs? In the UK, the National Health Service (NHS) asked a similar question. It was able to identify a range of services which did not necessarily require direct contact with the customer, such as standard health advice, and automated these using a website – NHS Direct. This helped to free resources for those operations that did require customer contact and are difficult to automate.

INNOVATION IN ACTION

Innovation in Services

The legal profession is not the most obvious place to find service innovation, but in 2006 the *Financial Times* invited submissions from lawyers and law firms in the UK and attracted 300 entries. The submissions were rated on the basis of rationale, originality and impact, and 33 were rated as 'outstanding'. The conclusion was that increased international competition, changes in regulation and the expectations of customers, were driving innovation in legal services. This has increased the commoditization of legal services.

Some law firms have responded to this by developing more standardized offerings, introducing more formal processes and investing in IT, while others have attempted to move away from these markets, and have begun to offer bundles of services, and more bespoke and customized services, similar to consultancy. Law firms can be innovative in the legal expertise and advise they offer (equivalent to product innovation), the way they deliver these services (service innovation), or they way they run their businesses (process innovation).

For example, Mishcon de Reya developed a new offering, the Tulip service, which combines the two distinct areas of legal expertise in financial fraud and intellectual property law, to assess whether and how best to pursue claims. Norton Rose has developed the Takaful insurance service product in compliance with sharia law aimed at the 20% of the population that is Muslim. Wragge developed a free service to offer unbiased strategic IT advice to the legal departments of client firms, which helps to add value to clients and deepen relationships. Withy King established a network of retail-style law centres, called Complete, to offer routine legal advice using non-lawyers. Pannone and Partners franchised its Connect2Law service which clusters local smaller firms around a larger main firm to provide a full range of services, and has recruited more than 500 law firms.

However, the report warns that these examples are not typical, and that most lawyers and law firms do not have a culture of innovation, and few have any formal processes or investments for innovation.

Source: *Financial Times Special Report: Innovative Lawyers*, 29 June 2006.

Products and Service Development Strategies: Success Factors

The main contribution new product and service development makes is to increase differentiation in the market. Differentiation measures the degree to which competitors differ from one another in a specific market. In general, higher differentiation is associated with higher market share and high return on investment at the product level.

These ideas were developed around the creation and development of new physical products – but with the rise in the service economy attention has moved to their application in service innovation. Sectors like financial services or retailing are increasingly concerned with offering variations on their existing range and also totally new service concepts – and with this has come a realization that managing these innovations requires a systematic process.

There have been numerous studies that have investigated the factors affecting the success of new products. Most have adopted a 'matched-pair' methodology in which similar new products are examined, but one is much less successful than the other. This allows us to discriminate between good and poor practice, and helps to control for other background factors.

These studies have differed in emphasis and sometimes contradicted each other, but despite differences in samples and methodologies it is possible to identify some consensus of what the best criteria for success are:

■ *Product advantage* Product superiority in the eyes of the customer, real differential advantage, high performance-to-cost ratio, delivering unique benefits to users – appears to be the primary factor separating winners and losers. Customer perception is the key.

■ *Market knowledge* The homework is vital: better pre-development preparation including initial screening, preliminary market assessment, preliminary technical appraisal, detailed market studies and business/financial analysis. Customer and user needs assessment and understanding are critical. Competitive analysis is also an important part of the market analysis.

■ *Clear product definition* This includes: defining target markets, clear concept definition and benefits to be delivered, clear positioning strategy, a list of product requirements, features and attributes or use of a priority criteria list agreed before development begins.

■ *Risk assessment* Market-based, technological, manufacturing and design sources of risk to the development project must be assessed, and plans made to address them. Risk assessments must be built into the business and feasibility studies so they are appropriately addressed with respect to the market and the firms' capabilities.

■ *Project organization* The use of cross-functional, multidisciplinary teams carrying responsibility for the project from beginning to end.

■ *Project resources* Sufficient financial and material resources and human skills must be available; the firm must possess the management and technological skills to design and develop the new product.

■ *Proficiency of execution* Quality of technological and production activities, and all pre-commercialization business analyses and test marketing; detailed market studies underpin new product success.

■ *Top management support* From concept through to launch. Management must be able to create an atmosphere of trust, coordination and control; key individuals or champions often play a critical role during the innovation process.

These factors have all been found to contribute to new product success, and should therefore form the basis of any formal process for new product development. Note from this list, and the factors illustrated in Figures 5.3 and 5.4,

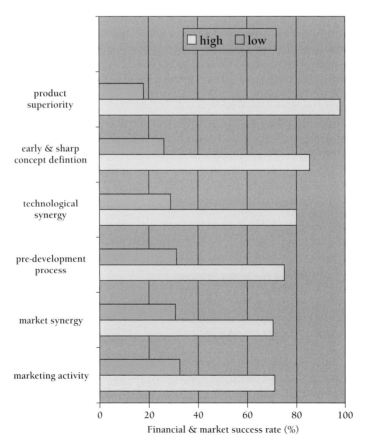

Figure 5.3   Factors influencing new product success.
Source: Derived from Cooper[3].

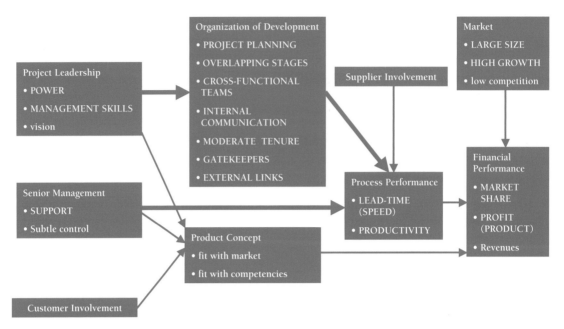

Figure 5.4   Key factors influencing the success of new products.

Source: Derived from Brown, S. L. and Eisenhardt K. M. (1995) Product development: Past research, present findings, and future directions, *Academy of Management Review*, **20**, 343–378.

that successful new product and service development requires the management of a blend of product or service characteristics, such as product focus, superiority and advantage, and organizational issues, such as project resources, execution and leadership. Managing only one of these key contributions is unlikely to result in consistent success.

The organizational issues appear to dominate even more in the case of more radical product or service offerings. This is probably because it is much more difficult in such cases to specify, in advance, the product or service characteristics in any detail, and instead managers have to rely more on getting the organization right and influencing the direction of development.

When we have asked managers to describe how radical products and services are developed, the answers include the mysterious and intuitive, and many highlight the importance of luck, accident and serendipity. Of course, there are examples of radical technologies or products that have begun life by chance, like the discovery of penicillin.

INNOVATION IN ACTION

Intangible Product Advantage

Engineers (and consumer associations) tend to focus too much on the measurable and tangible features of products and services, but as we saw in the case of services, intangibles can be important differentiators.

Branding and price can be a proxy for product or service quality, but more often it is much more profound than this. Customers associate brands with certain attributes which can create additional value by providing benefits such as 'comfort' or 'coolness'. For example, there are hundreds of competent MP3 players on the market, but in the USA at least, Apple's iPod still has 70% of the market partly because of its perceived 'coolness'.

Since 2001 the advertising consultancy CoolBrands, a spin-off from brand consultants SuperBrands, has created global rankings of brand 'coolness'. In the past this has been based on the views of a select band of 'style leaders', but in 2006 for the first time it also took into account an online poll of 1725 consumers. However, the results are still weighted 70:30 in favour the of nominated style leaders, so the results need to be interpreted with caution. The top ten ranks for 2006 were:

- Aston Martin
- Alexander McQueen
- iPod
- Agent Provocateur
- Bang & Olufsen
- Google
- Green & Black's
- Tate Modern
- Jimmy Choo
- Vivienne Westwood

Other members of CoolBrands include Asahi and Cobra beers, Boxfresh sportswear, Gaggia and DeLonghi coffee machines, PJ and Innocent's fruit drinks and Smile and First Direct banking. Make your own judgements about the precise rankings, but there is little doubt that each brand does create additional value by being 'cooler' in their respective markets.

Source: *Sunday Times*, Cool Brands, 24 September 2006; www.superbrands.uk.com.

Gary Lynn and Richard Reilly have tried to identify in a systematic way the most common factors that contribute to successful product development, focusing on what they call 'blockbuster' products – more radical and successful than most new products. Over 10 years they studied more than 700 teams and nearly 50 detailed cases of some of the most successful products ever developed, and compared and contrasted these organizations with less successful counterparts. They identify 5 key practices that contribute to the successful development of 'blockbuster' products:[4]

- Commitment of senior management;
- Clear and stable vision;
- Improvization;
- Information exchange;
- Collaboration under pressure.

All five practices operate as a system, and blockbuster development teams must adopt all five practices. Size of the organization did not seem to matter; neither did the type of product.

Commitment of Senior Management

Those teams that developed blockbusters had full support and cooperation from senior management. These senior managers functioned as sponsors for the project and took on an active and intimate role. Senior managers would often provide more of a 'hit and run' kind of involvement for those teams that did not produce blockbusters.

Clear and Stable Vision

It is important for the development team to have a clear and stable vision to guide them, with specific and enduring parameters, sometimes called 'project pillars', to guide the team. These pillars are the key requirements, or 'must-haves' for the new product. Mission awareness is a strong predictor of the success of R&D projects, the degree to which depends on the stage of the project. For example, in the planning and conceptual stage, mission awareness explains around two-thirds of the subsequent project success. Leadership clarity is also associated with clear team objectives, high levels of participation, commitment to excellence, and support for innovation. Leadership clarity, partly mediated by good team processes, is a good predictor of team innovation.

Improvization

A clear and stable vision is necessary, but nobody is so brilliant that they can see the end product from the beginning. They may have a vision of what the end product might look like or what the experience of using it will be (or must be) like. It's more like having a dialogue with the product – in trying to get the end results you may ditch what you've done and try something else. You may just have to accept that you may come up with something you never thought you would produce and you might be better off for it. Teams that produce blockbuster products complete the traditional stages of product development, but they take a different approach to the process. Although this may appear to be undisciplined, the teams nearly always have to meet a hard and fast deadline, and are more likely to monitor their progress and costs than the less successful teams.

Information Exchange

Effective communication and information exchange is another key practice. Many blockbuster outcomes require the use of cross-functional teams. Exchanging information openly and clearly on a cross-functional team can be challenging to say the least. Not only do specific functions have their own specialized language, they also often have conflicting interests. Team members call on each other through a variety of informal and personal ways like casual conversation, phone calls and meetings. In addition more formal knowledge exchange happens through a system for recording, storing, retrieving and reviewing information (see Chapter 6 for more on knowledge management). Both types of information exchange can be enabled for virtual team-working, but all teams need some face-to-face time.

Collaboration under Pressure

Blockbuster development teams are generally cross-functional, but must also often deal with outsiders to bring in a new perspective or expertise. Collaboration in the face of conflicting functions and other sources of internal and external pressure requires a number of facilitating factors. Teams that produce blockbuster products complete the traditional stages of product development, but take a different approach to the process. Rather than going through the gates step-by-step, waiting for a final decision to be made about going forward, they focus on getting an early prototype out quickly to learn how customers might respond. Once they learn how customers respond, they then continue to take new prototypes out for more continuous feedback. The teams need to be able to balance the insights they gain from the customers with the desired outcome. This constant balance allows them to adjust and fine-tune their understanding of both the market need and the product concept. This fast, iterative process is critical to their success.

To identify common characteristics of service innovators, we have examined over 100 service businesses from the PIMS (Profit Impact of Market Strategy) database, and separated out those which have the highest sustained new service content in their revenue (Table 5.1).

Table 5.1   Characteristics of high innovators

Business descriptor	Low innovators	High innovators
Innovation outcomes		
– % sales from services introduced < 3 years ago	<1%	17%
– % new services vs. competitors	>0%	5%
Customer base		
– Focus on key customers	Average	High
– Relative customer base	Similar to competitors	More focused than competitors
Value chain		
– Focus on key suppliers	Average	High/strategic
– Value-added/sales %	72%	60%
– Operating cost added/sales	36%	25%
– Vertical integration vs. competitors	Same or more	Same or less
Innovation input		
– 'What' R&D	0.1% sales	0.7% sales
– 'How' R&D	0.1% sales	0.5% sales
– Fixed assets/sales	growing at 10% p.a.	growing at >20% p.a.
– Overheads/sales %	8%	11%
Innovation context		
– Recent technology change	20%	40%
– Time to market	>1 year	<1 year

(continued overleaf)

Table 5.1 (continued)

Business descriptor	Low innovators	High innovators
Competition		
– Competitor entry	10%	40%
– Imports/exports vs. market	2%	12%
Quality of offer		
– Relative quality vs. competitors	Declining	Improving
– Value for money	Just below competitors	Better than competitors
Output		
– Real sales	9%	15%

Source: From Clayton (2003) in Tidd, J. and Hull, F.M. (eds) *Service Innovation: Organizational Responses to Technological Opportunities and Market Imperatives.* Imperial College Press, London.

Not surprisingly, high innovators spend more on R&D, to change both what they deliver to customers, and how they deliver it. In addition they have often experienced technology change, and invested in fixed assets to do so. They usually take less than a year to bring new service concepts to market. Competition is also an important factor. The highest innovating firms are more than likely to have experienced entry into their markets by a significant new competitor. They are also much more likely to compete in open markets where international trade – both imports and exports – plays an important role.

The data also indicate that focus is an important discriminating factor between high and low service innovators. First, those businesses with the highest level of new service content tend to avoid overcomplicating their customer base. They are usually firms for which fewer key customer segments account for a higher proportion of their total revenue. This suggests that customer complexity can be a barrier to effective innovation in service businesses. This 'focus' service strategy is well demonstrated by the rise of 'no frills' air services in the USA and Europe since the mid-1990s, such as South West, Ryanair and Easyjet. Second, it seems that focus in the procurement and service delivery process is also an aid to stronger innovation performance. High innovators tend to focus their purchases on fewer, larger suppliers and are less vertically integrated – and therefore focused on fewer internal processes within the overall value chain.

However, persuading customers to buy new services at a premium can be difficult. Most of our 'innovation winners' operate with a policy of parity pricing, with a policy of using their service advantage to go for growth, rather than to exploit it for maximum immediate profits. They grow real sales significantly faster, they grow share of their target markets faster than their direct competitors, and than non-innovators generally, and in addition they increase their returns on capital employed and assets.

INNOVATION IN ACTION

Charcol On-Line

As financial services move online, again the most successful are those with a very clear view of which customer segments to aim for. In the words of the MD of Charcol On-line (one of the UK's largest Internet mortgage companies): 'Segmentation is key to any business seeking to transform itself, and its market, through e-commerce. Understanding how groups of consumers behave, and what they are most likely to value, is a critically important factor for the business in gaining competitive advantage in constructing offers to customers'.

Charcol's strategy in creating a successful online business has been to move incrementally, from its original base in traditional mortgage broking, and maintaining its focus on higher net worth individuals, while developing methods for communicating with them in different ways. The firm has created relatively simple online advice systems, easy to use and designed to build trust in the brand, and then to offer a limited range of options, with selected, high-quality product suppliers.

Understanding customer needs, in terms of the preference for personal advice versus the ability or inclination to use 'self-service' is one important dimension for Charcol in filtering its customers to online purchasing or towards direct contact with a sales adviser. Another is the requirement for a simple transactional product versus more complex overall solutions, which depends on the client's circumstances. In the 'self-service/transactional product' corner of this matrix the possibilities of delivering reliable service are high, and the strategy behind Charcol's innovation approach is to offer this group the best value proposition in the market. Growing the business depends on new propositions to extend the envelope, rather than attacking directly the traditional customers with very different needs.

Source: From Clayton (2003) in Tidd, J. and Hull, F.M. (eds) *Service Innovation: Organizational Responses to Technological Opportunities and Market Imperatives.* Imperial College Press, London.

Organization for Development and Delivery of New Products and Services

We discussed the broader organizational factors to support innovation in Chapter 2, but here we explore the more specific needs of new product and service development. Successful product and service development requires much more than the application of a set of tools and techniques, and in addition requires an appropriate organization to support innovation and an explicit process to manage development. In this section we examine the critical role of organization, and the various options available in the case of new product and service development. The purpose of this section is not, however, to provide a more general overview of the theory and practice of organizational behaviour and development, and we assume that you are familiar with the basics of this field.

One of the key challenges facing the organization of new product and process development is that most organizations have not evolved or been designed to do this, but are structured for a different purpose, usually to serve some operational need. In most organizations new product or service development is a rather unusual and infrequent requirement, so in most organizations the first decision is what sort of team to put together to do this.

Essentially the choice is between functional teams, cross-functional project teams or some form of matrix between the two. For example, the team might be within a single function or department such as research, marketing or design. Alternatively, a special cross-functional team might be established, including representatives from many (but not all) functional groups. In a matrix organization a dedicated team is not formed, but rather members remain in their functional or departmental groups, but are designated to a project group. Studies of new product development suggest four main types of team structure:

■ *Functional structure* A traditional hierarchical structure where communication between functional areas is largely handled by function managers and according to standard and codified procedures.

■ *Lightweight product manager structure* Again a traditional hierarchical structure but where a project manager provides an over-arching coordinating structure to the inter-functional work.

■ *Heavyweight product manager structure* Essentially a matrix structure led by a product (project) manager with extensive influence over the functional personnel involved but also in strategic directions of the contributing areas critical to the project. By its nature this structure carries considerable organizational authority.

■ *Project execution teams* A full-time project team where functional staff leave their areas to work on the project, under project leader direction.

Project management structure is strongly correlated with product success, and of the available options the functional structures are the weakest. Associated with these different structures are different roles for team members and particularly for project managers. For example, the 'heavyweight project manager' has to play several different roles, which include extensive interpreting and communication between functions and players. Similarly, team members have multiple responsibilities. This implies the need for considerable efforts at team-building and development – for example, to equip the team with the skills to explore problems, to resolve the inevitable conflicts that will emerge during the project, and to manage relationships inside and outside the project.

More generally, different combinations of organizational structure, processes and tools create a number of possible coherent configurations with different properties and performance advantages as shown in the below box.

INNOVATION IN ACTION

Types of Service Organization and Innovation

Client Project-orientation

Project leaders organize the involvement of everyone early on to reduce hand-overs, the essence of concurrent product development. Structured processes, such as QFD (quality function deployment), are used to identify and influence customer requirements. Processes are mapped and continuously improved. The system is integrated by the voice of the customer and early involvement of the customer in need fulfilment. This configuration is strong on organization, but weaker on tools/technology, such as technological sophistication in either knowledge or IT. However, the art and craft of project management, which is somewhat analogous to batch production in goods industries, provides a strong yet flexible type of enabling control over the development and delivery of customer-focused services. It can achieve high levels of service delivery, and on time to market and cost reduction. These effects on performance are consistent with the inherent flexibility of project-based systems, and are effective in dynamic environments.

Many consultancies and technology-based firms fit this profile. For example, Arup is an international engineering consultancy firm that provides planning, designing, engineering and project management services. The business demands the simultaneous achievement of innovative solutions and significant time compression imposed by client and regulatory requirements. The organization has established a wide range of knowledge management initiatives to encourage sharing of know-how and experience across projects. These initiatives range from organizational processes and mechanisms, such as cross-functional communications meetings and skills networks, to technology-based approaches such as a project database and expert intranet. To date, the former have been more successful than the latter. This may be due to the difficulty of codifying tacit knowledge, which is difficult to store and retrieve electronically, and the unique environmental context of each project limiting the scope for the reuse of standardized knowledge and experience.

Mechanistic Customization

This is organized by the involvement of external customers in product development and delivery process decisions. Standardization is a key factor in controlling the relationship, and electronic links are used to exchange data with customers and suppliers. Setting standards for projects and products is a key method of process control, and customers help set these standards in conformance with their requirements. The electronic interchange with customers provides the capability for routinely adapting them to market demand. In addition, this type also has a significant positive effect on product innovation and quality, and the locus in both cases is external – the customer.

For example, in British Gas Trading (BGT) standardized documentation and processes are used as instruments of management control, and yet many different types of contract exist. Within BGT, there are formal procedures for assessing the financial performance of projects, and all projects over a certain threshold require the business owner to prepare a completion report within three months of completion. A project is complete when all physical work is completed, all costs relating to the work have been incurred, and all benefits have been delivered.

Hybrid Knowledge-sharing

In this type of organization, people are cross-trained and co-rewarded and organized in groups, which reinforces their team identity. Electronic tools are distributed to all and enable team members to map processes, share best practices and communicate lessons learned online. Group systems are typically rather self-contained which may be one reason companies in this factor are more likely to value knowledge, reuse it, and share it for achieving a balanced portfolio of performance advantages. It is strong in organization, tools, and system integration, but lacks formal processes. Its use of tools compensates for a lack of processes, and these focus on knowledge management (e.g. distributed databases, templates for process mapping, etc.). To the extent it represents a hybrid system, it can achieve different types of performance advantage simultaneously, but is not optimal for anything, and has only a weak association with product innovation and quality, time to market, and service delivery. The hybrid knowledge-sharing configuration enables a relatively self-contained group of people to become experts in developing and delivering products as quasi-professionals. This type of organization thereby provides some of the advantages of codified knowledge with far less hierarchical control by bureaucratic forms, consistent with the view that most service innovations demand greater knowledge-sharing than in conventional product development.

For example, Cable and Wireless Global Markets (CWGM), a division of the UK telecom operator Cable and Wireless, is a systems integrator and service provider which designs, integrates and operates telecommunications networks for multinational clients. CWGM was established to deal with the increasing number of non-standard and highly complex outsourcing projects. The common processes and standards developed by the parent company were found to be inappropriate for this type of business. In contrast to the formal business processes and matrix structure used for simpler management network services,

CWGM has adopted a more flexible teaming approach, which includes a 'war room' to help build relationships and promote communication between team members and customers. In this way teams can more easily work closely with customers to develop innovative service packages of standardized products and customized applications to achieve the required service level agreements for outsourcing.

Integrated Innovative

The integrated innovative organization is characterized by co-located, cross-functional teams in a flattened hierarchy. Communications are open regardless of rank, both face-to-face and via e-mail. Its technical base utilizes expert systems and management information systems. Responsibility for work is shared and partnering is practised throughout the value chain. The organic design has many advantages for creativity and innovation. They have dense communications facilitated by cross-functional teams and physical collocation. Cross-functional teaming, whereby different specialists are assigned to work on the same project simultaneously, has been advocated and widely adopted in many companies as a strategy to improve their product development process. Collaboration among diverse functions typically provides better solutions to complex design problems. Physical co-location involves aggregating project team members in common space to enhance rich communications among group members. Accordingly, it ranks significantly higher than other configurations in innovation, but lowest in all other performance measures.

For example, in BBC Worldwide (BBCW) speed/timeliness is essential to the processes given its strategic nature. Processes are strongly time-driven – indeed, diagrammatically they are captured in a timeline. A series of steps is defined, beginning with the initial receipt of programme treatment, to the final sign-off by a senior management committee. The process documentation at BBCW has in-built financial measures as well as benchmarks against the success of previous programmes. The quality of a bid is dependent on individuals and departments providing the required information on a timely basis, together with robust ROI analyses and sales projections. However, processes are able to evolve reactively to emergent business needs. For example, if a new means of exploiting programmes arises (video on demand, broadband video) these additional media can be included in the necessary documentation. In the case of an emergency item that requires urgent approval, informal contacts are exploited to minimize timescales, which is indicative of flexibility and the use of networking.

None of these different service organizations is optimal in every context, and instead different organizational configurations perform best in different cases or contingencies. The integrated-innovative is the most innovative; the mechanistic customization is the most cost-efficient; hybrid knowledge-sharing is best for overall performance; and the client project-orientated is best at service delivery.

Sources: Tidd, J. and Hull, F.M. (2006) Managing service innovation: the need for selectivity rather than 'best practice', *New Technology, Work and Employment*, **21** (2), 139–161; Tidd, J. and Hull, F.M. (2003) *Service Innovation: Organizational Responses to Technological Opportunities and Market Imperatives*. Imperial College Press, London.

All four configurations in the above box have one or more significant effects on performance. Each appears to have evolved or acquired sufficient good practices to be viable at least in niche markets. The client project-orientation reduces time to market and improves service delivery by focusing on customer requirements and project management; the mechanized customization reduces costs by setting standards and through the involvement of suppliers and customers; the hybrid knowledge-sharing provides a combination of innovation and efficiency by promoting team work and knowledge-sharing; and the integrated-innovative approach raises innovation and quality by means of cross-functional groups supported by groupware and other tools and technology, but this increased coordination raises the time and cost of service development.

Examination of the actual measures suggests that each of the four organizational configurations provide several common elements, including:

- Organizational mode of bringing people together;
- Control mechanisms, either impersonal (standards, documentation, common software) or interpersonal (collocated teams);
- Shared knowledge and/or technical information base;
- External linkages (e.g. customers and/or partners/suppliers).

In terms of performance, innovation and quality appear to be improved by cross-functional teams and sharing information, and raised by involvement with customers and suppliers, and by encouraging collaboration in teams. Service delivery is improved by customer focus and project management, and by knowledge-sharing and collaboration in teams. Time to market is reduced by knowledge-sharing and collaboration, and customer focus and project organization, but cross-functional teams can prolong the process. Costs are reduced by setting standards for projects and products, and by involvement of customers and suppliers, but can be increased by using cross-functional teams. Although individual practices can make a significant contribution to performance (Figure 5.5), it is clear that it is the coherent combination of practices and their interaction that creates superior performance in specific contexts.

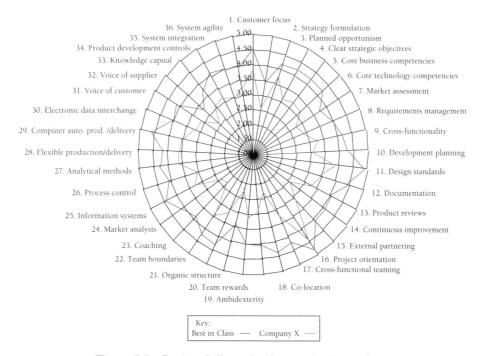

Figure 5.5   Factors influencing innovation in services.
Source: Derived from Tidd, J., Bessant, J. and Pavitt, K. (2005) *Managing Innovation*, John Wiley & Sons, Ltd, Chichester.

Processes for New Product and Service Development

The process of new product or service development – moving from idea through to successful products, services or processes – is a gradual process of reducing uncertainty through a series of problem-solving stages, moving through the phases of scanning and selecting and into implementation – linking market and technology-related streams along the way.

At the outset anything is possible, but increasing commitments of resources during the life of the project makes it increasingly difficult to change direction. Managing new product or service development is a fine balancing act, between the costs of continuing with projects which may not eventually succeed (and which represent opportunity costs in terms of other possibilities) and the danger of closing down too soon and eliminating potentially fruitful options. With shorter life cycles and demand for greater product variety, pressure is also placed upon the development process to work with a wider portfolio of new product opportunities and to manage the risks associated with progressing these through development to launch.

These decisions can be made on an ad hoc basis but experience and research suggests some form of structured development system, with clear decision points and agreed rules on which to base go/no-go decisions, is a more effective approach. Attention needs to be paid to reconfiguring internal mechanisms for integrating and optimizing the process such as concurrent engineering, cross-functional working, advanced tools, early involvement. To deal with this, attention has focused on systematic screening, monitoring and progression frameworks such as Cooper's stage-gate process (Figure 5.6).

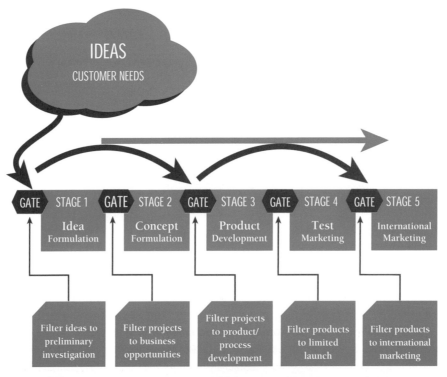

Figure 5.6　Stage-gate process for new product development.

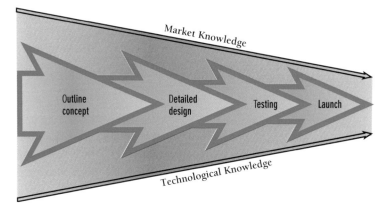

Figure 5.7 Development funnel model of new product development.

As Cooper suggests, successful product development needs to operate some form of structured, staging process. As projects move through the development process, there are a number of discrete stages, each with different decision criteria or 'gates' which they must pass. Many variations to this basic idea exist (e.g. 'fuzzy gates'), but the important point is to ensure that there is a structure in place which reviews both technical and marketing data at each stage. A common variation is the development funnel, which takes into account the reduction in uncertainty as the process progresses, and the influence of real resource constraints (Figure 5.7).[5]

The development of new products and services is inherently a complex and iterative process, and this makes it difficult to model for practical purposes. There are numerous models in the literature, incorporating various stages ranging from 3 to 13. Such models are essentially linear and unidirectional, beginning with concept development and ending with commercialization.

For ease of discussion and analysis, we will adopt a simplified four-stage model, which we believe is sufficient to discriminate between the various factors which must be managed at different stages:

- *Concept generation* Identifying the opportunities for new products and services;
- *Project assessment and selection* Screening and choosing projects which satisfy certain criteria;
- *Product development* Translating the selected concepts into a physical product;
- *Product commercialization* Testing, launching and marketing the new product.

Concept Generation

Much of the marketing and product development literature concentrates on monitoring market trends and customer needs to identify new product concepts. However, there is a well-established debate in the literature about the relative merits of 'market pull' versus 'technology push' strategies for new product development. A review of the relevant research suggests that the best strategy to adopt is dependent on the relative novelty of the new product. For incremental adaptations or product-line extensions, 'market pull' is likely to be the preferred route, as customers are familiar with the product type and will be able to express preferences easily. However, there are many 'needs' that the customer may be unaware of, or unable to articulate, and in these cases the balance shifts to a 'technology push' strategy. Nevertheless, in most cases customers do not buy a technology; they buy products for the benefits that they can receive from them; the 'technology push' must provide a solution for their needs. Thus some customer or market analysis is also important for more novel technological items. A number of tools are available to help systematically identify new product concepts, and these are described below.

Project Selection

This stage includes the screening and selection of product concepts prior to subsequent progress through to the development phase. Two costs of failing to select the 'best' project set are: the actual cost of resources spent on poor projects; and the opportunity costs of marginal projects which may have succeeded with additional resources.

There are two levels of filtering. The first is the aggregate product plan, in which the new product development portfolio is determined. The aggregate product plan attempts to integrate the various potential projects to ensure the collective set of development projects will meet the goals and objectives of the firm, and help to build the capabilities needed. The first step is to ensure resources are applied to the appropriate types and mix of projects. The second step is to develop a capacity plan to balance resource and demand. The final step is to analyse the effect of the proposed projects on capabilities, to ensure this is built up to meet future demands.

The second lower-level filters are concerned with specific product concepts. The two most common processes at this level are the development funnel and the stage-gate system. The development funnel is a means to identify, screen, review and converge development projects as they move from idea to commercialization. It provides a framework in which to review alternatives based on a series of explicit criteria for decision-making. Similarly, the stage-gate system provides a formal framework for filtering projects based on explicit criteria. The main difference is that where the development funnel assumes resource constraints, the stage-gate system does not.

Product Development

This stage includes all the activities necessary to take the chosen concept and deliver a product for commercialization. It is at the working level, where the product is actually developed and produced, that the individual R&D staff, designers, engineers and marketing staff must work together to solve specific issues and to make decisions on the details. Whenever a problem appears, a gap between the current design and the requirement, the development team must take action to close it. The way in which this is achieved determines the speed and effectiveness of the problem-solving process. In many cases this problem-solving routine involves iterative design–test–build cycles, which make use of a number of tools.

Product Commercialization and Review

In many cases the process of new product development blurs into the process of commercialization. For example, customer co-development, test marketing and use of alpha, beta and gamma test sites yield data on customer requirements and any problems in use, but also help to obtain customer buy-in and prime the market. It is not the purpose of this study to examine the relative efficacy of different marketing strategies, but rather to identify those factors which influence directly the process of new product development. We were primarily interested in what criteria firms use to evaluate the success of new products, and how these criteria might differ between low- and high-novelty projects. In the former case we expected more formal and narrow financial or market measures, but in the latter case we hoped to find a broader range of criteria to reflect the potential for organizational learning and future new product options.

Tools and Technology to Support Service Innovation

Despite their intangibility, many services are knowledge-based and/or are heavily dependent upon IT. Improvements in computers and software for storing and sharing information have increased capabilities for conceiving of new kinds of services as well as for managing development and delivery processes. Tools that were once hard to change and difficult to distribute are now soft, flexible and easily shared via electronic networks. IT can act as an enabler of continually updated processes and instant exchanges among cross-functional team members, regardless of distance.

Concept Generation

Most studies have highlighted the importance of understanding users' needs. Designing a product to satisfy a perceived need has been shown to be an important discriminator of commercial success. Common approaches include:

- *Surveys and focus groups* Where a similar product exists surveys of customers' preferences can be a reliable guide to development. Focus groups allow developers to explore the likely response to more novel products where a clear target segment exists.

- *Latent needs analysis* Are designed to uncover the unarticulated requirements of customers by means of their responses to symbols, concepts and forms.

- *Lead users* Are representative of the needs of the market, but some time ahead of the majority, and so represent future needs. Lead users are one of the most important sources of market knowledge for product improvements.

- *Customer-developers* In some cases new products are partly or completely developed by customers. In such cases the issue is how to identify and acquire such products.

- *Competitive analysis* Of competing products, by reverse engineering or benchmarking features of competing products.

- *Industry experts or consultants* Who have a wide range of experience of different users' needs. The danger is that they may have become too immersed in the users' world to have the breadth of vision required to assess and evaluate the potential of the innovation. The use of 'proxy experts' to help overcome the problem. They suggest selecting a specific group of respondents who have knowledge of the product category or usage context.

- *Extrapolating trends* In technology, markets and society to guess the short to medium-term future needs.

- *Building Scenarios* Alternative visions of the future based on varying assumptions to create robust product strategies. Most relevant to long-term projects and product portfolio development.

■ *Market experimentation* Testing market response with real products, but able to adapt or withdraw rapidly. Only practical where development costs are low, lead times short and customers tolerant of product under performance or failure. Sometimes referred to as 'expeditionary marketing', or more modestly 'test marketing'.

Project Selection

Different combinations of criteria are used to screen and assess projects prior to development. The most common are based on discounted cash flows, such as net present value/internal rate of return, followed by cost-benefit analysis, and simple calculations of the payback period. In addition to these financial criteria, most organization also use a range of additional measures:

■ *Ranking* A means of ordering a list of candidate projects in relative value or worthiness of support, broken down into several factors, so both objective and judgmental data can be assessed. These techniques are likely to be of most use in the early stages of the process, since they are fairly 'rough-cut' methods.

■ *Profiles* Projects are given scores on each of several characteristics, and are rejected if they fail to meet some predetermined threshold. The projects which dominate on all or most of the factor scores are selected. These methods can be used at all stages of the development process.

■ *Simulated outcomes* Alternative outcomes to which probabilities can be attached, or alternate paths depending on chance outcomes and when the projects have different pay-offs for different outcomes. The range of possible outcomes and the likelihood of a specific outcome are found. It is used especially in the analysis of sets of projects which are interdependent (the aggregate project plan).

■ *Strategic clusters* Projects not selected solely for maximization of some financial measure, but for the support they give to the strategic position. Groups are clustered according to their support for specific objectives, and then these groups are rated according to strategic importance and funded accordingly (again, this is important at the aggregate project plan level).

■ *Interactive* An iterative process between the R&D director and project managers, where project proposals are improved at each stage to more closely align with the objectives. The aim of this is to develop projects that more nearly fit the strategic and tactical objectives of the firm. These methods are used mainly at the aggregate project plan level, or at the early stages of specific projects.

Product Development

There are a number of tools, or methodologies, which have been developed to help solve the problems, and most require the integration of different functions and disciplines. The most significant tools and methods used are:

■ *Design for manufacture (DFM)* 'The full range of policies, techniques, practices and attitudes that cause a product to be designed for the optimum manufacturing cost, the optimum achievement of manufactured quality, and the optimum achievement of life-cycle support (serviceability, reliability and maintainability)'. It includes design for assembly (DFA), design for producibility (DFP) and other design rule approaches. Studies from the car industry indicate that up to 80% of the final production costs are determined at the design stage.

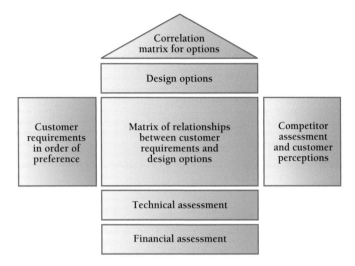

Figure 5.8   Quality Function Deployment (QFD) diagram for new product development.

■ *Rapid prototyping* Is the core element of the design–build–test cycle, and can increase the rate and amount of learning that occurs in each cycle. The first design is unlikely to be complete, and so designers go through several iterations learning more about the problem and alternative solutions each time. The number of iterations will depend on the time and cost constraints of the project. One study found that frequent proto-typing proved useful for intra-team communication, obtaining customer feedback and manufacturing process development. Having an actual prototype as a visual model enables more reliable assessment of preferences and suggestions.

■ *Computer-aided techniques (CAD/CAM)* Potential benefits include reduction in development lead times, economies in design, ability to design products too complex to do manually and the combination of CAD with production automation Computer-aided manufacture (CAM) to achieve the benefits of integration. However, these benefits are not always realized due to organizational shortcomings.

■ *Quality function deployment (QFD)* Is a set of planning and communications routines, which are used to identify critical customer attributes and create a specific link between these and design parameters (Figure 5.8); it focuses and coordinates the skills within the organization to design, manufacture and then market products that customers value. The aim is to answer three primary questions: What are the critical attributes for customers? What design parameters drive these attributes? What should the design parameter targets be for the new design?

Quality function deployment (QFD) is a useful technique for translating customer requirements into development needs, and encourages communication between engineering, production and marketing. Unlike most other tools of quality management, QFD is used to identify opportunities for product improvement or differentiation, rather than to solve problems. Customer-required characteristics are translated or 'deployed' by means of a matrix into language which engineers can understand. The construction of a relationship matrix – also known as 'the house of quality' – requires a significant amount of technical and market research. Great emphasis must be made on gathering market and user data in order to identify potential design trade-offs, and to achieve the most appropriate balance between cost, quality and performance. The construction of a QFD matrix involves the following steps:

■ Identify customer requirements, primary and secondary, and any major dislikes.

■ Rank requirements according to importance.

■ Translate requirements into measurable characteristics.

■ Establish the relationship between the customer requirements and technical product characteristics, and estimate the strength of the relationship.

■ Choose appropriate units of measurement and determine target values based on customer requirements and competitor benchmarks.

Symbols are used to show the relationship between customer requirements and technical specifications, and weights attached to illustrate the strength of the relationship. Horizontal rows with no relationship symbol indicate that the existing design is incomplete. Conversely, vertical columns with no relationship symbol indicate that an existing design feature is redundant as it is not valued by the customer. In addition, comparisons with competing products, or benchmarks, can be included. This is important because relative quality is more relevant than absolute quality: customer expectations are likely to be shaped by what else is available, rather than some ideal.

QFD was originally developed in Japan, and is claimed to have helped Toyota to reduce its development time and costs by 40%. More recently many leading American firms have adopted QFD, including AT&T, Digital and Ford, but results have been mixed: only around a quarter of projects have resulted in any quantifiable benefit. In contrast, there has been relatively little application of QFD by European firms. This is not the result of ignorance, but rather a recognition of the practical problems of implementing QFD.

In addition to these discrete techniques, the efficiency and effectiveness of new product development will also be influenced by the internal organization and relationships with other organizations. Both internal and external integrity determine the dynamic capability of the organization, in exploiting the existing technology and marketing capabilities in response to the changing market and technological environment. There is substantial agreement in the literature on the need for effective integration of all the stakeholders in the new product development process, and this is the rationale for multifunctional project teams. The other aspect of organization is concerned with the relationships with suppliers, customers and other external sources of innovation. For example, working closely with key suppliers may reduce the cost, time and effectiveness of product development, and exploiting other external sources of technology and market know-how allow a firm to focus on its own competencies.

Development projects range from simple improvements to existing products, through to radical 'new to the world' products. What matters to practising managers is how close a project is to their existing skills and past experience, which is a relative not an absolute matter. Clearly, what is novel for one firm may be routine for another, which is reflected in the common distinction between 'new to the firm', 'new to the market' and 'new to the world'. For example, the development of a new electronic control unit might be considered routine by a large electronics firm, but perceived as highly novel by a small manufacturer of machine tools, or large manufacturer of automobiles. This approach is consistent with the test of 'inventive step' for a new patent application, which is relative to the industry, being based on what is obvious to a 'skilled practitioner' in the same industry. Therefore we might expect managers to use different tools and approaches depending on the novelty of the products *relative* to the firm.

The use and usefulness of various techniques are shown in Table 5.2. In terms of frequency of use, the most common methods used for high-novelty projects are segmentation, market experimentation and industry experts, whereas for the less complex projects the most common methods are partnering customers, trend extrapolation

Table 5.2   Use and usefulness of techniques for product and service development

	High Novelty		Low Novelty	
	Usage (%)	Usefulness	Usage (%)	Usefulness
Segmentation*	89	3.42	42	4.50
Market experimentation	63	4.00	53	3.70
Industry experts	63	3.83	37	3.71
Surveys/focus groups*	52	4.50	37	4.00
User-practice observation	47	3.67	42	3.50
Partnering customers*	37	4.43	58	3.67
Lead users*	32	4.33	37	3.57
Probability of technical success	100	4.37	100	4.32
Probability of commercial success	100	4.68	95	4.50
Market share*	100	3.63	84	4.00
Core competencies*	95	3.61	79	3.00
Degree of internal commitment	89	3.82	79	3.67
Market size	89	3.76	84	3.94
Competition	89	3.76	84	3.81
Gap analysis	79	2.73	84	2.81
Strategic clusters*	42	3.63	32	2.67
Prototyping*	79	4.33	63	4.08
Trend extrapolation	47	4.00	47	3.44
QFD	47	3.33	37	3.43
Cross-functional teams*	63	4.47	37	3.74
Project manager (heavyweight)*	52	3.84	32	3.05

Notes: Usefulness scale: 1–5, 5 = critical, based on manager assessments of 50 development projects in 25 firms.

*denotes difference in usefulness rating is statistically significant at 5% level.

Source: Adapted from Tidd, J. and Bodley, K. (2002) The affect of project novelty on the new product development process, *R&D Management*, **32** (2), 127–138.

and segmentation. The use of market experimentation and industry experts might be expected where market requirements or technologies are uncertain, but reasons for the use of segmentation for such projects are less obvious. Segmentation is also commonly used for the low-novelty projects, but in this case technologies and market demand are more clearly defined, and therefore extrapolation of trends and customer requirements more reliable. In terms of usefulness, there are statistically significant differences in the ratings for segmentation, focus groups, customer partnerships and lead users. Segmentation is more useful for low-novelty projects, essentially product extensions where a reliable basis of segmenting markets is available, but for the novel projects deeper market analysis and closer relationships with lead customers are more important.[6]

In practice, most organizations use only three or four different techniques to support development, the most common being prototyping and market experimentation. Both of these techniques also received high ratings for usefulness, prototyping being even more critical for novel projects. In contrast, the relatively low use and usefulness rating of quality function deployment (QFD) is surprising. The low take-up may be due to the fact that QFD demands close integration between functional groups, in particular design, development and marketing, which is still not commonplace. The low rating for usefulness may reflect the difficulty in measuring some of the benefits of QFD, especially in the short term. QFD requires the compilation of a lot of marketing and technical data, and more importantly the close cooperation of the development and marketing functions. Indeed, the process of constructing the relationship matrix provides a structured way of getting people from development and marketing to communicate, and therefore is as valuable as any more quantifiable outputs. However, where relations between the technical and marketing groups are a problem, which is too often the case, the use of QFD may be premature.

Table 5.2 confirms that cross-functional teams are essential to new product and service development. However, there are significant differences in the management and usefulness of such teams. Heavyweight project managers and cross-functional teams appear to be a more effective combination for high-novelty projects, whereas lower-weight coordination mechanisms may be sufficient for more routine projects. The involvement of external organizations in different stages of the product development process is common. Customers are twice as likely to be involved in the development and commercialization of novel products and services, compared to low-novelty projects, and the involvement of lead users is significantly more effective in the development of novel products and services.

Developing Personal Capabilities

Problem-solving style is an important part of new product and service development. Information from different functions and disciplines needs to be integrated – especially the constant challenge of 'doing more with less,' and the always present need to anticipate, create, innovate, and manage change from both internal and external sources.

Problem-solving style can be defined as 'consistent individual differences in the ways people prefer to plan and carry out the generating and focusing of ideas, in order to gain clarity, or prepare for action when solving problems or managing change'.

An important dimension of problem-solving style is personal *orientation to change*, which focuses on a person's preferences for managing change and solving problems creatively. How someone perceives opportunities and challenges surrounding change is based on three main issues:

■ How much structure do you need in order to understand and deal effectively with the change?

■ How much will you need to have the guidance and direction from sources of authority?

■ What kind of novelty or originality do you prefer to pay attention to?

The two contrasting styles are the *explorer* and the *developer*. An 'explorer' is someone who prefers to venture into uncharted directions and follows possibilities wherever they might lead.

Explorers enjoy initiating many tasks. They thrive on novel, ambiguous situations and challenges. They seek to create many original options that, if developed and refined, might provide the foundation for valuable contributions. Explorers see unusual possibilities, patterns and relationships. These highly novel alternatives may not be very workable or easy to implement. Explorers often 'plunge right in', feeding on risk and uncertainty, and improvising as situations unfold. They often find externally imposed plans, procedures and structures confining.

Explorers prefer that sources of authority maintain their distance and limit their influence on their thinking and doing.

A 'developer' is someone who prefers to bring tasks to fulfilment, or who organizes, synthesizes, refines and enhances basic ingredients, shaping them into a more complete and useful result. Developers are concerned with practical applications and the reality of the task. They think creatively by emphasizing workable possibilities and successful implementation. They are usually careful and well organized, seek to minimize risk and uncertainty, and are comfortable with plans, details and structures. They are able to move tasks or projects forward efficiently and deliberately, and they appreciate close guidance from sources of authority.

Neither style is superior, but the two different perspectives result in different ways of seeing and solving problems. It is important to be aware of your own preferences and style so that you can compensate for this by forcing yourself to consider other perspectives and if necessary involving others with different styles.

Adapted from Isaksen, S. and Tidd, J. (2006) *Meeting the Innovation Challenge: Leadership for Transformation and Growth.* John Wiley & Sons, Ltd, Chichester.

ADVICE FOR FUTURE MANAGERS

Effective teamwork is critical for new product and service development. An effective team is one that has a mutual and shared accountability for its goal – the outcomes of the project will affect the evaluation of the individuals and the team as a whole.

When you work in a team, or are responsible for building or guiding a team, you will face a number of challenges and opportunities. To be effective, a team must be able to maintain collaboration, communication and positive interactions over a sustained period of time. One of the most significant issues is helping team members understand and deal effectively with differences, rather than viewing others with differing preferences as 'odd', 'wrong' or 'ineffective'. Team members need to understand that 'differences are not deficits'. Group members can also sustain their team's working relationship when they are able to celebrate each other's strengths and use their differences to complement each other. In general, if there is a need to provide for participation to increase acceptance, and to exploit a diverse range of experiences and perspectives, an effective development team needs:

- Competent team members, respectful of each other.
- Adequate, but not excessive resources.
- A clear, common and elevating goal.
- Unified commitment and shared standards.
- A collaborative climate and participation in decision-making.
- Principled leadership.
- External support and recognition.

Source: Adapted from Isaksen, S. and Tidd, J. (2006) *Meeting the Innovation Challenge: Leadership for Transformation and Growth.* John Wiley & Sons, Ltd, Chichester.

STRATEGIC AND SOCIAL IMPACT

The traditional model for many public services – in the UK and elsewhere – has been the vertically integrated 'command and control' model, in which organizations undertake most of the steps involved in delivering not just the service to final consumers, but also many of the intermediate and support services required. In addition, most public services are – in principle – available to all. The concept of customer selection is in many cases either inappropriate or difficult to enforce. Given the evidence we have shown about private-sector success rules for innovation, we should not be surprised if these structural characteristics of public-sector organizations have made the delivery of innovation difficult and slow.

In the process of privatizing UK public sector services, in energy, telecommunications and transport, and in attracting private capital into health, education and administrative support, some of these issues have been addressed. For example, in energy the electricity and gas industries have been 'vertically disintegrated', with primary energy assets separated from transmission, distribution and end-user supply. In transport, track ownership was split from maintenance, train ownership and train operation. The record of achievement across these examples has been – to say the least – mixed.

Comparing the successes with the failures, it seems at least arguable that the best-performing services are those which have used their new structures to innovate and improve customer value. This is true of some of the energy and telecommunications supply businesses, which have chosen to focus on specific customer groups through targeted marketing, and deliver a set of modular services which can be tailored through 'mass customization' and sourced from a limited range of suppliers.

The most spectacular failure – rail – was saddled with a new business structure which was itself much too complex, because of the number of relationships created by cutting the service into so many small entities. Some of the train-operating companies have succeeded in creating new and improved services by targeted investments and new operating practices. However, for the most part they have been handicapped by the strategy of the main infrastructure owner – Railtrack – to concentrate on cost reduction rather than value-creating innovation. Railtrack also miscalculated the importance of intangible assets – information, knowledge and skills – which were essential to improve the quality of its offer to immediate customers. The case of rail illustrates the necessity, in designing new business models for the public sector, to ensure that participants at every step in the value chain have clear incentives to innovate, and to develop the means to do so.

In health, the effects of recent changes in organization and governance are only now beginning to become apparent. The budget of the UK National Health Service is around £76 billion, larger than the GDP of 155 member states of the United Nations. It is a large, complex organization involving many stakeholders with diverse and sometimes conflicting goals. The initial simplistic approach of creating internal markets was replaced with a rather optimistic faith in the potential benefits of automation, using IT. The current, more integrated strategy of organizational change, service innovation and selected investment in technology may be more complex to plan and manage, but is more likely to yield improvements in performance.

From Clayton (2003) in Tidd, J. and Hull, F.M. (eds) *Service Innovation: Organizational Responses to Technological Opportunities and Market Imperatives.* Imperial College Press, London.

Chapter Summary

- There is a vast amount of management research on the subject of new product and service development, and we are now pretty certain what works and what does not. There are no guarantees that following the suggestions in this chapter will produce a blockbuster product, service or business, but if these elements are not managed well, your chances of success will be much lower. This is not supposed to discourage experimentation and calculated risk-taking, but rather to provide a foundation for evidence-based practice.

- Research suggests that a range of factors affect the success of a potential new product or service, including product advantage, clear target market and attention to pre-development activities.

- A formal process for new product and service development should consist of distinct stages, such as concept development, business case, product development, pilot and commercialization, separated by distinct decision points or gates, which have clear criteria such as product fit, product advantages and so on. Different stages of the process demand different criteria and different tools and methods. Useful tools and methods at the concept stage include segmentation, experimentation, focus groups and customer-partnering; and at the development stage useful tools include prototyping, design for production and QFD.

- Services and products are different in a number of ways, such as the tangibility of outputs, perceptions of performance, and the lag between production and consumption, and these will demand the adaptation of the standard models and prescriptions for new product development.

- If you want to develop blockbuster products and services, you will need to attend to all elements of the system. Only paying attention to one element of the system will decrease significantly the likelihood of success. You must be clear about the desired outcome, at least in terms of what needs to be done to meet consumers' needs and kind of innovation you desire as a result. You will need to establish and manage a deliberate process that promotes cross-functional teamwork and integrates the practices outlined above. The right people must be on the team and they need to be supported by appropriate leadership and sponsorship. The working environment must support the people and the process. The climate within the team is critical, but a broader organizational climate conducive to innovation is optimal.

Key Terms Defined

Development funnel An alternative to the stage-gate model, which takes into account the reduction in uncertainty as the process progresses, and the influence of real resource constraints.

Quality function deployment (QFD) A set of planning and communications routines, which are used to identify critical customer attributes and create a specific link between these and design parameters. It aims to answer three primary questions: What are the critical attributes for customers? What design parameters drive these attributes? What should the design parameter targets be for the new design?

Problem-solving style Individual differences in the ways people frame, perceive and attempt to solve problems: A 'developer' is someone who prefers to bring tasks to fulfilment, or who organizes, synthesizes, refines and enhances basic ingredients, shaping them into a more complete and useful result; an 'explorer' is someone who prefers to venture into uncharted directions and follows possibilities wherever they might lead.

Stage-gate process A structured process for new product or service development, which features a number of discrete stages, each with different decision criteria or 'gates' which they must pass.

Further Reading and Resources

The classic texts on new product development are those by Robert Cooper, for example, *Winning at New Products: Accelerating the Process from Idea to Launch* (Perseus Books, New York, 2001), or Cooper, R.G. (2000) 'Doing it right: winning with new products', *Ivey Business Journal*, **64**, (6), July/August, 1–7 [available online: http://www.iveybusinessjournal.com/article.asp?intArticle_ID=235], or anything by Kim Clark and Steven Wheelwright, such as: Wheelwright, S. C. and Clark, K. B. (1997). Creating project plans to focus product development, *Harvard Business Review*, September–October; or their book *Revolutionizing Product Development* (Free Press New York 1992). Paul Trott provides a good review of research in his text *Innovation Management and New Product Development* (3rd edn, 2005, FT Prentice Hall,), but for a more up-to-date review of the research see: Panne, G. van der, Beers, C. van and Kleinknecht, A. (2003). Success and failure of innovation: a literature review, *International Journal of Innovation Management*, 7 (3), 309–338.

For more focused studies of new service development, see the recent article: Berry, L.L., Shankar, V., Parish, J.T., Cadwallader, S. and Dotzel, T. (2006) Creating new markets through service innovation, *MIT Sloan Management Review*, **47** (2), Winter. More comprehensive overviews of service innovation are provided by Ian Miles in the Special Issue on Innovation in Services, *International Journal of Innovation Management*, December, 2000, or in the books: Tidd, J. and Hull, F.M. (2003) *Service Innovation: Organizational Responses to Technological Opportunities and Market Imperatives*. Imperial College Press, London; and Normann, R. (2001) *Service Management – Strategy and leadership in service business*, 3rd edn. John Wiley & Sons, Ltd, Chichester. For an excellent up-to-date review, please see Magnusson, P. et al (2007) Involving Customers in New Service Development. Imperial College Press, London.

References

1 Crespi, G., Criscuolo, C. and Haskel, J. (2006) Information technology, organisational change and productivity growth: evidence from UK firms. *The Future of Science, Technology and Innovation Policy: Linking Research and Practice*. SPRU 40th Anniversary Conference, Brighton, UK, September.

2 Tidd, J. and Hull, F.M. (2006) Managing service innovation: the need for selectivity rather than 'best-practice'. *New Technology, Work and Employment*, **21** (2), 139–161; Tidd, J. and Hull, F.M. (2003) *Service Innovation: Organizational Responses to Technological Opportunities and Market Imperatives*. Imperial College Press, London.

3 Cooper, R.G. (2000) Doing it right: winning with new products. *Ivey Business Journal*, **64** (6), July/August, 1–7; available online: http://www.iveybusinessjournal.com/article.asp?intArticle_ID=235.

4 Lynn, G.S. and Reilly, R.R. (2002) *Blockbusters: The Five Keys to Developing Great New Products*. HarperBusiness, New York.

5 Wheelwright, S.C. and Clark, K.B. (1997) Creating project plans to focus product development. *Harvard Business Review*, September–October.

6 Tidd, J. and Bodley, K. (2002) The affect of project novelty on the new product development process. *R&D Management*, **32** (2), 127–138.

Discussion Questions

1 What are the key differences between managing operations in services and manufacturing? Think of a business, and identify the relative contributions to value-added of the service and physical product components.

2 To what extent do you think that manufacturing and services are converging? Try to think of an example of a manufacturing operation that increasingly features a service. Conversely, identify a service operation that is becoming more product-based.

3 In what ways do you think the development of new products differs from the development of new services?

4 Identify the relative importance of product/service attributes and organizational factors in successful development.

5 In practice, how many stages and gates do you think a process for new product development should have?

6 What is the different between the 'stage-gate' and 'development funnel' models of the new product development process?

7 What effect does the novelty of the new product or service have on the development process?

Team Exercise

Apply QFD to a real example of a new product or service. In a group, take the following steps:

1 Identify the target customer requirements, by market research or in class by 'brain-storming'. Try to include both tangible and intangible elements.

2 Rank or weight these requirements, based on your best knowledge of the target market segment.

3 Where possible, translate the requirements into measurable characteristics

4 Identify different technical or design options to deliver these characteristics.

5 Compare or benchmark against real-life competing products.

See website for more information.

Assignment and Case Study Questions

Prepare a 20-minute presentation which critically assesses the reasons for the success or failure of a new product, service or technology. 'New' in this context means something which was launched within the past 5 years or so, so that sufficient data and material exists to assess its success. For these reasons please avoid very recent innovations, or generic non-proprietary technologies such as 'the Internet'. The product or service should be sufficiently well documented or known to you so that you can differentiate between controllable and uncontrollable factors:

Controllable	Uncontrollable
Technology or market strategy	Market potential
Product advantage	Market attractiveness
Pre-development activities	Competitor behaviour
Proficiency of development process	Capital requirements
Proficiency of marketing	Regulation or legislation

This should not simply be an assessment of the marketing and commercialization of the product or service, but should include an analysis of as many as possible of the factors listed.

CASE STUDY 5

Exploring Innovation in Action: The Development and Delivery of Digital TV Services

Digital TV allows more channels, higher-quality pictures and sound, and a level of interactivity with the programming. Digital television services can be delivered to homes in a number of different ways, including by satellite, cable, telephone lines, terrestrial broadcast (via an aerial) or via the Internet. In Europe digital TV in general has developed on pay-TV platforms, dominated by the powerful satellite companies and services, and in the USA by cable operators. Here we examine the initial failure and ultimate success of digital terrestrial television (DTT) in the UK.

The British Government was determined that Britain would become a leading developer and adopter of digital services, at the forefront of the next industrial revolution. It aimed to start the digital switchover in the regions in 2008 and to complete the switch from analogue to digital by 2012. Behind this worthy vision was a more direct financial calculation by the government, which would benefit from selling the frequencies freed up by the switch to digital (digital TV signals are compressed so they take up less of the broadcasting spectrum), estimated to be £20 billion.

By 2006 almost three-quarters (18 million) of UK households received digital television, the highest penetration in the world. The USA comes second at 55%, with some regions and cities in Germany and Sweden having already switched off analogue television broadcasting. In 2006 the number of households in the UK receiving DTT reached in excess of 7.1 million households, above analogue TV for the first time (6.4m), and fast approaching the reach of satellite with 7.7 million households. The service, now called Freeview, which offers more than 30 channels of free digital television and 20 radio stations through a rooftop aerial, has seen phenomenal growth over the past few years.

However, DTT has had many false starts in the UK. The first public demonstration of digital TV was in 1993, and the Broadcasting Act of 1996 provided the regulatory framework and goals. DTT really began in the UK in January 1997 with the formation of the British Digital Broadcasting (BDB) consortium by BSkyB, Carlton and Granada. BDB was renamed OnDigital and began broadcasting in November 1998. The consortium was clearly dominated by the concerns and needs of its members from the private sector, but the government hoped to use this to influence the rate and direction of development, delivery and adoption of DTT in the UK. This arrangement created tensions from the very beginning. BSkyB had to withdraw later because of anti-competition concerns, and immediately launched its own competing digital satellite service. OnDigital aimed to differentiate its services from those of BSkyB by offering a more limited but 'more discerning' range of channels and services, with 30 channels, rather than BSkyB's 200.

Both services struggled to attract new and to retain existing customers. Along with cable companies NTL and Telewest, BSkyB waived its charge for providing and installing the set-top boxes, and therefore OnDigital was forced to do the same. OnDigital planned to subsidize but to also charge £200 for each installation, and this move doubled its planned costs for equipment. BSkyB achieved 1 million subscribers to its digital services in 1999, but OnDigital did not achieve this level until 2001. By this time Sky had more than 5 million digital subscribers, and announced it is to turn off its analogue service.

The OnDigital service peaked at 1.2 million subscribers in December 2001, and struggled with accumulating losses. In 2001 Carlton and Granada relaunched the service as ITV Digital, in an effort to give it the kudos and reassurance of the ITV brand. This was the final attempt to make the service profitable, but it failed, and in 2002 ITV Digital went into administration. Its owners, Carlton and Granada, lost an estimated £1.2 billion they had invested in ITV Digital and OnDigital. Further, they now also faced legal action from many suppliers, creditors and subscribers, including the Football League, which took legal action against ITV Digital's owners Carlton and Granada with a claim for £678 million in outstanding payments and damages, and some 300 000 of ITV Digital's 1.2 million customers who had £200 pre-paid contracts.

A number of factors contributed to the failure of OnDigital/ITV Digital, some due to poor management, others influenced by government policy or inaction. For example, in some markets BSkyB's set-top giveaway could have been regarded as anti-competitive. DTT also experienced many signal and reception problems, which meant that the service could reach only 40% of homes instead of a projected 70%, equivalent to an additional 7 50 000 subscribers. Piracy was another problem. Their encryption codes were cracked and put on the Internet, costing the company a further £100 million. However, poor strategy and management also played a part. Despite its claim to target the 'more discerning' viewer, ITV Digital paid £315 million for rights to screen Football League games for three years, but these lacked the attraction and audiences of the Premier League football offered by Sky. ITV Digital had also agreed to pay BSkyB £17 million for encryption services and 'carriage rights', whereas others paid much less for these services.

The Independent Television Commission (ITC) assessed the bids for ITV Digital's multiplexes, including bids form the BBC, ITV, Channel 4, and Sky. The BBC's bid was for all free-to-air channels, but those from the commercial broadcaster included some pay-TV elements. The ITC also reduced the number of channels to help improve the broadcast coverage and signal strength and quality. The commercial broadcasters argued for their own system, with the BBC having another. Fortunately, the ITC had the wisdom (or luck) to reject this hybrid. In its decision, the ITC was convinced by commitments given by the BBC to promote digital terrestrial television, and by the technical and financial robustness of its bid. Licences were awarded for 12 years.

In October 2002 the Freeview consortium, which consisted of the BBC, BSkyB and the American transmitter company Crown Castle, launched its free-to-air digital service Freeview, available to anyone in an area of strong reception with a good rooftop aerial and a compatible set-top box, available for around £80, or a reconditioned ITV Digital box. Freeview reduced the number of channels from ITV Digital's 40 to 30, which allowed more households to receive them – around 70% of households at the launch of Freeview, compared to less than 50% for ITV Digital.

The initial service provided unlimited access to 30 free channels, which in addition to the 5 established terrestrial channels included 4 rolling news channels, including BBC News 24, Sky News and ITV News; all 8 of the BBC's current and forthcoming digital channels; 1 shopping, 1 lifestyle, 2 music and 2 travel channels; 11 public and commercial radio stations; and various interactive options. However, it had no channels dedicated either to sport or films, the 2 core subscription service offerings. The initial strategy was one of incremental market development, in an effort to build infrastructure and content and manage expectations of the new service. It began with a relatively modest marketing budget of £5 million, and a target penetration of 4–5 million households. However, the BBC spent £278 million on digital services in 2002, demonstrating its commitment.

There was still a fundamental question of the level of demand for such services. Surveys can be very unreliable guides to the demand for new products and services. Professional media research at that time claimed that 60% of people who did not have digital television said that 'nothing' would change their mind about getting it, with 45% of analogue users saying they were satisfied with existing analogue services. In 2001 the Digital Audience Research Tracking (DART) study suggested that only 3% of analogue homes planned to switch to digital. However, Freeview did rather better than the forecasts suggested. In its first year it achieved a total of 2 million users, and grew steadily after that.

By 2006 more than 10 million Freeview boxes had been purchased and the number of households in the UK receiving DTT exceeded 7 million households, and BSkyB had 7.7 million digital subscribers, but growth had slowed. BSkyB's plan assumes that the UK market will follow the USA, where more than four-fifths of households pay for TV. However, there appears to be a limit to the number of people in the UK willing to pay £40 a month for sport and movies, and in 2006 BSkyB was the first to launch high-definition (HD) TV services in an effort to attract new customers. In the future, Freeview plans to compete further with BSkyB by launching Freeview Playback, its personal video recorder brand. PVRs are digital devices that allow easy recording of digital television broadcasting. BSkyB has been offering its subscribers Sky+, its own digital recorders. There are estimated to be 34 million VCRs in use in the UK, which will cease to be of use once the analogue television signal starts to be switched off in 2008.

Conditional access technology incorporated in some set-top boxes and almost all new digital televisions now allow a 'mixed economy' of free-to-air and subscription channels. For example, Top Up TV was launched in March 2004 to offer access to 11 pay-subscription channels, albeit at restricted times, in return for a connection fee and monthly subscription. No contract was required, but a card had to be purchased at the outset.

Top Up TV was founded in 2003 by David Chance and Ian West, who together had more than 35 years' experience in pay-TV. David Chance is also a non-executive director of ITV plc and Chairman of the Scandinavian media company MTG, owner of leading channel TV3 and the Viasat pay-TV platform. He was deputy managing director of BSkyB 1993–1998. Ian West is an Advisory Board Member of Kabel Deutschland, Germany's largest cable company, and was previously Managing Director of Sky Entertainment, and a strategic advisor to NTL, the US-owned cable TV company in the UK.

Top Up TV needed to reach 250 000 subscribers to break even, which it achieved by March 2006, two years after launch, but at the cost of initial losses of £7 million. In May 2006 the holding company changed its name to Minds 1 Limited and restructured into three separate companies: Top Up TV 1 Limited, Top Up TV 2 Limited, and Top Up TV 3 Limited. In July 2006 Channel Five in the UK announced two new channels to be broadcast on capacity currently used by Top Up TV's channels as part of a £20 million investment made in Top Up TV since November 2005.

A growing coalition of the public (BBC) and private commercial broadcasters is now emerging, offering more free-to-air channels, including channels dedicated to films and children. However, there are potential problems with this strategy, because the commercial companies are increasingly concerned that the BBC is going beyond its public service role to encourage the growth of digital television and using its public funding to compete in their markets. Nonetheless, a growing number of the commercial terrestrial broadcasters have begun to support this strategy, partly because it reduces their dependence on BSkyB and the cable companies to distribute their programmes when the analogue broadcasting signal is finally switched off in 2012. With no clear direction from either government policy-makers or industry, the debate continues on how further growth will be funded – if free-to-air services dominate, can advertising funding continue to support all the new content, or will public money be used to support DTT, or will the market return to more subscription services?

Case Study Questions

1 What were the main reasons for the initial failure of the development and diffusion of digital TV services?

2 What were the critical differences which contributed to the subsequent success of digital TV?

3 In what ways did the interaction of products, services and infrastructure influence success and failure in this case, and what lessons can be learned?

Part 3
Practice

Chapter 6

Creating and Sharing Knowledge and Intellectual Property

This chapter

- Looks at generating and acquiring knowledge.

- Explores processes for identifying and codifying knowledge.

- Reviews mechanisms for sharing and distributing knowledge.

- Examines ways of translating knowledge into innovation.

- Looks at ways of exploiting intellectual property.

Learning Objectives

When you have completed this chapter you will be able to:

- Describe the different types of knowledge that exist at the individual and organizational levels.

- Understand the relationships between knowledge, learning and innovation.

- Identify the potential for improving knowledge management in an organization, and recommend appropriate mechanisms.

- Describe the main types of formal intellectual property rights (IPR) that exist, and their main uses to help protect and exploit innovation.

In this chapter we discuss how individuals and organizations identify 'what they know' and how best to exploit this. We examine the related fields of knowledge management, organizational learning and intellectual property. Key issues include the nature of knowledge, for example, explicit versus tacit knowledge; the locus of knowledge, for example individual versus organizational; and the distribution of knowledge across an organization. More narrowly, knowledge management is concerned with identifying, translating, sharing and exploiting the knowledge within an organization. One of the key issues is the relationship between individual and organizational learning, and how the former is translated into the latter, and ultimately into new processes, products and businesses. Finally, we review different types of formal intellectual property, and how these can be used in the development and commercialization of innovations.

In essence managing knowledge involves five critical tasks:

- Generating and acquiring new knowledge.

- Identifying and codifying existing knowledge.

- Storing and retrieving knowledge.

- Sharing and distributing knowledge across the organization.

- Exploiting and embedding knowledge in processes, products and services.

Generating and Acquiring Knowledge

We have discussed the generation and acquisition of knowledge in Chapters 1, 2 and 3, so here we provide only a summary of the issues. Organizations can acquire knowledge by experience, experimentation or acquisition.

Of these, learning from experience appears to be the least effective. In practice, organizations do not easily translate experience into knowledge. Moreover, learning may be unintentional or it may not result in improved effectiveness. Organizations can incorrectly learn, and they can learn that which is incorrect or harmful, such as learning faulty or irrelevant skills or self-destructive habits. This can lead an organization to accumulate experience of an inferior technique, and may prevent it from gaining sufficient experience of a superior procedure to make it rewarding to use, sometimes called the 'competency trap'.

Experimentation is a more systematic approach to learning. It is a central feature of formal R&D activities, market research and some organizational alliances and networks, as we examined in Chapter 3. When undertaken with intent, a strategy of learning through incremental trial and error acknowledges the complexities of existing technologies and markets, as well as the uncertainties associated with technology and market change and in forecasting the future. The use of alliances for learning is less common and requires an intent to use them as an opportunity for learning, a receptivity to external know-how and partners of sufficient transparency. Whether the acquisition of know-how results in organizational learning depends on the rationale for the acquisition and the process of acquisition and transfer. For example, the cumulative effect of outsourcing various technologies on the basis of comparative transaction costs may limit future technological options and reduce competitiveness in the long term.

A more active approach to the acquisition of knowledge involves scanning the internal and external environments. As we discussed in Chapter 1, scanning consists of searching, filtering and evaluating potential opportunities from outside the organization, including related and emerging technologies, new markets and services, which can be exploited by applying or combining with existing competencies. Opportunity recognition, which is a precursor to entrepreneurial behaviour, is often associated with a flash of genius, but in reality is probably more often the end result of a laborious process of environmental scanning. External scanning can be conducted at various levels. It can be an operational initiative with market- or technology-focused managers becoming more conscious of new developments within their own environments, or a top-driven initiative where venture managers or professional capital firms are used to monitor and invest in potential opportunities.

INNOVATION IN ACTION

Identifying Different Types of Knowledge

The concept of disembodied knowledge can become a very abstract idea, but it can be assessed in practice. Here are some types of knowledge identified in a study of the biotechnology and telecommunications industries:

- Variety of knowledge;
- Depth of knowledge;
- Source of knowledge, internal and external;
- Evaluation of knowledge and awareness of competencies;
- Knowledge management practices, the capability to identify, share and acquire knowledge;
- Use of IT systems to store, share and reuse knowledge;
- Identification and assimilation of external knowledge;
- Commercial knowledge of markets and customers;
- Competitor knowledge, current and potential;
- Knowledge of supplier networks and value chain;
- Regulatory knowledge;
- Financial and funding stakeholder knowledge;
- Knowledge of intellectual property (IPR), own and others;
- Knowledge practices, including documentation, intranets, work organization and multidisciplinary teams and projects.

The study concluded that each of these contributed to the intellectual assets and innovative performance of companies, but in different ways. In general, the less tangible and more tacit knowledge of individuals, groups and practices are necessary to exploit the more explicit and tangible types of knowledge, such as R&D and IPR, and these in turn can lead to better use of and access to external sources of knowledge, due to a strengthening of position, reputation and trust.

Source: Derived from Marques, D.P., Simon, F.J.G. and Caranana, C.D. (2006) The effect of innovation on intellectual capital: an empirical evaluation in the biotechnology and telecommunications industries, *International Journal of Innovation Management*, **10** (1), 89–112.

Identifying and Codifying Knowledge

It is useful to begin with a clearer idea of what we mean by 'knowledge'. It has become all things to all people, ranging from corporate IT systems to the skills and experience of individuals. There is no universally accepted typology, but the following hierarchy is helpful:

- *Data* are a set of discrete raw observations, numbers, words, records and so on. Typically easy to structure, record, store and manipulate electronically.

- *Information* is data that has been organized, grouped or categorized into some pattern. The organization may consist of categorization, calculation or synthesis. This organization of data endows information with relevance and purpose, and in most cases adds value to data.

- *Knowledge* is information that has been contextualized, given meaning and therefore made relevant and easier to use. The transformation of information into knowledge involves making comparisons and contrasts, identifying relationships and inferring consequences. Therefore knowledge is deeper and richer than information, and includes framed expertise, experience, values and insights.

There are essentially two different types of knowledge, each with different characteristics:

- Explicit knowledge, which can be codified, that is expressed in numerical, textual or graphical terms, and therefore is more easily communicated; for example, the design of a product

- Tacit or implicit knowledge, which is personal, experiential, context-specific and hard to formalize and communicate; for example, how to ride a bicycle.

Note that the distinction between explicit and tacit is not necessarily the result of the difficulty or complexity of the knowledge, but rather how easy it is to express that knowledge. Blacker develops a finer typology of knowledge, which identifies five types:[1]

- *Embrained* knowledge, which depends on conceptual skills and cognitive abilities, and emphasizes the value of abstract knowledge.

- *Embodied* knowledge, which is action-oriented but likely to be only partly explicit – for example, problem-solving ability and learning by doing – and is highly context-specific.

- *Encultured* knowledge, which is the process of achieving shared understanding and meaning. It is socially constructed and open to negotiation, and involves socialization and acculturation.

- *Embedded* knowledge, which resides in systematic routines and processes. It includes resources and relationships between roles, procedures and technologies and is related to the notion of organizational capabilities or competencies.

- *Encoded* knowledge, which is represented by symbols and signs, and includes designs, blueprints, manuals and electronic media.

None of these types of knowledge is inherently superior, and the most relevant type will be contingent upon the organizational and environmental needs. It is also possible to add a sixth type of knowledge, *commodified* knowledge, which is embodied in the outputs of an organization, for example products and services (see box on page 187). This is a critical point, because much of the writing and practice of knowledge management treats the creation and sharing of knowledge as an end in itself. However, in most organizations, perhaps with the exceptions of (some) schools and universities, this is not the case. Knowledge is simply an input or means to achieve some organizational goal.

It is useful to distinguish between learning 'how' and learning 'why'. Learning 'how' involves improving or transferring existing skills, whereas learning 'why' aims to understand the underlying logic or causal factors with a view to applying the knowledge in new contexts.

Neither form of learning is inherently superior, and each will be important in different circumstances. For example, learning 'how' is more relevant where speed or quality is critical, but learning 'why' will be necessary to apply skills and know-how in new situations.

Much of the research on innovation management and organizational change has failed to address the issue of organizational learning. Instead, it has focused on learning by individuals within organizations: 'It is important to recognize that organizations do not learn, but rather the people in them do';[2] 'An organization learns in only two ways: (i) by the learning of its members; or (ii) by ingesting new members.'[3]

Clearly, individuals do learn within the context of organizations. This context affects their learning which, in turn, may affect the performance of the organization. However, individuals and organizations are very different entities, and there is no reason why organizational learning should be conceptually or empirically the same as learning by individuals or individuals learning within organizations. Existing theory and research on organizational learning has been dominated by a weak metaphor of human learning and cognitive development, but such simplistic and inappropriate anthropomorphizing of organizational characteristics has contributed to confused research and misleading conclusions.

Using the dimensions of individual versus collective knowledge, and routine versus novel tasks, it is possible to identify four organizational configurations (Figure 6.1). This framework is useful because rather than advocate a simplistic universal trend towards 'knowledge workers', it allows different types of knowledge to be mapped onto different organizational and task requirements.

For example, this framework suggests that, under conditions of environmental uncertainty, embrained and encultured knowledge are more relevant than embedded or embodied knowledge. The choice between the two

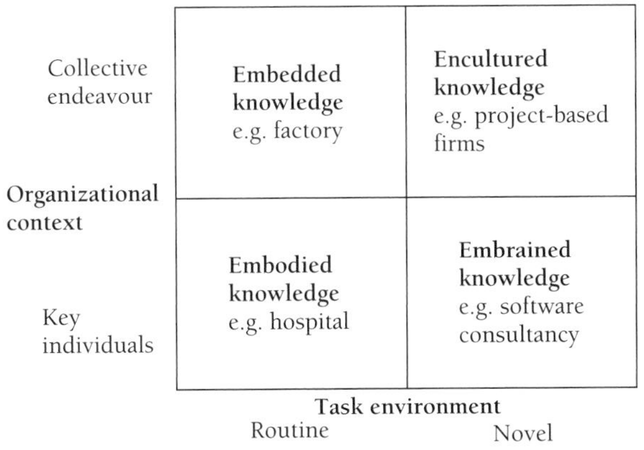

Figure 6.1   Task environment, organizational context and knowledge types.
Source: Derived from Blackler[1].

approaches will depend on the organizational culture and context. We might expect a small, entrepreneurial firm to rely more on embrained knowledge, and a large established firm on encultured knowledge.

As we have seen, knowledge can be embodied in people, organizational culture, routines and tools, technologies, processes and systems. Organizations consist of a variety of individuals, groups and functions with different cultures, goals and frames of reference. Knowledge management consists of identifying and sharing knowledge across these disparate entities. There is a range of integrating mechanisms which can help to do this. Mobilizing and managing knowledge should become a primary task and many of the recipes offered for achieving this depend upon mobilizing a much higher level of participation in innovative problem-solving and on building such routines into the fabric of organizational life.

Nonaka and Takeuchi argue that the conversion of tacit to explicit knowledge is a critical mechanism underlying the link between individual and organizational knowledge. They argue that all new knowledge originates with an individual, but that through a process of dialogue, discussion, experience-sharing and observation such knowledge is amplified at the group and organizational levels. This creates an expanding community of interaction, or *knowledge network*, which crosses intra- and inter-organizational levels and boundaries. Such knowledge networks are a means to accumulate knowledge from outside the organization, share it widely within the organization, and store it for future use. This transformation of individual knowledge into organizational knowledge involves four cycles:[4]

- ■ *Socialization* – tacit to tacit knowledge, in which the knowledge of an individual or group is shared with others. Culture, socialization and communities of practice are critical for this.

- ■ *Externalization* – tacit to explicit knowledge, through which the knowledge is made explicit and codified in some persistent form. This is the most novel aspect of Nonaka's model. He argues that tacit knowledge can be transformed into explicit knowledge through a process of conceptualization and crystallization. Boundary objects are critical here.

- ■ *Combination* – explicit to explicit knowledge, where different sources of explicit knowledge are pooled and exchanged. The role of organizational processes and technological systems are central to this.

- ■ *Internalization* – explicit to tacit, whereby other individuals or groups learn through practice. This is the traditional domain of organizational learning.

Max Boisot has developed the similar concept of C-Space (culture space) to analyse the flow of knowledge within and between organizations. It consists of two dimensions: codification, the extent to which information can be easily expressed; and diffusion, the extent to which information is shared by a given population. Using this framework he proposes a social learning cycle which involves four stages: scanning, problem-solving, diffusion and adsorption (Figure 6.2).[5]

C-Space (culture-space) is a useful conceptual framework for this analysis. It focuses on the structuring and flow of knowledge within and between organizations. It consists of two dimensions: *codification* and *diffusion*. Codifying knowledge involves taking information that human agents carry in their heads and find hard to articulate, and structuring it in such a way that its complexity is reduced (see box overleaf). This enables it to be incorporated into physical objects or described on paper. Once this has occurred, it will develop a life of its own and can diffuse quite rapidly and extensively. Knowledge moves around the C-Space in a cyclical fashion as shown in Figure 6.2.

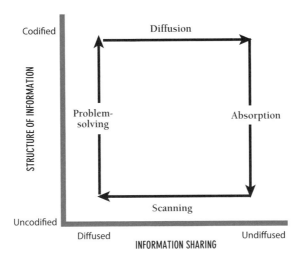

Figure 6.2   A model of knowledge structuring and sharing.
Source: Boisot, M. and Griffiths, D. in Tidd, J. (2006) *From Knowledge Management to Strategic Competencies*, 2nd edn. Imperial College Press, London**.**

INNOVATION IN ACTION

An Example of Codification and Diffusion Scales

Codified

Can be totally automated

Can be partially automated

Can be systematically described

Can be described and put down on paper

Can be shown and described verbally

Can be shown

Inside someone's head

Uncodified

Diffused

Known by all firms in all industries

Known by many firms in all industries

Known by many firms in many industries

Known by many firms in a few industries

Known by a handful of firms in a few industries

Known by only a handful of firms in one industry

Known only by one firm in one industry

Undiffused

This methodology can be used to map knowledge in an organization or industry. This framework can help define what an organization needs to do over time to maintain and renew resources and competencies. Effective management is about knowing where to locate knowledge resources and the organizational linkages that integrate them together to create competencies. The objectives of the framework are:

■ To enable an organization to map its resources and the key linkages between them onto the C-Space;

■ To act as an elicitation device to facilitate a discussion about the meaning and action required – in terms of core competencies and knowledge resources.

Storing and Retrieving Knowledge

Storing knowledge is not a trivial problem, even now that the electronic storage and distribution of data is so cheap and easy. The biggest hurdle is the codification of tacit knowledge. The other common problem is to provide incentives to contribute, retrieve and reuse relevant knowledge. Many organizations have developed excellent knowledge intranet systems, but these are often underutilized in practice as shown in the box below.

INNOVATION IN ACTION

Knowledge Management at Arup

Arup is an international engineering consultancy firm which provides planning, designing, engineering and project management services. The business demands the simultaneous achievement of innovative solutions and significant time compression imposed by client and regulatory requirements.

Since 1999 the organization has established a wide range of knowledge management initiatives to encourage sharing of know-how and experience across projects. These initiatives range from organizational processes and mechanisms, such as cross-functional communications meetings and skills networks, to technology-based approaches such as the Ovebase database and intranet.

To date, the former have been more successful than the latter. For example, a survey of engineers in the firm indicated that, in design and problem-solving, discussions with colleagues were rated as being twice as valuable as knowledge databases, and consequently engineers were four times as likely to rely on colleagues. Two primary reasons were cited for this. First, the difficulty of codifying tacit knowledge. Engineering consultancy involves a great deal of tacit knowledge and project experience which is difficult to store and retrieve electronically. Second, the complex engineering and unique environmental context of each project limits the reuse of standardized knowledge and experience.

In practice, there are two common but distinct approaches to knowledge management. The first is based on investments in IT, usually based on groupware and intranet technologies. These are the favoured approach of many management consultants. But introducing knowledge management into an organization consists of much more than technology and training. It can require fundamental changes to organizational structure, processes and culture. The second approach is more people- and process-based, and attempts to encourage staff to identify, store, share and use information throughout the organization. Research suggests that, as in previous cases of process innovation, the benefits of the technology are not fully realized unless the organizational aspects are first dealt with.[6]

Therefore the storage, retrieval and reuse of knowledge demands much more than good IT systems. It also requires incentives to contribute to and use knowledge from such systems, whereas many organizations instead encourage and promote the generation and use of new knowledge.

Organizational memory is the process by which knowledge is stored for future use. Such information is stored either in the memories of members of an organization or in its operating procedures and routines. The former suffers from all of the shortcomings of human memory, with the additional organizational problem of personnel loss or turnover. However, over time, these behavioural routines create and are reinforced by artefacts such as organizational structures, procedures and policies. In these terms, competencies become highly firm-specific combinations of behavioural routines and artefacts. This specificity questions the validity of the current fashion for benchmarking 'best practice' processes and structures: what works for one firm may not work for another. Conversely, the difficulty in anticipating future needs.

Richard Hall goes some way towards identifying the components of organizational memory. His main purpose is to articulate intangible resources and he distinguishes between intangible assets and intangible competencies. Assets include intellectual property rights and reputation. Competencies include the skills and know-how of employees, suppliers and distributors, as well as the collective attributes which constitute organizational culture. His empirical work, based on a survey and case studies, indicates that managers believe that the most significant of these intangible resources are the company's reputation and employees' know-how, both of which may be a function of organizational culture. These include:[7]

- Intangible, off-balance-sheet assets; such as patents, licences, trademarks, contracts and protectable data.

- Positional, which are the result of previous endeavour; that is, with a high path-dependency, such as processes and operating systems, and individual and corporate reputation and networks.

- Functional, which are either individual skills and know-how or team skills and know-how, within the company, at the suppliers or distributors.

- Cultural, including traditions of quality, customer service, human resources or innovation.

The key questions in each case are:

- Are we making the best use of this resource?

- How else could it be used?

- Is the scope for synergy identified and exploited?

- Are we aware of the key linkages which exist between the resources?

Sharing and Distributing Knowledge

In practice, large organizations often do not know what they know. Many organizations now have databases and groupware to help store, retrieve and share data and information, but such systems are often confined to 'hard' data and information, rather than more tacit knowledge. As a result functional groups or business units with potentially synergistic information may not be aware of where such information could be applied.

Knowledge-sharing and distribution is the process by which information from different sources is shared and, therefore, leads to new knowledge or understanding. Greater organizational learning occurs when more of an organization's components obtain new knowledge and recognize it as being of potential use. Tacit knowledge is not easily imitated by competitors because it is not fully encoded, but for the same reasons it may not be fully visible to all members of an organization. As a result, organizational units with potentially synergistic information may not be aware of where such information could be applied. The speed and extent to which knowledge is shared between members of an organization is likely to be a function of how codified the knowledge is.

There is a large number of permutations of the processes required for converting and connecting knowledge from different parts of an organization:[8]

- *Converting data and information to knowledge* – for example, identifying patterns and associations in databases.

- *Converting text to knowledge* – through synthesis, comparison and analysis.

- *Converting individual to group knowledge* – sharing knowledge requires a supportive culture, appropriate incentives and technologies.

- *Connecting people to knowledge* – for example, through seminars, workshops or software agents.

- *Connecting knowledge to people* – pushing relevant information and knowledge through intranets, agent systems.

- *Connecting people to people* – creating expert and interest directories and networks, mapping who knows what and who knows who.

- *Connecting knowledge to knowledge* – identifying and encouraging the interaction of different knowledge domains; for example, through common projects.

This process of conversion and connection is underpinned by *communities of practice*. A community of practice is a group of people related by a shared task, process or the need to solve a problem, rather than by formal structural or functional relationships.[9] Through practice, a group within which knowledge is shared becomes a community of practice through a common understanding of what it does, how to do it and how it relates to other communities of practice.

Within communities of practice, people share tacit knowledge and learn through experimentation. Therefore the formation and maintenance of such communities represents an important link between individual and organizational learning. These communities naturally emerge around local work practice and so tend to reinforce functional or professional silos, but also can extend to wider, dispersed networks of similar practitioners.

The existence of communities of practice facilitates the sharing of knowledge within a community, due to both the sense of collective identity, and the existence of a significant common knowledge base. However, the sharing of knowledge between communities is much more problematic, due to the lack of both these elements. Thus the dynamics of knowledge-sharing within and between communities of practice are likely to be very different, with the sharing of knowledge between communities typically much more complex, difficult and problematic.

Taking the issue of identity first, differences between different communities of practice will complicate the process of knowledge-sharing because of perceived or real differences of interest between communities, resulting in potential conflict. We discussed the benefits and drawbacks of conflict in Chapter 2. If conflict is too high, you may see information-hoarding, open aggression, or people lying or exaggerating about their real needs. These conditions could be caused by power struggles of both a personal and professional nature. However, if conflict is too low, individuals and groups may lack motivation or interest in their tasks, and meetings are about one-way communication or reporting, rather than discussion and debate.

The other factor which can prevent the sharing of knowledge between communities of practice is the distinctiveness of different knowledge bases, and the lack of common knowledge, goals, assumptions and interpretative frameworks. These differences significantly increase the difficulty not just of sharing knowledge between communities, but appreciating the knowledge of another community.

There are a few proven mechanisms to help knowledge transfer between different communities of practice:[10]

- An organizational knowledge translator, who is an individual able to express the interests of one community in terms of another community's perspective. Therefore the translator must be sufficiently conversant with both knowledge domains and trusted by both communities. Examples of translators include the 'heavyweight product manager' in new product development, who bridges different technical groups and the technical and marketing groups.

- A knowledge broker, who differs from a translator in that they participate in different communities rather than simply mediate between them. They represent overlaps between communities, and are typically people loosely linked to several communities through *weak ties* who are able to facilitate knowledge flows between them.[11] An example might be a quality manager responsible for the quality of a process that crosses several different functional groups.

- A boundary object or practice, which is something of interest to two or more communities of practice. Different communities of practice will have a stake in it, but from different perspectives. A boundary object might be a shared document, for example, a quality manual; an artefact, for example, a prototype; a technology, for example, a database; or a practice, for example, a product design. A boundary object provides an opportunity for discussion, debate (and conflict) and therefore can encourage communication between different communities of practice.

For example, formally appointed 'knowledge brokers' can be used to systematically scavenge the organization for old or unused ideas, to pass these around the organization and imagine their application in different contexts. For example, Hewlett-Packard created a SpaM group to help identify and share good practice among its 150 business divisions. Before the new group was formed, divisions were unlikely to share information because they often competed for resources and were measured against each other. Similarly, Skandia, a Swedish insurance company active in overseas markets, attempts to identify, encourage and measure its intellectual capital, and has appointed a 'knowledge manager' who is responsible for this. The company has developed a set of indicators that it uses both to manage knowledge internally, and for external financial reporting.

More generally, cross-functional team-working can help to promote this inter-communal exchange. Functional diversity tends to extend the range of knowledge available and increase the number of options considered, but also can have a negative effect on group cohesiveness and the cost of projects and efficiency of decision-making.

However, a major benefit of cross-functional team-working is the access it provides to the bodies of knowledge that are external to the team. In general a high frequency of knowledge-sharing outside of a group is associated with improved technical and project performance, as gatekeeper individuals pick up and import vital signals and knowledge. In particular, cross-functional composition in teams is argued to permit access to disciplinary knowledge outside. Therefore cross-functional team-working is a critical way of promoting the exchange of knowledge and practice across disciplines and communities.

A wide range of strategies for introducing knowledge management are available, and no single approach will be appropriate in all circumstances. The most appropriate strategy will depend on the existing organizational culture, structure and processes, the nature of knowledge, and the availability of resources and urgency of action.

It follows from this that developing a climate conducive to knowledge-sharing is not a simple matter since it consists of a complex web of behaviours and artefacts. And changing this culture is not likely to happen quickly or as a result of single initiatives, such as restructuring or mass training in a new technique. Given this, it is clear that management cannot directly change culture but it can intervene at the level of artefacts – by changing structures or processes – and by providing models and reinforcing preferred styles of behaviour. Instead, building a culture supportive of knowledge management involves systematic development of organizational structures, communication policies and procedures, reward and recognition systems, training policy, accounting and measurement systems and deployment of strategy.

One useful way of understanding the advantages and disadvantages of different ways of implementing knowledge management, and identifying five different strategies for introducing knowledge management to an organization (Table 6.1):[12]

Table 6.1   Knowledge management strategies

Strategy	Characteristics	Requirements	Risks
Ripple	Bottom-up, continuous improvement, e.g. quality management	Process tools, sustained motivation	Isolation from technical excellence
Flow	Integration of functional knowledge within processes, e.g. product development	Improved interfaces, early involvement, overlapping phases	Conformity, coordination burden
Embedding	Coupling of systems, products and services, e.g. enterprise resource planning (ERP)	Common information systems and technology, motivation and rewards	Loss of autonomy, system complexity
Bridge	New knowledge by novel combination of existing competencies, e.g. architectural innovations	Common language and objectives	High control needs, technical feasibility, market failure
Transfer	Exploiting existing knowledge in a new context, e.g. related diversification	New market knowledge	Inappropriate technology, customer support and service

Source: Adapted from Friso den Hertog, J. and Huizenga, E. (2000) *The Knowledge Enterprise*. Imperial College Press, London.

■ Ripple

■ Flow

■ Embedding

■ Bridge

■ Transfer.

The *ripple* approach is the most basic, and consists of a knowledge centre or core of one specific discipline, technology or skill, which is developed incrementally over time. An example might be quality management, or the experience curve in mass production, or robust designs. The impact over time can be great, but the danger is that the knowledge will become detached from market needs and technological opportunities.

The *flow* approach involves projects being handed from one knowledge centre to another, often sequentially. This is similar to the traditional new product or service development process, and one of the biggest problems is managing the interfaces and integration between the knowledge centres; for example, the design, production and marketing functions.

The *embedding* approach brings different knowledge centres into a broader framework, without any major changes to the centres. An example would be the electronic data interchange (EDI) between a supplier and retailer to reduce stocks and improve responsiveness. Potential problems include asymmetric cost and benefits between the centres, and fear of control or leakage of information.

The *bridge* approach merges two or more different knowledge centres to create a whole new knowledge domain. This may be a merger of disciplines; for example, mechanical and electrical engineering to form mechatronics, which is sometimes referred to as *technology fusion*, or may involve the combination of two organizations in a joint venture or merger. This is a very risky strategy, as such bridges typically have significant technological, organizational and commercial uncertainties, but when successful can result in radically new knowledge and high rewards.

The *transfer* approach is more selective, and consists of taking a useful element of one knowledge domain and adapting it for use in another. The knowledge transferred might be technology, market knowledge or organizational know-how or processes. Process benchmarking is an example of a knowledge-transfer strategy.

This framework is useful because it helps us to understand better the needs and limits of different approaches to knowledge management, beyond the usual, but often unsuccessful 'technology and training' approach.

Translating Knowledge into Innovation

Knowledge management has all the characteristics of a management fad or fashion (see box overleaf). However, successful management practice is never fully reproducible. In a complex world, neither the most scrupulous practising manager nor the most rigorous management scholar can be sure of identifying – let alone evaluating – all the necessary ingredients in real examples of successful management practice. In addition, the conditions of any (inevitably imperfect) reproduction of successful management practice will differ from the original, whether in terms of firm, country, sector, physical conditions, state of technical knowledge, or organizational skills and cultural norms. Therefore in real life there are no easily applicable recipes for successful management practice. This is one of the reasons why there are continuous swings in management fashion.

INNOVATION IN ACTION

Management Fads and Fashion Statements Versus Behavioural Change in Organizations

The problem with routines is that they have to be learned – and learning is difficult. It takes time and money to try new things, it disrupts and disturbs the day-to-day working of the firm, it can upset organizational arrangements and require efforts in acquiring and using new skills. Not surprisingly most firms are reluctant learners – and one strategy which they adopt is to try and short-cut the process by borrowing ideas from other organizations.

While there is enormous potential in learning from others, simply copying what seems to work for another organization will not necessarily bring any benefits and may end up costing a great deal and distracting the organization from finding its own ways of dealing with a particular problem. The temptation to copy gives rise to the phenomenon of particular approaches becoming fashionable – something which every organization thinks it needs in order to deal with its particular problems.

Over the past 20 years we have seen many apparent panaceas for the problems of becoming competitive. Organizations are constantly seeking for new answers to old problems, and the scale of investment in the new fashions of management thinking have often been considerable. The *original* evidence for the value of these tools and techniques was strong, with case studies and other reports testifying to their proven value within the context of origin, But there is also extensive evidence to suggest that these changes do not always work, and in many cases lead to considerable dissatisfaction and disillusionment.

Examples include:

■ Advanced manufacturing technology (AMT – robots, flexible machines, integrated computer control, etc.), lean and agile production.

■ Quality circles, total quality management (TQM), ISO9000.

■ Business process re-engineering (BPR), enterprise resource planning (ERP).

■ Benchmarking best practice.

■ Networking/clustering.

■ Knowledge management.

What is going on here demonstrates well the principles behind behavioural change in organizations. It is not that the original ideas were flawed or that the initial evidence was wrong. Rather it was that other organizations assumed they could simply be copied, without the need to adapt them, to customize them, to modify and change them to suit their circumstances. In other words, there was no learning, and no progress towards making them become routines, part of the underlying culture within the firm.

However, innovation and entrepreneurship are about knowledge – creating new possibilities through combining different knowledge sets. These can be in the form of knowledge about what is technically possible or what particular configuration of this would meet an articulated or latent need. Such knowledge may already exist in our

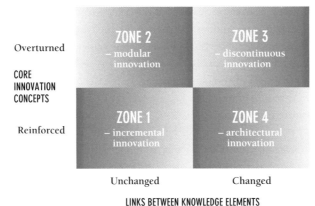

Figure 6.3   Architectural innovation and knowledge components.
Source: Tidd, J., Bessant, J. and Pavitt, K. (2005) *Managing Innovation*. John Wiley & Sons, Ltd, Chichester.

experience, based on something we have seen or done before. Or it could result from a process of search – research into technologies, markets, competitor actions and so on. And it could be in explicit form, codified in such a way that others can access it, discuss it, transfer it and so on – or it can be in tacit form, known about but not actually put into words or formulae.

The process of weaving these different knowledge sets together into a successful new process, product or business is one which takes place under highly uncertain conditions. We often don't know what the final configuration will look like, or precisely how we will get there. In such cases managing knowledge is about committing resources to reduce the uncertainty.

A key contribution to our understanding here comes from the work of Henderson and Clark who looked closely at the kinds of knowledge involved in different kinds of innovation. They argue that innovation rarely involves dealing with a single technology or market but rather a bundle of knowledge which is brought together into a configuration. Successful innovation management requires that we can get hold of and use knowledge about *components* but also about how those can be put together – what they termed the *architecture* of an innovation (Figure 6.3).

Figure 6.3 highlights the issues for managing innovation. In zone 1 the rules of the game are clear – this is about steady-state improvement to products or processes and uses knowledge accumulated around core components.

In zone 2 there is significant change in one element but the overall architecture remains the same. Here there is a need to learn new knowledge but within an established and clear framework of sources and users – for example, moving to electronic ignition or direct injection in a car engine, the use of new materials in airframe components, the use of IT systems instead of paper-processing in key financial or insurance transactions. None of these involve major shifts or dislocations.

In zone 3 we have discontinuous innovation where neither the end state nor the ways in which it can be achieved are known about – essentially the whole set of rules of the game changes and there is scope for new entrants.

In zone 4 we have the condition where new combinations – architectures – emerge, possibly around the needs of different groups of users (as in the disruptive innovation case). Here the challenge is in reconfiguring the knowledge sources and configurations. We may use existing knowledge and recombine it in different ways or we may use a combination of new and old. Examples might be low-cost airlines and direct-line insurance.

We can see this more clearly with an example. Change at the component level in building a flying machine might involve switching to newer metallurgy or composite materials for the wing construction or the use of fly-by-wire controls instead of control lines or hydraulics. But the underlying knowledge about how to link aerofoil shapes, control systems, propulsion systems and so on at the *system* level is unchanged – and being successful at both requires a different and higher order set of competencies.

One of the difficulties with this is that innovation knowledge flows – and the structures which evolve to support them – tend to reflect the nature of the innovation. So if it is at component level then the relevant people with skills and knowledge around these components will talk to each other – and when change takes place they can integrate new knowledge. But when change takes place at the higher system level – 'architectural innovation' – then the existing channels and flows may not be appropriate or sufficient to support the innovation and the firm needs to develop new ones. This is another reason why existing incumbents often fare badly when major system-level change takes place – because they have the twin difficulties of learning and configuring a new knowledge system and 'unlearning' an old and established one.

A variation on this theme comes in the field of 'technology fusion', where different technological streams converge, such that products which used to have a discrete identity begin to merge into new architectures. An example here is the home automation industry, where the fusion of technologies like computing, telecommunications, industrial control and elementary robotics is enabling a new generation of housing systems with integrated entertainment, environmental control (heating, air conditioning, lighting, etc.) and communication possibilities.

Similarly, in services a new addition to the range of financial services may represent a component product innovation, but its impacts are likely to be less far-reaching (and the attendant risks of its introduction lower) than a complete shift in the nature of the service package – for example, the shift to direct-line systems instead of offering financial services through intermediaries.

David Tranfield and his colleagues map the different phases of the innovation process to identify the knowledge routines in each of three innovation phases – discovery, realization and nurture (Figure 6.4):[13]

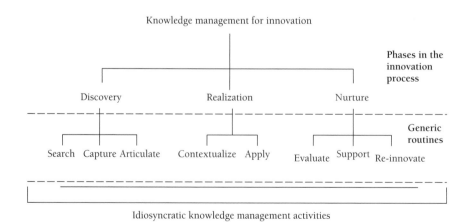

Figure 6.4   Hierarchical process model of knowledge management for innovation.
Source: From Tranfield, D., Young, M., Partington, D., Bessant, J. and Sapsed, J. Knowledge management routines for innovation projects: developing a hierarchical process model, in J. Tidd (2006) *From Knowledge Management to Strategic Competence*, Imperial College Press, London.

Table 6.2   Process model linking innovation phase to knowledge management activities

Phase in the innovation process	Generic routines	Description	Examples of detailed knowledge management activities
Discovery	Search	The passive and active means by which potential knowledge sources are scanned for items of interest	Active environmental scanning (technological, market, social, political, etc.) Active future scanning Experiment (R&D, etc.)
	Capture	The means by which knowledge search outcomes are internalized within the organization	Picking up relevant signals and communicating them within and across the organization to relevant players
	Articulate	The means by which captured knowledge is given clear expression	Concept definition – what might we do? Strategic and operational planning cycles – from outline feasibility to detailed operational plan
Realization	Contextualize	The means by which articulated knowledge is placed in particular organizational contexts	Resource planning and procurement – inside and outside the organization Prototyping and other concept refining activities Early mobilization across functions – design for manufacture, assembly, quality, etc.
	Apply	The means by which contextualized knowledge is applied to organizational challenges	Project team mobilization Project planning cycles Project implementation and modification – 'cycles of mutual adaptation' in technological, market, organizational domains Launch preparation and execution
Nurture	Evaluate	The means by which the efficacy of knowledge applications is assessed	Post-project review Market/user feedback Learning by using/making, etc.
	Support	The means by which knowledge applications are sustained over time	Feedback collection Incremental problem-solving and debugging
	Re-innovate	The means by which knowledge and experience are re-applied elsewhere within the organization	Pick up relevant signals to repeat the cycle Mobilize momentum for new cycle

Source: From Tranfield, D., Young, M., Partington, D., Bessant, J. and Sapsed, J. Knowledge management routines for innovation projects: developing a hierarchical process model, in J. Tidd (2006) *From Knowledge Management to Strategic Competence*, Imperial College Press, London

■ *Discovery* – scanning and searching the internal and external environments, to pick up and process signals about potential innovation. These could be needs of various kinds, opportunities arising from research activities, regulative pressures, or the behaviour of competitors.

■ *Realization* – how the organization can successfully implement the innovation, growing it from an idea through various stages of development to final launch as a new product or service in the external marketplace or a new process or method within the organization. Realization requires selecting from this set of potential triggers for innovation those activities to which the organization will commit resources.

■ *Nurturing* the chosen option by providing resources, developing (either by creating through R&D or acquiring through technology transfer) the means for exploration. It involves not only codified knowledge formally embodied in technology, but also tacit knowledge in the surrounding social linkage which is needed to make the innovation work. The nurture phase involves maintaining and supporting the innovation through various improvements and also reflecting upon previous phases and reviewing experiences of success and failure in order to learn about how to manage the process better, and capture relevant knowledge from the experience. This learning creates the conditions for beginning the cycle again, or 're-innovation'.

Exploiting Intellectual Property

In some cases knowledge, in particular in its more explicit or codified forms, can be commercialized by licensing or selling the intellectual property rights (IPR), rather than the more difficult and uncertain route of developing new processes, products or businesses.

For example, in one year IBM reported licence income of US$1 billion, and in the USA the total royalty income of industry from licensing is around US$100 billion. Much of this is from payments for licenses to use software, music or films. For example, in 2005 the global sales of legal music downloads exceeded US$1 billion (although illegal downloads are estimated to be worth 3 to 4 times this figure), still only around 5% of all music company revenue, with music downloaded to mobile phones accounting for almost a quarter of this. Patterns of use vary by country; for example, in Japan 99.8% of all music downloads are to mobile phones, rather than to dedicated MP3 players. However, despite the growth of legal sites for downloading music and an aggressive programme of pursuing users of illegal file-sharing sites, the level of illegal downloads has not declined.

This clearly demonstrates two of the many problems associated with intellectual property: these may provide some legal rights, but such rights are useless unless they can be effectively enforced; and, once in the public domain, imitation or illegal use is very likely. For these reasons, secrecy is often a more effective alternative to seeking IPR.

However, IPR can be highly effective in some circumstances and, as we will argue later, can be used in less obvious ways to help to identify innovations and assess competitors. A range of IPRs exist, but those most applicable to technology and innovation are patents, copyright and design rights and registration.

Patents

All developed countries have some form of patent legislation, the aim of which is to encourage innovation by allowing a limited monopoly, usually for 20 years, and more recently many developing and emerging economies have been encouraged to signup to the Trade Related Intellectual Property System (TRIPS). Legal regimes differ in the detail, but in most countries the issue of a patent requires certain legal tests to be satisfied:

- *Novelty* – no part of 'prior art', including publications, written, oral or anticipation. In most countries the first to file the patent is granted the rights, but in the USA it is the first to invent. The American approach may have the moral advantage, but results in many legal challenges to patents, and requires detailed documentation during R&D.

- *Inventive step* – 'not obvious to a person skilled in the art'. This is a relative test, as the assumed level of skill is higher in some fields than others. For example, Genentech was granted a patent for the plasminogen activator t-PA which helps to reduce blood clots, but despite its novelty, a Court of Appeal revoked the patent on the grounds that it did not represent an inventive step because its development was deemed to be obvious to researchers in field.

- *Industrial application* – utility test requires the invention to be capable of being applied to a machine, product or process. In practice a patent must specify an application for the technology, and additional patents sought for any additional application. For example, Unilever developed Ceramides and patented their use in a wide range of applications. However, it did not apply for a patent for application of the technology to shampoos, which was subsequently granted to a competitor.

- *Patentable subject* – for example, discoveries and formula cannot be patented, and in Europe neither can software (the subject of copyright) nor new organisms, although both these are patentable in the USA. For example, contrast the mapping of the human genome in the USA and Europe: in the USA the research is being conducted by a commercial laboratory which is patenting the outcomes, and in Europe by a group of public laboratories which is publishing the outcomes on the Internet.

- *Clear and complete disclosure* Note that a patent provides only certain legal property rights, and in the case of infringement the patent holder needs to take the appropriate legal action. In some cases secrecy may be a preferable strategy. Conversely, national patent databases represent a large and detailed reservoir of technological innovations which can be interrogated for ideas.

Apart from the more obvious use of patents as IPR, they can be used to search for potential innovations, and to help identify potential partners or to assess competitors. For example, the TRIZ system developed by Genrich Altshuller identifies standard solutions to common technical problems distilled from an analysis of 1.5 million patents, and applies these in different contexts. Many leading companies use the system, including 3M, Rolls-Royce and Motorola.

Patents can also be used to identify and assess innovation, at the firm, sector or national level. However, great care needs to be taken when making such assessments, because patents are only a partial indicator of innovation.

The main advantages of patent data are that they reflect the corporate capacity to generate innovation, are available at a detailed level of technology over long periods of time, are comprehensive in the sense that they cover small as well as large firms, and are used by practitioners themselves. However, patenting tends to occur early in the development process, and therefore can be a poor measure of the output of development activities, and tells us nothing about the economic or commercial potential of the innovation.

Crude counts of the number of patents filed by a firm, sector or country reveal little, but the quality of patents can be assessed by a count of how often a given patent is cited in later patents. This provides a good indicator of its technical quality, albeit after the event, although not necessarily commercial potential. Highly cited patents are generally of much greater importance than patents which are never cited, or are cited only a few times. The reason for this is that a patent which contains an important new invention – or major advance – can set off a stream of follow-on inventions, all of which may cite the original, important invention upon which they are building.

Using such patent citations, the quality distribution of patents tends to be very skewed: there are large numbers of patents that are cited only a few times, and only a small number of patents cited more than 10 times. For example, half of patents are cited 2 or fewer times, 75% are cited 5 or fewer times, and only 1% of the patents are cited 24 or more times. Overall, after 10 or more years, the average cites/patent is around 6.[14]

The most useful indicators of innovation based on patents are:

■ *Number of patents* Indicates the level of technology activity, but crude patent counts reflect little more than the propensity to patent of a firm, sector or country.

■ *Cites per patent* Indicates the impact of a company's patents.

■ *Current impact index (CII)* This is a fundamental indicator of patent portfolio quality; it is the number of times the company's previous five years of patents, in a technology area, were cited from the current year, divided by the average citations received.

■ *Technology strength (TS)* Indicates the strength of the patent portfolio, and is the number of patents multiplied by the current impact index; that is, patent portfolio size inflated or deflated by patent quality.

■ *Technology cycle time (TCT)* Indicates the speed of invention, and is the median age, in years, of the patent references cited on the front page of the patent.

■ *Science linkage (SL)* Indicates how leading edge the technology is, and is the average number of science papers referenced on the front page of the patent.

■ *Science Strength (SS)* Indicates how much the patent applies basic science, and is the number of patents multiplied by science linkage; that is, patent portfolio size inflated or deflated by the extent of science linkage (see Table 6.3).

Table 6.3   Patent indicators for different sectors

	Current impact index (expected value 1.0)	Technology life cycle (years)	Science linkage (science references/patents)
Oil and gas	0.84	11.9	0.8
Chemicals	0.79	9.0	2.7
Pharmaceuticals	0.79	8.1	7.3
Biotechnology	0.68	7.7	14.4
Medical equipment	2.38	8.3	1.1
Computers	1.88	5.8	1.0
Telecoms	1.65	5.7	0.8
Semiconductors	1.35	6.0	1.3
Aerospace	0.68	13.2	0.3

Source: Derived from Narin (2006) in Tidd, J. (ed.), *From Knowledge Management to Strategic Competence*, 2nd edn. Imperial College Press, London

Companies whose patents have above-average current impact indices (CII) and science linkage indicators (SL) tend to have significantly higher market-to-book ratios and stock market returns. However, having a strong intellectual property portfolio does not, of course, guarantee a company's success. Many additional factors influence the ability of a company to move from quality patents to innovation and financial and market performance. The decade of troubles at IBM, for example, is certainly illustrative of this, since IBM has always had very high-quality and highly cited research in its laboratories. As Chris Evans, founder of Chiroscience and Merlin Ventures notes: 'Academics and universities…have no management, no muscle, no vision, no business plan and that is 90% of the task of exploiting science and taking it to the marketplace. There is a tendency for universities to think, "we invented the thing so we are already 50% there." The fact is they are 50% to nowhere' (*Times Higher*, 27 March 1998).

At the firm level, rather than at the industry level, there is a lot of variability in the productivity of technological inputs; that is, how effectively these are translated into technological outputs. Research suggests at least three reasons for the differences in the ability of firms to translate inputs into outputs: scale, technological opportunity and organization and management. However, few managers are interested in improved measures of technological inputs, and instead need ways to assess the *efficiency* and *effectiveness* of the innovation process: efficiency in the sense of how well companies translate technological and commercial inputs into new products, processes and businesses; effectiveness in the sense of how successful such innovations are in the market and their contribution to financial performance. Our own research, using various combinations of inputs, outputs and indicators of performance, suggests that some ratio of outputs (e.g. new product announcements) to input (e.g. patents or R&D) provides a good proxy for innovation efficiency, and is associated with a range of financial and market measures of performance, such as value-added and market-to-book value.

Therefore care needs to be taken when using patent data as an indicator of innovation. The main advantages of patents are:

- Patents represent the output of the inventive process, specifically those inventions which are expected to have an economic benefit.

- Obtaining patent protection is time-consuming and expensive. Hence applications are only likely to be made for those developments which are expected to provide benefits in excess of these costs.

- Patents can be broken down by technical fields, thus providing information on both the rate and direction of innovation.

- Patent statistics are available in large numbers and over very long time series.

The main disadvantages of patents as indicators of innovation are:

- Not all inventions are patented. Firms may chose to protect their discoveries by other means, such as through secrecy. It has been estimated that firms apply for patents for 66–87% of patentable inventions.

- Not all innovations are technically patentable – for example, software development (outside the USA), and some organisms.

- The propensity to patent varies considerably across different sectors and firms. For example, there is a high propensity to patent in the pharmaceutical industry, but a low propensity in fast-moving consumer goods.

- Firms have a different propensity to patent in each national market, according to the attractiveness of markets.

- A large proportion of patents are never exploited, or are applied for simply to block other developments. It has been estimated that 40–60% of all patents issued are used.

There are major inter-sectoral differences in the relative importance of patenting in achieving its prime objective, namely, to act as a barrier to imitation. For example, patenting is relatively unimportant in automobiles, but critical in pharmaceuticals. Moreover, patents do not yet fully measure technological activities in software since copyright laws are often used as the main means of protection against imitation, outside the USA.

There are also major differences among countries in the procedures and criteria for granting patents. For this reason, comparisons are most reliable when using international patenting or patenting in one country. The US patenting statistics are a particularly rich source of information, given the rigour and fairness of criteria and procedures for granting patents, and the strong incentives for firms to get IPR in the world's largest market. More recently, data from the European Patent Office are also becoming more readily available.

Copyright

Copyright is concerned with the expression of ideas, and not the ideas themselves. Therefore the copyright exists only if the idea is made concrete; for example, in a book or recording. There is no requirement for registration, and the test of originality is low compared to patent law, requiring only that 'the author of the work must have used his own skill and effort to create the work'. Like patents, copyright provides limited legal rights for certain types of material for a specific term. For literary, dramatic, musical and artistic works copyright is normally for 70 years after the death of the author, 50 in the USA, and for recordings, film, broadcast and cable programmes 50 years from their creation. Typographical works have 25 years copyright. The types of materials covered by copyright include:

- 'Original' literary, dramatic, musical and artistic works, including software and in some cases databases;

- Recordings, films, broadcasts and cable programmes;

- Typographical arrangement or layout of a published edition.

Design Rights

Design rights are similar to copyright protection, but mainly apply to three-dimensional articles, covering any aspect of the 'shape' or 'configuration', internal or external, whole or part, but specifically excluding integral and functional features, such as spare parts. Design rights exist for 15 years and 10 years if commercially exploited. Design registration is a cross between patent and copyright protection, is cheaper and easier than patent protection, but more limited in scope. It provides protection for up to 25 years, but covers only visual appearance – shape, configuration, pattern and ornament. It is used for designs that have aesthetic appeal; for example, consumer electronics and toys. For example, the knobs on top of Lego bricks are functional, and would therefore not qualify for design registration, but were also considered to have 'eye appeal', and therefore granted design rights.

INNOVATION IN ACTION

Open Source Software

Proprietary software usually restricts imitation by retaining the source code and by enforcing intellectual property rights such as patents (mainly the USA) or copyright (elsewhere). However, open source software (OSS) has many characteristics of a public good, including non-excludability and non-rivalry, and developers and users of OSS have a joint interest in making OSS free and publicly available. The open software movement has grown since the 1980s when the programmer Richard Stallman founded the Free Software Foundation, and the General Public License (GPL) is now widely used to promote the use and adaptation of OSS. The GPL forms the legal basis of three-quarters of all OSS, including Linux.

Therefore firms active in the field of OSS have to create value and appropriate private benefits in different ways. The ineffectiveness of traditional intellectual property rights in such cases means that firms are more likely to rely on alternative ways of appropriating the benefits of innovation, such as being first to the market or by using externalities to create value. More generic strategies include product and service approaches:

- *Products* – adding a proprietary part to the open code and licensing this, or black-boxing by combining several pieces of OSS into a solution package.

- *Services* – consultancy, training or support for OSS.

Linux is a good example of a successful OSS which firms have developed products and services around. It has been largely developed by a network of voluntary programmers, often referred to as the 'Linux community'. Linus Torvalds first suggested the development of a free operating system to compete with the DOS/Windows monopoly in 1991, and quickly attracted the support of a group of volunteer programmers: 'Having those 100 part-time users was really great for all the feedback I got. They found bugs that I hadn't because I hadn't been using it the way they were . . . after a while they started sending me fixes or improvements . . . this wasn't planned, it just happened.' Thus Linux grew from 10 000 lines of code in 1991 to 1.5 million lines by 1998. Its development coincided with and fully exploited the growth of Internet and later Web forms of collaborative working. The provision of the source code to all potential developers promotes continuous incremental innovation, and the close and sometimes indistinguishable developer and user groups promote concurrent development and debugging. The weaknesses are potential lack of support for users and new hardware, availability of compatible software and forking in development.

By 1998 there were estimated to be more than 7.5 million users and almost 300 user groups across 40 countries. Linux has achieved a 25% share of the market for server operating systems, although its share of the PC-operating system market was much lower, and Apache, a Linux application Web server programme, accounted for half the market. Although Linux is available free of charge, a number of businesses have been spawned by its development. These range from branding and distribution of Linux, development of complementary software and user support and consultancy services. For example, although Linux can be downloaded free of charge, Red Hat Software provides an easier installation programme and better documentation for around US$50, and in 1998 achieved annual revenues of more than US$10 million. Red Hat was floated in 1999. In China, the lack of legacy systems, low costs and government support have made Linux-based systems popular on servers and desktop applications. In

2004 Linux began to enter consumer markets, when Hewlett-Packard launched its first Linux-based notebook computer, which helped to reduce the unit cost by US$60.

Source: L. Dahlander, Appropriation and appropriability in open source software (2005), *International Journal of Innovation Management*, **9** (3), 259–286. See also Muffatto, M (2006) *Open Source: A Multidisciplinary Approach*. Imperial College Press, London.

Licensing IPR

Once you have acquired some form of formal legal IPR, you can allow others to use it in some way in return for some payment (a licence), or sell the IPR outright (or assign it). Licensing IPR can have a number of benefits:

■ Reduce or eliminate production and distribution costs and risks;

■ Reach a larger market;

■ Exploit in other applications;

■ Establish standards;

■ Gain access to complementary technology;

■ Block competing developments;

■ Convert competitor into defender.

Considerations when drafting a licensing agreement include degree of exclusivity, territory and type of end use, period of licence and type and level of payments – royalty, lump sum or cross-licence. Pricing a licence is as much an art as a science, and depends on a number of factors such as the balance of power and negotiating skills. Common methods of pricing licences are:

■ Going market rate – based on industry norms, for example, 6% of sales in electronics and mechanical engineering;

■ 25% rule – based on licensee's gross profit earned through use of the technology;

■ Return on investment – based on licensor's costs;

■ Profit-sharing – based on relative investment and risk. First, estimate total life-cycle profit. Next, calculate relative investment and weight according to share of risk. Finally, compare results to alternatives; for example, return to licensee, imitation, litigation.

There is no 'best' licensing strategy, as it depends on the strategy of the organization and the nature of the technology and markets (see box overleaf). For example, Celltech licensed its asthma treatment to Merck for a single payment of US$50 million, based on sales projections. This isolated Celltech from the risk of clinical trials and commercialization, and provided a much-needed cash injection. Toshiba, Sony and Matsushita license DVD technology for royalties of only 1.5% to encourage its adoption as the industry standard. Until the recent legal proceedings, Microsoft applied a 'per processor' royalty to its original equipment manufacturer (OEM) customers for Windows to discourage its customers from using competing operating systems.

INNOVATION IN ACTION

ARM Holdings

ARM Holdings designs and licenses high-performance, low-energy-consumption 16- and 32-bit reduced instruction set computing (RISC) chips, which are used extensively in mobile devices such as cellphones, cameras, electronic organizers and smart cards. ARM was established in 1990 as a joint venture between Acorn Computers in the UK and Apple Computer. Acorn did not pioneer the RISC architecture, but it was the first to market a commercial RISC processor in the mid-1980s. Perhaps ironically, the first application of ARM technology was in the relatively unsuccessful Apple Newton Personal Digital Assistant (PDA). One of the most recent successful applications has been in the Apple iPod. ARM designs but does not manufacture chips, and receives royalties of between 5 cents and US$2.50 for every chip produced under licence. Licensees include Apple, Ericsson, Fujitsu, HP, NEC, Nintendo, Sega, Sharp, Sony, Toshiba and 3Com. In 1999 it announced joint ventures with leading chip manufacturers such as Intel and Texas Instruments to design and build chips for the next generation of hand-held devices. It is estimated that ARM-designed processors were used in 10 million devices in 1996, 50 million in 1998, 120 million devices sold in 1999, and a billion sold in 2004, and more than 2 billion in 2006, representing around 80% of all mobile devices. In 1998 the company was floated in London and on the Nasdaq in New York, and it achieved a market capitalization of £3 billion in December 1999, with an annual revenue growth of 40% to £15.7 million. The company employs around 400 staff, 250 of which are based in Cambridge in the UK, with an average age of 27. It spends almost 30% of revenues on R&D. The company has created 30 millionaires among its staff.

Since the mid-1980s the universities have increasingly used IPR in an effort to commercialize technology and increase income. Changes in funding and law have clearly encouraged many more universities to establish licensing and technology transfer departments, but while the level of patenting has increased significantly as a result, the income and impact have been relatively small. The number of patents granted to US universities doubled between 1984 and 1989, and doubled again between 1989 and 1997. In 1979 the number of patents granted to US universities was only 264, compared to 2436 in 1997.

There are a number of explanations for this significant increase in patent activity. Changes in government funding and intellectual property law played a role, but detailed analysis indicates that the most significant reason was technological opportunity. For example, there is strong evidence that the scientific and commercial quality of patents has fallen since the mid-1980s as a result of these policy changes, and that the distribution of activity has a very long tail.

Measured in terms of the number of patents held or exploited, or by income from patent and software licenses, commercialization of technology is highly concentrated in a small number of elite universities which were highly active prior to changes to funding policy and law: the top 20 US universities account for 70% of the patent activity. Moreover, at each of these elite universities a very small number of key patents account for most of the licensing income; the 5 most successful patents typically account for 70–90% of total income. The average income from a university license is only around US$60 000, whereas the average return from a university spin-out firm was more than 10 times this.

This suggests that a (rare) combination of research excellence and critical mass is required to succeed in the commercialization of technology. Nonetheless, technological opportunity has reduced some of the barriers to commercialization. Specifically, the growing importance of developments in the biosciences and software present new opportunities for universities to benefit from the commercialization of technology.

The successful exploitation of IPR also incurs costs and risks:

■ Cost of search, registration and renewal;

■ Need to register in various national markets;

■ Full and public disclosure of your idea;

■ Need to be able to enforce.

In most countries the basic registration fee for a patent is relatively modest, but in addition applying for a patent includes the cost of professional agents, such as patent agents, translation for foreign patents, official registration

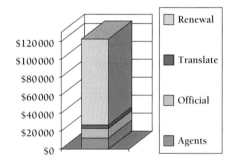

Figure 6.5   Typical lifetime cost of a single patent from the European Patent Office.

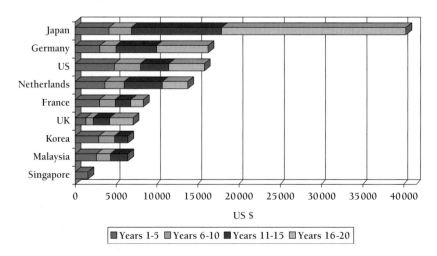

Figure 6.6   Lifetime patent costs in different national markets.

fees in all relevant countries and renewal fees. As a result the lifetime cost for a single non-pharmaceutical patent in the main European markets would be around £80 000, and the addition of the USA and Japan some £40 000 more. Patents in the other Asian markets are cheaper, at up to £5000 per country, but the cumulative cost becomes prohibitive, particularly for lone inventors or small firms. Pharmaceutical patents are much more expensive, up to 5 times more, due to the complexity and length of the documentation. In addition to these costs, firms must consider the competitive risk of public disclosure, and the potential cost of legal action should the patent be infringed (Figure 6.5). Costs vary by country, because of the size and attractiveness of different national markets, and also because of differences in government policy. For example, in many Asian countries the policy is to encourage patenting by domestic firms, so the process is cheaper. An exception is Japan, which historically has discouraged patenting to allow local firms to legally develop and exploit technologies from overseas (Figure 6.6).

Developing Personal Capabilities

We have argued in this chapter that knowledge is created, shared and exploited by interaction with different groups or communities of practice, both within and external to an organization. It is all too easy to mix with those with similar backgrounds, education or professions to our own, but this is unlikely to stimulate innovation and entrepreneurship. Here are 100 different ways of interacting with other individuals and groups, to help stimulate knowledge creation and transfer:

1 One-on-one conversation	18 Phone conversations one-on-one	35 Braille
2 A small group	19 Video conferences	36 Audio tapes
3 Multiple small groups	20 Telephone conferences	37 Compact disc (CD)
4 Across functions	21 Web or internet	38 Within cultures
5 Within functions	22 Bookmarks	39 Across cultures
6 Organization-wide	23 Signs	40 On pens
7 Across organizations	24 Clothing	41 Paging systems
8 At workplaces	25 Flipcharts	42 Cell phones
9 Between workplace and home	26 Music	43 Answering machines
10 At homes	27 Dance	44 Voice mail
11 Conferences	28 Games	45 Articles
12 Training courses	29 Role-playing	46 Fax
13 Workshops	30 Arena or stadium events	47 Intercom
14 Conventions	31 Out-of-doors	48 FedEx
15 Trade shows	32 Indoors	49 DHL
16 E-mail	33 Smoke signals	50 UPS
17 Letters through the mail	34 Sign language	51 Networks (people)

52 Bulletin boards	69 Flyers	86 LAN
53 Mailboxes	70 Parties	87 Carrier pigeons
54 Notes	71 PowerPoint presentations	88 Focused on self
55 AOL instant message	72 Paintings, art and sculpture	(introspection)
56 Group ware	73 Drawings and illustrations	89 Focused on others
57 Body language	74 Graphic images and icons	90 Talking
58 Newsletters	75 Cafes	91 Listening
59 Brochures	76 Over meals	92 Whispering
60 Place mats	77 On planes	93 Shouting
61 Advertisements	78 On trains	94 Seeing
62 Magazines	79 On buses	95 Tasting
63 Books	80 In cars	96 Smelling
64 Billboards	81 On boats	97 With content
65 TV	82 Lounges, pubs and bars	98 With silence
66 Radio	83 Sending messages with flowers	99 With meaning
67 Whiteboards	84 Singing telegrams	100 Storytelling.
68 Posters	85 Telex	

Source: From Isaksen, S. and Tidd, J. (2006) *Meeting the Innovation Challenge: Leadership for Transformation and Growth.* John Wiley & Sons, Ltd, Chichester.

ADVICE FOR FUTURE MANAGERS

When you need to contact a potential financial backer, manufacturer or other partner, or need to share your ideas with someone about a new product, process or business, you should consider a confidentiality or non-disclosure agreement (NDA) of some kind.

Such confidential ideas, or 'trade secrets', cannot be patented, but can be equally important commercially. Also, outside the USA (which has a 'first to invent' system, rather than the more common 'first to file' patent system), if you tell anyone about your invention before a patent application has been filed then this will invalidate the application.

An NDA is a legally binding document that records the terms under which you exchange secret information. This does not mean that a duty of confidence does not arise in the absence of an NDA, but a written agreement gives added legal weight. Also, having a signed NDA means you will be able to share more with a potential partner, and are therefore more likely to secure their support.

However, some professional advisers and organizations will be unable or unwilling to sign a NDA. This is often because they do not want to receive any confidential information which might prejudice or conflict with projects they may already be working on. In such cases it is best to describe and discuss a potential innovation in more general terms of its business benefits, rather than in more detailed technical features and functions.

If you do decide to apply for a patent, the process in most countries is relatively simple, but can be time-consuming and will require the involvement (and payment!) of professional advisers, including the services of a registered patent agent. The basic process is as follows:

- First prepare a *patent specification*, including drawings if these are useful in describing the invention. The specification should contain a full description of your invention, and it is important that this is as complete a description as possible, as you cannot make any changes to your specification once you have filed your application.

- Complete a *formal application* form, with two copies of your patent specification and, with the appropriate fees, request a search. This must be done by a given date, usually within a year of your filing date, to avoid the application being terminated.

- The Patent Office conducts a *preliminary examination* to make sure your application meets certain formal requirements, and searches through published patents to assess whether or not the invention is new and inventive. This can take time, typically many months, and in some countries the backlog is years.

- If you satisfy the formal requirements, you pay another fee and the Patent Office *publishes your patent application* around 18 months from your filing date (or sooner if you have requested a priority date).

- Finally, you complete and file an *examination form*, together with the appropriate fee, within six months of publication of the application. The Patent Office then examines your application, and advises you of any necessary revisions. If your application meets all the requirements of the relevant Patents Acts, they will grant your patent, publish your application in its final form and send you a certificate. So from start to finish the process will take two or more years.

For further advice in the UK see www.patent.gov.uk, or the relevant patent office in your country.

STRATEGIC AND SOCIAL IMPACT

The UK Treasury established the agency Partnerships UK (PUK) in 2000 to help commercialize public sector knowledge. It is a public–private venture, 49% owned by the UK government and 51% by the private sector firms, including Abbey, British Land, Group 4 Securicor, Prudential, Serco and Sun Life. It has acted as an adviser in many public–private partnerships infrastructure projects in the health and education sectors, but has also made more targeted investments in higher-risk technologies from the biotechnology and defence sectors. For example, medical diagnostics technologies from the defence science and technology labs have received funding of £1–2 million per project, and innovations from various universities have received similar levels of funding, such as £1.5 million for the Smart Hologram project to development of sensor holograms at Cambridge and £750 000 to the CellTran project to develop skin-regeneration technology at Sheffield.

In the UK, the Lambert Review of Business–University Collaboration reported in December 2003. It reviewed the commercialization of intellectual property by universities in the UK, and also made international comparisons of policy and performance. The UK has a similar pattern of concentration of activity to the USA: in 2002 80% of UK universities made no patent applications, whereas 5% filed 20 or more patents; similarly, 60% of universities issued no new licences, but 5% issued more than 30. However, in the UK there has been a bias towards spin-outs rather than licensing, which the Lambert Report criticizes. It argues that spin-outs are often too complex and unsustainable, and of low quality – a third in the UK are fully funded by the parent university and attract no external private funding. In 2002 universities in the UK created over 150 new spin-out firms, compared to almost 500 by universities in the USA; the respective figures for new licences that year were 648 and 4058. As a proportion of R&D expenditure, this suggests that British universities place greater emphasis on spin-outs than their North American counterparts, and less on licensing. Lambert argues that universities in the UK may place too high a price on their intellectual property, and that contracts often lack clarity of ownership. Both of these problems discourage businesses from licensing intellectual property from universities, and may encourage universities to commercialize their technologies through wholly owned spin-outs.

Chapter Summary

- The generation, acquisition, sharing and exploitation of knowledge are central to the successful practice of innovation and entrepreneurship. However, there is a wide range of different types of knowledge, and each plays a different role.

- Tacit knowledge is critical, but is difficult to capture, and draws upon individual expertise and experience. Therefore, where possible, tacit knowledge needs to be made more explicit and codified to allow it to be more readily shared and applied to different contexts.

- One of the key challenges in innovation is to identify and exchange knowledge across different groups and organizations, and a number of mechanisms can help, mostly social in nature, but supported by technology.

- In some cases, codified knowledge can form the basis of legal intellectual property rights (IPR), and these can form a basis for the commercialization of knowledge. A range of IPR exist, but those most applicable to technology and innovation are patents, copyright and design rights and registration.

- Care needs to be taken when using IPR, as these can divert scarce management and financial resources, and can expose an organization to imitation and illegal use of IPR.

Key Terms Defined

Boundary object or practice Something of interest to two or more communities of practice. Different communities of practice will have a stake in it, but from different perspectives. A boundary object might be a shared document, for example, a quality manual; an artefact, for example, a prototype; a technology, for example, a database; or a practice, for example, a product design.

Codified knowledge Knowledge that has been structured and simplified, which facilitates its transfer and use in different contexts.

Community of practice A group of people related by a shared task, process or the need to solve a problem, rather than by formal structural or functional relationships.

Copyright Legal rights associated with the *expression* of ideas, and not the ideas themselves, only available if the idea is made explicit or codified, for example, in a book or recording, and can demonstrate some effort or skill used. There is no requirement for registration, and the test of originality is low compared to patent law.

Explicit knowledge Can be codified, that is expressed in numerical, textual or graphical terms, and therefore is more easily communicated, for example, the design of a product.

Intellectual property rights (IPR) Includes all formal legal means of identifying or registering rights, including patents, copyright design rights and trademarks.

Knowledge translator An individual able to express the interests of one community in terms of another community's perspective. Therefore the translator must be sufficiently conversant with both knowledge domains and trusted by both communities.

Knowledge broker Differs from a translator in that they participate in different communities rather than simply mediating between them. They represent overlaps between communities, and are typically people loosely linked to several communities and are able to facilitate knowledge flows between them. An example might be a quality manager responsible for the quality of a process that crosses several different functional groups.

Patent A limited legal monopoly, usually for 20 years, provided an invention satisfies certain requirements, including novelty, inventive step and application.

Tacit or implicit knowledge Personal, experiential, context-specific and hard to articulate, formalize and communicate.

TRIZ – a system of problem-solving and opportunity-seeking developed by Genrich Altshuller identifies standard solutions to common technical problems distilled from an analysis of 1.5 million patents, and applies these in different contexts.

Further Reading and Resources

Knowledge management and intellectual property are both very large and complex subjects. For knowledge management, we would recommend the books by Friso den Hertog, *The Knowledge Enterprise* (Imperial College Press, London, 2000) for applications and examples; and for theory Nonaka's *The Knowledge Creating Company* (Oxford University Press, Oxford, 1995). We provide a good combination of theory, research and practice of knowledge management in *From Knowledge Management to Strategic Competence*, edited by Joe Tidd (Imperial College Press, London, 2006, 2nd edn), which tries to establish the links between knowledge, innovation and performance. For a more structured approach to the subject, see DeFillippi, R., Arthur, M. and Lindsay, V. (2006) *Knowledge at work*, Blackwell Publishing.

More critical accounts of the concept and practice of knowledge management can be found in the editorial by Jack Swan and Harry Scarbrough (2001), Knowledge management: concepts and controversies, *Journal of Management Studies*, **38** (7), 913–921; Storey, J. and Barnett, E. (2000), Knowledge management initiatives: learning from failure, *Journal of Knowledge Management*, **4** (2), 145–156; and Pritchard, C., Hull, R., Chumer, M. and Willmott, H. (2000) *Managing Knowledge: Critical Investigations of Work and Learning*, Macmillan, London.

For understanding the role and limitations of intellectual property, we like the theoretical approach adopted by David Teece, for example, in his book *The Transfer and Licensing of Know-how and Intellectual Property* (World Scientific Publishing, London, 2006), or for a more applied treatment of the topic see *Licensing Best Practices: Strategic, Territorial and Technology Issues*, edited by Robert Goldscheider and Alan Gordon (John Wiley & Sons, Ltd, Chichester, 2006), which includes practical case studies of licensing from many different countries and sectors. The open source movement is covered widely, but often in a partisan way, and a good balanced discussion which links this to innovation can be found in *Open Source: A Multidisciplinary Approach*, by Moreno Muffatto (Imperial College Press, London, 2006).

References

1 Blackler, F. (1995) Knowledge, knowledge work organizations: an overview and interpretation. *Organization Studies*, **16** (60), 1021–1046.

2 Bessant, J. (2003) *High-Involvement Innovation*. John Wiley & Sons, Ltd, Chichester.

3 Simon, H.A. (1996) Bounded rationality and organizational learning, in Cohen, M.D. and Sproull, L.S. (eds) *Organizational Learning*, 175–187. Sage, London.

4 Nonaka, I. and Takeuchi, H. (1995). *The Knowledge Creating Company*. Oxford University Press, Oxford.

5 Boisot, M. and Griffiths, D. Are there any competencies out there? Identifying and using technical competencies, in Tidd, J. (ed.), *From Knowledge Management to Strategic Competence*, 2nd edn. 249–307. Imperial College Press, London.

6 Crespi, G., Criscuolo, C., and Haskel, J. (2006). Information technology, organisational change and productivity growth: evidence from UK firms, *The Future of Science, Technology and Innovation Policy: Linking Research and Practice*, SPRU 40th Anniversary Conference, Brighton, UK, September.

7 Hall, R. (2006). What are strategic competencies?, in Tidd, J. (ed.), *From Knowledge Management to Strategic Competence*, 2nd edn, 26–49. Imperial College Press, London.

8 O'Leary, D. (1998). Knowledge management systems: converting and connecting, *IEEE Intelligent Systems*, **13** (3), 30–33; Becker, M. (2001). Managing dispersed knowledge: organizational problems, managerial strategies and their effectiveness, *Journal of Management Studies*, **38** (7), 1037–1051.

9 Brown, J.S. and Duguid, P. (2001). Knowledge and organization: a social practice perspective, *Organization Science*, **12** (2), 198–213; Brown, J.S. and Duguid, P. (1991). Organizational learning and communities of practice: towards a unified view of working, learning and organization, *Organizational Science*, **2** (1), 40–57; Hildreth, P., Kimble, C. and Wright, P. (2000). Communities of practice in the distributed international environment, *Journal of Knowledge Management*, **4** (1), 27–38.

10 Star, S.L. and Griesemer, J.R. (1989). Institutional ecology, translations and boundary objects, *Social Studies of Science*, **19**, 387–420; Carlile, P.R. (2002). A pragmatic view of knowledge and boundaries: boundary objects in new product development, *Organization Science*, **13** (4), 442–455.

11 Granovetter, M. (1976). The strength of weak ties, *American Journal of Sociology*, 1360–1380; Cummings, J.N. (2004). Work groups, structural diversity, and knowledge sharing in a global organization, *Management Science*, **50** (3), 352–364.

12 Den Hertog, J.F. and Huizenga, E. (2000). *The Knowledge Enterprise*. Imperial College Press, London.

13 Tranfield, D., Young, M., Partington, D., Bessant, J. and Sapsed, J. (2006). Knowledge management routines for innovation projects: developing a hierarchical process model, in Tidd, J. (ed.), *From Knowledge Management to Strategic Competence*, 2nd edn, 126–149. Imperial College Press, London; Coombs, R. and Hull, R. (1998). Knowledge management practices and path-dependency in innovation, *Research Policy*, 237–253.

14 Narin, F (2006). Assessing technological competencies, in Tidd, J. (ed.), *From Knowledge Management to Strategic Competence*, 2nd edn, 179–219. Imperial College Press, London.

Discussion Questions

1 Consider a university. What types of data, information and knowledge might be relevant to its management and performance?

2 For an organization with which you are familiar, identify an example of each of these six types of knowledge.

Embrained:_____

Embodied:_____

Encultured:_____

Embedded:_____

Encoded:_____

Commodified:_____

3 In what ways can tacit knowledge be made explicit and codified?

4 What mechanisms exist to help the sharing and transfer of knowledge within an organization?

5 What are the similarities and differences between Nonaka's and Boisot's models of knowledge generation and transfer?

6 What are the advantages and disadvantages of using formal IPR to commercialize an innovation?

Team Exercise

For each of the following cases suggest a possible boundary object or practice to encourage knowledge sharing:

1 The design and production groups in a car company;

2 The operations and marketing groups in a service organization;

3 Different research groups in a technical centre.

Assignment and Case Study Questions

Using the framework in Figure 6.1, identify the most important types of knowledge in the following cases.

1 a hospital

2 a factory

3 a construction company

4 a software consultancy.

CASE STUDY 6

Exploring Innovation in Action – Evolving Knowledge Needs of a New Venture

Helax AB was founded in 1986 by 3 staff of Uppsala University in Sweden. The three founders had degrees in physics, mathematics and computer science, and had experience of using IT in medical applications, in particular radiotherapy. The founders successfully raised US$3 million of venture capital from private and government sources, enough for three years of working capital without any additional revenues.

The idea for the business originated in a public-funded research project called CART (Computer-Aided Radio Therapy), which aimed to create an integrated information management system for the records of cancer patients. This was believed to be desirable because such patients usually undertook a wide range of different examinations, scans, diagnosis and treatments over an extended period. By combining and tracking these data, it was hoped that the overall effectiveness of the therapy would be improved. The CART project successfully demonstrated that the success of therapy could be improved through better management of the patient data, identified user requirements for such a system, and had developed a number of the software sub-systems and components necessary to begin building a more integrated information management system. However, CART did not go as far as hoped, and never developed a functioning integrated system. Helax AB was created to take the work further, and to develop commercial applications.

So at start-up the three founders of the company inherited knowledge of the problem area, user requirements, and most importantly had formal knowledge relevant to potential solutions within the combined fields of computer science, mathematics and physics. Based on the results of the CART project, a process map of the clinical process was developed, independent of any systems design. This was circulated to 30 international cancer centres for feedback, and this quasi-Delphi survey also helped to create potential customer awareness and buy-in for the future. The feedback was positive, and provided the basis for further development of the system. In 1988 the technology was installed in 2 hospitals for clinical trials and evaluation. At the core of this design was the dose-planning system, later to be renamed the

TMS (Treatment Management System). This architecture allowed Helax AB to act as a systems integrator by adding further components from other providers and partners.

The potential solution had two very different components. The first was specific to radiotherapy and concerned the planning of dosage levels. Dose-planning requires knowledge of the relationship between radiation levels and patterns and their effects on biological tissues and cells. This subject had been explored in a PhD project jointly funded by Helax AB and Uppsala University. The second area of knowledge was more generic, and concerned with information management. These two fields of knowledge evolved in different ways as the new venture developed. The first was based on the knowledge generated and accumulated from the CART research, plus access to an extended external network of scientific research and clinical expertise. The second was more internal, but required extension by further recruitment.

Development was grouped into 3 different areas: hardware and operating systems architecture; software for the user interfaces; and quite separately, the development of the algorithms for calculating the doses, which required access to more basic science. Within a year the whole CART project group of 13 from Uppsala University had joined Helax AB, and in addition engineers with product development and commercial experience were recruited to help in design and development, bringing the total number of employees to 20 by 1990. Almost all employees had degrees, mainly in the physical sciences or engineering, but the company decided not to recruit medical expertise. Instead, it relied on a network of contacts in the medical community. By this time the original venture capital funding had been exhausted, and arguments between the founders and venture capital owners over the future direction of the firm resulted in the founders buying out the venture capitalists' interest in the firm.

By 1994 the company had installed its system in 11 of the 15 radiotherapy centres in Sweden, and had also achieved some sales in Germany and the UK. During this period the company developed some new knowledge and capabilities in production, and had an annual capacity to build 12 systems. However, in product development most of the knowledge-seeking effort was within the existing system design, and was aimed at fixing bugs and improving performance of the existing system by refining the dose algorithms. To extend its sales and international reach further, it established partnerships with Siemens, Philips and General Electric. This was rather too successful, and in the first 6 months of the Siemens partnership 60 new systems were ordered, equivalent to 5 years of production. Therefore Helax had to fundamentally change how it produced and installed the systems, and the increasing customer base demand created a need for maintenance, service and support for the installed systems. Initially the system developers undertook the new service and support function, but this placed strains on product development, and so the firm had to create a new service division and recruit new personnel with the relevant skills and experience.

The additional revenues from these sales allowed Helax to invest in research and development, and two product extensions were successfully launched between 1994 and 1998. Customers were demanding more standard interfaces compatible with Windows PCs, rather than the purpose-built and non-standard interface offered. These more fundamental attempts to upgrade and change the software failed, and Helax experienced significant problems recruiting and retaining the necessary staff experienced in more structured software development The legacy of the unstructured development approach of the original founders and CART team resulted in underinvestment in formal software engineering, and attempts to outsource this development had also failed.

The company continued to develop sales subsidiaries in Northern Europe, and extended its product market into other fields such as oncology with the development of the HOME (Helax Oncology Management Environment) system. However, efforts to enter the critical USA market were not successful, and in return for access to North America Helax sold out to the Canadian firm MDS Nordion. Helax in Uppsala is now a division of MDS Nordion, and a centre of excellence for the development of the HOME concept. The identity and knowledge of the founding group remains, but autonomy and control do not:

> *The 20 first employees have become, and still are, the core of the company. [But they have not] broadened their core function since they started, but have become mentors in the company's main process, i.e. the development of a system of radiography . . . but I don't think it is possible to break up and get the individuals to work together in a different perspective. (p. 422)*

Therefore over its 15-year life as an independent new venture, the knowledge needs of Helax have changed significantly. The new venture was founded based on the formal knowledge outputs of the CART research project, and the explicit knowledge of the 3 founders in the fields of physics, computer science and mathematics, plus their experience in the domains of informatics and radiography. The core knowledge base of the new venture was, and largely remained, a detailed knowledge of the whole radiography process, combined with the specific knowledge of dose-planning. Over time, the need for new internal knowledge of production systems and formal software development and engineering grew, and to a great extent these had to be satisfied by the recruitment of new staff with knowledge and experience of these fields. In addition, a wide range of external sources of knowledge had to be utilized to help translate the technology into a successful commercial venture. These included the local networks within medical research and clinical practice, and international networks for cancer treatment. The need for specialist national and product market knowledge and access demanded partnerships with large multinationals, and culminated in the sale of the company and loss of control.

Case Study Questions

1 Identify the different types of knowledge needed throughout the growth of the new venture.

2 What was the balance of internal and external sources of knowledge at different stages of the venture's development?

3 How else might Helax have commercialized its knowledge?

Source: From Saemundsson, R.J. (2004). Technical knowledge-seeking in a young and growing technology-based firm, *International Journal of Innovation Management*, **8** (4), 399–430.

Chapter 7
Exploiting Discontinuous Innovation

This chapter

- Introduces the concept of discontinuous innovation and its role in changing the rules of the game.

- Looks at the threats and the opportunities when such disruption occurs.

- Explores the ways in which new entrant organizations and established players can anticipate and deal with the challenge of discontinuous innovation.

- Reviews experience in trying to manage discontinuous innovation alongside 'steady-state' innovation.

- Underlines the continuing importance of entrepreneurial behaviour in new start-ups and in established organizations in dealing with discontinuities.

Learning Objectives

By the end of this chapter you will develop an understanding of:

- What discontinuous innovation is and how it represents a key strategic challenge.
- The different ways in which disruption can occur to established markets.
- The challenges in managing discontinuous innovation – in spotting emerging changes early and in organizing and acting to deal with them.
- Triggers of disruptive innovation.
- The difficulties in managing what is an uncertain and risky process.
- The key themes in thinking about how to manage this process effectively.

INNOVATION IN ACTION

Innovation in the Glass Industry

It's particularly important to understand that change doesn't come in standard-sized jumps. For much of the time it is essentially incremental, a process of gradual improvement over time on dimensions like price, quality, choice. For long periods of time nothing much shifts in either product offering or the way in which this is delivered (product and process innovation is incremental). But sooner or later someone somewhere will come up with a radical change which upsets the apple cart.

For example, the glass window business has been around for at least 600 years and is – since most houses, offices, hotels and shops have plenty of windows – a very profitable business to be in. But for most of those 600 years the basic process for making window glass hasn't changed. Glass is made in approximately flat sheets which are then ground down to a state where they are flat enough for people to see through them. The ways in which the grinding takes place have improved – what used to be a labour-intensive process became increasingly mechanized and even automated, and the tools and abrasives became progressively more sophisticated and effective. But underneath the same core process of grinding down to flatness was going on.

Then in 1952 Alastair Pilkington working in the UK firm of the same name began working on a process which revolutionized glass-making for the next 50 years. He got the idea while washing up when he noticed that the fat and grease from the plates floated on the top of the water – and he began thinking about producing glass in such a way that it could be cast to float on the surface of some other liquid and then be allowed to set. If this could be accomplished it might be possible to create a perfectly flat surface without the need for grinding and polishing.

Five years, millions of pounds and over 100 000 tonnes of scrapped glass, later the company achieved a working pilot plant and a further 2 years on began selling glass made by the float glass process. The process advantages included around 80% labour and 50% energy savings plus those which came because of the lack of need for abrasives, grinding equipment and so on. Factories could be made smaller and the overall time to produce glass dramatically cut. So successful was the process that it became – and still is – the dominant method for making flat glass around the world.

When change of this kind happens, the rules change and there is a scramble for position – some people fall off and new ones come on board. Eventually things settle down until the next discontinuous shift. The message in this for strategic innovation management is that we have to watch both trends and be able to contribute to continuous incremental improvement while also watching for and working on more radical and discontinuous shifts. Far from falling asleep, firms need to be wide awake and actively seeking the changes which will change the way their industry works. They shouldn't sleep too soundly anyway because history tells us that this pattern is common – someone somewhere *will* come up with a new product or process which will render current experience and capabilities redundant.

Introduction

Innovation matters – of course. As we've already seen, unless organizations change what they offer the world and the ways in which they create and deliver those offerings they risk falling behind in today's turbulent and complex environment. Smart firms know this and they invest time and take trouble to create systems, structures and processes to ensure a sustained flow of innovation.

But while they are highly competent at what we could call 'steady-state' innovation (essentially doing what they do but better) problems can occur when they confront the need for *discontinuous* innovation. History tells us that when technologies shift, new markets emerge, the regulatory rules of the game move or someone introduces a new business model then established players can suddenly become vulnerable. When confronted with the need to explore doing something radically different many fail the test.

INNOVATION IN ACTION

One of the founding fathers of the study of innovation was Joseph Schumpeter – a one-time finance minister of Austria and a prolific writer on the theme of innovation. His theory is essentially based on this story – he saw the role of the entrepreneur as one constantly seeking out opportunities to do something different and, through being the only one, to secure monopoly profit. Of course, as soon as others see him doing so they will desperately try to imitate and get a piece of this action for themselves – with the result that the game gradually loses its interest and so our entrepreneur goes off to seek the next new big and different thing. This cycle of entrepreneurial search and exploitation of ideas as innovations is what Schumpeter saw as driving the economy. And at its heart was the principle he termed 'creative destruction' – the quest for the killer application which doesn't just offer something dramatically new but in the process overturns the tables on the established ways of doing that thing.

A key part of the problem is that dealing with discontinuity requires a very different set of capabilities for organizing and managing innovation. Searching in unlikely places, building links to strange partners, allocating resources to high-risk ventures, exploring new ways of looking at the business – all of these challenge the 'normal' way we approach the innovation problem. And while we know a lot about how to manage the steady-state kind of innovation we're much less clear about where and how to start building discontinuous innovation capability.

INNOVATION IN ACTION

The cosy world of telecommunications hadn't changed much until the 1990s when mobile communications became a reality. As cellular systems proliferated, so did competition – and faced with dramatically expanding technological and market boundaries, there were winners and losers. But no sooner had this technology-led revolution begun to settle down with a few players coming to dominate than the game was on the move again, this time driven by the potential of using voice-over-Internet-protocol (VOIP) to offer effectively free calls anywhere in the world. As with the early days of mobiles there were plenty of players and many competing services, standards and business models – from new entrants but increasingly from fixed line and mobile players fighting back. One of the early winners has been Skype – a concept born out of experience in peer-to-peer networking (Kazaa) and using viral marketing across the Internet to drive early awareness. Skype managed to attract around 54 million users to its model and was eventually sold to eBay for an estimated US$2.6 billion.

So what do we know? Let's go back to basics and remind ourselves of two types of innovation – that which is primarily about 'doing what we do, but better' and that which involves something completely different. The former tends to be about building on what we already know, incrementally improving along product or process trajectories. That kind of innovation tends, not surprisingly, to favour the established players – they're the ones with the experiences, the resources, the wherewithal to manage technical and market research to push the boundaries. Small and new entrant firms have a hard time breaking into this.

But when something shocks the cosy set-up it can shatter – and in the process open up opportunities for new players to enter what becomes a new game. In fact it often favours them because they don't have the prior commitments to the old market or technology framework, they're not scared of cannibalizing their established businesses with the new one, since they don't have one to cannibalize! In short they have nothing to lose and a lot to gain.

History suggests that when such shocks happen – be they technological shifts, the emergence of totally new markets or the bringing in of a new business model which reframes the rules of the game – they favour the new entrant over the established incumbent. But this is not a hard and fast rule – there are plenty of examples of established players who take on the new and use it to enhance their competitive position. Think of firms like 3M, Philips, Siemens or General Electric which have been in business for over a century – their track record is one of managing both continuous (do what we do, better) and discontinuous innovation, often pioneering or riding on the front of the waves of change. Equally we hear about the successful new entrants when a wave of change breaks – but we don't know about the many others who tried and failed to build something out of the new opportunity. What is clear is that standing still in the face of discontinuous change is not an option. Firms need to rediscover and use entrepreneurial flair to find and exploit high-risk new opportunities – and they need some very different approaches to managing the conversion of those weak signals into successful and ground-breaking innovations.

This chapter looks at the challenge of managing discontinuous innovation and what individual entrepreneurs and established organizations might do to take advantage of the opportunities it throws up.

The Problem and the Opportunity in Discontinuous Innovation

Back in the 1880s there was a thriving industry in the north-eastern United States in the lucrative business of selling ice. The business model was deceptively simple – work hard to cut chunks of ice out of the frozen northern wastes, wrap the harvest quickly and ship it as quickly as possible to the warmer southern states – and increasingly overseas – where it could be used to preserve food. In its heyday this was a big industry – in 1886 the record harvest ran to 25 million tons – and it employed thousands of people in cutting, storing and shipping the product. And it was an industry with strong commitment to innovation – developments in ice-cutting, snow ploughs, insulation techniques and logistics underpinned the industry's strong growth.[1]

Meanwhile in another part of the universe – or at least in laboratories around the globe – researchers like the young Carl von Linde were working on the emerging problems of refrigeration. It wasn't long before artificial ice-making became a reality and by 1873 a patented commercial refrigeration system was on the market. In the years which followed the industry grew – in 1879 there were 35 plants and 10 years later 222 making artificial ice. Effectively this development signposted the end of the road for the ice-harvesting industry – although for a while both industries grew alongside each other, learning and innovating and together expanding the overall market for ice. Eventually the ice-harvesting industry was replaced by the new refrigeration industry dominated by new entrant firms.

From Freezers to Servers – the Pattern's the Same

This pattern of long periods of innovation under relatively steady conditions punctuated by dramatic shifts is a common one. Let's wind the film forwards to the last part of the twentieth century and a very different industry – the computer disk-drive business. Just like the ice industry it was a thriving sector in which the voracious demands of the growing mini-computer industry for powerful machines for engineering, banking and other industries meant there was a booming market for disk-drive storage units. Firms in the industry worked closely with their customers, understanding the particular needs and demands for more storage capacity, faster access times, smaller footprints and so on. All fine – until a discontinuous change rocked the happily sailing boat of the industry.

INNOVATION IN ACTION

We shouldn't be surprised at this – new markets do not emerge in their full scale or with clearly identifiable needs but start out as messy, uncertain and risky places with small size and dubious growth prospects. The early days of the PC industry were characterized by enthusiasm among a group of nerds and geeks running small and highly speculative ventures. These hardly represented a serious alternative market to the multi-billion-dollar business of supplying the makers of mainstream mini-computers. As Steve Jobs described their attempts to engage interest, 'So we went to Atari and said, "Hey, we've got this amazing thing, even built with some of your parts, and what do you think about funding us? Or we'll give it to you. We just want to do it. Pay our salary, we'll come work for you." And they said, "No." So then we went to Hewlett-Packard, and they said, "Hey, we don't need you. You haven't got through college yet." '

In this case the dramatic shift wasn't due to technology but triggered by the emergence of a new market with very different expectations. While the emphasis in the mini-computer world was on high performance and the requirement for storage units correspondingly technologically sophisticated, the emerging market for personal computers had a very different shape. These were much less clever machines, capable of running much simpler software and with massively inferior performance – but at a price which a very different set of people could afford. Importantly although simpler they were capable of doing most of the basic tasks which a much wider market was interested in – simple arithmetical calculations, word processing and basic graphics. As the market for these grew so the learning effects meant that these capabilities improved – but from a much lower cost base. This shift affected not only the makers of the new personal computers but also the new firms who supplied them with simpler and lower-cost disk-drives. In the end there was the same pattern as we saw in the ice industry–but from a different direction. Of the major manufacturers in the disk-drive industry in the 1990s only a handful survived – and leadership in the new industry shifted to new entrant firms working with a very different model (Christensen, 1997).

These are not isolated examples but typical of a pattern in innovation. Think about the revolution in flying which the low-cost carriers have brought about. Here the challenge came via a new business model rather than technology – based on the premise that if prices could be kept low a large new market could be opened up. In order to make low prices pay a number of problems needed solving – keeping load factors high, cutting administration costs, enabling rapid turnaround times at terminals – but once the model began to work it attracted not only new customers but increasingly established flyers who saw the advantages of lower prices.

What these – and many other examples – have in common is that they represent the challenge of *discontinuous* innovation. None of the industries were lacking in innovation or a commitment to further change. But the ice harvesters, mini-computer disk companies or the established airlines all carried on their innovation on a stage covered with a relatively predictable carpet. But shifts in technology, in new market emergence or in new business models pulled this carpet out from under the firms – and created a new set of conditions on which a new game would be played out. The trouble is that under such conditions, it is the new players who tend to do better because they don't have to wrestle with learning new tricks and letting go of their old ones. This is why discontinuous changes can often be *disruptive* to established players.

INNOVATION IN ACTION

Technological Excellence May Not Be Enough

In the 1970s Xerox was the dominant player in photocopiers, having built the industry from its early days when it was founded on the radical technology pioneered by Chester Carlsen and the Battelle Institute. But despite their prowess in the core technologies and continuing investment in maintaining an edge it found itself seriously threatened by a new generation of small copiers developed by new entrants linking several Japanese players. Despite the fact that Xerox had enormous experience in the industry and a deep understanding of the core technology it took them almost eight years of mishaps and false starts to introduce a competitive product. In that time Xerox lost around half its market share and suffered severe financial problems. As Henderson and Clark put it, in describing this case, 'Apparently modest changes to the existing technology ... have quite dramatic consequences'.[2]

In similar fashion in the 1950s the electronics giant RCA developed a prototype portable transistor-based radio using technologies which it had come to understand well. However it saw little reason to promote such an apparently inferior technology and continued to develop and build its high-range devices. By contrast Sony used it to gain access to the consumer market and to build a whole generation of portable consumer devices – and in the process acquired considerable technological experience which enabled them to enter and compete successfully in higher-value, more complex markets.

Innovation Life Cycles – from Discontinuity to Steady-state

In their pioneering work on this theme two US researchers (William Abernathy and James Utterback) developed a model describing the pattern in terms of three distinct phases.[3] Initially, under discontinuous conditions, there is what they term a fluid phase during which there is high uncertainty along two dimensions:

- The target – what will the new configuration be and who will want it?
- The technical – how will we harness new technological knowledge to create and deliver this?

No one knows what the 'right' configuration of technological means and market needs will be and so there is extensive experimentation (accompanied by many failures) and fast learning by a range of players including many new entrepreneurial businesses.

Gradually these experiments begin to converge around what they call a dominant design – something which begins to set up the rules of the game. This represents a convergence around the most popular (importantly not necessarily the most technologically sophisticated or elegant) solution to the emerging configuration. At this point a 'bandwagon' begins to roll and innovation options become increasingly channelled around a core set of possibilities – what another researcher, Giovanni Dosi, calls a 'technological trajectory'. It becomes increasingly difficult to explore outside this space because entrepreneurial interest and the resources which that brings increasingly focus on possibilities within the dominant design corridor.[4]

This can apply to products or processes; in both cases the key characteristics become stabilized and experimentation moves to getting the bugs out and refining the dominant design. For example, the nineteenth-century chemical industry moved from making soda ash (an essential ingredient in making soap, glass and a host of other products) from the earliest days where it was produced by burning vegetable matter through to a sophisticated chemical reaction which was carried out on a batch process (the Leblanc process) which was one of the drivers of the Industrial Revolution. This process dominated for nearly a century but was in turn replaced by a new generation of continuous processes which used electrolytic techniques and which originated in Belgium where they were developed by the Solvay brothers. Moving to the Leblanc process or the Solvay process did not happen overnight; it took decades of work to refine and improve the processes, and to fully understand the chemistry and engineering required to get consistent high quality and output.

The same pattern can be seen in products. For example, the original design for a camera is something which goes back to the early nineteenth century and – as a visit to any science museum will show – involved all sorts of ingenious solutions. The dominant design gradually emerged with an architecture which we would recognize – shutter and lens arrangement, focusing principles, back plate for film or plates, and so on. But this design was then modified still further – for example, with different lenses, motorized drives, flash technology – and, in the case of George Eastman's work, to creating a simple and relatively 'idiot-proof' model camera (the Box Brownie) which opened up photography to a mass market. More recent development has seen a similar fluid phase around digital-imaging devices.

ADVICE FOR FUTURE MANAGERS

The pattern can be seen in many studies and its implications for innovation management are important. In particular it helps us understand why established organizations often find it hard to deal with discontinuous change. Organizations build capabilities around a particular trajectory and those who may be strong in the later (specific) phase of an established trajectory often find it hard to move into the new one. (The example of the firms which successfully exploited the transistor in the early 1950s is a good case in point – many were new ventures, sometimes started by enthusiasts in their garage, yet they rose to challenge major players in the electronics industry like Raytheon.

So one important management skill is to develop the ability to look with more than one pair of eyes at the industry in which you operate. What's going on at the edges? How could someone else reframe this line of business and create a new fluid state? If such a state starts to emerge can we develop an approach more like that of a new entrant firm?

The period in which the dominant design emerges and emphasis shifts to imitation and development around it is termed the 'transitional phase' in the Abernathy and Utterback model. Activities move from radical concept development to more focused efforts geared around product differentiation and to delivering it reliably, cheaply, with higher quality, extended functionality and so on.

As the concept matures still further so incremental innovation becomes more significant and emphasis shifts to factors like cost – which means efforts within the industries which grow up around these product areas tend to focus increasingly on rationalization, on scale economies and on process innovation to drive out cost and improve productivity. Product innovation is increasingly about differentiation through customization to meet the particular needs of specific users. Abernathy and Utterback term this the 'specific phase'.[5]

INNOVATION IN ACTION

A good example of this can be seen in the case of bicycles which went through an extended period of fluidity in design options before the dominant diamond frame emerged which has characterized the industry for the past century. You can find out more in Walsh, V., Roy, R., Potter, S. and Bruce, M. (1992). *Winning by Design: Technology, Product Design and International Competitiveness.* Basil Blackwell, Oxford.

Finally the stage is set for change – the scope for innovation becomes smaller and smaller while outside – for example, in the laboratories and imaginations of research scientists – new possibilities are emerging. Eventually a new technology emerges which has the potential to challenge all the by now well-established rules – and the game is disrupted. In the camera case, for example, this is happening with the advent of digital photography which is having an impact on cameras and the overall service package around how we get, keep and share our photographs.

Table 7.1   Stages in the innovation life cycle

Innovation characteristic	Fluid pattern	Transitional phase	Specific phase
Competitive emphasis placed on . . .	Functional product performance	Product variation	Cost reduction
Innovation stimulated by . . .	Information on user needs, technical inputs	Opportunities created by expanding internal technical capability	Pressure to reduce cost, improve quality, etc.
Predominant type of innovation	Frequent major changes in products	Major process innovations required by rising volume	Incremental product and process innovation
Product line	Diverse, often including custom designs	Includes at least one stable or dominant design	Mostly undifferentiated standard products
Production processes	Flexible and inefficient – aim is to experiment and make frequent changes	Becoming more rigid and defined	Efficient, often capital-intensive and relatively rigid.

In our chemical case this is happening with biotechnology and the emergence of the possibility of no longer needing giant chemical plants but instead moving to small-scale operations using live organisms genetically engineered to produce what we need.

Although originally developed for manufactured products the model also works for services – for example, the early days of Internet banking were characterized by a typically fluid phase with many options and models being offered. This gradually moved to a transitional phase, building a dominant design consensus on the package of services offered, the levels and nature of security and privacy support, the interactivity of websites, and so on. The field has now become mature with much of the competition shifting to marginal issues like relative interest rates.

Table 7.1 sets out the main elements of this model.

Discontinuous Can Be *Disruptive*

The term disruptive innovation is particularly associated with the work of Clayton Christensen, a US scholar who looked at the patterns of change in a number of industries including computer disk-drives (outlined above), earthmoving equipment, and steelmaking.[6] He noticed a pattern which seemed to run through all of these cases – and one which he has subsequently applied to over 50 industries. For much of the time there is a stability around markets where innovation of the 'do better' variety takes place and is well-managed. Close relationships with existing customers are fostered and the system is configured to deliver a steady stream of what the market wants – and usually a great deal more! What he terms 'technology overshoot' is often a characteristic of this, where markets are offered more and more features which they may never use or place much value on but which come as part of the package. (Think about software like Microsoft Word and ask whether you really do make use of all the features or just a small but very useful subset? What some programmers call 'bloatware' is another way of thinking about technology overshoot.)

But somewhere else there is another group of potential users who have very different needs – usually for something much simpler and cheaper – which will help them get something done. For example, the emergent home computer industry began among a small group of hobbyists who wanted simple computing capabilities at a much lower price than was available from the mini-computer suppliers. In turn the builders of those early PCs wanted disk drives which were much simpler technologically but – importantly – much cheaper and so were not really interested in what the existing disk-drive industry had to offer. It was too high-tech, massively over-engineered for their needs and, most important, much too expensive.

Although they approached the existing drive makers none of them was interested in making such a device – not surprisingly since they were doing very comfortably supplying expensive high-performance equipment to an established mini-computer industry. Why should they worry about a fringe group of hobbyists as a market? Consequently the early PC makers had to look elsewhere – and found entrepreneurs willing to take the risks and experiment with trying to come up with a product which did meet their needs. It didn't happen overnight and there were plenty of failures on the way – and certainly the early drives were very poor performers in comparison with what was on offer in the mainstream industry. But gradually the PC market grew, moving from hobbyists to widespread home use and from there – helped by the emergence and standardization of the IBM PC – to the office and business environment. And as it grew and matured so it learned and the performance of the machines became much more impressive and reliable – but coming from a much lower cost base than mini-computers. The same thing happened to the disk drives within them – the small entrepreneurial firms who began in the game grew and learned and became large suppliers of reliable products which did the job – but at a massively lower price.

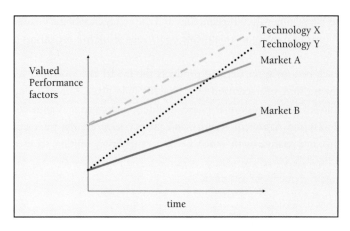

Figure 7.1   The pattern of disruptive innovation.

Eventually the fringe market which the original disk-drive makers had ignored because it didn't seem relevant or important enough to worry about grew to dominate – and by the time they realized this it was too late for many of them. The best they could hope for would be to be late-entrant imitators, coming from behind and hoping to catch up.

This pattern is essentially one of *disruption* – the rules of the game changed dramatically in the marketplace with some new winners and losers. Figure 7.1 shows the transition where the new market and suppliers gradually take over from the existing players. It can be seen in many industries – think about the low-cost airlines, for example. Here the original low-cost players didn't go head to head with the national flag carriers who offered the best routes, high levels of service and prime airport slots – all for a high price. Instead they sought new markets at the fringe – users who would accept a much lower level of service (no food, no seat allocation, no lounges, no frills at all) but for a basic safe flight would pay a much lower price. As these new users began to use the service and talk about it, so the industry grew and came to the attention of existing private and business travellers who were interested in lower-cost flights at least for short haul because they met their needs for a 'good enough' solution to their travel problem. Eventually the challenge hit the major airlines who found it difficult to respond because of their inherently much higher cost structure. Even those – like BA and KLM – which set up low-cost subsidiaries found themselves unable to manage with the very different business model that low-cost flying involved.

Importantly this is only one way to upset the market apple-cart. Low end market disruption is a potent threat – think what a producer in China might do to an industry like pump manufacturing if they began to offer a simple, low-cost 'good enough' household pump for US$10 instead of the high-tech, high-performance variants available from today's industry at prices 10 to 50 times as high? Or medical devices like asthma inhalers once they have come off-patent?

But disruption can also come when technology shifts – as in the ice industry – and opens up new possibilities. It can come through shifts in thinking around the dominant business model. It can come when external agencies like government change the regulatory rules of the game. The end effect is the same – the carpet is pulled out from beneath the market and a new set of rules comes into play. How new and established players handle the disruption is the challenge – but they should begin by recognizing that there is an increasing likelihood of disruption happening (Table 7.2).

Table 7.2   Sources of discontinuity

Triggers/sources of discontinuity	Explanation	Problems posed	Examples (of good and bad experiences)
New market emerges	Most markets evolve through a process of growth, segmentation, etc. But at certain times completely new markets emerge which cannot be analysed or predicted in advance or explored through using conventional market research/analytical techniques	Established players don't see it because they are focused on their existing markets May discount it as being too small or not representing their preferred target market – fringe/cranks dismissal Originators of new product may not see potential in new markets and may ignore them, – e.g. text-messaging	Disk-drives, excavators, mini-mills Mobile phone/SMS where market which actually emerged was not the one expected or predicted by originators
New technology emerges	Step change takes place in product or process technology – may result from convergence and maturing of several streams (e.g. industrial automation, mobile phones) or as a result of a single breakthrough (e.g. LED as new white light source)	Don't see it because beyond the periphery of technology search environment Not an extension of current areas but completely new field or approach Tipping point may not be a single breakthrough but convergence and maturing of established technological streams, whose combined effect is underestimated 'Not invented here' effect – new technology represents a different basis for delivering value – e.g. telephone vs. telegraphy	Ice-harvesting to cold storage Valves to solid-state electronics Photos to digital images Voice over Internet protocol telephony Filament light bulbs to LED sources
New political rules emerge	Political conditions which shape the economic and social rules may shift	Old mindset about how business is done, rules of the game, etc. are challenged and	Centrally planned to market economy e.g. former Soviet Union Apartheid to

(*continued overleaf*)

Table 7.2 (continued)

Triggers/sources of discontinuity	Explanation	Problems posed	Examples (of good and bad experiences)
	dramatically – for example, the collapse of communism meant an alternative model – capitalist, competition – as opposed to central planning – and many ex-state firms couldn't adapt their ways of thinking	established firms fail to understand or learn new rules	post-apartheid South Africa Free trade/globalization results in dismantling protective tariff and other barriers and new competition basis emerges
Running out of road	Firms in mature industries may need to escape the constraints of diminishing space for product and process innovation and the increasing competition of industry structures by either exit or by radical reorientation of their business	Current system is built around a particular trajectory and embedded in a steady-state set of innovation routines which militate against widespread search or risk-taking experiments	*Encyclopaedia Britannica* finally running out of road as it is displaced by first CD-based, then online and now open source encyclopaedias like Wikipedia Sometimes the firm manages to break out and establish a new trajectory – e.g. Nokia from timber products to mobile phones or Preussag, from metals and commodities to tourism
Sea change in market sentiment or behaviour	Public opinion or behaviour shifts slowly and then tips over into a new model – e.g. the music industry is in the midst of a (technology-enabled) revolution in delivery systems from buying records, tapes and CDs to direct download of tracks in MP3 and related formats Long-standing issues of concern to a minority accumulate momentum (sometimes through the action of pressure	Don't pick up on it or persist in alternative explanations – cognitive dissonance – until it may be too late Rules of the game suddenly shift and then new pattern gathers rapid momentum, wrong-footing existing players working with old assumptions	Apple, Napster, Dell, Microsoft vs. traditional music industry McDonalds, Burger King and obesity concerns Tobacco companies and smoking bans Oil/energy and others and global warming Opportunity for new energy sources like wind-power where Danish firms have come to dominate

Table 7.2 (*continued*)

Triggers/sources of discontinuity	Explanation	Problems posed	Examples (of good and bad experiences)
	groups) and suddenly the system switches/tips over – for example, social attitudes to smoking or health concerns about obesity levels and fast foods		
Deregulation/shifts in regulatory regime	Political and market pressures lead to shifts in the regulatory framework and enable the emergence of a new set of rules – e.g. liberalization, privatization or deregulation	New rules of the game but old mindsets persist and existing player unable to move fast enough or see new opportunities opened up	Old monopoly positions in fields like telecommunications and energy were dismantled and new players/combinations of enterprises emerged. In particular, energy and bandwidth become increasingly viewed as commodities. Innovations include skills in trading and distribution – a factor behind the considerable success of Enron in the late 1990s as it emerged from a small gas pipeline business to becoming a major energy trader
Business model innovation	Established business models are challenged by a reframing, usually by a new entrant who redefines/reframes the problem and the consequent 'rules of the game'	New entrants see opportunity to deliver product/service via new business model and rewrite rules – existing players have at best to be fast followers	Amazon.com in retailing Charles Schwab in share trading Southwest and other low-cost airlines Direct Line insurance
Unthinkable events	Unimagined and therefore not prepared for events which – sometimes literally – change the	New rules may disempower existing players or render competencies unnecessary	9/11

(*continued overleaf*)

Table 7.2 *(continued)*

Triggers/sources of discontinuity	Explanation	Problems posed	Examples (of good and bad experiences)
	world and set up new rules of the game		
Shifts in 'techno-economic paradigm' – systemic changes which impact whole sectors or even whole societies	Change takes place at system level, involving technology and market shifts. This involves the convergence of a number of trends which result in a 'paradigm shift' where the old order is replaced.	Hard to see where new paradigm begins until rules become established. Existing players tend to reinforce their commitment to old model, reinforced by 'sailing ship' effects	Industrial Revolution Mass production

Managing Discontinuous Innovation

Discontinuous innovation offers threats and opportunities for both new and established players. By changing the rules of the game it puts a premium on entrepreneurial behaviour – being able to spot an emerging opportunity and exploit it. For new entrants it is the 'classic' entrepreneurs challenge of being able to manage the growth of a business from a bright but often high-risk idea – and doing it from a weak asset base. For established players the challenge is one of reinventing themselves to allow at least a part of the business to behave as if it were an entrepreneurial start-up – and of holding back the conservative forces of the mainstream organization to let this happen.

The problem is not that discontinuity happens – it is a near-certainty that disruption will come from somewhere at some time, as we saw in Table 7.2. What do we do about it – and can we do it early enough – to exploit the opportunities rather than be threatened by the disruptive changes? And – for existing players – this raises the question of whether what we have already learned to do about managing innovation is still the right thing to do under the new circumstances.

For example, the problem for the firms in the disk-drive industry wasn't that they didn't listen to customers but rather that they listened too well. They built a virtuous circle of demanding customers in their existing marketplace with whom they developed a stream of improvement innovations – continuously stretching their products and processes to do what they were doing better and better. The trouble was that they were getting very close to the wrong customers – the discontinuity which got them into trouble was the emergence of a completely different set of users with very different needs and values.

INNOVATION IN ACTION

Thomas Edison's bulb has been with us since 1886 so we shouldn't be surprised that, like ice-harvesting, there are limits to how much further it can go in terms of product or process improvement. But new developments in the field of light-emitting diodes mean that there is a new set of light sources which last 20 times as long as a light bulb and offer energy savings of 85% – and that's at the start of their innovation careers. Needless to say this could pose a problem for established lighting firms like Siemens, Philips or General Electric, especially since the original patents around such solid-state devices were held by a small Japanese chemical company. But it is clear that a combination of licensing and R&D plus a commitment running into billions of dollars means that the major players will be able to exploit their experience, brands, distribution channels and other assets to ensure this innovation is competence-enhancing.

Not all technological revolutions do upset the established players. If they see the new developments early enough and pick up on their significance they can often strengthen their position. Two US researchers studied discontinuous technological shifts across a wide range of industries over an extended time period and noted that under some conditions major technological shifts could be 'competence destroying' – at which point new entrants would dominate the new industries enabled by radical technology (Tushman and Anderson, 1987[7]). But under other conditions the radical technologies were 'competence enhancing' and strengthened the hand of existing incumbents. This suggests that disruption is not always a 'changing of the guard' between existing incumbents and new entrants.

Figure 7.2 shows two kinds of innovation space which organizations have to operate in. Type 1 is essentially one where the challenge is innovating within a relatively stable framework – the rules of the game are clear, the

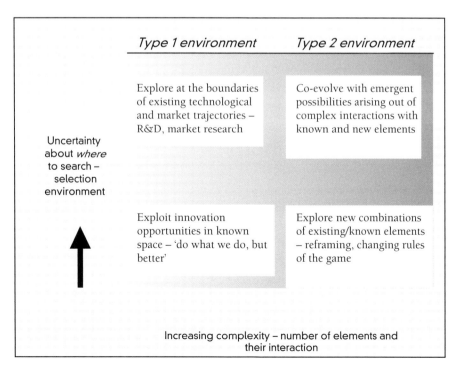

Figure 7.2   Mapping innovation space.

Table 7.3   Different archetypes for steady-state and discontinuous innovation

Type 1 Innovation organization	Type 2
Operates within mental framework based on clear and accepted set of rules of the game	No clear rules – these emerge over time High tolerance for ambiguity
Strategies path-dependent	Path-independent, emergent, probe and learn
Clear selection environment	Fuzzy, emergent selection environment
Selection and resource allocation linked to clear trajectories and criteria for fit	Risk-taking, multiple parallel bets, tolerance of (fast) failure
Operating routines refined and stable	Operating patterns emergent and 'fuzzy'
Strong ties and knowledge flows along clear channels	Weak ties and peripheral vision important

identity and nature of competitors is known, the sources of ideas and the relationships along which they flow (for example with customers or suppliers, universities and others) are well established and the underlying requirement is essentially around 'doing what we do, but better'. This may not be easy but it clearly is something which established players have much more experience in – so we'd expect them to have learned how best to structure and operate the innovation process for this relatively steady state.

By contrast Type 2 is a volatile, unpredictable and essentially fluid state – on the edge of chaos. New games emerge here – triggered by discontinuous shifts in markets, technologies or external regulations – but quite what the rules are, or even the precise nature of the game is not clear.

Table 7.3 contrasts the innovation management challenges posed by these two very different environments. Type 1 organizations are – not surprisingly – something which established players are good at creating and operating – geared to 'doing what we do better' and to repeating the innovation trick – structures and procedures to enable a steady stream of product, process and service innovations. But Type 2 organizations are much more like new entrants – agile and flexible, able to switch directions, to experiment around the emergent new rules of the game.

Dealing with Discontinuity

Working in Type 2 mode means a new set of approaches to organizing and managing innovation – for example, how the firm searches for weak signals about potential discontinuities, how it makes strategic choices in the face of high uncertainty, how it resources projects which lie far outside the mainstream of its innovation operations. And it's a problem which extends beyond the firm – discontinuous innovation is often problematic because it may involve building and working with a significantly different set of partners. 'Strong ties' – close and consistent relationships with regular partners in a network – may be important in enabling a steady stream of continuous improvement innovations, but where firms are seeking to do something different they may need links across a very different population in order to gain access to new ideas and different sources of knowledge and expertise.

For new entrants this isn't an issue – they can set up their organization and networks from scratch. But what does an established player do? One option is to set up their own version of new entrant firms, simply spinning off entities which they hope will be able to colonize and settle the new world of a Type 2 environment. This is a low-risk option but also means that there may be little synergy or leverage to and from the core business. Another option is to try and develop a parallel innovation management capability within the mainstream business – but in order to do this a number of new approaches will be needed.

In practice there are many options between these two poles, including setting up special units within an established business or managing more 'open innovation' operations which leverage the entrepreneurial strengths of smaller players. A number of large firms – for example, Microsoft, Intel Cisco Siemens and GSK – have developed sophisticated 'fishing' strategies looking around for smaller smart players to buy or at least link up with to help them keep an edge.

Do We Need a New Model for Managing Innovation?

However they choose to set it up, organizations wanting to manage discontinuous innovation will need to develop ways of organizing and managing innovation. We've been using a model in the book which looks like the figure nearby.

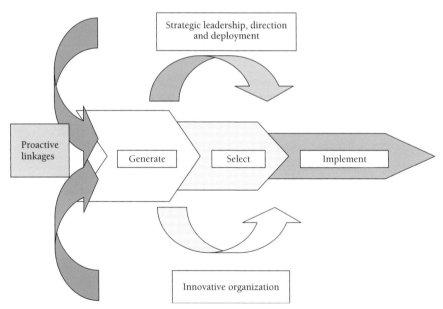

The questions facing organizations trying to deal with discontinuity can be summarized as:

- What do we need to do more of and extend?

- What do we need to do less of, or stop?

- What new approaches do we need to add?

How to Search for the Unexpected?

This isn't as easy as it looks – think about the 'search' challenge, for example. Rather like the drunk who has lost his keys on the way home and is desperately searching for them under the nearest lamp post 'because there is more light there', firms have a natural tendency to search in spaces which they already know and understand. But we know that the weak early warning signals of the emergence of totally new possibilities – radically different technologies, new markets with radically different needs, changing public opinion or political context – won't happen under our particular lamp post. Instead they are out there in the darkness – so we have to find new ways of searching in space we aren't familiar with. To make it even worse we have no real idea what we are looking for – it will only become clear as it emerges and the best we can hope for is to spot it early in its emergence and develop our response alongside it.

So what we need to develop is three sets of skills:

- the capability to be in the space where emergence of something new is likely to happen;

- The capability to 'hear' or sense the emergence of something new against the background noise, in a position to pick up on emerging trends early;

- The capability to act – to mobilize enough around us to capture and shape the innovation opportunities before others become aware of the new 'rules of the game'.

INNOVATION IN ACTION

The problem of 'not invented here' is essentially one of reframing. Alexander Bell originally looked for a partner to commercialize his invention of the telephone and approached Western Union, at the time the major player in the late-nineteenth-century communications industry in the USA. Their reaction is worth noting: in a letter they said, 'After careful consideration of your invention, which is a very interesting novelty, we have come to the conclusion that it has no commercial possibilities.'

How can this be done? By luck, sometimes – except that simply being in the right place at the right time doesn't always help. History suggests that even when the new possibility is presented to the firm on a plate its internal capacity to see and act on the possibilities is often lacking. For example, the famous 'not invented here' effect has been observed on many occasions where an otherwise well-established and successful innovative firm rejects a new opportunity which turns out to be of major significance

The problem of framing is a big one – it takes insight and courage to see a mistake or failure as an opportunity – although when this does happen it can have spectacular results. Viagra, for example, began life as a failure in terms of its original indication as a vasoconstrictor while 3M's Post-it notes are based on an adhesive with decidedly non-sticky properties! What emerges from stories like these is that firms need more than luck – they need to be prepared and equipped to do something about unexpected opportunities when they emerge.

INNOVATION IN ACTION

Of course the challenge is not simply one of picking up on a wide variety of signals- it's also in building a parallel capacity in which interesting – but apparently 'off-message' signals can be processed into a form where they can be communicated to the rest of the organization. Medproducts – an award-winning Danish medical devices firm – has recognized this difficulty, drawing a parallel with an immune system which detects alien organisms and rejects them. In their sophisticated product development system they have a series of filters which effectively screen out at a very early stage any signals about innovation possibilities outside of a focused mainstream. As one interviewee put it, 'Round here we don't have a product development funnel, we have a tube!' In an attempt to extend their capability to deal with discontinuous innovation they have set up a small team of technology and market 'scouts' whose task is not simply to pick up on potential weak signals but also to explore and process them into a form in which the rest of the organization can be made aware of them without the instant rejection they would normally receive. Building what they called the 'business case lite' (i.e. a business case without the level of detail normally expected by the company) for such ideas requires a sophisticated understanding not only of the new possibilities but also of the internal context (political as well as resources) into which they will be introduced. Much of the work of this team is around building coalitions of support for the new ideas before they are brought into the formal strategic-planning process.

So if it's not just luck but some more purposive action, how might we do it? One answer is to try and match the variety which is out there, cover all the bases – so firms should put lots of resource into building rich intelligence networks to detect and give early warning about possible shifts in their environment. At first sight this would seem a non-starter on the grounds of prohibitive cost – but increasingly firms are experimenting with tools like the Internet to help provide some kind of wide-scanning early warning system. The Internet has become a powerful amplifier for making such connections and an increasing number of organizations are developing search strategies (and accompanying 'gatekeeper' skills) to work with it. IBM, for example, uses an approach called Web fountain to help it monitor a wide range of potential triggers. Even the CIA makes use of an internal group called In-Q-Tel to act as a 'venture catalyst' to facilitate trend spotting in key technology areas!

Processing the data from such an array is another big issue but again we are seeing some creative responses – such as IBM's use of pattern-recognition tools to make sense out of large data sets or Procter & Gamble's use of retired employees (in the 'Encore' programme, who have not only the time to act as Internet scanners but also the experience and insight into the firm's needs and means to act as highly relevant gatekeepers).

Another problem to be addressed is that of escaping the dominant frame of reference in the business – what C. K. Prahalad calls 'the blinders of dominant logic'.[8] If you have traditionally worked with one set of users, chances are you'll develop better ways of listening to them and people like them. But emergence is often driven by people with different needs or wants – as Christensen's work showed. For example, much of the development of the mobile phone industry has been on the back of the different uses to which schoolchildren put their phones and delivering innovations which support this. Examples include text-messaging, image/video exchange and downloadable personal ring tones where the clues to the emergence of these innovation trajectories were picked up by monitoring what such children were doing or aspiring towards. Yet school playgrounds isn't where most market research would normally get done.

The concept of 'communities of practice' stresses not only the power of formal and informal networking as a source of knowledge but also the importance of bringing unconnected elements together – most new knowledge emerges at such interfaces. In Xerox, for example, 23 000 technical reps from around the world are linked into a network of communities of practice to share knowledge about unusual machine faults and heuristics for finding and fixing them. In industries like computer games the role of user groups and online communities becomes central – as an executive of Westwood Studios (producers of successful games like Command and Conquer and Red Alert) commented: 'The online communities are the way to get the feedback we need … and these guys, they help us ultimately to better our product.'

INNOVATION IN ACTION

The Danish pharmaceutical firm Novo Nordisk is exploring future models which might involve a much higher level of care services wrapped around a core set of products for treating chronic diseases like diabetes. Its activities include working with health education programmes in Tanzania, carrying out extensive psychosocial research on diabetes sufferers to establish actual needs and problems in diagnosis and treatment, and contributing to multi-stakeholder groups like the Oxford Health Alliance set up in 2003 with members drawn from an international set of academics, health professionals, government agencies and private-sector firms sharing a common goal – 'to raise awareness among influencers and educate critical decision-makers so that the pressing case for preventative measures can advance, and we can begin to combat chronic disease'.

CEO Lars Rebien Sørensen doesn't underestimate the mindset change this represents:

> In moving from intervention to prevention – that's challenging the business model where the pharmaceut- icals industry is deriving its revenues! …We believe that we can contribute to solving some major global health challenges – mainly diabetes – and at the same time create business opportunities for our company.

Another strategy is what might be termed 'total immersion' in a potentially interesting new context. Researcher Peter Koen calls this approach a 'deep dive' as part of the 'fuzzy front end' of new product/service development, a chance to tune in to emerging needs and match them to potential means to create radical innovations. The challenge here is to ensure sufficient openness to new and emerging stimuli rather than focusing too quickly on a particular target. The Danish medical devices producer, Coloplast, is employing this approach, exploring not only new medical needs in their home country markets but also in a number of developing countries in which the starting and operating context is radically different.

The difficulty of such strategies is that they depend still on some form of targeting – of knowing where to start looking. In an earlier era of the music business, skilled A&R staff knew which smoky clubs to go and sit in to pick up on new artists and musical trends and sign them to the record label. But 'cool hunting' of this kind is a lot more tricky in the Internet era where MP3, peer-to-peer networking and a host of other technological enablers mean that the emergence of new musical directions comes from many different sources and along many different channels.

Getting in early is another strategy which is becoming increasingly important. As US professor Eric von Hippel has noted over many years, users can be active innovators, playing a key role in developing and shaping early stage innovations.[9] His recent work in fields as diverse as sports equipment and open-source software underlines the power of building such networks and working with them in the co-evolution of novel and influential innovations. (Chapter 10 picks up in more detail this theme of working with lead users.)

ADVICE FOR FUTURE MANAGERS

All of this experimental experience suggests some principles around which innovation strategies for picking up on discontinuities might be built. They are:

Strategic principle	Why it matters	Why it's hard to do
Being there	New things don't arrive fully formed – they emerge but you won't be able to play a part unless you're in the space where they are likely to develop. For many firms this means recognizing that this emergence space may well be a long way from their existing turf.	But being in there means making investments in exploring spaces which may be far from the core business and may not offer any short-term prospects. And no firm can be everywhere at once – so how to target your presence?
Get in early	Discontinuous shifts do not emerge fully formed but emerge over time. So the earlier an organization can pick up key signals about threats, opportunities and potential actions to climb the learning curve, the better.	Where and when do you start committing resources? Maintaining an early-warning system is expensive and most of it may be redundant most of the time.
Diversity – enabling odd conversations	Discontinuity is often the result of unexpected conjunctions – not necessarily radical shifts at the technological or market frontier. Recombinant innovation – packaging existing things up by making new connections between elements, or linking users' needs to technological means – can often be the trigger.	Maintaining existing networks is expensive but returns justify this. Building speculative linkages is less easy to justify. But the limitation is that while strong ties support exploitation innovation, 'the ties that bind can become the ties that blind' when it comes to discontinuous.
Try things out – probe and learn	Discontinuous innovation doesn't involve a binary switch from one dominant design to another but rather a transitional process of multiple experiments, most of which fail. But there is learning and each experiment helps clarify the emerging trajectory.	Risk aversion and difficulty of justifying radical experiments – no organizational slack. Low tolerance for failure – mistakes are not welcome, organizational systems try to avoid or cover them up rather than use them to learn.
Make early bets	Active co-evolution rather than passive waiting for the trend to develop.	Risk aversion and project selection systems which favour the safe bets.

Strategic principle	Why it matters	Why it's hard to do
Work with the 'fuzzy front end'	Emergence is a process which is high on ambiguity – multiple views and approaches need to be held simultaneously.	Low tolerance of ambiguity.
Think along different tracks	Need to reframe to see the relevance of emerging phenomena – and may need to do this from several different reference points.	Linear thinking, inability to view with alternative perspectives, dominant logic blinders.

Developing Alternative Strategic Frames

Another significant problem is a reluctance to reframe the underlying models of the business. The example of Polaroid is a good illustration – their inability to see the move to digital-imaging as a completely new game rather than just a technological shift led to the company's downfall. They aren't alone – as writers like Foster and Kaplan point out in many examples of firms which lose by being too heavily committed to defending a status quo. The problem is compounded by the presence of many aspects of organizational life which reinforce old models – for example, reward systems which favour working with established customers or knowledge flows which underpin established product architectures.

In order to escape this trap, organizations seek to develop alternative ways of framing their activities. One route for this is to explore alternative scenarios for the future and to look at ways in which the current resource base could be reconfigured to provide an alternative but viable business model. For example, Shell has developed its long-established capabilities in scenario-planning into an approach called Gamechanger, in which detailed alternative future scenarios are developed and used to provide challenging reframing possibilities. In turn these help identify relevant domains within which 'targeted hunting' for new opportunities can take place. Such exploration provides a mechanism for pursuing several 'parallel future' development projects without compromising mainstream activities and helps maintain a tolerance for ambiguity suited to discontinuous conditions.

Extending Resource Allocation Approaches

A significant problem around discontinuous innovation occurs when well-developed strategic resource allocation and review systems are confronted with radical challenges. While such systems evolve as a robust way of managing a stream of projects under steady-state innovation conditions they may not be suited to discontinuities. For this reason a number of organizations decentralize the funding process for high-risk/radical venturing and make use of various forms of corporate venturing approach. These arrangements range from completely separate venture units to internal venture capital sources for which project owners can make bids. The intention – although not always the outcome – is to provide an alternative and parallel channel for exploring radical options and allocating at least early stage funding.

ADVICE FOR FUTURE MANAGERS

An Emergent 'Good Practice' Model Outline for Discontinuous Innovation

Element in innovation model	Type 2 characteristics
Search – firms need to scan and search their environments (internal and external) to pick up and process signals about potential innovation. These could be needs of various kinds, or opportunities arising from research activities somewhere, or pressures to conform to legislation, or the behaviour of competitors – but they represent the bundle of stimuli to which the organization must respond	Search at the periphery – pick up and amplify weak signals Use multiple and alternative perspectives Manage the idea-generation process inside the firm – enable systematic and high-involvement in innovation Develop an external scanning capability – scouts and hunters Use technological antennae to seek out potential new technologies Tune in to weak market signals – e.g. working with fringe users, early trend locations (such as chat rooms on Internet) Develop future exploring capability – scenario and alternatives Explore at periphery of firm – subsidiaries, joint ventures, distributors as sources of innovation Bring in outside perspectives
Strategic selection – from this set of potential triggers for innovation, firms need to choose what they will commit resources to doing. Even the best-resourced organization can't do everything, so the challenge lies in selecting those things which offer the best chance of developing a competitive edge.	Build pluralism into decision-making processes Create 'markets for judgement' Decentralize seed funding for new ideas – e.g. via internal venture funds or development budgets Build dual structures for innovation development and decision-making Develop 'fuzzy front end' approaches
Implementation – having chosen an option, organizations need to grow it from an idea through various stages of development to final launch – as a new product or service in the external marketplace or a new process or method within the organization. On the way they have to solve a host of problems (like where to get hold of the knowledge they	Build flexible project-development organizations – emphasize probe and learn rather than predictive project-planning Work actively with users on co-evolution of innovation Build parallel resource networks

Element in innovation model	Type 2 characteristics
need, how to find and integrate different groups of people with key skills, how to get the bugs and wrinkles out of the emerging innovation, how to steer the project against tight budgets of time and cost, etc.) and they have to do all this against a background of high uncertainty!	
Innovation strategy – innovation is about taking risks, about going into new and sometimes completely unexplored spaces. We don't want to gamble – simply changing things for their own sake or because the fancy takes us. No organization has resources to waste in that scattergun fashion – innovation needs a strategy. But equally we need to have a degree of courage and leadership, steering the organization away from what everyone else is doing or what we've always done and into new spaces.	Explore alternative future scenarios and consider parallel possibilities Identify strategic domains within which targeted hunting can take place Build capacity for ambiguity/multiple parallel strategies Actively explore 'how to destroy the business' to enable reframing
Innovative organization – firms need a structure and climate which enables people to deploy their creativity and share their knowledge to bring about change. It's easy to find prescriptions for innovative organizations which highlight the need to eliminate stifling bureaucracy, unhelpful structures, brick walls blocking communication and other factors stopping good ideas getting through. But we must be careful not to fall into the chaos trap – not all innovation works in organic, loose, informal environments or 'skunk works' – and these types of organization can sometimes act against the interests of successful innovation. Too little order and structure may be as bad as too much.	Build a culture which supports and encourages diversity and curiosity-driven behaviour. Set up appropriate incentive structures Enable complex knowledge flows
Proactive linkages – firms need to build bridges across boundaries inside the organization and to the many external agencies who can play a part in the innovation process – suppliers, customers, sources of finance, skilled resources and of knowledge, etc.	Develop non-committal exploratory supply relationships in addition to longer-term strategic alliances – 'strategic dalliances' Explore and develop parallel 'weak ties'

Managing Discontinuous Innovation

One thing is inevitable – all organizations will confront discontinuities in their worlds from time to time. Sometimes these will be separated by long periods of calm where innovation is just a case of 'doing what we do but better' – as was the case for nearly 300 years of banking before the storms of the Internet forced radical change on the sector. At other times it's as if there is a new model every day – as is the case in the turbulent waters of the telecommunications ocean. Discontinuities come from all sorts of causes – technological shifts, emergence of new markets, political pressures or just unforeseen dramatic events. Their result, however, is the same – a rewriting of the rules of the game.

Under these conditions all the old recipes for organizing and managing an efficient innovation process come into question. What we really need is the ability to deal with a 'fluid' state in which as the new rules emerge so there are rich opportunities in the game. But in order to exploit them we need to harness the basic entrepreneurial spirit – risk-taking, agile, quick to spot and follow through on opportunities – and to reshape what we do as we learn fast about the new situation. This kind of behaviour is second nature to a start-up or new entrant – it's what they are in the game for. But for existing organizations there is a real challenge – how can they – or at least a part of their organization – get back to their roots and rediscover how to be an entrepreneurial player?

STRATEGIC AND SOCIAL IMPACT

One of the characteristics of discontinuous innovation – DI – is that it often changes the rules of the game. And in doing so it can have an impact beyond the individual enterprise or indeed the sector in which the firm is based. 'Revolutions' like low-cost flying are a good example of a DI which began with an alternative business model but which is having profound wider implications – for example, on personal mobility, on regeneration of towns around newly activated airports and, on the negative side, noise pollution and climate change associated with emissions of greenhouse gases. This is only the latest in a long line – think, for example, of the profound social changes which the emergence of mechanization technologies and the growing use of steam power brought about – not for nothing was the period called the Industrial Revolution.

Work by a Russian economist, Nikolai Kondratiev, suggested that there are periodic 'long waves' of change in the economy occurring every 50 to 60 years and associated with major technological changes. The current Internet-led revolution is part of a Kondratiev wave which started breaking in the 1980s with the growing developments around information and communication technologies. Previous waves included steam and electric power, the rise of mass transportation and the emergence of synthetic materials. Other researchers have looked at this and point out that it is not simply technological change but a wider shift in the socio-economic framework in which people live. The moves to the cities in the Industrial Revolution, the opening up of mass markets following the development of the motor car, the emergence of giant multinational enterprises around core technologies and the gradual rise of social networking across the millions of Internet users are all examples of this.

Given developments across technological fields like nanotechnology, biotechnology/genetics and communications, and trends towards market fragmentation, never mind segmentation, it seems likely that DI will increasingly have a significant 'knock-on' effect on wider society – and thus pose some significant management challenges. Anticipating the wide impacts and the role of different stakeholders will increasingly become a necessity for players wanting to exploit the new opportunities successfully.

Developing Personal Capabilities

One of the key skills in dealing with discontinuous innovation (DI) is seeing it coming. A famous study in cognitive psychology involves showing a video of a group of students playing basketball inside a building. People are asked to watch the students carefully – who passes to whom, how they handle the ball, etc. In the middle of the film a man in a gorilla suit walks through the middle of the action, pauses to beat his breast and then walks off again. Hard to miss, you'd think – yet the experiment regularly shows that around half the people watching the video don't see the gorilla!

The answer to this conundrum is, of course, that they are too focused on watching the students to notice something they are not expecting. It's a powerful metaphor for the challenge of dealing with DI and highlights the need for peripheral vision.

Among the ways of developing peripheral vision are:

■ Scan at the edges of the business;

■ Develop what law enforcement professionals call 'splatter vision' – (unfocused wide-ranging searches across a field);

■ Search into the future;

■ Talk with different stakeholders, including those with views opposed to yours;

■ Develop multiple ways of finding out – for example, don't just ask people in carrying out market research, watch what they actually do (as anthropologists do when trying to learn about different societies);

■ Probe and learn – try experiments with new and alternative approaches;

■ Develop skills in reframing – how else could this business or this problem or this market be seen?

■ Explore alternative futures and how things might develop – and try and identify the underlying drivers for creating such alternative possibilities.

For more on this, see Day, G. and Schoemaker, P. (2006). *Peripheral Vision*. Harvard Business School Press, Boston, Mass.

Chapter Summary

■ Whilst organizations may be highly competent at what we could call 'steady-state' innovation (essentially doing what they do but better) problems can occur when they confront the need for *discontinuous* innovation.

■ A key part of the problem is that dealing with discontinuity requires a very different set of capabilities for organising and managing innovation. Searching in unlikely places, building links to strange partners, allocating resources to high risk ventures, exploring new ways of looking at the business – all of these challenge the 'normal' way we approach the innovation problem.

■ History suggests that when such shocks happen—be they technological shifts, the emergence of totally new markets or the bringing in of a new business model which reframes the rules of the game – it favours the new entrant over the established incumbent. But this is not a hard and fast rule – there are plenty of examples of established players who take on the new and use it to enhance their competitive position.

- Triggers for discontinuous shifts – where the rules of the game are changed – can be radical technological developments, the emergence of new markets, changes in the political or regulatory framework, shifts in public opinion or simply unexpected and sometimes catastrophic events.

- Changing the rules of the game puts a premium on entrepreneurial behaviour – being able to spot an emerging opportunity and exploit it. For new entrants it is the 'classic' entrepreneur's challenge of being able to manage the growth of a business from a bright but often high-risk idea – and doing it from a weak asset base. For established players the challenge is one of reinventing themselves to allow at least a part of the business to behave as if it were an entrepreneurial start-up – and of holding back the conservative forces of the mainstream organization to let this happen.

Key Terms Defined

Co-evolution Where innovations emerge out of a fluid set of technological and market possibilities.

Competence-destroying technological change Innovations which remove the basic source of a company's competitive strength – for example, online retailing or digital photography.

Competence-enhancing technological change Innovations which established players can use to strengthen their existing position – for example Philips using its marketing and product knowledge about lighting to exploit new LED technology.

Discontinuous innovation Occasional shifts in the environment which require or make possible a radically different innovation response.

Disruptive innovation A change in the rules of the game which can happen when entrepreneurs take advantage of discontinuous conditions.

Dominant design Emerging concept which comes out of a fluid phase in the innovation life cycle and defines the trajectory of future development.

Fluid phase Early stage in the innovation life cycle where a wide range of new possibilities in technology and market configurations are possible.

Peripheral vision Search processes used by firms to look outside their normal selection environment.

Selection environment The space which firms explore to find triggers for innovation – technological fields, market possibilities, competitor behaviour, government and other influences, and so on.

Technological trajectory Pathway along which development tends to focus, a kind of 'bandwagon' which sets the direction for innovation after a dominant design has emerged.

Further Reading and Resources

A number of researchers are actively exploring questions raised by discontinuous innovation – what it is, and how can it be anticipated and dealt with. See, for example, Bessant, J., Birkinshaw, J. et al. (2004). One step beyond – building a climate in which discontinuous innovation will flourish, *People Management*, **10**, 28–32; Day, G. and Schoemaker P. (2000). *Wharton on Managing Emerging Technologies.* John Wiley & Sons, New York. Inc.; Day, G. and Schoemaker, P. (2006). *Peripheral Vision: Detecting the Weak Signals that Will Make or Break*

Your Company. Harvard Business School Press; Boston, Mass. Hamel, G. (2000). *Leading the Revolution*, Harvard Business School Press; Boston, Mass. Philips, W., Noke, H. et al. (2006). Beyond the steady state: managing discontinuous product and process innovation, *International Journal of Innovation Management*, **10** (2).

Case studies of firms or sectors which have faced these challenges can be found in Evans, P. and Wurster, Y. (2000). *Blown to Bits: How the New Economics of Information Transforms Strategy.* Cambridge, Mass., Harvard Business School Press; Foster, R. and Kaplan, S. (2002). *Creative Destruction.* Cambridge, Harvard University Press; Utterback, J. (1994). *Mastering the Dynamics of Innovation.* Harvard Business School Press, Boston, Mass.

References

1 Utterback, J. (1994). *Mastering the Dynamics of Innovation.* Harvard Business School Press, Boston, Mass.

2 Henderson, R. and Clark, K. (1990). Architectural innovation: the reconfiguration of existing product technologies and the failure of established firms, *Administrative Science Quarterly*, **35**, 9–30.

3 Abernathy, W. and Utterback, J. (1975). A dynamic model of product and process innovation, *Omega*, **3** (6), 639–656.

4 Dosi, G. (1982). Technological paradigms and technological trajectories, *Research Policy*, **11**, 147–162.

5 Abernathy, W. and Utterback, J. (1978). Patterns of industrial innovation, *Technology Review*, **80**, 40–47.

6 Christensen, C. (1997). *The Innovator's Dilemma.* Harvard Business School Press, Boston, Mass.

7 Tushman, M. and Anderson, P. (1987). Technological discontinuities and organizational environments, *Administrative Science Quarterly*, **31** (3), 439–465.

8 Prahalad, C. (2004). The blinders of dominant logic. *Long Range Planning*, **37** (2), 171–179.

9 Von Hippel, E. (2005). *The Democratization of Innovation.* MIT Press, Cambridge.

Discussion Questions

1 Give some examples of discontinuous innovation and show how this differs from 'doing what we do but better', steady-state innovation.

2 What different challenges does discontinuous innovation pose for management of the process?

3 A paradox in innovation is that sometimes 'smart' firms – especially those which have been successful innovators in the past – find themselves in difficulties under discontinuous conditions. Why does this happen – and what might they do to avoid it?

4 Using examples from disk drives, mini-mill steelmaking, mechanical excavators or other sectors, show how Christensen's disruptive innovation theory operates.

5 Give an example of a 'dominant design' – and explain why.

6 Why do existing incumbents in an industry do badly and new entrants do well when fluid conditions characterize the environment?

Team Exercises

1 Competence-destroying and competence-enhancing innovation:

Read the case study in Chapter 1 about the changing nature of the music industry. Then try and review it in terms of the following questions.

■ To what extent are the changes involved competence-enhancing or competence-destroying innovations?

■ And for whom? (Think about the different players in the music industry – who are the likely winners and losers?)

■ What strategies might a firm use to exploit the opportunities? (Again think about the different players in the industry and how they might defend their positions or open up new opportunities.)

Use the following framework to capture your answers.

	An established record company	A newcomer wanting to offer entertainment on the Web	A music publishing company (responsible for copyrights on sheet music, etc.)	Other examples...
Is the change competence-enhancing? Why?				
Is the change competence-destroying? Why?				
What might you do about this to secure and improve your position?				

2 Patterns of discontinuity – past, present, future.

Every sector goes through periods of relative calm when innovation is about doing what you do better. But these are punctuated by disruptions where the rules of the game get rewritten – for example, by the emergence of a new technology or by external market changes. The trouble is that firms are pretty good at the first kind of innovation management but less so at the second – with the result that when discontinuous change happens not all firms survive the transition. At the same time many new entrants see that the rules of the game have changed and that they now have a chance to join the sector.

In this activity think about your firm (or one with which you are familiar) and the sector in which it operates. Looking back over the past 50 years or so, try and plot where there has been major disruption or discontinuity and what caused it. What response did existing firms have to make to ensure they survived and continued in the sector?

Having looked backwards, try and project forwards over the next 50 years and think of factors – perhaps only on the horizon at the moment – which might disrupt the sector. What will firms need to do to ensure they survive and develop with the changes rather than being left behind by them?

You will probably have to talk to people about this and read some background to the firm. Try and capture the key points of your research in a short summary. You might want to use the framework below.

Looking back – what disruptions occurred – and why?	What did survivors do to adapt and stay in the game?	Looking forward – what disruptions might occur – and why?	What should survivors do to stay in the game?

Assignment and Case Study Questions

1 Using an example of an industry with which you are familiar, show how the innovation life cycle operates, moving from fluid, through transition to mature phases.

2 Begin by reviewing a sector which you are familiar with and the particular configuration of technologies and markets which it involves. Now try and think about what *disruptive* technologies might emerge which would:
   ■ Threaten and undermine your existing competence-base; and/or
   ■ Open up significant new opportunities if you could acquire these.

(As an example, consider Kodak – their traditional competence base of wet chemistry-based imaging has been radically undermined by the new digital-imaging technologies. But at the same time these technologies are opening up significant new horizons in e-business, etc.)

Now try and present your view of these challenges in a couple of paragraphs or a list of bullet points. Try doing it in the style of a science-fiction story, looking back from a position in the year 2050 and telling others about the big change of direction this meant for your company, how it identified and explored the new technology, how it changed its structures and processes to take advantage of it, the difficulties involved in making the transition and so on.

CASE STUDY 7
Exploring Innovation in Action: the Dimming of the Light Bulb

In the Beginning . . .

. . . God said, 'Let there be light.' And for a long time this came from a rather primitive but surprisingly effective method – the oil lamp. From the early days of putting simple wicks into congealed animal fats, through candles to more sophisticated oil lamps, people have been using this form of illumination. Archaeologists tell us this goes back at least 40 000 years so there has been plenty of scope for innovation to improve the basic idea! Certainly by the time of the Romans, domestic illumination – albeit with candles – was a well-developed feature of civilized society.

Not a lot changed until the late eighteenth century when the expansion of the mining industry led to experiments with uses for coal gas – one of which was as an alternative source of illumination. One of the pioneers of research in the coal industry – Humphrey Davy – invented the carbon arc lamp and ushered in a new era of safety within the mines – but also opened the door to alternative forms of domestic illumination, and the era of gas lighting began.

But it was not until the middle of the following century that researchers began to explore the possibilities of using a new power source and some new physical effects. Experiments by Joseph Swan in England and Farmer in the USA (among others) led to the development of a device in which a tiny metal filament enclosed within a glass envelope was heated to incandescence by an electric current. This was the first electric light bulb – and it still bears more than a passing resemblance to the product found hanging from millions of ceilings all around the world.

By 1879 it became clear that there was significant commercial potential in such lighting – not just for domestic use. Two events occurred during that year which were to have far-reaching effects on the emergence of a new industry. The first was that the city of Cleveland – although using a different lamp technology (carbon arc) – introduced the first public street lighting. And the second was that patents were registered for the incandescent filament light bulb by Joseph Swan in England and one Thomas Edison in the USA.

Needless to say the firms involved in gas supply and distribution and the gas lighting industry were not taking the threat from electric light lying down and they responded with a series of improvement innovations which helped retain gas lighting's popularity for much of the late nineteenth century. Much of what happened over the next 30 years is a good example of what is sometimes called the 'sailing ship effect'. That is, just as in the shipping world the invention of steam power did not instantly lead to the disappearance of sailing ships but instead triggered a whole series of improvements in that industry, so the gas lighting industry consolidated its position through incremental product and process innovations.

But electric lighting was also improving and the period 1886–1920 saw many important breakthroughs and a host of smaller incremental performance improvements. In a famous and detailed study (carried out by an appropriately named researcher called Bright) there is evidence to show that little improvements in the design of the bulb and in the process for manufacturing it led to a fall in price of over 80% between 1880 and 1896. Examples of such innovations include the use of gas instead of vacuum in the bulb (1913, Langmuir) and the use of tungsten filament.

Innovation theory teaches us that after an invention there is a period in which all sorts of designs and ideas are thrown around before finally a 'dominant design' settles out and the industry begins to mature. So it was with the light bulb; by the 1920s the basic configuration of the product – a tungsten filament inside a glass gas-filled bulb – was established and the industry began to consolidate. It is at this point that the major players with whom we associate the industry – Philips, General Electric, Westinghouse – become established.

Technological Alternatives

Although the industry then entered a period of stability in the marketplace there was still considerable activity in the technology arena. Back in the nineteenth century Henri Becquerel invented the fluorescent lamp and in 1911 Claude invented the neon lamp – both inventions which would have far-reaching effects in terms of the industry and its segmentation into different markets.

The neon lamp started a train of work based on forming different glass tubes into shapes for signs and in filling them with a variety of gases with similar properties to neon but which gave different colours.

The fluorescent tube was first made commercially by Sylvania in the USA in 1938 following extensive development work by both GE and Westinghouse. The technology had a number of important features including low power consumption and long life – factors which led to their widespread use in office and business environments although less so in the home. By the 1990s this product had matured alongside the traditional filament bulb and a range of compact and shaped fittings were available from the major lighting firms.

Meanwhile, in Another Part of the World...

While neon and fluorescent tubes were variations on the same basic theme of lights, a different development began in a totally new sector in the 1960s. In 1962 work on the emerging solid-state electronics area led to the discovery of a light-emitting diode – LED – a device which would, when a current passed through it, glow in red or green colour. These lights were bright and used little power; they were also part of the emerging trend towards miniaturization. They quickly became standard features in electronic devices and today the average household will have hundreds of LEDs in orange, green or red to indicate whether devices such as TV sets, mobile phones or electric toothbrushes are on and functioning.

Development and refinement of LEDs took place in a different industry for a different market and in particular one line of work was followed in a small Japanese chemical company supplying LEDs to the major manufacturers like Sony. Nichia Chemical began a programme of work on a type of LED which would emit blue light – something much more difficult to achieve and requiring complex chemistry and careful process control. Eventually they were successful and in 1993 produced a blue LED based on gallium arsenide technology. The firm then committed a major investment to development of both product and process technology, amassing around 300 patents along the way. Their research culminated in the development in 1995 of a white light LED – using the principle that white light is made up of red, green and blue light mixed together.

So what? The significance of Shuji Nakamura's invention may not be instantly apparent – and at present the only products which can be bought utilizing it are small high-power torches. But think about the significance of this discovery. White LEDs offer the following advantages:

■ 85% less power consumption;

■ 16 times brighter than normal electric lights;

■ Tiny size;

■ Long life – tests suggest the life of an LED could be 100 000 hours – about 11 years;

■ Can be packaged into different shapes, sizes and arrangements;

■ Will follow the same economies of scale in manufacturing that led to the continuing fall in the price of electronic components so will become very cheap very quickly.

If people are offered a low-cost, high-power, flexible source of white light they are likely to adopt it – and for this reason the lighting industry is feeling some sense of threat. The likelihood is that the industry as we know it will be changed dramatically by the emergence of this new light source – and while the names may remain the same they will have to pay a high price for licensing the technology. They may try and get around the patents – but with 300 already in place and the experience of the complex chemistry and processing which go into making LEDs Nichia have a long head start. When Dr Nakamura left Nichia Chemical for a chair at the University of California, Santa Barbara, sales of blue LEDs and lasers were bringing the firm more than US$200 million a year and the technology is estimated to have earned Nichia nearly US$2 billion.

Things are already starting to happen. Many major cities are now using traffic lights which use the basic technology to make much brighter green and red lights since they have a much longer life than conventional bulbs. One US company, Traffic Technology Inc., has even offered to give away the lights in return for a share of the energy savings the local authority makes! Consumer products like torches are finding their way into shops and online catalogues while the automobile industry is looking at the use of LED white light for interior lighting in cars. Major manufacturers such as GE are entering the market and targeting mass markets such as street lighting and domestic applications, a market estimated to be worth US$12 billion in the USA alone.

Some of the advantages of solid-state lighting include the fact that there is no filament to break – so product life is much longer. Another advantage is that, as it is essentially a programmable electronic device, software can make it do all kinds of things rather than simply be turned on and off. With a life as long as some of these new LED products it is possible to produce sealed products and units which can be guaranteed for a certain period of time. We also shouldn't forget the 'do what we do better' effect – US estimates suggest that the average selling price of light bulbs between 2000 and 2003 declined by approximately 10% and that price competition essentially represented a commoditization and internationalization of the industry.

Having a discontinuous innovation doesn't necessarily mean that the major players lose out but they do need to pick it up quickly and to be aware what the weak signals might mean and to be prepared to change what they do and what they offer. Phillips for example carried out a variety of experiments with solid-state lighting to try and see what might emerge as acceptable and interesting uses ranging from things which looked like LED candles to the successful ambient lighting system product for hospitals. They adopted what Guba Rao, Vice President, called a launch-and-learn strategy: 'By creating pilots we minimize risks . . . if we make mistakes we keep them small and learn quickly.' Some of their experiments included looking at how to retrofit LED lighting into existing lighting sockets rather than transforming the plug system.

Their LED candle offers a lighting product which is like a candle but without the danger. The new technology also enabled them to develop ambient lighting, sensitive to users' needs and preferences. An experiment at Chicago's Lutheran General Hospital used LED panels which allow patients to choose different themes and to change the lights and theme as they move around the room.

A key issue in the unfolding of this innovation is that since all the lighting companies are facing the same challenge there is a strong pressure to do collaborative work. In 2003 a project was launched called Bridges in Light, which involved the major stakeholders in the industry exploring the future.

Case Study Questions

How is the technological revolution in lighting likely to affect the strategic 'rules of the game' in the lighting market? What would you do to preserve or create strategic advantage if you were:

- A major manufacturer of 'traditional' incandescent light bulbs (like Philips or GTE)?

- A firm specializing in 'designer' light fittings for up-market flats and houses?

- A firm involved in the children's entertainment industry – computer games and toys?

- Nichia Chemicals themselves?

Make some notes summarising your key points – the actions you would take and why. Use the frame below to help. Remember there are no 'right' answers!

Company	Strategic actions	Why?
Light bulb maker – Philips, GE, etc.	e.g. get out of the business	Because the competence around making light bulbs has changed – it's a new product and we're late entrants to the race.
Interior designer		
Children's toy maker		
Nichia Chemicals		
Light fittings maker		
Others???		

Chapter 8

Entrepreneurship and New Ventures

This chapter

- ■ Looks at the characteristics of entrepreneurs.

- ■ Examines the context for entrepreneurship.

- ■ Reviews the process and stages for creating a new venture:
    - ■ Developing the business plan;
    - ■ Acquiring the resources and funding.

- ■ Explores ways of harvesting the venture.

- ■ Looks at growth and exit strategies.

Learning Objectives

When you have completed this chapter you will be able to:

- ■ Understand the key characteristics of an entrepreneur.

- ■ Identify the contextual factors which influence the creation of new ventures.

- ■ Identify key stages of the process of creating an innovative new venture.

- ■ Describe harvesting the venture: growth and exit strategies.

In the UK, between 400 000 and 500 000 new businesses are created each year. At the same time, each year around 300 000 firms fail, suggesting a net annual rate of new business creation of some 100 000 to 200 000 firms. However, most of these new businesses are not very creative or innovative, and entrepreneurship is much more than the creation of a new business.

Contrary to popular belief, the majority of small firms are not particularly innovative. The goal of most entrepreneurs is to achieve independence of employment, rather than the creation of innovative businesses. However, here we focus on the creation and development of *innovative* new ventures, those which aim to offer new products or services, or are based on novel processes or ways of creating value. These are not necessarily, or even frequently, based on inventions, new technology or scientific breakthroughs. Instead, the entrepreneur has chosen or been forced to create a new business in order to exploit the innovation.[1]

People create new ventures for many different reasons, and it is critical to understand the different motives and mechanisms of entrepreneurship:

- *Lifestyle entrepreneurs* – those who seek independence, and wish to earn a living based around their personal circumstances and values, for example, individual professional consulting practices, or home-based craft businesses. Statistically speaking, these are the most common types of new venture, and are an important source of self-employment in almost all economies. Contrary to popular belief, the majority of such small firms are not particularly creative or innovative, and instead are simply exploiting an asset (e.g. a shop), or expertise (e.g. IT consulting).

- *Growth entrepreneurs* – those who aim to become wealthy and powerful through the creation and aggressive growth of new businesses (plural, as they are often serial entrepreneurs who create a string of new ventures). They are more likely to measure their success in terms of wealth, influence and reputation. Although we tend to think of people like Bill Gates or Steve Jobs, more typical examples are in relatively conservative, capital-intensive and well-understood sectors such as retail, property and commodities. Successful growth entrepreneurs tend to create very large corporations through acquisitions, which may dominate national markets, and the founders may become very wealthy and influential.

- *Innovative entrepreneurs* – individuals who are driven by the desire to create or change something, whether in the private, public or third sectors. Independence, reputation and wealth are not the primary goals in such cases, although they are often achieved anyway. Rather, the main motivation is to actually change or create something new. Innovative entrepreneurs include technological entrepreneurs and social entrepreneurs, but such ventures are rarely based on inventions, new technology or scientific breakthroughs. Instead, the entrepreneur has chosen or been forced to create a new venture in order to create or change something. These are the focus of this chapter.

Characteristics of Entrepreneurs

To try to explain entrepreneurial behaviour, researchers tend to examine either personal traits and characteristics, or the influence of contextual factors, such as the availability of support and finance. Clearly, any complete understanding of entrepreneurship requires both perspectives to be integrated: no matter how entrepreneurial an individual might be, they will require a context which provides access to appropriate resources (Figure 8.1). Conversely, the availability of support and venture capital may be a necessary condition for entrepreneurship, but will not be sufficient to result in the creation of new ventures.

Figure 8.1   Factors influencing the creation of new ventures.
Source: Tidd, J., Bessant, J. and Pavitt, K. (2005) *Managing Innovation*. John Wiley & Sons, Ltd, Chichester**.**

Much of the US research on entrepreneurs tends to emphasize the background and characteristics of a typical entrepreneur, whereas research in Europe and elsewhere places equal or more emphasis on the context.[2] Personal factors found to affect the likelihood of establishing a venture include:

■ Family and religious background;

■ Formal education and early work experience;

■ Psychological profile.

A number of studies confirm that both family background and religion affect an individual's propensity to establish a new venture. A significant majority of entrepreneurs have a self-employed or professional parent. The most common explanation for this observed bias is that the parent acts as a role model and may provide support for self-employment. The effect of religious background is more controversial, but it is clear that certain religions are over-represented in the population of technical entrepreneurs. For example, in the USA and Europe, Jews are more likely to establish a new venture, and Chinese are more likely to in Asia. Whether this observed bias is the result of specific cultural or religious norms, or the result of minority status, is the subject of much controversy but little research. The US studies suggest that dominant cultural values are more important than minority status, but even this work indicates that the effect of family background is more significant than religion. In any case, and perhaps more importantly, there appears to be no significant relationship between family and religious background and the subsequent probability of success of a new venture.

The relationships between education and entrepreneurship are also complex. The influences of the *level* and *type* of education appear to be different. In terms of the general level of formal education, entrepreneurs tend to be less educated than the average of the population. The usual explanation is similar to the minority status one for religion: under-education encourages or sometimes forces ambitious individuals to seek personal fulfilment and public recognition outside conventional jobs and professions. However, there are important exceptions to this tendency which are discussed below. Technological and social entrepreneurs are often more highly educated than the population average. The type of education and early work experiences can have a more profound effect. Although many schools, colleges and universities now have classes and courses on entrepreneurship, the traditions of pedagogy and learning often still reflect the needs of employment, and emphasize content and the acquisition of knowledge, rather than skills and practice.

Much of the research on the psychology of entrepreneurs is based on the experience of small firms in the USA, so the generalizability of the findings must be questioned. Two of the common characteristics appear to be an internal locus of control and a high need for achievement. The former characteristic is common in scientists and engineers, but the need for high levels of achievement is less common. Entrepreneurs are typically motivated by a high need for achievement (so-called 'nAch'), rather than a general desire to succeed. This behaviour is associated with moderate risk-taking, but not gambling or irrational risk-taking. A person with a high nAch:

■ Likes situations where it is possible to take personal responsibility for finding solutions to problems.

■ Has a tendency to set challenging but realistic personal goals and to take calculated risks.

■ Needs concrete feedback on personal performance.

The most common view is that certain inherent personality traits result in entrepreneurial behaviour. Some typical characteristics of an entrepreneur are:[3]

■ Passionately seek to identify new opportunities and ways to profit from change and disruption.

■ Pursue opportunities with discipline and focus on a limited number of projects, rather than opportunistically chasing every option.

■ Focus on action and execution, rather than endless analysis.

■ Involve and energize networks of relationships, exploiting the expertise and resources of others, while helping others to achieve their own goals.

The conventional explanation is that such personality traits result in specific behaviours, but more recent studies indicate that this is only an association, rather than a simple cause and effect relationship. In other words, training, practice, experience and support can influence behaviour. This suggests that entrepreneurship is not simply an inherited trait but, to a significant extent, can be learned and developed. Of course, like any endeavour, personality does play a role, but interacts with development, context and opportunity. In any case, there are very few 'ideal types' who exhibit the full range of such traits or behaviours, and much of the research and evidence is heavily biased towards Anglo-Saxon cultures and does not travel very well.

In addition to these important qualifications to the idea of an ideal entrepreneurial type, there are two important variations on the more typical profile presented. These are social entrepreneurs, and technological entrepreneurs.

Social Entrepreneurs

There are numerous definitions of social entrepreneurship, but most include two critical elements:

■ The aim is to create social change and value, rather than commercial innovation and financial value. Conventional commercial entrepreneurship often results in new products and services and growth in the economy and employment, but social benefits are not the explicit goal.

■ It involves business, public and third-sector organizations to achieve this aim. Conventional commercial entrepreneurship tends to focus on the individual entrepreneur and new venture, which occupy the business sector, although organizations in the public or third sectors may be stakeholders or customers.

Examples of applications of social entrepreneurship include:

■ Poverty relief.

■ Community development.

■ Health and welfare.

■ Environment and sustainability.

■ Arts and culture.

■ Education and employment.

However, social entrepreneurship is not simply entrepreneurship in a different context. Traditional, public and third-sector organizations have often failed to deliver improvement or change because of the constraints of organization, culture, funding or regulation. For example, in many public and third-sector organizations the needs of the funders or employees may become more important to satisfy than the needs of their target community.

Therefore social entrepreneurs share most of the characteristic of entrepreneurs, but are different is some important respects:

■ *Motives and aims* – less concerned with independence and wealth, and more on social means and ends.

■ *Timeframe* – less emphasis on short-term growth and longer-term harvesting of the venture, and more concern on long-term change and enduring heritage.

■ *Resources* – less reliance on the firm and management team to execute the venture, and greater reliance on a network of stakeholders and resources to develop and deliver change.

Key characteristics which appear to distinguish social entrepreneurs from their commercial counterparts include a high level of empathy and a need for social justice. The concept of empathy is complex, but includes the ability to recognize and emotionally share the feelings and needs of others, and is associated with a desire to help. However, while empathy and a need for social justice may be necessary attributes of a social entrepreneur, they are not sufficient. These may make a social venture desirable, but not necessarily feasible.[4] The feasibility will be influenced by the more conventional personal characteristics of an entrepreneur, such as background and personality, but also some contextual factors more common in public and third sector. Potential barriers to social entrepreneurship:

■ Access to and support of local networks of social and community-based organizations, for example, relationships and trust in informal networks.

■ Access to and support of government and political infrastructure, for example, nationality or ethnic restrictions.

(Chapter 9 looks at social entrepreneurship in more detail.)

ENTREPRENEURSHIP IN ACTION

Marc Koska and Star Syringe

Marc Koska founded Star Syringe in 1996 to design and develop disposable, single-use or so-called 'auto-disable syringes' (ADS) to help prevent the transmission of diseases like HIV/AIDS. For example, over 23 million infections of HIV and hepatitis are given to otherwise healthy patients through syringe reuse every year.

Marc had no formal training in engineering, but had relevant design experience from previous jobs in modelling and plastics design. He designed the ADS according to the following basic principles:

- Cheap: the same price as a standard disposable plastic syringe.

- Easy: manufactured on existing machinery, to cut set-up costs.

- Simple: used as closely as possible in the same way as a standard disposable plastic syringe.

- Scalable: licensed to local manufacturers, leveraging resources in a sustainable way.

The ADS is not manufactured in-house, but by Star licensees based all over the world. Koska now licenses the technology to international aid agencies and is recognized by the UNICEF and the World Health Organization (WHO). Star Alliance is the network which connects the numerous manufacturing licensees to the global marketplace. The Alliance includes 19 international manufacturing partners, and serves markets in over 20 countries. The combined capacity of the alliance licensees is close to 1 billion annual units.

His dedication and persistent drive over the last 20 years have earned him respect from leaders in state health services as well as industry: in February 2005 for example the Federal Minister for Health in Pakistan presented Marc with an award for Outstanding Contribution to Public Health for his work on safer syringes, and in 2006 the company won the UK Queen's Award for Enterprise and International Trade.

Source: www.starsyringe.com, web.mac.com/marckoska/

Technological Entrepreneurs

The creation of a technology venture is the interaction of individual skills and disposition and the technological and market characteristics. The US studies emphasize the role of personal characteristics, such as family background, goal orientation, personality and motivation, whereas the European studies stress the role of the environment, including institutional support and resources.[5]

The decision to start a technology venture typically begins with a desire to gain independence and to escape the bureaucracy of a large organization, whether it is in the public or private sector. Thus the background, psychological profile and work and technical experience of a technical entrepreneur all contribute to the decision to create a new venture.

Education and training are major factors that distinguish the founders of technology ventures from other entrepreneurs. The median level of education of technical entrepreneurs in the US study was a master's degree, and with the important exception of biotechnology-based ventures, a doctorate was superfluous. Significantly, the levels of education of technical entrepreneurs do not differentiate them from other scientists and engineers. However, potential technical entrepreneurs tend to have higher levels of productivity than their technical work colleagues, measured in terms of papers published or patents granted. This suggests that potential entrepreneurs may be more driven than their corporate counterparts.

In addition to a master's-level education, on average, a technical entrepreneur will have around 13 years of work experience before establishing a new venture. In the case of Route 128, the entrepreneur's work experience is typically with a single incubator organization, whereas technical entrepreneurs in Silicon Valley tend to have gained their experience from a larger number of firms before establishing their own business. This suggests that there is no ideal pattern of previous work experience. However, experience of development work appears to be more important than work in basic research. As a result of the formal education and experience required, a typical technical entrepreneur will be aged between 30 and 40 years when establishing his or her first technology venture. This is relatively late in life compared to other types of venture, and is due to a combination of ability and opportunity. On the one hand, it typically takes between 10 and 15 years for a potential entrepreneur to attain the necessary technical and business experience. On the other hand, many people begin to have greater financial and family responsibilities at this time. Thus there appears to be a window of opportunity to start a technology venture, some time in the mid-thirties. Moreover, different fields of technology have different entry and growth potential. Therefore the choice of a potential entrepreneur will be constrained by the dynamics of the technology and markets. The capital requirements, product lead times and potential for growth are likely to vary significantly between sectors.

Unlike general entrepreneurs, technology entrepreneurs appear to have only moderate nAch, but a low need for affiliation (nAff). This suggests that the need for independence, rather than success, is the most significant motivator for technical entrepreneurs. Technology entrepreneurs also tend to have an internal locus of control. In other words, they believe that they have personal control over outcomes, whereas someone with an external locus of control believes that outcomes are the result of chance, powerful institutions or others. More sophisticated psychometric techniques such as the Myers–Briggs type indicators (MBTI) confirm the differences between technology entrepreneurs and other scientists and engineers.

Numerous surveys indicate that most technology entrepreneurs claim to have been frustrated in their previous job as shown in the box below. This frustration appears to result from the interaction of the psychological predisposition of the potential entrepreneur and poor selection, training and development by the parent organization. Specific events may also trigger the desire or need to establish a technology venture, such as a major reorganization or downsizing of the parent organization (Figure 8.1).

ENTREPRENEURSHIP IN ACTION

Mike Lynch and Autonomy

Mike Lynch founded the software company Autonomy in 1994, a spin-off from his first start-up Neurodynamics. Lynch, a grammar school graduate, studied information science at Cambridge where he carried out PhD research on probability theory. He rejected a conventional research career as he had found his summer job at GEC Marconi a 'boring, tedious place'. In 1991, aged 25, he approached the banks to raise money for his first venture, Neurodynamics, but 'met a nice chap who laughed a lot and admitted that he was only used to lending money to people to open newsagents'. He subsequently raised the initial £2000 from a friend of a friend. Neurodynamics developed pattern recognition software which it sold to specialist niche users such as the UK police force for matching fingerprints and identifying disparities in witness statements, and banks to identify signatures on cheques.

Autonomy was spun off in 1994 to exploit applications of the technology in Internet, intranet and media sectors, and received the financial backing of venture capitalists Apax, Durlacher and Enic. Autonomy was floated on the Easdaq in July 1998, on the Nasdaq in 1999, and in February 2000 was worth US$5 billion, making Lynch the first British software billionaire. Autonomy creates software which manages unstructured information, which accounts for 80% of all data. The software applies Bayesian probabilistic techniques to identify patterns of data or text, and compared to crude keyword searches can better take into account context and relationships. The software is patented in the USA, but not in Europe as patent law does not allow patent protection of software. The business generates revenues through selling software for cataloguing and searching information direct to clients such as the BBC, Barclays, BT, Eli Lilly, General Motors, Merril Lynch, News Corporation, Nationwide, Proctor & Gamble and Reuters. In addition, it has more than 50 licence agreements with leading software companies to use its technology, including Oracle, Sun and Sybase. A typical licence will include a lump sum of US$100 000 plus a royalty on sales of 10–30%. By means of such licence deals Autonomy aims to become an integral part of a range of software and the standard for intelligent recognition and searching. In the financial year ending March 2000 the company reported its first profit of US$4 40 000 on a turnover of US$11.7 million. The company employs 120 staff, split between Cambridge in the UK and Silicon Valley, and spends 17% of its revenues on R&D. In 2004 sales were around US$60 million, with an average licence costing US$3 60 000, and high gross margins of 95%. New customers include AOL, BT, CitiBank, Deutsche Bank, Ford, the 2004 Greek Olympics, and the defence agencies in the USA, Spain, Sweden and Singapore. Repeat customers account for 30% of sales.

Context for Entrepreneurship

Most of what we know about innovative new ventures is based on the experience of start-up firms in the USA, in particular, the growth of biotechnology, semiconductor and software firms. Many of these originated from a parent or 'incubator' organization, typically either an academic institution or large well-established firm. Examples of university incubators include Stanford which spawned much of Silicon Valley, the Massachusetts Institute of Technology (MIT) which spawned Route 128 in Boston, and Imperial College, London, and Cambridge University in the UK. MIT in particular has become the archetype academic incubator, and in addition to the creation of Route 128, its alumni have established some 200 new ventures in northern California, and account for more than a fifth of employment in Silicon Valley (see box overleaf). The so-called MIT model has been adopted worldwide, so far with limited success. For example, in 1999 Cambridge University in the UK formed a UK government-sponsored joint venture with MIT to help develop spin-offs in the UK. However, to put such initiatives into perspective, Hermann Hauser, a venture capitalist, notes 'Stanford alumni have produced companies worth a trillion dollars. MIT half a trillion dollars. If Cambridge is getting to $20bn we will be lucky.' One reason is the differences in scale. Mike Lynch, founder of the software company Autonomy, observes: 'Silicon Valley is 60 miles long and in the last few months there will have been 70 to 80 money raisings in the $50 million to $200 million range. In Cambridge we might think of one, perhaps.'

ENTREPRENEURSHIP IN ACTION

Boston's Route 128

The cluster of universities in Boston and Cambridge in the USA, which includes the Massachusetts Institute of Technology (MIT), Harvard, Boston University and 70 other colleges and universities, has a long tradition of spawning spin-off firms. The success of the region can be traced back to the defence-related investments in computing and software which helped to create incubator firms such as Compaq, Digital, Data General, Lucent, Lotus, Raytheon and Wang in the 1970s, and more recently the creation of many life sciences-based ventures in biotechnology and medical devices.

For several decades now, the venture capital industry has consistently funded the creation or growth of around 200–300 new firms each year with annual funding of around US$2 billion (this more than quadrupled during the Internet boom/bubble of 1998/2000). To date MIT alone has helped to create 4000 new firms worldwide with total revenues of US$232 billion, with more than a thousand of these firms still based in Massachusetts.

Source: Wonglimpiyarat, J. (2006). The Boston Route 128 model of high-tech industry development, *International Journal of Innovation Management*, **10** (1), 47–64.

Examples of large incubator firms include the Xerox PARC and Bell Laboratories in the USA which spawned Fairchild Semiconductor which in turn led to numerous spin-offs including Intel, Advanced Memory Systems, Teledyne and Advanced Micro-Devices. Similarly, Engineering Research Associates (ERA) led to more than 40 new firms, including Cray, Control Data Systems, Sperry and Univac as shown in box below. In many cases, incubator firms provide the technical entrepreneurs, and the associated academic institutions provide the additional qualified manpower.

ENTREPRENEURSHIP IN ACTION

Spin-off Companies from Xerox's PARC Labs

Xerox established its Palo Alto Research Center (PARC) in California in 1970. PARC was responsible for a large number of technological innovations in the semiconductor lasers, laser printing, Ethernet networking technology and Web indexing and searching technologies, but it is generally acknowledged that many of its most significant innovations were the result of individuals who left the company and firms which spun off from PARC, rather than developed via the Xerox itself. For example, many of the user-interface developments at Apple originated at Xerox, as did the basis of Microsoft's Word package. By 1998 Xerox PARC had spun out 24 firms, including 10 which went public such as 3Com, Adobe, Documentum, and SynOptics. By 2001 the value of the spin-off companies was more than twice that of Xerox itself.

A debate continues as to the reasons for this, most attributing the failure to retain the technologies in-house to corporate ignorance and internal politics. However, most of the technologies did not simply 'leak out', but instead were granted permission by Xerox, which often provided non-exclusive licences and an equity stake in the spin-off firms. This suggests that Xerox's research and business managers saw little potential for exploiting these technologies in its own businesses. One of the reasons for the failure to commercialize these technologies in-house was that Xerox had been highly successful with its integrated product-focused strategy, which made it more difficult to recognize and exploit potential new *businesses*.

Source: Chesbrough, H. (2003). *Open Innovation: The New Imperative for Creating and Profiting from Technology*. Harvard Business School Press, Boston, Mass.

Spin-off firms tend to cluster around their respective incubator organizations, forming regional networks of expertise. The firms tend to remain close to their parents for a number of technical and personal reasons. Most spin-offs retain contacts with their parent organizations to gain financial and technical support, and are often reluctant to disrupt their social and family lives while establishing a new venture. Perhaps surprisingly, the mortality rate of spin-offs is lower than that of most types of new firm, around 20–30% in 10 years compared to more than 80% for other types of new business. One explanation for their higher survival rate is that the barriers to entry are higher than for many other businesses, in terms of expertise and capital. Therefore those new ventures that are able to overcome such barriers are more likely to survive. The concentration of start-ups in a region can create positive feedback, through demonstration effects and by increasing the demand for, and experience of, supporting institutions, such as venture capitalists, legal services and contract research and production, thereby improving the environment and probability of success of subsequent start-ups. Failures are an inherent part of such a system and, providing a steady stream of new venture proposals exists and venture capitalists maintain diverse investment portfolios and are ruthless with failed ventures, the system continues to learn from both good and bad investments.

However, the unique circumstances of the US environment in the 1970s and 1980s call into question the generalizability of the lessons of Silicon Valley and Route 128. Specifically, the role of the defence industry investment, liberal tax regimes and sources of venture capital were unique. In addition, it is important to distinguish the evolutionary growth of such regional clusters of innovative new ventures, from more recent attempts to establish science parks based around universities. For example, the success of science parks in Europe and Asia in the 1990s, and other attempts to emulate the early US experiences, has been limited, and studies comparing firms located on and off university science parks conclude that there were no statistically significant differences between their technological inputs, such as expenditure on R&D, and outputs, such as new products and patents. Often such science parks provide little more than cheap, short-term leases and a prestigious address.

In addition to individual entrepreneurs, a successful entrepreneurial system needs the broad participation of a diversity of entrepreneurial actors and institutions, including small and larger firms, universities, and sources of funding and support.

Broad participation refers to the need for an inclusive system of development, production and consumption of innovations. Early innovations can be traced to individual inventors or more often a combination of an inventor and entrepreneur, and their efforts were often only affordable by the wealthy elite. This system is often referred to as the Schumpeter Model 1 of innovation, after the economic historian Joseph Schumpeter. However, as Schumpeter and others noted, innovation became more and more the province of larger organizations, characterized by greater economies of research, development, production and sales. This is often referred to as the Schumpeter Model 2 of innovation. It is characterized by mass production and consumption, but more fundamentally by workers and consumers who believe that growth and innovation are both inevitable and desirable. In this system the sources of innovation are more distributed, for example, it is difficult to trace individual inventors, and educated users play a more significant part in the development and evolution of innovations.

The diversity of the entrepreneurial species refers to the co-existence of both Schumperian models of innovation. Individual inventors and entrepreneurs, small and large firms co-exist and make different contributions. For example, in the computer games industry, large firms are necessary to test, distribute and support games, but the design, development and improvement of games is the result of inputs of numerous developers and users.

Roles of Small and Large Firms

The relationship between the size of firm and degree of innovation is unclear. In theory, large and small firms have different advantages and disadvantages:[6]

- Larger firms are more able to exploit economies of scale and scope in innovation, including research, development, production and sales. For example, large firms dominate where large expenditures on R&D are necessary, such as in aerospace or pharmaceuticals, where there are significant production economies of scale, as in automobile or consumer electronics, or where high-volume global sales are necessary, as in fast-moving consumer goods (FMCGs). However, larger firms suffer from high levels of bureaucracy and may neglect higher risk or lower volume opportunities.

- Small firms are less bureaucratic, and are able to flourish in smaller market niches which may be unattractive to larger firms. Motivation is typically much higher in such organizations. However, they lack internal resources and must therefore rely more on external sources of innovation and partnerships to develop and exploit innovations.

In practice, this means that neither large nor small firms are inherently more or less innovative. Instead, they tend to exhibit different patterns of innovation due to these different relative advantages.

In terms of innovation, the performance of small and medium enterprises (SMEs) is easily exaggerated. Early studies based on innovation counts consistently indicated that, when adjusted for size, smaller firms created more new products than their larger counterparts. However, methodological shortcomings appear to undermine this clear message. When the divisions and subsidiaries of larger organizations are removed from such samples, and the innovations weighted according to their technological merit and commercial value, the relationship between firm size and innovation is reversed: larger firms create proportionally more significant innovations than SMEs.

Research over the past decade or so suggests that the innovative activities of SMEs exhibit broadly similar characteristics across sectors. They:

- Are more likely to involve product innovation than process innovation;

- Are focused on products for niche markets, rather than mass markets;

- Will be more common among producers of final products, rather than producers of components;

- Will frequently involve some form of external linkage;

- Tend to be associated with growth in output and employment, but not necessarily profit.

Unlike large firms, small firms tend to be specialized rather than diversified in their technological competencies and product range. However, as with large firms, it is impossible to make robust generalizations about their technological trajectories and innovation strategies. Kurt Hoffman and his colleagues have recently pointed out that relatively little research has been undertaken on innovation in small firms: what research has been done tends to concentrate on the small group of spectacular high-tech successes (or failures) rather than the much more numerous run-of-the-mill small firms coping (say) with the introduction of IT into their distribution systems.[7]

Table 8.1 tries to categorize these differences. Until recently, attention has been focused on the left-hand side of the table – the spectacular and visible successes among small innovating firms: in particular, the 'superstars' that became big, and those of the technology-based firms that often want to become big. As we have seen earlier in this chapter, recent more systematic surveys of innovative activities and of small firms show two other classes of small firm with less spectacular innovation strategies, but of far greater importance to the overall economy: specialized suppliers of production inputs, and firms whose sources of innovation are mainly their suppliers.

Superstars are large firms that have emerged from small beginnings, through high rates of growth based on the exploitation of a major invention (e.g. instant photography, reprography), or a rich technological trajectory (e.g. semiconductors, software), enabling small firms to exploit first-mover advantages like patent protection (see Chapter 6). Successful innovators often either accumulated their technological knowledge in large firms before leaving to start their own, or they offered their invention to large firms but were refused (e.g. Polaroid, Xerox). Few superstars have emerged either in the chemical industry over the past 50 years, or – contrary to expectations – out of biotechnology firms over the past 15 years, probably because the barriers to entry (in R&D, production, or marketing) remain high.

The examples in Table 8.1 show that many superstars are from the USA, although we can find European and Japanese examples. Experience suggests that one of the main challenges facing the management of superstars is their transition from the original innovator and the original innovation to new management and a new line of products. Beyond the period of spectacular growth, the characteristics behind the original success can become sources of 'core rigidities'. Successful innovators are often strong characters who do not necessarily encourage diversity in ideas and approaches within the firm. Successful innovations are often well protected by patents and other first-comer

Table 8.1   Categories of innovating small firms

	Superstars: small firms into big since 1950	New technology-based firms (NTBFs)	Specialized	Supplier-dominated
Examples	Polaroid, DEC, TI, Xerox, Intel, Microsoft, Compaq, Sony, Casio, Benetton	Start-ups in electronics, biotechnology and software	Producer of goods (machines, components, instruments, software)	Traditional products (e.g. textiles, wood products, food products) and many services
Sources of competitive advantage	Successful exploitation of major invention or technological trajectory	1. Product or process development in fastmoving and specialized area 2. Privatizing academic research	Combining technologies to meet user's needs	Integration and adaptation of innovations by suppliers
Main tasks of innovation strategy	Preparing replacements for the original invention (or inventor)	1. 'Superstar' or 'specialized supplier'? 2. Knowledge or money?	Links to advanced users and pervasive technologies	Exploiting new IT-based opportunities in design, distribution and co-ordination

advantages, which can blunt the drive for improvement and change. These difficulties have beset companies like DEC, Polaroid and Xerox. An interesting exercise is to speculate about the future of today's superstars: what will happen to Microsoft after Bill Gates, or Apple after Steve Jobs?

New technology-based firms (NTBFs) are small firms that have emerged recently from large firms and large laboratories in such fields as electronics, software and biotechnology. They are usually specialized in the supply of a key component, subsystem, service or technique to larger firms, who may often be their former employers. Contrary to a widespread belief, most of the NTBFs in electronics and software have emerged from corporate or government laboratories involved in development and testing activities. It is only with the advent of biotechnology (and, more recently, software), that university laboratories have become regular sources of NTBFs, thereby strengthening the strong direct links that have always existed between university-based research and the pharmaceutical industry. However, some observers criticize this trend, and fear the 'privatization' of university research in biotechnology will in the long term reduce the rate of scientific progress and innovation and their contribution to economic and social welfare.

The management of NTBFs faces two sets of strategic problems:

- The first relates to long-term prospects for growth. Very few technology-based small firms can become superstars, since they provide mainly specialized 'niche' products with no obvious or spectacular synergies with other markets. How far the firm will grow, or how long it will survive, will often depend on its ability to negotiate the transition from the first to the second (improved) generation of products, and to develop the supporting managerial competencies.

- How far the NTBF will grow depends on the second strategic choice: whether the management is aiming to maximize long-term value of the business, or merely seeking an increase in income and independence. Thus, owners of small firms often sell their firms after a few years and live off their investments. And university researchers set up consultancy firms, either to increase their personal income (the BMW effect), or to find supplementary income for their university-based research and teaching activities in times of increasing financial stringency.

Specialized supplier firms design, develop and build specialized inputs into production, in the form of machinery, instruments and (increasingly) software, and interact closely with their (often large) technically progressive customers. They perform relatively little formal R&D, but are nonetheless a major source of the active development of significant innovations, with major contributions being made by design and production staff.

Finally, most small firms fall into the *supplier-dominated* category, with their suppliers of production inputs as their main sources of new technology. These firms depend heavily on their suppliers for their innovations, and therefore are often unable to appropriate firm-specific technology as a source of competitive advantage. Technology will become more important in future, with the growing range of potential IT applications offered by suppliers, especially in service activities like distribution and coordination. An increasing range of small firms will therefore need to obtain the technological competencies to be able to specify, purchase, install and maintain software systems that help increase their competitiveness. Whether these competencies will become distinctive, *core* competencies is less clear, given that they can be adopted by all small firms. Distinctive advantage will emerge only where the software competencies are difficult to imitate, namely in developing and operating complex systems. Among small firms, such competencies are less likely to emerge in those *using* software, than among those *supplying* software services.

Role of University Incubators

The creation and sharing of intellectual property is a core role of a university, but managing it for commercial gain is a different challenge. Most universities with significant commercial research contracts understand how to license, and the roles of all parties – the academics, the university and the commercial organization – are relatively clear. In particular, the academic will normally continue with the research while possibly having a consultancy arrangement with the commercial company. However, forming an independent company is a different matter. Here both the university and the scientist must agree that spin-out is the most viable option for technology commercialization and must negotiate a spin-out deal. This may include questions of, for example, equity split, royalties, academic and university investment in the new venture, academic secondment, identification and transfer of intellectual property and use of university resources in the start-up phase. In short, it is complicated. As Chris Evans, founder of Chiroscience and Merlin Ventures notes: 'Academics and universities – have no management, no muscle, no vision, no business plan and that is 90% of the task of exploiting science and taking it to the marketplace. There is a tendency for universities to think, "we invented the thing so we are already 50% there". The fact is they are 50% to nowhere' (*Times Higher*, 27 March 1998). A characteristically provocative statement, but it does highlight the gulf between research and successful commercialization.

Many universities have accepted and followed the fashion for the commercial exploitation of technology, but typically put too much emphasis on the importance of the technology and ownership of the intellectual property, and 'fail to recognize the importance and sophistication of the business knowledge and expertise of management and other parties who contribute to the non-technical aspects of technology shaping and development . . . the linear model gives no insight into the interplay of technology push and market pull'.[8]

Since the mid-1980s the role of universities in the commercialization of technology has increased significantly. For example, the number of patents granted to US universities doubled between 1984 and 1989, and doubled again between 1989 and 1997. In 1979 the number of patents granted to US universities was only 264, compared to 2436 in 1997. There are a number of explanations for this significant increase in patent activity. Changes in government funding and intellectual property law played a role, but detailed analysis indicates that the most significant reason was technological opportunity.

Changes in funding and law in the 1980s clearly encouraged many more universities to establish licensing and technology transfer departments, but the impact of these has been relatively small. For example, there is strong evidence that the scientific and commercial quality of patents has fallen since the mid-1980s as a result of these policy changes, and that the distribution of activity has a very long tail. Measured in terms of the number of patents held or exploited, or by income from patent and software licences, commercialization of technology is highly concentrated in a small number of elite universities which were highly active prior to changes to funding policy and law: the top 20 US universities account for 70% of the patent activity. Moreover, at each of these elite universities a very small number of key patents account for most of the licensing income; the 5 most successful patents typically account for 70–90% of total income.[9] This suggests that a (rare) combination of research excellence and critical mass is required to succeed in the commercialization of technology. Nonetheless, technological opportunity has reduced some of the barriers to commercialization. Specifically, the growing importance of developments in the biosciences and software present new opportunities for universities to benefit from the commercialization of technology.

University spin-outs are an alternative to exploitation of technology through licensing, and involve the creation of an entirely new venture based upon intellectual property developed within the university. Estimates vary, but 3–12% of all technologies commercialized by universities are via new ventures. As with licensing, the propensity and success of these ventures varies significantly. For example, MIT and Stanford University each create around 25 new start-ups each year, whereas Columbia and Duke Universities rarely generate any start-up companies. Studies in the USA suggest that the financial returns to universities are much higher from spin-out companies than from the more common licensing approach. One study estimated that the average income from a university licence was US$63 832, whereas the average return from a university spin-out was more than 10 times this – US$692 121. When the extreme cases were excluded from the sample, the return from spin-outs was still US$139 722, more than twice that for a licence.[10] Apart from these financial arguments, there are other reasons why forming a spin-out company may be preferable to licensing technology to an established company:

- No existing company is ready or able to take on the project on a licensing basis.

- The invention consists of a portfolio of products or is an 'enabling technology' capable of application in a number of fields.

- The inventors have a strong preference for forming a company and are prepared to invest their time, effort and money in a start-up.

As such they involve the 'academic entrepreneur' more fully in the detail of creating and managing a market entry strategy than is the case for other forms of commercialization. They also require major career decisions for the participants. Consequently, they highlight most clearly the dilemmas faced as the scientist tries to manage the interface between academe and industry. The extent to which an individual is motivated to attempt the launch of a venture depends upon three related factors – antecedent influences, the incubator organization and environmental factors:

- *Antecedent influences*, often called the 'characteristics' of the entrepreneur, include genetic factors, family influences, educational choices and previous career experiences, all of which contribute to the entrepreneur's decision to start a venture.

- *Individual incubator experiences* immediately prior to start-up include the nature of the physical location, the type of skills and knowledge acquired, contact with possible fellow founders, the type of new venture or small business experience gained.

- *Environmental factors* include economic conditions, availability of venture capital, entrepreneurial role models, availability of support services.

There are relatively few data on the characteristics of the academic entrepreneur, partly due to the low numbers involved, but also because the traditional context within which they have operated, particularly as they apply to IPR and equity sharing, has meant that many have been unwilling to be researched. It is also probable that this is compounded by inadequate university data capture systems. Nevertheless, it is clear that, in the USA, scientists and engineers working in universities have long become disposed towards the commercialization of research. Studies in the USA reveal an increasing legitimization of university–industry research interactions. However, academic entrepreneurs are still not the norm, even in the USA. A study of 237 scientists working in 3 large national laboratories in the USA found clear differences between the levels of education in inventors in national laboratories and those in a study of technical entrepreneurs from MIT. The study found significant differences between entrepreneurs and non-entrepreneurs in terms of situational variables such as the level of involvement in business activities outside the laboratory or the receipt of royalties from past inventions.[11] Studies of academic scientists and engineers in the UK identify similar relationships between attitudes to industry, number of industry links and commercial activity.[12] This begs the question: What is the direction of causation? Do entrepreneurial researchers seek more links outside the organization, or do more links encourage entrepreneurial behaviour?

Entrepreneurs, academic or otherwise, require a supportive environment. Surveys indicate that two-thirds of university scientists and engineers now support the need to commercialize their research, and half the need for start-up assistance. There are two levels of analysis of the university environment: the formal institutional rules, policies and structures, and the 'local norms' within the individual department. There are a number of institutional variables which might influence academic entrepreneurship:

■ Formal policy and support for entrepreneurial activity from management.

■ Perceived seriousness of constraints to entrepreneurship, for example, IPR issues.

■ Incidence of successful commercialization, which demonstrate feasibility and provide role models.

Formal policies to encourage and support entrepreneurship can have both intended and unintended consequences. For example, a university policy of taking an equity stake in new start-ups in return for paying initial patenting and licensing expenses seems to result in a higher number of start-ups, whereas granting generous royalties to academic entrepreneurs appears to encourage licensing activity, but tends to suppress significantly the number of start-up companies.[13] In addition, some very common university policies appear to have little or no positive effect on the number of subsequent successful start-ups, including university incubators and local venture capital funding. Moreover, badly targeted and poorly monitored financial support may encourage 'entrepreneurial academics', rather than academic entrepreneurs – scientists in the public sector who are not really committed to creating start-ups, but rather are seeking alternative support for their own research agendas. This can result in start-ups with little or no growth prospects, remaining in incubators for many years. Simply encouraging commercially oriented or industry-funded research also appears to have no effect on the number of start-ups, whereas a university's intellectual eminence has a very strong positive effect.[14] There are two explanations for this effect: more prestigious universities typically attract better researchers and higher funding; and other commercial investors use the prestige or reputation of the institution as a signal or indicator of quality.

Formal policies may send a signal to staff, but the effect on individual behaviour depends very much on whether these policies are reinforced by behavioural expectations. Individual characteristics and local norms appear to be equally effective predictors of entrepreneurial activity, but only provide weak predictions of the forms of entrepreneurship. Where successful, this can create a virtuous circle, the demonstration effect of a successful spin-out encouraging others to try. This leads to clusters of spin-outs in space and time, resulting in entrepreneurial departments or universities, rather than isolated entrepreneurial academics. Local norms or culture at the departmental level will influence the effectiveness of formal policies by providing a strong mediating effect between the institutional context and individual perceptions. Local norms evolve through self-selection during recruitment, resulting in staff with similar personal values and behaviour, and reinforced by peer pressure or behavioural socialization resulting in a convergence of personal values and behaviour. However, there is a potential conflict between the pursuit of knowledge and its commercial exploitation, and a real danger of lowering research standards exists. Therefore it is essential to have explicit guidelines for the conduct of business in a university environment:

■ Specific guidelines on the use of university facilities, staff and students and intellectual property rights.

■ Specific guidelines for, and periodic reviews of, the dual employment of scientist-entrepreneurs, including permanent part-time positions.

■ Mechanisms to resolve issues of financial ownership and the allocation of research contracts between the university and the venture.

ENTREPRENEURSHIP IN ACTION

License or Spin-out? The Lambert Review of Business–University Collaboration in the UK

In the UK, the Lambert Review of Business–University Collaboration reported in December 2003. It reviewed the commercialization of intellectual property by universities in the UK, and also made international comparisons of policy and performance. The UK has a similar pattern of concentration of activity as the USA: in 2002 80% of UK universities made no patent applications, whereas 5% filed 20 or more patents; similarly, 60% of universities issued no new licences, but 5% issued more than 30. However, in the UK there has been a bias towards spin-outs rather then licensing, which the Lambert Report criticizes. It argues that spin-outs are often too complex and unsustainable, and of low quality – a third in the UK are fully funded by the parent university and attract no external private funding. In 2002 universities in the UK created over 150 new spin-out firms, compared to almost 500 by universities in the USA; the respective figures for new licenses that year were 648 and 4058. As a proportion of R&D expenditure, this suggests that British universities place greater emphasis on spin-outs than their North American counterparts, and less on licensing. Lambert argues that universities in the UK may place too high a price on their intellectual property, and that contracts often lack clarity of ownership. Both of these problems discourage businesses from licensing intellectual property from universities, and may encourage universities to commercialize their technologies through wholly owned spin-outs.

Process and Stages for Creating a New Venture

Typical stages of creating a new venture include:

- Assessing the opportunity for a new venture – generating, evaluating and refining the business concept.

- Developing the business plan and deciding the structure of the venture.

- Acquiring the resources and funding necessary for implementation – including expert support and potential partnerships.

- Growing and harvesting the venture – how to create and extract value from the business.

A new venture will face different challenges at different stages in order to make a successful transition to the next stage, what the researchers call 'critical junctures':

- *Opportunity recognition* – at the interface of the research and opportunity framing phases. This requires the ability to connect a specific technology or know-how to a commercial application, and is based on a rather rare combination of skill, experience, aptitude, insight, and circumstances. A key issue here is the ability to synthesize scientific knowledge and market insights, which increases with the entrepreneur's social capital – linkages, partnerships and other network interactions.

- *Entrepreneurial commitment* – acts and sustained persistence that bind the venture champion to the emerging business venture. This often demands difficult personal decisions to be made, for example, whether or not to remain an academic, as well as evidence of direct financial investments to the venture.

■ *Venture credibility* – is critical for the entrepreneur to gain the resources necessary to acquire the finance and other resources for the business to function. Credibility is a function of the venture team, key customers and other social capital and relationships. This requires close relationships with sponsors, financial and other, to build and maintain awareness and credibility. Lack of business experience, and failure to recognize their own limitations are a key problem here. One solution is to hire the services of a 'surrogate entrepreneur'. As one experienced entrepreneur notes: 'The not so smart or really insecure academics want their hands over everything. These prima donnas make a complete mess of things, get nowhere with their companies and end up disappointed professionally and financially.'

Assessing the Opportunity

One of the failures of many discussions of entrepreneurship is that they assume that the opportunity has already been identified, and all that remains is to develop and resource this. However, in practice a budding entrepreneur may have only a vague idea of the basis of a new venture. Common sources of ideas for new ventures include:

■ Extensions or adaptations of existing products or services.

■ Application of existing products or services in different or newly created market segments, or at different price points, for example, low-cost airlines such as Ryanair and Easyjet, or Dyson's household cleaner which adapted centrifugal technology from industrial applications.

■ Adding value to an existing product or service, for example, Web search engines for specialist fields like travel and insurance, such as TravelJungle.co.uk or Confused.com.

■ Developing a completely new product or service.

The more fundamental drivers of opportunities for new ventures are:

■ Economic factors – for example, changes in disposable income;

■ Technological developments – which may reduce (or increase) barriers to entry;

■ Demographic trends – for example, the ageing population, more leisure time;

■ Regulatory changes – for example, environmental requirements, health and safety.

All of these potential sources can be more readily identified and assessed by using the systematic approaches to scanning and searching that we advocated in Chapters 1 and 2. One useful source of ideas is to examine how potential users live and work, and identify unmet needs or better ways of providing existing products and services as shown in box below. We introduced quality function deployment in Chapter 5, but it is also useful here to help to assess opportunities and compare these with existing competing offerings as shown in the box overleaf.

ENTREPRENEURSHIP IN ACTION

Learning from Users at IDEO

IDEO is one of the most successful design consultancies in the world, based in Palo Alto, California and London, UK. It helps large consumer and industrial companies worldwide to design and develop innovative new products and services. Behind its rather typical Californian wackiness lies a tried and tested process for successful design and development:

■ Understand the market, client and technology.

■ Observe users and potential users in real-life situations.

■ Visualize new concepts and the customers who might use them, using prototyping, models and simulations.

■ Evaluate and refine the prototypes in a series of quick iterations.

■ Implement the new concept for commercialization.

The first critical step is achieved through close *observation* of potential users in context. As Tom Kelly of IDEO argues:

> We're not big fans of focus groups. We don't much care for traditional market research either. We go to the source. Not the 'experts' inside a (client) company, but the actual people who use the product or something similar to what we're hoping to create . . . we believe you have to go beyond putting yourself in your customers' shoes. Indeed we believe it's not even enough to ask people what they think about a product or idea . . . customers' may lack the vocabulary or the palate to explain what's wrong, and especially what's missing.

The next step is to develop prototypes to help evaluate and refine the ideas captured from users. 'an iterative approach to problems is one of the foundations of our culture of prototyping . . . you can prototype just about anything – a new product or service, or a special promotion. What counts is moving the ball forward, achieving some part of your goal.'

Source: Kelly, T. (2002). *The Art of Innovation: Lessons in Creativity from IDEO*, HarperCollins Business, New York.

ENTREPRENEURSHIP IN ACTION

Using Quality Function Deployment to Assess Opportunities

Quality function deployment (QFD) is a useful technique for translating customer requirements into development needs, and encourages communication between engineering, production and marketing. Unlike most other tools of quality management, QFD is used to identify opportunities for product improvement or differentiation, rather than to solve problems. Customer-required characteristics are translated or 'deployed' by means of a matrix into language which engineers can understand. The construction of a relationship matrix – also known as 'the house of quality' – requires a significant amount of technical and market research. Great emphasis must be made on gathering market and user data in order to identify potential design trade-offs, and to achieve the most appropriate balance between cost, quality and performance. The construction of a QFD matrix involves the following steps:

■ Identify customer requirements, primary and secondary, and any major dislikes.

■ Rank requirements according to importance.

■ Translate requirements into measurable characteristics.

■ Establish the relationship between the customer requirements and technical product characteristics, and estimate the strength of the relationship.

■ Choose appropriate units of measurement and determine target values based on customer requirements and competitor benchmarks.

Symbols are used to show the relationship between customer requirements and technical specifications, and weights attached to illustrate the strength of the relationship. Horizontal rows with no relationship symbol indicate that the existing design is incomplete. Conversely, vertical columns with no relationship symbol indicate that an existing design feature is redundant as it is not valued by the customer. In addition, comparisons with competing products, or benchmarks, can be included. This is important because relative quality is more relevant than absolute quality: customer expectations are likely to be shaped by what else is available, rather than some ideal.

In some cases potential users may have latent needs or requirements which they cannot articulate. In such cases three types of user need can be identified: 'must-bes', 'one-dimensionals' and attractive features or 'delighters'. Must-bes are those features which must exist before a potential customer will consider a product or service. For example, in the case of an executive car it must be relatively large and expensive. One-dimensionals are the more quantifiable features which allow direct comparison between competing products. For example, in the case of an executive car, the acceleration and braking performance. Finally, the delighters, which are the most subtle means of differentiation. The inclusion of such features delights the target customers, even if they do not explicitly demand them. For example, delighters in the case of an executive car include ultrasonic parking aids, rain-sensitive windscreen wipers and photochromatic mirrors. Such features are rarely demanded by customers or identified by regular market research. However, indirect questioning can be used to help identify latent requirements.

Developing the Business Plan

The primary reason for developing a formal business plan for a new venture is to attract external funding. However, it serves an important secondary function. A business plan can provide a formal agreement between founders regarding the basis and future development of the venture. A business plan can help reduce self-delusion on the part of the founders, and avoid subsequent arguments concerning responsibilities and rewards. It can help to translate abstract or ambiguous goals into more explicit operational needs, and support subsequent decision-making and identify trade-offs. Of the factors *controllable* by entrepreneurs, business planning has the most significant positive effect on new venture performance. However, there are of course many *uncontrollable* factors, such as market opportunity, which have an even more significant influence on performance.

A typical formal business plan will include the following sections:

■ Details of the product or service.

■ Assessment of the market opportunity.

■ Identification of target customers.

- Barriers to entry and competitor analysis.

- Experience, expertise and commitment of the management team.

- Strategy for pricing, distribution and sales.

- Identification and planning for key risks.

- Cash-flow calculation, including break-even points and sensitivity.

- Financial and other resource requirements of the business.

No standard business plan exists, but in many cases venture capitalists will provide a pro forma for the business plan. Typically a business plan should be relatively concise, say no more than 10–20 pages, begin with an executive summary, and include sections on the product, markets, technology, development, production, marketing, human resources, financial estimates with contingency plans, and the timetable and funding requirements. Most business plans submitted to venture capitalists are strong on the technical considerations, often placing too much emphasis on the technology relative to other issues. As Ed. Roberts notes, 'Entrepreneurs propose that they can do *it* better than anyone else, but may forget to demonstrate that anyone wants *it*.' He identifies a number of common problem areas with business plans submitted to venture capitalists: marketing plan, management team, technology plan and financial plan. The management team will be assessed against their commitment, experience, and expertise, normally in that order. Unfortunately, many potential entrepreneurs place too much emphasis on their expertise, but have insufficient experience in the team, and fail to demonstrate the passion and commitment to the venture.

There are common serious inadequacies in all four of these areas, but the worst are in marketing and finance. Less than half of the plans examined provide a detailed marketing strategy, and just half include any sales plan. Three-quarters of the plans fail to identify or analyse any potential competitors. As a result most business plans contain only basic financial forecasts, and just 10% conduct any sensitivity analysis on the forecasts. The lack of attention to marketing and competitor analysis is particularly problematic as research indicates that both factors are associated with subsequent success.

For example, in the early stages many new ventures rely too much on a few major customers for sales, and are therefore very vulnerable commercially. As an extreme example, around half of technology ventures rely on a single customer for more than half of their first-year sales. This over-dependence on a small number of customers has three major drawbacks:

- Vulnerability to changes in the strategy and health of the dominant customer.

- A loss of negotiating power, which may reduce profit margins.

- Little incentive to develop marketing and sales functions, which may limit future growth.

Acquiring the Resources and Funding

The potential sources of initial funding for creating a new venture include:

- Self-funding.

- Family and friends.

- Business angels.

- Bank loans.

- Government schemes.

The initial funding to establish a new venture is rarely a major problem. Almost all are funded from personal savings or loans from family or friends. At this stage few professional sources of capital will be interested, with the possible exception of government support schemes. However, a new venture is likely to require financial restructuring every three years, if it is to develop and grow. Studies identify stages of development, each having different financial requirements:

- Initial financing for launch.

- Second-round financing for initial development and growth.

- Third-round financing for consolidation and growth.

- Maturity or exit.

In general, professional financial bodies are not interested in initial funding because of the high risk and low sums of money involved. It is simply not worth their time and effort to evaluate and monitor such ventures. However, as the sums involved are relatively small, typically of the order of tens of thousands of pounds, personal savings, remortgages and loans from friends and relatives are often sufficient. In contrast, third-round finance for consolidation is relatively easy to obtain, because by that time the venture has a proven track record on which to base the business plan, and the venture capitalist can see an exit route.

Given their strong desire for independence, most entrepreneurs seek to avoid external funding for their ventures. However, in practice this is not always possible, particularly in the latter growth stages. The initial funding required to form a new venture includes the purchase of accommodation, equipment and other start-up costs, plus the day-to-day running costs such as salaries, heating, light and so on – usually referred to as the working capital. For these reasons, many ventures begin life as part-time businesses, and are funded by personal savings, loans from friends and relatives, and bank loans, in that order. Around half also receive some funding from government sources, but in contrast receive next to nothing from venture capitalists. Venture capital is typically only made available at later stages to fund growth on the basis of a proven development and sales record.

Technology ventures are different from other new ventures in that there is often no marketable product available before or shortly after formation. Therefore, initial funding of the venture cannot normally be based on cash flow derived from early sales. The precise cash-flow profile will be determined by a number of factors, including development time and cost, and the volume and profit margin of sales. Different development and sales strategies exist, but to some extent these factors are determined by the nature of the technology and markets. For example, biotechnology ventures typically require more start-up capital than electronics or software-based ventures, and have longer product development lead times. Therefore, from the perspective of a potential entrepreneur, the ideal strategy would be to conduct as much development work as possible within the incubator organization before starting the new venture. However, there are practical problems with this strategy, in particular ownership of the intellectual property on which the venture is to be based.

The extent of the need for external funding will depend on the nature of the technology and the market strategy of the venture. For example, software-based ventures typically require less start-up capital than either electronics or biotechnology ventures, it is more common for such firms to rely solely on personal funding; but an electronics or software-based venture will also demand high initial funding if a strategy of aggressive growth is to be achieved. Biotechnology firms tend to have the highest R&D costs, and consequently most require some external funding. In contrast, software firms typically require little R&D investment, and are less likely to seek external funds. Almost three-quarters of software start-ups were funded by profits after three years, whereas only a third of the biotechnology firms had achieved this.

Venture capitalists are keen to provide funding for a venture with a proven track record and strong business plan, but in return will often require some equity or management involvement. Moreover, most venture capitalists are looking for a means to make capital gains after about five years. However, almost by definition technical entrepreneurs seek independence and control, and there is evidence that some will sacrifice growth to maintain control of their ventures. For the same reason, few entrepreneurs are prepared to 'go public' to fund further growth. Thus many entrepreneurs will choose to sell the business and found another. In fact, the typical technical entrepreneur establishes an average of three new ventures. Therefore the biggest funding problem is likely to be for the second-round financing to fund development and growth. It can be a time-consuming and frustrating process to convince venture capitalists to provide finance. The formal proposal is critical at this stage. Professional investors will assess the attractiveness of the venture in terms of the strengths and personalities of the founders, the formal business plan and the commercial and technical merits of the product, probably in that order.

ENTREPRENEURSHIP IN ACTION

Reuters' Corporate Venture Funds

Reuters established its first fund for external ventures, Greenhouse 1, in 1995. It has since added a further two venture funds, which aim to invest in related businesses such as financial services, media and network infrastructure. By 2001 it had invested US$432 million in 83 companies, and these investments contributed almost 10% to its profits. However, financial return was not the primary objective of the funds. For example, it invested US$1 million in Yahoo in 1995, and consequently Yahoo acquired part of its content from Reuters. This increased the visibility of Reuters in the growing Internet markets, particularly in the USA where it was not well known, and resulted in other portals following Yahoo's lead with content from Reuters. By 2001 Reuters' content was available on 900 Web services, and had an estimated 40 million users per month.

Source: Loudon, A. (2001). *Webs of Innovation: The Networked Economy Demands New Ways to Innovate*, Pearson Education, Harlow.

Venture Capital

An important issue is the influence of venture capitalists on the success of new ventures. They can play two distinct roles. The first is to identify or select those ventures that have the best potential for success; that is 'picking winners' or 'scouting'. The second role is to help develop the chosen ventures, by providing management expertise and access to resources other than financial; that is a 'coaching' role. Distinguishing between the effects of these two roles is critical for both the management of and policy for business. For managers, it will influence the choice of venture capital firm, and for policy, the balance between funding and other forms of support.

When selecting start-ups to invest in, the most significant criteria used by venture capitalists are a broad, experienced top management team, a large number of recent patents, and downstream industry alliances (but not upstream research alliances, which had a negative effect on selection). The strongest effect on the decision to fund was the first criterion, and the human capital in general. However, subsequent analysis of venture performance

Table 8.2 Criteria used by venture capitalists to assess proposals

Criteria	European (n = 195)	American (n = 100)	Asian (n = 53)
Entrepreneur able to evaluate and react to risk	3.6	3.3	3.5
Entrepreneur capable of sustained effort	3.6	3.6	3.7
Entrepreneur familiar with the market	3.5	3.6	3.6
Entrepreneur demonstrated leadership ability*	3.2	3.4	3.0
Entrepreneur has relevant track record*	3.0	3.2	2.9
Product prototype exists and functions*	3.0	2.4	2.9
Product demonstrated market acceptance*	2.9	2.5	2.8
Product proprietary or can be protected*	2.7	3.1	2.6
Product is 'high technology'*	1.5	2.3	1.4
Target market has high growth rate*	3.0	3.3	3.2
Venture will stimulate an existing market	2.4	2.4	2.5
Little threat of competition within three years	2.2	2.4	2.4
Venture will create a new market*	1.8	1.8	2.2
Financial return >10 times within 10 years*	2.9	3.4	2.9
Investment is easily made liquid* (e.g. made public or acquired)	2.7	3.2	2.7
Financial return >10 times within 5 years*	2.1	2.3	2.1

1 = irrelevant, 2 = desirable, 3 = important, 4 = essential. * Denotes significant at the 0.05 level.

Source: Adapted from Knight, R. (1992) Criteria used by venture capitalists, in Khalil, T. and Bayraktar, B. (eds), *Management of Technology III: The key to global competitiveness*. Industrial Engineering & Management Press, Georgia, 574–583.

indicates that this factor has limited effect on performance, and that the few significant effects are split equally between improving and impeding the performance of a venture. The effects of technology and alliances on subsequent performance are much more significant and positive. In short, in the *selection* stage, venture capitalists place too much emphasis on human capital, specifically the top management team. In the development or coaching stages, venture capitalists do contribute to the success of the chosen ventures, and tend to introduce external professional management much earlier than if the venture is not funded by venture capital. Taken together, this suggests that the coaching role of venture capitalists is probably as important, if not more so, than the funding role, although policy interventions to promote the creation of venture often focus on the latter.

While there is general agreement about the main components of a good business plan, there are some significant differences in the relative weights attributed to each component. General venture capital firms typically only accept 5% of the ventures they are offered, and the specialist technology venture funds are even more selective, accepting around 3%. The main reasons for rejecting proposals are the lack of intellectual property, the skills of the management team, and size of the potential market. A survey of venture capitalists in North America, Europe and Asia found major similarities in the criteria used, but also identified several interesting differences in the weights attached to some criteria (Table 8.2). The criteria are similar to those discussed earlier, grouped into 5 categories:

- The entrepreneur's personality.
- The entrepreneur's experience.
- Characteristics of the product.
- Characteristics of the market.
- Financial factors.

ENTREPRENEURSHIP IN ACTION

Andrew Rickman and Bookham Technology

Andrew Rickman founded Bookham Technology in 1988, aged 28. Rickman has a degree in mechanical engineering from Imperial College, London, a PhD in integrated optics from Surrey University and an MBA, and has worked as a venture capitalist. Unlike many technology entrepreneurs, he did not begin with the development of a novel technology and then seek a means to exploit it. Instead, he first identified a potential market need for optical-switching technology for the then fledgling optical fibre networks, and then developed an appropriate technological solution. The market for optical components is growing fast as the use of Internet and other data-intensive traffic grows. Rickman aimed to develop an integrated optical circuit on a single chip to replace a number of discrete components such as lasers, lenses and mirrors. He chose to use silicon rather than more exotic materials to reduce development costs and exploit traditional chip production techniques. The main technological developments were made at Surrey University and the Rutherford Appleton Laboratory, where he had worked, and 27 patents were granted and a further 140 applied for. Once the technology had been proved, the company raised US$110 million over several rounds of funding from venture capitalist 3i, and leading electronics firms Intel and Cisco. The most difficult task was scale-up and production: 'Taking the technology out of the lab and into production is unbelievably tough in this area. It is infinitely more difficult than dreaming up the technology'. Bookham

Technology floated in London and on the Nasdaq in New York in April 2000 with a market capitalization of more than £5 billion, making Andrew Rickman, with 25% of the equity, a paper billionaire. Bookham is based in Oxford, and employs 400 staff. The company acquired the optical component businesses of Nortel and Marconi in 2002, and in 2003 the US optical companies Ignis Optics and New Focus, and the latter included chip production facilities in China. This puts Bookham in the top three in the global opto-electronics sector.

Overall, a bundle of personal, market and financial factors are consistently ranked as being most significant: a proven ability to lead others and sustain effort; familiarity with the market; and the potential for a high return within 10 years (Table 8.2). The personality and experience of the entrepreneurs are consistently ranked as being more important than either product or market characteristics, or even financial considerations. However, there were a number of significant differences between the preferences of venture capitalists from different regions. Those from the USA place a greater emphasis on a high financial return and liquidity than their counterparts in Europe or Asia, but less emphasis on the existence of a prototype or proven market acceptance. Perhaps surprisingly, all venture capitalists are averse to technological and market risks. Being described as a 'high-technology' venture was rated very low in importance by the US venture capitalists, and the European and Asian venture capitalists rated this characteristic as having a negative influence on funding. Similarly, having the potential to create an entirely new market is considered a drawback because of the higher risk attached. In short, venture capitalists are not particularly adventurous.

Venture capital in the UK invests relatively little in technology-based ventures. Over a 15-year period, 1990–2005, investment in technology-based firms as a percentage of total venture capital remained stable at around 10% of the total by value (Table 8.3). In absolute terms this still represents a significant sum, almost £7 billion in 2005, as the UK has a very large venture capital market. Of the total venture capital investment in UK of £6.8 billion in the year 2005, only 5% was for early stage funding (by value, or 38% by number of firms), 29% for expansion (by value, or 44% by number of firms), and the rest for management buy-outs or buy-ins (MBO/MBI). The average funds for a start-up or early stage venture was £800 000 (in 2005). The USA has the largest venture capital industry with investments of around US$340 billion in 2004 (Figure 8.2).

Table 8.3   Structure of venture capital in the UK, by stage and sector

	All ventures	Software	E-commerce	Biotechnology	Telecoms
Early/start-up	£382m (5%) n = 491 (38%)	£52m n = 88	£21m n = 46	£34m n = 36	£12m n = 27
Expansion	£1951m (29%) n = 573 (44%)	£82m n = 82	£24m n = 81	£23m n = 28	£24m n = 23
Management buy-out/in	£4480m (66%) n = 308 (24%)	£16m n = 14	£117m n = 31	£1m n = 3	£161m n = 9
Totals	£6813m n = 1307	£150m n = 180	£162m n = 157	£58m n = 67	£197m n = 58

Note: Totals do not always sum to 100% as firms may receive multiple funding.
Source: British Venture Capital Association (2006).

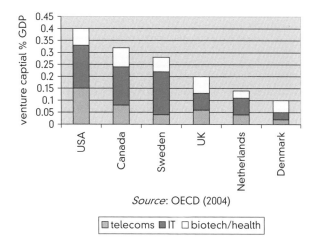

Figure 8.2 Breakdown of main venture funding capital by country and field.

As venture capital firms have gained experience of this type of funding, and the opportunities for flotation have increased due to the new secondary financial markets in Europe such as the AIM, TechMARK and Neur Market, their returns on investment have increased significantly as shown in the box below.

ENTREPRENEURSHIP IN ACTION

Alternative Investment Market

The Alternative Investment Market (AIM) was established in London, UK, in 1995 as an alternative to the London Stock Exchange (LSE). It is designed to be simpler and cheaper than the main market, and to have a less restrictive regulatory regime than the main exchange, and therefore is more suited to smaller firms at an earlier stage of development. AIM began with just 10 UK-based companies in 1995, but by 2006 had 1500 firms listed, including 250 from overseas. The total market capitalization was £72 billion in 2006. About half of all firms on the AIM have a market capitalization of less than £15 million, and a quarter of firms less than £5 million.

Listing on AIM is easier and cheaper than on most other exchanges, and costs around 5% of the funds raised on flotation. Admission to AIM takes around 4 months, and involves a number of prescribed steps:

- Development of the business plan.
- Appointment of the advisers – Nomad (nominated adviser), broker, accountant and lawyer. The Nomad is a unique and critical feature of AIM, and these are regulated by the LSE.
- Nomad prepares the timetable for admission.
- Accountants prepare financial due diligence, including historical trading record.
- Lawyers conduct the legal due diligence, including a review of all contracts, titles and any litigation.
- Accountants prepare the 18-month working capital requirements for the admission document.

> ■ Formal admission document is developed.
>
> ■ Marketing and completion, including institutional road-show and public relations.
>
> There is no minimum capitalization or trading record requirement, and no minimum proportion of shares which have to be held by the public. Institutional investors have been attracted to invest in AIM companies because of the many tax breaks available to investors, such as venture capital trusts. However, a listing on AIM requires greater transparency than a private company, for example, in terms of accounting standards, corporate governance and communication with investors.
>
> In 2005, 29 Chinese or China-focused firms were listed on the London AIM, but regulation, language and distance can make this more difficult and expensive than for local firms. The cost of listing is typically between £500 000 and £1 million, around twice that of a UK-based firm. AIM-style markets have been launched in Asia, including the SESDAQ in Singapore, Growth Enterprise Market in Hong Kong, and Mother Market in Japan.

Business Angels

Business angels are successful entrepreneurs who wish to reinvest in others' new ventures, usually in return for some management role. The sums involved are usually relatively small (by venture capital standards), in the range £100 000–250 000, but in addition they can bring experience and expertise to a new venture. They are usually able to introduce a venture to an established network of professional advisors and business contacts. In this way they can provide a critical knowledge bridge between the venture and potential customers and investors.

Government Funding

There are a number of reasons why governments become involved in promoting and providing resources for new ventures:[15]

■ There is an 'equity gap' between the costs and risks involved in assessing and funding a new venture, and its potential return. The costs associated with the 'due diligence' of assessing a venture and its subsequent management are relatively high and fixed, therefore professional venture capitalists are unlikely to consider proposals below a certain threshold, typically £0.5–1 million. Similarly, where the risk of a new venture exceeds the expected return, professional venture capital is unlikely to be available. Table 8.4 indicates that this is a common problem, particularly in the UK and the rest of Europe. This suggests that government schemes may provide support and funding for smaller or higher risk ventures.

Table 8.4   Comparative venture capital structures

Country	% funding for seed/start-up	% funding for technology ventures
Singapore	40	85
USA	31	80
EU	13	26
UK	8	13

■ Professional venture capital tends to gravitate to fashionable fields, for example IT or biotechnology, and favour established centres of excellence, for example, Cambridge and Oxford in the UK, or Boston in the USA. Table 8.4 indicates that this is a common problem, particularly in the USA and some emerging economies, where venture capital quickly follows technology trends and fads. This suggests there is a role for policy to broaden the availability of funding for ventures in a wider range of fields and regions.[16]

■ Broader need to promote an entrepreneurial culture within a country or region, to provide management support and to establish equity funding (as opposed to debt) as a legitimate source of venture funding. This includes the non-financial support often provided by venture capitalists, including advice and mentoring.[17]

Harvesting the Venture: Growth and Exit Strategies

A high proportion of new ventures fail to grow and prosper. Estimates vary by type of business and national context, but typically 40% of new businesses fail in their first year, and 60% within the first 2. In other words, around 40% survive the first two years. Common reasons for failure include:

■ Poor financial control;

■ Lack of managerial ability or experience;

■ No strategy for transition, growth or exit.

There are many ways that a new venture can grow and create additional value:

■ Organic growth through additional sales and diversification.

■ Acquisition of or merger with another company.

■ Sale of the business to another company, or private equity firm.

■ An initial public offering (IPO) on a stock exchange.

Table 8.5   Some of the fastest-growing private firms in the UK

Name	Date founded	Business	Profit, 2005, £ million	Annual growth, %
Betfair	1999	Online bookmaker	23.2	146
Invotec	2001	Circuit boards	3.4	88
Azzurri	2000	Telecoms services	8.0	77
Unicom	1998	Telecoms services	3.3	86
Regard	1994	Care homes	4.0	76
Spearhead	2000	Farm produce	5.2	74
Baxter	2000	Contract caterer	4.1	66
Ingenious media	1998	Media adviser	35.7	56
Ineos	1998	Chemicals	191	56
Esri	1993	Software	5.2	79

Source: Sunday Times Profit Track, April 2006.

For example, The UK *Sunday Times* Profit Track estimates that of the 500 fastest growing private firms in the UK, over 5 years around 100 have merged with or been acquired by other companies or private equity firms, but only 10 or so have been floated (Table 8.5).

ENTREPRENEURSHIP IN ACTION

Chris Evans and Chiroscience

Chiroscience plc is 1 of the nearly 20 biotechnology firms founded by the microbiologist/entrepreneur Chris Evans. Evans, PhD and since OBE, formed his first new venture, Enzymatix Ltd, in 1987, aged 30. His business plan was rejected by venture capitalists, so he was forced to sell his house for £40 000 to raise the initial finance. Subsequent finance of £1 million was provided by the commodities group Berisford International, but following financial problems in the property market, the company was divided into Celsis plc, which makes contamination-testing equipment, and Chiroscience, which exploits chiral technology, the basis of which is that most molecules have mirror images that have different properties, essentially a right-hand sense and a left-hand sense. Isolating the more effective mirror image in an existing drug formulation can improve its efficacy, or reduce unwanted side effects.

Chiroscience was formed in 1990, other directors being recruited from large established pharmaceutical firms such as Glaxo, SmithKlineBeecham and Zeneca. The company was floated on the London Stock Exchange in 1994. This was only possible because in 1992 the Stock Exchange relaxed its requirements for market entry, and no longer required three consecutive years' profits before listing. The biotechnology company applies chiral technology to the purification of existing drugs and design of new drugs. Chiroscience has three potential applications of chiral technology: first, and most immediately, the improvement of existing drugs by isolating the most effective sense of molecules; second, the development of alternative processes for the production of existing drugs as they come off-patent; and finally, the design of new drugs by means of single-isomer technology.

Chiroscience was the first British biotechnology firm to be granted approval for sale of a new product, Dexketoprofen, in 1995. This is a non-steroidal anti-inflammatory drug, based on a right-handed version of the older drug ketoprofen. The drug is marketed by the Italian firm Menarini. Chiroscience has been involved in a number of collaborative development and marketing deals. In 1995 it formed an alliance with the Swedish pharmaceutical group, Pharmacia, to develop and market its local anaesthetic, Levobupivacaine. It also forged a more general strategic alliance with Medeva, the pharmaceutical group which performs no primary research, but specializes in taking products to market.

Biotechnology stocks are more volatile than most other investments, and it is difficult to use conventional techniques to assess their current value or future potential. Expenditure on R&D in the initial years typically results in significant losses, and sales may be negligible for up to 10 years. Therefore there are no price–earnings ratios or future revenues to discount. For example, in its first 2 years after flotation Chiroscience reported cumulative losses of £3.7 million, due largely to research spending of £12.4 million. Nevertheless, Chiroscience has outperformed the financial markets, and most other biotechnology stock. The company was floated in 1994 at 150p, and quickly fell to below 100p. However, by December 1995 shares had reached 364p. As a result, Chris Evans's personal fortune was estimated to have reached £50 million by 1995.

In January 1999 Chiroscience merged with Celltech to form Celltech Chiroscience, which subsequently acquired Medeva to become the Celltech Group. The new company has some 400 research staff, an R&D

budget of £51 million and adds much-needed sales and marketing competencies with a sales force of 550. Celltech Group is 3 times the size of Chiroscience, and reached a market capitalization of £3 billion in 2000. It is one of the few British biotechnology companies to gain regulatory approval for its products in the USA, and the first to achieve profitability. Sir Chris Evans (he was knighted in 2001) now runs the biotechnology venture capital firm Merlin Biosciences.

Successful, high-growth new ventures are associated with:

- Strong emphasis on design and innovation, but not necessarily technology or formal R&D.
- Extensive external links, including contract research organizations, suppliers, customers and universities.

Design and Innovation

Innovation, broadly defined, is found to be statistically three times more important to growth than other attributes or factors. Innovativeness, including a propensity to engage in new idea-generation and experimentation, is associated with performance, and so is proactiveness, defined as the firm's approach to market opportunities through active market research and the introduction of new products and services. The amount of expenditure by a new venture on design and engineering generally has a positive effect on the share of exports in sales, but formal R&D appears to be only weakly associated with profitability, and is not correlated with growth. Moreover, expenditure on R&D and investment in technology do not appear to discriminate between the success and failure of ventures. Instead, other factors have been found to have a more significant effect on profitability and growth, in particular the contributions of technically qualified owner managers and their scientific and engineering staff, and attention to product planning and marketing.

Where a new venture has a niche product strategy and relies too much on close relationship with a small number of customers, it may have little incentive or scope for further innovation, and therefore may pay relatively little attention to formal product development or marketing. Such ventures form dependent relationships and are likely to have limited potential for future growth, and may remain permanent infants or subsequently be acquired by competitors or customers.

External links

Innovative new ventures are likely to have diverse and extensive linkages with a variety of external sources of innovation, and in general there is a positive association between the level of external scientific, technical and professional inputs and the performance of an SME. The sources of innovation and precise types of relationship vary by sector, but links with contract research organizations, suppliers, customers and universities are consistently rated as being highly significant, and constitute the 'social capital' of the firm. However, such relationships are not without cost, and the management and exploitation of these linkages can be difficult for an SME, and can overwhelm the limited technical and managerial resources of SMEs. As a result, in some cases the cost of collaboration may outweigh the benefits and in the specific case of collaboration between SMEs and universities there is an inherent mismatch between the short-term, near-market focus of most SMEs and the long-term, basic research interests of universities.[18]

Links with sponsors, including venture capital, play an important developmental role, as discussed earlier. The size and location of new ventures also has an effect on performance. Geographic closeness increases the likelihood of informal linkages and encourages the mobility of skilled labour across firms. However, the probability of a start-up benefiting from such local knowledge exchanges appears to decrease as the venture grows. This growing inability to exploit informal linkages is a function of organizational size, not the age of the venture, and suggests that as ventures grow and become more complex, they begin to suffer many of the barriers to innovation faced by larger firms.

In general, larger SMEs are associated with a greater spatial reach of innovation-related linkages, and with the introduction of more novel product or process innovations for international markets. In contrast, smaller SMEs are more embedded in local networks, and are more likely to be engaged in incremental innovations for the domestic market. It is always difficult to untangle cause and effect relationships from such associations, but it is plausible that as the more innovative start-ups begin to outgrow the resources of their local networks, they actively replace and extend their networks, which both creates the opportunity and demand for higher levels of innovation. Conversely, the less innovative start-ups fail to move beyond their local networks, and therefore are less likely to have either the opportunity or need for more radical innovation.

However, different contingencies will demand different innovation strategies. For example, for software start-ups five factors appear to influence success most strongly: level of R&D expenditure, how radical new products were, the intensity of product upgrades, use of external technology and management of intellectual property.[19] In contrast, in biotechnology start-ups three factors are associated with success: location within a significant concentration of similar firms, quality of scientific staff (measured by citations) and the commercial experience of the founder. In biotechnology ventures, the number of scientific staff in the top management team had a negative association, suggesting that the scientists are best kept in the laboratory. Other studies of biotechnology start-ups confirm this pattern, and suggest that maintaining close links with universities reduces the level of R&D expenditure needed, increases the number of patents produced, and moderately increases the number of new products under development. However, as with more general alliances, the *number* of university links has no effect on the success or performance of biotechnology start-ups, but the *quality* of such relationships does.[20]

ENTREPRENEURSHIP IN ACTION

Technology-based High-growth Ventures

Since 2001 the Oxford-based research company Fast Track has compiled a report for the *Sunday Times* newspaper on the top 100 technology-based new ventures in the UK, sponsored by consultants PriceWaterhouseCoopers and Microsoft.

Following the collapse of the dot-com boom and bust, the annual survey provides an excellent barometer of the more robust and consistent technology-based new ventures, which, without reaching the headlines, continue to be created, grown and prosper.

Of the 100 firms studied, 48 have been funded by venture capital or private equity funds. As might be expected, many of the most successful new ventures are based on software or telecommunications technologies, so-called information communication telecommunications (ICT) technologies, but the commercial applications are increasingly dynamic and diverse, including gaming, gambling, music, film, fashion and education. Although most of these firms are only 5 or 6 years old, annual sales average £5 million, with annual growth of 60%. Examples include:

- Gamesys, a gaming website operator created in 2001, now with 50 staff and sales of £9.4 million.

- The Search Works, an advertising consultant for search engines, founded in 1999, now employing more than 50 staff, with sales of $18.6 million.

- Redtray, an e-learning software developer, formed in 2002, now has 30 staff and sales of £4.5 million.

- Ocado, the delivery business for online orders to supermarket Waitrose, created in 2000, and now employing almost 1000, with 3 million deliveries each week, and turnover of $143 million.

- Wiggle, an online retailer of sports goods, founded in 1998, now with 50 staff and sales of £9.2 million.

- Betfair, an online bookmaker and betting website, established in 1999, with turnover of £107 million and employing more than 400.

Source: *Sunday Times* Tech Track 100, 24 September 2006. www.fasttrack.co.uk;www.pwc.com

Developing Personal Capabilities

The framework shown in Table 8.6 is useful for structuring the assessment and development of ideas for a new business.

One of the early decisions an entrepreneur will have to make is the type of business structure to use. When deciding what type of company to form, the entrepreneur needs to consider:

- How much capital is needed to start the business?

- How much control and ownership do you want?

- How much risk are you willing to take on, in the case of failure?

- How large could the business become, and how fast?

- What are the registration, reporting and tax implications of different structures?

- What are the proposed harvest strategies or exit routes?

- Who might become the beneficiary of the business?

The basic options are:

- *Sole proprietorship* – the advantages are: relatively light regulation and reporting, autonomy of decision-making and total control, direct personal incentive to succeed, and ease of exit. However, this exposes the owner to unlimited personal liability, provides only limited access to external capital and development, and relies on the skills and talent of only one person.

■ *Partnership* – the advantages are: it is easy to establish, larger pool of expertise and capital, partners share all profits, flexibility to extend partnerships as the business develops. However, potential for personality and decision-making conflicts, buying out partners who wish to leave, joint unlimited liability of partners.

■ *Company* – easy and cheap to establish, better access to capital for growth, and exposes owners to only a limited liability. The disadvantages are the reporting requirements, rules of operations, different shareholder interests and restrictions on the sale and transfer of assets.

Table 8.6   New business opportunities

Criterion	Initial opportunity	Stronger opportunity
Customers and market segments		
Needs		
Benefits		
Differentiation		
Competition		
Industry structure		
Barriers to entry		
Regulation/IPR		
Market size		
Market growth		
Potential market share		
Gross margins		
Profits		
Return on capital		
Break-even time		
Capital requirements		
Cash-flow needs		
Management team		
Contacts and networks		
Exit options		
Assumptions		
Critical risks		

Source: Derived from Kaplan, J.M. and Warren, A.C. (2007). *Patterns of Entrepreneurship*. John Wiley & Sons, Inc, New York.

ENTREPRENEURSHIP IN ACTION

UnLtd – The UK Foundation for Social Entrepreneurs

UnLtd aims to support social entrepreneurs by providing funding and support to help these individuals start up and run projects that deliver social benefit. It was established in 2000 through a partnership between 7 leading UK non-profit organizations, including the School for Social Entrepreneurs, Ashoka, Senscot, the Scarman Trust, the Community Action Network, Comic Relief, and Changemakers, and funded by an endowment of £100 million from the UK Millennium Commission Award Scheme. The Foundation invests the money awarded to generate an income of £5 million a year to provide grants to individuals with projects to improve their community. These individual grants were launched in 2002, and range from £2500 to £15 000.

In addition to funding, UnLtd provides advice, training and support, using its extensive network of resources and partner organizations throughout the UK. It has formed an Institute for Social Entrepreneurs to help to raise the effectiveness of the sector by building a deeper understanding of what works and what does not, translating that understanding into tools and performance measures, and promoting public and media awareness.

In future UnLtd plans to establish a social venture fund to link social investors to more mature social entrepreneurs, whose projects have the potential to develop in scope and/or geography with significant financial backing. Current plans range from becoming a broker between different venture philanthropy funds to establishing its own VP fund.

Sources: www.unltd.org.uk, www.aworldconnected.org, www.howtochangetheworld.org, www.socialent.org

Chapter Summary

- Entrepreneurs have many different motives, but typically an innovative entrepreneur will establish a venture primarily to create something new or to change something, rather than to achieve independence or wealth, although both of these may follow as a consequence.

- A range of factors influence the creation of innovative new ventures, some contextual such as institutional support, availability of capital and culture, other are more personal, such as personality, background and relevant skills and experience. Therefore entrepreneurship is not simply an individual act, driven by psychology, but also a profoundly social process.

- The process of creating an innovative new venture requires careful business planning, and also the systematic assessment and acceptance of opportunities and risks. Innovative entrepreneurs need to be able to identify and exploit a broader range of external resources and sources of knowledge than their more conventional counterparts, including diverse networks stakeholders and resources in the private, public and third sectors.

■ A primary benefit of developing a formal business plan is to clarify the aims and means of a new venture, and a secondary advantage is to raise support and external finance.

■ Most new ventures are initially funded from personal sources, such as savings, but in later stages external sources of finance become more interested and relevant.

Key Terms Defined

Alternative Investment Market (AIM) – Was established as a simpler and cheaper alternative to the London Stock Exchange (LSE).

Business angels – Successful entrepreneurs who wish to reinvest in new ventures, usually in return for some management role. They are usually able to introduce a venture to an established network of professional advisors and business contacts.

Incubator organization – A private firm, university or public organization which provides resources and support for the generation of spin-out firms.

New technology-based firms (NTBFs) – Small firms that have emerged recently from large firms or public laboratories in such fields as electronics, software and biotechnology. They are usually specialized in the supply of a key component, subsystem, service or technique to larger firms, who may often be their former employers.

Social entrepreneur – Aim is to create social change and value, rather than commercial innovation and financial value. Involves business, public and third-sector organizations to achieve this aim.

Superstars – Large firms that have grown rapidly from small beginnings, through high rates of growth based on the exploitation of a major invention.

Further Reading and Resources

There are many books and journal articles on the subject of entrepreneurship, but relatively little has been produced on the more specific subject of innovative new ventures. We believe one of the best general texts on entrepreneurship is Jack Kaplan's *Patterns of Entrepreneurship,* written with A.C. Warren (2007, New York, John Wiley & Sons, Inc., 2nd edn), which adopts a very practical approach. The second edition is strong on the links between entrepreneurship and innovation, and the practicalities of venture structure and resources, but has little on technology-based ventures and sources of innovation. Alex Nicholls (2006). *Social Entrepreneurship: New Paradigms of Sustainable Social Change* (Oxford University Press, Oxford), and Mair, J., Robinson, J. and Hockets, K. (2006). *Social Entrepreneurship* (Palgrave Macmillan, Basingstoke) are both edited texts and rather academic, but both discuss the definitions, boundaries and some of the problems of research and practice in the emerging field of social entrepreneurship.

For a more specialist treatment of technology-based entrepreneurship, Ed. Roberts's *Entrepreneurs in High Technology: Lessons from MIT and Beyond* (1991, Oxford University Press, Oxford) is an excellent study of the MIT experience, albeit a little dated, but perhaps places too much emphasis on the characteristics of individual entrepreneurs rather than the unique context. The broader role of the Boston Route 128 is discussed in the paper 'The Boston Route 128 model of high-tech industry development', by J. Wonglimpiyarat (2006), *International*

Journal of Innovation Management, **10** (1), 47–64. For a more comprehensive study of technology-based new ventures in the USA see Martin Kenny (ed.) (2000). *Understanding Silicon Valley: Anatomy of an Entrepreneurial Region*. Stanford University Press, CA. For a review of recent research on the broader issue of innovative small firms see 'Small firms, R&D, technology and innovation: a literature review' by Kurt Hoffman et al. (1998), published in *Technovation*, **18** (1), 39–55. A special issue of the *Strategic Management Journal* (July 2001, **22**) examined entrepreneurial strategies, and includes a number of papers on technology-based firms; and a special issue of the journal *Research Policy* (2003, **32**) features papers on technology spin-offs and start-ups.

The literature in this field is dominated by the US experience, but other models exist. Ray Oakey's *High-technology New Firms* (1995, Paul Chapman, London) is a study of technology-based new ventures in the UK, and places greater emphasis on how different technologies constrain the opportunities and success. Acs, Z.J. and Audretsch, D.B. (2005) Entrepreneurship, Innovation and Technological Change, *Foundations and Trends in Entrepreneurship*, **1**(4), 1–49, provide a short but excellent review of the theories and evidence linking the fields of entrepreneurship and innovation; and in Audretsch, D.B, Keilbach, M.C. and Lehman, E.E. (2006). *Entrepreneurship and Economic Growth*, (Oxford University Press, Oxford) they examine the evidence in Germany. Vinig, T. and Van der Voort, R. (2005). *The Emergence of Entrepreneurial Economics*, Amsterdam, Elsevier, is an edited book, with a strong historical perspective in Part 1, and recent country studies in Part 2, including less commonly studied countries such as Russia, New Zealand and France. *Country Studies in Entrepreneurship*, edited by Y. Cassis and I.P. Minoglou (2006, Palgrave Macmillan, Basingstoke), includes case studies of the USA, UK, France, Italy, Germany, and most interesting of all, Singapore. Simon Barnes, with Rupert Pearce, gives an up-to-date and practitioner's account of the workings of venture capital in *Venture Capital: Fuel for the Entrepreneurial Engine* (2006). John Wiley & Sons, Ltd, Chichester.

References

1 Cosh, A., Fu, X. and Hughes, A. (2006). Management Characteristics, managerial ownership and innovative efficiency in high-technology industry, *The Future of Science, Technology and Innovation Policy: Linking Research and Practice*, SPRU 40th Anniversary Conference, Brighton, UK, 11–13 September.

2 Acs, Z.J. and Audretsch, D.B. (2005). Entrepreneurship, Innovation and Technological Change. *Foundations and Trends in Entrepreneurship*, **1**(4) 1–49; Vinig, T. and Van der Voort, R. (2005). *The Emergence of Entrepreneurial Economics*. Amsterdam, Elsevier; Roberts, E.B. (1991). *Entrepreneurs in High Technology: Lessons from MIT and Beyond*. Oxford University Press, Oxford.

3 Kaplan, J.M. and Warren, A.C. (2007). *Patterns of Entrepreneurship*. New York, John Wiley & Sons, Inc.

4 Mair, J., Robinson, J. and Hockets, K. (2006). *Social Entrepreneurship*. Basingstoke, Palgrave Macmillan. An edited book which discusses the definitions, boundaries and some of the problems of research and practice in the emerging field of social entrepreneurship.

5 Wonglimpiyarat, J. (2006). The Boston Route 128 Model of high-tech industry development, *International Journal of Innovation Management*, **10** (1), 47–64; Kenny, M. (2000). *Understanding Silicon Valley: Anatomy of an Entrepreneurial Region*. California, Stanford University Press; Roberts, E.B. (1991). *Entrepreneurs in High Technology: Lessons from MIT and Beyond*. Oxford University Press, Oxford.

6 Audretsch, D.B, Keilbach, M.C. and Lehman, E.E. (2006). *Entrepreneurship and Economic Growth*. Oxford, Oxford University Press.

7 Hoffman, K., Parejo, M., Bessant, J. and Perren, L. (1998). Small firms, R&D, technology and innovation in the UK: a literature review, *Technovation*, **18** (1), 39–55.

8 Bower, J. (2003). Business model fashion and the academic spinout firm, *R&D Management*, **33**(2), 97–106.

9 Mowery, D.C., Nelson, R.R., Sampat, B.N. and Ziedonis, A.A. (2001). The growth of patenting and licensing by U.S. universities: an assessment of the effects of the Bayh–Dole Act of 1980, *Research Policy*, **30**; Henderson, R., Jaffe, A.B. and Trajtenberg, M. (1998). Universities as a source of commercial technology: a detailed analysis of university patenting 1965–1988, *Review of Economics and Statistics*, 119–127.

10 Bray, M.J. and Lee, J.N. (2000). University revenues from technology transfer: licensing fees versus equity positions, *Journal of Business Venturing*, 15, 385–392.

11 Kassicieh, S.K., Radosevich, R. and Umbarger, J. (1996). A comparative study of entrepreneurship incidence among inventors in national laboratories, *Entrepreneurship Theory and Practice*, Spring, 33–49.

12 Meyer, M. (2004). Academic entrepreneurs or entrepreneurial academics? Research-based ventures and public support mechanisms, *R&D Management*, **33** (2), 107–115; Butler, S. and Birley, S. (1999). Scientists and their attitudes to industry links, *International Journal of Innovation Management*, **2** (1), 79–106.

13 Lee, Y.S. (1996). Technology transfer and the research university: a search for the boundaries of university–industry collaboration, *Research Policy*, **25**, 843–863.

14 Di Gregorio, D. and Shane, S. (2003). Why do some universities generate more start-ups than others?, *Research Policy*, **32**, 209–227.

15 Harding, R. (2000). *Venturing Forward: The Role of Venture Capital in Enabling Entrepreneurship*. London, Institute for Public Policy Research.

16 Lockett, A., Murray, G. and Wright, M. (2002). Do UK venture capitalists still have a bias against investment in new technology firms?, *Research Policy*, **31**, 1009–1030.

17 Baum, J.A.C. and Silverman, B.S. (2004). Picking winners or building them? Alliance, intellectual and human capital as selection criteria in venture financing and performance of biotechnology startups, *Journal of Business Venturing*, **19**, 411–436.

18 Almeida, P., Dokko, G. and Rosenkopf, L. (2003). Startup size and the mechanisms of external learning: increasing opportunity and decreasing ability?, *Research Policy*, **32**, 301–315; Freel, M.S. (2003). Sectoral patterns of small firm innovation, networking and proximity, *Research Policy*, **32**, 751–770; Lee, C., Lee, K. and Pennings, J.M. (2000). Internal capabilities, external networks, and performance: a study of technology-based ventures, *Strategic Management Journal*, **22**, 615–640.

19 Gans, J.S. and Stern, S. (2003). The product and the market for 'ideas': commercialization strategies for technology entrepreneurs, *Research Policy*, **32**, 333–350; Zahra, S.A. and Bogner, W.C. (2000). Technology strategy and software new ventures performance, *Journal of Business Venturing*, 15 (2), 135–173.

20 Deeds, D.L., DeCarolis, D. and Coombs, J. (2000). Dynamic capabilities and new product development in high technology ventures: an empirical analysis of new biotechnology firms, *Journal of Business Venturing*,

15 (3), 211–229; George, G., Zahra, S.A. and Robley Wood, D. (2002). The effects of business-university alliances on innovative output and financial performance: a study of publicly traded biotechnology companies, *Journal of Business Venturing*, **17**, 577–609.

Discussion Questions

1 What are the typical personal characteristics of an entrepreneur?

2 How does the organizational and national context influence entrepreneurship?

3 In what ways do social entrepreneurs and technology entrepreneurs differ from other types of entrepreneur?

4 What are the main funding options for a new venture, and what are the advantages and disadvantages of each?

5 What should be included in a business plan, and what do venture capitalists look for?

6 In each of the different stages in the development of a new venture, what are the different management requirements?

7 What factors affect the decision of what type of company to form?

Team Exercise

Identify an idea for a new venture, and develop a business plan to attract external funding. This should include:

1 Details of the product or service.

2 Assessment of the market opportunity.

3 Identification of target customers.

4 Barriers to entry and competitor analysis.

5 Experience, expertise and commitment of the management team.

6 Strategy for pricing, distribution and sales.

7 Identification and planning for key risks.

8 Cash-flow calculation, including break-even points and sensitivity.

9 Financial and other resource requirements of the business.

Assignment and Case Study Questions

In your university, find out what the policies, incentives, resources and support are for commercializing technology, including patenting, licensing and the creation of new venture firms. Identify a recent new venture and interview the founders to find out why and how they created the business, and what their plans are for its development and growth.

CASE STUDY 8

Electronic Gaming

The global market for videogames has grown within a decade to US$40 billion, and in the UK, the handheld games market alone is worth £250 million a year. Although it can cost several million dollars to develop and distribute a new computer or console game, the industry still reflects its origins with individual users/developers and small groups of developers, but they now work with global manufacturers such as Sony, Nintendo and Microsoft, and major corporate publishers like Electronic Arts and Universal. The industry consists of a diverse 'eco-system', which has evolved as the industry has grown rapidly:

- *Super developers* – who develop games across different platforms and have their own intellectual property and brands.

- *Original IP developers* – who develop and seek to own their own intellectual property, but self- publish, or publish through other companies.

- *Specialist niche developers* – who specialize in a particular platform or genre.

- *Work-for-hire* – who compete for games development contracts from the publishers, and have no ownership of intellectual property.

- *Service providers* – who provide a range of services to developers and publishers throughout the development process.

This emerging sector integrates the combined creativity of individual and groups of developers and users, with the more formal innovation processes of the hardware and publishing firms. The challenge is to translate creative ideas into commercially successful products on a consistent basis, which demands a systemic approach to entrepreneurship and innovation. As one analyst notes:

> *Developers are highly regarded by the wider community for their creativity, originality and technical achievement . . . developers have the potential to leverage these technical and creative abilities, but only through the development of a range of complimentary business, management and personal competencies.*

Few of these firms have the critical strategic, commercial and financial capabilities needed to grow and prosper. The super developers may have up to five development teams and projects at any time, but the original IP and specialist niche developers may have only one team. For example, most rely on advances from publishers to fund development, rather than debt or equity funding.

Although the design of any innovative game can often be traced to the creativity of just 1 or 2 people, its development into a commercially successful product involves the continuous improvement of the content that can only be achieved through the collaboration and frequent, continuous prototyping by a much bigger group of developers. The initial idea for any new game usually comes from 1 or 2 designers who outline the central concept and map out the game structure. If this is promising, it is developed by a larger team over a few months to create a more formal proposal that will normally include a prototype of a section with art and code. This is pitched to a potential publisher for funding, and if accepted will be developed by a large team over 1 or 2 years. Around two-fifths of these pitches are funded, and each proposal, whether or not successful, can cost a developer US$200 000. If funded, the development budget is US$350 000–6 million, the average being around US$2 million. The main cost is labour, around 70% of total costs, but the dedicated gamer/developers work long hours for modest income, with teams of 20–30 developers working on a typical development project.

The process of developing an electronic game is characterized by multiple design iterations and frequent milestones and testing. It is a strong combination of technology, creative games design and artistic content, and therefore demands complex concurrent multifunctional team development and the interaction and integration of design, content and technology. A typical profile for staff in a development team of 20 might be half working on artistic content, a third on programming and the rest on design. These interactions and interdependencies between design, content and technology require a highly iterative and evolutionary approach to games development, and can cause many problems in game function and development scheduling. Teams need to be coordinated on an almost daily basis; the integration of these components is critical. These relatively large, multidisciplinary teams require significant leadership, to maintain the vision and direction and to overcome the many decision deadlocks. This is a similar role to the producer in film or music development, what Baba refers to as a 'benevolent dictator keen on sustaining both the product's integrity and the egalitarian relationship among the project members'.

The game play experience and interactivity are crucial to success, and can be tested and tuned only by experience. The technical and creative nature of developers has restricted their ability to grow and evolve the game business. The predominately male, 20–30 year-old developers are increasingly isolated from broader market needs. For example, the traditional gamer/developer hero, such as Shigeru Miyamoto, the creator of classic Nintendo games such as *Donkey Kong* and *Super Mario Brothers*, may be less relevant exemplars than more sophisticated marketing approaches. Nintendo has recently targeted those who do not currently play computer games, and has explicitly developed games beyond the typical 18–35 male demographic market. The value of this central market has continued to grow with the development of new consoles and games, but the number of core users has stabilized at around a third of the population. Therefore any further growth will demand expanding beyond the core gamer community. For example, games for the DS handheld console have been developed specifically for female users, such as *Nintendogs*, and the brain-testing and -developing game *Brain Training* for older users. *Nintendogs* sold 4 million units in 2005, and *Brain Training*, aimed at the over-45-year olds, was launched in the UK in 2006, following a successful launch in Japan in May 2005.

The increasing cost of development and need for global sales has resulted in a significant consolidation of the sector. For example, the development of a game for the Playstation 3 platform is estimated to cost around US$12 million. As a result major console manufacturers and independent publishers currently dominate the industry, and these largely dictate what games will reach the market, and drive the cost, quality and development times. However, the industry continues to evolve, which presents further opportunities for entrepreneurship and innovation:

- Potentially disruptive innovations, such as Web-based and mobile interactive gaming, which may challenge the big publisher business model.

- New software automation modules, middleware, which may change relationships and create new specialist niche suppliers.

- The availability of low-cost but experienced software development talent from India and Eastern Europe, leading to new models of development and new markets and competitors in the games industry.

Case Study Questions

1 In the computer games industry, what are the respective roles of individual developers, small firms and large international companies?

2 What are the potential conflicts between the need for creativity and more formal development processes in the industry?

3 Given trends in the structure and funding of the industry, what future opportunities are there for innovation and entrepreneurship?

Sources: Andrew Grantham and Raphael Kaplinsky (2005). Getting the measure of the electronic games industry: developer and the management of innovation, *International Journal of Innovation Management*, **9** (2), 183–214; F. Ted Tschang (2005). Videogames as interactive experiential products and their manner of development, *International Journal of Innovation Management*, **9** (1), 103–131; Yasonori Baba and F. Ted Tschang (2001). Product development in Japanese TV game software, *International Journal of Innovation Management*, **5** (4), 487–515.

Chapter 9

Social Entrepreneurship and Innovation

This chapter

- Introduces the concept social entrepreneurship (SE) – a form of innovation which pursues social rather than financial goals.

- Looks at the challenge of managing this innovation process.

- Explores the ways in which social entrepreneurship works through a variety of examples.

Learning Objectives

By the end of this chapter you will develop an understanding of:

- What social entrepreneurship is and how it can contribute to sustainable innovation.

- Social entrepreneurship as an organized and disciplined process rather than well-meaning but unfocused intervention.

- The difficulties in managing what is just as much an uncertain and risky process as 'conventional' economically motivated innovation.

- The key themes in thinking about how to manage this process effectively.

Thinking about Innovation

Throughout the book we've been looking at the challenge of change – and how individuals and groups of entrepreneurs, working alone or inside organizations, try and bring this about. We've seen that innovation is not a simple flash of inspiration but an extended and organized process of turning bright ideas into successful realities – changing the offering (product/service), the ways in which it is created and delivered (process innovation), the context and the ways in which it is introduced to that context (position innovation), and the overall mental models for thinking about what we are doing (business model or 'paradigm' innovation).

INNOVATION IN ACTION

The Aravind Eye Care System has become the largest eye care facility in the world with its headquarters in Madurai, India. Its doctors perform over 200 000 cataract operations per year – and with such experience have developed state-of-the art techniques to match their excellent facilities. Yet the cost of these operations runs from US$50 to US$300, with over 60% of patients being treated free. Despite only 40% paying customers the company is highly profitable and the average cost per operation (across free and paying patients) at US$25 is the envy of most hospitals around the world.

Aravind was founded by Dr G. Venkataswamy back in 1976 on his retirement from the Government Medical College and represents the result of a passionate concern to eradicate needless blindness in the population. Within India there are an estimated 9 million (and worldwide 45 million) people who suffer from needless blindness which could be cured via corrective glasses and simple cataract or other surgery. Building on his experience in organizing rural eye camps to deal with diagnosis and treatment, he set about developing a low-cost high-quality solution to the problem, originally aiming at the treatment of needless blindness in his home state of Tamil Nadu.

One of the key building blocks in developing the Aravind system has been transferring the ideas of another industry concerned with low-cost, high- and consistent quality provision – the hamburger business pioneered by the Croc brothers and underpinning McDonalds. By applying the same process innovation approaches to standardization and workflow, and tailoring tasks to skills he created a system which not only delivered high quality but was also reproducible. The model has now diffused widely – there are now 5 hospitals within Tamil Nadu offering nearly 4000 beds, the majority of which are free. It has moved beyond cataract surgery to education, lens manufacturing, research and development and other linked activities around the theme of improving sight and access to treatment.

In making this vision come alive Dr V has not only demonstrated considerable entrepreneurial flair – he has created a template which others, including health providers in the advanced industrial economies, are now looking at very closely.

Above all we've seen that getting innovation to happen depends on a focused and determined drive – a passion to change things, which we call 'entrepreneurship'. Essentially this is about being prepared to challenge and change, to take (calculated) risks and put energy and enthusiasm into the venture, picking up and enthusing other supporters along the way.

ENTREPRENEURSHIP IN ACTION

> *Social entrepreneurs are not content just to give a fish or teach how to fish. They will not rest until they have revolutionized the fishing industry.*

Bill Drayton, CEO, chair and founder of Ashoka, a global non-profit organization devoted to developing the profession of social entrepreneurship

If we think about successful entrepreneurs they are typically ambitious, mission-driven, passionate, strategic (not just impulsive), resourceful, results-oriented. And we can think of plenty of names to fit this frame – Bill Gates (Microsoft), Richard Branson (Virgin), James Dyson, Larry Page and Sergey Brin (Google) or Jeff Bezos (Amazon). But we could also apply these terms to describe people like Florence Nightingale, Elizabeth Fry or Albert Schweizer. And while less famous than Gates or Bezos, there are some impressive individuals around today who have made a significant mark on the world through getting their ideas into action. For example Muhammad Yunus revolutionized economics by founding the Grameen Bank, or 'village bank', in Bangladesh in 1976 to offer 'micro loans' to help impoverished people attain economic self-sufficiency through self-employment – a model that has now been replicated in 58 countries around the world. Or Dr V whose passion for finding ways of giving eyesight back to people with cataracts in his home state of Tamil Nadu eventually led to the development of an eye care system which has helped thousands of people around the country.

Table 9.1 Characteristics of social entrepreneurs

- *Ambitious* Social entrepreneurs tackle major social issues – poverty, healthcare, equal opportunities and so on – with the underlying desire, passion even – to make a change. They may work alone or from within a wide range of existing organizations including those which mix elements of non-profit and for-profit activity.

- *Mission-driven* Their primary concern is generating social value rather than wealth – wealth creation may be part of the process but it is not an end in itself. Just like business entrepreneurs, social entrepreneurs are intensely focused and hard-driving – even relentless – in their pursuit of a social vision.

- *Strategic* Like business entrepreneurs, social entrepreneurs see and act upon what others miss: opportunities to improve systems, create solutions and invent new approaches that create social value.

- *Resourceful* Social entrepreneurs often work in contexts where they have limited access to capital and traditional market support systems. As a result, they must be exceptionally skilled at mustering and mobilizing human, financial and political resources.

- *Results-oriented* Again, like business entrepreneurs, social entrepreneurs are motivated by a desire to see things change and to produce measurable returns. The results they seek are essentially linked to 'making the world a better place' – for example, through improving quality of life, access to basic resources, supporting disadvantaged groups.

These are people who undoubtedly fit our entrepreneur mould – as Table 9.1 shows – but target their efforts in a different, socially valuable direction. Wikipedia, quoting the Ashoka Foundation (non-profit organization for encouraging social entrepreneurship) defines a social entrepreneur as:

> *someone who recognizes a social problem and uses traditional entrepreneurial principles to organize, create, and manage a venture to make social change. Whereas business entrepreneurs typically measure performance in profit and return, social entrepreneurs often start nonprofits and citizen groups.*

> *Unlike traditional business entrepreneurs, social entrepreneurs primarily seek to generate 'social value' rather than profits. And unlike the majority of non-profit organizations, their work is targeted not only towards immediate, small-scale effects, but sweeping, long-term change.*

> *Veronica Khosa was frustrated with the system of healthcare in South Africa. A nurse by trade, she saw sick people getting sicker, elderly people unable to get to a doctor and hospitals with empty beds that would not admit patients with HIV. So Veronica started Tateni Home Care Nursing Services and instituted the concept of 'home care' in her country. Beginning with practically nothing, her team took to the streets providing care to people in a way they had never received it – in the comfort and security of their homes. Just years later, the government had adopted her plan and through the recognition of leading health organizations the idea is spreading beyond South Africa.*

(Ashoka Foundation website)

Importantly this is not just philanthropy or good works but rather the mobilization of sound entrepreneurial principles – of the kind we've been looking at in this book – in pursuit of a different or parallel end. It's more than the basic human concern to give to others less fortunate – it is targeted at making long-term sustainable change rather than short-term alleviation of problems. And – if delivered in a much more systematic fashion – less 'good works' and more creating enabling structures which provide viable alternative models.

In many cases it is an individual-driven thing, where a passion for change leads to remarkable and sustainable results. They include people like:

■ Amitabha Sadangi of International Development Enterprises-India, who develops low-cost irrigation technologies to help subsistence farmers survive dry seasons.

■ Victoria Hale of Institute for OneWorld Health, who taps existing but abandoned pharmaceutical research to bring new drugs to the world's poorest people.

■ William Foote, who promotes a more equitable and sustainable model of international trade for a range of commodities, including coffee.

■ Gillian Caldwell of WITNESS, who uses video and communications technology to document human rights abuses.

But social entrepreneurship of this kind is also an increasingly important component of 'big business', as large organizations realize that they secure a licence to operate only if they can demonstrate some concern for the wider communities in which they are located. (The recent backlash against the pharmaceutical firms as a result of their perceived policies in relation to drug provision in Africa is an example of what can happen if firms don't pay attention to this agenda.) Corporate social responsibility (CSR) is becoming a major function in many businesses and many make use of formal measures – such as the triple bottom line – to monitor and communicate their focus on more than simple profit-making.

This chapter looks at how we might approach this challenge – how to mobilize the principles and practices of successful entrepreneurship and innovation to create social as well as economic value. (There are some clear connections to the entrepreneurship theme in Chapter 8 and 'sustainability' issues which we look at in Chapter 10.)

Uncommon Heroes

So far in this book we've assumed a profit-driven version of innovation – which is understandable, since it represents a powerful force for economic growth. As Karl Marx argued, innovation is 'the flywheel of capitalism' and many economists – notably Joseph Schumpeter – have helped us understand the powerful links between innovation and the pursuit of profits. Of course these profits are not simply about making entrepreneurs and shareholders richer – they are also the fuel for future growth. It's the argument for spending on research and development (R&D) and on its relatives in market research – without it there may simply be no long-term future for the business. For example, in the pharmaceutical industry future growth depends on reinvesting up to 25% of the sales in order to create the next wave of possibilities.

INNOVATION IN ACTION

Joseph Schumpeter – the 'Godfather' of Innovation Studies

The 'godfather' of this area of economic theory was Joseph Schumpeter who wrote extensively on the subject. He had a distinguished career as an economist and served as Minister for Finance in the Austrian Government. His argument was simple; entrepreneurs will seek to use technological innovation – a new product/service or a new process for making it – to get strategic advantage. For a while this may be the only example of the innovation so the entrepreneur can expect to make a lot of money – what Schumpeter calls 'monopoly profits'. But of course other entrepreneurs will see what he has done and try to imitate it – with the result that other innovations emerge, and the resulting 'swarm' of new ideas chips away at the monopoly profits until an equilibrium is reached. At this point the cycle repeats itself – our original entrepreneur or someone else looks for the next innovation which will rewrite the rules of the game, and off we go again. Schumpeter talks of a process of 'creative destruction' where there is a constant search to create something new which simultaneously destroys the old rules and establishes new ones – all driven by the search for new sources of profits

In his view:

> [What counts is] competition from the new commodity, the new technology, the new source of supply, the new type of organization . . . competition which . . . strikes not at the margins of the profits and the outputs of the existing firms but at their foundations and their very lives.[1]

But the same core principles of innovation and entrepreneurship apply if we switch the motivating driver to something else – to build social enterprises. Just like mountaineers climb peaks simply 'because they are there', sometimes the motivation for innovating comes because of a desire to make a difference. Psychological studies of entrepreneurs suggest they often have high need for achievement – nAch – a technical term which measures how far they want to make their mark on the world. High nAch requires some evidence that a mark has been made – but this doesn't have to be in terms of profit or loss on a balance sheet. As we saw earlier, many people find entrepreneurial satisfaction through social value creation – and even those with a long track record of building successful businesses may find themselves drawn into this territory. For example, Bill Gates' withdrawal from running Microsoft to concentrate on the Gates Foundation and other activities is the latest in a long line going back at least to the great industrial barons like Carnegie and Rockefeller.

INNOVATION IN ACTION

One of the biggest problems facing people living below the poverty line is the difficulty of getting access to banking and financial services. As a result they are often dependent on moneylenders and other unofficial sources – and are often charged at exorbitant rates if they do borrow. This makes it hard to save and invest – and puts a major barrier in the way of breaking out of this spiral through starting new entrepreneurial ventures. Awareness of this problem led Muhammad Yunus, Head of the Rural Economics Program at the University of Chittagong, to launch a project to examine the possibility of designing a credit delivery system to provide banking services targeted at the rural poor. In 1976 the Grameen Bank Project (Grameen means 'rural' or 'village' in the Bangla language) was established, aiming to:

- Extend banking facilities to the poor;
- Eliminate the exploitation of the poor by moneylenders;
- Create opportunities for self-employment for unemployed people in rural Bangladesh;
- Offer the disadvantaged an organizational format which they can understand and manage by themselves;
- Reverse the age-old vicious circle of 'low income, low saving and low investment', into the virtuous circle of 'low income, injection of credit, investment, more income, more savings, more investment, more income'.

The original project was set up in Jobra (a village adjacent to Chittagong University) and some neighbouring villages and ran during 1976–1979. The core concept was of 'micro-finance' – enabling people (and a major success was with women) to take tiny loans to start and grow tiny businesses. With the sponsorship of the central bank of the country and support of the nationalized commercial banks, the project was extended to Tangail district (a district north of Dhaka, the capital city of Bangladesh) in 1979. Its further success there led to the model being extended to several other districts in the country and in 1983 it became an independent bank as a result of government legislation. Today Grameen Bank is owned by the rural poor whom it serves. Borrowers of the bank own 90% of its shares, while the remaining 10% is owned by the Government. It now serves over 5 million clients, and has enabled 10 000 families to escape the poverty trap every month.

There are many heart-warming stories about individuals who have had the vision, creativity and drive to make something exceptional happen which creates social value. But we should be careful – just because there is no direct profit motive doesn't take the commercial challenges out of the equation. If anything it becomes harder to be an entrepreneur when the challenge is not only to convince people that it can be done (and use all the tricks of the entrepreneur's trade to do so) but also to do so in a form which makes it commercially sustainable. Bringing a radio within reach of rural poor across Africa is a great idea – but someone still has to pay for raw materials, build and run a factory, arrange for distribution – and collect the small money from the sales. None of this comes cheap – and setting up such a venture faces economic, political and business obstacles every bit as hard as a bright start-up company in medical devices or computer software working in a developed country environment.

Big can be Beautiful Too

Of course it is not simply a matter of individuals and start-up ventures. As we've seen throughout the book, entrepreneurial behaviour can be found in any organization and is central to its ability to develop and reinvent themselves. In the field of social entrepreneurship a growing number of businesses are recognizing the possibilities of pursuing parallel and complementary trajectories, targeting both conventional profits and also social value creation.

INNOVATION IN ACTION

BT, the UK telecommunications firm, has – under strong pressure from the regulator – a responsibility to provide services for all elements of society but it has used the connections in this 'stakeholder network' to move early into understanding and creation of services for what will be a major expansion in the future with an ageing population. By 2026, 30% of the UK population will be more than 60 years old. The pilot innovation is based on placing sensors in the home to monitor movement and the use of power and water – if something goes wrong it triggers an alarm. It has already begun to generate significant revenues for BT but has also opened up the possibility of relieving pressure on the NHS for beds and services – estimates suggest savings of around £700 million of this kind if fully deployed. Most significantly, the initial project can be seen as a stepping stone, a transitional object to help BT learn about what will be a huge and very different market in the future.

By engaging stakeholders directly, companies are also better able to avoid conflicts, or to resolve them when they arise. In some cases, this involves directly engaging activists who are leading campaigns or protests against a company. For example, Starbucks responded to customers' concerns and activist protests about the impact of coffee-growing on songbirds by partnering with leading activist groups to improve organic, bird-friendly coffee production methods, setting up a pilot sourcing programme, and further increasing public awareness. The conflict was resolved, and Starbucks established itself as a leader on this issue.

INNOVATION IN ACTION

The UK 'do-it-yourself' home and garden retailer B&Q has been honoured for its work on disability where it has used corporate social responsibility to drive improvements in customer services. What in retrospect looks like a successful business strategy has in fact evolved through real-time learning from partnerships between individual stores and local disability organizations. Following on from its pioneering experiments in having stores entirely staffed by older people, B&Q wanted to ensure that disabled people are able to shop in confidence and that they will be able to access goods and services easily. In the UK alone there are 8 million disabled people; it is estimated that the 'disabled pound' is worth £30 billion and is growing. However B&Q also saw this initiative as a way to improve wider customer care competencies: 'If we can get it right for disabled people we can get it right for most people.' To begin the process of understanding what it was like to shop and work in B&Q as a disabled person they started by talking to disabled people in a single store. They have now established 300 partnerships between store 'disability champions' and local disability groups to understand local needs and develop training on disability awareness and service provision. They see these partnerships as a way for B&Q to access 'the incredible amount of knowledge, commitment and enthusiasm which exists in this wide variety of organizations'. As a result all B&Q staff now take part in disability awareness training, they are improving store design and provide printed material in Braille, audio type, large print and CD-Rom. They are also developing their 'Daily Living Made Easier' range of products from grab rails and bath chairs through to visual smoke alarms and lightweight garden tools.

Ahold, the largest retailer in the Netherlands, has also used stakeholder engagement to enable it to expand its operations into under-served urban areas. The company realized that on its own it would not be able to operate successfully and would need to work with government and other companies to create a 'sound investment climate' locally. With the local government and nine other retailers it developed a comprehensive development plan for the Dutch town of Enschede.

Sometimes there is scope for social entrepreneurship to spin out of mainstream innovative activity. Procter & Gamble's PUR water purification system offers radical improvements to point-of-use drinking-water delivery. Estimates are that it has reduced intestinal infections by 30–50%. The product grew out of research in the mainstream detergents business but the initial conclusion was that the market potential of the product was not high enough to justify investment; by reframing it as a development aid the company has improved its image but also opened up a radical new area for working.

In some cases the process begins with an individual but gradually a trend is established which other players see as relevant to follow, in the process bringing their resources and experience to the game. Examples here might include 'Fair Trade' products which were originally a minority idea but have now become a mainstream item in any supermarket, or the wind-up radio which provided a model which highlighted the needs – but also the opportunities – for communications in developing countries.

There is also increasing pressure on established businesses to work to a more socially responsible agenda – with many operating a key function around corporate social responsibility (CSR). The concept is simple – firms need to secure a 'licence to operate' from the stakeholders in the various constituencies in which they work. Unless they take notice of the concerns and values of those communities they risk passive – and increasingly active – resistance and their operations can be severely affected. CSR goes beyond public relations in many cases with genuine efforts to ensure social value is created alongside economic value, and that stakeholders benefit as widely as possible and not simply as consumers. CSR thinking has led to the development of formal measures and frameworks like the double or even 'triple bottom line' which many firms use as a way of expanding the traditional company reporting framework to take into account not just financial outcomes but also environmental and social performance.

It is easy to become cynical about CSR activity, seeing it as a cosmetic overlay on what are basically the same old business practices. But there is a growing recognition that pursuing social entrepreneurship-linked goals may not be incompatible with developing a viable and commercially successful business. For example, in 2004 a survey by the consultants Arthur D. Little of around 40 technology firms in Europe, Japan and the USA suggested that a focus on the sustainability question was beginning to be recognized as a key way of creating new market space, products and processes. In particular 95% felt that it had potential to bring business value and almost a quarter felt it definitely would deliver such value. This value is in both intangible domains like brand and reputation but increasingly in bottom-line benefits like market share and product/service innovation. Significantly there has been considerable acceleration in these trends compared to the last time the survey was conducted, in 1999. When asked where they saw the benefits coming in 5 years' time, 90% believed they would come through new products and services and 75% in new markets and new business models.

The A.D. Little survey suggests that an increasing number of firms are looking to develop new opportunities via social innovation. They use the metaphor of a journey which begins with simple compliance innovation – the 'licence to operate' argument. Many companies have now moved into the 'foothills' of the 'beyond compliance' area where they are realizing that they have to deal with key stakeholders and that in the process some interesting innovation opportunities can emerge. But the real challenge is to move on to the innovation high ground of full-scale stakeholder innovation, 'creating new products and services, processes and markets which will respond to the needs of future as well as current customers'.

> *We've put more emphasis on serving an even broader base of consumers. We have the goal of serving the majority of the world's consumers someday. Today, we probably serve about 2 billion-plus consumers around the globe, but there are 6 billion consumers out there. That has led us to put increased emphasis on low-end markets and in mid- and low-level pricing tiers in developed geographies. That has caused us to put a lot more attention on the cost aspects of our products. We call this cost innovation.*

G. Gilbert Cloyd, Chief Technology Officer, Procter & Gamble, in a *Business Week* interview, 2005

INNOVATION IN ACTION

The Danish pharmaceutical firm Novo Nordisk is deploying stakeholder innovation through expansion and reframing of the role of its corporate stakeholder relations (CSR) activities. It has been consistently highly rated on this, not least because it is a board-level strategic responsibility (specified in the company's articles of association) with significant resources committed to projects to sustain and enhance good practice. It was one of the first companies to introduce the concept of the triple-bottom-line performance measurement, recognizing the need to take into account wider social and societal concerns and to be clear about its values.

But there is now growing recognition that this investment is also a powerful innovation resource. It offers a way of complementing the compound pipeline R&D with special relevance to the challenges of discontinuous innovation. As we saw in Chapter 7, the questions here are:

- How do the organizations pick up on emergent phenomena?

- How do they get in the game early?

- And if they do manage that, how might they position themselves to shape the emergent new game?

Investing in stakeholder relations represents a powerful way of doing this by involving the company closely in learning from a wide range of actors. Two examples will help highlight this process.

The DAWN (Diabetes Attitudes, Wishes and Needs) Programme

The objective of DAWN, initiated in 2001, was to explore attitudes, wishes and needs of both diabetes sufferers and healthcare professionals to identify critical gaps in the overall care offering. Its findings showed in quantitative fashion how people with diabetes suffered from different types of emotional distress and poor psychological well-being, and that such factors were a major contributing factor to impaired health outcomes. Insights from the programme opened up new areas for innovation across the system. For example, a key focus was on the ways in which healthcare professionals presented therapeutic options involving a combination of insulin treatment and lifestyle elements – and on developing new approaches to this.

A DAWN Summit in 2003 brought together representatives from 31 countries and key agencies such as the World Health Organization; it was widely publicized in specialist and non-specialist journals and via the International Diabetes Federation (IDF). The result has been to establish a common framework within which an understanding of the issues is combined with relationships with key players who could become involved in the design and delivery of relevant innovations. DAWN's value is as an independent, evidence-based platform on which extended discussion and exploration can take place around the future of diabetes management as a holistic system – not simply the treatment via insulin or other specific therapies. It has helped mobilize a global community of practice across which there is significant sharing of learning and interactive changing of perspectives.

Søren Skovlund, senior adviser, Corporate Health Partnerships, sees the key element as:

> the use of the DAWN study as a vehicle to get all the different people round the same table . . . to bring patients, health professionals, politicians, payers, the media together to find new ways to work more effectively together on the same task . . . You can't avoid getting some innovation because you're bringing together different baskets of knowledge in the room!

Why do it? One reason is a growing sense that the rules of the game around chronic disease management are shifting. For example the WHO estimate that diabetes is a bigger killer than AIDS with around 3.2 million deaths attributable to the disease – and its complications – every year. In developing countries the figures are particularly alarming where 1 in 10 deaths of adults aged 35 to 64 are due to diabetes (in some countries the figure is as high as 1 in 5). Chronic diseases like diabetes represent a time bomb around which major activity is likely to happen in the near future. Healthcare systems are increasingly focusing their efforts on reducing the socio-economic burden of disease through reorganization of the care process and structure. These major shifts pose the risk that the product-focused pharmaceutical industry is falling behind.

DAWN is a learning investment for Novo Nordisk about the whole system of diabetes care, not just the drug side. It opens up possibilities around emergent models – for example, in integrated service solutions provision around chronic healthcare management.

National Diabetes Programmes

DAWN provides an input to a set of activities operated by Novo Nordisk under the banner of National Diabetes Programmes (NDPs). These programmes bring the company into close and continuing proximity with key and diverse players in that field. Beyond the PR value of showing the company's commitment to improving diabetes care it creates presence/positioning for emergence.

This initiative began in 2001 when the company set about building a network of relationships in key geographical areas, helping devise and configure relevant holistic care programmes. Rather than a product focus, NDPs offer a range of inputs – for example, supporting education of healthcare professionals or establishing clinics for care of diabetic ulcers. CEO Lars Rebien Sørensen argues that 'only by offering and advocating the right solutions for diabetes care will we be seen as a responsible company. If we just say "drugs, drugs, drugs", they will say "give us a break!"'[1] This is clearly good CSR practice – but the potential learning about new approaches to care, especially under resource-constrained conditions, also represents an important 'hidden R&D' investment.

Typically the NDP process involves identifying needs with key partners and developing a National Diabetes Healthcare Plan – with Novo Nordisk providing resources to help with implementation. The NDPs are closely linked to another initiative, the World Diabetes Foundation, established in 2003 with an initial pledge of US$100 million over a 10-year period. It operates in over 40 countries trying to raise awareness and improve care especially in areas – such as India and China – where diabetes is seriously under-diagnosed.

The core underlying principle is one of developing and testing generic prototype plans which can then be 'customized' for a variety of other countries. For example, Tanzania was an early pilot. It was initially difficult to convince authorities to take chronic diseases like diabetes into account since they had no budget for them and were already fighting hard with infectious diseases. With little likelihood of new investment Novo Nordisk began working with local diabetes associations to establish demonstration projects. It set up clinics in hospitals and villages, trained staff and provided relevant equipment and materials. This gave visibility to the possibilities in a chronic disease management approach – for example, before the programme someone with diabetes might have had to travel 200 km to the major hospital in Dar-es-Salaam whereas now they can be dealt with locally. The value to the national health system is significant in terms of savings on the costs of treating complications such as blindness and amputations, which are tragic and expensive results of poor and delayed treatment. As a result the Ministry of Health is able to deal with diabetes management without the need for new investment in hospital capacity or recruitment of new doctors and nurses. Novo Nordisk is essentially a facilitator here – but in the process is very much centrally involved in an emerging and shifting healthcare system.

NDPs represent an experience-sharing network across over 40 countries. Much of the learning is about the context of different national healthcare systems and how to work within them to bring about significant change – essentially positioning the company for co-evolution. One of the big lessons has been the recognition of the problem of under-diagnosis. Typically around 80% of diabetes sufferers in developing countries remain undiagnosed, and as a result most attention (of the healthcare system and the pharmaceutical companies working with them) goes on the 20% who are identified. The move is now towards finding the undiagnosed and developing ways to manage their diabetes in such a way that they don't get complications, which is where the major costs arise. This has implications not only for expanding the potential market for insulin treatment but also moving the company into much broader areas of healthcare management and delivery.

In his powerful book, *The Fortune at the Bottom of the Pyramid*, C.K. Prahalad points out that most of the world's population – around 4 billion people – live close to or below the poverty line, with an average income of less than

US$2/day. It is easy to make assumptions about this group along the lines of 'they can't afford it so why innovate?'[2] In fact the challenge of meeting their basic needs for food, water, shelter and healthcare require high levels of creativity – but beyond this social agenda lies a considerable innovation opportunity. But it requires a reframing of the 'normal' rules of the market game and a challenging of core assumptions. Table 9.2 gives some examples.

Meeting the needs of people at the bottom of the pyramid is not about charity but rather about a fundamental rethink of the business model – 'paradigm innovation' – to create sustainable alternative systems.[3]

Table 9.2   Challenging assumptions about the bottom of the pyramid

Assumption	Reality – and opportunity
The poor have no purchasing power and do not represent a viable market.	Although low income the sheer scale of this market makes it interesting. Additionally the poor often pay a premium for access to many goods and services – e.g. borrowing money, clean water, telecommunications and basic medicines – because they cannot address 'mainstream' channels like shops and banks. The innovation challenge is to offer low-cost, low-margin but high-quality goods and services across a potential market of 4 billion people.
The poor are not brand-conscious.	Evidence suggests a high degree of brand and value consciousness – so if an entrepreneur can come up with a high-quality, low-cost solution it will be subject to hard testing in this market. Learning to deal with this can help migrate to other markets – essentially the classic pattern of 'disruptive innovation'.
The poor are hard to reach.	By 2015 there are likely to be nearly 400 cities in the developing world with populations over 1 million and 23 with over 10 million; 30–40% of these will be poor. So the potential market access is considerable. Innovative thinking around distribution – via new networks or agents (such as the women village entrepreneurs used by Hindustan Lever in India or the 'Avon ladies' in rural Brazil) – can open up untapped markets.
The poor are unable to use and not interested in advanced technology.	Experience with PC kiosks, low-cost mobile phone-sharing and access to the Internet suggests that rates of take-up and sophistication of use are extremely fast among this group. In India the e-choupal (e-meeting place) set up by software company ITC enabled farmers to check prices for their products at the local markets and auction houses. Very shortly after that the same farmers were using the Web to access prices of their soya beans at the Chicago Board of Trade and strengthen their negotiating hand!

INNOVATION IN ACTION

Pretty high on anyone's list of wants is a quality home – but financing more than basic shelter is often beyond the means of most of the world's population. But CEMEX, the Mexican cement and building materials producer – has pioneered an innovative approach to changing this. Triggered by a domestic financial crisis in the mid-1990s, CEMEX saw a big drop in sales in Mexico. But closer inspection revealed that the market segment of do-it-yourself, especially among the less wealthy, had sustained demand levels. In fact the market was worth a great deal – nearly 1 billion dollars per year – but it was made up of many small purchases rather than large construction projects. Since over 60% of the Mexican population earn less than US$5/day the challenge was to find ways to work with this market in the future.

The response was a novel financing approach, built on the fact that many communities oper-ate a 'savings club' type of scheme to help finance major purchases – the tanda network. CEMEX set up Patrimonio Hoy – a version of the tanda system which allowed poor people to save and access credit for building projects. It relies on social networks, replacing traditional distributors with 'promoters' who work on a commission but who also help set up and run the tandas; signific-antly 98% of these promoters are women. The scheme allows access not just to materials but to architects and other support services; it has effectively changed the way a large segment of soci-ety can manage its own construction projects. Success with the home improvements area has led to its extension to village infrastructure projects linked to drainage, lighting and other community facilities.

INNOVATION IN ACTION

ITC is one of India's largest private-sector firms, with a turnover of around US$4 billion. It operates in a variety of markets including agri-trading, dealing with a variety of Indian commodities including pepper, edible nuts and fruits and grains. It has been active in trying to improve its relationships with local farmers and pioneered the e-choupal – village information centre – as a route for doing so. (Choupal is a Hindi word meaning 'traditional gathering place'.) Some 2000 computer kiosks have been located in villages and linked to a wider network across the country, allowing access to information about weather, prices, agricultural advice, etc. It helps ITC plan its logistics more effectively but also brings benefits to the farmers – e-choupals allow them to find out about prices at local markets and reduces the high transaction costs which the traditional (and often corrupt) manual system of intermediaries and auctions carried. Uptake has been rapid and the farmers soon learn to use the system to strengthen their position – indeed one group began not only looking at local markets but at the Chicago Stock Exchange to monitor soya bean prices and futures!

In addition to direct benefits e-choupals also provide villages with access to educational and information resources.

Challenges in Managing Social Entrepreneurship and Innovation

We've seen throughout the book how innovation doesn't simply happen – it is a process which can be organized and managed. The model we have been working with looks something like this:

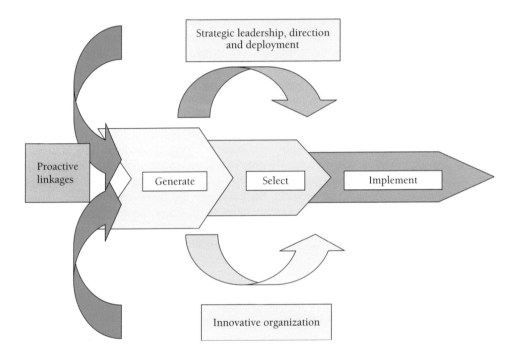

The process happens through seeking out opportunities – often new or different combinations which no one else has seen, and working them up into viable concepts which can be taken forward. It's then a matter of persuading various people – venture capitalists, senior management and so on – to choose to put resources behind the idea rather than backing off or backing something else. If we get past this hurdle the next step is to begin to transform the idea into reality, weaving together a variety of different knowledge and resource streams before finally launching the new thing – product, process or service – onto a market. Whether they choose to adopt and use it, and spread the word to others so the innovation diffuses depends a lot on how we manage using other knowledge and resource streams to understand, shape and develop the market. We also know that the whole process is influenced and shaped by having clear strategic direction and support, an underlying innovative and enthusiastic organization willing to commit its creativity and energy, and extensive and rich links to other players who can help with the knowledge and resource flows we need. Fuelling the whole is the underlying creativity, drive, foresight and intuition to make it happen – entrepreneurship – to undertake and take the risks.

So how does this play out in the case of social entrepreneurship? Table 9.3 gives some examples of the challenges.

Table 9.3   Challenges in social entrepreneurship

What has to be managed . . .	Challenges in social entrepreneurship
Search for opportunities	Many potential social entrepreneurs (SEs) have the passion to change something in the world – and there are plenty of targets to choose from, like poverty, access to education, healthcare and so on. But passion isn't enough – they also need the classic entrepreneur's skill of spotting an opportunity, a connection, a possibility which could develop. It's about searching for new ideas which might bring a different solution to an existing problem – for example, the micro-finance alternative to conventional banking or street-level moneylending. As we've seen elsewhere in the book the skill is often not so much discovery – finding something completely new – as connection – making links between disparate things. In the SE field the gaps may be very wide – for example, connecting rural farmers to high-tech international stock markets requires considerably more vision to bridge the gap than spotting the need for a new variant of futures trading software. So SEs need both passion and vision, plus considerable broking and connecting skills.
Strategic selection	Spotting an opportunity is one thing – but getting others to believe in it and, more importantly, back it is something else. Whether it's an inventor approaching a venture capitalist or an internal team pitching a new product idea to the strategic management in a large organization, the story of successful entrepreneurship is about convincing other people. In the case of SE the problem is compounded by the fact that the targets for such a pitch may not be immediately apparent. Even if you can make a strong business case and have thought through the likely concerns and questions, who do you approach to try and get backing? There are some foundations and non-profit organizations but in many cases one of the important skill sets of a SE is networking, the ability to chase down potential funders and backers and engage them in their project. Even within an established organization the presence of a structure may not be sufficient. For many SE projects the challenge is that they take the firm in very different directions, some of which fundamentally challenge its core business. For example, a proposal to make drugs cheaply available in the developing world might sound a wonderful idea from an SE perspective – but it poses huge challenges to the structure and operations of a large pharmaceutical firm with complex economics around R&D funding, distribution and so on. It's important to build coalitions of support – securing support for social innovation is very often a distributed process – but power and resources are often not concentrated in the hands of a single decision-maker. There may also not be a 'board' or venture capitalist to pitch the ideas to – instead it is a case of building momentum and groundswell.

(continued overleaf)

Table 9.3   *(continued)*

What has to be managed . . .	Challenges in social entrepreneurship
	It's very important to provide practical demonstrations of what otherwise might be seen as idealistic 'pipedreams'. Role of pilots which then get taken up and gather support is well-proven – for example, the Fair Trade model or micro-finance.
Implementation	Social innovation requires extensive creativity in getting hold of the diverse resources to make things happen – especially since the funding base may be limited. Networking skills become critical here – engaging different players and aligning them with the core vision.
Innovation strategy	Here the overall vision is critical – the passionate commitment to a clear vision can engage others–but social entrepreneurs can also be accused of idealism and head in the clouds. Consequently there is a need for a clear plan to translate the vision step by step into reality.
Innovative organization	Social innovation depends on loose and organic structures where the main linkages are through a sense of shared purpose. At the same time there is a need to ensure some degree of structure to allow for effective implementation.
Rich linkages	The history of many successful social innovations is essentially one of networking, mobilizing support and accessing diverse resources through rich networks. This places a premium on networking and broking skills.

STRATEGIC AND SOCIAL IMPACT

Innovation is about change – the word comes from the Latin and means changing, making new. One way in which change becomes a part of everyday life is through entrepreneurs finding and making available new products or services and new ways of creating and delivering them. They don't do this out of the goodness of their hearts – they do so because there is a strong economic imperative. If they can offer something which no one else can they will have a monopoly and be able to make a lot of money selling something which is scarce and desirable. Of course others will see the attractions of this and jump in with their imitations – and gradually the advantages will get competed away. At this point our entrepreneur will get fed up and go and look for the next opportunity to get ahead in the economic race.

So far, so obvious – and as an explanation for what drives the capitalist system it has been well developed by writers like Joseph Schumpeter. But not all entrepreneurs want to create wealth, either for themselves of the companies they work for. Social entrepreneurship is about using the same set of skills and following the same core innovation process to bring about change – the difference is that this is socially valuable, 'concerned in some way with making the world a better place'.

The two are not necessarily incompatible – increasingly we are seeing 'win–win' combinations of innovative projects which both improve social well-being and also deliver profits. There may well be a 'fortune at the bottom of the pyramid' as C.K. Prahalad suggests – and smart firms would do well to look at how they might open up this 4 billion-person market. But there may also be no option – large firms won't continue to hold a 'licence to operate' unless they address wider social concerns among their stakeholders – as major pharmaceutical, food and other firms have been finding out. Innovating only along economically attractive pathways may well be profitable – but in the face of energy shortages, climate change, waste accumulation and depletion of natural resources we may find that the current models for doing business simply become unsustainable – as we will see in the next chapter. Social entrepreneurship isn't simply a 'feel good' aspect of the innovation puzzle to occupy the more idealistic players in the game. It is increasingly becoming a central component of successful and sustainable business. But making it happen will require learning and absorbing a new set of skills to sit alongside our current ways of thinking about and managing innovation. How do we find opportunities which deliver social as well as economic benefits? How do we identify and engage a wide range of stakeholders – and understand and meet their very diverse expectations? How do we mobilize resources across networks? How do we build coalitions of support for socially valuable ideas? One thing is already clear from studies of successful social entrepreneurship – it needs organizing and managing in an even more professional fashion than 'conventional' business innovation.

Developing Personal Capabilities

Social entrepreneurs (SEs) need to possess – or develop – the same set of capabilities as commercial entrepreneurs. That means being prepared to take risks, spot and seize opportunities and build networks. Some of the key 'tips' for SEs offered by experienced players are:

- Spot a gap in the market and try to fill it. For example, gaps exist where the private and public sectors fail to provide a service or product.

- Be clear why you want to do it – many social entrepreneurs have the passion but lack enough patience in researching for constructive or feasible ideas.

- Be able to network with a variety of people and communities.

- Be good at spotting and reusing resources that are underused or abandoned, such as buildings and open spaces.

- Don't be afraid to make mistakes – but do be prepared to learn from them.

- Manage the cash flow – the commonest cause of any business failure is simply running out of cash. (Interestingly women are often key players in SE stories – perhaps because in most households they manage the family finances.)

- Use 'viral marketing' – unlike well-resourced business with access to marketing and advertising budgets SEs often need to mobilize low-cost options – and word of mouth is often powerful, especially via the Internet.

- Identify your skills needs – and map your existing and required network. What do you need in the way of management, financial, sales and marketing, production, distribution, service? Can you link to specialist organizations like the Ashoka Foundation or Skoll Centre?

- Get someone expert to review your plan – business plans don't need to be long but they do need to contain critical components, and to pass scrutiny by people who know what will work and what won't in the business world.

■ Have an exit strategy – deciding ahead of time how you will react when/if things get tough. It may be a good idea to share your ideas with other social organizations – to spread the risks and costs and also because your idea may be a big catalyst in getting another organization off the ground.

Chapter Summary

■ Innovation is not a simple flash of inspiration but an extended and organized process of turning bright ideas into successful realities. Getting innovation to happen depends on a focused and determined drive – a passion to change things which we call 'entrepreneurship'. Essentially this is about being prepared to challenge and change, to take (calculated) risks and put energy and enthusiasm into the venture, picking up and enthusing other supporters along the way.

■ There are people who undoubtedly fit this entrepreneur mould but target their efforts in a different, socially valuable direction. 'Social entrepreneurs' recognize a social problem and use traditional entrepreneurial principles to organize, create and manage a venture to make social change.

■ Just because there is no direct profit motive doesn't take the commercial challenges out of the equation. If anything it becomes harder to be an entrepreneur when the challenge is not only to convince people that it can be done (and use all the tricks of the entrepreneur's trade to do so) but also to do so in a form which makes it commercially sustainable.

■ Social entrepreneurship of this kind is also an increasingly important component of 'big business', as large organizations realize that they only secure a licence to operate if they can demonstrate some concern for the wider communities in which they are located.

■ Increasingly we are seeing 'win–win' combinations of innovative projects which both improve social well-being and also deliver profits. There may well be a 'fortune at the bottom of the pyramid' – the estimated 4 billion people on less than US$2/day income.

■ Making social entrepreneurship happen will require learning and absorbing a new set of skills to sit alongside our current ways of thinking about and managing innovation. How do we find opportunities which deliver social as well as economic benefits? How do we identify and engage a wide range of stakeholders – and understand and meet their very diverse expectations? How do we mobilize resources across networks? How do we build coalitions of support for socially valuable ideas?

Key Terms Defined

Double bottom line – Assessing an organization's performance against financial and social goals.

Social enterprise – An organization that tries to pursue a double bottom line or a triple bottom line.

Social entrepreneurship – Applying entrepreneurship to achieve social goals rather than (but not excluding) financial reward.

Triple bottom line – Simultaneous assessment of a company's performance against its financial and share-holder performance, its internal and external stakeholder expectations and responsibilities and its environmental responsibilities.

Further Reading and Resources

There is a wealth of information about social entrepreneurship including useful websites for the Ashoka Foundation (www.ashoka.org), the Skoll Foundation (www.skollfoundation.com), and the Institute for Social Entrepreneurs http://www.socialent.org/. Chapter 8 has a case example of the UK organization UnLtd and weblinks to their site. Stanford University's Entrepreneurs website has a number of resources including videos of social entrepreneurs explaining their projects – http://edcorner.stanford.edu

A number of books describing approaches and tools include Bornstein, David (2004). *How to Change the World: Social Entrepreneurs and the Power of New Ideas*, Oxford University Press, Oxford; Brinckerhoff, Peter (2000). *Social Entrepreneurship: The Art of Mission-Based Venture Development*. John Wiley & Sons, Ltd, Chichester; Dees, G., Emerson, J. and Economy, P. (2001). *Enterprising Nonprofits: A Tool-kit for Social Entrepreneurs*. John Wiley & Sons, Ltd, Chichester.

Case studies of projects like Grameen Bank (www.grameen-info.org) and the wind-up radio (www.freeplayenergy. com) also give insights into the process and the difficulties confronting social entrepreneurs. A useful website here is http://www.howtochangetheworld.org/, as is the Ashoka Foundation. Prahalad's book, *The Fortune at the Bottom of the Pyramid*, is a useful collection of cases in this direction.

References

1 Schumpeter, J. (1950). *Capitalism, Socialism and Democracy*. Harper & Row, New York.

2 Prahalad, C.K. (2006). *The Fortune at the Bottom of the Pyramid*. Wharton School Publishing, New Jersey.

3 Forbes, N. and Wield, D. (2002). *From Followers to Leaders*. Routledge, London.

Discussion Questions

1 Give a man a fish, and you feed him for a day. Teach a man to fish and he can feed himself for life. How might you put this principle into practice through a social entrepreneurship venture – and what might stop you making a success of this?

2 'Some problems have no solution' is a somewhat pessimistic Japanese saying. How might a social entrepreneur challenge this?

3 Jasmine Chang has approached you as an innovation advisor with a novel treatment for childhood diarrhoea. How would you advise her to take this idea forward to make a difference?

4 In many ways taking a socially valuable concept to market has much in common with 'conventional' new product development. Where do you see the similarities and differences?

Team Exercise

Dragons' Den is a popular BBC TV programme in which successful entrepreneurs and venture capitalists listen to would-be entrepreneurs pitch for money to fund their business ideas. Appoint several team members to be the (tough, hard-nosed and business-minded) 'Dragons' and the remainder of the group should prepare 'pitches' setting out how they would carry through a social innovation. Groups should spend a few minutes brainstorming around key areas of social need – and at the same time the Dragons should think of the key questions to ask of any entrepreneur to assess whether and how far they have thought through their business idea.

Assignment and Case Study Questions

Identify an area of social need and develop some ideas for possible innovative solutions which might help deal with this challenge. Then think about how you would turn this into a business plan and convince other people to back your idea or help you take it forward. Think about the likely questions they would ask and how you would make a strong case to convince the more sceptical members of your audience. Write your ideas up as an outline business plan.

CASE STUDY 9

Exploring Innovation in Action: Power to the People – Freeplay Energy

Trevor Baylis was quite a swimmer in his youth, representing Britain at the age of 15. So it wasn't entirely surprising that he ended up working for a swimming-pool firm in Surrey before setting up his own company. He continued his swimming passion – working as a part-time TV stuntman doing underwater feats – but also followed an interest in inventing things. One of the projects he began work on in 1991 was to have widespread impact despite – or rather because of – being a 'low tech' solution to a massive problem.

Having seen a documentary about AIDS in Africa he began to see the underlying need for something which could help communication. Much of the AIDS problem lies in the lack of awareness and knowledge across often isolated rural communities – people don't know about causes or prevention of this devastating disease. And this reflects a deeper problem – of *communication*. Experts estimate that fewer than 20% of the world's population have access to a telephone, while even fewer have a regular supply of electricity, much less television or Internet access. Very low literacy levels exclude most people from reading newspapers and other print media.

Radio is an obvious solution to the problem – but how can radio work when the receivers need power and in many places mains electricity is simply non-existent? An alternative is battery power – but batteries are equally problematic – even if they were of good quality and freely available via village stores people couldn't afford to buy them regularly. In countries where US$1 a day is the standard wage, batteries can cost from a day's to a week's salary. The HIV/AIDS pandemic also means that household incomes are under increased pressure as earners become too ill to work while greater expenditure goes towards healthcare, leaving nothing for batteries.

What was needed was a radio which ran on some different source of electricity. In thinking about the problem Baylis remembered the old-fashioned telephones of pre-war days which had wind-up handles to generate power. He began experimenting, linking together odd items such as a hand brace, an electric motor and a small radio. He found that the brace turning the motor would act as a generator that would supply sufficient electricity to power the radio. By adding a clockwork mechanism he found that a spring could be wound up – and as it unwound the radio would play. This first working prototype ran for 14 minutes on a 2-minute wind. Trevor had invented a clockwork (wind-up) radio! As a potential solution to the communication problem the idea had real merit. The trouble was that, like thousands of entrepreneurs before him, Trevor couldn't convince others of this. He spent nearly 4 years approaching major radio manufacturers like Philips and Marconi but to no avail. But luck often plays a significant part in the innovation story – and this was no exception. The idea came to the attention of some TV researchers and the product was featured in 1994 on a BBC TV programme, *Tomorrow's World*, which showcased interesting and exciting new inventions.

Among those who saw it and whose interest was taken by the wind-up radio were a corporate finance expert, Christopher Staines, and a South African entrepreneur, Rory Stear. They bought the rights from Baylis and received a UK government grant to help develop the product further, including the addition of solar panel options. In South Africa, the details of the invention were featured in a new broadcast and heard by Hylton Appelbaum, head of an organization called the Liberty Life Foundation, who saw the potential. Even in relatively rich South Africa, half the homes have no electricity, and elsewhere in Africa the problem is even more severe.

Liberty Life is a body set up by a major South African insurance company, and Anita and Gordon Roddick, the socially conscious owners of the Body Shop. Part of the work of the Foundation is in providing access to employment for the disabled and a third of the company's factory workers are blind, deaf, in wheelchairs or mentally ill. Through Applebaum, Liberty Life provided the US$1.5 million in venture capital that founded the company. Baygen Power Industries (from *Bay*lis *Gen*erator) was set up by Staines and Stear in 1995, in Cape Town; 60% of the shares were held by a group of organizations for the disabled, a condition of Liberty's support. Technical development was provided by the Bristol University Electronics Engineering Department. Shortly thereafter production of the radio began in Cape Town by BayGen Products PTY South Africa.

It came on the market at the beginning of 1996 and one year later around 160 000 units had been sold. Much of the early production was purchased by aid charities working in Rwanda and other African countries where relief efforts were underway.

This was not a glamorous product – as a *New York Times* article described it,

> It is no threat to a Sony Walkman. It weighs six pounds, it's built like an overstuffed lunch box, and it has a tinny speaker. But its wholesale price is only $40 and it gets AM, FM, and shortwave, meaning it can pick up the British Broadcasting Corporation or the Voice of America, so a circle of mud huts can zip back into the Information Age with a twist of the wrist. (Donald G. McNeil Jr., New York Times News Service, 1996)

The impact was significant. In 1996 another BBC TV programme, *QED*, featured the radio and at one point showed footage of Baylis, Staines and Stear together with Nelson Mandela who commented that this was a 'fantastic product that can provide an opportunity for those people who have been despised by society'.

Although appearing basic and low-tech, there is a surprising amount of invention in the product. Baylis filed no less than 13 patents covering the mainspring and gears that drive a little dynamo. The spring mechanism is not a simple clockwork but is more closely related to the kind used in rewinding auto seat belts. A double-spool mechanism keeps its tension constant, which is crucial, and the gearing is sophisticated.

Baygen continued to develop products around the energy needs of developing countries including wind-up torches and small generators. The company renamed itself in 1999 as the Freeplay Energy Group and have taken the original concepts into a wide range of new product areas.

Although founded on strong social entrepreneurship principles the business has grown through expanding markets in both developing and advanced economies. At an early stage in their life they realized that dependence on government, international and charitable aid providers posed problems in terms of business sustainability and in 1997, following investment by the US General Electric Company, they began diversifying into commercial markets, modifying the product designs to suit this shift. One of the casualties in this shift has been the Cape Town factory – after five years manufacturing was outsourced to plants in China where labour costs are lower.

The company is now commercially successful, having sold over 3 million units of their basic radio models, and has raised an additional US$45 million in capital. Product development has embraced a wider range of power options including solar cells, and an increasing range of applications including torches and lighting, small-scale generators and mobile-phone chargers. Emphasis remains on replacing battery and fixed-line power applications with rechargeable or self-generating approaches – an approach which, given increasing concerns about sustainability in the advanced industrial economies, is opening new possibilities for market growth.

Typical of their current products is the Lifeline radio, a multi-band, self-powered radio,

> *designed specifically for providing dependable access to information across a broad range of humanitarian projects. The radio does not require batteries or mains electricity and can be used practically anywhere. Engineered to operate in the harshest of rural conditions, it is rugged, robust and easy to operate. It offers excellent FM/AM/SW reception and runs on wind-up energy and solar power. Fully charged, it can play for up to 24 hours. The Lifeline radio was field-tested in various developing countries as part of an extensive research and development programme to identify and create a radio that truly meets the requirements of these unique and diverse applications.*

The declared mission of Freeplay Energy plc is 'To make energy available to everybody all of the time', and it continues to do this through product development and strategic alliances with partners that bring compatible technology and market leadership.

On their website they set out their social entrepreneurship goals:

> *We are committed to balancing the imperatives of both profit and social justice, by providing excellent returns to our shareholders and stakeholders, whilst maintaining complete integrity and contributing to the personal fulfilment of our employees, the communities in which we operate, and beneficiaries of our products.*

All of Freeplay's business practices are shaped by our Six Core Ideologies:

- *Results Orientated* – Delivering on promises to shareholders and partners.

- *Leading-edge* – On the edge of technology and business practice.

- *Proactive* – Showing leadership and taking the initiative wherever possible.

- *Empowering* – Seeking to enable all our stakeholders to achieve their goals.

■ *Responsible* – Being responsible towards our employees, the environment and the communities we touch.

■ *A Friend and Partner* – Taking a positive attitude to developing partnerships and friendships based on trust.

In 1998 the Freeplay Foundation was established as an extension of the Group's commitment to empowerment and development. The Foundation operates as an independent organization with its own board of trustees but it still receives an annual grant from the Freeplay Energy Group with which it shares some managerial and administration resources. The balance of funding is raised from various donors and used to support a wide range of development and implementation projects. Working primarily in Africa, the Freeplay Foundation promotes access to radio broadcasting in rural and remote areas through alternative energy solutions. It seeks 'to advance economic progress, promote community development and help eradicate disease, famine and conflict'. It does this by continuing the original wind-up radio mission – supporting or initiating projects that harness appropriate and alternative energy solutions that deliver information and education through radio broadcasting.

The Foundation facilitates access to specialists who can provide the four components vital to the sustainable success of any radio communication initiative:

■ *Software* – quality radio programming directed at a targeted audience.

■ *Hardware* – radios that allow sustainable listening access to all groups.

■ *Structured distribution* – a planned and coordinated distribution of radios, in consultation with communities.

■ *Project-monitoring and evaluation* – measuring effectiveness against set objectives.

Using the Products

The scope for application is wide since it meets the basic human need for communication and enables a wide range of information, education and community-building activities. Some examples from the radio side of the business include:

■ A project (funded by various development agencies) using communication satellites and FM radio technology to communicate weather, agricultural and health information to nomadic communities and villages across Africa. The pilot is built on a model in the village of Bankilare, outside Niger's capital, Niamey, and combines a WorldSpace satellite receiver, a laptop, Freeplay radios, a transmitter, solar panels and other equipment. Information is downloaded from the Internet via a satellite connection. It is then rebroadcast via a community FM radio station powered by solar energy. Villagers, nomads and farmers living in remote and poorly served areas receive broadcasts on Freeplay radios. The aim of this project is to provide timely information on the weather, with implications for crop-planting and livestock care, availability of water, market prices for crops, associated diseases, health and disaster mitigation. This is just as important for the nomad as for the farmer. As stated by a nomad: 'I do not depend on the rain that falls on my head, but on streams running from the hills when they flood. So just tell me when it will rain in that distant land and I will know what to do.'

■ In Madagascar the Ministries of Communication and Health, working with various aid agencies, developed a radio drama series for women's listening clubs in Madagascar. Wind-up radios, funded by Rotary, were distributed to clubs who provided regular feedback on the programmes. The series is aimed at improving health education, family planning and AIDS prevention. Similarly in Ethiopia people living in remote communities in Ethiopia's Harar Province are tuning in twice weekly to a radio serial drama aimed at creating awareness and prevention of HIV/AIDS – a project funded by the Centres for Disease Control and Prevention.

■ According to the Zambian Ministry of Education (MOE) 800 000 Zambian children are unable to attend school. They cannot afford it, are orphans, live too far to walk to school or are girls who are kept at home. The attrition rate of teachers poses another problem – 2 teachers are dying of AIDS for every one who is trained. The MOE, together with the Educational Broadcasting Services, is using interactive radio instruction to help fill the educational void. Each morning thousands of primary school learners listen to the lively English and maths programme, *Learning at Taonga Market*, on the radio. To assist with the lesson, adult mentors from the community are trained to use radio as a teaching aid. The Peace Corps in Zambia purchased Freeplay radios for their volunteers to distribute. These volunteers are trained in the mentoring process and then train community mentors, enabling the programme to reach deep rural areas. In addition, Rotary UK is helping to raise funds to bring more radios to community schools.

■ In early 2000, hundreds of thousands of Mozambicans were displaced by catastrophic flooding. One of the items that people lost were radios – often the only access to information. Various donor agencies including the Freeplay Foundation distributed over 7000 radios and a daily programme called *Ndhambi* was created in the local language, Shangani. *Ndhambi* covered information on health, sanitation, hygiene, the location of landmines, obtaining lost ID documents and title deeds, governance, tracing and contacting lost family members, as well as agricultural assistance, all of which were of great importance during the post-flood period.

■ During the crisis in Kosovo in 1999, DFID and the ICRC purchased over 40 000 Freeplay radios to distribute to refugees on the move and in camps in Albania and Montenegro. Here they played a part in helping to find missing relatives and to inform of the location of landmines, contaminated water supplies and booby-trapped villages.

Case Study Questions

1 How could you reconcile the social agenda – make radios freely available – with the commercial challenges of running a business? What problems do you think Freeplay face in trying to sustain the business?

2 Jennifer Peters has an idea for water treatment which could help provide clean drinking water to millions of people in Africa. Using ideas from the Freeplay story, what advice would you give her to help her take this forward? And what should she watch out for?

3 Do you think it's easier or harder to create a sustainable business venture with a social entrepreneurship idea? Why?

Chapter 10

Innovation for Growth and Sustainability

This chapter

- ◼ Explores the question of innovation for sustainability.

- ◼ Reviews the concept of open systems of innovation.

- ◼ Examines diffusion and adoption of innovations.

- ◼ Looks at some tools for forecasting and influencing future innovation.

Learning Objectives

When you have completed this chapter you will be able to:

- ◼ Understand the relationships between innovation and sustainable development.
- ◼ Appreciate how different types of innovation can contribute to sustainability.
- ◼ Describe the factors that influence the diffusion and adoption of innovations.
- ◼ Construct and assess forecasts of future innovations using different methods.

Innovation for Sustainability

Social and political concerns about the environment and sustainability present a critical, but often subtle, influence on the *rate*, and more importantly *direction* of innovation. Science and technology do have their own internal logics, but development paths and applications are influenced and shaped by broader political, social and commercial imperatives. In most cases there are numerous potential technological trajectories, most of which will not be pursued, or will fail to become established. For example, nuclear power as a technological innovation has evolved in very different ways in countries like the USA, UK, France and Japan. Similarly, innovation in genetically-modified crops and foods has taken radically different paths in the USA and Europe, mainly due to public concerns and pressure. The box below discusses some of the more general issues related to managing sustainable innovation.

INNOVATION IN ACTION

Managing Innovation for Sustainability

In their review of the field, Frans Berkhout and Ken Green argue that:

> technological and organizational innovation stands at the heart of the most popular and policy discourses about sustainability. Innovation is regarded as both a cause and solution...yet, very little attempt has been made in the business and environment, environmental management and environmental policy literatures to systematically draw on the concepts, theories and empirical evidence developed over the past three decades of innovation studies.

They identify a number of limitations in the innovation literature, and suggest potential ways to link innovation and sustainability research, policy and management:

■ A focus on managers, the firm or the supply chain is too narrow. Innovation is a distributed process across many actors, firms and other organizations, and is influenced by regulation, policy and social pressure.

■ A focus on a specific technology or product is inappropriate. Instead the unit of analysis must be on technological systems or regimes, and their evolution rather than management.

■ The assumption that innovation is the consequence of coupling technological opportunity and market demand is too limited. It needs to include the less obvious social concerns, expectations and pressures. These may appear to contradict stronger but misleading market signals.

They present empirical studies of industrial production, air transportation and energy to illustrate their arguments, and conclude that 'greater awareness and interaction between research and management of innovation, environmental management, corporate social responsibility and innovation and the environment will prove fruitful'.

Source: From *International Journal of Innovation Management*, 2002, **6** (3), Special Issue on Managing Innovation for Sustainability, edited by Frans Berkhout and Ken Green

The most conventional approach to innovation and sustainability focuses on how to influence the development and application of innovations through regulation and control. In this approach, formal policies are used in an attempt to direct innovation by using systems of regulation, targets, incentives and usually punishments for non-compliance. This can be effective, but is a rather blunt instrument to encourage change, and can be slow and incremental.

A more balanced and effective approach tries to understand how technology, markets and society co-evolve through a process of negotiation, consultation and experimentation with new ways of doing things. This perspective demands a better appreciation of how firms and innovation work, and highlights the need to better understand all the organizations involved – the policy-makers, consumers, firms, institutions and other stakeholders that can influence the rate and direction of innovation.[1] By focusing on policy and regulation the innovation–environment debate and research has not really fully understood or engaged with the motivations and actions of individual entrepreneurs or innovative organizations.

Innovation is often presented as a major contribution to the degradation of the environment, through its association with increased economic growth and consumption.[2] However, innovation must also be a large part of any potential solution to a range of environmental issues, including:

- *Cleaner products* – with a lower environmental impact over their life cycle;

- *More efficient processes* – to minimize or treat waste, to reuse or recycle;

- *Alternative technologies* – to reduce emissions, provide renewable energy;

- *New services* – to replace or reduce consumption of products;

- *Systems innovation* – to measure and monitor environmental impact, new socio-technical systems.

Figure 10.1 presents a typology of the different ways in which innovation can contribute to sustainability. One dimension is the novelty of the knowledge, and the other dimension is the novelty of the application of that knowledge. In the bottom left quadrant the innovation focuses on the improvement of existing technologies, products and services. This is not necessarily incremental, and may at times involve radical innovation, but the goals and performance criteria remain the same – for example, increasing the fuel efficiency of a power station or car engine. This is the most common type of innovation, and we have discussed this throughout this book. The top left-hand quadrant represents the development of new knowledge, but its application to existing problems.

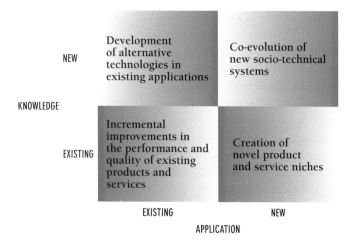

Figure 10.1   A typology of sustainable innovations.

This includes alternative materials, processes or technologies used in existing products. For example, in energy production and packaging of goods there are often many alternative competing technologies, with very different properties and benefits. In food-packaging, glass, different plastics, aluminum and steel are all viable alternatives, but each has different energy requirements over their life cycle in their production and reuse or recycling.

Moving to the right-hand column, the bottom quadrant represents the application of existing knowledge to create new market niches. These are sometime called *architectural* innovations (see Chapter 10), because they reuse different components and sub-systems in new configurations. These are very important for sustainable innovation, as typically such innovations emerge and are developed in niches which initially co-exist with the existing mass market, but these niches can mature and grow to influence demand and development in the dominant market. For example, in the car industry safety was not a significant feature until the early 1980s. Up until that point the assumption was that 'safety did not sell', and manufacturers were reluctant to develop such features. Corning was initially unable to convince any US manufacturer to adopt laminated windscreens (windshields). However, local demand for improved safety in Scandinavia, especially Sweden, encouraged local manufacturers such as Volvo and Saab to develop and incorporate new safety technologies. These slowly became popular in overseas markets, and competing manufacturers had to respond with similar features. As a result today almost all cars have a range of active and passive safety technologies, such as airbags, side-impact protection, crumple zones, anti-lock brakes and electronic stability systems.

The top-right quadrant is probably the most fundamental contribution of innovation to sustainability. It is here that new socio-technical systems co-evolve. Developers and users of innovation interact more closely, and many more actors are involved in the process of innovation. In this case firms are not the only, or even the most important, actor, and the successful development and adoption of such systems innovation demand a range of externalities, such as supporting infrastructure, complementary products and services, finance and new training and skills. For example, the micro-generation of energy requires much more than technological innovation and product development. It requires changes in energy pricing and regulation, an infrastructure to allow the sale of energy back to the grid, and new skills and services in the installation and service of generators. Such innovations typically evolve by a combination of top-down policy change and coordination, and bottom-up social change and firm behaviour.

Alternative Technologies

Alternative innovations are characterized by the application of new technologies to existing needs or applications. In this case the key issue is to identify existing applications where an alternative may have a performance advantage.

The first and most critical distinction to make is between a technology and a product. Technologists are typically concerned with developing devices, whereas potential customers buy products, which marketing must create from the devices. Developing a product is much more costly and difficult than developing a device. Devices that do not function or are difficult to manufacture are relatively easy to identify and correct compared to an incomplete product offering. A product may fail or be difficult to sell due to poor logistics and branding, or difficult to use because insufficient attention has been paid to customer training or support. Therefore attempting to differentiate a product on the basis of its functionality or the performance of component devices can be expensive and futile.

For example, a personal computer (PC) is a product consisting of a large number of devices or sub-systems, including the basic hardware and accessories, operating system, application programmes, languages, documentation, customer training, maintenance and support, advertising and brand development. Therefore a development in microprocessor technology, such as reduced instruction set computing (RISC) may improve product performance in certain circumstances, but may be undermined by more significant factors such as lack of support for developers of software and therefore a shortage of suitable application software.

The traditional literature on industrial marketing has a bias towards relatively low-technology products, and has failed largely to take into account the nature of high-technology products and their markets. In the case of alternative technologies it is not sufficient to carry out a simple technical comparison of the performance of technological alternatives, and conventional market segmentation is unlikely to reveal opportunities for substituting a new technology in existing applications. It is necessary to identify why a potential customer might look for an alternative to the existing solution. It may be because of lower costs, superior performance, greater reliability or simply fashion. In such cases there are two stages to identify potential applications and target customers: technical and behavioural.

Statistical analysis of existing customers is unlikely to be of much use because of the level of detail required. Typically technical segmentation begins with a small group of potential users being interviewed to identify differences and similarities in their requirements. The aim is to identify a range of specific potential uses or applications. Next, a behavioural segmentation is carried out to find three or four groups of customers with similar situations and behaviour. Finally, the technical and behavioural segments are combined to define specific groups of target customers and markets that can then be evaluated commercially.

Several features are unique to the promotion of alternative technologies, and affect buying behaviour:

- *Buyers' perceptions of differences in technology affect buying behaviour.* In general, where buyers believe technologies to be similar, they are likely to search for longer than when they believe there to be significant differences between technologies.

- *Buyers' perceptions of the rate of change of the technology affects buying behaviour.* In general, where buyers believe the rate of technological change is high, they put a lot of effort into the search for alternatives, but search for a shorter time. In non-critical areas a buyer may postpone a purchase.

- *Organizational buyers may have strong relationships with their suppliers, which increases switching costs.* In general, the higher the supplier-related switching costs, the lower the search effort, but the higher the compatibility-related switching costs, the greater the search effort.

Novel Niches

Novel niches or architectural innovations consist of novel configurations of existing knowledge that serve new needs or applications. In such cases the critical issue is to identify or create new market segments. A fundamental issue in novel niches is the need to identify the need to change the architecture or configuration, rather than just the components within an existing system.[3]

Clayton Christensen distinguishes between two fundamental types of innovation.[4] The first is *sustaining* innovation, which continues to improve existing product functionality for existing customers and markets. The term is unfortunate, as it refers to sustaining in the sense of sustaining existing markets and performance characteristics, rather than sustaining the environment. The second, *disruptive* innovation, provides a different set of functions which are likely to appeal to a very different segment of the market. As a result, existing firms and their customers are likely to undervalue or ignore disruptive innovations, as these are likely to underperform existing technologies in terms of existing functions in established markets. This illustrates the danger of simplistic advice such as 'listening to customers', and the limitations of traditional management and marketing approaches. Therefore established firms tend to be blind to the potential of disruptive innovation, which is more likely to be exploited by new entrants. Segmentation of current markets and close relations with existing customers will tend to reinforce sustaining innovation, but will fail to identify or wrongly reject potential disruptive innovations. Instead firms must develop and maintain a detailed understanding of potential applications and changing user needs.

Critical to this process is how to identify or help to create new market segments. Market or buyer segmentation is simply the process of identifying groups of customers with sufficiently similar purchasing behaviour so that they can be targeted and treated in a similar way. This is important because different groups are likely to have different needs. By definition the needs of customers in the same segment will be highly homogeneous. In formal statistical terms the objective of segmentation is to maximize across-group variance and to minimize within-group variance.

In such cases many of the standard marketing tools and techniques are of limited utility for the development and commercialization of truly novel niches. A number of weaknesses can be identified:

- *Identifying and evaluating novel product characteristics.* Marketing tools such as conjoint analysis have been developed for variations of existing products or product extensions, and therefore are of little use for identifying and developing novel products or applications.

- *Identifying and evaluating new markets or businesses.* Marketing techniques such as segmentation are most applicable to relatively mature, well-understood products and markets, and are of limited use in emerging, ill-defined markets.

- *Promoting the purchase and use of novel products and services.* The traditional distinction between consumer and business marketing is based on the characteristics of the customers or users, but the characteristics of the innovation and the relationship between developers and users is more important in the case of novel and complex products and services.

In many cases potential users may have latent needs or unarticulated requirements. In such cases three types of user need can be identified:

- *Must-haves, or pre-qualifiers* – those features which must exist before a potential customer will consider a product or service. For example, in the case of an executive car it must be relatively large and expensive.

- *One-dimensionals* – the more quantifiable features which allow direct comparison between competing products. For example, in the case of an executive car, the acceleration and braking performance.

- *Delighters, or order-winners* – the most subtle means of differentiation. The inclusion of such features delights the target customers, even if they do not explicitly demand them. For example, delighters in the case of an executive car include ultrasonic parking aids, rain-sensitive windscreen wipers and photochromatic mirrors. Such features are rarely demanded by customers or identified by regular market research. However, indirect questioning can be used to help identify latent requirements.

In practice segmentation is conducted by analysing customers' buying behaviour and then using factor analysis to identify the most significant variables influencing behaviour – descriptive segmentation – and then using cluster analysis to create distinct segments which help identify unmet customer needs – prescriptive segmentation. The principle of segmentation applies to both consumer and business markets, but the process and basis of segmentation is different in each case.

Segmenting Consumer Markets

Much of the research on the buying behaviour of consumers is based on theories adapted from the social and behavioural sciences. Utilitarian theories assume that consumers are rational and make purchasing decisions by comparing product utility with their requirements. This model suggests a sequence of phases in the purchasing decision: problem recognition, information search, evaluation of alternatives and finally the purchase. However, such rational processes do not appear to have much influence on actual buying behaviour. For example, in the UK the Consumers' Association routinely tests a wide range of competing products, and makes buying recommendations based on largely objective criteria. If the majority of buyers were rational, and the Consumers' Association successfully identified all relevant criteria, these recommendations would become best-sellers, but this is not the case.

Behavioural approaches have greater explanatory power. These emphasize the effect of attitude, and argue that the buying decision follows a sequence of changing attitudes to a product – awareness, interest, desire and finally action. The goal of advertising is to stimulate this sequence of events. However, research suggests that attitude alone explains only 10% of decisions, and can rarely predict buyer behaviour.

In practice the balance between rational and behavioural influences will depend on the level of customer involvement. Clearly, the decision-making process for buying an aircraft or machine tool is different from the process of buying a toothpaste or shampoo. Many purchasing decisions involve little cost or risk, and therefore low involvement. In such cases consumers try to minimize the financial, mental and physical effort involved in purchasing. Advertising is most effective in such cases. In contrast, in high-involvement situations, in which there is a high cost or potential risk to customers, buyers are willing to search for information and make a more informed decision. Advertising is less effective in such circumstances, and is typically confined to presenting comparative information between rival products. Assessing the level of involvement is absolutely critical in the case of developing and promoting novel niches for sustainable innovations. For example, surveys routinely suggest that consumers would be willing to pay a premium price for organic produce, but actual sales fall far short of expectations.

There are many bases of segmenting consumer markets, including by socio-economic class, life-cycle groupings and by lifestyle or psychographic (psychological–demographic) factors. An example of psychographic segmentation is the Taylor–Nelson classification that consists of self-explorers, social registers, experimentalists, achievers, belongers, survivors and the aimless. Better-known examples include the *Yuppy* (young upwardly mobile professional) and *Dinky* (dual income, no kids), and the more recent *Yappy* (young affluent parent), *Sitcoms* (single income, two children, oppressive mortgage), and *Skiers* (spending the kid's inheritance). There is often a strong association between a segment and preferences for particular attributes, products and services.

Segmenting Business Markets

Business customers tend to be better informed than consumers and, in theory at least, make more rational purchasing decisions. Business customers can be segmented on the basis of common buying factors or purchasing processes. The basis of segmentation should have clear operational implications, such as differences in preferences, pricing, distribution or sales strategy. For example, customers could be segmented on the basis of how experienced, sophisticated or price-sensitive they are. However, the process is complicated by the number of people involved in the buying process:

- The actual customer or buyer, who typically has the formal authority to choose a supplier and agree terms of purchase.

- The ultimate users of the product or service, who are normally, but not always, involved in the initiation and specification of the purchase.

- Gatekeepers, who control the flow of information to the buyers and users.

- Influencers, who may provide some technical support to the specification and comparison of products.

Therefore it is critical to identify all relevant parties in an organization, and determine the main influences on each. For example, technical personnel used to determine the specification may favour performance, whereas the actual buyer may stress value for money.

The most common basis of business segmentation is by the benefits customers derive from the product, process or service. Customers may buy the same product for very different reasons, and attach different weightings to different product features. For example, in the case of a new numerically controlled machine tool, one group of customers may place the greatest value on the reduction in unit costs it provides, whereas another group may place greater emphasis on potential improvements in precision or quality of the output.

It is difficult in practice to identify distinct segments by benefit because these are not strongly related to more traditional and easily identifiable characteristics such as firm size or industry classification. Therefore benefit segmentation is only practical where such preferences can be related to more easily observable and measurable customer characteristics. For example, in the case of the machine tool, analysis of production volumes, batch sizes, operating margins and value-added might help differentiate between those firms which value higher efficiency from those which seek improvements in quality. This suggests a three-stage segmentation process for identifying new business markets:

■ A segmentation based on the functionality of the technology, mapping functions against potential applications.

■ Behavioural segmentation to identify potential customers with similar buying behaviour, for example regarding price or service.

■ Finally, combine the functional and behavioural segmentations in a single matrix to help identify potential customers with relevant applications and buying behaviour.

In addition, analysis of competitors' products and customers may reveal segments not adequately served, or alternatively an opportunity to redefine the basis of segmentation. For example, existing customers may be segmented on the basis of size of company, rather than the needs of specific sectors or particular applications. However, in the final analysis, segmentation provides only a guide to behaviour as each customer will have unique characteristics.

There is likely to be a continuum of customer requirements, ranging from existing needs to emerging requirements and latent expectations, and these must be mapped on to existing and emerging technologies. Whereas much of conventional market research is concerned with identifying the existing needs of customers and matching these to existing technological solutions, in this case the search has to be extended to include emerging and new customer requirements. There are three distinct phases of analysis:

■ Cross-functional teams including customers are used to generate new product concepts by means of brainstorming, morphology and other structured techniques.

■ These concepts are refined and evaluated, using techniques such as QFD.

■ Parallel prototype development and market research activities are conducted. Prototypes are used not as 'master models' for production, but as experiments for internal and external customers to evaluate.

Where potential customers are unable to define or evaluate product design features, in-depth interview clinics must be carried out with target focus groups or via antenna shops. In antenna shops market researchers and engineers conduct interactive customer interviews, and use marketing research tools and techniques to identify and quantify perceptions about product attributes. Product-mapping can be used to expose the technological and market drivers of product development, and allows managers to explore the implications of product extensions. It helps to focus development efforts and limit the scope of projects by identifying target markets and technologies. This helps to generate more detailed functional maps for design, production and marketing.

New product introduction is, up to a point, associated with higher sales and profitability, but very high rates of product introduction become counterproductive as increases in development costs exceed additional sales revenue. This was the case in the car industry, when Japanese manufacturers reduced the life cycle to just four years in the 1990s, but then had to extend it again. Alternatively, expectations of new product introductions can result in users skipping a generation of products in anticipation of the next generation. This has happened in both the PC and cellphone markets, which has had knock-on effects in the chip industry. Put another way, there is often a trade-off between high rates of new product introduction and product life. The development of common product platforms and increased modularity is one way to try to tackle this trade-off in new product development. Incremental product innovation within an existing platform can either introduce benefits to *existing* customers, such as lower price or improved performance, or additionally attract *new* users and enter new market niches. A critical issue in managing architectural innovation is the precise balance between the frequency of radical change of product platform, and incremental innovation within these platforms. This suggests that a strategy of ever-faster new product development and introduction is not sustainable, but rather the aim should be to achieve an optimum balance between platform change and new product based on existing platforms. This logic appears to apply to both manufactured products and services.

INNOVATION IN ACTION

The Evolution of Electric and Hybrid Cars

The car industry is an excellent example of a large, complex, socio-technical system which has evolved over many years, such that the current system of firms, products, consumers and infrastructure interact to restrict the degree and direction of innovation. Since the 1930s the dominant design has been based around a gasoline (petrol)- or diesel-fuelled reciprocating combustion engine/Otto-cycle, mass-produced in a wide variety of relatively minimally differentiated designs. This is no industrial conspiracy, but rather the almost inevitable industrial trajectory, given the historical and economic context. This has resulted in car companies spending more on marketing than on research and development. However, growing social and political concerns over vehicle emissions and their regulation have forced the industry to reconsider this dominant design, and in some cases to develop new capabilities to help to develop new products and systems. For example, zero- and low-emissions targets and legislation have encouraged experimentation with alternatives to the combustion engine, while retaining the core concept of personal, rather than collective or mass travel.

For example, the zero-emission law passed in California in 1990 required manufacturers selling more than 35 000 vehicles a year in the State to have 2% of all vehicle sales zero-emission by 1998, 5% by 2001 and 10% by 2003. This most affected GM, Ford, Chrysler, Toyota, Honda and Nissan, and potentially BMW and VW, if their sales increased sufficiently over that period. However, the US automobile industry subsequently appealed, and had the quota reduced to a maximum of 4%. As fuel cells were still very much a longer-term solution, the main focus was on developing electric vehicles. At first sight this would appear to represent a rather 'autonomous' innovation, that is the simple substitution of one technology (combustion engine) for another (electric). However, the shift has implications for related systems such as power storage, drive-train, controls, weight of materials used and the infrastructure for refuelling/recharging and servicing. Therefore it is much more of a 'systemic' innovation than it first seems.

Moreover, it challenges the core capabilities and technologies of many of the existing car manufacturers. The US manufacturers struggled to adapt, and early vehicles from GM and Ford were not successful. However, the Japanese were rather more successful in developing the new capabilities and technologies, and new products from Toyota and Honda have been particularly successful.

However, zero-emissions legislation was not adopted elsewhere, and more modest emission-reduction targets were set. Since then, hybrid petrol–electric cars have been developed to help to reduce emissions. These are clearly not long-term solutions to the problem, but do represent valuable technical and social prototypes for future systems such as fuel cells. In 1993, Eiji Toyoda, Toyota's chairman, and his team embarked on the project code-named G21. G stands for global and 21, the twenty-first century. The purpose of the project was to develop a small hybrid car that could be sold at a competitive price in order to respond to the growing needs and eco awareness of many consumers worldwide. A year later a concept vehicle was developed called the Prius, taken from the Latin for 'before'. The goal was to reduce fuel consumption by 50%, and emissions by more than that. To find the right hybrid system for the G21, Toyota considered 80 alternatives before narrowing the list to 4. Development of the Prius required the integration of different technical capabilities including, for example, a joint venture with Matsushita Battery.

The prototype was revealed at the Tokyo Motor Show in October 1995. It is estimated that the project cost Toyota US$1 billion in R&D. The first commercial version was launched in Japan in December 1997, and after further improvements such as battery performance and power-source management, introduced to the US market in August 2000. For urban driving the economy is 60 mpg, and 50 for motorways – the opposite consumption profile of a conventional vehicle, but roughly twice as fuel-efficient as an equivalent Corolla. From the materials used in production, through driving, maintenance, and finally its disposal, the Prius reduced CO_2 emissions by more than a third, and has a recyclability potential of approximately 90%. The Prius was launched in the USA at a price of US$19 995, and sales in 2001 were 15 556 in the USA, and 20 119 in 2002. However, industry experts estimate that Toyota was losing some US$16 000 for every Prius it sold because it costs between US$35 000 and US$40 000 to produce. Toyota did make a profit on its second-generation Prius launched in 2003, and other hybrid cars such as the Lexus range in 2005, because of improved technologies and lower production costs.

The Hollywood celebrities soon discovered the Prius: Leonardo DiCaprio bought one of the first in 2001, followed by Cameron Diaz, Harrison Ford and Calista Flockhart at the 2003 Academy Awards. British politicians took rather longer to jump on the hybrid bandwagon, with the leader of the Conservative Party, David Cameron, driving a hybrid Lexus in 2006. In 2005, 107 897 cars were sold in the USA, about 60% of global Prius sales, and 4 times more than the sales in 2000, and twice as many in 2004. Toyota plans to sell 1 million hybrids by 2010.

In addition to the direct income and indirect prestige the Prius and other hybrid cars have created for Toyota, the company has also licensed some of its 650 patents on hybrid technology to Nissan and Ford, which are expected to develop hybrid vehicles for 2007, and Ford plans to sell 2 50 000 hybrids by 2010. Mercedes-Benz showed a diesel–electric S-class at the Frankfurt auto show in autumn 2005, and Honda has developed its own technology and range of hybrid cars, and is also probably the world leader in fuel-cell technology for vehicles.

Sources: Pilkington A. and Dyerson R. (2004) Incumbency and the disruptive regulator: the case of the electric vehicles in California, *International Journal of Innovation Management*, **8** (4), 339–354; Why the future is hybrid, *The Economist*, 4 December 2004; Too soon to write off the dinosaurs, *Financial Times*, 18 November 2005; *Fortune*, 21 February 2006; Toyota: the birth of the Prius, *Wall Street Journal*, 13 February, 2006.

New Socio-technical Systems

New socio-technical systems are a special case of innovation because neither the technology nor applications are well-defined or understood. Therefore technology and markets co-evolve over time, as developers, potential users and other stakeholders interact. The main differences between systems innovation and novel niches are the scale and scope of the innovation. Systems innovation involves more actors than novel niches do, and typically requires greater coordination of these different actors, by some institutional or policy intervention, rather than relying only on market mechanisms.[5]

In such cases the process of development, implementation and diffusion of innovations has certain unique characteristics:

- Systems are likely to consist of a complex configuration of new technologies, products, services, institutions and infrastructure, interacting at various levels and interfaces, which complicates development and implementation.

- The role and knowledge of users is likely to be much more significant, but there is a burden on developers to educate potential users. This requires close links between developers and users.

- Adoption is likely to involve a long-term commitment, involving many different actors, and therefore the cost of failure to perform is likely to be high.

- The development and diffusion process is often lengthy and uncertain, and adoption may lag years behind availability and receipt of the initial information.

Systems innovations will consist of a number of components, or sub-systems. Depending on how open the standards are for interfaces between the various components, products may be offered as bundled systems, or as sub-systems or components. For bundled systems, customers evaluate purchases at the system level, rather than at the component level. For example, many pharmaceutical firms are now operating managed healthcare services, rather than simply developing and selling specific drugs. Similarly, robot manufacturers offer 'manufacturing solutions', rather than stand-alone robot manipulators. Bundled systems can offer customers enhanced performance by allowing a package of optimized components using proprietary interfaces of 'firmware', and in addition may provide the convenience of a single point of purchase and after-sales support. For example, many utility companies now offer services for domestic customers which include an environmental assessment, advice on insulation and appliances, as well as more traditional energy provision.

The growth of general service providers and systems integrators and 'turnkey' solutions suggests that there is additional value to be gained by developing and marketing systems rather than components: typically, the value added at the system level is greater than the sum of the value added by the components. There is, however, an important exception to this rule. In cases where a particular component or sub-system is significantly superior to competing offerings, unbundling is likely to result in a larger market. The increased market is due to additional customers who would not be willing to purchase the bundled system, but would like to incorporate one of the components or sub-systems into their own systems. Moreover, bundled systems may not appeal to customers with idiosyncratic needs, or knowledgeable customers able to configure their own systems. In such cases the trick is to identify the specific needs of such users. For example, in the case of micro-generation discussed earlier, it is very unlikely to become a dominant energy system because of the particular characteristics of the technologies and potential users.

Links between Developers and Users

The development and adoption process for systems innovations is particularly difficult. The benefits to potential users may be difficult to identify and value, and because there are likely to be few direct substitutes available, the market may not be able to provide any benchmarks. The choice of suppliers is likely to be limited, more an oligopolistic market than a truly competitive one. In the absence of direct competition, price becomes less important than other factors such as reputation, performance and service and support.

Innovation research has long emphasized the importance of 'understanding user needs' when developing new products but, in the special case of complex products and services, potential users may not be aware of, or may be unable to articulate, their needs. In such cases it is not sufficient simply to understand or even to satisfy existing customers, but rather it is necessary to lead existing customers and identify potential new customers. Conventional market research techniques are of little use, and there will be a greater burden on developers to work with potential users, in what has been called expeditionary or agnostic marketing, to reflect the emergent nature of the development and diffusion process. The main issue is how to learn as quickly as possible through experimentation with real products and users, and thereby anticipate future requirements and pre-empt future trends and demand.

The relationship between developers and users will change throughout the development and adoption process. Three distinct processes need to be managed, each demanding different linkages: development, adoption and interfacing. The processes of development and adoption are relatively well understood, but managing the critical interface between developers and potential users is more problematic.

Two dimensions help determine the most appropriate relationship between developers and users: the range of different applications for an innovation; and the number of potential users of each application:[6]

- *Few applications and few users.* In this case direct face-to-face negotiation regarding the technology design and use is possible.

- *Few applications, but many users.* This is the classic marketing case, which demands careful segmentation, but little interaction with users.

- *Many applications, but few users.* In this case there are multiple stakeholders among the user groups, with separate and possibly conflicting needs. This requires skills to avoid optimization of the technology for one group at the expense of others. The core functionality of the technology must be separated and protected, and custom interfaces developed for the different user groups.

- *Many applications and different users.* In this case developers must work with multiple archetypes of users and therefore aim for the most generic market possible, customized for no one group.

The interface between developers and users can be thought of as consisting of two flows: information flows and resource flows. Developers and adopters will negotiate the inflows and outflows of both information and resources. Therefore developers should recognize that resources committed to development and resources committed to aiding adoption should not be viewed as independent or 'ring-fenced'. Both contribute to the successful commercialization of complex products, processes and services. Developers should also identify and manage the balance and direction of information and resource flows at different stages of the process of development and adoption. For example, at early stages managing information inflows may be most important, but at later stages managing outflows of information and resources may be critical. In addition, learning will require the management of knowledge flows, involving the exchange or secondment of appropriate staff.

In *Democratizing Innovation* Eric von Hippel builds on his concept of lead users in innovation, and argues that innovation is becoming more democratic, with users increasingly being capable of developing their own new products and services.[7] He believes that such user innovation can have a positive impact on social welfare as innovating users – both individuals and firms – often freely share their innovations with others, creating user-innovation communities and a rich intellectual commons. Examples range from surgical equipment to surfboards to software security.

Role of Lead Users

Lead users are critical to the development and adoption of novel niches and systems innovations. As the title suggests, lead users demand new requirements ahead of the general market of other users, but are also positioned in the market to significantly benefit from the meeting of those requirements. Where potential users have high levels of sophistication, for example in business-to-business markets such as scientific instruments, capital equipment and IT systems, lead users can help to co-develop innovations, and are therefore often early adopters of such innovations. The initial research by Von Hippel suggests lead users adopt an average of seven years before typical users, but the precise lead time will depend on a number of factors, including the technology life cycle. Characteristics of lead users include:[8]

- ■ *Recognizing requirements early* – being ahead of the market in identifying and planning for new requirements.

- ■ *Expecting high level of benefits* due to their market position and complementary assets.

- ■ *Developing their own innovations and applications* – having sufficient sophistication to identify and capabilities to contribute to development of the innovation.

- ■ *Perceived to be pioneering and innovative* by themselves and their peer group.

This has two important implications. First, those seeking to develop novel niches or system innovations should identify potential lead users with the above characteristics to contribute to the co-development and early adoption of the innovation. Second, that lead users, as early adopters, can provide insights into forecasting the diffusion of innovations. Clayton Christensen and Michael Raynor make a similar point in their book, *The Innovator's Solution*, and argue that conventional segmentation of markets by product attributes or user types cannot identify potentially disruptive innovations, as shown in the box below.

INNOVATION IN ACTION

Identifying Potentially Disruptive Innovations

In their book, *The Innovator's Solution: Creating and Sustaining Successful Growth,* (Harvard Business School Press, Boston, Mass., 2003), Clayton Christensen and Michael Raynor argue that segmentation of markets by product attributes or type of customer will fail to identify potentially disruptive innovations. Building on the seminal marketing work of Theodore Levitt, they recommend *circumstance*-based segmentation, which focuses on the 'job to be done' by an innovation, rather than product attributes or type of users. This perspective is likely to result in very different new products and services than traditional ways of segmenting markets. One of the insights this approach provides is the idea of innovations from *non-consumption*. So instead of comparing product attributes with competing products, identify target customers who are trying to get a job done, but due to circumstances – wealth, skill, location – do not have access to existing solutions. These potential customers are more likely to compare the disruptive innovation with the alternative of having nothing at all, rather than existing offerings. This can lead to the creation of whole new markets, for example, the low-cost airlines in the USA and UK, such as Southwest and Ryanair, or Intuit's QuickBooks. Similarly, in the MBA market, distance learning programmes were once considered inferior to conventional programmes, and instead leading business schools competed (and many still do) for funds for larger and ever more expensive buildings in prestigious locations. However, improvements to technology, combined with other forms of learning to create 'blended' learning environments, have created whole new markets for MBA programmes, for those who are unable or unwilling to pursue more conventional programmes.

The adoption process for systems innovation is likely to be lengthy due to the difficulty of evaluating risk and subsequent implementation. Perceived risk is a function of a buyer's level of uncertainty and the seriousness of the consequences of the decision to purchase. There are two types of risk: the performance risk, that is the extent to which the purchase meets expectations; and the psychological risk associated with how other people in the organization react to the decision. Low-risk decisions are likely to be made autonomously, and therefore it is easier to target decision-makers and identify buying criteria. For complex products there is greater uncertainty, and the consequences of the investment are more significant, and therefore some form of joint or collective decision-making and responsibility is more likely.

In the case of organizational decision-making and investment, the expectations, perceptions, roles and perception of risk of the main decision-makers may vary. Therefore we should expect and identify the different buying criteria used by various decision-makers in an organization. For example, a production engineer may favour the reliability or performance of a piece of equipment, whereas the finance manager is likely to focus on life-cycle costs and value for money. Three factors are likely to affect the purchase decision in an organization:

- *Political and legal environment.* This may affect the availability of, and information concerning, competing products. For example, government legislation might specify the tender process for the development and purchase of new equipment.

- *Organizational structure and tasks.* Structure includes the degree of centralization of decision-making and purchasing; tasks include the organizational purpose served by the purchase, the nature of demand derived from the purchaser's own business, and how routine the purchase is.

- *Personal roles and responsibilities.* Different roles need to be identified and satisfied. Gatekeepers control the flow of information to the organization, influencers add information or change-buying criteria, deciders choose the specific supplier or brand, and the buyers are responsible for the actual purchase. Therefore the ultimate users may not be the primary target.

Open Systems of Innovation

In this section we expand upon the discussion of open innovation and networks which we began in Chapter 3. Here we are concerned with the enabling routines for building effective linkages outside the organization in order to identify, resource and implement innovations for sustainability. This is a good example of what has been called networked or 'open' innovation, in contrast to 'closed innovation', which primarily takes place within the firm.[9]

Increasingly, networks of relationships are the most appropriate unit of analysis for understanding the innovation process. A network is as much a process as a structure, which both constrains firms, and in turn is shaped by firms. In these terms collaboration can be understood as an attempt to cope with the increasing complexity and interrelatedness of different technologies and markets. We examine the technological and market motives for collaboration, and identify the organizational processes necessary to exploit it as an opportunity for knowledge acquisition and learning.

Organizations collaborate for many reasons, including efficiency and flexibility, but here we are concerned with gaining access to technological and market knowledge. Such relationships may take many forms, ranging from simple licensing agreements, loose coalitions or so-called strategic alliances, to more formal joint ventures. Therefore the technological and market competencies of a specific firm may be a less reliable indicator of innovative potential than its position in a network.

The concept of innovation networks has become popular in recent years, as it appears to offer many of the benefits of internal development, but with few of the drawbacks of collaboration. Networks have been claimed by some to be a new hybrid form of organization that has the potential to replace both firms (hierarchies) and markets, in essence the 'virtual corporation', whereas others believe them to be simply a transitory form of organization, positioned somewhere between internal hierarchies and external market mechanisms. Whatever the case, there is little agreement on what constitutes a network, and the term and alternatives such as 'web' and 'cluster' have been criticized for being too vague and all-inclusive.

Different authors adopt different meanings, levels of analysis and attribute networks with different characteristics. For example, academics on the Continent have focused on social, geographical and institutional aspects of networks, and the opportunities and constraints these present for innovation. In contrast, Anglo-Saxon studies have tended to take a systems perspective, and have attempted to identify how best to design, manage and exploit networks for innovation. Figure 10.2 presents a framework for the analysis of different network perspectives in innovation studies.

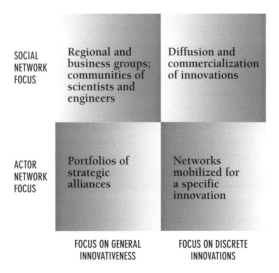

Figure 10.2   Types of innovation network.

Source: Jones, O., Conway, S. and Steward, F (2001) *Social Interaction and Organizational Change: Aston perspectives on innovation networks*. Imperial College Press, London.

A network can be thought of as consisting of a number of positions or nodes, occupied by individuals, firms, business units, universities, governments, customers or other actors, and links or interactions between these nodes. A network perspective is concerned with how these economic actors are influenced by the social context in which they are embedded and how actions can be influenced by the position of actors. A network is more than an aggregation of bilateral relationships or dyads, and therefore the configuration, nature and content of a network impose additional constraints and present additional opportunities.

Innovations networks can exist at any level: global, national, regional, sector, organizational or individual. For example, a national system of innovation, which we will examine in Chapter 11, is an example of an innovation network at a high level of aggregation – the country. Whatever the level of analysis, the most interesting attribute of an innovation network is the degree and type of interaction between actors, which results in a dynamic but inherently unstable set of relationships. Innovation networks are an organizational response to the complexity or uncertainty of technology and markets, and as such innovations are not the result of any linear process. This makes it very difficult, if not impossible, to predict the path or nature of innovation resulting from network interactions. The generation, application and regulation of an innovation within a network is unlike the trial-and-error process within a single firm or venture, or variation and selection within a market. Instead, actors in an innovation network attempt to reduce the uncertainty associated with complexity through a process of recursive learning and testing, as shown in the box below.

INNOVATION IN ACTION

An Environmental Innovation Network for IKEA

The catalogue of IKEA has one of the world's highest circulations, with a print run of more than 100 million per year, needing 50 000 tonnes of high-quality paper each year. However, in the 1990s there were growing environmental concerns about the discharge of chlorinated compounds from the processes used to create the relatively high-quality paper used in such promotional materials, as well as the more general issue of paper recycling. In response to these concerns, in 1992 IKEA introduced 2 new goals for the production of its catalogue: be printed on paper that was totally chlorine-free (TCF), and to include a high proportion of recycled paper.

However, these goals demanded significant innovation. No such paper product existed at the time, and the dominant industry suppliers believed the combination of no chlorine and high levels of recycled pulp to be impossible. To achieve the necessary paper brightness for catalogue printing, a minimum of 50% chlorine-dioxide-bleached pulp had been used. Chlorine had been used for 50 years as the bleaching agent for high-quality paper. Moreover, the high-quality paper used for such catalogues consisted of a very thin paper base, which is coated with clay, which makes the insertion of recycled fibre very difficult. The manager of R&D at Svenska Cellulosa Aktiebolaget (SCA), one of Europe's largest producers of high-quality paper, argued that 'the high-quality demands and the large volume of filling substances is the main reason that it is neither realistic nor necessary to use recycled fibre'. SCA reinforced this view with the decision to build a new SEK 2.4 billion plant to produce conventional high-quality coated paper. At that time SCA was not a supplier to IKEA.

In Sweden, the paper manufacturer Aspa worked with the chemical firm Eka Nobel to develop an environmentally acceptable bleaching process with less damaging discharges, but this was still based on chlorine dioxide and failed to achieve the necessary brightness for use in high-quality paper, and was marketed as 'semi-bleached'. Following customer demand for a true TCF product, including a request from Greenpeace for TCF paper for production of its newsletter, Aspa was forced to develop a stable product with secure supplies. At this stage the pulp and fibre company Sodra Cell became involved, and identified the need to reach full brightness to create a broader market for TCF paper. Sodra worked with the German company Kvaerner to develop an alternative but equally effective bleaching process, and Kvaerner established a research project on ozone bleaching with Lenzing and STORA Billerud. The ozone bleaching process was adapted from an established process for water purification with the help of AGA Gas. However, the use of ozone in place of chlorine for bleaching required the quality of the pulpwood to be improved, so the harvesting system had to be changed to ensure that wood was better sorted and available within weeks of harvesting. To improve the brightness and strength of the paper, the impurities in the pulp from de-inked recycled paper had to be reduced, which required a new washing process. The changes in the chemistry of the pulp subsequently reduced the strength of the paper, which required changes in the paper-production process. The printing processes had to be adapted to the characteristics of the new paper. Initially Sodra Cell supplied the new product to SCA through its relationship with Aspa, but also to the Italian paper producer Burgo, which provided the paper for the IKEA catalogue.

Thus the organization evolved beyond a simple industrial supply relationship, to an innovation network including customers, printers, paper manufacturers, pulp and fibre producers, forestry companies, research institutes, environmental and lobby groups across many different countries. At the same time, the intended innovation shifted from a high-quality TCF clay-coated paper, to a TCF uncoated fresh pulp and 10% de-inked recycled pulp product.

Source: Hakansson, H. and Waluszewski, A. (2003) *Managing Technological Development: IKEA, the Environment and Technology*. Routledge, London.

A network can influence the actions of its members in two ways. First, through the flow and sharing of information within the network. Second, through differences in the position of actors in the network, which causes power and control imbalances. Therefore the position an organization occupies in a network is a matter of great strategic importance, and reflects its power and influence in that network. Sources of power include technology, expertise, trust, economic strength and legitimacy. Networks can be tight or loose, depending on the quantity (number), quality (intensity) and type (closeness to core activities) of the interactions or links. Such links are more than individual transactions, and require significant investment in resources over time. Types of interaction include:

- *Product interactions* – products and groups of products and services interact, are adapted and evolve.

- *Process interactions* – the interdependencies between product and process, and between different processes and production facilities are another interaction within a network, together with their use and utilization.

- *Social interaction within the organization* – for example, business units are more than a combination of product and process facilities. They consist also of social interactions, with knowledge of and an ability to work with other business units within the organization.

- *Social interaction between organizations* – business relationships both restrict and provide opportunities for innovation, particularly for systemic innovations.

Historically, networks have evolved from long-standing business relationships. Any firm will have a group of partners that it does regular business with – universities, suppliers, distributors, customers and competitors.

Over time mutual knowledge and social bonds develop through repeated dealings, increasing trust and reducing transaction costs. Therefore a firm is more likely to buy or sell technology from members of its network. Firms may be able to access the resources of a wide range of other organizations through direct and indirect relationships, involving different channels of communication and degrees of formalization. Typically, this begins with a stronger relationship between a firm and a small number of primary suppliers, which share knowledge at the concept-development stage. The role of the technology gatekeeper, or heavyweight project manager, is critical in this respect. In many cases organizational linkages can be traced to strong personal relationships between key individuals in each organization. These linkages may subsequently evolve into a full network of secondary and tertiary suppliers, each contributing to the development of a sub-system or component technology, but links with these organizations are weaker and filtered by the primary suppliers. However, links among the primary, secondary and tertiary supplier groups may be stronger to facilitate the exchange of information.

This process is path-dependent in the sense that past relationships between actors increase the likelihood of future relationships, which can lead to inertia and constrain innovation. Indeed much of the early research on networks concentrated on the constraints networks impose on members, for example preventing the introduction of 'superior' technologies or products by controlling supply and distribution networks. Organizational networks have two characteristics that affect the innovation process: activity cycles and instability. The existence of activity cycles and transaction chains creates constraints within a network. Different activities are systematically related to each other and through repetition are combined to form transaction chains. This repetition of transactions is the basis of efficiency, but systemic interdependencies create constraints to change.

For example, the Swiss watch industry was based on long-established networks of small firms with expertise in precision mechanical movements, but as a result was slow to respond to the threat of electronic watches from Japan. Similarly, in Japan the formal business groups dominate many traditional sectors, originally the family-based *zaibatsu*, and more recently the more loosely connected *keiretsu* such as Mitsui, Mitsubishi, Sumitomo, Fuji, Sanwa and Dal Ichi Kangyo (DKB). Benefits of membership of a *keiretsu* include access to low-cost, long-term capital, and access to the expertise of firms in related industries. In practice, membership of *keiretsu* is associated with below-average profitability and growth, and independent firms like Honda and Sony are often cited as being more innovative than established members of *keiretsu*.

Networks are most appropriate where the benefits of sharing of joint infrastructure and standards and other network externalities outweigh the costs of network governance and maintenance. Where there are high transaction costs involved in purchasing technology, a network approach may be more appropriate than a market model, and where uncertainty exists a network may be superior to full integration or acquisition.

However, no network can ever be optimal in any generic sense, as there is no single reference point. Therefore any network is inherently instable, but these imperfections mean that networks can evolve over time, for example, the evolution of innovation networks in a range of traditional industries in Italy. There are two distinct dynamics of formation and growth. The first type of network emerges and develops as a result of environmental interdependence, and through common interests – an *emergent* network. However, the other type of network requires some triggering entity to form and develop – an *engineered* network. In an engineered network a nodal firm actively recruits other members to form a network, without the rationale of environmental interdependence or similar interests. Different types of network may present different opportunities for learning. In a closed network, a company seeks to develop proprietary standards through scale economies and other actions, and thereby to lock customers and other related companies into its network.

In such cases established companies are able to reinforce their positional advantage by adopting new technologies which have implications for compatibility, whereas new entrants or existing firms at the periphery of the network will find it extremely difficult to gain a positional advantage through innovation. Obvious examples include Microsoft in operating systems and Intel in microprocessors for PCs. In the case of open networks, complex products, services and businesses have to interface with others and it is in everyone's interest to share information and to ensure compatibility. Open networks or systems often involve multiple hierarchical levels or sub-systems, each controlled by a different technical community. Therefore innovations in one technical sub-field may influence some relationships within the network, but not the whole network. Therefore innovation by established firms at the periphery of the network or by new entrants is more common. Examples include many large socio-technical systems, such as telephony and power generation and distribution.

Diffusion and Adoption of Innovations

Much of the knowledge and many of the technologies necessary to improve the environment already exist or would soon be developed if the demand was demonstrated. However, there are many barriers to the widespread adoption of such innovations, including:

- *Economic* – personal costs versus social benefits, access to information, insufficient incentives;
- *Behavioural* – priorities, motivations, rationality, inertia, propensity for change or risk;
- *Organizational* – goals, routines, power and influence, culture and stakeholders;
- *Structural* – infrastructure, sunk costs, governance.

For these reasons, historically, large complex socio-technical systems tend to change only incrementally. However, more radical transformations can occur, but these often begin in strategic niches, with different goals, needs, practices and processes. As these niches demonstrate and develop the innovations, through social experimentation and learning, they may begin to influence or enter the mainstream. This may be through whole new market niches, or by forming hybrid markets between the niche and mainstream.

Rogers' (2003) definition of diffusion is used widely: 'The process by which an innovation is communicated through certain channels over time among members of a social system. It is a special type of communication, in that the messages are concerned with new ideas' (p. 5). However, there are no generally accepted definitions of associated terms such as 'technology transfer', 'adoption', 'implementation' or 'utilization'. Diffusion usually involves the analysis of the spread of a product or idea in a given social system, whereas technology transfer is usually a point-to-point phenomenon. Technology transfer usually implies putting information to use, or more specifically moving ideas from the laboratory to the market. The distinction between adoption, implementation and utilization is less clear. Adoption is generally considered to be the decision to acquire something, whereas implementation and utilization imply some action and adaptation.

The literature on diffusion is vast and highly fragmented. However, a number of different approaches to diffusion research can be identified, each focusing on particular aspects of diffusion and adopting different methodologies. The main contributions have been from economics, marketing, sociology and anthropology. Economists have developed a number of econometric models of the diffusion of new products and processes in an effort to explain past behaviour and to predict future trends. Prediction is a common theme of the marketing literature. Marketing studies have adopted a wide range of different research instruments to examine buyer behaviour, but most recent research focused on social and psychological factors. Development economics and rural sociology have both examined the adoption of agricultural innovations, using statistical analysis of secondary data and collection of primary data from surveys. Much of the anthropological research has been based on case studies of the diffusion of new ideas in tribes, villages or communities. Most recently, there has been a growing number of multidisciplinary studies which have examined the diffusion of educational, medical and other policy innovations.

Numerous variables have been identified as affecting the diffusion and adoption of innovations, but these can be grouped into three clusters: characteristics of the innovation itself; characteristics of individual or organizational adopters; and the characteristics of the environment. Characteristics of an innovation found to influence adoption include relative advantage, compatibility, complexity, observability and trialability. Individual characteristics include age, education, social status and attitude to risk. Environmental and institutional characteristics include economic factors such as the market environment and sociological factors such as communications networks. However, while there is general agreement regarding the relevant variables, there is very little consensus on the relative importance of the different variables, and in some cases disagreements over the direction of relationships.

A great deal of research has been conducted to try to identify what factors affect the rate and extent of adoption of an innovation. In this section we examine three issues relevant to the marketing of innovations:

- How the characteristics of an innovation affect adoption.

- How the process of commercialization and diffusion affects adoption.

- What techniques are available for forecasting future patterns of adoption.

Characteristics of an Innovation

A number of characteristics of an innovation have been found to affect diffusion and adoption:[10]

- Relative advantage

- Compatibility

- Complexity

- Trialability

- Observability.

Relative advantage

Relative advantage is the degree to which an innovation is perceived as better than the product it supersedes, or competing products. Relative advantage is typically measured in narrow economic terms, for example cost or financial payback, but non-economic factors such as convenience, satisfaction and social prestige may be equally important. In theory, the greater the perceived advantage, the faster the rate of adoption.

It is useful to distinguish between the primary and secondary attributes of an innovation. Primary attributes, such as size and cost, are invariant and inherent to a specific innovation irrespective to the adopter. Secondary attributes, such as relative advantage and compatibility, may vary from adopter to adopter, being contingent upon the perceptions and context of adopters. In many cases, a so-called 'attribute gap' will exist. An attribute gap is the discrepancy between a potential user's perception of an attribute or characteristic of an item of knowledge and how the potential user would prefer to perceive that attribute. The greater the sum of all attribute gaps, the less likely a user is to adopt the knowledge. This suggests that preliminary testing of an innovation is desirable in order to determine whether significant attribute gaps exist. Not all attribute gaps require changes to the innovation itself – a distinction needs to be made between knowledge content and knowledge format. The idea of pre-testing information for the purposes of enhancing its value and acceptance is not widely practised.

Compatibility

Compatibility is the degree to which an innovation is perceived to be consistent with the existing values, experience and needs of potential adopters. There are two distinct aspects of compatibility: existing skills and practices; and values and norms. The extent to which the innovation fits the existing skills, equipment, procedures and performance criteria of the potential adopter is important, and relatively easy to assess.

However, compatibility with existing practices may be less important than the fit with existing values and norms. Significant misalignments between an innovation and an adopting organization will require changes in the innovation or organization, or both. In the most successful cases of implementation, mutual adaptation of the innovation and organization occurs. However, few studies distinguish between compatibility with value and norms, and compatibility with existing practices. The extent to which the innovation fits the existing skills, equipment, procedures and performance criteria of the potential adopter is critical. Few innovations initially fit the user environment into which they are introduced. Significant misalignments between the innovation and the adopting organization will require changes in the innovation or organization or, in the most successful cases of implementation, mutual adaptation of both. Initial compatibility with existing practices may be less important, as it may provide limited opportunity for mutual adaptation to occur.

In addition, so-called 'network externalities' can affect the adoption process. For example, the cost of adoption and use, as distinct from the cost of purchase, may be influenced by: the availability of information about the technology from other users, of trained skilled users, technical assistance and maintenance, and of complementary innovations, both technical and organizational.

Complexity

Complexity is the degree to which an innovation is perceived as being difficult to understand or use. In general, innovations which are simpler for potential users to understand will be adopted more rapidly than those which require the adopter to develop new skills and knowledge.

However, complexity can also influence the *direction* of diffusion, not only the rate of adoption. Evolutionary models of diffusion focus on the affect of 'network externalities', that is the interaction of consumption, pecuniary and technical factors which shape the diffusion process. For example, within a region the cost of adoption and use, as distinct from the cost of purchase, may be influenced by: the availability of information about the technology from other users, of trained skilled users, technical assistance and maintenance, and of complementary innovations, both technical and organizational.

Trialability

Trialability is the degree to which an innovation can be experimented with on a limited basis. An innovation that is trialable represents less uncertainty to potential adopters, and allows learning by doing. Innovations which can be trialled will generally be adopted more quickly than those which cannot. The exception is where the undesirable consequences of an innovation appear to outweigh the desirable characteristics. In general, adopters wish to benefit from the functional effects of an innovation, but avoid any dysfunctional effects. However, where it is difficult or impossible to separate the desirable from the undesirable consequences trialability may reduce the rate of adoption.

Developers of an innovation may have two different motives for involving potential users in the development process. First, to acquire knowledge from the users needed in the development process, to ensure usability and to add value. Second, to attain user 'buy-in', that is user acceptance of the innovation and commitment to its use. The second motive is independent of the first, because increasing user acceptance does not necessarily improve the quality of the innovation. Rather, involvement may increase users' tolerance of any inadequacies. In the case of point-to-point transfer, typically both motives are present.

However, in the case of diffusion it is not possible to involve all potential users, and therefore the primary motive is to improve usability rather than attain user buy-in. But even the representation of user needs must be indirect, using surrogates such as specially selected user groups. These groups can be problematic for a number of reasons. First, because they may possess atypically high levels of technical knowledge, and therefore not be representative. Second, where the group must represent diverse user needs, such as both experienced and novice users, the group may not work well together. Finally, when user representatives work closely with developers over a long period of time they may cease to represent users, and instead absorb the developer's viewpoint. Thus, there is no simple relationship between user involvement and user satisfaction. Typically, very low levels of user involvement are associated with user dissatisfaction, but extensive user involvement does not necessarily result in user satisfaction.

Observability

Observability is the degree to which the results of an innovation are visible to others. The easier it is for others to see the benefits of an innovation, the more likely it will be adopted. The simple epidemic model of diffusion assumes that innovations spread as potential adopters come into contact with existing users of an innovation.

Peers who have already adopted an innovation will have what communication researchers call 'safety credibility', because potential adopters seeking their advice will believe they know what it is really like to implement and utilize the innovation. Therefore early adopters are well positioned to disseminate 'vicarious learning' to their colleagues. Vicarious learning is simply learning from the experience of others, rather than direct personal experimental learning. However, the process of vicarious learning is neither inevitable nor efficient because, by definition, it is a decentralized activity. Centralized systems of dissemination tend to be designed and rewarded on the basis of being the source of technical information, rather than for facilitating learning among potential adopters.

Over time, learning and selection processes foster both the evolution of the technologies to be adopted and the characteristics of actual and potential adopters. Thus an innovation may evolve over time through improvements made by early users, thereby reducing the relative cost to later adopters. In addition, where an innovation requires the development of complementary features, for example a specific infrastructure, late adopters will benefit. This suggests that instead of a single diffusion curve, a series of diffusion curves will exist for the different environments. However, there is a potential drawback to this model. The short-term preferences of early adopters will have a disproportionate impact on the subsequent development of the innovation, and may result in the establishment of inferior technologies and abandonment of superior alternatives. In such cases interventionalist policies may be necessary to postpone the lock-in phenomenon.

From a policy perspective, high visibility is often critical. However, high visibility, at least initially, may be counterproductive. If users' expectations about an innovation are unrealistically high and adoption is immediate, subsequent disappointment is likely. Therefore in some circumstances it may make sense to delay dissemination or to slow the rate of adoption. However, in general researchers and disseminators are reluctant to withhold knowledge.

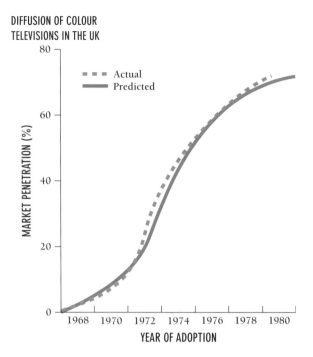

DIFFUSION OF COLOUR
TELEVISIONS IN THE UK

Figure 10.3   Typical Diffusion S-curve: Predicted and actual adoption of colour televisions.
Source: Data from Meade, N. (1984) The use of growth curves in forecasting market development: a review and appraisal, *Journal of Forecasting*, **3** 429–451.

Processes of Diffusion

Research on diffusion attempts to identify what influences the rate and direction of adoption of an innovation. The diffusion of an innovation is typically described by an S-shaped (logistic) curve (Figure 10.3). Initially, the rate of adoption is low, and adoption is confined to so-called 'innovators'. Next to adopt are the 'early adopters', then the 'late majority', and finally the curve tails off as only the 'laggards' remain. Such taxonomies are fine with the benefit of hindsight, but provide little guidance for future patterns of adoption.[11]

Hundreds of marketing studies have attempted to fit the adoption of specific products to the S-curve, ranging from television sets to new drugs. In most cases mathematical techniques can provide a relatively good fit with historical data, but research has so far failed to identify robust generic models of adoption. In practice the precise pattern of adoption of an innovation will depend on the interaction of demand-side and supply-side factors:

- *Demand-side factors* – direct contact with or imitation of prior adopters, adopters with different perceptions of benefits and risk.

- *Supply-side factors* – relative advantage of an innovation, availability of information, barriers to adoption, feedback between developers and users.

The epidemic S-curve model is the earliest and is still the most commonly used. It assumes a homogeneous population of potential adopters, and that innovations spread by information transmitted by personal contact, observation and the geographical proximity of existing and potential adopters. This model suggests that the emphasis should be on communication, and the provision of clear technical and economic information. However, the epidemic model has been criticized because it assumes that all potential adopters are similar and have the same needs, which is unrealistic.

The Probit model takes a more sophisticated approach to the population of potential adopters. It assumes that potential adopters have different threshold values for costs or benefits, and will only adopt beyond some critical or threshold value. In this case differences in threshold values are used to explain different rates of adoption. This suggests that the more similar potential adopters are, the faster the diffusion.

However, adopters are assumed to be relatively homogeneous, apart from some difference in progressiveness or threshold values. They do not consider the possibility that the rationality and the profitability of adopting a particular innovation might be different for different adopters. For example, local 'network externalities' such as the availability of trained skilled users, technical assistance and maintenance, or complementary technical or organizational innovations are likely to affect the cost of adoption and use, as distinct from the cost of purchase.

Also, it is unrealistic to assume that adopters will have perfect knowledge of the value of an innovation. Therefore Bayesian models of diffusion introduce lack of information as a constraint to diffusion. Potential adopters are allowed to hold different beliefs regarding the value of the innovation, which they may revise according to the results of trials to test the innovation. Because these trials are private, imitation cannot take place and other potential adopters cannot learn from the trials. This suggests better-informed potential adopters may not necessarily adopt an innovation earlier than the less well informed, which was an assumption of earlier models.

Slightly more realistic assumptions, such as those of the Bass model, include two different groups of potential adopters: innovators, who are not subject to social emulation; and imitators, for whom the diffusion process takes the epidemic form. This produces a skewed S-curve because of the early adoption by innovators, and suggests that different marketing processes are needed for the innovators and subsequent imitators. The Bass model is highly influential in economics and marketing research, and the distinction between the two types of potential adopters is critical in understanding the different mechanisms involved in the two user segments.

Bandwagons may occur where an innovation is adopted because of pressure caused by the sheer number of those who have already adopted an innovation, rather than by individual assessments of the benefits of an innovation. In general, as soon as the number of adopters has reached a certain threshold level, the greater the level of ambiguity of the innovation's benefits, the greater the subsequent number of adopters. This process allows technically inefficient innovations to be widely adopted, or technically efficient innovations to be rejected. Examples include the QWERTY keyboard, originally designed to prevent professional typists from typing too fast and jamming typewriters; and the DOS operating system for personal computers, designed by and for computer enthusiasts.

Bandwagons occur due to a combination of competitive and institutional pressures. Where competitors adopt an innovation, a firm may adopt because of the threat of lost competitiveness, rather than as a result of any rational evaluation of benefits. For example, many firms adopted flexible manufacturing systems (FMS) in the 1980s in response to increased competition, but most failed to achieve significant benefits. The main institutional pressure is the threat of lost legitimacy, for example, being considered by peers or customers as being less progressive or competent. For example, in the early 1990s most leading firms established websites on the World Wide Web (WWW) because it was perceived to be progressive, rather than because of any immediate commercial benefits.[12]

The critical difference between bandwagons and other types of diffusion is that they require only limited information to flow from early to later adopters. Indeed, the more ambiguous the benefits of an innovation, the more significant bandwagons are on rates of adoption. Therefore the process of diffusion must be managed with as much care as the process of development. In short, better products do not necessarily result in more sales. Not everybody requires a better mousetrap.

Finally, there are more sociological and psychological models of adoption, which are based on interaction between and feedback between the developers and potential adopters. These perspectives consider how individual psychological characteristics such as attitude and perception affect adoption. Individual motivations, perceptions, likes and dislikes determine what information is reacted to and how it is processed. Potential adopters will be guided and prejudiced by experience, and will have 'cognitive maps' which filter information and guide behaviour. Social context will also influence individual behaviour. Social structures and meaning systems are locally constructed, and therefore highly context-specific. These can distort the way in which information is interpreted and acted upon. The perceived value of an innovation, and therefore its subsequent adoption, is not some objective fact, but instead depends on individual psychology and social context. These factors are particularly important in the later stages of diffusion.

Initially, the needs of early adopters or innovators dominate, and therefore the characteristics of an innovation are most important. Innovations tend to evolve over time through improvements required by these early users, which may reduce the relative cost to later adopters. However, early adopters are almost by definition 'atypical', for example, they tend to have superior technical skills. As a result the preferences of early adopters can have a disproportionate impact on the subsequent development of an innovation, and result in the establishment of inferior technologies or abandonment of superior alternatives.

The choice between the different models of diffusion will depend on the characteristics of the innovation and nature of potential adopters. The simple epidemic model appears to provide a good fit to the diffusion of new processes, techniques and procedures, whereas the Bass model appears to best fit the diffusion of consumer products. However, the mathematical structure of the epidemic and Bass models tends to overstate the importance of differences in adopter characteristics, but tends to underestimate the effect of macroeconomic and supply-side factors. In general, both these models of diffusion work best where the total potential market is known, that is for derivatives of existing products and services, rather than totally new innovations.

Diffusion research and practice has been criticized for an increasingly limited scope and methodology. Rogers (2003) identifies a number of shortcomings of research and practice:

- Diffusion has been seen as a *linear, unidirectional communication* activity in which the active source of research or information attempts to influence the attitudes and/or behaviours of essentially passive receivers. However, in most cases diffusion is an interactive process of adaptation and adoption.

- Diffusion has been viewed as a *one-to-many communication* activity, but point-to-point transfer is also important. Both centralized and decentralized systems exist. Decentralized diffusion is a process of convergence as two or more individuals exchange information in order to move toward each other in the meanings they ascribe to certain events.

- Diffusion research has been preoccupied with an *action-entered and issue-entered* communication activity, such as selling products, actions, or policies. However, diffusion is also a social process, affected by social structure and position and inter-personal networks.

- Diffusion research has used *adoption as the dependent variable* – the decision to use the innovation, rather than implementation itself – the consequences of the innovation. Most studies have used attitudinal change as the dependent variable, rather than change in overt behaviour.

- Diffusion research has suffered from an implicit *pro-innovation bias*, which assumes that an innovation should be adopted by all members of a social system as rapidly as possible. Therefore the process of adaptation or rejection of an innovation has been overlooked, and there have been relatively few studies of how to prevent the diffusion of 'bad' innovations.

Forecasting and Influencing Future Innovation

Forecasting can help to identify what might be required in the future, and to estimate how many products are likely to be required in a given time period. However, in the case of innovative products, service and systems forecasting is difficult, as the products and markets will not be well defined or clearly articulated.

The most appropriate choice of forecasting method will depend on:

- What we are trying to forecast;
- Rate of technological and market change;
- Availability and accuracy of information;
- The company's planning horizon;
- The resources available for forecasting.

In practice there will be a trade-off between the cost and robustness of a forecast. The more common methods of forecasting such as trend extrapolation and time series are of limited use for new products, because of the lack of past data. However, regression analysis can be used to identify the main factors driving demand for a given product, and therefore provide some estimate of future demand, given data on the underlying drivers.

For example, a regression might express the likely demand for the next generation of digital mobile phones in terms of rate of economic growth, price relative to competing systems, rate of new business formation, and so on. Data are collected for each of the chosen variables and coefficients for each derived from the curves which best describe the past data. Thus the reliability of the forecast depends a great deal on selecting the right variables in the first place. The advantage of regression is that, unlike simple extrapolation or time series analysis, the forecast is based on cause and effect relations. Econometric models are simply bundles of regression equations, including their interrelationship. However, regression analysis is of little use where future values of an explanatory value are unknown, or where the relationship between the explanatory and forecast variables may change.

Leading indicators and analogues can improve the reliability of forecasts, and are useful guideposts to future trends in some sectors. In both cases there is a historical relationship between two trends. For example, new business start-ups might be a leading indicator of the demand for fax machines in six months' time. Similarly, business users of mobile telephones may be an analogue for subsequent patterns of domestic use.

Such 'normative' techniques are useful for estimating the future demand for existing products, or perhaps alternative technologies or novel niches, but are of limited utility in the case of more radical systems innovation. Exploratory forecasting, in contrast, attempts to explore the range of future possibilities. The most common methods are:

- Customer or market surveys
- Internal analysis, for example, brainstorming
- Delphi or expert opinion
- Scenario development.

Customer or Market Surveys

Most companies conduct customer surveys of some sort. In consumer markets this can be problematic simply because customers are unable to articulate their future needs. For example, Apple's iPod was not the result of extensive market research or customer demand, but was largely the result of the vision and commitment of Steve Jobs. In industrial markets, customers tend to be better equipped to communicate their future requirements, and consequently, business-to-business innovations often originate from customers. Companies can also consult their direct sales force, but these may not always be the best guide to future customer requirements. Information is often filtered in terms of existing products and services, and biased in terms of current sales performance rather than long-term development potential.

There is no 'one best way' to identify novel niches, but rather a range of alternatives. For example, where new products or services are very novel or complex, potential users may not be aware of or able to articulate their needs. In such cases traditional methods of market research are of little use, and there will be a greater burden on developers of radical new products and services to 'educate' potential users.

Our own research confirms that different managerial processes, structures and tools are appropriate for routine and novel development projects. We discussed this in detail in Chapter 5. For example, in terms of frequency of use, the most common methods used for high-novelty projects are segmentation, prototyping, market experimentation and industry experts, whereas for the less novel projects the most common methods are partnering customers, trend extrapolation and segmentation. The use of market experimentation and industry experts might be expected where market requirements or technologies are uncertain, but the common use of segmentation for such projects is harder to justify. However, in terms of usefulness, there are statistically significant differences in the ratings for segmentation, prototyping, industry experts, market surveys and latent needs analysis. Segmentation is the only method more effective for routine development projects; and prototyping, industry experts, focus groups and latent needs analysis are all more effective for novel development projects.[13]

Internal Analysis – Brainstorming

Structured idea generation, or brainstorming, aims to solve specific problems or to identify new products or services. Typically, a small group of experts is gathered together and allowed to interact. A chairman records all suggestions without comment or criticism. The aim is to identify, but not evaluate, as many opportunities or solutions as possible. Finally, members of the group vote on the different suggestions. The best results are obtained when representatives from different functions are present, but this can be difficult to manage. Brainstorming does not produce a forecast as such, but can provide useful input to other types of forecasting.

We discussed a range of approaches to creative problem-solving and idea generation in Chapter 2. Most of these are relevant here, and include ways to:

- *Understand the problem* – the active construction by the individual or group through analysing the task at hand (including outcomes, people, context and methodological options) to determine whether and when deliberate problem-structuring efforts are needed. This stage includes constructing opportunities, exploring data and framing problems.

- *Generate ideas* – to create options in answer to an open-ended problem. This includes a generating and focusing phase. During the generating phase of this stage, the person or group produces many options (fluent thinking), a variety of possible options (flexible thinking), novel or unusual options (original thinking), or a number of detailed or refined options (elaborative thinking). The focusing phase provides an opportunity for examining, reviewing, clustering and selecting promising options.

■ *Plan for action* – is appropriate when a person or group recognize a number of interesting or promising options that may not necessarily be useful, valuable or valid. The aim is to make or develop effective choices, and to prepare for successful implementation and social acceptance.

External Assessment – Delphi or Expert

The opinion of outside experts, or Delphi method, is useful where there is a great deal of uncertainty or for long time horizons. Delphi is used where a consensus of expert opinion is required on the timing, probability and identification of future technological goals or consumer needs and the factors likely to affect their achievement. It is best used in making long-term forecasts and revealing how new technologies and other factors could trigger discontinuities in technological trajectories. The choice of experts and the identification of their level and area of expertise are important; the structuring of the questions is even more important. The relevant experts may include suppliers, dealers, customers, consultants and academics. Experts in non-technological fields can be included to ensure that trends in economic, social and environmental fields are not overlooked.

The Delphi method begins with a postal survey of expert opinion on what the future key issues will be, and the likelihood of the developments. The response is then analysed, and the same sample of experts resurveyed with a new, more focused questionnaire. This procedure is repeated until some convergence of opinion is observed, or conversely if no consensus is reached. The exercise usually consists of an iterative process of questionnaire and feedback among the respondents; this process finally yields a Delphi forecast of the range of experts' opinions on the probabilities of certain events occurring by a quoted time. The method seeks to nullify the disadvantage of face-to-face meetings at which there could be deference to authority or reputation, a reluctance to admit error, a desire to conform or differences in persuasive ability. All of these could lead to an inaccurate consensus of opinion. The quality of the forecast is highly dependent on the expertise and calibre of the experts; how the experts are selected and how many should be consulted are important questions to be answered. If international experts are used, the exercise can take a considerable length of time, or the number of iterations may have to be curtailed. Although seeking a consensus may be important, adequate attention should be paid to views that differ radically 'from the norm' as there may be important underlying reasons to justify such maverick views. With sufficient design, understanding and resources, most of the shortcomings of the Delphi technique can be overcome and it is a popular technique, particularly for national foresight programmes.

In Europe, governments and transnational agencies use Delphi studies to help formulate policy, usually under the guise of 'foresight' exercises. In Japan, large companies and the government routinely survey expert opinion in order to reach some consensus in those areas with the greatest potential for long-term development. Used in this way, the Delphi method can to a large extent become a self-fulfilling prophecy.

Scenario Development

Scenarios are internally consistent descriptions of alternative possible futures, based upon different assumptions and interpretations of the driving forces of change. Inputs include quantitative data and analysis, and qualitative assumptions and assessments, such as societal, technological, economical, environmental and political drivers.

Scenario development is not strictly speaking prediction, as it assumes that the future is uncertain and that the path of current developments can range from the conventional to the revolutionary. It is particularly good at incorporating potential critical events which might result in divergent paths or branches being pursued.

Scenario development can be normative or explorative. The normative perspective defines a preferred vision of the future and outlines different pathways from the goal to the present. For example, this is commonly used in energy futures and sustainable futures scenarios. The explorative approach defines the drivers of change, and creates scenarios from these without explicit goals or agendas.

For scenarios to be effective they need to be inclusive, plausible and compelling (as opposed to being exclusive, implausible or obvious), as well as being challenging to the assumptions of the stakeholders. They should make the assumptions and inputs used explicit, and form the basis of a process of discussion, debate, policy, strategy and ultimately action. The output is typically two or three contrasting scenarios, but the process of development and discussion of scenarios is much more valuable.

Scenario development may involve many different forecasting techniques, including computer-based simulation. Typically, it begins with the identification of the critical indicators, which might include use of brainstorming and Delphi techniques. Next, the reasons for the behaviour of these indicators is examined, perhaps using regression techniques. The future events which are likely to affect these indicators are identified. These are used to construct the best, worst and most likely future scenarios. Finally, the company assesses the impact of each scenario on its business. The goal is to plan for the outcome with the greatest impact or, better still, retain sufficient flexibility to respond to several different scenarios. Scenario development is a key part of the long-term planning process in those sectors characterized by high capital investment, long lead times and significant environmental uncertainty, such as energy, aerospace and telecommunications.

Developing Personal Capabilities

When building scenarios, the team first needs to decide whether to adopt an exploratory or normative approach. Next it must identify the drivers of changes, and how these factors interact. Finally, any critical events or uncertainties should be identified as these often create potential branching points between alternative futures. The basic steps include:

1 *Identify the drivers of change* – workshops can be useful for this, and should include a mix of stakeholder groups.

2 *Develop a model of how the drivers and stakeholders interact and influence each other.* This is probably the most difficult step.

3 *Produce draft scenarios* – perhaps 6 to 10 broad scenarios. These are then clustered and reduced to 2 or three larger and internally consistent scenarios. This process involves considerable debate, but creates fundamental insights into the drivers, assumptions, models and scenarios.

4 *Test the scenarios* – developing scenarios is an iterative process. Challenge the underlying assumptions and models.

5 *Validate the scenarios* – once written up, a wider range of stakeholders need to be consulted. This can be done by using workshops or by Delphi-type processes. This helps to refine and gain approval for the final scenarios. Otherwise some audiences may become defensive and reject the scenarios.

For scenarios to be effective they need to be incorporated into a project, strategy or policy. This demands they are challenging, but also plausible and compelling.

Source: www.strategy.gov.uk/downloads/survivalguide/skills/eb_scenarios.htm

ADVICE FOR FUTURE MANAGERS

The process of developing and communicating scenarios and Delphi studies is as important as the outcomes for helping to build consensus across different communities, and for expressing and discussing alternative future visions and expectations. Visions can influence expectations and outcomes in profound ways, by encouraging the development or acquisition of competencies relevant to planned paths or goals of innovation:

- *Motivation* which serves to focus attention and to direct energy, and encourages the concentration of resources. It requires senior management to communicate the importance of radical innovation, and to establish and enforce challenging goals to influence the *direction* of innovative efforts.

- *Insight* represents the critical connection between technology and potential application. For radical technological innovations, such insight is rarely from the marketing function, customers or competitors, but is driven by those with extensive technical knowledge and expertise with a sense of both market needs and opportunities.

- *Elaboration* involves the demonstration of technical feasibility, validating the idea within the organization, prototyping and the building and testing of different business models. At this point the concept is sufficiently well elaborated to work with the marketing function and potential customers.

There were multiple ways for a vision to take hold of an organization ... our expectation was that a single individual would create a vision of the future and drive it across the organization. But just as we discovered that breakthrough innovations don't necessarily arise simply because of a critical scientific discovery, neither do we find that visions are necessarily born of singular prophetic individuals. (O'Connor and Veryzer, 2001: 239–244)[14]

STRATEGIC AND SOCIAL IMPACT

The World Economic Forum compiled a pilot Environmental Performance Index (EPI) league table for the first time in 2006. The table is based on data collected by researchers at Columbia and Yale Universities in the USA, and uses 16 indicators, including greenhouse-gas emissions, air and water quality, health and habitat quality, and sustainable energy. Clearly the overall index depends very much on the weights attributed to these different components of the index, but the top 10 ranks were: New Zealand (first), Sweden, Finland, Czech Republic, UK, Austria, Denmark, Canada, Malaysia and Ireland. Significantly, major economies such as the USA were ranked a lowly 28th, mainly due to energy policy and high emissions. The worst performers were the world's poorest countries, mainly in Africa, which lack the resources and political stability to make such environmental commitments.

Like scenario-planning, the real value of the EPI comes from careful analysis of the underlying data and indicators, but by creating ranks by issue, policy category, peer group and country, it helps to identify leaders and to expose laggards, and therefore focus debate and improvement.

See http://www.yale.edu/epi/

Chapter Summary

- Innovation is too often portrayed as antagonistic to sustainability. However, in this chapter we have argued that innovation has a central role to play in helping to create sustainable futures through conventional means such as new processes, products and services, but also through promoting change in organization, business and behaviour.

- By better understanding the dynamics of innovation, including development, adoption and diffusion, the rate and direction of innovation can be influenced, and more sustainable trajectories explored. The process of innovation is much more complex than technology responding to market signals.

- The adoption and diffusion of an innovation depends on the characteristics of the innovation, the nature of potential adopters, and the process of communication. The relative advantage, compatibility, complexity, trialability and observability of an innovation all affect the rate of diffusion.

- The skills, psychology, social context and infrastructure of adopters also affect adoption. Epidemic models assume that innovations spread by communication between adopters, but bandwagons do not require this. Instead, early adopters influence the development of an innovation, but subsequent adopters may be more influenced by competitive and peer pressures.

- Forecasting the development and adoption of innovations is difficult, but participative methods such as Delphi and scenario planning are highly relevant to innovation and sustainability. In such cases the process of forecasting, including consultation and debate, is probably more important than the precise outcomes of the exercise.

Key Terms Defined

Bandwagons – May occur where an innovation is adopted because of pressure caused by the sheer number of those who have already adopted an innovation, rather than by individual assessments of the benefits of an innovation.

Expeditionary marketing – With complex products and services, potential users may not be aware of, or may be unable to articulate, their needs. In such cases it is not sufficient simply to understand or even to satisfy existing customers, but rather it is necessary to lead existing customers and identify potential new customers. Conventional market research techniques are of little use, and there will be a greater burden on developers to work with potential users.

Externalities – Factors which influence the adoption and diffusion of an innovation, such as supporting infrastructure, complementary products and services, finance and new training and skills, or are created by the adoption of an innovation, for example, pollution. Therefore externalities can be positive or negative.

Lead users – Demand new requirements ahead of the general market of other users, but are also positioned in the market to significantly benefit from the meeting of those requirements. Lead users are critical to the development and adoption of novel niches and systems innovations.

Further Reading and Resources

For a general introduction to the key issues in sustainable development, our favourite text is *The Principles of Sustainability* by Simon Dresner (Earthscan Publications, London, 2002). Unlike most of the literature on the subject, this treatment is well-balanced and even includes some humour. Jennifer Elliott's *An Introduction to Sustainable Development* (Routledge, London, 2nd edn, 2005) is a more conventional academic approach, and focuses on the implications for developing nations. However, neither text is strong on the links between sustainability and innovation. The Special Issue of the *International Journal of Innovation Management* (2002), **6** (3), on Innovation for Sustainability is a useful place to begin, and is edited by two leading scholars in the field, Frans Berkhout and Ken Green.

The Natural Advantage of Nations: Business Opportunities, Innovations and Governance in the 21st Century by Amory B. Lovins (Earthscan Publications, London, 2005) is a collection of papers by leading authors including Michael Porter, and makes the business case for sustainable development, including technological, structural and social change. The book has a useful companion website. *Sustainable Business Development: Inventing the Future through Strategy, Innovation, and Leadership* by David L. Rainey (Cambridge University Press, Cambridge, 2006) provides a practical analysis of what sustainable business development (SBD) is and how companies do it, and includes many case studies from the USA, Europe, Pacific Rim and South America. *Sustainable Innovation: The Organizational, Human and Knowledge Dimension* by Rene J. Jorna (Greenleaf Publishing, Sheffield, 2006) is a more theoretical and philosophical book, and the human, social and management challenges and responses. The book argues that it is impossible to achieve the appropriate balance between the needs of people, planet and profit, and advocates a process of 'making sustainable', instead of trying to achieve 'sustainability'.

More generally, the problems of forecasting the future development, adoption and diffusion of innovations is dealt with by many authors in the innovation field. Everett Roger's classic text, *The Diffusion of Innovations*, first published in 1962, remains the best overview of this subject, the most recent and updated edition being published in 2003 (Simon & Schuster International, New York). In *Democratizing Innovation* (MIT Press, Cambridge, Mass., 2005, and free online) Eric von Hippel builds on his earlier concept of 'lead users' in innovation, and argues that innovation is becoming more democratic, with users increasingly being capable of developing their own new products and services. He believes that such user innovation has a positive impact on social welfare as innovating users – both individuals and firms – often freely share their innovations with others, creating user-innovation communities and a rich intellectual commons. Examples provided range from surgical equipment to surfboards to software security.

Clayton Christensen's (with S. D. Anthony and E. A. Roth) *Seeing What's Next: Using the Theories of Innovation to Predict Industry Change* (Harvard Business School Press, Boston, Mass., 2005) is a useful, up-to-date review of methods for forecasting radical and potentially disruptive innovations. A Special Issue of the journal *Long Range Planning* (2004), **37** (2), is devoted to forecasting, and provides a good overview of current thinking. *Scenario Planning* by Gill Ringland (John Wiley & Sons, Ltd, Chichester, 2nd edn, 2006) and *Scenario Planning: The Link between Future and Strategy* by Mats Lindgren (Palgrave Macmillan, Basingstoke, 2002) are both detailed and practical guides to conducting scenario-planning, which is probably one of the more relevant methods for understanding innovation and sustainability.

References

1 Geels, F.W. (2002) Technological transitions as evolutionary reconfiguration processes: a multi-level perspective and a case study. *Research Policy*, **31** (8–9), 1257–1274.

2 Porter, M.E. and Van der Linde, C. (1995) Green and competitive: ending the stalemate. *Harvard Business Review*, **73** (5), 120–134.

3 Smith, A. (2004) Alternative technology niches and sustainable development. *Innovation: Management, Policy and Practice*, **6** (2), 220–235; Smith, A., Stirling, A. and Berkhout, F. (2005) The governance of sustainable socio-technical transitions. *Research Policy*, **34** (10), 1491–1510.

4 Christensen, C.M. (2000) *The Innovator's Dilemma*. HarperCollins, New York.

5 Kemp, R., Schot, J. and Hoogma, R. (1998) Regime shifts to sustainability through processes of niche formation. *Technology Analysis and Strategic Management*, **10** (2), 175–195.

6 Leonard-Barton, D. and Sinha, D.K. (1993) Developer–user interaction and user satisfaction in internal technology transfer. *Academy of Management Journal*, **36** (5), 1125–1139; More, P.L.A. (1986) Developer/adopter relationships in new industrial product situations. *Journal of Business Research*, **14**, 501–517.

7 Von Hippel, E. (2005) *Democratizing Innovation*. MIT Press, Cambridge, Mass.

8 Morrison, P.D., Roberts, J.H. and Midgley, D.F. (2004) The nature of lead users and measurement of leading edge status. *Research Policy*, **33**, 351–362; Von Hippel, E. (1986) Lead users: a source of novel product concepts. *Management Science*, **32** (7), 791–805; Von Hippel, E. (1988) *The Sources of Innovation*. Oxford University Press, Oxford.

9 Chesborough, H. (2003) *Open Innovation: The New Imperative for Creating and Profiting from Technology*. Harvard Business School Press, Boston, Mass.

10 Rogers, E.M. (2003) *Diffusion of Innovations*. Simon & Schuster, New York.

11 Geroski, P.A. (2000) Models of technology diffusion', *Research Policy*, **29**, 603–625.

12 Abrahamson, E. and Plosenkopf, L. (1993) Institutional and competitive band-wagons: using mathematical modelling as a tool to explore innovation diffusion. *Academy of Management Journal*, **18** (3), 487–517.

13 Tidd, J. and Bodley, K. (2002) Effect of novelty on new product development processes and tools. *R&D Management*, **32** (2), 127–138.

14 O'Connor, G.C. and Veryzer, R.W. (2001) The nature of market visioning for the technology-based radical innovation. *Journal of Product Innovation Management*, **18**, 231–246.

Discussion Questions

1 In what ways can innovation contribute to or potentially constrain sustainability?

2 What are the differences between 'open' and 'closed' types of innovation?

3 What are 'novel niches', and why are they important for sustainable innovation?

4 What is special about changes in socio-technical systems?

5 What characteristics do 'lead users' have, and why are they important?

6 What factors influence the adoption and diffusion of innovations?

7 What are the differences between Delphi and scenario methods of forecasting, and in what circumstances might you use each?

Team Exercise

Using Figure 10.1, identify a sustainable innovation for each of the four quadrants.

Assignment and Case Study Questions

Develop three alternative scenarios for the future of the micro-generation of energy over the next five years for a specific country. You will need to identify the relevant technological, social and regulatory drivers, and potential branching events.

CASE STUDY 10

Innovation in the Micro-generation of Energy

Innovation in the generation and distribution of energy is not driven by developments in technology or politics alone. Instead it is the product of the interaction of emerging technology possibilities, political and societal pressures, economics, decision-making and resource commitment by firms, and behavioural changes in demand. Macroeconomic issues such as the price and security of supply are important influences, as are international policies such as the Kyoto agreement and European Emissions Trading Scheme, and national infrastructure, industry structure and regulation. However, innovation and change also require the involvement and participation of firms creating new products and services, and markets and people willing to purchase and use these.

One potential development path is the decentralization of energy production, which can help to reduce losses in transmission, reduce emissions and create opportunities for a range of new technologies, products and services to support the micro-generation of energy, including renewable sources. Options include active and passive solar systems, micro-turbines (or 'windmills'), fuel cells or more conventional engineered products such as Otto- or Stirling-type engines. The common characteristic of all these technologies is the aim to generate power for a single household or building, typically generating less than 15 kW (electricity), or up to 50 kW in commercial or industrial applications, and in the case of the engines, combined heat and power (CHP) can be generated. This can minimize the loss of energy through the distribution system or grid, which in Europe is estimated to account for 6–9% of all electricity generated, and in the USA 3–13%.

Fuel cells convert the chemical energy of a fuel, usually hydrogen, and oxygen into electricity. Natural gas can be used as a fuel, and emissions are very low. However, although the technology is proven, and has been used in space and automotive applications, low-temperature cells suitable for micro-generation typically achieve low electrical and thermal efficiencies, typically around 30%. Forecasts suggest commercially viable fuel cells for micro-generation are probably 8–10 years away.

Reciprocating engine micro-generators have more immediate potential. These convert fuel, usually gas, into CHP using the Otto-combustion cycle like the engine in a car, but rather than waste the heat it is used to heat water via a heat exchanger. The combined efficiency depends on a number of factors, such as the air/fuel mix and load, but is usually 80–90% or more. Most commercial micro-generators currently available are around 5 kW (electricity) plus 15 kW (thermal), which are suitable for small commercial or public buildings or larger houses. In Japan Honda has co-developed with Osaka Gas a 1 kW system for single-family households, which sold more than 10 000 units in 2004. In Europe, the British utility company Powergen, part of Germany's EON, committed to the production of 80 000 WhisperGen systems. These were developed by the New Zealand firm WhisperTech, based on a Stirling engine which can generate 1.2 kW (electricity) and 8 kW (thermal). The advantage of the Stirling over the reciprocating engine is its ability to use a wider range of fuel types, including biomass and solar, because combustion can take place in a separate furnace. Its main relative disadvantage is its complexity of manufacture, as it demands higher-precision components and assembly than the reciprocating engine, and this can increase costs and may reduce reliability.

However, the radical change and transformation of large technical systems is not simply a matter of economic competition between different technologies. Rather, it is a highly dynamic and uncertain process, involving the interaction of many actors, including regulators, energy utility companies, appliance manufacturers and service providers, end-users and those involved in designing, developing, building and supporting the infrastructure and structures. Therefore the process of development, diffusion and adoption is multi-actor and multi-level, and consists of the co-evolution of technology and society – a socio-technical system of change. So innovation and change is about much more than new technology or products. It is likely to demand alliances between these different actors, and will result in compromises and failures before any dominant design or configuration becomes established. Alliances have begun to emerge between the developers of micro-generators and boiler manufacturers and gas utilities, but some tensions exist because, for example, a gas supplier may favour a different technology and system to a boiler-maker or building company.

Innovation in such cases often begins in a favourable niche within an existing system or regime and, as the technology matures and complementary innovations are developed, support begins to grow and broaden, and slowly new institutions, standards and regulations are developed to promote the innovations. This is similar to the notion of disruptive innovation, discussed later, but with much stronger feedback to existing technologies and competing innovations. For example, a utility company might lose revenue and profit because of micro-generation, and therefore have no incentive to promote this. In contrast, a more vertically integrated utility might promote micro-generation to maintain the provision of gas, to lock in customers and to create new support services as sources of additional revenue.

Many different scenarios have been developed for the future of micro-generation, some indicating it will become much more significant, others less so, but all agree that a wide range of technologies and systems are possible. Delphi, expert-based studies tend to emphasize improvements in proven technologies such as fuel cells and engines, but policy scenarios based on sustainability assumptions put more weight on renewable sources such as solar, micro-turbines and biomass. For example, the European demand for micro-generation is estimated to reach 730 000 units a year (equivalent to 3.5 GW, or 3% of total energy demand) by 2010, and the boiler manufacture Vaillant is planning for annual sales in Europe of 250 000 micro-generators by then.

Users and potential adopters of micro-generators have a distinct socio-demographic profile, usually males in their forties or fifties with families, living in rural areas or smaller towns. However, different segments appear to favour different technologies. Studies indicate that farmers, skilled manual workers and lower educational groups appear to prefer biomass or (passive) solar thermal collectors, whereas higher income and education groups prefer (active) solar photo-voltaics and fuel-cell technology. The reasons for this split is not clear, but one explanation is the former group desire to understand and maintain the technology, but the latter are more conscious of the 'pioneer status' the more sophisticated technologies might confer upon them, and are unlikely to be concerned with the maintenance (or understanding!) of the underlying technologies. This logic suggests that reciprocating engine micro-generators would appeal more to the skilled segment, but that stirling-engine micro-generators might satisfy the higher income and education segment.

In addition national markets differ in their attractiveness for innovation and diffusion of micro-generation. Climate, energy markets and prices, energy mix and building and housing stock are the main factors influencing demand. For example, in the UK there is a relatively large potential market. The Energy Savings Trust estimates that micro-generation has the potential to provide 30–40% of all UK energy needs by 2010. Most of the 23 million households have central heating of some type, but the majority are relatively low-efficiency conventional gas or oil-fired boilers, typically less than 80% efficient, or less than 70% if older (although since 2005 all new boiler installed have to be at least 86% efficient i.e. condensing boilers). A moderate climate, average floor spaces of 85 square metres, typical consumptions of 18 000 kWh of space heating and 5000 kWh of water heating and 3500 kW of electricity and a running time of 2000–4000 hours each year are ideal conditions for micro-generation. The annual market for new or replacement boilers in the UK is around 300 000. Powergen launched its WhisperGen unit in 2005, and following a further £14 million on development, re-launched it in 2007 and plans to install 80 000 micro-generators in UK homes by 2010. It estimates that each household adopting the technology will reduce carbon emission by 1.5 tonnes per year. British Gas and the boiler-maker Baxi are also to enter the UK market in 2007, but regulation, prices, distribution and installation and maintenance networks remain a barrier. In Europe, Germany and the Netherlands also represent attractive markets, but more extreme climates may not be suitable for micro-generation. Japan has a small but growing market, led by Honda's 1 kW reciprocating generator, but there has so far been less interest in the USA or Canada because of the low price of fuel and dominance of forced-air heating systems.

Case Study Questions

1 What are the technological and organizational options for micro-generation, and what are the relative advantages of each approach?

2 Identify all the organizations which influence the development and adoption of micro-generation technologies?

3 Identify the human barriers to adoption of micro-generation technologies, and suggest ways to overcome these.

Sources: Pehnt, M., Cames, M., Fischer, C., Praetorius, B., Schneider, L., Schumacher, K. and Vob J.P. (2006) *Micro Co-Generation: Towards Decentralized Energy Systems*. Springer, Berlin; Tidd, J. (1995) The development of novel products through intra- and inter-organizational networks: the case of home automation. *Journal of Product Innovation Management*, **12** (4), 307–322; Tidd, J. (1994) *Home Automation: Market and Technology Networks*. Whurr, London.

Chapter 11

Innovation, Globalization and Development

This chapter

- ■ Looks at globalization of innovation.

- ■ Explores the theme of national systems of innovation.

- ■ Reviews how to position in international value chains.

- ■ Examines ways of building capabilities and creating value.

Learning Objectives

When you have completed this chapter you will be able to:

- ■ Understand the reasons for, and implications of, the uneven global distribution of innovation.

- ■ Identify the main components of a national system of innovation, and how these interact to influence the degree and direction of innovation in a country.

- ■ Describe how the position of a firm in an international value chain may constrain the opportunities for innovation and entrepreneurship.

- ■ Define dynamic capabilities, and understand how these can contribute to the development and growth of firms and nations.

Innovation and enterprise are central to the development and growth of emerging economies, and yet their contribution is usually considered in terms of the most appropriate national policy and institutions, or the regulation of international trade. Macroeconomic issues are important, and national systems of innovation, including formal policy, institutions and governance, can have a profound influence on the degree and direction of innovation and enterprise in a country or region, but it is also critical to consider a more micro perspective, in particular innovation by firms and the entrepreneurship of individuals. Therefore in this chapter we examine the respective roles of national systems and policy, the capabilities of firms, and initiative of individual entrepreneurs, and the interactions between these three perspectives.

The largest of the emerging economies – the so-called BRIC nations of Brazil, Russia, India and China – face similar challenges, but begin from very different historical, geographic and political starting points. As a result, the potential of each nation is very different, and the likely trajectories of innovation and development will be different in each case. In the main text we identify some common denominators or generic good practices of emerging economies, but we will use the four BRIC cases to illustrate the different constraints and opportunities in each country. We begin with the case of innovation and entrepreneurship in China.

Four factors have a major influence on the ability of a firm to develop and create value through innovation:

- The *national system of innovation* in which the firm is embedded, and which in part defines its range of choices in dealing with opportunities and threats.

- Its power and *market position* within the international value chain, which in part defines the innovation-based opportunities and threats that it faces.

- The *capability and processes* of the firm, including research, design, development, production, marketing and distribution.

- Its ability to identify and exploit *external sources of innovation*, especially international networks.

Globalization of Innovation

In his best-selling book, *The World is Flat: The Globalized World in the 21st Century* (Penguin, London, 2006), Thomas Friedman argues that developments in technology and trade, in particular information and communications technologies (ICTs), are spreading the benefits of globalization to the emerging economies, promoting their development and growth. This optimistic thesis is appealing, but the evidence suggests the picture is rather more complex.

First, because technology and innovation are not evenly distributed globally, and are not easily packaged and transferred across regions or firms. For example, only about a quarter of the innovative activities of the world's largest 500, technologically active firms are located outside their home countries.[1] Second, different national contexts influence significantly the ability of firms to absorb and exploit such technology and innovation. For example, state-ownership and availability of venture capital both influence entrepreneurship.[2] Third, the position of firms in international value chains can constrain profoundly their ability to capture the benefits of their innovation and entrepreneurship. Many firms in emerging economies have become trapped in dependent relationships as low-cost providers of low-technology, low-value manufactured goods or services, and have failed to develop their own design or new products.[3]

Since the 1980s, some analysts and practitioners have argued that, following the 'globalization' of product markets, financial transactions and direct investment, large firms' R&D activities should also become globalized – not only in their traditional role of supporting local production, but also in order to create interfaces with specialized skills and innovative opportunities at a world level. However, although striking examples of the internationalization of R&D can be found (e.g. the large Dutch firms, particularly Philips, and some more progressive German firms, such as Siemens), more comprehensive evidence casts doubt on the strength of such a trend. The evidence from patent files and R&D data suggest that innovation remains unevenly distributed across the world:

- The world's largest firms perform about only 25% of their innovative activities outside their home country. Overall, the proportion of R&D expenditure made outside the home nation is growing, albeit slowly, from less than 15% in 1995, to 22% by 2001.

- The most important factor explaining each firm's share of foreign innovative activities is its share of foreign production. Firms from smaller countries in general have higher shares of foreign innovative activities. On average, foreign production is less innovation-intensive than home production. Most of the foreign innovative activities are performed in the USA and Europe (in fact, Germany). They are not 'globalized'.

- Since the late 1990s, European firms – and especially those from France, Germany and Switzerland – have been performing an increasing share of their innovative activities in the USA, in large part in order to tap into local skills and knowledge in such fields as biotechnology and IT.

Controversy remains both in the interpretation of this general picture, and in the identification of implications for the future. Our own views are as follows:[4]

- There are major efficiency advantages in the geographic concentration in one place of strategic R&D for *launching major new products and processes* (first model and production line). These include dealing with unforeseen problems, since proximity allows quick, adaptive decisions; and integrating R&D, production and marketing, since proximity allows integration of tacit knowledge through close personal contacts.

- The nature and degree of international dispersion of R&D will also depend on the company's major technological trajectory, and the strategically important points for integration and learning that relate to it. Thus, whereas automobile firms find it difficult to separate their R&D geographically from production when launching a major new product, drug firms can do so, and instead locate their R&D close to strategically important basic research and testing procedures.

- In deciding about the internationalization of their R&D, managers must distinguish between becoming part of global *knowledge networks* – in other words, being aware of and able to absorb the results of R&D being carried out globally. Practising scientists and engineers have always done this, and it is now easier with modern IT. However, business firms are finding it increasingly useful to establish relatively small laboratories in foreign countries in order to become strong members of local research networks and thereby benefit from the person-embodied knowledge behind the published papers; and the *launching of major innovations*, which remains complex and costly, and depends crucially on the integration of tacit knowledge. This remains difficult to achieve across national boundaries. Firms therefore still tend to concentrate major product or process developments in one country. They will sometimes choose a foreign country when it offers identifiable advantages in the skills and resources required for such developments, and/or access to a lead market.

- Matching global knowledge networks with the localized launching of major innovations will require increasing international mobility among technical personnel, and the increasing use of multinational teams in launching innovations.

■ Advances in IT will enable spectacular increases in the international flow of codified knowledge in the form of operating instructions, manuals and software. They may also have some positive impact on international exchanges of tacit knowledge through teleconferencing, but nowhere near to the same extent. The main impact will therefore be at the second stage of the 'product cycle', when product design has stabilized, and production methods are standardized and documented, thereby facilitating the internationalization of production. Product development and the first stage of the product cycle will still require frequent and intense personal exchanges, and be facilitated by physical proximity. Advances in IT are therefore more likely to favour the internationalization of production than of the process of innovation.

Until recently, a useful rule of thumb for deciding where R&D should be performed was the following:

■ *R&D supporting existing businesses* (i.e. products, processes, divisions) should be located in established divisions.

■ *R&D supporting new businesses* (i.e. products, processes, divisions) should initially be located in central laboratories, then transferred to divisions (established or newly created) for exploitation.

■ *R&D supporting foreign production* should be located close to that foreign production, and concerned mainly with adapting products and processes to local conditions.

The main factors influencing the decision where to locate R&D globally are, in order of importance:

■ The availability of critical competencies for the project;

■ The international credibility (within the organization) of the R&D manager responsible for the project;

■ The importance of external sources of technical and market knowledge (e.g. sources of technology, suppliers and customers);

■ The importance and costs of internal transactions (e.g. between engineering and production);

■ Cost and disruption of relocating key personnel to the chosen site.

There are two broad logics of organizing innovation globally, *specialization-based* and *integration-based*, or network structure. In the specialization-based structure the firm develops global centres of excellence in different fields, which are responsible globally for the development of a specific technology or product or process capability. The advantage of such global specialization is that it helps to achieve a critical mass of resources and makes coordination easier. As one R&D director notes: 'The centre of excellence structure is the most preferable. Competencies related to a certain field are concentrated, coordination is easier, and economies of scale can be achieved. Any R&D director has the dream to structure R&D in such a way. However, the appropriate conditions seldom occur' (Tidd, Bessant and Pavitt, 2005). In addition, it may allow location close to a global innovation cluster. The main disadvantages of global specialization are the potential isolation of the centre of excellence from global needs, and the subsequent transfer of technologies to subsidiaries worldwide.

In contrast, in the integration-based structure, different units around the world each contribute to the development of technology projects. The advantage of this approach is that it draws upon a more diverse range of capabilities and international perspectives. In addition, it can encourage competition among different units. However, the integrated approach suffers from very high costs of coordination, and commonly suffers from duplication of efforts and inefficient use of scarce resources. In practice, hybrids of these two extreme structures are common, often as a result of practical compromises and trade-offs necessary to accommodate history, acquisitions and politics. For example, specialization by centre of excellence may include contributions from other units, and integrated structures may include the contribution of specialized units.

The histories of major firms in technology-based industries suggest there is no right answer, and that finding and maintaining the proper balance is not easy. Nonetheless, we can identify four sets of factors that will influence the proper balance:

- *The firm's main technological trajectory.* This gives strong guidance on the appropriate balance. At one extreme, the corporate initiatives are very important in the chemically based – and particularly the pharmaceutical – industry, where fundamental discoveries at the molecular level are often directly applicable in technological development. At the other extreme, corporate-level laboratories are less important in sectors – like aircraft and automobiles – that are based on complex products and production systems, where the benefits of basic advances are more indirect (e.g. the use of simulation technologies), and the critical interface is between R&D and design, on the one hand, and production, on the other.

- *The degree of maturity of the technology.* The examples of opto-electronics and biotechnology show that, after the emergence of a fundamental technological breakthrough, extended periods of trial, error and learning are necessary before specific technological opportunities begin to emerge. During the early 'incubation' stage, there are advantages in isolating such learning processes from immediate commercial pressure by locating them in the corporate laboratory, before transfer to a more market-oriented framework in an established division or internal venture group.

- *Corporate strategic style.* The corporate R&D laboratory will have low importance in firms whose strategies are entirely driven by short-term financial performance in existing products. Such 'market-led' strategies will concentrate on the division-level funding, but miss the opportunities emerging from the development and exploitation of radical new technologies.

- *Links to 'new science'-based technologies.* New forms of corporate linkages with basic and academic research are emerging in the 'new sciences' that have grown out of recent advances in molecular biology, nanotechnology and IT. Advances in these fields are the basis of the growth of firms spun off from universities, since they have reduced the costs of technical experimentation to a level where university-type laboratories and research methods can make significant technical advances. This has also had the effect of increasing both the range of technological opportunities that large firms can exploit, and the uncertainties surrounding their eventual usefulness. Large firms therefore prefer to explore these opportunities through collaborations until the uncertainties are reduced.

Learning from Foreign Systems of Innovation

While information on competitors' innovations is relatively cheap and easy to obtain, corporate experience shows that knowledge of how to replicate competitors' product and process innovations is much more costly and time-consuming to acquire. Useful and usable knowledge does not come cheap. Such imitation typically costs 60–70% of the original, and typically takes 3 years to achieve. These conclusions are illustrated by the examples of Japanese and Korean firms, where very effective imitation has been sustained by heavy and firm specific investments in education, training and R&D.

Firms have at least three reasons for monitoring and learning from the development of technological, production and organizational competencies of national systems of innovation other than those in which they are embedded themselves, and especially from those that are growing and strong:

- They will be the sources of firms with a strong capacity to compete through innovation. For example, beyond Japan, other East Asian countries are developing strong innovation systems. In particular, business firms in South Korea and Taiwan now spend more than 2% of GDP on R&D, which puts them up with the advanced OECD countries. By the early 1990s, Taiwan was granted more patents in the USA than Sweden, and together with South Korea, is catching up fast with Italy, the Netherlands and Switzerland. Other Asian countries like Malaysia are also developing strong technological competencies. Following the collapse of the Russian Empire, we can also anticipate the re-emergence of strong systems of innovation in the Czech Republic and Hungary.

- There are also potential sources of improvement in the corporate management of innovation, and in national systems of innovation. However, as we shall see below, understanding, interpreting and learning general lessons from foreign systems of innovation is a difficult task. Effectiveness in innovation has become bound up with wider national and ideological interests, which makes it more difficult to separate fact from belief. Both the business press and business education are dominated by the English language and Anglo-Saxon examples: very little is available in English on the management of innovation in Germany; and much of the information about the management of innovation in Japan has been via interpretations of researchers from North America.

- Finally, firms can benefit more specifically from the technology generated in foreign systems of innovation. A high proportion of large European firms attach great importance to foreign sources of technical knowledge, whether obtained through affiliated firms (i.e. direct foreign investment) and joint ventures, links with suppliers and customers, or reverse engineering. In general, they find it is more difficult to learn from Japan than from North America and elsewhere in Europe, probably because of greater distances – physical, linguistic and cultural. Perhaps more surprising, European firms find it most difficult to learn from foreign publicly funded research. This is because effective learning involves more subtle linkages than straightforward market transactions: for example, the membership of informal professional networks. This public knowledge is often seen as a source of potential world innovative advantage and, as we discussed in Chapter 3, firms are increasingly active in trying to access foreign sources. In contrast, knowledge obtained through market transactions and reverse engineering enables firms to catch up, and keep up, with competitors. East Asian firms have been very effective over the past 25 years in making these channels an essential feature of their rapid technological learning (see box overleaf).

The slow but significant internationalization of R&D is also a means of firms learning from foreign systems of innovation. There are many reasons why multinational companies choose to locate R&D outside their home country, including regulatory regime and incentives, lower cost or more specialized human resources,

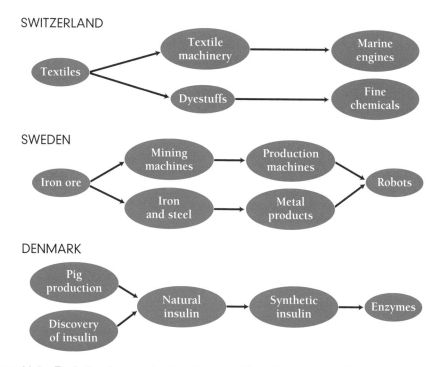

Figure 11.1   Evolution from natural endowment to national specialization of innovation.

proximity to lead suppliers or customers, but in many cases a significant motive is to gain access to national or regional innovation networks. However, some countries are more advanced in internationalizing their R&D than others (Figure 11.1). In this respect European firms are the most internationalized, and the Japanese the least.

INNOVATION IN ACTION

Technology Strategies of Latecomer Firms in East Asia

The spectacular modernization in the past 25 years of the East Asian 'dragon' countries – Hong Kong, South Korea, Singapore and Taiwan – has led to lively debate about its causes. Michael Hobday has provided important new insights into how business firms in these countries succeeded in rapid learning and technological catch-up, in spite of underdeveloped domestic systems of science and technology, and of lack of technologically sophisticated domestic customers.

Government policies provided the favourable general economic climate: export orientation; basic and vocational education, with strong emphasis on industrial needs; and a stable economy, with low inflation and high savings. However, of major importance were the strategies and policies of specific business firms for the effective assimilation of foreign technology.

The main mechanism for catching up was the same in electronics, footwear, bicycles, sewing machines and automobiles, namely the original equipment manufacture (OEM) system. OEM is a specific form of subcontracting, where firms in catching-up countries produce goods to the exact specification of a foreign transnational company (TNC) normally based in a richer and technologically more advanced country. For the TNC, the purpose is to cut costs, and to this end offer assistance to the latecomer firms in quality control, choice of equipment, and engineering and management training. OEM began in the 1960s, and became more sophisticated in the 1970s. The next stage in the mid-1980s was own design and manufacture (ODM), where the latecomer firms learned to design products for the buyer. The last stage was own brand manufacture (OBM) when latecomer firms market their own products under their own brand name (e.g. Samsung, Acer) and compete head-on with the leaders.

For each stage of catching up, the company's technology position must be matched with a corresponding market position, as is shown below:

Stage	Technology position	Market position
1	Assembly skills	Passive importer pull
	Basic production	Cheap labour
	Mature products	Distribution by buyers
2	Incremental process change	Active sales to foreign buyer
	Reverse engineering	Quality and cost-based
3	Full production skills	Advanced production sales
	Process innovation	International marketing department
4	Product design	Markets own design
	R&D	Product marketing push
	Product innovation	Own brand product range and sales
5	Frontier R&D	Own brand push
	R&D linked to market needs	In-house market research
	Advanced innovation	Independent distribution

Source: Hobday, M. (1995) *Innovation in East Asia: The Challenge to Japan*. Edward Elgar, Cheltenham.

Managers report that the most important methods of learning about competitors' innovations were independent R&D, reverse engineering and licensing, all of which are expensive compared to reading publications and the patent literature. More formal approaches to technology intelligence-gathering are less widespread, and the use of different approaches varies by company and sector (Figure 11.2). For example, in the pharmaceutical sector, where much of the knowledge is highly codified in publications and patents, these sources of information are scanned routinely, and the proximity to the science base is reflected in the widespread use of expert panels. In electronics, product technology roadmaps are commonly used, along with the lead users. Surprisingly long-established and proven methods such as Delphi-studies, S-curve analysis and patent citations are not in widespread use.

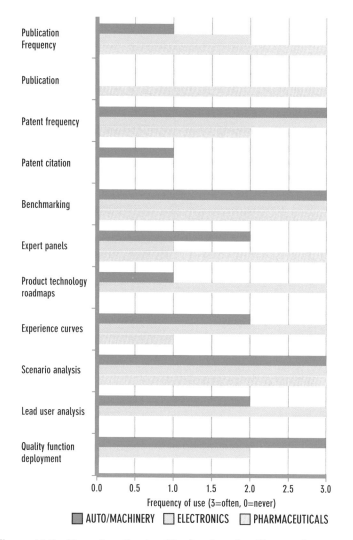

Figure 11.2   Use of methods of technology intelligence by sector.
Source: Derived from Lichtenthaler, E. (2004) Technology intelligence processes in leading European and North American multinationals, *R&D Management*, **34**(2), 121–134.

INNOVATION IN ACTION

Building BRICs – Capabilities in India

India has a population of around 1.1 billion, a large proportion of which is English-speaking, a relatively stable political and legal regime, and a good national system of education, especially in science and engineering. It has some 250 universities and listed 1500 R&D centres (although care needs to be taken in the definitions used in both cases), and this has translated into international strengths in the fields of biotechnology, pharmaceuticals and software. As a result Indian firms have benefited greatly by the increasing international division of labour in some services and the support and development of software and services. India is now a global centre for outsourcing and offshoring. Until the mid-1980s the software industry was dominated by government and public research organizations, but the introduction of export processing zones provided tax breaks and allowed the import of foreign computer technology for the first time. The market liberalization of 1991 accelerated development and inward investment, and in 2005 India attracted inward investment of US$6 billion (significant, but still only around a tenth of that attracted by China). Since then the software and services industry in India has grown by around 50% each year to reach US$8.3 billion by 2000, and employing 400 000, second only to the USA. The industry is forecast to grow to US$50 billion by 2008. Unusually for India, which has historically pursued a policy of national self-reliance, the industry is very export-oriented, with around 70% of output being traded internationally.

There are 3 broad types of software firms in India. First, those that specialize in a specific sector or domain, for example accounting, gaming or film production, and these develop capabilities and relationships specific to those users. Second, those that develop methods and tools to provide low-cost and timely software support and solutions. The majority of the industry is in this lower-value-added part of the supply chain, and is involved in low-level coding, maintenance and design, and relies on a large pool of English-speaking talent which costs around 10% of those in the USA or EU. However a third segment of firms is emerging that is more involved with new product and service development.

India's version of Silicon Valley is around the southern city of Bangalore. This is home to a large number of firms from the USA, as well as indigenous Indian firms. Large employers include Infosys, and call and service centres here employ 250 000 operatives, including support services for firms such as Cisco, Microsoft and Dell. IBM, Intel, Motorola, Oracle, Sun Microsystems, Texas Instruments and GE all now have technology centres here. Texas Instruments was 1 of the few major foreign firms to start up a development unit in 1985, prior to the opening up of the Indian economy in 1991. GE Medical Systems followed in the late 1980s, and established a development centre in Bangalore in 1990, which later resulted in a joint venture with the Indian firm Wipro Technologies. GE now employs 20 000 people in India, who generate sales of US$500 million. IBM was 1 of the first investors in India, but later withdrew because of the onerous government policy and restrictions in the 1980s. It returned after the government liberalized the economy, and its Indian operations contributed US$510 million in sales in 2005, employing 43 000 in India following the acquisition of the Indian outsourcing company Daksh in 2004. In 2006 it announced that it would triple its investment from US$2 billion to US$6 billion by 2009, including further service delivery centres to support computer networks worldwide and a new telecommunications research centre. Similarly, Adobe is to invest US$50 million in India over the next 5 years, and to recruit 300 software developers. Each year Adobe India contributes 10 of the 60 patents which Adobe files each year.

One of the challenges of the software and services industry in India is to increase value-added through product and service development. To date the impressive growth has been based on winning more outsourcing business from overseas and employing more staff, rather than by increasing the value-added by new services and products. For example, the Indian software and service firm Tata plans to increase the proportion of its revenue from new products from around 5% to 40%, to make it less reliant on low-cost human capital, which is likely to become more expensive and more mobile. Ramco Systems developed an ERP system in the 1990s, which cost 1 billion rupees to develop and involved 400 developers. By 2000 the company was profitable, with 150 customers, half overseas. It has established sales and support offices in the USA, Europe and Singapore. In 2006 the Indian outsourcing company Genpact (40% owned by GE of the USA) launched a joint venture with New Delhi Television (NDTV) to digital video editing, post-production and archiving services to media firms. The industry is worth US$1 trillion, and 70% of all media work is now digital.

Based on patent citations, Indian firms rely much more on linkages with the science base and technology from the developed countries, whereas China has a broader reliance which includes its Asian neighbours in other emerging economies, and specializes in more applied fields of technology. Indian firms rely on technologies from US firms most – about 60% of all patent citations, followed by (in order of importance) Japan, Germany, France and the UK. In many cases these linkages have been reinforced by inward investment by MNCs, but in other cases they are the result of Indians trained or employed overseas who have returned to India to create new ventures.

Infosys was 1 of the first and is now 1 of the largest software and IT services firms in India. It was created by entrepreneur N.R. Narayana Murthy with 6 colleagues in 1981 with only US$250, but by 2006 it was worth US$13.7 billion, with annual profits of US$345 million. Murthy believes that 'entrepreneurship is the only instrument for countries like India to solve the problem of its poverty . . . it is our responsibility to ensure that those who have not made that kind of money have an opportunity to do so'.

Sources: Forbes, N. and Wield, D. (2002) *From Followers to Leaders: Managing Technology and Innovation*. Routledge, London; IEEE (2006) International Conference on Management of Innovation and Technology, Singapore; Friedman, T.L. (2006) *The World is Flat: The Globalized World in the Twenty-First Century*. Penguin, London.

National Systems of Innovation

In this section we examine how the national and market environment of a firm shapes its innovation strategy. We first show that the *home country* positions of even global firms have a strong influence on their innovation strategies. The national influences can be grouped into three categories: *competencies* (workforce education, research), *economic inducement mechanisms* (local demand and input prices, competitive rivalry) and *institutions* (methods of funding, controlling and managing business firms). For example, the largest numbers of European firms among the technical leaders were to be found in the technological fields of industrial and fine chemicals, and defence-related technologies (e.g. aerospace), which are fields of national technological strength, while the reverse is the case in electronics, capital equipment and consumer goods. Japanese firms predominate in consumer electronics and motor vehicle technologies, and US firms in fine chemicals and in raw materials-based (e.g. oil, gas and food) and defence-related technologies, again reflecting the technological strengths of their home countries.[5]

The strategic importance to corporations of home countries' technological competencies would matter little if they were all more or less the same, but they are not. Patterns of sectoral specialization differ greatly: for example, the Japanese pattern of strengths and weaknesses is almost the opposite of that in the USA. In addition, countries differ in both the level and the rate of increase in the resources devoted by business firms to innovative activities. This captures corporate innovative activities only imperfectly, but remains one of the best available indicators of aggregate innovative investments, and international differences significantly influence national economic growth and trade performance. Importantly, the rate of increase in corporate commitment to R&D in a country is not closely related to its industrial structure. Compare Finland and Canada, both of whose economies rely heavily on natural resources; Finland's R&D expenditures have increased even more rapidly than Japan's as a share of GDP, while Canada's increased only slightly.

Contrary to what many observers continue to assume, Europe and Japan did not progressively and smoothly catch up with the USA, which was the technological leader in the period after the Second World War. Switzerland has always been among the leaders and remains so. As early as 1971, Germany and Japan overtook the USA and progressively increased their lead until the late 1980s. This was reflected in the relative performance in R&D and sales growth of the large firms based in these countries. Since then, the trend has changed, with the shares of business-funded R&D in GDP stabilizing in Japan, declining in Germany and increasing in the USA. At the same time, the three Scandinavian countries have continued to increase their shares, with the growth of major firms in pharmaceuticals and telecommunications. The other early leaders of the late 1960s – the UK and the Netherlands – have not reacted to the growing competition like the USA in the 1990s. The share of business-funded R&D in GDP in both countries declined considerably in the 1970s, and has not recovered to earlier levels.

A recent study of the innovation capabilities of European countries based on two Community Innovation Surveys (which are conducted every four years by all nation states within the EU) and other data estimated the effects of different macro and micro factors on innovation. Table 11.1 provides a summary of the results. Using patents as an indicator of innovation, innovation at the national level is positively influenced by the size of the economy, foreign competition in the domestic market, public expenditure on R&D and the availability of venture capital; it is negatively influenced by the presence of a relatively large number of small and medium-sized firms, high company tax and a high level of economic prosperity. Using relative sales of innovative products as an indicator of innovation, firm-level effects become more evident: national innovation is positively influenced by the size of the economy, R&D expenditure of firms, use of external sources of innovation and the presence of small and medium-sized firms, but negatively influenced by economic prosperity and foreign competition in the home market. Put another way, macroeconomic conditions in a country and the structure of the national economy have significant effects on innovation, measured by patenting and sales of innovative products. At the national level, the innovative activities of firms appear to have a stronger influence on sales of innovative products, than patenting.

In conclusion, the national system of innovation in which a firm is embedded matters greatly, since it strongly influences both the direction and the vigour of its own innovative activities. However, managements still have ample influence over their firms' innovation strategies, and firms can benefit from foreign systems of innovation through

Table 11.1   European national systems of innovation and innovation capability

NIS variable	Regression coefficient on:	
	Patents granted	Sales of new products
Public R&D expenditure	+0.839	
Firm expenditure on R&D		+0.421
Gross domestic product (GDP)	+0.691	+0.310
Openness of national economy	+0.319	−0.454
Availability of venture capital	+0.200	
Presence of SMEs	−0.146	+0.621
External sources of innovation		+0.688
Presence of innovative firms		+0.591

Source: Derived from Faber, J. and Hesen A.B. (2004) Innovation capabilities of European nations, *Research Policy*, **33**, 193–207.

a variety of mechanisms. Next we will identify and discuss the main national factors that influence the rate and direction of technological innovation in a country: more specifically, the national market *incentives and pressures* to which firms have to respond, and the *institutions of corporate governance*.

Incentives and Pressures: National Demand and Competitive Rivalry

Patterns of National Demand

Those concerned to explain international patterns of innovative activities have long recognized the important influence of local demand and price conditions on patterns of innovation in local firms. Strong local 'demand pull' for certain types of product generates innovation opportunities for local firms, especially when the demand depends on face-to-face interactions with customers.

In Table 11.2 we identify the main factors that influence local demands for innovation, and give some examples. In addition to the obvious examples of local buyers' tastes, we identify:

- Local (private and public) investment activities, which create innovative opportunities for local suppliers of machinery and production inputs, where competence is accumulated mainly through experience in designing, building and operating machinery.

- Local production input prices, where international differences can help generate very different pressures for innovation (e.g. the effects of different petrol prices on the design and related competencies in automobiles in

Table 11.2 Local factors that influence the rate and direction of innovation

Factors in	*Examples*
Local buyers' tastes	■ Quality food and clothing in France and Italy ■ Reliable machinery in Germany
Private investment activities	■ Automobile and other downstream investments stimulating innovation in computer-aided design and robots in Japan, Italy, Sweden and Germany
Public investment activities	■ Railways in France ■ Medical instruments in Sweden ■ Coal-mining machinery in the UK (<1979)
Input prices	■ Labour-saving innovations in the USA ■ Europe–USA differences in automobile technology ■ Environmental technology in Scandinavia ■ Synthetic fertilizers in Germany
Local natural resources	■ Innovations in oil and gas, mineral ores, and food and agriculture in North America, Scandinavia and Australia

the USA and Europe). High prices can also generate pressure for substitute products, like synthetic fertilizers in Germany at the beginning of the twentieth century.

■ Local natural resources, which create opportunities for innovation in both upstream extraction and downstream processing.

A more subtle, but increasingly significant influence is the role of social concerns and pressure about the environment, safety and governance. For example, nuclear power as a technological innovation has evolved in very different ways in countries like the USA, UK, France and Japan. Similarly, innovation in genetically modified crops and foods has taken radically different paths in the USA and Europe, mainly due to public concerns and pressure.

Competitive Rivalry

Innovation is always difficult and often upsetting to established interests and habits, so that local demands by themselves do not create the necessary conditions for innovation. Both case studies and statistical analysis show that competitive rivalry stimulates firms to invest in innovation and change, since their very existence will be threatened if they do not. For example, comparison of public policies towards the pharmaceutical industries in the UK and France show that the former was more successful in creating a demanding local competitive environment conducive to the emergence of British firms among the world leaders. German strength in chemicals is based on three large and technologically dynamic firms, BASF, Bayer and Hoechst, rather than on one super-large national champion. Similarly, the Japanese strengths in consumer electronics and automobiles is based on numerous technologically active firms rather than a few giants (despite the early efforts of the Ministry of International Trade and Industry (MITI) to promote national champions and mergers – however, neither Sony or Honda were members of the Japanese industrial groups, or *zaibatsu*). Relatively smaller size also reduces the severity of the task of management to maintain corporate entrepreneurship. This is because managers can spend more time familiarizing themselves with the innovative potentialities of the various businesses, and can thereby avoid the dangers of managing divisions purely through financial indicators.

Thus although corporate policy-makers in large firms might often be tempted in the short term to avoid strong competition – and to reap extra monopoly profits – by merging with their competitors, the long-term costs could be considerable. Public policy-makers should be persuaded by the evidence that creating gigantic national champions does not increase innovation, quite the contrary, and therefore take countervailing measures. Lack of competitive rivalry makes firms less fit to compete on global markets through innovation.

In many countries, national advantages in natural resources and traditional industries have been fused with related competencies in broad technological fields that then become the basis for technological advantage in new product fields. For example, in Denmark, Sweden and Switzerland linkages with established fields of strength were the basis of local technological accumulation. This accumulation reinforced corporate and national competencies and created the potential for entry and competitiveness in new product fields. Firm-specific investments in technology and related basic research and training in universities led to the mastery of broad technological fields with multiple potential applications: metallurgy and materials in Sweden, machinery in Switzerland and Sweden, and chemistry and (more recently) biology in Switzerland and Denmark. Another example is the development of chemical engineering in the USA, in response to the challenges and opportunities of refining petrol.

These differences in national endowments of research and education influence managers in their search to identify technological fields and related product markets where specific national systems of innovation are likely to be most supportive to corporate innovative activities. For example, firms in the UK and USA are particularly strong in software and pharmaceuticals, both of which require strong basic research and graduate skills, but few production skills; they are therefore particularly well matched to local skill structures. Similarly, Japanese strength in consumer electronics and automobiles is particularly well matched to its local strength in production skills, as are the German strengths in mechanical engineering.

Institutions: Finance, Management and Corporate Governance

Firms' innovative behaviours are strongly influenced by the competencies of their managers and the ways in which their performance is judged and rewarded (and punished). Methods of judgement and reward vary considerably among countries, according to their national systems of *corporate governance*: in other words, the systems for exercising and changing corporate ownership and control. In broad terms, we can distinguish two systems: one practised in the USA and UK, and the other in Japan, Germany and its neighbours, such as Sweden and Switzerland. In his book *Capitalism against Capitalism*, Michel Albert calls the first the 'Anglo-Saxon' and the second the 'Nippon–Rhineland' variety. A lively debate continues about the essential characteristics and performance of the two systems, in terms of innovation and other performance variables. Table 11.3 is based on a variety of sources, and tries to identify the main differences that affect innovative performance.

   In the UK and the USA, corporate ownership (shareholders) is separated from corporate control (managers), and the two are mediated through an active stock market. Investors can be persuaded to hold shares only if there is an expectation of increasing profits and share values. They can shift their investments relatively easily. On the other hand, in countries with governance structures like those of Germany or Japan, banks, suppliers and customers are more heavily locked into the firms in which they invest. Until the 1990s, countries strongly influenced by German and Japanese traditions persisted in investing heavily in R&D in established firms and technologies, while

Table 11.3   National governance structures and innovation

Characteristics	Anglo-Saxon	Nippon–Rhineland
Ownership	Individuals, pension funds, insurers	Companies, individuals, banks
Control	Dispersed, arm's length	Concentrated, close and direct
Management	Business schools (USA), accountants (UK)	Engineers with business training
Evaluation of R&D investments	Published information	Insider knowledge
Strengths	■ Responsive to radically new technological opportunities	■ Higher priority to R&D than to dividends for shareholders
	■ Efficient use of capital	■ Remedial investment in failing firms
Weaknesses	■ Short-termism	■ Slow to deal with poor investment choices
	■ Inability to evaluate firm-specific intangible assets	■ Slow to exploit radically new technologies

the US system has since been more effective in generating resources to exploit radically new opportunities in IT and biotechnology.

During the 1980s, the Nippon–Rhineland model seemed to be performing better. R&D expenditures were on a healthy upward trend, and so were indicators of aggregate economic performance. Since then, there have been growing doubts. The technological and economic indicators have been performing less well. Japanese firms have proved unable to repeat in telecommunications, software, microprocessors and computing their technological and competitive successes in consumer electronics. German firms have been slow to exploit radically new possibilities in IT and biotechnology, and there have been criticisms of expensive and unrewarding choices in corporate strategy, like the entry of Daimler Benz into aerospace. At the same time, US firms appear to have learned important lessons, especially from the Japanese in manufacturing technology, and to have reasserted their eminence in IT and biotechnology. The 1990s have also seen sustained increases in productivity in US industry. According to *The Economist* in 1995, in a report entitled 'Back on top?', one professor at the Harvard Business School believed that people will look back at this period as 'a golden age of entrepreneurial management in the USA'.

However, some observers have concluded that the strong US performance in innovation cannot be satisfactorily explained simply by the combination of entrepreneurial management, a flexible labour force and a well-developed stock exchange. They argue that the groundwork for US corporate success in exploiting IT and biotechnology was laid initially by the US Federal Government, with the large-scale investments by the Defense Department in California in electronics, and by the National Institutes of Health in the scientific fields underlying biotechnology. In addition, we should not write off Germany and Japan too soon. The former is now dealing with the dirt and inefficiency of the former East Germany, and Japanese firms like Sony are world leaders in exploiting in home electronics the opportunities opened up by advances in digital technology. And Scandinavian countries are now well ahead of the rest of the world (including the USA) in mobile telephony, as well as in more general indicators of skills and knowledge. The influences institutions, incentives and competition have on innovation and entrepreneurship are complex, as illustrated in the box below by the case of Russia.

INNOVATION IN ACTION

Building BRICs – Capabilities in Russia

Industry in Russia is still dominated by heavy industry, including oil, gas, defence and aerospace. Consumer and service sectors are relatively poorly developed, reflecting national endowments and the legacy of the communist, centrally planned era. For example, in 2001 oil and energy accounted for about 70% of all industrial output, and 40% of total GDP. Similarly, hydrocarbons account for more than half of exports, followed by metals, which make up about a quarter of overseas sales. Some higher-technology sectors have emerged from the earlier specialization of the Soviet economy, such as space-launches, aviation and lasers, but these remain relatively small niches. This absence of significant innovations is an interesting paradox, given the strong national emphasis given to investment and training in science and technology.

In the year 2000, Russia had more than 4000 formal organizations dedicated to science and technology, including 2600 public R&D centres employing almost 1 million qualified scientists and engineers. However, historically the focus of these numerous organizations has been on basic scientific research, rather than technological or commercial innovation. The focus has been on 'big science' and the science-push model of innovation and growth, rather than a market- or demand-coupled model. On the supply side, the prestigious national Academy of Sciences dominates this system, and these emphasize traditional Soviet strengths in the theoretical and physical sciences such as mathematics, chemistry and physics. The Academy has never had the responsibility or role to commercialize scientific research, or to support the development of new processes or products. While overall investment in science and technology has declined in Russia, the investment in basic sciences has proportionally declined far less than investment in the applied sciences and technologies. On the demand side, the traditional, centrally planned, target-based structure did not provide incentives or resources for firms to develop or seek such innovations. Given this industrial structure and political legacy, the industrial research and design centres have failed to flourish: in 2000 there were less than 300 industrial R&D enterprises, and around 400 design organizations.

Russia also has an unusual industrial structure by the size of enterprise. Compared to other industrial economies, very large firms and very small enterprises are relatively under-represented, and instead in Russia medium-sized firms are the most common and economically significant. In most advanced economies the very large firms are the main investors in formal R&D and development of commercially significant innovations, whereas the micro businesses provide a continuous outlet for more entrepreneurial behaviour. Typically medium-sized enterprises are less important as they lack sufficient resources, but suffer from most of the disadvantages of size. They are also less likely to participate in international joint ventures and alliances, or to receive foreign direct investment (FDI).

Unlike the case of many other emerging economies, FDI and international joint ventures have played only a minor part in the development of the Russian economy. They account for only around 5% of total investment in Russia, compared to more than 20% in other former Soviet economies of Hungary, Poland and Romania. The main foreign investments and associated transfers of technological and managerial know-how have been in the oil industry, because of its significance to the Russian economy, and the food industry, which historically has been a low national priority and has performed poorly. However, in most manufacturing and service sectors there have been little foreign investment or influence, and little improvement or innovation. There are many reasons for this relative isolation from international investment and innovation, including problems of governance, including legal restrictions on ownership and the dominance of dynastic insiders in the main industries. Therefore the institutional structure of Russia continues to constrain domestic and international innovation and entrepreneurship.

There are many cases of transfer of hard technologies in the oil and aerospace industries, both into and out of Russia, but these are usually rather conventional licensing agreements, with very little transfer or upgrading of critical managerial or commercial know-how. However, there are examples of successful innovation, often as a result of individual technical entrepreneurs or spin-offs from public research organizations, working with firms overseas. For example, the Moscow Centre for SPARC Technology, founded by Boris Babayan, is funded by Sun Microsystems and is active in the workstation market, but is based on supercomputer technology used in the Soviet space and nuclear industries. Similarly, ParaGraph, a Russian software company, is based on technology used by the military for pattern recognition, but worked with Apple to commercialize the technology.

Sources: Derived from Dyker, D.A. (2006) *Closing the EU East-West Productivity Gap*. Imperial College Press, London; and (2004) *Catching Up and Falling Behind: Post-Communist Transformation in Historical Perspective*. Imperial College Press, London.

Positions in International Value Chains

Development of firms from emerging economies is much more than simply 'catching up' with those in the more advanced economies, and is not (only) the challenge of moving from 'followers' to 'leaders'. Global standards and position in international value chains can constrain the ability of firms based in emerging economies to upgrade their capabilities and appropriate greater value, but they also present ways in which these firm can innovate to overcome these hurdles, for example, by using international standards as a catalyst for change, or by repositioning themselves in local clusters or global networks. By position, we refer to the current endowment of technology and intellectual property of a firm, as well as its relations with customers and suppliers.

According to Porter, firms must also decide between two broad innovation strategies:[6]

- Innovation 'leadership' – where firms aim at being first to market, based on technological leadership. This requires a strong corporate commitment to creativity and risk-taking, with close linkages both to major sources of relevant new knowledge, and to the needs and responses of customers.

- Innovation 'followership' – where firms aim at being late to market, based on imitating (learning) from the experience of technological leaders. This requires a strong commitment to competitor analysis and intelligence, to reverse engineering (i.e. testing, evaluating and taking to pieces competitors' products, in order to understand how they work, how they are made and why they appeal to customers), and to cost-cutting and learning in manufacturing.

However, in practice the distinction between 'innovator' and 'follower' is much less clear. For example, market pioneers often continue to have high expenditures on R&D, but this is most likely to be aimed at minor, incremental innovations. A pattern emerges where pioneer firms do not maintain their historical strategy of innovation leadership, but instead focus on leveraging their competencies in minor incremental innovations. Conversely, late-entrant firms appear to pursue one of two very different strategies. The first is based on competencies other than R&D and new product development, for example, superior distribution or greater promotion or support. The second, more interesting, strategy is to focus on major new product-development projects in an effort to compete with the pioneer firm.

It is not necessarily a great advantage to be a technological leader in the early stages of the development of radically new products, when the product performance characteristics and features valued by users are not always clear, either to the producers or to the users themselves. Especially for consumer products, valued features emerge only gradually through a process of dynamic competition, that involves a considerable amount of trial, error and learning by both producers and users. New features valued by users in one product can easily be recognized by competitors and incorporated in subsequent products. This is why market leadership in the early stages of the development of personal computers was so volatile, and why pioneers are often displaced by new entrants. In such circumstances, product development must be closely coupled with the ability to monitor competitors' products and to learn from customers. In fact, pioneers in radical consumer innovations rarely succeed in establishing long-term market positions. Success goes to so-called 'early entrants' with the vision, patience and flexibility to establish a mass consumer market. For example, studies of the Profit Impact of Market Strategy (PIMS) database indicate that (surviving) product pioneers tend to have higher quality and a broader product line than followers, whereas followers tend to compete on price, despite having a cost disadvantage. A pioneer strategy appears more successful in markets where the purchasing frequency is high, or distribution important (e.g. fast-moving consumer goods), but confer no advantage where there are frequent product changes or high advertising expenditure (e.g. consumer durables).

Therefore technological leadership in firms does not necessarily translate itself into economic benefits. The capacity of the firm to appropriate the benefits of its investment in technology depends on: its ability to translate its technological advantage into commercially viable products or processes, for example, through complementary assets or capabilities in marketing and distribution; and its capacity to defend its advantage against imitators, for example, through secrecy, standards or intellectual property. Some of the factors that enable a firm to benefit commercially from its own technological lead can be strongly shaped by its management: for example, the provision of complementary assets to exploit the lead. Other factors can be influenced only slightly by the firm's management, and depend much more on the general nature of the technology, the product market and the regime of intellectual property rights: for example, the strength of patent protection. We identify below some of the key factors which influence the firm's capacity to benefit commercially from its technology:

INNOVATION IN ACTION

Globetronics Evolution of Global Supply Chains

Globetronics Bhd. was formed in 1990 by two Malaysians formerly employed by Intel. The Malaysian Technology Development Corporation (MTDC) provided 30% of the venture capital, and the company was subsequently floated in 1997 to raise additional capital for growth. The company's primary activities are similar to the majority of transnational semiconductor firms based in Malaysia, and involve post-fabrication manufacture of semiconductors, including assembly and packaging. Indeed, the company's main customers are US and Japanese transnationals. The significant difference is that domestic ownership and management have allowed Globetronics more easily to capture value-added activities such as development and marketing.

The company now has 7 business divisions and a new plant in the Philippines. Two of the businesses are joint ventures with the Japanese firm, Sumitomo. The relationship with Sumitomo began as a simple subcontracting agreement, but over the years a high level of trust has been achieved and two joint ventures have been established. The first, SGT, was created in 1994, and is 49% owned by Globetronics. It is the largest manufacturer in the world and the only company outside of Japan to produce ceramic substrate semiconductor packages. The second joint venture, SGTI, was created in 1996, and is 30% owned by Globetronics. In both cases the Japanese partner has maintained majority ownership, but it is clear that the Malaysian partner has made some progress in assimilating the technological and design capabilities. This provides a promising model for companies in developing countries, to escape dependent subcontracting relationships by using joint ventures to upgrade their technological and market competencies.

Source: Tidd, J. and Brocklehurst, M. (1999) Routes to technological learning and development: an assessment of Malaysia's innovation policy and performance. *Technological Forecasting and Social Change*, **63** (2), 239–257.

Translating Technology into Innovations

The following are important mechanisms for capturing value by translating technology into innovations:

- *Complementary assets.* The effective commercialization of an innovation very often depends on assets (or competencies) in production, marketing and after-sales to complement those in technology.

■ *Accumulated tacit knowledge* can be long and difficult to imitate, especially when it is closely integrated in specific firms and regions. Examples include product-design skills, ranging from those of Benetton and similar Italian firms in clothing design, to those of Rolls-Royce in aircraft engines.

■ *The learning curve* in production generates both lower costs, and a particular and powerful form of accumulated and largely tacit knowledge that is well recognized by practitioners. In certain industries and technologies (e.g. semiconductors, continuous processes), the first-comer advantages are potentially large, given the major possibilities for reducing unit costs with increasing cumulative production. However, such 'experience curves' are not automatic, and require continuous investment in training, and learning.

■ *Lead times and after-sales service* are considered by practitioners as major sources of protection against imitation, especially for product innovations. Taken together with a strong commitment to product development, they can establish brand loyalty and credibility, accelerate the feedback from customer use to product improvement, generate learning-curve cost advantages (see below) and therefore increase the costs of entry for imitators.

Protecting Innovations against Imitators

We discussed IPR in more detail in Chapter 6. Here we begin with those over which management has some degree of discretion for action, and move on to those where its range of choices is more limited.

■ *Secrecy* is considered an effective form of protection by industrial managers, especially for process innovations. However, it is unlikely to provide absolute protection, because some process characteristics can be identified from an analysis of the final product, and because process engineers are a professional community, who talk to each other and move from one firm to another, so that information and knowledge inevitably leak out. Moreover, there is evidence that in some sectors firms that share their knowledge with their national system of innovation outperform those that do not, and that those that interact most with global innovation systems have the highest innovative performance. Specifically, firms that regularly have their research (publications and patents) cited by foreign competitors are rated more innovative than others, after controlling for the level of R&D. In some cases this is because sharing knowledge with the global system of innovation may influence standards and dominant designs (see below), and can help attract and maintain research staff, alliance partners, and other critical resources.

■ *Product complexity.* Product complexity is recognized by managers as an effective barrier to imitation. For example, IBM could rely on the size and complexity of their mainframe computers as an effective barrier against imitation, given the long lead times required to design and build copy products. With the advent of the microprocessor and standard software, these technological barriers to imitation disappeared and IBM was faced in the late 1980s with strong competition from IBM 'clones', made in the USA and in East Asia. Boeing and Airbus have faced no such threat to their positions in large civilian aircraft, since the costs and lead times for imitation remain very high.

■ *Standards.* The widespread acceptance of a company's product standard widens its own market and raises barriers against competitors. Among other things the marker leader normally has the advantage in a standards war, but this can be overturned through radical technological change, or a superior response to customers' needs. Competing firms can adopt either 'evolutionary' strategies minimizing switching costs for customers (e.g. backward compatibility with earlier generations of the product), or 'revolutionary' strategies based on greatly superior performance–price characteristics, such that customers are willing to accept higher switching costs. Standards wars are made less bitter and dramatic when the costs to the losers of adapting to the winning standard are relatively small. Different factors will have an influence at different phases of the standards process. In the early phases, aimed at demonstrating technical feasibility, factors such as the technological superiority, complementary assets and credibility of the firm are most important, combined with the number and nature of other firms and appropriability regime. In the next phase, creating a market, strategic manoeuvring and regulation are most important. In the decisive phase, the most significant factors are the installed base, complementary assets, credibility and influence of switching costs and network effects. Where strong appropriability regimes exist, compatibility standards may be less important than customer interface standards, which help to 'lock in' customers. Apple's graphic user interface is a good example of this trade-off.

- *Strength of intellectual property.* As we have already seen in the examples described above, strength of IP is a strong determinant of the relative commercial benefits to innovators and imitators. On the whole, European firms value patent protection more than their US counterparts. However, with one exception (cosmetics), the variations across industry in the strength of patent protection are very similar in Europe and the USA. Patents are judged to be more effective in protecting product innovations than process innovations in all sectors except petroleum-refining, probably reflecting the importance of improvements in chemical catalysts for increasing process efficiency. It also shows that patent protection is rated more highly in chemical-related sectors (especially drugs) than in other sectors. This is because it is more difficult in general to 'invent round' a clearly specified chemical formula than round other forms of invention. Radically new technologies are now posing new problems for the protection of intellectual property, including the patenting system. The number of patents granted to protect software technology is growing in the USA, and so are the numbers of financial institutions getting involved in patenting for the first time. Debate and controversy surround important issues, such as the possible effects of digital technology on copyright protection, the validity of patents to protect living organisms, and the appropriate breadth of patent protection in biotechnology.

Finally, we should note that firms can use more than one of the above factors to defend their innovative lead. For example, in the pharmaceutical industry secrecy is paramount during the early phases of research, but in the later stages of research patents become critical. Complementary assets such as global sales and distribution become more important at the later stages. Despite all the mergers and acquisitions in this sector, these factors, combined with the need for a significant critical mass of R&D, have resulted in relatively stable international positions of countries in pharmaceutical innovation over a period of some 70 years. By any measure, firms in the USA have dominated the industry since the 1940s, followed by a second division consisting of Switzerland, Germany, France and the UK. Some of the methods are mutually exclusive: for example, secrecy precludes patenting, which requires disclosure of information, although it can precede patenting. However, firms typically deploy all the useful means available to them to defend their innovations against imitation.

INNOVATION IN ACTION

Chip Design in Asia

In the case of complex innovations, physical proximity is normally an advantage in the organization and location of design and development. However, a study of 60 electronics firms and 15 research organizations found that in the design and development of electronic chips there has been a growing geographic dispersion of organization and location. Over a decade, Asia's share of world chip design has grown from almost nothing to around a third. It is forecast to reach a 50% world share by 2008, led by Japan, South Korea, Taiwan and Singapore, with Malaysia, India and China following fast.

The study concludes that two of the drivers of this trend are specific to the technology: changes in design methodology, which allow the de-coupling of design stages and the design of related components and sub-systems; and greater outsourcing and vertical specialization within global innovation systems. Therefore any generalizations regarding the globalization of innovation are unwise.

Source: Derived from Ernst, D. (2005) Complexity and internationalisation of innovation – why is chip design moving to Asia? *International Journal of Innovation Management*, **9** (1), 47–74.

Building Capabilities and Creating Value

In this section we discuss the importance of developing firm-level capabilities. Firms in emerging economies may pursue different routes to upgrading through innovation:[7]

- *Process upgrading* – incremental process improvements to adapt to local inputs, reduce costs or to improve quality.

- *Product upgrading* – through adaptation, differentiation, design and product development.

- *Capability upgrading* – improving the range of functions undertaken, or changing the mix of functions, for example, production versus development or marketing.

- *Inter-sectoral upgrading* – moving to different sectors, for example, to those with higher value-added.

To some extent firms in emerging economies face a 'reverse product–process innovation life cycle'. We saw in Chapter 1 that the most common pattern of evolution of technological innovation in the industrialized world has been from product to process innovation, on the one hand, and from radical to incremental innovation, on the other. Initially a series of different radical product innovations emerge and compete in the market, but as the innovations and markets evolve together a 'dominant design' begins to emerge, and the locus of innovation shifts from product to process, and from radical to more incremental improvements in cost and quality. However, in emerging economies, the path of evolution is often reversed, and begins with incremental process innovations, to produce an existing product at a lower cost or at a lower quality for different market needs. As firms improve their capabilities they may then begin to make product adaptations and changes in design, and eventually move towards more radical product innovation. This has important implications for the type of capabilities firms needs to develop. For example, at first, the emphasis should be on incremental process improvement and development, which suggests innovation in production and organization, rather than technological development or formal R&D. This suggests a hierarchy of capabilities or learning, each adding greater value.

C.K. Prahalad and Gary Hamel have had a major influence on management thinking by showing that the capacity to open up new product markets requires distinctive core competencies, coupled with methods of corporate organization and evaluation that explicitly recognize the importance of these competencies, and top management visions that identify future opportunities.[8] Experience shows that, along some technological trajectories, the opportunities for product diversification are abundant but uncertain, while along others they hardly exist at all. It also shows that companies also need background competencies to coordinate and integrate changes coming from outside the firm, and that corporate visions can be wrong. Their basic ideas can be summarized as follows:

- The sustainable competitive advantage of firms resides not in their products but in their *core competencies*: 'The real sources of advantage are to be found in management's ability to consolidate corporate-wide technologies and production skills into competencies that empower individual businesses to adapt quickly to changing opportunities' (Prahalad and Hamel, 1990, p. 81).

- Core competencies feed into more than one core product, which in turn feed into more than one business unit. They use the metaphor of the tree:
  - End products   = Leaves, flowers and fruit
  - Business units   = Smaller branches
  - Core products   = Trunk and major limbs
  - Core competencies = Root systems

  Examples of core competencies include Sony in miniaturization, Philips in optical media, 3M in coatings and adhesives and Canon in the combination of the precision mechanics, fine optics and microelectronics technologies that underlie all their products. Examples of core products include Honda in lightweight, high-compression engines, and Apple in product design and user-interfaces.

- The importance of associated organizational competencies is also recognized: 'Core competence is communication, involvement, and a deep commitment to working across organisational boundaries' (Prahalad and Hamel, 1990, p. 82).

- Core competencies require focus: 'Few companies are likely to build world leadership in more than five or six fundamental competencies. A company that compiles a list of 20 to 30 capabilities has probably not produced a list of core competencies' (Prahalad and Hamel, 1990, p. 84). The notion of core competencies suggests that large and multidivisional firms should be viewed not only as a collection of strategic business units, but as bundles of competencies that do not necessarily fit tidily in one business unit.

According to Hamel and Prahalad, the concept of the corporation based on core competencies should not replace the traditional one, but a commitment to it will inevitably influence patterns of diversification, skill deployment, resources allocation priorities, and approaches to alliances and outsourcing. David Teece and Gary Pisano integrate the various dimensions of innovation strategy into what they call the 'dynamic capabilities' approach, which underlines the importance of dynamic change and corporate learning.[9] This emphasizes the key role of strategic management in appropriately adapting, integrating and reconfiguring internal and external organizational skills, resources and functional competencies towards a changing environment. To be strategic, a capability must be honed to a user need (so that there are customers), unique (so that the products/services can be priced without too much regard for the competition), and difficult to replicate (so that profits will not be competed away).

Technological development does have its own internal logic, which helps define where firms will find innovative opportunities. Thus, we can marvel at the rapid rate of improvement in the performance–price ratio of the electronic chip and at the economic and social changes it has made possible. But we can also be frustrated that our laptop computers can rarely be made to run independently for more than a few hours, or that battery-driven cars are so heavy, limited in range and slow to recharge: in spite of extensive private investments, existing knowledge of battery technology has not enabled us to do much better. The energy density of gasoline fuel (i.e. energy generated per unit weight) remains 100 times higher than electric batteries. Similarly, we can speculate that a set of technologies that could convert deep-mined coal into oil and gas at the same price, and with lesser adverse environmental consequences, than existing supplies would have economic, social and political effects at least equal to those of the microchip. But it will remain speculation, since the present state of knowledge does not enable it to be done.

In addition to the constraints of knowledge, there are those of competence: in other words, of what specific firms are capable of learning and exploiting. Innovation requires improvements and changes in the operation of complex technical and organizational systems. This involves trial, error and learning. Learning tends to be incremental, since major step changes in too many parameters both increase uncertainty and reduce the capacity to learn. As a consequence, firms' learning processes are path-dependent, with the directions of search strongly conditioned by the competencies accumulated for the development and exploitation of their existing product base. Moving from one path of learning to another can be costly, even impossible, given cognitive limits – think of the problems of learning a foreign language from scratch.

Furthermore, firms cannot easily jump from one major path to another through hiring individuals with the required competencies. Corporate competencies are rarely those of an individual, and most often those of specialized, interdependent and coordinated groups, where tacit technical and organizational knowledge accumulated through experience are of central importance. This is why firms perform most of their innovative activities in-house. And even when competencies come from outside the firm as part of a corporate acquisition, different practices and cognitive structures may make their assimilation costly or impossible. For example, it is no accident that electrical firms find it much easier to master and exploit semiconductor technology than chemical firms: the fields of technological competencies required are much closer.

The ability of firms to track and exploit technological trajectories depends on their specific technological and organizational competencies, and on the difficulties that competitors have in imitating them. The notion of firm-specific competencies has become increasingly influential among economists, trying to explain why firms are different, and how they change over time, and also among business practitioners and consultants, trying to identify the causes of competitive success. In the 1990s, management began to shift interest from improvements in short-term operational efficiency and flexibility (through 'de-layering', 'downsizing', 'outsourcing' and 'business process re-engineering', etc.), to a concern that – if taken too far – the 'lean corporation' could become the 'anorexic corporation', without any capacities for longer-term change and survival.

This has led to much confusion about the characteristics and implications of the 'new' or 'knowledge' economy. The more traditional notion of the knowledge economy included the broad opportunities created by developments in science and technology, and the role of intellectual capital and innovation for competitive advantage. The more recent and narrower perspective focuses exclusively on the potential of information and communications technologies. However, these two views are based on contradictory assumptions and suggest different implications. The latter ICT perspective emphasizes the low marginal costs of reproduction and near instantaneous transmission of such technologies, but too often assumes that the exchange and transfer of knowledge is almost effortless and unrestricted. The former, broader view highlights the difficulties of capturing and transferring knowledge due to its tacit nature and context-specificity.

Limits of the Core Competence Approach

The notions of core competence and dynamic capabilities are useful as they emphasize the importance of developing firm-level resources. However, there are a number of limitations to these approaches:

Differing Potentials for Technology-based Diversification

It is not clear whether the corporate core competencies in all industries offer a basis for product diversification. Compare the recent historical experience of most large chemical and electronics firms, where product diversification based on technology has been the norm, with that of most steel and textile firms, where technology-related product diversification has proved very difficult (see, for example, the unsuccessful attempts to diversify by the Japanese steel industry in the 1980s).

Multi-technology Firms

Recommendations that firms should concentrate resources on a few fundamental (or 'distinctive') world-beating technological competencies are potentially misleading. Large firms are typically active in a wide range of technologies, in only a few of which do they achieve a 'distinctive' world-beating position. In other technological fields, a *background* technological competence is necessary to enable the firm to coordinate and benefit from outside linkages, especially with suppliers of components, sub-systems, materials and production machinery. In industries with complex products or production processes, a high proportion of a firm's technological competencies are deployed in such background competencies. In addition, firms are constrained to develop competencies in an increasing range of technological fields (e.g. IT, new materials, biotechnology in order to remain competitive as products become even more 'multi-technological').

In-house competencies in background (enabling) technologies are necessary for the effective coordination of changes in production and distribution systems, and in supply chains. In industries with complex product systems (like automobiles), background technologies can account for a sizeable proportion of corporate innovative activities. Background technologies can also be the sources of revolutionary and disruptive change. For example, given the major opportunities for improved performance that they offer, all businesses today have no choice but to adopt advances in IT technology, just as all factories in the past had no choice but to convert to electricity as a power source. However, in terms of innovation strategy, it is important to distinguish firms where IT is a core technology and a source of distinctive competitive advantage (e.g. CISCO, the supplier of Internet equipment) from firms where it is a background technology, requiring major changes but available to all competitors from specialized suppliers, and therefore unlikely to be a source of distinctive and sustainable competitive advantage (e.g. Tesco, the UK supermarket chain).

In all industries, emerging (key) technologies can end up having pervasive and major impacts on firms' strategies and operations (e.g. software). A good example of how an emerging/key technology can transform a company is provided by the Swedish telecommunications firm Ericsson, and the accumulation of technological competencies, with successive generations of mobile cellphones and telecommunication cables. In both cases, each new generation required competencies in a wider range of technological fields, and very few established competencies were made obsolete. The process of accumulation involved both increasing links with outside sources of knowledge, and greater expenditures on R&D, given greater product complexity. This was certainly not a process of concentration, but of diversification in both technology and product. For these reasons, the notion of 'core competencies' should perhaps be replaced for technology by the notion of 'distributed competencies'.

Core Rigidities

As Dorothy Leonard has pointed out, 'core competencies' can also become 'core rigidities' in the firm, when established competencies become too dominant. In addition to sheer habit, this can happen because established competencies are central to today's products, and because large numbers of top managers may be trained in them. As a consequence, important new competencies may be neglected or underestimated (e.g. the threat to mainframes from mini- and microcomputers by management in mainframe companies). In addition, established innovation strengths may overshoot the target. Many examples show that, when 'core rigidities' become firmly entrenched, their removal often requires changes in top management.

Developing and Sustaining Competencies

The final question about the notion of core competencies is very practical: how can management identify and develop them?

There is no widely accepted definition or method of measurement of competencies, whether technological or otherwise. One possible measure is the level of *functional performance* in a generic product, component or sub-system: in, for example, performance in the design, development, manufacture and performance of compact, high-performance combustion engines. As a strategic technological *target* for a firm like Honda, this obviously makes sense. But its achievement requires the combination of technological competencies from a wide variety of *fields* of knowledge, the composition of which changes (and increases) over time. Twenty years ago, they included mechanics (statics and dynamics), materials, heat transfer, combustion, fluid flow. Today they also include ceramics, electronics, computer-aided design, simulation techniques and software.

Thus, the functional definition of competencies bypasses two central tasks of corporate strategy: first, to identify and develop the range of disciplines or fields that must be combined into a functioning technology; second (and perhaps more important) to identify and explore the new competencies that must be added if the functional capability is not to become obsolete. This is why a definition based on the measurement of the combination of competencies in different fields is more useful for formulating innovation strategy, and is in fact widely practised in business.

Richard Hall goes some way towards identifying and measuring core competencies (see Chapter 6). He distinguishes between intangible assets and intangible competencies. Assets include intellectual property rights and reputation. Competencies include the skills and know-how of employees, suppliers and distributors, and the collective attributes which constitute organizational culture. His empirical work, based on a survey and case studies, indicates that managers believe that the most significant of these intangible resources are company reputation and employee know-how, both of which may be a function of organizational culture. Thus organizational culture, defined as the shared values and beliefs of members of an organizational unit, and the associated artefacts, becomes central to organizational learning.

However, dynamic capabilities typically involve long-term commitments to specialized resources, and consist of patterned activity to relatively specific objectives. Therefore dynamic capabilities involve both the exploitation of existing competencies and the development of new ones. For example, leveraging existing competencies through new product development can consist of de-linking existing technological or commercial competencies from one set of current products, and linking them in a different way to create new products. However, new product development can also help to develop new competencies. For example, an existing technological competence may demand new commercial competencies to reach a new market, or conversely a new technological competence might be necessary to service an existing customer.

The trick is to get the right balance between exploitation of existing competencies and the exploitation and development of new competencies. Research suggests that over time some firms are more successful at this than others, and that a significant reason for this variation in performance is due to difference in the ability of managers to build, integrate and reconfigure organizational competencies and resources. These 'dynamic' managerial capabilities are influenced by managerial cognition, human capital and social capital (see Chapter 2). Cognition refers to the beliefs and mental models which influence decision-making. These affect the knowledge and assumptions about future events, available alternatives and association between cause and effect. This will restrict a manager's field of vision, and influence perceptions and interpretations. Human capital refers to the learned skills that require some investment in education, training experience and socialization, and these can be generic, industry- or firm-specific. It is the firm-specific factors that appear to be the most significant in dynamic managerial capability, which can lead to different decisions when faced with the same environment. Social capital refers to the internal and external relationships which affect a manager's access to information, their influence, control and power.

INNOVATION IN ACTION

Building BRICs – Capabilities in Brazil

In his research, Fernando Perini examined the structure and dynamics of the knowledge networks in the IT and telecommunications sectors in Brazil. The Brazilian government promoted the development of the industry between 1997 and 2003 by the 'ICT Law' which provided tax incentives for collaborative R&D, following the liberalization of the economy in the early 1990s and the unsuccessful period of import substitution. This policy promoted an overall private investment of more than US$2 billion in innovation supporting partnerships in innovation projects inside a network of 216 companies and 235 universities and research institutes, but the lasting effects on firm and national capabilities are more mixed. While the policy of tax incentives promoted a higher level of investments in innovation, it did not determine the direction or organization of innovation in the sector.

The study concludes that the effect of the tax incentives depends on the nature of the technology and industry structure. They were important in helping to create knowledge networks in system and software technologies where multinational companies were key players, but much less successful in equipment, semiconductors, production process and hardware, where MNCs relied most on internal R&D and their own international networks. However, the MNCs did develop new partnerships in product development in IT systems and software, mainly with new private research institutes, rather than with established universities and research centres. Many of these private research institutes have become network integrators in the Brazilian ICT sector, and act as technological partners in activities such as training, technological services and research.

However, a small number of multinational companies still dominate the Brazilian market. More than 70% of the total investments under the ICT Law were conducted by the top 15 MNC subsidiaries.

For example, Lucent entered Brazil through the acquisition of 2 main national telecom companies, Zetax and Batik. It benefited from the ICT Law incentives between 2000 and 2002, but now invests more than 3 times the amount required by the original legislation, and the laboratory in Brazil had around 105 employees in 2005. The lab has competencies in both hardware and software, but there has been a shift toward software because it is less influenced by the regulation of international trade. The lab includes a new group of 50 engineers created in 2004 to develop competences in optical access, specifically, an optical concentrator for public commutation networks. The interaction with the global R&D community is very strong, in particular through the exchange of personnel. For example, the new optical unit involved the exchange of 35 people for two months. In addition, Lucent has developed local supply and research networks, and approximately 85% of its external activities are out-sourced to FITEC. FITEC has facilities throughout Brazil, including Campinas, Belo Horizonte and Recife.

Siemens Mercosur has the longest and largest MNC presence in Brazil. The subsidiary has developed technological capabilities mainly in telecommunications, and since the ICT Law still invests more than twice the required by that legislation. R&D at the subsidiary is divided into 6 groups; the largest, in Manaus, has 300 technical staff and specializes in mobile handsets that supply global markets. In addition, the networks development group in Curitiba has around 120 engineers, and the enterprise group 100 engineers. In relation to local technological partners, Siemens has focused on the upgrading of partnerships in the south, including 2 local universities (UTF-PR and PUC-PR) and one private institute (CITS), but the removal of public incentives and shifts in the technology have increased the importance of the partnership with the private research institute, CITS. However, the subsidiary has also invested in enabling institutes and postgraduate courses, for example, it helped to create a new postgraduate degree in computer science in Manaus. One recent development was the announcement in 2006 of a new €4 million development centre in Brazil, to develop digital TV technologies for the Brazilian market. Another initiative is the creation of an innovation portal to register and process innovative ideas from Brazilian companies and researchers.

Source: Perini, F. (2006) The structure and dynamics of the knowledge networks: incentives to innovation and R&D spillovers in the Brazilian ICT Sector. *The Future of Science, Technology and Innovation Policy: Linking Research and Practice*, SPRU 40th Anniversary Conference, Brighton, UK, September 2006.

Developing Personal Capabilities

There is no substitute for experiencing first-hand the national differences in contexts and capabilities. This suggests a good personal strategy is to seek systematic exposure to work or study overseas. If we can be excused a promotional opportunity, the University of Sussex in the UK has for more than 40 years been an international centre for excellence in the fields of innovation and development. Sussex University is home to 2 renowned global research centres, the Institute of Development Studies (www.ids.ac.uk) and the Science and Technology Research Unit (SPRU), www.sussex.ac.uk/spru. Both offer the opportunity for postgraduate and post-experience study and research. Here are some comments about the SPRU experience:

> *My particular interest was to study the challenges that developing countries face regarding technological and productive development. In particular, I looked for a deeper understanding of the challenges and options of resource-based development*

strategies in the case of Latin American countries. After almost a year of study, I can say that my expectation was fulfilled ... the programme maps the key issues in science, technology and production policy arenas, giving a systematic vision of such a complex field. – Osvaldo Urzua

Following family visits to Bangladesh, I discovered that the diseases which dominate the agendas there (such as malaria and typhoid) were not the diseases that my biochemistry degree emphasised (such as cancer). I became interested in the forces which direct research and wanted a better understanding of how such a situation can persist, where the diseases that burden the world most are also the most neglected. At SPRU I found that it had an international reputation which attracted a wide range of students from many nationalities and academic disciplines. The rich diversity exposes you to different perspectives and makes for a very productive intellectual environment. – Obid Yaqub

I decided to study at SPRU because of its high reputation as a first-class and innovative research centre. I worked for the United Nations Economic Commission for Latin America and the Caribbean doing research on science and technology policy. A great percentage of the literature I read when working for the UN had been written by SPRU's researchers. – Ramon Padilla-Perez

ADVICE FOR FUTURE MANAGERS

The competence or resource-based view is concerned essentially with identifying and building on strengths, preferably those which, for whatever reason, are unique to the firm. Every firm is unique by virtue of its history, value-chain configuration, organizational culture and so on. The challenge is to make the firm's uniqueness the source of its sustainable competitive advantage.

At one level the identification of competence appears to pose few difficulties. There are many cases which refer, for example, to the core competence of Honda in engines or Sony in miniaturization and which explore why and how these firms have developed and maintain these competencies. But for core competence to be a tool of strategic analysis what is also required is a means for firms to analyse rigorously their own and their competitors' competencies. Yet, despite all the effort and attention, core competencies remain elusive.

Few managers we have talked to could claim to have utilized core competence to achieve success in the marketplace, and even fewer to have built a core competence from scratch. Indeed, most were uncertain as to exactly what qualifies as a core competence ... it is like a mirage: something that from a distance appears to offer hope ... but turns to sand when approached.

Our own experience in working with the concept of core competence supports their view. Competencies disappear all too easily under close examination. A careful scrutiny of competence claims reveals, all too often, that they are neither firm-specific nor sustainable, that they do not convey functionality to the customer nor generic qualities to the firm. A proven methodology to help to identify and assess the elusive competencies consists of three parts:

- Identify the key attributes of the most successful products and services offered by the organization;
- Map these attributes to the resources or competencies of the organization, including tangible and intangible resources;
- Assess the potential for sustaining, protecting and exploiting these resources, including knowledge management.

1 Identifying Key Attributes

A pragmatic view of the nature of competitive advantage was advanced by Coyne (1986) whose argument starts with the observation that any company which is making repeat sales in a competitive market must enjoy an advantage in the eyes of the customers who are making the repeat purchases. He went on to argue that for a *sustainable* competitive advantage to exist three conditions must apply:

■ Customers must perceive a consistent difference in important attributes between the producer's product/service and the attributes offered by competitors.

■ This difference is the direct consequence of a capability gap between the producer and its competitors.

■ Both the difference in important attributes and the capability gap can be expected to endure over time.

Types of resource capability:

■ *Regulatory*: the possession of legal entities (e.g. patents and trademarks);

■ *Positional*: the results of previous endeavour (e.g. reputation, trust, value-chain configuration);

■ *Business systems*: the ability to do things well (e.g. consistent conformance to specification);

■ *Organizational characteristics* (e.g. the ability to manage change).

It is now possible to ask the question 'What is the nature of the package of product/delivery system attributes which customers value?' and to go on to ask the question 'What is responsible for producing the valued attributes?'. The product/delivery system attributes will include factors such as: price, quality, specification, image.

The Valued Attributes

In answering the questions posed in Table 11.4, it may be necessary to identify different rankings for different categories of customers, such as new as opposed to long-standing customers, retailers as opposed to end-users. In carrying out this analysis of attributes it is appropriate to seek consensus between the relevant executives with respect to questions such as:

■ Can executives agree an importance weighting for each attribute?

■ Can executives agree a benchmark score for each attribute compared with the competition?

■ Can executives agree the *sustainability* of the advantage represented by each attribute?

Table 11.4   Typical product/delivery system attributes which define competitive advantage

Image	What is the image of the product range? Is it important?
Price	Is a low selling price a key buying criterion?
User friendliness	Is it important for the product to be user-friendly?
Availability	Is product range availability crucial?

Table 11.4 (*continued*)

Rapid response to enquiry	Is it important to produce designs, quotations and so on very quickly?
Quick response to customer demand	Will sales be lost to the competition if they respond more quickly than you?
Width of product range	Is it important to offer a wide range of products and/or services to customers?
New product to market time	How important is the product development time?
Quality – the product's fitness for purpose	Does the product, or service, deliver exactly the benefits which the customers want?
Quality – the consistent achievement of defined specification	Is constant conformance to spec. vital?
Safety	Is safety in use a major concern?
Regulatory requirements	Does meeting regulatory requirements earlier/better than the competition give a competitive advantage?
Degree of innovation	Is it important for the product or service to represent 'state of the art'?
Ability to vary product specification	Is it important to produce product or service modifications easily and quickly?
Ability to vary product volume	Is it important to be able to increase, or decrease, production volume easily?
Customer service	Is the quality of the overall service which customers receive a key to winning business?
Pre- and after-sales service	Is the supply of advice, spares and so on a key aspect of winning business?

The degree of congruence, or dissonance, in executives' perceptions of these issues can in itself be illuminating. In addition to identifying the current strengths in the marketplace it is also appropriate at this stage to identify known deficiencies in the product offering.

2 Mapping Attributes to Resources and Competencies

The important characteristics of strategic competencies are that they:

- are responsible for delivering a significant benefit to customers.
- are idiosyncratic to the firm.
- take time to acquire.
- are sustainable because they are difficult and time-consuming to imitate.
- comprise *configurations* of resources.
- have a strong tacit content and are socially complex - they are the product of experiential learning.

The resources which produce product/delivery system attributes can now be placed in a framework of capabilities:

Regulatory capability – resources which are legal entities.

■ Tangible, on balance sheet, assets, Intangible, off balance sheet, assets:
   Patents
   Licences
   Trademarks
   Contracts
   Protectable data, and so on.

Positional capability – resources which are not legal entities and which are the result of previous endeavour, that is, with a high path-dependency:

■ Reputation of company

■ Reputation of product

■ Corporate networks

■ Personal networks

■ Unprotectable data

■ Distribution network

■ Supply chain network

■ Formal and informal operating systems

■ Processes.

Functional capability – comprises resources which are either individual skills and know-how, or team skills and know-how, within the company, at suppliers or at distributors, and so on.

■ Employee know-how and skills in: Operations
   Finance
   Marketing
   R&D, and so on.

■ Supplier know-how

■ Distributor know-how

■ Professional advisors' expertise, and so on.

Cultural capability – comprises resources which are the characteristics of the organization:

■ Perception of quality standards

■ Tradition of customer service

■ Ability to manage change

- Ability to innovate
- Team-working ability
- Ability to develop staff, suppliers and distributors
- Automatic response mechanisms.

While it is possible for a valued product/delivery system attribute to be the result of a tangible asset such as a building or a specialist manufacturing capability, research and experience suggest intangible resources such as product reputation and employee know how are the factors most often responsible for producing the attributes which are valued by customers. The resources which occur frequently in the body of the matrix are those which, either by themselves, or in combination with others, constitute the organization's strategic competencies.

3 Sustaining, Protecting and Exploiting Competencies

Having identified the key resources it is appropriate to examine development scenarios in terms of protection, sustenance, enhancement, and leverage (Table 11.5).

Table 11.5   Issues with respect to the development of intangible resources

With respect to *protection*

- Do all concerned recognize value of this intangible resource to the company?
- Can the resource be protected in law?

With respect to *sustainability*

- How long did it take to acquire this resource? Is it unique because of all that has happened in creating it?
- How durable is the resource? Will it decline with time?
- How easily may the resource be lost?
- How easily and quickly can others identify and imitate the resource?
- Can others easily 'buy' the resource?
- Can others easily 'grow' the resource?
- How appropriable is the resource? Can it 'walk away'?
- Is the resource vulnerable to substitution?

With respect to *enhancement*

- Is the 'stock' of this resource increasing?
- How can we ensure that the 'stock' of this resource *continues* to increase?

(continued overleaf)

Table 11.5 *(continued)*

With respect to *exploitation*

■ Are we making the best use of this resource?

■ How else could it be used?

■ Is the scope for *synergy* identified and exploited?

■ Are we aware of the key linkages which exist between the resources?

Source: Adapted from Tidd, J. (ed.) (2006) *From Knowledge Management to Strategic Competence.* Imperial College Press, London; in particular the chapter by Richard Hall.

STRATEGIC AND SOCIAL IMPACT

Since the beginning of the new millennium, the performance of the world economy has been shaped by the rapid growth of China and India, which has spilled over to many other developing countries.

The growth dynamics in China and other Asian economies have positive effects for many other developing countries. This is true for those countries that benefit directly from the surge in import demand from the fast-growing Asian economies. It is also true for those that benefit indirectly through the positive growth effects in the economies of their main trading partners. Still others have achieved higher export and income growth as a result of the rise in commodity prices, even though their exports to the fast-growing Asian economies are relatively small.

Growth in the developing countries has been rapid and more broad-based than it had been for many years. Latin America has seen a rebound from its deep economic crisis, and a return to faster growth, fuelled by export expansion. Africa again reached a growth rate of more than 4.5% in 2004. However, this relatively strong growth in many African countries is only likely to be short term, based on strong demand for a number of their primary commodities.

However, China's increasing participation in international trade poses new challenges for many developing and developed countries. Its dominance of some international markets will contribute to a fall in the export prices of manufactures that it produces and exports along with other developing countries, such as clothing, footwear and certain types of information and communication technology products.

Therefore international initiatives to alleviate poverty and achieve development goals need to also promote a smooth correction of these global imbalances to ensure the sustainability of this rapid growth and the positive spillovers to other developing countries.

Source: United Nations Conference on Trade and Development – UNCTAD (2005) *Trade and Development Report 2005: New Features of Global Interdependence.*

Chapter Summary

- Factors that have a major influence on the ability of a firm to develop and create value through innovation include the national system of innovation, the market position or power within the international value chain, the capability and processes of the firm, including research, design, development, production, marketing and distribution, and ability to identify and exploit external sources of innovation, especially international networks.

- The distribution of innovation globally is uneven, and the location of innovative activities is influenced by the local availability of critical competencies, international credibility of the R&D, importance of external sources of technical and market knowledge, and the importance and costs of internal transactions, e.g. between engineering, production, distribution and marketing.

- In formulating and executing their development and innovation strategies, business firms cannot ignore the national systems of innovation and international value chains in which they are embedded. Through their strong influences on demand and competitive conditions, the provision of human resources, and forms of corporate governance, national systems of innovation both open opportunities and impose constraints on what firms can do.

- Although firms' strategies are *influenced* by their own national systems of innovation, and their position in international value chains, they are not *determined* by them. Learning (i.e. assimilating knowledge) from competitors and external sources of innovation is essential for developing capabilities, but does require costly investments in R&D, training and skills development in order to develop the necessary absorptive capacity.

- The innovation challenges facing the emerging and developing economies, such as the so-called BRIC nations of Brazil, Russia, India and China, are similar, but every country begins with very different historical, geographic and political origins. As a result, the potential of each nation is very different, and the likely trajectories of innovation and development will be different in each case.

- The innovation strategies open to most emerging and developing economies include process upgrading, product upgrading, capability upgrading, and inter-sectoral upgrading.

- Capturing the benefits of innovation also depends upon on what management itself does, by way of investing in complementary assets in production, marketing, service and support, and its position in local and international systems of innovation. It also depends on a variety of contextual factors that make it more or less difficult to appropriate the benefits from innovation, such as intellectual property and international trading regimes, and over which management can sometimes have very little influence.

Key Terms Defined

Corporate governance The systems for exercising and changing corporate ownership and control.

Position The current endowment of technology and intellectual property of a firm, as well as its relations with customers and suppliers.

Spillovers A term used by economists to describe the flow of know-how and other benefits from firm-specific investments, for example by MNCs, to the broader economy, for example, between firms and between sectors. This is often presented as being automatic, but demands a significant effort by domestic firms.

Value chain or value network The system of relationships to create and capture value, for example, between suppliers and customers. These can constrain profoundly the ability to capture the benefits of their innovation and entrepreneurship.

Further Reading and Resources

There are a number of texts which describe and compare different systems of national innovation policy, including *National Innovation Systems* (Oxford University Press, Oxford, 1993), edited by Richard Nelson; *National Systems of Innovation* (Pinter, London, 1992) edited by B.A. Lundvall; and *Systems of Innovation: Technologies, Institutions and Organisations* (Pinter, London, 1997) edited by Charles Edquist. The former is stronger on US policy, the other two on European, but all have an emphasis on public policy rather than corporate strategy. Michael Porter's *The Competitive Advantage of Nations* (Macmillan, London, 1990) provides a useful framework in which to examine the direct impact on corporate behaviour of innovation systems. At the other extreme, David Landes' *Wealth and Poverty of Nations* (Little Brown, London, 1998), takes a broad (and stimulating) historical and cultural perspective. In *Globalisation, Poverty and Inequality* (Polity Press, Cambridge, UK, 2005), Raphie Kaplinsky argues that macroeconomic conditions can overwhelm the efforts of firms' countries to benefit from globalization, and that global excess capacity in production and the terms of international trade mean that emerging economies may not benefit from further globalization.

Comprehensive and balanced reviews of the arguments and evidence for product leadership versus follower positions is provided by G.J. Tellis and P.N. Golder, *Will and Vision: How Latecomers Grow to Dominate Markets* (McGraw Hill, New York, 2002) and *Fast Second: How Smart Companies Bypass Radical Innovation to Enter and Dominate New Markets* (Jossey-Bass San, Francisco, CA, 2004) by Constantinos C. Markides. More relevant to firms from emerging economies, and our favourite text on the subject, is Naushad Forbes and David Wield's *From Followers to Leaders: Managing Technology and Innovation* (Routledge, London, 2002), which includes numerous case examples. *Local Enterprises in the Local Economy: Issues of Governance and Upgrading* (Edward Elgar, Cheltenham, 2004), edited by Hubert Schmitz of the Institute of Development Studies, provides a summary of recent research on the influence of global standards and value chains on the development of firms from emerging economies. For recent reviews of the core competence and dynamic capability perspectives see David Teece's *Essays in Technology Management and Policy: Selected Papers* (World Scientific Publishing, London, 2004) and Connie Helfat's *Dynamic Capabilities: Understanding Strategic Change in Organizations* (Blackwell, Oxford, 2006).

References

1 Cantwell, J. and Molero, J. (2003) *Multinational Enterprises, Innovative Systems and Systems of Innovation.* Edward Elgar, Cheltenham; Granstrand, O., Hêakanson, L. and Sjèolander, S. (1992) *Technology Management and International Business: Internationalization of R&D and Technology.* John Wiley & Sons, Ltd, Chichester,

especially the chapter by Patel, P. and Pavitt, K., Large firms in the production of the world's technology: an important case of non-globalization.

2 Kim, L. and Nelson, R.R. (2000) *Technology, Learning and Innovation: Experiences of Newly Industrializing Economies.* Cambridge University Press, Cambridge, UK; Viotti, E.B. (2002) National learning systems: a new approach on technological change in late industrializing economies and evidences from the cases of Brazil and South Korea. *Technological Forecasting and Social Change*, **69**, 653–680; Bell, M. and Pavitt, K. (1993) Technological accumulation and industrial growth: contrasts between developed and developing countries. *Industrial and Corporate Change*, **2** (2), 157–210.

3 Schimtz, H. (2004) *Local Enterprises in the Global Economy.* Edward Elgar, Cheltenham; Sahay, A. and Riley, D. (2003) The role of resource access, market conditions, and the nature of innovation in the pursuit of standards in the new product development process. *Journal of Product Innovation Management*, **20**, 338–355.

4 Tidd, J., Bessant, J. and Pavitt, K. (2005) *Managing Innovation: Integrating Technological, Market and Organizational Change*, 3rd edn. John Wiley & Sons, Ltd, Chichester.

5 Nelson, R. (1993) *National Innovation Systems.* Oxford University Press, Oxford; Edquist, C. (1997) *Systems of Innovation: Technologies, Institutions and Organisations* (Pinter, London); Lundvall, B.A. (1992) *National Systems of Innovation* (Pinter, London).

6 Porter, M. (1990) *The Competitive Advantage of Nations.* Macmillan, London.

7 Forbes, N. and Wield, D. (2002) *From Followers to Leaders: Managing Technology and Innovation.* Routledge, London.

8 Prahalad, C.K. and Hamel, G. (1990) The core competence of the corporation. *Harvard Business Review*, May/June, 79–91.

9 Teece, D. (2004) *Essays in Technology Management and Policy: Selected Papers.* World Scientific Press, London; Helfat, C.E. (2006) *Dynamic Capabilities: Understanding Strategic Change in Organizations.* Blackwell.

Discussion Questions

1 What factors influence the location of innovation, and how might these constrain the globalization of innovation?

2 What are the main components of a national innovation system, and how do these interact?

3 How can firms learn from overseas sources of innovation?

4 How can firms limit the scope for competitors imitating their innovations, and therefore better appropriate the benefits of their innovations?

5 Beyond formal R&D investment, what types of capabilities and competencies do firms need in order to innovate?

6 Compare the development of capabilities in China and India. What are the key lessons for developing economies?

Team Exercise: Identifying Capabilities

Using the framework in *Advice for Future Managers*, identify the capabilities and intangible resources of a chosen company. The exercise consists of three parts:

1 Identify the key attributes of the most successful products and services offered by the organization;

2 Map these attributes to the resources or competencies of the organization, including tangible and intangible resources;

3 Assess the potential for sustaining, protecting and exploiting these resources, including knowledge management.

Example of the matrix of attributes and resources:

	The resources which produce, or do not produce, the key attributes:			
Key product/ delivery attributes	Regulatory capability	Positional capability	Functional capability	Cultural capability
Strengths				
1 e.g. Availability		Value-chain configuration	Forecasting skills	
2 e.g. Quality				High perception of quality
3 e.g. Specification	Patent 'abc'		Technology 'xyz'	
Etc.				
Weaknesses				
1				
2				
Summary of the key resources				

Assignment and Case Study Questions

Choose a country, industrialized or developing, and identify the key aspects of the national innovation system. Compare these with any observed sectoral patterns of performance. What do you conclude about the respective role of government policy, national institutions and firm capabilities and behaviour?

CASE STUDY 11
Building BRICs – Innovation Capabilities in China

Since economic reform began in 1978, the Chinese economy has grown by about 9–10% each year, compared to 2–3% for the industrialized countries. As a result its GDP overtook Italy in 2004, France and

UK in 2005 and is expected to overtake Germany in 2008. China has a population of around 1.3 billion, and an economy valued at US$2.3 trillion in 2006 (for comparison, the UK was US$2.1 trillion, the USA US$11.7 trillion, and Japan US$4.9 trillion). China now has the world's second largest economy after the USA on a purchasing power (PPP) basis.

The Chinese government has followed a twin-track policy of exporting relatively low-technology products, while using various measures to protect its domestic economy, and providing subsidies to support selected state-owned firms, to build technological capability. This activist technology policy will be tightly constrained in future, with the completion of entry to the World Trade Organization in 2005, and implementation of the Trade Related Intellectual Property System (TRIPS) in 2006. These will require stricter laws on intellectual property laws and their enforcement, and limit subsidies and interference with trade.

After 2 decades of providing the world economy with inexpensive labour, China is now starting to become a platform for innovation, research and development. The actual formal R&D expenditure is still comparatively small, about 1.3% of GDP (compared to an average of 2.3% of GDP in the advanced economies of the OECD, although Japan exceeds 3%), but the Chinese Government aims to make China an 'innovation nation' by 2010, and a scientific power by 2050, and in 2006 increased government funding in R&D by 25% to US$425 million. It plans to increase R&D expenditure to 2.5% of GDP by 2020, in line with expenditure in developed economies. China's science and technology output is already increasing, and was ranked fifth globally in terms of science papers produced between 2002 and 2005, which is impressive given the language disadvantage.

China's policy has followed the East Asian model in which success has depended on technological and commercial investment by and collaboration with foreign firms. Typically companies in the East Asian tiger economies such as South Korea and Taiwan developed technological capabilities on a foundation of manufacturing competence based on low-tech production, and developed higher levels of capability such as design and new product development, for example, through own equipment manufacture (OEM) production for international firms. However, the flow of technology and development of capabilities are not automatic. Economists refer to 'spillovers' of know-how from foreign investment and collaboration, but this demands a significant effort by domestic firms.

Most significantly, China has encouraged foreign multinationals to invest in China, and these are now also beginning to conduct some R&D in China. Motorola opened the first foreign R&D lab in 1992, and estimates indicate there were more than 700 R&D centres in China in 2005, although care needs to be taken in the definitions used. The transfer of technology to China, especially in the manufacturing sector, is considered to be a major contributor to its recent economic growth. Around 80% of China's inward foreign direct investment (FDI) is 'technology' (hardware and software), and FDI inflows have continued to grow, to US$72 billion in 2005 (for comparison, this is around 10 times that attracted by India, whereas some advanced economies continue to attract significant FDI, for example, US$165 billion was invested in the UK in 2005). However, we must distinguish between technology transferred by foreign companies into their wholly or majority-owned subsidiaries in China, versus the technology acquired by indigenous enterprises. It is only through the successful acquisition of technological capability by indigenous enterprises, many of which still remain state-owned, that China can become a really innovative and competitive economic power.

The import of foreign technology can have a positive impact on innovation and, for large enterprises, the more foreign technology is imported, the more conducive to its own patenting. However, for the small and medium-sized enterprises this is not the case. This probably implies that larger enterprises possess certain absorptive capacity to take advantage of foreign technology which in turn leads to an enhancement of innovation capacity, whereas the small- and medium-sized enterprises are more likely to rely on foreign technology due to the lack of appropriate absorptive capacity and the possibly huge gap between imported and its own technology. Buying bundles of technology has been encouraged. These included *embodied* and *codified* technology: hardware and licences. If innovation expenditure is broken down by class of innovative activity, the costs of acquisition for *embodied* technology, such as machines and production equipment, account for about 58% of the total innovation expenditures, compared with 17% internal R&D, 5% external R&D, 3% marketing of new product, 2% training cost and 15% engineering and manufacturing start-up.

It is clear that the large foreign MNCs are the most active in patenting in China. Foreign patenting began around 1995 and, since 2000, patent applications have increased annually by around 50%. MNCs' patenting activities are highly correlated with total revenue, or the overall Chinese market size. This strongly supports the standpoint that foreign patents in China are largely driven by demand factors. China's specialization in patenting does not correspond to its export specialization. Automobiles, household durables, software, communication equipments, computer peripherals, semiconductors, telecommunication services are the primary areas. The semiconductor industry in 2005, for example, was granted as many as fourfold inventions of the previous year. Patents by foreign MNCs account for almost 90% of all patents in China, the most active being firms from Japan, the USA and South Korea. Thirty MNCs have been granted more than 1000 patents, and 8 of these each have more than 5000: Samsung, Matsushita, Sony, LG, Mitsubishi, Hitachi, Toshiba and Siemens. Almost half of these patents are for the application of an existing technology, a fifth for inventions, and the rest for industrial designs. Among the 18 000 patents for inventions with no prior overseas rights, only 924 originate from Chinese subsidiaries of these MNCs, accounting for only 0.75% of the total. The average lag between patenting in the home country and in China is more than 3 years, which is an indicator of the technology lag between China and MNCs.

One reason for this pattern is the very low level of industry-funded R&D, as opposed to public-funded, but there has also been a failure of corporate governance in the large state-owned enterprises selected for support. When the economic reform programme began in 1978 it inherited the advantages and disadvantages of Maoist autarchy. China had enterprises producing across a very wide range of products, having spent heavily from the late 1950s to give itself a high degree of technological independence. The main disadvantage was that its technologies were out of date. The government promoted FDI through joint ventures, 51% owned by a 'national team' of about 120 large domestic state-owned enterprises. Pressures on and incentives for management in state-owned firms have encouraged them to rely on external sources of technology, rather than to develop their own internal capabilities. At the same time private Chinese firms have been constrained by a shortage of finance. However, in 2000 the government reviewed its policy and began to restructure the state-owned firms and to support the most successful private firms. There is a clear link between such restructuring and the development of capabilities.

Examples of companies which have gone through significant changes in governance or financial structure include Xiali, which was transformed into a joint venture with Toyota; TPCO, where debt-funding was changed into equity and shareholding, which allowed higher investment in production capacity and technology development; and Tianjin Metal Forming, restructured to remove debt and in a stronger position to invest and be a more attractive candidate for a foreign investment. Private firms like Lenovo, TCL (Ningbo) Bird and Huawei have since prospered and, with belated government help, are successful overseas: in 2004 Huawei gained 40% of its over-US$5 billion revenues outside China; Haier has overseas revenues of over US$1 billion from its home appliances; Lenovo bought IBM's PC division in 2005; TCL made itself the largest TV maker in the world by buying Thomson of France's TV division in 2004; Wanxiang, a motor components manufacturer started by a farmer's son as a bicycle repair shop, had US$2 billion annual sales by 2004.

However, there are significant differences of innovation and entrepreneurial activity in different areas of China. The eastern coastal region is higher than the other regions, especially in Shanghai, Beijing and Tianjin, whose entrepreneurial activity level is higher and continues to grow. Beijing and the Tianjin Region, the Yangtze River Delta Region (Shanghai, Jiangsu, Zhejiang),and the Zhu Jiang Delta Region (Guangdong) are the most active regions. Shanghai ranks first in most surveys, followed by Beijing, but the disparity of the 2 areas has been expanding. For example, the local city government in Shanghai provides funds of US$12 million each year to fund 'little giants', small high-technology firms which it hopes will contribute annual sales of US$12 billion by 2010. In the middle region and the northeast region, entrepreneurial activity level is lower than in the eastern coastal region, but is increasing. The western and north-west region is the lowest and least improving area for entrepreneurial activity level, and shows little change. Econometric models indicate that the main determinants for entrepreneurial activity are explained by regional market demand, industrial structure, availability of financing, entrepreneurial culture and human capital. Technology innovation and rate of consumption growth do not have significant effects on entrepreneurship in China. Although some 200 million Chinese still live on US$1 a day, China is also the largest market in the world for luxury goods. China is estimated to have 300 000 dollar millionaires, 400 entrepreneurs valued at US$60 million each, and 7 billionaires. Such disparities in income can create huge social and political tensions, and may result in a reaction against further growth unless governance and distribution are improved further.

Case Study Questions

1 In China, how has state policy promoted and constrained innovation?

2 What roles have MNCs had in the development of local capabilities?

3 In future, how might innovation and entrepreneurship contribute to development in China?

Sources: East meets West: 15th International Conference on Management of Technology, Beijing, May 2006; *R&D Management* (2004), **34** (4). Special Issue on Innovation in China.

Part 4
Action

Chapter 12

Taking the Next Steps – Making it Happen

This chapter

■ Reviews the main themes we have covered in the book.

■ Looks at the question of how we can organize and manage the process of innovation.

■ Focuses on key success factors at each stage in the process – search, select and implement – and at creating the supporting conditions for success.

■ Explores key tools, techniques and mechanisms to help make it effective.

■ Provides an audit framework for reviewing and thinking about innovation.

Learning Objectives

By the end of this chapter you will have:

■ Reviewed and consolidated the key themes in the book.

■ Explored key influences on how to manage the innovation process effectively.

■ Developed the ability to review how well an organization manages the process.

■ Practised taking an audit approach to improving innovation management.

Introduction

Let's take stock of where we've been going in this book and the key themes we've tried to introduce. Chapter 1 introduced the idea of innovation not as some luxury to be thought about occasionally but as a business imperative. Unless established businesses change what they offer the world and the ways they create and deliver that offering they are likely to fall behind their competitors and even disappear. On a more positive side creating new business through coming up with and deploying ideas is well established as a powerful source of economic growth – not to mention a great way to make the successful entrepreneurs behind those ideas very wealthy!

This process works right across the economy – whether we are talking about cars, clothes or silicon chips. It isn't confined to manufacturing – it works just as powerfully for the services which make up the majority of most economies – banks, insurance companies, shops and airlines all have to look hard and often at the innovation challenge if they are to stay ahead. For public services the same is true – but here we begin to see that it isn't always money which drives the entrepreneurial wheels. Innovation here is targeted at improving education, saving lives, making people more secure and addressing other basic needs. And while some innovation is about taking costs and waste out of established service-delivery processes, much is about coming up with new and better ways of improving the quality of human life. Whether in a start-up or across a large public sector department there is a strong thread of social entrepreneurship running through driven less by a desire for profits than literally wanting to change the world.

But whatever drives innovation and wherever it happens – big firm, small firm, start-up business – one thing is clear. Successful innovation won't happen simply by wishing for it. The complex and risky process of transforming ideas into something which makes a mark needs organizing and managing in strategic fashion. Passion and energy aren't enough – if we are to do more than just gamble enthusiastically then we need to organize and focus the process. And we need to be able to repeat the trick – anyone might get lucky once but being able to deliver a steady stream of innovations requires something a bit more structured and robust.

As we saw in Part 1 of the book, innovation is a generic process, running from ideas through to their implementation. Despite the many different ways in which we see it playing out in manufacturing or services, at heart the process is about weaving knowledge and resources together. And it's this creative tapestry that we have to organize and manage as we move through three core stages from getting hold of the ideas in the first place, choosing the best candidates to put our resources into and then making them into successful innovations.

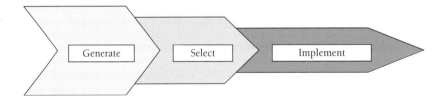

We know that this process is influenced along the way by several things which can help or hinder, and Part II of the book looked particularly at some of the levers we could use as architects and managers of the process. How can we construct innovative organizations which allow creative ideas to come through, let people build on and share knowledge and feel motivated and rewarded for doing so? How can we harness the power of networks, making rich and extensive connections to deliver a stream of innovations? Figure 12.1 illustrates the complete model.

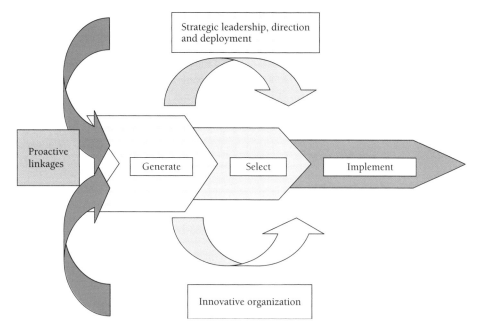

Figure 12.1 Simplified model for innovation management.

The energy and passion that drive through the process is *entrepreneurship* – the seeing and making real of opportunities. It is clearly involved in a start-up where a new business requires an individual or a small group to channel their creative energy and drive to make something new. But it's also needed in an established company where renewal comes through stimulating and enabling the same drive and creativity to deliver both a stream of improvement innovations and also the occasional inspired leap which helps reinvent the business. And increasingly such drive, energy and enthusiasm are being harnessed to more than economic growth – in start-ups and established organizations where the challenges of sustainability are being picked up. Such social entrepreneurship is literally about changing the world – but it uses the same basic engine.

Of course the context for innovation and entrepreneurship varies hugely. The particular pattern of threats and opportunities from which ideas emerge and are selected isn't a case of 'one size fits all' but an incredibly rich and diverse environment including manufacturing and service sectors and small to giant firm players. It's happening on a global stage which is placing increasing emphasis on networks and extended and often virtual connections. Innovation takes place against a backdrop of increasing concern about sustainability in terms of energy, resources and meeting basic human needs in a more balanced and better-distributed fashion – and this has brought many different and sometimes opposing actors into the play. And there is the long-standing tension between innovation aimed at sustaining what we already have (doing what we do but better) and innovation aimed at creating something completely different – *discontinuous* innovation.

But despite this richly varied context we still have to make it happen. How? This chapter looks at the key lessons learned about organizing and managing the process of innovation and entrepreneurship – and how we might use those lessons to review and strengthen our capability.

Making Innovation Happen

Rather than the cartoon image of a light bulb flashing on above someone's head, we need to think about innovation as an extended sequence of activities – a *process*. To make innovation happen we need to generate, select and implement ideas – so how can we best organize to make these activities happen?

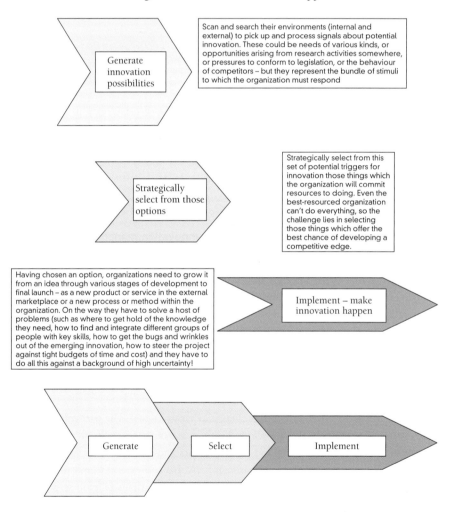

Measuring Innovation Performance

In reviewing innovative performance we can look at a number of possible measures and indicators:

■ Measures of specific outputs of various kinds – for example, patents and scientific papers as indicators of knowledge produced, or number of new products introduced (and percentage of sales and/or profits derived from them) as indicators of product innovation success.

- Output measures of operational or process elements, such as customer satisfaction surveys to measure and track improvements in quality or flexibility.

- Output measures which can be compared across sectors or enterprises – for example, cost of product, market share, quality performance.

- Output measures of strategic success, where the overall business performance is improved in some way and where at least some of the benefit can be attributed directly or indirectly to innovation – for example, growth in revenue or market share, improved profitability, higher value-added.

We could also consider a number of more specific measures of the internal workings of the innovation process or particular elements within it. For example:

- Number of new ideas (product/service/process) generated at start of innovation system.

- Failure rates – in the development process, in the marketplace.

- Number or percentage of overruns on development time and cost budgets.

- Customer satisfaction measures – was it what the customer wanted?

- Time to market (average, compared with industry norms).

- Development person-hours per completed innovation.

- Process innovation average lead time for introduction.

- Measures of continuous improvement – suggestions per employee, number of problem-solving teams, savings accruing per worker, cumulative savings and so on.

There is also scope for measuring some of the influential conditions supporting or inhibiting the process – for example, the 'creative climate' of the organization or the extent to which strategy is clearly deployed and communicated.. And there is value in considering inputs to the process – for example, percentage of sales committed to R&D, investments in training and recruitment of skilled staff.

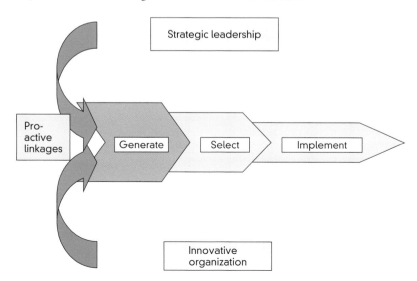

Generating Ideas

Ideas – as we've seen – can come from anywhere. Some boffin in a lab may have a 'Eureka!' moment. Or someone talking with a customer may see a need which hasn't been met. A competitor might start offering a service we haven't got in our repertoire. A civil servant may change the rules of the particular game our business is playing and force us to rethink what we do. Or a newcomer from a different industry might spot a way to reframe the game and bring in a completely new way of looking at it – as we see every day on the Internet.

ADVICE FOR FUTURE MANAGERS

When looking for triggers for innovation, smart players try and cover as many bases as possible, looking at things like exploring:

- The technology space – finding opportunities but also checking who else is innovating.

- The market space – finding out if there is a market and how big, how fast it's growing, and so on. But also finding out about competitors real and potential and about barriers to entry, and so on.

- What others are doing. Who else is or could be playing – and could we learn from them?

- Future space – look ahead at how threats and opportunities might develop and affect both technical and market space.

- With others – bringing different stakeholders into the process, using their perspectives and ideas to enrich the variety and generate new directions.

Wherever the ideas come from the challenge for us is to make sure we pick up on them and harness them to provide the fuel of the innovation process. Entrepreneurship may give us the drive but without ideas the engine will be running on empty. So how do successful organizations organize and manage what is essentially a search process? Needless to say there isn't a standard recipe but in a well-developed organization there will be a number of parallel mechanisms used to make sure the search is carried out in systematic and extensive fashion. How do they organize and manage these?

Exploring the Technology Space

One option is, of course, to do some research and development (R&D) – which has the big advantage of letting you keep and exploit whatever you find out. But R&D is risky and expensive – in the case of pharmaceutical firms it can cost as much as 20% of the turnover of the business yet there is still only a tiny chance of success in terms of coming up with a new blockbuster drug.

Formal R&D on this scale is mainly something which larger or highly focused small firms undertake but many others do experiment and explore the technological knowledge underpinning their products/services and processes. Much of this is incremental improvement innovation – for example, getting their operating processes to be leaner

INNOVATION IN ACTION

To make 'open innovation' work firms need two things – some way of finding out what is 'out there' and also the ability to see and understand what is relevant. For the former they are making increasing use of scouts – people specifically tasked with going out looking. For example, Procter & Gamble employs around 80 'technology entrepreneurs' whose job it is to hunt for interesting connections, and they back this up with an extensive Web-based search system. This recently paid off for them – they had decided that one way of improving their share of the market for snack foods might be to find ways of printing images on to their 'Pringles' product. But where was the knowledge that might enable this complex task to be carried out? Eventually one of their technology entrepreneurs found a small printing firm in Bologna, Italy, which had developed a system for this kind of application.

or faster – and it may not show up in formal statistics although it does have a positive impact on the bottom line. But even those major R&D players are beginning to recognize the arguments for a more 'open innovation' approach which also links up with sources of research elsewhere.

If organizations are going down the 'open innovation' road then they need to have a well-developed network of external sources which can supply it, and the ability to put that externally acquired technology to effective use. This is rarely a simple shopping transaction – it involves abilities like those listed in Table 12.1.

Table 12.1   **Key abilities in technology transfer**

Ability	Why?
Building and maintaining a network of technology sources	To ensure a wide range of choice and availability, rather than being forced to take inappropriate solutions
Selecting	To ensure a good fit between internal needs and external offer
Negotiating	To ensure that what is transferred includes the knowledge and experience surrounding the technology and not simply the hardware or licence
Implementing	To ensure the process of transfer is effectively managed
Learning	To ensure that once transferred the development and internalization of the technology takes place

A number of tools have been developed to help with strategic decision-making around this issue. They usually make some classification of technologies in terms of their open availability and the ease with which they can be protected and deployed to strategic advantage. For example, the consultancy Arthur D. Little uses a matrix which groups technological knowledge into four key groups – base, key, pacing and emerging.

- Base technologies represent those on which product/service innovations are based and which are vital to the business. However they are also widely known about and deployed by competitors and offer little potential competitive advantage.

- Key technologies represent those which form the core of current products/ services or processes and which have a high competitive impact – they are strategically important to the organization and may well be protectable through patent.

■ Pacing technologies are those which are at the leading edge of the current competitive game and may be under experimentation by competitors – they have high but as yet unfulfilled competitive potential.

■ Emerging technologies are those which are at the technological frontier, still under development and whose impact is promising but not yet clear.

Making this distinction helps in thinking about where it might make sense to do some internal R&D and where it makes more sense to use the wider market. For base technologies it may make sense to source outside whereas for key technologies an in-house or carefully selected strategic alliance may seem more sensible in order to preserve the potential competitive advantage. Emerging technologies may be best served by a watching strategy, perhaps through some pilot project links with universities or technological institutes. A fast-growing new market may require extensive investment in the pacing technology in order to be able to build on the opportunities being created whereas a mature or declining market may be better served by a strategy which uses base technology to help preserve a position but at low cost.

Of course it's not simply a matter of generating ideas through your own research or shopping around for someone else's which you can use. As Table 12.2 shows, there's a spectrum of possibilities, each with its own strengths and weaknesses.

Picking up on technology opportunities requires active search and scanning, and sources with which links can be made include suppliers, universities, research/technology institutions, other users and producers, trade associations, international bodies (e.g. for standards), and so on. The principle behind this is to multiply the range of channels along which technological intelligence can flow. The Web has become a powerful amplifier for making such connections and an increasing number of organizations are developing search strategies (and accompanying 'gatekeeper' skills) to work with it. IBM, for example, uses an approach called 'Web fountain' to help it monitor a wide range of potential triggers. Even the CIA makes use of an internal group called In-Q-Tel to act as a 'venture catalyst' to facilitate trend-spotting in key technology areas!

INNOVATION IN ACTION

'Mistakes Management'

Sometimes great ideas lie in mistakes and apparent failures which open up completely new directions for innovation. For example, the famous story of 3M's 'Post-it' notes began when a polymer chemist mixed an experimental batch of what should have been a good adhesive but which turned out to have rather weak properties – sticky but not very sticky. This failure in terms of the original project provided the impetus for what has become a billion-dollar product platform for the company. Henry Chesbrough calls this process 'managing the false negatives' and draws attention to a number of cases. For example, in the late 1980s, scientists working for Pfizer began testing what was then known as compound UK-92,480 for the treatment of angina. Although promising in the lab and in animal tests, the compound showed little benefit in clinical trials in humans. Despite these initial negative results the team pursued what was an interesting side effect which eventually led to UK-92,480 becoming the blockbuster drug Viagra.

But using mistakes as a source of ideas only happens if the conditions exist to help it emerge. For example Xerox developed many technologies in its laboratories in Palo Alto which did not easily fit their image of themselves as 'the document company'. These included Ethernet (later successfully commercialized by 3Com and others) and PostScript language (taken forward by Adobe Systems). Chesborough reports that 11 of 35 rejected projects from Xerox's labs were later commercialized with the resulting businesses having a market capitalization of twice that of Xerox itself.

Table 12.2   Different ways of getting hold of technological ideas

Mechanism	Strengths	Weaknesses
Mobilizing tacit knowledge	Internal, highly specific knowledge Hard to copy	Hard to mobilize Needs processes to articulate and capture
In-house formal R&D	Strategically directed Under full control Knowledge remains inside the firm Learning by doing	High cost and commitment Risks – no guarantee of success
In-house R&D and network links outside	As above but with less control over knowledge unless there is a clear contract on intellectual property rights	Costs and risks
Reverse engineering	Lower costs Offers insight into competitors' processes and products Knowledge can be inferred, but needs a level of skill to do so	Depends on ability to infer knowledge Knowledge may be protected anyway, e.g. in patent or copyright
Covert acquisition (industrial espionage!) plus internal R&D	Fast access to knowledge and relevance of that knowledge can be managed through internal capability	Illegal Costs of internal R&D
Technology transfer and absorption	Easier access to knowledge – someone else has developed and packaged it	Risk of not being able to translate external knowledge to internal needs Costs Risk of not understanding or being able to make full use of technology May be prohibited from further exploration and learning by terms of licence, etc.
Contract R&D	Speed and focus	Costs Lack of control Lack of learning effect – someone else is carrying out the experimentation and learning process
Strategic R&D partnership	Links complementary knowledge sets Enables complex problems to be addressed	Costs Risks in partnership not working Lack of learning since technology development is carried out by other parties
Licensing	Fast access to knowledge	Costs Restricted learning – may also be prohibited by terms of licence
Purchasing	Fast access	Costs Lack of learning

(continued overleaf)

Table 12.2 *(continued)*

Mechanism	Strengths	Weaknesses
Joint venture	Links complementary knowledge sets Enables complex problems to be addressed	Costs Risks in partnership not working Lack of learning since technology development is carried out by other parties
Acquisition of a company with the knowledge	Fast access to knowledge Control over knowledge	Costs May not be able to absorb knowledge

Needless to say firms need to make sure they aren't just searching close to home but also at the periphery – not only looking in the places where developments might be expected to occur but also exploring at the edges where something unexpected might take off. It's also clear that bringing unconnected elements together is often important in innovation – after all, most new knowledge emerges at such interfaces. In Xerox, for example, 23 000 technical reps from around the world are linked into a network of communities of practice to share knowledge about unusual machine faults and heuristics for finding and fixing them.

INNOVATION IN ACTION

Involving insiders

In looking for signals about possible innovation triggers it is important not to neglect those which originate inside the organization. We shouldn't neglect the considerable resource which 'ordinary' employees represent in terms of their ideas, particularly for incremental improvement innovations. Tapping into such high-involvement innovation potential has been demonstrably helpful to a wide range of organizations- for example:

■ A prison guard in Massachusetts suggested a way of using digital cameras which saved around US$56 000 when applied across all prisons in the state.

■ A major investment bank saved around US$1 million per year through savings suggested by a team in its back-office operations in Hong Kong.

■ A worker in a large European communications firm found ways to improve the billing software in the firm and saved around US$26 million in lost revenues.

■ Toyota has risen to become the world's number one auto-maker not so much through radical innovation as through a regular stream of incremental innovation ideas from its workforce. Since 1960 when records began they have received on average 2 million ideas per year from their workforce.

Communication and Connection

Using ideas from outside is powerful – but only if the right connections are made back into the organization. For example, in assessing technological opportunities it's also important that the user perspective is communicated to all the different functions and disciplines within the organization. Among recipes for achieving this are to rotate staff so that they spend some time out working with and listening to customers, and the introduction of the concept that 'everybody is someone's customer'.

An increasing number of tools and structured frameworks are now available for trying to identify, clarify, articulate and communicate 'the voice of the customer' throughout the organization. Based on the principles of quality function deployment (QFD) these tools usually take as their starting point the customer needs as expressed in the customer's own words or images and gradually and systematically decompose them into tasks for the various elements within the organization. (There's a description of QFD in Chapter 5 and it's also described – along with many other tools – on the John Wiley & Sons website: www.managing-innovation.com.)

We're also making much more use of our understanding of social networks and how ideas flow within and across organizations. Of particular significance in this context is the role played by various forms of 'gatekeeper' in the organization. This concept – which goes back to the pioneering work of Thomas Allen in his studies within the aerospace industry – relates to a model of communication in which ideas flow via key individuals to those who can make use of them in developing innovation.[1]

Gatekeepers are often well-positioned in the informal communication networks and have the facility to act as translators and brokers of key information. Studies of the operation of such communication networks stress the informal flows of knowledge and have led to a variety of architectural changes in research laboratories and other knowledge environments. These are essentially variants around the 'village pump' idea where environments are configured to allow plenty of space for informal encounter (such as by the coffee machine or in a relaxation area) where key exchange of information can take place. Significantly the rise of distributed working and the use of virtual teams have spawned an extension to these ideas making use of advanced communications to enable such networking across geographical and organizational boundaries.

Exploring the Market Space

Defining the boundaries of the marketplace – what business are we in? This sounds obvious – but sometimes innovation can take the form of repositioning – offering the same basic product or service but addressed in a new way to different markets. For example, Amazon.com is seen as an online retailer but is trying to broaden its business by positioning itself also as a software developer and supplier.

Another key element is to use market research tools to understand the shape, size and dynamics of the market. For example, the cellphone business has moved from a specialist, high-price business tool into the general marketplace as a result of both technological and cultural change. Similarly low-cholesterol and other healthy foods are increasingly becoming relevant to a large segment of the population as a result of changing social attitudes and education. Building up such understanding of the changing marketplace requires various forms of communication and interaction, from monitoring through to customer panels and surveys. Firms like Zara and Benetton have sophisticated IT systems installed in each of their shops such that they can quickly identify which lines are selling well on a daily basis – and tailor production to this.

Learning from Others

Another group of approaches deals with comparisons against competitor organizations to generate new ideas. Search techniques of this kind include competitor analysis ('what are they doing in terms of product range, service proposition, process performance?') and variants on the theme of 'reverse engineering'. For example much of the early growth in Korean manufacturing industries in fields like machine tools came from adopting a strategy of 'copy and develop' – essentially learning (often as a result of taking licences or becoming service agents) by working with established products and understanding how they might be adapted or developed for the local market. Subsequently this learning was used to develop new generations of products or services.

INNOVATION IN ACTION

Learning from Outside the Box

For example, Southwest Airlines became the most successful carrier in the USA by dramatically reducing the turnaround times at airports – an innovation which it learned from studying pit stop techniques in the Formula 1 Grand Prix events. Similarly the Karolinska Hospital in Stockholm made significant improvements to its cost and time performance through studying inventory management techniques in advanced factories.

A powerful variation on this theme is the concept of benchmarking. In this process enterprises make structured comparisons with others to try and identify new ways of carrying out particular processes or to explore new product or service concepts. The learning triggered by benchmarking may arise from comparing between similar organizations (same firm, same sector, etc.), or it may come from looking outside the sector but at similar products or processes. Benchmarking of this kind is increasingly being used to drive change across the public sector, both via 'league tables' linked to performance metrics which aim to encourage fast transfer of good practice between schools or hospitals and also via secondment, visits and other mechanisms designed to facilitate learning from other sectors managing similar process issues such as logistics and distribution.

Exploring Future Space

A wide range of techniques are available for trying to understand the likely dynamics of new markets, running from simple extrapolation of current trends through to complex techniques for handling discontinuous change, such as Delphi panels and scenario-writing. Such forecasting needs to move beyond sales-related information to include other features which will influence the potential market – for example, demographic, technological, political and environmental issues. For example, the present concern for environmentally friendly 'green' products is likely to increase and will be shaped by a variety of these factors. From this information come valuable clues about the type of performance which the market expects from a particular manufacturer or service provider – and hence the targets for process innovation.

One difficulty in exploring a market space arises when the market does not exist or where it suddenly takes a turn in a new direction. Developing antennae to pick up on the early warnings of trends is important, particularly in consumer-related innovation. For example, much of the development of the mobile phone industry has been on the back of the different uses to which schoolchildren put their phones and delivering innovations which support this. Examples include text-messaging, image/video exchange and downloadable personal ring tones where the clues to the emergence of these innovation trajectories were picked up by monitoring what such children were doing or aspiring towards.

Technological Forecasting

As we saw in Chapter 10, various techniques exist for exploring technological futures, ranging from simple extrapolation of performance parameters and rates of development to complex, nonlinear techniques. Some, like Delphi panels and scenarios, are similar to market-forecasting techniques, while others are more closely aligned to technological development models. An important approach here is the use of 'S' curves to try and identify the point at which an emerging new technological trajectory takes over from an existing one. But we also need to be careful – new opportunities may also emerge from making different use of existing technologies configured in new ways.

Integrated Future Search

Another approach is to take an integrated view of what different futures might look like and then explore innovation triggers within those spaces. Typical of this approach is the work which Shell and other organizations do with scenarios where a number of people work together to build up pictures of alternative parallel futures. These are usually richly woven backgrounds which describe technologies, markets, politics, social values and other elements in the form of a 'storyline' which can then be explored as a rich space of future opportunities and challenges.

INNOVATION IN ACTION

A recent Shell publication looked at possible scenarios for 2020 in terms of two alternatives – 'Business class' and 'Prism'. The former offers a vision of 'connected freedom' in which cities and regions become increasingly powerful at the expense of central government, and where there is increasing mobility among a 'global elite'; while the latter describes a different world in which people increasingly look to their roots and reorientate towards values as the focus around which to organize their lives. Neither is necessarily the 'right' answer to what the world will look like by 2020 but they do offer a richly described space within which to explore and simulate, and to search for threats and opportunities which might affect the company. In particular they allow an organization to define particular 'domains' – spaces within the bigger scenario where it can think about deploying its particular competencies to advantage – and to carry out a kind of 'targeted hunting' in its search for innovation possibilities.

Integrated futures exercises of this kind do not have to be organization-specific – indeed, there is much value in getting a diverse picture which brings different perspectives into play and explores the resulting search space from different angles. It is an approach increasingly used at sectoral and national level – for example, in the many 'Foresight' programmes which are in place. In the UK, for example, the Department of Trade and Industry has coordinated such activity for over a decade using panels made up of a wide range of interest and expertise. (See http://www.foresight.gov.uk/ for more details on their current programmes.)

Involving Stakeholders

Another key approach is to bring key stakeholders into the process – for example, by involving customers in providing information about the kinds of products and services which they require. This can be done through regular surveys, through customer panels and other forms of involvement. In similar fashion there is a growing trend towards shared *process* innovation, where customers and suppliers work together to reduce costs or increase quality or some other performance parameter.

INNOVATION IN ACTION

Working with users can often offer important insights or new directions. For example, the Danish pharmaceutical company Novo-Nordisk developed a highly successful range of insulin delivery devices to revitalize the market for diabetes treatments by pioneering the 'Novopen' concept. In 1981 the marketing director had read an article in The *Lancet* which described a young English girl with diabetes who each morning filled a disposable syringe with enough insulin for the rest of the day. This enabled her to administer the doses she needed over the course of the day without having to refill the syringe. She had always felt that it was cumbersome and indiscreet to administer a dose of insulin from a vial using a disposable syringe.

This led him to ask the development team if it would be possible to produce a device that looked like a fountain pen, was easy to use, which could hold a week's supply of insulin and administer two units of insulin at the touch of a button. The pen had to be simple and discreet, and preferably look like an actual fountain pen. After extensive development work the device was successfully produced and marketed and has become a key product platform for the firm.

An important variation on the theme of involving customers in concept development is the idea of working with *lead users*. In industries like semiconductors and instrumentation research suggests that the richest understanding of needed new products is held by only a few organizations, who are ahead of the majority of firms in the sector. Equally, finding the most demanding customer in a particular sector is a valuable approach; stretching the concept to meet their needs will ensure that most other potential users come within the envelope. (There is more discussion of this theme in Chapter 10.)

In similar fashion, successful innovation depends on maintaining a strong user perspective over time: this argues for mechanisms which emphasize continuing interaction rather than a one-off information-gathering exercise. Mechanisms for doing so include involvement of users in the project team and two-way visiting between sites.

HOW WELL DO WE DO IT?

These are all approaches which an organization could take to managing the challenge of generating ideas to trigger the innovation process. How well it does it is another matter – but one way we could tell might be to listen to the things people said in describing 'the way we do things around here' – in other words, the pattern of behaviour and beliefs which creates the climate for innovation. And if we walked around the organization we'd expect to hear people talking about the methods they actually use. We should hear things like:

Around here . . .

■ We have good 'win–win' relationships with our suppliers and we pick up a steady stream of ideas from them.

- We are good at understanding the needs of our customers/end-users.

- We work well with universities and other research centres to help us develop our knowledge.

- Our people are involved in suggesting ideas for improvements to products or processes.

- We look ahead in a structured way (using forecasting tools and techniques) to try and imagine future threats and opportunities.

- We systematically compare our products and processes with other firms.

- We collaborate with other firms to develop new products or processes.

- We try to develop external networks of people who can help us – for example, with specialist knowledge.

- We work closely with 'lead users' to develop innovative new products and services.

Dealing with the Unexpected

Of course, part of the search question is about picking up rather weak signals about emerging – and sometimes radically different – triggers for innovation (as we saw in Chapter 7). So people in smart firms might also say things like:

Around here . . .

- We deploy 'probe and learn' approaches to explore new directions in technologies and markets.

- We make connections across industry to provide us with different perspectives.

- We have mechanisms to bring in fresh perspectives – for example, recruiting from outside the industry.

- We use make regular use of formal tools and techniques to help us think 'out of the box'.

- We focus on 'next practices' as well as 'best practices'.

- We use some form of technology scanning/intelligence gathering – we have well-developed technology antennae.

- We work with 'fringe' users and very early adopters to develop our new products and services.

- We use technologies like the Web to help us become more agile and quick to pick up on and respond to emerging threats and opportunities on the periphery.

- We deploy 'targeted hunting' around our periphery to open up new strategic opportunities.

- We are organized to deal with 'off-purpose' signals (not directly relevant to our current business) and don't simply ignore them.

- We have active links into the long-term research and technology community – we can list a wide range of contacts.

- We recognize users as a source of new ideas and try and 'co-evolve' new products and services with them.

Selection

The trouble with ideas is that you can have too much of a good thing. A well-developed search process will throw up all sorts of possible opportunities – interesting ideas which are all waiting to take flight if only they had the resources to help them get off the ground. But no organization has infinite resources so the next stage in the process involves making some tough decisions about which ideas to back – and why. Inevitably this is a risky process – we have to take decisions about ideas which are in their earliest stages and which could become the best thing since sliced bread, but which could equally crash into oblivion and take us down with them!

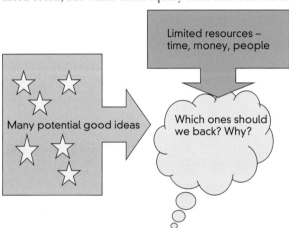

For the entrepreneur the challenge is daunting – like taking part in a high-stakes competition. The test is one of how to put across your wonderful idea to a panel of judges who seem determined to find fault with everything. Passion and energy are all very well but they are looking for the impossible – guarantees that the idea will work, that people will want to buy and use it when it is developed and – most important – that they will get a return on their investment in you and your idea. Whether you are trying to convince a venture capitalist, a group of business angels or some close friends who might be interested in backing you, the same problem will emerge – can you marshal enough to convince them that they are taking a well-calculated risk rather than a wild gamble? Putting the business plan together is critical – and it doesn't hurt to have a sense of the kind of questions they might be thinking of asking you.

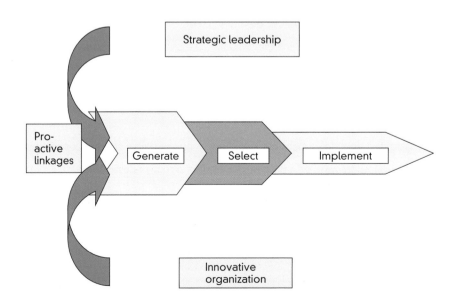

Which brings us to the other side of the fence. How do those responsible for judging ideas and selecting the best for further investment actually think? What are their concerns and how do they go about building an effective and balanced portfolio of ideas? The judges may be venture capitalists specialized in examining and taking risks with innovative ideas. But they could also be the management board reviewing the company's portfolio of new products or services, or a department manager considering a new process to implement across her group. Or a hospital administrator looking for new ways to reduce costs or increase quality of service being delivered.

As with the previous stage we have learned quite a bit about the ways in which this task of selection can be organized and managed – a 'good practice' model which we can learn from and adapt. Smart organizations don't simply gamble – they make choices on the basis of some clear ground rules. Does the idea have promise? Is it a good fit with where we are trying to go in our wider business strategy? Does it build on things that we know and can take advantage of – or if not, can we get hold of this knowledge to make it work? They make use of techniques and structures to help them in the selection process – and make sure these are flexible enough to help monitor and adapt projects over time as ideas move towards more concrete innovations. And if they aren't going as well as expected – because of unexpected developments on the technological or market front, they have mechanisms in place to stop the process and either go back to the drawing board or kill it altogether. (Chapter 5 describes many of these approaches in more detail.)

If we are talking about the single 'big idea' then some quite specific judgements will need to be made around risk versus reward. But in most cases the problem is comparing one set of innovation opportunities against another – and this poses the question of *which* projects, and the subsidiary one of ensuring a balance between risk, reward, novelty, experience and many other elements of uncertainty. The challenge of building a portfolio is as much an issue in non-commercial organizations – for example, should a hospital commit to a new theatre, a new scanner, a new support organization around integrated patient care, or a new sterilization method?

Approaches to deal with 'portfolio management' range from simple judgements about risk and reward to complex quantitative tools based on probability theory. But the underlying purpose is the same – to provide a coherent basis on which to judge which projects should be undertaken, and to ensure a good balance across the portfolio of risk and potential reward. Failure to make such judgements can lead to a number of problem issues, as Table 12.3 indicates.

Table 12.3   Problems arising from poor portfolio management. (Source: based on Cooper)

Without portfolio management there may be ...	Impacts
No limit to projects taken on	Resources spread too thinly
Reluctance to kill-off or 'de-select' projects	Resource starvation and impacts on time and cost – overruns
Lack of strategic focus in project mix	High failure rates, or success of unimportant projects and opportunity cost against more important projects
Weak or ambiguous selection criteria	Projects find their way into the mix because of politics or emotion or other factors – high downstream failure rates and resource diversion from other projects
Weak decision criteria	Too many 'average' projects selected, little impact downstream in market

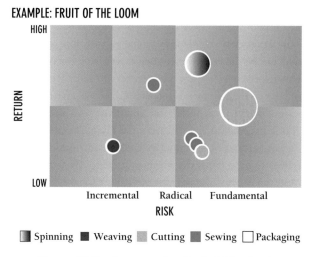

EXAMPLE: FRUIT OF THE LOOM

■ Spinning ■ Weaving ■ Cutting ■ Sewing □ Packaging

Figure 12.2   An example of a bubble chart.

Three main approaches are generally used in portfolio management – benefit measurement techniques, economic models and portfolio models. Benefit measurement approaches are usually based on relatively simple subjective judgements – for example, checklists which ask whether certain criteria are met or not. More advanced versions attempt some kind of scoring or weighting so that projects can be compared in terms of their overall attractiveness. The main weakness here is that they consider each project in relative isolation.

Economic models attempt to put some financial or other quantitative data into the equation – for example, by calculating a payback time or discounted cash flow arising from the project. Once again these suffer from only treating single projects rather than reviewing a bundle, and they are also heavily dependent on the availability of good financial data – not always the case at the outset of a risky project. The third group – portfolio methods – tries to deal with the issue of reviewing across a set of projects and look for balance. A typical example is to construct some form of matrix measuring risk versus reward – for example, on a 'costs of doing the project' versus expected returns. Other possible axes include ease of entry versus market attractiveness (size or growth rate), the competitive position of the organization in the project area versus the attractiveness of the market, or the expected time to reach the market versus the attractiveness of the market.

A useful variant on this set of portfolio methods is the 'bubble chart' in which the different projects are plotted but represented by 'bubbles' – circles whose diameter varies with the size of the project (for example, in terms of costs). This approach gives a quick visual overview of the balance of different sized projects against risk and reward criteria. Figure 12.2 shows an example.

Pitching the Idea

For entrepreneurs – whether looking to start their own business or operating inside an organization – pitching their ideas to others to get support involves the other side of this judgement process. Smart players don't simply throw their ideas over the wall and hope they land safely – instead they develop a convincing businesses case, anticipating the questions and concerns of their audience. The purpose is to move an outline idea to something with clearer shape and form, a concept which can be tested in the marketplace, explored within design, development and manufacturing, compared with competing offerings, and so on. It can be used to provide the vision for the development team; the clearer the vision, the more focused the development activity can be. In the case of process innovation the concept can be tested on the 'internal market' – those users likely to be affected by the change who need to 'buy in' to it in order for the innovation to succeed. Perhaps the most important principle in preparing a business case is to understand the questions likely to be worrying the potential supporters – and answer them in advance!

Several techniques are available to support this process – for example, 'product-mapping' and 'focus groups' to explore the market potential – and there is a powerful armoury of tools for simulation and prototyping which allow for much higher levels of experimentation on the technological side without incurring time or cost penalties. Examples of such tools include advanced computer modelling which allows for simulation and large-scale experiments, rapid prototyping which offers physical representations of form and substance, and simulation techniques which allow the workings of different options to be explored. Most important, these tools can help build a more complete picture of what the innovation might look like – helping make the concept real and allowing potential supporters to understand and explore it.

HOW WELL ARE WE DOING IT?

If we visited such a smart organization we'd expect to find evidence that these ways of helping the selection process were widely used. People we approached would tell us things like:
Around here . . .

- We have a clear system for choosing innovation projects and everyone understands the rules of the game in making proposals.
- When someone has a good idea they know how to take it forward.
- We have a selection system which tries to build a balanced portfolio of low- and high-risk projects.
- We focus on a mixture of product, process, market and business model innovation.
- We balance projects for 'do better' innovation with some efforts on the radical, 'do different' side.
- We recognize the need to work 'outside the box' and there are mechanisms for handling 'off-message' but interesting ideas.
- We have structures for corporate venturing.

Concept-testing can equally be applied to process innovation. Pilot plant trials are often used in developing and scaling up processes while there is increasing use of advanced simulation technology to explore various dimensions with key users.

Process-mapping is a widely used technique in ensuring effective design, especially of cross-functional processes where the workflow is not always clearly understood. Again there is plenty of scope for tools like simulation and prototyping – for example, in introducing new production management software a common practice is to 'walk through' the operation of core processes using computer and organizational simulation.

Implementation

Having decided on which ideas to back the organization has one small problem left – how to actually make them happen? Moving from a gleam in some entrepreneur's eye to a product or service people use and value, or a business process which employees buy into and work with can be a somewhat difficult journey! It isn't usually a simple matter of project management, balancing resources against a budget of time and money – the big difference with innovation is that we don't know whether or not things will work until we start doing them. So it's a case of developing something against a background of uncertainty. The only way we reduce the uncertainty is by trying things out and learning, even if what we learn is that it isn't going to work after all!

We're also weaving together different strands of knowledge about the innovation – the 'technological' (Will it work as an idea?) and the 'market' (Is there a need for this idea and do we understand and meet that need?). So a key aspect of implementation is making sure the threads come together and intertwine successfully – which in practice means making sure the right people get to talk with each other at the right time and for long enough to make something happen.

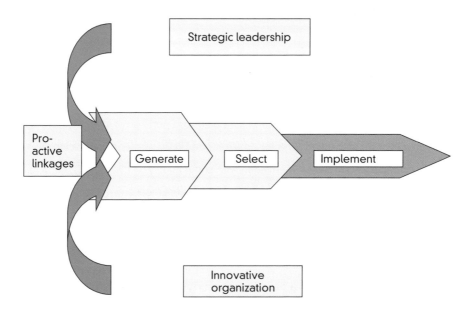

Innovation is often described in terms of the metaphor of a journey – and this helps us particularly think about the implementation phase. What stages does our idea need to go through before it becomes a successful innovation as a product/service in the marketplace or a process in everyday use within the business? And what structures and techniques do smart entrepreneurs and firms use to help their innovation along this journey – and to check its progress? It would be foolish to throw good money after bad so most organizations make use of some kind of risk management as they implement innovation projects. By installing a series of 'gates' as the project moves from a gleam in the eye to an expensive commitment of time and money it becomes possible to review – and if necessary redirect or even stop something which is going off the rails.

Models of this kind (Figure 12.3) have been widely applied in different sectors, both in manufacturing and services. Needless to say it's a matter of horses for courses – adapting a system to the particular circumstances of the business. We need to recognize the importance here of configuring the practice system to the particular contingencies of the organization – for example, a highly-procedural system which works for a global multi-product software and hardware company like Siemens or Lucent will be far too big and complex for many small organizations. And not every project needs the same degree of scrutiny – for some there will be a need to develop parallel 'fast tracks' where monitoring is kept to a light touch to ensure speed and flow in development.

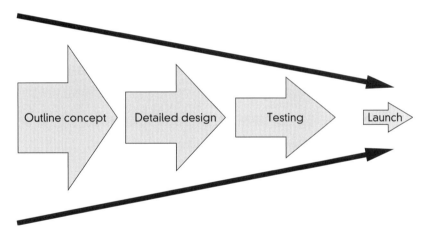

Figure 12.3   The new product development funnel[3].

INNOVATION IN ACTION

Accelerating Ideas to Market – the AIM Process

Coloplast is a Danish company involved in manufacture of a wide range of medical products. Their stage-gate process is called AIM and the basic structure is given in Figure 12.4.

AIM's purpose can be expressed as being:

- ■ To provide common rules of the game for product development within Coloplast.

- ■ To make clear decisions at the right moment.

- ■ To clarify responsibility.

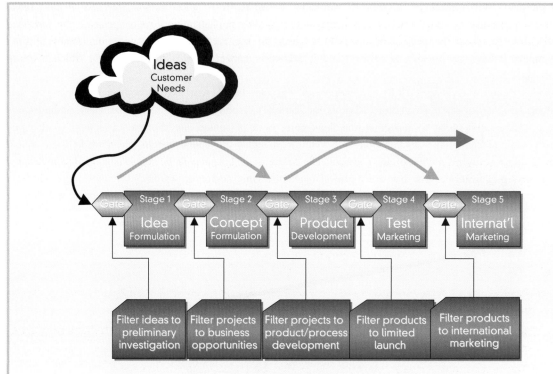

Figure 12.4 Accelerating aims to market

The objective of the AIM process is to ensure a high, uniform level of professionalism in product development yielding high-quality products. It is based on the view that Coloplast must increase the success rate and reduce the development time for new products in order to become a 'world-class innovator'.

The AIM process divides the development of new products into five manageable 'stages'. Each stage contains a number of parallel and coordinated activities designed to refine the definitions of customer needs and to develop technological solutions and capacity for efficient manufacturing.

Each stage is followed by a 'gate', a decision point at which the project is reviewed by the 'gatekeepers', senior managers with authority to keep worthy projects moving ahead quickly. The gates serve as the critical quality-control checkpoints between the stages. A 'go' decision is made when the gatekeepers decide that a project is likely, technically and economically, to meet the needs of the customers as well as to comply with Coloplast's high standards for return on investment, quality and environmental impact.

Much of the work in product development is carried out by project teams consisting of selected specialists from marketing (from both product divisions and subsidiaries), R&D, clinical affairs and manufacturing. Each project team will work under the leadership of a skilled and enthusiastic project manager, and the AIM process defines the rules to be followed by the project team.

Managing innovation projects is more than simply scheduling resources against time and budget. Dealing with unexpected and unpredictable events and gradually bringing projects into being requires high levels of flexibility and creativity – and in particular it involves integrating knowledge sets from across organizational, functional and disciplinary boundaries. And we've learned a lot about how to do this – for example, through using cross-boundary teams, through various forms of parallel or concurrent working, and through the use of simulation and other exploration technologies to anticipate downstream problems and reduce time and resource costs while enhancing innovation quality.

INNOVATION IN ACTION

In a report to the Product Development Management Association Griffin[3] indicated that, across a sample of 380 US firms:

- Progress had been made on reducing NPD cycle times. For example, the average time to market for more innovative projects was down to 24 months, a 30% decrease from 5 years ago.

- The best performers had better commercialization success rates (nearly 80% vs. 53% for the rest) and had higher revenue contribution from new products (nearly 50% vs. 25%).

- Nearly 60% of firms now use some form of stage and gate process but 39% still have no formal process for managing NPD.

- More sophisticated versions of this approach are in use. For example, the best performers were more likely to use a facilitated stage and gate process or a process with flexible gates.

- The best performers were also more likely to drive NPD with a specific strategy.

- Multi-functional teams are in common use with 84% using them for more innovative projects.

- The best companies were more likely to use these team structures on less innovative projects as well.

- Two types of tools were in common use, market research tools to make development more customer-driven and engineering tools to automate design, analysis and prototyping.

- The best performers do significantly more qualitative market research and are more likely to use engineering design tools.

Table 12.4 gives some examples of the mechanisms, tools and structures which smart firms and entrepreneurs use.

Building the 'better mousetrap which no one wants' is one of the prime reasons for failure in innovation – even if the product/service is technically excellent there is no guarantee that people will adopt it or continue its use over the long term. So how can we improve the chances of successful adoption and diffusion? Part of the puzzle can be solved by taking into account the various influences on adoption behaviour, and a wide range of studies on buyer behaviour and influences on the adoption decision are available to help with this. We can use this information to anticipate likely aspects of the innovation and the ways in which it is launched which will help dispose potential adopters favourably. And we can also deploy strategies like early and active user-involvement to help build confidence in emerging innovations.

Table 12.4   Mechanisms, tools and structures to assist innovation project development

Key needs/issues on the journey	Key mechanisms
Systematic process for progressing new products	Stage-gate model Close monitoring and evaluation at each stage
Early involvement of all relevant functions	Bringing key perspectives into the process early enough to influence design and prepare for downstream problems Early detection of problems leads to less rework
Overlapping/parallel working	Concurrent or simultaneous engineering to aid faster development while retaining cross-functional involvement
Appropriate project management structures	Choice of structure – e.g. matrix/line/project/heavyweight project management – to suit conditions and task
Cross-functional team-working	Involvement of different perspectives, use of team-building approaches to ensure effective team-working and develop capabilities in flexible problem-solving
Advanced support tools	Use of tools – such as CAD, rapid prototyping, computer-supported cooperative work aids – to assist with quality and speed of development
Learning and continuous improvement	Carrying forward lessons learned – via post-project audits, etc. Development of continuous improvement culture

INNOVATION IN ACTION

The Ford Edsel was one of the best-researched product concepts in the company's history. The final product failed disastrously – mainly because the market had moved on in terms of customer tastes in the time it took to develop the production model.

Some useful approaches here include taking out prototypes of the product/service to users (or bringing the users in to test them out). It is particularly important in ensuring that the original concept still holds at the end of the development phase. Such tests can also be used to explore customer preferences which provide important information about pricing policy, advertising strategy, and so on. For more complex products it may be necessary to allow the user an extended period of use to permit learning and familiarization with the product and how to make the best use of it.

Test marketing involves a trial sale of the new product to a controlled group of customers; effectively it is a pilot of the full marketing launch. Such testing can reveal actual as opposed to simulated data on acceptance, concerns, adoption rates and speeds, and so on. It also offers the opportunity to test different launch strategies – for example, two different regions could be used, each employing a different launch strategy. Sometimes different releases (alpha, beta, etc.) of the product under development are issued to controlled groups of users. This strategy allows feedback of positive and negative responses which can be built into the final version; it is simultaneously a good way of enhancing product quality and user-need fit while also pre-advertising/'warming up' the marketplace. This approach is extensively used in the area of computer software, where user feedback is an important source of product improvement and final development.

HOW WELL ARE WE DOING IT?

We can use this kind of 'good practice' model to compare against – and identify where and how we could improve the ways we manage the implementation of innovation. If we visited a smart organization we'd find many of these structures and techniques in use to help make the process happen well – and if we asked people we'd find evidence that they were using them. We'd hear things like:

Around here . . .

■ We have clear and well-understood formal processes in place to help us manage new product development effectively from idea to launch.

■ Our innovation projects are usually completed on time and within budget.

■ We have effective mechanisms for managing process change from idea through to successful implementation.

■ We have mechanisms in place to ensure early involvement of all departments in developing new products/processes.

■ There is sufficient flexibility in our system for product development to allow small 'fast track' projects to happen.

■ Our project teams for taking innovation forward involve people from all the relevant parts of the organization.

■ We involve everyone with relevant knowledge from the beginning of the process.

We'd also expect them to have some provision for the wilder and more radical kind of project which might need to go on a rather different route in making its journey. People might say about that things like:

Around here . . .

■ We have alternative and parallel mechanisms for implementing and developing radical innovation projects which sit outside the 'normal' rules and procedures.

■ We have mechanisms for managing ideas that don't fit our current business – for example, we license them out or spin them off.

■ We make use of simulation, rapid prototyping tools, etc. to explore different options and delay commitment to one particular course.

■ We have strategic decision-making and project-selection mechanisms which can deal with more radical proposals outside of the mainstream.

■ There is sufficient flexibility in our system for product development to allow small 'fast track' projects to happen.

Launching into an Internal Market – the Question of 'Change Management'

Within process innovation the question of launch takes on particular significance. Not only must the project be managed along what may be a complex development funnel (as with product innovation) but the market into which it will be launched is an internal one, often involving the same people. Since many process innovations represent major changes in 'the way we do things round here' the question of managing cultural change and overcoming resistance to innovation needs to be addressed.

Trying to introduce changes in the ways in which products are made or services delivered is a cooperative effort which requires inputs of knowledge and expertise from across the organization. Extensive work on successful implementation of IT systems – probably the most widely used class of process innovations over the past 40 years – repeatedly stresses the need to involve users in order to get better-designed systems and to get commitment to making them work.

Managing organizational change is problematic largely because human beings are programmed to resist or at least be cautious about change. Change is often perceived as threatening, painful, disruptive and sometimes dangerous; resistance has both cognitive and emotional components. Some of this resistance can be dealt with in formal ways – by training, communicating information, etc. – but emotional responses (anxieties about loss of status, power, influence, fear of risk-taking, etc.) cannot be addressed directly. Instead it is necessary to create a climate in which these concerns can surface, issues and conflicts can be addressed and in which individuals can find reassurance.

Key elements associated with effective change management are:

- *Establish a clear change-management strategy at top level* and communicate this shared vision to the rest of the organization – essentially this will involve a cascade process down through the organization during which opportunities are set up for others to challenge and take 'ownership' of the same shared vision.

- *Communication* – active, open (rather than allowing information to flow on a 'need-to-know' basis), timely (in advance of change – the informal communication network will disseminate this information anyway and a slow formal system will undermine credibility), and above all, two-way in operation. Unless there are channels through which people can express their responses and ideas and voice their concerns then no amount of top-down communication will succeed in generating commitment.

- *Early involvement* – there are two important benefits to allowing participation and allowing it to take place as early as possible in the change process. The first is that without it – even if attempts have been made to consult or to inform – people will not develop a sense of 'ownership' of the project or commitment to it – and may express their lack of involvement later in various forms of resistance. And the second is that involvement and encouragement of participation can make significant improvements in the overall project design.

- *Create an open climate*, in which individual anxieties and concerns can be expressed and the ideas and knowledge held within the organization can be used to positive effect. Once again, this involves generating a sense of 'ownership' of the project and commitment to the shared goals of the whole organization – rather than an 'us and them' climate.

- *Set clear targets* – with major change programmes it is especially important to set clear targets for which people can aim. People need feedback about their performance and the establishment of clear milestones and goals is an important way of providing this. In addition, one of the key features in successful organizational development is to create a climate of continuous improvement in which the achievement of one goal is rewarded but is also accompanied by the setting of the next.

■ Invest in training – seeing it far more as an investment in developing not only specific skills but also in creating an alternative type of organization – one which understands why changes are happening and one which is capable of managing some of the behavioural processes involved in change.

Strategic Leadership

Innovation doesn't take place in a vacuum – it is subject to a range of internal and external influences which shape what is possible and what actually emerges. In particular it needs clear strategic leadership and direction, plus the commitment of resources to make this happen. Innovation is about taking risks, about going into new and sometimes completely unexplored spaces. We don't want to gamble – simply changing things for their own sake or because the fancy takes us. And passion, drive and energy are critical entrepreneurial characteristics but they carry the risk that we might point them in the wrong direction. No organization has resources to waste in that scattergun fashion – innovation needs a strategy. But equally we need to have a degree of courage and leadership, steering the organization away from what everyone else is doing or what we've always done and into new spaces.

Again we've learned that successful entrepreneurs and innovating organizations use a range of structures, tools and techniques to help them create, articulate, communicate and deploy a clear strategy. For example, many organizations take time – often off-site and away from the day-to-day pressures of their 'normal' operations – to reflect and develop a shared strategic framework for innovation. The underlying question this framework has to answer is about balancing fit with business strategy: Does the innovation we are considering help us reach the strategic goals we have set ourselves (for growth, market share, profit margin, etc)? With the underlying

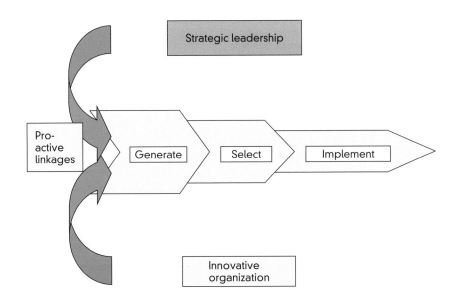

competencies: Do we know enough about this to pull it off (or if not do we have a clear idea of how we would get hold of and integrate such knowledge?). Much can be gained through taking a systematic approach to answering these questions; a typical approach might be to carry out some form of competitive analysis which looks at the position of the organization in terms of its environment and the key forces acting upon competition. Within this picture, questions can then be asked about how a proposed innovation might help shift the competitive positioning favourably – by lowering or raising entry barriers, by introducing substitutes to rewrite the rules of the game, and so on.

In carrying out such a systematic analysis it is important to build on multiple perspectives. Reviews can take an 'outside in' approach, using tools for competitor and market analysis, or they can adopt an 'inside out' model, looking for ways of deploying competencies. They can build on explorations of the future such as the scenarios described earlier in this chapter, and they can make use of techniques like 'technology road-mapping' to help identify courses of action which will deliver broad strategic objectives. But in the process of carrying out such reviews it is critical to remember that strategy is not an exact science so much as a process of building shared perspectives and developing a framework within which risky decisions can be located.

Innovation Strategy Deployment

It is also important not to neglect the need to communicate and share this strategic analysis. Unless people within the organization understand and commit to the analysis it will be hard for them to use it to frame their actions. The issue of innovation strategy deployment – communicating and enabling people to use the framework – is essential if the organization is to avoid the risk of having 'know how' but not 'know why' in its innovation process. Deployment of this kind comes to the fore in the case of focused incremental improvement activities common to implementations of the 'lean' philosophy or of *kaizen*. In principle it is possible to mobilize most of the people in an organization to contribute their ideas and creativity towards continuous improvement, but in practice this often fails. A key issue is the presence – or absence – of some strategic focus within which they can locate their multiple small-scale innovation activities. This requires two key enablers – the creation of a clear and coherent strategy for the business and the deployment of it through a cascade process which builds understanding and ownership of the goals and sub-goals.

INNOVATION IN ACTION

Policy deployment is a characteristic feature of many Japanese *kaizen* systems and may help explain why there is such a strong 'track record' of strategic gains through continuous improvement. In such plants overall business strategy is broken down into focused three-year mid-term plans (MTPs); typically the plan is given a slogan or motto to help identify it. This forms the basis of banners and other illustrations, but its real effect is to provide a backdrop against which efforts over the next three years can be focused. The MTP is specified not just in vague terms but with specific and measurable objectives – often described as pillars. These are, in turn, decomposed into manageable projects which have clear targets and measurable achievement milestones, and it is to these that workplace innovation activities are systematically applied.

Policy deployment of this kind requires suitable tools and techniques and examples include *hoshin* (participative) planning, how–why charts, 'bowling charts' and briefing groups.

Stretching Leadership

Challenging the way the organization sees things – the corporate mindset – can sometimes be accomplished by bringing in external perspectives. IBM's recovery was due in no small measure to the role played by Lou Gerstner who succeeded at least in part *because* he was a newcomer to the computer industry, and was able to ask the awkward questions that insiders were oblivious to. And when Intel was facing strong competition from Far Eastern producers, Groves and Noyce reported on the need to 'think the unthinkable', that is, get out of memory production (the business on which Intel had grown up) and to contemplate moving into other product niches. They trace their subsequent success to the point where they found themselves 'entering the void' and creating a new vision for the business.

Doing this may need mechanisms for legitimating challenge to the dominant vision. This may come from the top – such as Jack Welch's challenge to 'destroy your business' memo. Perhaps building on their earlier experiences Intel now has a process called 'constructive confrontation', which essentially encourages a degree of dissent. The company has learned to value the critical insights which come from those closest to the action rather than assume senior managers have the 'right' answers every time.

The same pattern holds for the start-up entrepreneur. Unless he or she has the sense of compelling vision – and the ability to communicate this passion to others – then getting the early stage support for their idea is unlikely to happen. Equally it is precisely because of their willingness to push the frontiers that major and exciting changes get to happen. George Bernard Shaw, the famous playwright, got pretty close to it when he observed that: 'The reasonable man adapts himself to the conditions that surround him . . . The unreasonable man adapts surrounding conditions to himself . . . All progress therefore depends on the unreasonable man' (*Mrs Warren's Profession*, 1893).

HOW WELL ARE WE DOING IT?

Statements we'd expect to hear around such a strategically focused and led organization might include:

- People in this organization have a clear idea of how innovation can help us compete.
- There is a clear link between the innovation projects we carry out and the overall strategy of the business.
- We have processes in place to review new technological or market developments and what they mean for our firm's strategy.
- There is top management commitment and support for innovation.
- Our top team have a shared vision of how the company will develop through innovation.
- We look ahead in a structured way (using forecasting tools and techniques) to try and imagine future threats and opportunities.
- People in the organization know what our distinctive competence is – what gives us a competitive edge.
- Our innovation strategy is clearly communicated so everyone knows the targets for improvement.

And we'd also expect some stretching strategic leadership, getting the organization to think well outside its box and anticipate very different challenges for the future – expressed in statements like:

- ■ Management create 'stretch goals' that provide the direction but not the route for innovation.

- ■ We actively explore the future, making use of tools and techniques like scenarios and foresight.

- ■ We have capacity in our strategic thinking process to challenge our current position – we think about 'how to destroy the business'!

- ■ We have strategic decision-making and project-selection mechanisms which can deal with more radical proposals outside of the mainstream.

- ■ We are not afraid to 'cannibalize' things we already do to make space for new options.

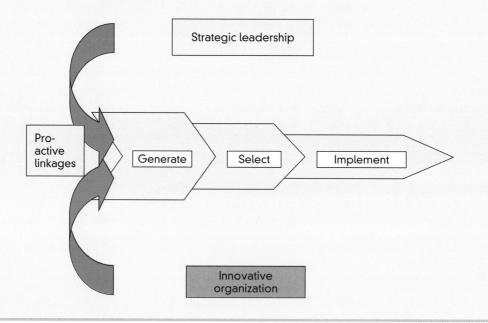

Building an Innovative Organization

The key to innovation and entrepreneurship is, of course, people. And the simple challenge is how to enable them to deploy their creativity and share their knowledge to bring about change. It's easy to find prescriptions for innovative organizations which highlight the need to eliminate stifling bureaucracy, unhelpful structures, brick walls blocking communication and other factors stopping good ideas getting through. But we must be careful not to fall into the chaos trap – not all innovation works in organic, loose, informal environments or 'skunk works' – and these types of organization can sometimes act against the interests of successful innovation. We need to determine *appropriate* organization – that is, the most suitable organization given the operating contingencies. Too little order and structure may be as bad as too much.

Successful entrepreneurs and innovative organizations recognize this – and make use of a range of structures, tools and techniques to help them achieve this balance. We explored this theme in Chapter 2 so we'll just summarize the key issues here. Table 12.5 gives a list of key components in building an innovative organization.

Table 12.5   Components of the innovative organization

Component	Key features
Shared vision, leadership and the will to innovate	Clearly articulated and shared sense of purpose Stretching strategic intent 'Top management commitment'
Appropriate structure	Organization design which enables creativity, learning and interaction. Not always a loose 'skunk works' model; key issue is finding appropriate balance between 'organic and mechanistic' options for particular contingencies
Key individuals	Promoters, champions, gatekeepers and other roles which energize or facilitate innovation
Effective team-working	Appropriate use of teams (at local, cross-functional and inter-organizational level) to solve problems. Requires investment in team selection and building
Continuing and stretching individual development	Long-term commitment to education and training to ensure high levels of competence and the skills to learn effectively
Extensive communication	Within and between the organization and outside. Internally in three directions – upwards, downwards and laterally
High-involvement in innovation	Participation in organization-wide continuous improvement activity
External focus	Internal and external customer orientation. Extensive networking
Creative climate	Positive approach to creative ideas, supported by relevant motivation systems
Learning organization	High levels of involvement within and outside the firm in proactive experimentation, finding and solving problems, communication and sharing of experiences and knowledge capture and dissemination

HOW WELL DO WE DO IT?

If we visited such an organization we'd find evidence of these approaches being used widely and people would say things like:

Around here . . .

■ Our organization structure does not stifle innovation but helps it to happen.

- People work well together across departmental boundaries.
- There is a strong commitment to training and development of people.
- People are involved in suggesting ideas for improvements to products or processes.
- Our structure helps us to take decisions rapidly.
- Communication is effective and works top-down, bottom-up and across the organization.
- Our reward and recognition system supports innovation.
- We have a supportive climate for new ideas – people don't have to leave the organization to make them happen.
- We work well in teams.

We'd also find a recognition that one size doesn't fit all and that innovative organizations need the capacity – and the supporting structures and mechanisms – to think and do very different things from time to time. So we'd also expect to find people saying things like:

- Our organization allows some space and time for people to explore 'wild' ideas.
- We have mechanisms to identify and encourage 'intrapreneurship' – if people have a good idea they don't have to leave the company to make it happen.
- We allocate a specific resource for exploring options at the edge of what we currently do – we don't load everyone up 100%.
- We value people who are prepared to break the rules.
- We have high-involvement from everyone in the innovation process.
- Peer pressure creates a positive tension and creates an atmosphere to be creative.
- Experimentation is encouraged.

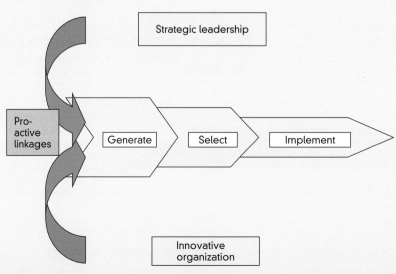

Networking for Innovation

We've always known that innovation is not a solo act; successful players working hard to build links across boundaries inside the organization and to the many external agencies who can play a part in the innovation process – suppliers, customers, sources of finance, skilled resources and of knowledge, and so on – twenty-first-century innovation is increasingly about 'open innovation', a multi-player game where connections and the ability to find, form and deploy creative relationships is of the essence.

Table 12.6   Challenges in managing innovation networks

Set-up stage	Operating stage	Sustaining (or closure) stage
Issues here are around providing the momentum for bringing the network together and clearly defining its purpose. It may be crisis-triggered – for example, perception of the urgent need to catch up via adoption of innovation. Equally, it may be driven by a shared perception of opportunity – the potential to enter new markets or exploit new technologies. Key roles here will often be played by third parties – network brokers, gatekeepers, policy agents and facilitators.	The key issues here are about trying to establish some core operating processes about which there is support and agreement. These need to deal with: ■ Network boundary management – how the membership of the network is defined and maintained. ■ Decision-making – how decisions (where, when, who) get taken at the network level. Conflict resolution – how conflicts are resolved effectively. ■ Information-processing – how information flows among members and is managed. Knowledge management – how knowledge is created, captured, shared and used across the network. ■ Motivation – how members are motivated to join/remain within the network. Risk/benefit sharing – how the risks and rewards are allocated across members of the network. ■ Coordination – how the operations of the network are integrated and coordinated.	Networks need not last forever – sometimes they are set up to achieve a highly specific purpose (e.g. development of a new product concept) and once this has been done the network can be disbanded. In other cases there is a case for sustaining the networking activities for as long as members see benefits. This may require periodic review and 're-targeting' to keep the motivation high. For example, CRINE, a successful development programme for the offshore oil and gas industry, was launched in 1992 by key players in the industry such as BP, Shell and major contractors with support from the UK Government with the target of cost reduction. Using a network model, it delivered extensive innovation in product/services and processes. Having met its original cost-reduction targets, the programme moved to a second phase with a focus aimed more at capturing a bigger export share of the global industry through innovation.

Innovation networks can be broken down into three stages of a life cycle. Table 12.6 looks at some of the key management questions associated with each stage.

As we saw in Chapter 3, making this happen requires skills in finding network partners, building relationships with them and finally linking their contributions with others so that the whole becomes greater than the sum of the parts. The challenges include:

■ How to manage something we don't own or control;

■ How to see system level effects, not narrow self-interests;

■ How to build trust and shared risk-taking without tying the process up in contractual red tape;

■ How to avoid 'free riders' and information 'spillovers'.

HOW WELL DO WE DO IT?

If we were to visit a successful innovative player we'd get a sense of how far they had developed these capabilities for networking by asking around. People would typically say things like:

■ We have good 'win–win' relationships with our suppliers.

■ We are good at understanding the needs of our customers/end-users.

■ We work well with universities and other research centres to help us develop our knowledge.

■ We work closely with our customers in exploring and developing new concepts.

■ We collaborate with other firms to develop new products or processes.

■ We try to develop external networks of people who can help us – for example, with specialist knowledge.

■ We work closely with the local and national education system to communicate our needs for skills.

■ We work closely with 'lead users' to develop innovative new products and services.

And there would be some evidence of their increasing efforts to create wide-ranging 'open innovation' type links – with statements like:

■ We make connections across industry to provide us with different perspectives.

■ We have mechanisms to bring in fresh perspectives – for example, recruiting from outside the industry.

■ We have extensive links with a wide range of outside sources of knowledge – universities, research centres, specialized agencies – and we actually set them up even if not for specific projects.

■ We use technology to help us become more agile and quick to pick up on and respond to emerging threats and opportunities on the periphery.

■ We have 'alert' systems to feed early warnings about new trends into the strategic decision-making process.

- We practice 'open innovation' – rich and widespread networks of contacts from whom we get a constant flow of challenging ideas.

- We have an approach to supplier management which is open to strategic 'dalliances'.

- We have active links into the long-term research and technology community – we can list a wide range of contacts.

- We recognize users as a source of new ideas and try and 'co-evolve' new products and services with them.

Learning to Manage Innovation

No individual or organization is born with the perfect set of capabilities to make innovation happen. Instead they learn and develop these over time and through trial and error. In this chapter we've looked at a range of 'good practices' which are commonly found across very different entrepreneurial organizations – and they give us a helpful framework for thinking about how we could organize and manage the innovation process. We've tried to give some examples and also to suggest how we might diagnose how well (or badly) an organization managed the process by asking some focused questions of the people working within it. The core questions are basically:

- Do we have a clear process for making innovation happen and effective enabling mechanisms to support it?

- Do we have a clear sense of shared strategic purpose and do we use this to guide our innovative activities?

- Do we have a supportive organization whose structures and systems enable people to be creative and share and build on each other's creative ideas?

- Do we build and extend our networks for innovation into a rich open innovation system?

HOW WELL DO WE MANAGE LEARNING?

Smart firms do – and the kinds of thing people might say in such organizations would be that 'around here':

- We take time to review our projects to improve our performance next time.

- We learn from our mistakes.

- We systematically compare our products and processes with other firms.

- We meet and share experiences with other firms to help us learn.

- We are good at capturing what we have learned so that others in the organization can make use of it.

- We use measurement to help identify where and when we can improve our innovation management.

- We learn from our periphery – we look beyond our organizational and geographical boundaries.

- Experimentation is encouraged.

To this we can add a final but central question: Do we actively try and learn to develop our capabilities for innovation? Learning isn't easy – organizations are usually too busy *doing* to find time to stop and think about how they might do things better. But assuming they did manage to get offline and reflect on how they might improve their innovation management they would probably find some structured framework for thinking about the process helpful. We can use the idea of comparing against what we've learned about good practice to develop simple audit frameworks which could be used for diagnosis. How well do we do things compared to what the 'good practice' is? How far would we agree with the kinds of statements we've listed in the chapter associated with good innovators? Where are our strengths? And where would we want to focus our efforts to improve the organization? This kind of audit and review process doesn't carry any prizes but it can help with making the organization more effective in the ways it deals with the innovation challenge. And that might lead to some pretty important outcomes – like survival or growth!

There is no single framework for doing an innovation audit – and no 'right' answer at the end of the process. But using such frameworks can be helpful and we have included some on the website accompanying this book. There are audits which look in general terms, those which focus on capabilities to manage the more radical end of innovation, those which deal with sector differences like how to manage innovation in services. And there are those which focus on aspects of the organization – like how well it is able to engage its whole workforce in the innovation process. Audits can be targeted at the individual – for example Chapter 2 provides a framework for reflecting on 'How creative are you?'

There is also an increasing number of online audit resources available, and a growing consultancy industry built around providing this kind of 'mirror' on how well an organization is doing at innovation together with some advice on how it might do it better. But it's not the audits so much as using them in the *process* of questioning and developing innovation capability which matters. As the quality guru, W. Edwards Deming, pointed out, 'If you don't measure it you can't improve it!'

Managing Innovation and Entrepreneurship

We began the book by talking about innovation as a survival imperative. Quite simply, if organizations don't change what they offer the world, and the ways they create and deliver those offerings, then they may not be around in the long term. But simply saying 'We believe in innovation' isn't likely to get us very far – it's going to need a considerable amount of action to make it happen. Getting a good idea into widespread and successful use is hard enough – but growing and sustaining a business requires the ability to repeat the trick. Even serial entrepreneurs, whose philosophy is to make this happen and then make their (hopefully wealthy) exit, only do so in order to repeat the process with another good idea.

Success isn't about luck – although there is probably some truth to the old saying attributed to various famous sportsmen and women that 'the more I practice the luckier I get!' Innovation is about managing a structured and focused process, engaging and deploying creativity throughout but also balancing this with an appropriate degree of control. No organization or individual starts out with this – it's essentially something they learn and develop over time. This learning can come through trial and error – but it can also come through learning from others and building on their hard-won experience. And it can come through using tools and models to help understand and engage with managing innovation more effectively. We hope that the lessons we've tried to capture in the book provide some helpful input to this process.

Developing Personal Capabilities

'Those who don't learn from history are condemned to repeat it.' That quote – attributed to various writers – throws down an important challenge in innovation and entrepreneurship. If we don't learn from our mistakes, we're likely to repeat them and get increasingly frustrated in the process. Of course we don't have to learn by our own mistakes; another option is to learn from others – whether their mistakes or their successes. And we can learn from trying things out – designing experiments to see if something works or not, rather than assuming there is one 'best' way to do things.

If we are to learn effectively we will need:

■ Structured and challenging reflection on the process – what happened, what worked well, what went wrong, etc.

■ Conceptualizing – capturing and codifying the lessons learned into frameworks and eventually procedures to build on lessons learned.

■ Experimentation – the willingness to try and manage things differently next time, to see if the lessons learned are valid.

■ Honest capture of experience (even if this has been a costly failure) so we have raw material on which to reflect.

In fact the key to effective learning is to use a variety of approaches – but at the centre, to ensure we reflect on what we or others have learned and use this to drive different approaches in the future. Among the ways in which we might improve our learning capabilities are:

Reflect	Conceptualize	Experiment	Experience
Post-project reviews	Theories and models	Pilot projects	Capture experience – on video, via diaries, project records, photographs, etc.
Benchmarking	New structures and process designs	Testing and prototyping	
Structured audits	Formal planning reviews	R&D activities	
Project evaluation		Designed experiments and simulations	Sharing experience – via display, direct exchange, etc.
Measurement	Training and development		
			Documentation and display
			Measurement

Chapter Summary

■ Whatever drives innovation and wherever it happens – big firm, small firm, start-up business – one thing is clear. Successful innovation won't happen simply by wishing for it. This complex and risky process of transforming ideas into something which makes a mark needs organizing and managing in strategic fashion.

■ It's a generic process, running through three core stages – getting hold of the ideas in the first place, choosing the best candidates to put our resources into and then making them into successful innovations.

■ We know that this process is influenced along the way by several things which can help or hinder it. Is there clear strategic leadership and direction? How can we construct innovative organizations which allow creative ideas to come through, let people build on and share knowledge and feel motivated and rewarded for doing so? How can we harness the power of networks, making rich and extensive connections to deliver a stream of innovations?

■ A wide range of structures, tools and techniques exist for helping think about and manage these elements of the innovation process. The challenge is to adapt and use them in a particular context – essentially a learning process.

■ Developing innovative capability needs to begin with an audit of where we are now – and there are many ways of asking and exploring the core questions:
  ■ Do we have a clear process for making innovation happen and effective enabling mechanisms to support it?
  ■ Do we have a clear sense of shared strategic purpose and do we use this to guide our innovative activities?
  ■ Do we have a supportive organization whose structures and systems enable people to be creative and share and build on each other's creative ideas?
  ■ Do we build and extend our networks for innovation into a rich open innovation system?

Key Terms Defined

Innovation audit Structured review of innovation capability across an organization.

Innovation strategy Statement of how innovation is going to take the business forward – and why.

Innovation strategy deployment Communicating and enabling people to use the framework.

Further Reading and Resources

A number of books offer more detailed discussion of managing innovation – see for example:

Burgelman, R., Christensen, C. et al. (eds.) (2004) *Strategic Management of Technology and Innovation*. McGraw Hill Irwin, Boston.

Dodgson, M. (2000) *The Management of Technological Innovation*. Oxford University Press, Oxford.

Dodgson, M., Gann, D. et al. (2005) *Think, Play, Do: Technology and Organization in the Emerging Innovation Process*. Oxford University Press, Oxford.

Ettlie, J. (1999) *Managing Innovation*. John Wiley & Sons, Inc., New York.

Jones, T. (2002) *Innovating at the Edge*. Butterworth Heinemann, London.

Schilling, M. (2005) Strategic Management of Technological Innovation. McGraw Hill, New York.

Tidd, J., Bessant, J. et al. (2005). *Managing Innovation: Integrating Technological, Market and Organizational Change*, 3rd edn. John Wiley & Sons, Ltd, Chichester.

Tidd, J. and Hull, F (eds.) (2003) Service Innovation: *Organizational Responses to Technological Opportunities and Market Imperatives*. Imperial College Press, London.

Trott, P. (2004) *Innovation Management and New Product Development*. Prentice-Hall, London.

Van de Ven, A. (1999) *The Innovation Journey*. Oxford University Press, Oxford.

Von Stamm, B. (2003) *Managing Innovation, Design and Creativity*. John Wiley & Sons, Ltd, Chichester.

There are plenty of sites which look at aspects of managing innovation so just typing the phrase into a search engine should get you started! But these are some useful links which offer research and related support:

Advanced Institute of Management Research http://www.aimresearch.org/

Academy of Management (which has a TIM special interest group) http://www.aomtim.org/

SPRU http://www.sussex.ac.uk/spru/

CENTRIM http://centrim.mis.brighton.ac.uk/

Imperial College Innovation Studies Centre http://www3.imperial.ac.uk/portal

McMaster University (they run an excellent newsletter) http://mint.mcmaster.ca/mint/mint.htm

International Association for the Management of Technology (IAMOT) http://www.iamot.org/

Innovation auditing is increasingly popular and a number of websites offer frameworks for carrying this out – see, for example, www.innovationdoctor.htm, www.thinksmart.htm, www.jpb.com/services/audit.php,

www.innovation-triz.com/innovation/, www.cambridgestrategy.com/page_c5_summary.htm, and www.innovationwave.com/

References

1 Allen, T. (1977) *Managing the Flow of Technology*. MIT Press, Cambridge, Mass.

2 Cooper, R. (2001) *Winning at New Products*, 3rd edn. Kogan Page, London.

3 Griffin, A. (1998) Overview of PDMA survey on best practices. *PDMA Visions*, January.

Discussion Questions

1 Is innovation manageable – or just a random, gambling process? If it is manageable, what factors are important?

2 What lessons can we derive from studies of innovation success and failure about key principles on which to focus management attention?

3   If you were trying to ensure an innovation project had no hope of succeeding, what would you recommend?

4   How can innovation be measured?

5   The managing director of your company has asked you to give her some clear guidance on what the company should measure to ensure its investment in innovation is worthwhile. What would you suggest as possible measurement targets, and why?

Assignment and Case Study Questions

1   Using one of the innovation audits on the website (www.managing-innovation.com), review a case of an organization and develop a perspective on how well you think they manage innovation. Why? And where do they need to concentrate their development efforts to enhance their capability for the future?

(If you need a case to focus on there are several on the Wiley website www.managing-innovation.com – for example, Corning, Marshalls, Coloplast.)

2   Although innovation is a generic process we need to configure the ways we organize and manage it for different circumstances. How might such an innovation process look for:
   ■ A fast-food restaurant chain?
   ■ An electronic test equipment maker?
   ■ A hospital?
   ■ An insurance company?
   ■ A new entrant biotechnology firm?

3   Jane Smith was a bright young PhD scientist with a patent on a new algorithm for monitoring brainwave activity and predicting the early onset of a stroke. She was convinced of the value of her idea and took it to market having sold her car, borrowed money from family and friends and taken out a large loan. She went bankrupt despite having a demonstration version which doctors she showed it to were impressed by. Why might her failure be linked to having a partial model of how innovation works – and how could she avoid making the same mistake in the future?

4   All organizations have their own particular approach to managing innovation – even those who don't formally try and manage it at all! It's a bit like having a particular personality – even firms in the same sector often approach innovation in very different ways. These represent the results of their own learning processes and the way they manage things accumulates by trial and error.

Think about an organization with which you are familiar and try and map its 'innovation personality' – its particular approach – on to our generic framework model. How do they search, select, implement, etc.?

5   Think about an innovation success story with which you are familiar – or from a case-study example. Try and identify what factors helped that to happen. What key influences made for success? And if you were trying to repeat the trick, what would you take from that experience and apply again?

Now do the same with a failure story – what factors are associated with negative outcomes? What would you try and do if you were determined to stop an innovation succeeding?

List these two sets of factors alongside each other – there will be many that are mirror images of each other. But this exercise will often begin to highlight some of the key success/failure factors which have also emerged consistently in the literature.

CASE STUDY 12

Innovation at 3M

3M began life just over 100 years ago as the Minnesota Mining and Manufacturing Corporation. Its beginnings weren't entirely auspicious – the original idea was to make sandpapers to supply the growing automobile industry of the time. But the property which they had bought to mine for carborundum (the key abrasive in sandpaper) turned out not to contain any, so they had to go back to the drawing board! Despite this setback they grew a business based on supplying abrasives and made an important breakthrough early on when they introduced the first wet and dry papers – which meant that the problems of dust associated with dry papers could be avoided. Perhaps the first key breakthrough – which took them beyond the abrasives product and into many other markets – was the innovation of masking tape in 1925.

Since those days as an abrasives producer they have grown to a global business with around 70 000 employees, operations in over 200 countries and a turnover around US$15 billion. Their product range has also expanded – currently running at around 50 000 items across the range. Significantly there is still a competence around key fields like coatings which goes back to their days as a sandpaper maker – the difference is that they have deployed their skills in surface coatings in fields like magnetic oxides (for recording tape, computer drives, etc.), adhesives (with the famous Post-it range) and optical coatings for lenses.

Innovation 'Claim to Fame'

During its lifetime 3M has established a clear reputation as a major innovator. Their technical competence has been built up by a long-term commitment to R&D on which they currently spend around US$1 billion per year; this has yielded them a regular position among the top 10 in US patents granted. They have launched a number of breakthrough products which have established completely new markets and they have set themselves a consistent stretch target of getting 30% of sales turnover from products launched during the past 4 years. Their success can be measured in the many household name breakthrough products they have introduced – Scotch tape, Scotchgard carpet protection, Post-its are all well-known examples – but also in their regular presence as award winners. For example they were in the top 3 of *Business Week*'s most innovative companies in the world in 2005 and 2006.

How Do They Manage Innovation?

The company presents a consistent picture in interviews and in publications – innovation success is a consequence of creating the culture in which it can take place – it becomes 'the way we do things around here' in a very real sense. This philosophy is borne out in many anecdotes and case histories – the key to their success has been to create the conditions in which innovation can arise from any one of a number of directions, including lucky accidents, and there is a deliberate attempt to avoid putting too much structure in place since this would constrain innovation.

Innovation Strategy and Leadership

3M has always valued innovation and this has been a consistent and key theme since their inception; their 'hero' figures among previous CEOs have been strongly associated with enacting and supporting the innovation culture which characterizes the firm. (In particular William McKnight who ran the firm from 1929 until 1966 laid down many of the core principles by which the firm still operates.) Their overall innovation strategy is focused on two core themes – deep technological competence and strong product development capabilities. They combine these to enable them to offer a steady stream of breakthrough products and line extensions/product improvements. A great strength is the integrated input from the technical and marketing sides which enables 'creative association', coming up with new and often powerful combinations of needs and means.

A number of key strategic enablers are worth flagging:

■ Setting stretch targets – such as 'x% of sales from products introduced during the past y years' provides a clear and consistent message and a focus for the whole organization.

■ Investing in R&D to support this – typical spend is US$1 billion per year, or around 6% of sales – high for their type of business.

■ Allocating resources as 'slack' – space and time in which staff can explore and play with ideas, build on chance events or combinations, and so on.

■ Encouragement of 'bootlegging' employees working on innovation projects in their own time and often accessing resources in an informal way – the 'benevolent blind eye' effect.

■ Provision of staged resource support for innovators who want to take an idea forward – effectively different levels of internal venture capital for which people can bid (against increasingly high hurdles) – this encourages 'intrapreneurship' – internal entrepreneurial behaviour – rather than people feeling they have to leave the firm to take their good ideas forward.

In recent years they have seen their momentum falter, in part because of the sheer scale of the operation and the range of competition. Their response has been to identify a series of 'pacing plus' programmes which attempt to focus priorities around 30 key areas for development across the business – essentially an innovation strategy.

Enabling the Process

The high spend on R&D gives them a strong position in their field – they claim to have deep knowledge of 42 diverse technologies, for example. Much of their philosophy involves making sure there is cross-linkage across the firm – so for example technology originally developed for layered plastic lenses is also applied in reflective road signs, durable abrasives and golf gloves which allow tighter grip without having to squeeze harder.

Having been working on innovation for so long they have developed a set of structures and policies to guide innovative activity from picking up signals through to implementation. Importantly they allow for parallel routes through their system so that innovations can come from close market interactions or from deep technology research in their labs or from various forms of collaboration, or from serendipitous discovery by their staff. As they put it, 'We don't have a skunk-works – round here everyone is a skunk!' Their skill in enabling *association* is particularly relevant; many of their breakthrough products have come because staff with technical knowledge have worked alongside those with awareness of real or latent market needs and the result has been a creative combination.

There is a formal stage-gate system for innovations and extensions based on established products but in addition there is a clear progress route for more radical ideas, moving from an incubator stage where they are encouraged and where development funds are available against loose targets through to much more rigorous business plan appraisal for projects further down the line. The 'trial by fire' approach is well known but carries with it a strong element of encouraging innovation champions to take nonlinear ideas through the system. Effectively they run parallel systems which all involve funnels and clear gateways through which ideas pass into narrower parts of the funnel and which also commit more extensive resources – and although the mechanisms differ the intent is the same.

Building an Innovative Organization

McKnight's strong legacy can particularly be felt in the underlying values which drive the organization. He is famous for summarizing his philosophy for success as being: 'Hire good people and let them do their job in their own ways. And tolerate mistakes'.

- Recognition and reward – throughout the company there are various schemes which acknowledge innovative activity – for example, their Innovator's Award which recognizes effort rather than achievement.

- Reinforcement of core values – innovation is respected – for example, there is a 'hall of fame' whose members are elected on the basis of their innovative achievements.

- Sustaining 'circulation' – movement and combination of people from different perspectives to allow for creative combinations – a key issue in such a large and dispersed organization.

- Allocating 'slack' and permission to play – allowing employees to spend a proportion of their time (typically 15%) in curiosity-driven activities which may lead nowhere but which have sometimes given them breakthrough products.

- Patience – acceptance of the need for 'stumbling in motion' as innovative ideas evolve and take shape. Breakthroughs like Post-its and Scotchgard were not overnight successes but took two to three years to 'cook' before they emerged as viable prospects to put into the formal system.

- Acceptance of mistakes and encouragement of risk-taking – another famous quote from McKnight, is often cited in this connection:

> Mistakes will be made, but if a person is essentially right, the mistakes he or she makes are not as serious, in the long run, as the mistakes management will make if it's dictatorial and undertakes to tell those under its authority exactly how they must do their job ... Management that is destructively critical when mistakes are made kills initiative, and it is essential that we have many people with initiative if we are to continue to grow.

■ Encouraging 'bootlegging' – giving employees a sense of empowerment and turning a blind eye to creative ways which staff come up with to get around the system – acts as a counter to rigid bureaucratic procedures.

■ Policy of hiring innovators – recruitment approach is looking for people with innovator tendencies and characteristics.

■ Operate a dual career ladder so that technically skilled people can progress to the highest levels rather than get diverted into management roles in order to gain promotion.

Linkages and Networking

■ Recognition of the power of association – deliberate attempts not to separate out different functions but to bring them together in teams and other groupings.

■ Encouraging broad perspectives – for example, in developing their overhead projector business it was close links with users made by getting technical development staff to make sales calls that made the product so user-friendly and therefore successful.

■ Strong culture dating back to 1951 of encouraging informal meetings and workshops in a series of groups, committees, and so on, under the structural heading of the Technology Forum – established 'to encourage free and active interchange of information and cross-fertilization of ideas'. The model persists and every year the 9700 staff meet to share and explore ideas. This is a voluntary activity although the company commits support resources – but it enables a company-wide 'college' with fluid interchange of perspectives and ideas. Smaller-scale versions run across different labs and make extensive use of webcasts and intranets to consolidate links. Larry Wendling, vice-president for corporate research, calls networking '3M's secret weapon', and formal and informal linkages are encouraged.

■ Recruiting volunteers – particularly in trying to open up new fields, involvement of customers and other outsiders as part of a development team is encouraged since it mixes perspectives.

■ Linking research closely with customers, with many staff spending time out of the labs working with users to understand their needs. Post-it Photo Paper was a typical result of this – a product which emerged from understanding what people do with digital photos. Typically they take many photos but fail to print them or else put the batch in a drawer. Making the photos easy to print and then stick up – on walls, fridge doors, car dashboards, and so on – opens up a new market space to use a well-established 3M technology.

Case Study Question

Carry out a critical review of the ways in which the 3M organization manages innovation. Some frameworks for this have been developed throughout the book, and the 'innovation audit' frameworks on the website provide a structured aid. Use this review to argue whether or not you think 3M will still be around for another 100 years.

This can be an individual reflection or a group review and presentation.

INDEX